Research Anthology on Machine Learning Techniques, Methods, and Applications

Information Resources Management Association
USA

Volume III

Published in the United States of America by
    IGI Global
    Engineering Science Reference (an imprint of IGI Global)
    701 E. Chocolate Avenue
    Hershey PA, USA 17033
    Tel: 717-533-8845
    Fax: 717-533-8661
    E-mail: cust@igi-global.com
    Web site: http://www.igi-global.com

Library of Congress Cataloging-in-Publication Data

Names: Information Resources Management Association, editor.
Title: Research anthology on machine learning techniques, methods, and
  applications / Information Resources Management Association, editor.
Description: Hershey, PA : Engineering Science Reference, an imprint of IGI
  Global, [2022] | Includes bibliographical references and index. |
  Summary: "This reference set provides a thorough consideration of the
  innovative and emerging research within the area of machine learning,
  discussing how the technology has been used in the past as well as
  potential ways it can be used in the future to ensure industries
  continue to develop and grow while covering a range of topics such as
  artificial intelligence, deep learning, cybersecurity, and robotics"--
  Provided by publisher.
Identifiers: LCCN 2022015780 (print) | LCCN 2022015781 (ebook) | ISBN
  9781668462911 (h/c) | ISBN 9781668462928 (ebook)
Subjects: LCSH: Machine learning--Industrial applications. | Computer
  security--Data processing. | Medical care--Data processing. | Data
  mining. | Artificial intelligence.
Classification: LCC Q325.5 .R46 2022 (print) | LCC Q325.5 (ebook) | DDC
  006.3/1--dc23/eng20220628
LC record available at https://lccn.loc.gov/2022015780
LC ebook record available at https://lccn.loc.gov/2022015781

British Cataloguing in Publication Data
A Cataloguing in Publication record for this book is available from the British Library.

The views expressed in this book are those of the authors, but not necessarily of the publisher.

For electronic access to this publication, please contact: eresources@igi-global.com.

List of Contributors

Table of Contents

Volume III

Section 6
Emerging Trends

Preface

Machine learning, due to its many uses across fields and disciplines, is becoming a prevalent technology in today's modern world. From medicine to business, machine learning is changing the way things are done by providing effective new techniques for problem solving and strategies for leaders to implement. Machine learning is driving major improvements in society including the promotion of societal health, sustainable business, and learning analytics. The possibilities for this technology are endless, and it is critical to further investigate its myriad of opportunities and benefits to successfully combat any challenges and assist in its evolution.

Staying informed of the most up-to-date research trends and findings is of the utmost importance. That is why IGI Global is pleased to offer this three-volume reference collection of reprinted IGI Global book chapters and journal articles that have been handpicked by senior editorial staff. This collection will shed light on critical issues related to the trends, techniques, and uses of various applications by providing both broad and detailed perspectives on cutting-edge theories and developments. This collection is designed to act as a single reference source on conceptual, methodological, technical, and managerial issues, as well as to provide insight into emerging trends and future opportunities within the field.

The *Research Anthology on Machine Learning Techniques, Methods, and Applications* is organized into six distinct sections that provide comprehensive coverage of important topics. The sections are:

1. Fundamental Concepts and Theories;
2. Development and Design Methodologies;
3. Tools and Technologies;
4. Utilization and Applications;
5. Organizational and Social Implications; and
6. Emerging Trends.

The following paragraphs provide a summary of what to expect from this invaluable reference tool.

Section 1, "Fundamental Concepts and Theories," serves as a foundation for this extensive reference tool by addressing crucial theories essential to understanding the concepts and uses of machine learning in multidisciplinary settings. Opening this reference book is the chapter "Introduction to Machine Learning and Its Implementation Techniques" by Profs. Sathiyamoorthi V. and Arul Murugan R. from Sona College of Technology, India, which aims in giving a solid introduction to various widely adopted machine learning techniques and serves as a simplified guide for the aspiring data and machine learning enthusiasts. This first section ends with the chapter "Machine Learning Applications in Nanomedicine and Nanotoxicology: An Overview" by Prof. Gerardo M. Casañola-Martin from North Dakota State

University, USA and Prof. Hai Pham-The of Hanoi University of Pharmacy, Vietnam, which discusses the recent advances in the conjunction of machine learning with nanomedicine.

Section 2, "Development and Design Methodologies," presents in-depth coverage of the design and development of machine learning techniques for their use in different applications. This section starts with the chapter "Classification and Machine Learning" by Prof. Damian Alberto from the Indian Institute of Technology Bombay, India, which addresses the classification concept in detail and discusses how to solve different classification problems using different machine learning techniques. This section ends with "A Process for Increasing the Samples of Coffee Rust Through Machine Learning Methods" by Prof. David Camilo Corrales from the University of Cauca, Colombia & Carlos III University of Madrid, Spain and Profs. Juan Carlos Corrales and Jhonn Pablo Rodríguez from the University of Cauca, Colombia, which describes how coffee rust has become a serious concern for many coffee farmers and manufacturers and provides a process about coffee rust to select appropriate machine learning methods to increase rust samples.

Section 3, "Tools and Technologies," explores the various tools and technologies utilized in the implementation of machine learning for various uses. This section begins with "Artificial Intelligence and Machine Learning Algorithms" by Prof. Amit Kumar Tyagi from Vellore Institute of Technology, India and Prof. Poonam Chahal of MRIIRS, India, which considers how machine learning and deep learning techniques and algorithms are utilized in today's world. This section closes with the chapter "Identifying Patterns in Fresh Produce Purchases: The Application of Machine Learning Techniques" by Profs. Malgorzata W. Korolkiewicz, Timofei Bogomolov, and Svetlana Bogomolova from the University of South Australia, Australia, which applies machine learning techniques to examine consumer food choices, specifically purchasing patterns in relation to fresh fruit and vegetables.

Section 4, "Utilization and Applications," describes how machine learning is used and applied in diverse industries for various technologies and applications. The opening chapter in this section, "Machine Learning Algorithms," by Profs. Namrata Dhanda and Stuti Shukla Datta from Amity University, India and Prof. Mudrika Dhanda from Royal Holloway University, UK, introduces the concept of machine learning and the commonly employed learning algorithm for developing efficient and intelligent systems. The closing chapter in this section, "Classification of Traffic Events in Mexico City Using Machine Learning and Volunteered Geographic Information," by Profs. Magdalena Saldana-Perez, Miguel Torres-Ruiz, and Marco Moreno-Ibarra from Instituto Politecnico Nacional, Mexico, implements a traffic event classification methodology to analyze volunteered geographic information and internet information related to traffic events with a view to identify the main traffic problems in a city and to visualize the congested roads.

Section 5, "Organizational and Social Implications," includes chapters discussing the impact of machine learning on society and business. The opening chapter, "Challenges and Applications for Implementing Machine Learning in Computer Vision: Machine Learning Applications and Approaches," by Prof. Hiral R. Patel from Ganpat University, India; Prof. Ajay M. Patel of AMPICS, India; and Prof. Satyen M. Parikh from FCA, India, discusses the fundamentals of machine learning and considers why it is important. The closing chapter, "Machine Learning Based Program to Prevent Hospitalizations and Reduce Costs in the Colombian Statutory Health Care System," by Prof. Alvaro J. Riascos from the University of los Andes and Quantil, Colombia and Prof. Natalia Serna of the University of Wisconsin-Madison, USA, suggests a hospitalization prevention program in which the decision of whether to intervene on a patient depends on a simple decision model and the prediction of the patient risk of an annual length-of-stay using machine learning techniques.

Section 6, "Emerging Trends," highlights areas for future research within the machine learning field. Opening this final section is the chapter "Current Trends: Machine Learning and AI in IoT" by Profs. Jayanthi Jagannathan and Anitha Elavarasi S. from Sona College of Technology, India, which addresses the key role of machine learning and artificial intelligence for various applications of the internet of things. The final chapter in this section, "The Role and Applications of Machine Learning in Future Self-Organizing Cellular Networks," by Profs. Muhammad Ali Imran, Paulo Valente Klaine, and Oluwakayode Onireti from the University of Glasgow, UK and Prof. Richard Demo Souza of Federal University of Santa Catarina (UFSC), Brazil, provides a brief overview of the role and applications of machine learning algorithms in future wireless cellular networks, specifically in the context of self-organizing networks.

Although the primary organization of the contents in this multi-volume work is based on its six sections, offering a progression of coverage of the important concepts, methodologies, technologies, applications, social issues, and emerging trends, the reader can also identify specific contents by utilizing the extensive indexing system listed at the end of each volume. As a comprehensive collection of research on the latest findings related to machine learning, the *Research Anthology on Machine Learning Techniques, Methods, and Applications* provides computer scientists, managers, researchers, scholars, practitioners, academicians, instructors, and students with a complete understanding of the applications and impacts of machine learning techniques. Given the vast number of issues concerning usage, failure, success, strategies, and applications of machine learning, the *Research Anthology on Machine Learning Techniques, Methods, and Applications* encompasses the most pertinent research on the applications, impacts, uses, and development of machine learning.

Chapter 52

A Comparative Review of Various Machine Learning Approaches for Improving the Performance of Stego Anomaly Detection

Hemalatha Jeyaprakash
Thiagarajar College of Engineering, India

KavithaDevi M. K.
Thiagarajar College of Engineering, India

Geetha S.
VIT University, India

ABSTRACT

In recent years, steganalyzers are intelligently detecting the stego images with high detection rate using high dimensional cover representation. And so the steganographers are working towards this issue to protect the cover element dependency and to protect the detection of hiding secret messages. Any steganalysis algorithm may achieve its success in two ways: 1) extracting the most sensitive features to expose the footprints of message hiding; 2) designing or building an effective classifier engine to favorably detect the stego images through learning all the stego sensitive features. In this chapter, the authors improve the stego anomaly detection using the second approach. This chapter presents a comparative review of application of the machine learning tools for steganalysis problem and recommends the best classifier that produces a superior detection rate.

DOI: 10.4018/978-1-6684-6291-1.ch052

INTRODUCTION

Steganographers aim is to conceal some undisclosed message inside an innocuous cover file known as digital images, and later it could be send via an unconfident channel as a stego file. In contrary, the anomaly detection called steganalysis aims to detect the presence of steganogram. In the last two decades, both the steganography and steganalysis experienced a precipitous development. There are three reasons are there why the research on steganalysis has attained a greater attention. Originally, sensing the occurrence of hidden messages, that can be castoff as a clandestine communication among terrorists or illegal groups. Then the greater achievement of steganalysis aids to increase the security of information hiding/steganography and watermarking. Steganalysis finds to be helpful in computer forensics, cyber warfare, criminal activities and etc. At last, it stimulates the researchers to construct the enhanced numerical model for multimedia which leads to the great successful application on other fields such as digital forensics. In the recent works, the best detectors are known to be the supervised learning for detecting the steganographic methods. In this chapter, we propose to study several recent machine learning algorithms available for steganalysis of images. The objective of this chapter is to present the efficiency of using machine learning algorithms in detecting stego objects.

Since many image formats are hugely available on the communication networks, JPEG images are the utmost frequently castoff images for data hiding purpose. The primarily steganographic procedures opted for the JPEG format was JSteg (Upham, n.d.), Outguess (Provos et al., 2001), F5 (Westfeld et al. 2001), Steghide (Hetzl et al., 2005) followed by Model-based Steganography (Sallee et al., 2005). Thereby Outguess and JSTEG obviously alters the DCT coefficient histogram, whereas the ancient attacks purely depended on first-order statistics of DCT (Discrete Cosine Transform) coefficients (Zhang et al., 2003). After, substantially more promising detectors were designed as possibility ratio trials with an id of well DCT coefficient cover models (Thai et al., 2015; Hastie et al, 2009).

The promising detectors for F5 and nsF5 (Fridrich et al., 2007) along with for Steghide, Model-Based Steganography are presently designed as classifiers skilled on features since DCT-quantized coefficients, the JRM (JPEG Rich Model) (Kodovský et al., 2012). When the features are mined from the residuals in the spatial domain, namely JPEG – phase – aware features, J-UNIWARD and UED (Guo et. 2012; Lerch-Hostalot et al., 2016) are perfectly detected by using such a feature-based model. Example of such features is GFR (Song et al., 2015), PHARM (Holub et al., 2015), DCTR (Holub et al., 2015) and etc. The concept of such a design is the JPEG phase notion, which is, the residual location in the 8*8 grid of JPEG. By rending the informations gathered from the residuals by their segment, further promising stego detector can be built.

Steganographic Methods

- **Steghide:** The practical LSB implementation for images and audios are dome by Steghide. It may modify the original algorithm by adds a graph to lessen the amount of pixel modification. To enhance the hiding security, the hidden messages are properly encrypted and compressed before the message is embedded. Following that pseudo-random sequence is generated equation the passphrase as seed. This corresponding sequence belongs to the image pixels and the LSB bits are modified the sequence message bits. To enhance the visual imperceptibility, the LBS bit that differ from the message bit is considered for exchange. This may handle by a graph where every vertex represents the change and every 20 edges is a successful exchange. At the end, the balanced message bits are hidden y replacing the corresponding LSB.

- **LSB matching Revisited:** It customs the couple of pixels as an entrenching part. Binary function (decrement or increment) is used to hide a bit pairs.

- **Model-Based:** The research based on Model-Based steganographic algorithm will preserve the distribution of an image as well as the distribution coefficients. The distribution values have been estimated by using the conditional probability.

- **Edge Adaptive LSB Matching Revisited:** This approach is same as pixel pair, where the data embedding is carried out by regions. At first, the given image is divided by random block size. The random rotation is applied to the block for improving the security. Pixel pair in the threshold is considered and binary function is used for hiding the message.

- **F5 Steganography:** F5 steganography is a transform domain hiding algorithm where password starts a pseudo-random number generator used for permuting DCT coefficients. Then bits are embedded in the certain coefficients based on matrix encoding. To perform such an operation image coefficients are used as a code word with modifiable bits for message bits. Then by using a hash function, the message bits are entrenched with the XOR operation, in the sequence manner. When the message is embedded each time, when the sum is not zero then is the corresponding result the index of the coefficient that must be changed and also the consistent value is decrement, on the other hand, the code word remains are the same. At last, JPEG compression continues followed by the reverted permutation.

- **Spread Spectrum:** Spread spectrum is mainly developed for the purpose of military appliances to reduce the signal jam and interruptions. An example of spread spectrum is frequency hopping. In the case of frequency hopping, message bits are divided and sent via various frequencies controlled by a key. Using spread spectrum in an image, the message bits are modulated as independent and distributed as the Gaussian sequence then the embedding takes place.

Approaches of Steganalysis

The steganalysis finder can be constructed by means of two approaches. The initial approach is numerical signal detection. From the arithmetical perfect of the concealment source, the detector is derived and detector performance error will be obtained. Normalized statistical detection is less sensitive in finding differences among cover sources. Instead adopted cover model is used but it confines the indicator optimality and rationality error to the chosen cover model (Ker et al., 2006). Hence by using this simple model, we could not capture the entire associations between the separate image basics acquired using image sensors. Moreover, it has been successful in detecting the simple embedding operations such as LSB embedding and matching (Hostalot et al., 2013;Zhang et al., 2010; Chen et al., 2016). But it quite difficult in detecting complex and content adaptive steganographic algorithms such as wavelet obtained weights (WOW) (Fridrich et al., 2011), Highly undetectable SteGo HUGO (HUGO) (Pevny et al., 2010), HUGO BD, Universal Wavelet Relative Distortion (UNIWARD) (Houlb et al., 2014), edge adaptive because it is infeasible to measure the local model parameters for highly non-stationary natural images.

Another approach is to consider as a classification problem (stego/clean), it does not need any cover distribution. Individually, the image is characterized as a feature vector and hence it is a heuristic dimensionality reduction. Later by using any machine learning tool, the database consists of both stego and clean image is trained and testing. The key advantage of this approach is constructing detector for arbitrary embedding algorithms is easy. The disadvantage is that the classifiers may be imprecise when examining a particular image of unknown origin. Because it is not possible to have several samples from the concealment source and detect the steganographic channel for a time length.

Designing a practical steganalysis benchmark requires many choices. The first choice is to extract the statistical features (Ho et al., 1995) from each image. The goal of such extraction is to decrease the dimensionality of the space to analyze. It is known that extraction information is a destructive process because the projection is taken place from the image space to lower dimensional space this may cause the information destruction. In the steganalysers point of view, the extracted feature contains the most important relevant features. The second choice is to choose the most appropriate model in order to discriminate the stego image based on the useful devised features. In many cases supervised machine learning model is used for stego image classification.

General Classes of Steganalysis

Since the steganalysis aim is to notice the mere existence of message concealed in a suspicious medium, the field has developed towards improvements. The general types of steganalysis can be categorized as follows

Specific / Targeted Steganalysis

The hypothesis of this method is the steganographic embedding algorithm is already known before detection. It tries to analyze the images for detecting the hidden message and focus on the statistics/features which are modified by the steganographic algorithm.

In more detail, this type of techniques is recognized by examining the entrenching process and finding the image statistics. Accordingly such methods quietly in need of the meticulous embedding process. Hence such a method yields an actual precise result once used in contradiction of the target steganographic technique. Specific steganalysis techniques (Xiong et al., 2010) are used for detecting the secret messages from stego images undergone by steganographic embedding such as LSBM matching, JPEG compression, spread spectrum, and also for other transform domain (Chanu et al., 2012; Qian et al., 2015). Chi-Square is a first specific statistical steganalysis tool for detecting the message bits.

Blind/ Universal Steganalysis

Blind steganalysis aims to detect the stego images and it has been undergone with any type of steganographic algorithms. Blind steganalysers are restricted by the training data. Computational complexity is the severe problem as the training set grows. The limitation of such steganalysers depends on machine learning is that it depends on a range of training set characteristics. For example, for a JPEG image, the characteristics are the resolution, compression ratio, sensor noise and etc. Anyhow with the possible set of cover images, accurately the steganalysers should train.

Quantitative Steganalysis

Quantitative steganalysis intentions to predict the length of the clandestine communication that has been concealed in the cover medium. It is quite difficult to find the hidden message length other than the stego detection. This concept was familiarized by Chandramouli and Memon (2001). In detail, this method inventions to excerpt the further information around the hidden communication in the covert communication. So for many quantitative steganalysis in the literature aimed to goal a specific entrenching algorithm and successfully excerpt the payload information by means of some structural paradigm. In addition to that to calculate the stego message payload, modern steganalysers use supervised machine learning by using some useful set of features.

In the literature, many methods have been proposed for envisaging the stego payload. Nearly of the powerful methods are Sample Pair Analysis (SPA), Regular- Singular steganalysis (RS), Triple/ Quadruple and Difference Image Histogram (DIH) (Fridrich et al., 2001; Sorina et al., 2003; Tao et al., 2003). These methods are mainly focused on image structural correlation based on neighbor pixels characteristics and hence it is called as structural steganalysis. The basic knowledge for all these approaches is that the LSB flipping due to stego communication embedding which may affect the penetrating information of sample pair of signals. Likewise weighted stego (Fridrich et al., 2006), which finds the payload by using estimated cover version. To estimate the cover version, attributes such as local variance, saturation and etc. are used. The main problem of these algorithms is, even though it attains high accuracy, it targets only specific steganographic algorithm.

On the other hand, universal quantitative steganalysis, irrespective of the embedding algorithm used to embed and domain used to embed the stego message, it endeavors to find the secret message length. These works by extracting the useful set of image features and learn such a feature using supervised learning. Many research works have been done for extracting the sophisticated features (Shi et al., 2012; Xiaz et al., 2016) to find the advanced steganographic algorithms. These steganographic algorithms lead to disturbing the weaker enslavements among cover elements and later to find these, there is a need for complex statistical descriptors. But the problem is, the dimensionality is relatively high for such feature sets. A strong framework (Hou et al., 2016; Lerch-Hostalot et al., 2016; Sajedi et al., 2016) is required for handling such a dimensionality problem. Only a fewer research works have been proposed for universal quantitative steganalysis (Guan et al., 2011; Pevny et al., 2012).

Forensic Steganalysis

In addition to the quantitative steganalysis, forensic steganalysis target to obtain the actual concealed message. The first step needs for such a forensic steganalysers is their algorithm should support for universal steganalysis. Because once the detection is done on the corresponding image, then it is a need to know about the hiding algorithm of the particular image to extract the hidden message. In this case, forensic steganalysis is merely close to cryptanalysis.

Using a brute force search is the best method for determining the stego key. That is the dictionary attack and mining the allege communication when searching for a recognized leader as a sign that can originate athwart the stego key. Anyhow this will be unsuccessful when the entrenched informations does not have any detectable arrangement, and also it is very difficult to find because of the stego key, also entirely possible encryption key should be tested. Consequently the complexity of both encryption key space and product of stego size is proportional.

For the stego key search method Fridrich et al. (2012) show the embedding paradigm and whose entrenching device involves of the subsequent points.

1.   Hiding laterally a pseudo-random path engendered equation the stego key

2.   Bits are hidden as equivalences of separate pixels.

3.   In the needed case, pixels parity is change by means of an entrenching process.

By using PRNG (Pseudo Random Number Generator), random path selection has done that is broadcasted with a kernels consequent equation a passphrase or user defied stego key. PRNG (Pseudo Random Number Generator) output is used to create a pseudo-random walk over the pixels. Along the pseudo-random walk, the secret message is embedded as a bitstream element parity. This helps to change the element parity and hence it may probabilistic or deterministic (Shrivastava et al., 2013).

Feature Extraction

When designing classifier using machine learning, it is very helpful to represent images in some manner. Because signal dimensions are high and the stego-signal-to-noise ratio is very low. In the case of feature extraction, images are represented using features. For an effective steganalysis, this feature should sensitively react to steganographic embedding and it should be very insensitive to the image content. In this section, we introduce the most famous feature set done by the existing steganalysers especially in the image domain of spatial and JPEG.

Feature Extraction in Spatial Domain

Fundamentally noise residual values highly depend on the content other than the pixel values. For every pixel, noise residuals are calculated as differences among the pixel value and its predicted value obtained from the pixel neighbors. Based on this idea, from the spatial domain noise residuals, images are represented. Also, the noise residual has a limited dynamic range other than the pixels and hence the stego noise uses a larger SNR. Likewise, it has an advantage of easy in finding a well-fitting model. But the problem is the dimension of this signal is very high, proportional to the original image.

Due to steganographic embedding, the dependency of neighboring samples is disturbed. Hence it is not enough to extract a first order static from the residuals, needs to extract the joint statistics of residuals. To do this the residuals are first quantized into the small number of samples following that co-occurrence matrix (joint probability mass function) are formed. The problem with co-occurrence matrix is the number of co-occurrence bins will increase exponentially with the dimension of co-occurrence. In this section, we are going to discuss the two strong spatial domain feature sets.

Spatial Rich model (SRM) (Kodovsky et al., 2012; Fridrich et al., 2007) is a very strong and promising statistical descriptor of images. Four-dimensional co-occurrence matrices are formed with the quantized residuals and detection is done in a diverse content. Likewise, from the spatial domain, several feature sets are extracted. Subtractive pixel adjacency matrix and subtractive DCT coefficient adjacency matrix (SDAM) (Farsi et al., 2014) LLT histogram coefficient textural features and co-occurrence matrix (Xian et al., 2012) textural features of LLT coefficient histogram, co-occurrence matrix and etc.

Feature Extraction in Transform Domain

In this segment, we provide an evaluation of the feature mining methods for image universal steganalysis. Also, we mainly absorbed on the arithmetical characteristics mined as of the wavelet sub-band of an image. Then, Universal steganalysis is designed built on two choices namely 1. Feature extraction 2.

Classifier used for stego detection. So for numerous feature mining systems has been described based on discrete wavelet transform. In 2002, Farid et al. proposed the first universal steganalysis method. A examination image is disintegrated at three stages via QMF (Quadrature Mirror Filter). PDF (Probability distribution function) moments of each subband are mined from the sophisticated frequency wavelet subband coefficient, and also from log-linear prediction fault subband. And hence 72-dimensional features are generated and given as input to the FLD (Fisher Linear Discriminant) classifier for stego detection. Later Farid's feature set has been extended by Lfu and Farid et al (2004), to extract 216 features from first and higher order color wavelet statistics. The classifier used to discriminate the stego image is one- class SVM (Support Vector Machine). Similarly, four-level dwt has used to (Shunquan Tan et al., 2014) to capture PDF moment of wavelet coefficient subband and log-linear prediction error subband.

Guoming et al (2012) extracted the wavelet transformation based features by decomposing an image into three levels using Haar discrete wavelet transform. Likewise, Xiangyand et al. (2011) decomposed an image into three levels to gather 255 features collected of absolute characteristic function moment of histograms obtained from 85 coefficient of each subband. To distinguish the stego images from cover, a back propagation neural network was used.

To capture the first three CF (characteristic Function) moment of wavelet subband, Xuan et al. (2005) disintegrated an image into three stages and the resulting 39 features are given as input to Bayes classifier to organize the stego images. The method proposed by Holotyak et al. (2005) calculated the stego wavelet subband by using message estimation method. PDF moment of higher frequency wavelet coefficient subbands of stego version is mined as 33-dimensional features. Finally FLD 9Filsher Linear Discriminant) is used as a classifier for discriminating the stego version from the clean one. Moreover, Yang et al. (2011) estimated the absolute CF (Characteristic Function) and PDF moments by hypothetical examination and to finding the more sensitive feature to embed the stego message. And their experimental founding's shown that CF moments attained from prediction subband, high-frequency wavelet subband, prediction error subband or wavelet coefficient subband of image noise are additional complex to stego message embedding's rather than the PDF moments. Also aimed at the log prediction fault subband, first order CF moments are not healthier than the PDF moments.

Machine Learning

Support Vector Machine

Support vector machines are a good and more promising algorithm for detecting the stego images. Basically, SVM is a linear and binary learner, when to solve the nonlinear problems; the kernel is used to convert it to linear which can map the feature vector into high dimensional spaces. SVM enlarges the margin of the data samples in two different classes. The success of SVM purely depends on the kernel function. Kernels are used to convert the input data into higher dimensional space; hence decision boundaries are made. The problem of SVM is, for the moderate six problems, the SVM training complexity slows down the development cycle and kernels gram matrix is

Gran matrix = (Feature dimension × size of training set)^2.

This may restrict the steganalyst to deliberately project the features set that fitting in the involvedness problems. In other words, training an SVM classifier their complexity cultivates by means of the cube of the amount of features and training examples. The easily solvable problem need of fewer support vectors and thus training process is quick, but in the case of highly overlapped features number of support, vectors are needed to train the samples and hence it is very time-consuming. For a classification problem, based on the amount of features and support vectors complexity grows linearly. As alternative ensemble classifiers significantly give freedom to the steganalyst without any concern about the feature dimension, the training set size and build detectors with a faster development cycle.

Deepa et al. (2016) proposed the steganalysis scheme for wow stego images. Using SPAM and CC-CHEN features set the stego images created by WOW steganographic scheme are detected. To classify the stego images SVM classifier has been used. In Muthuramalingam et al. proposed the steganalysis system built on low dimensional informative features. With the idea of curvelet, sub band image representation provides the discrimination ability; features are formed from the empirical moments. Support vector machine has been employed to distinguish the stego images from the clean images. And their results are outperforming than the previous steganalysis methods. Likewise, support vector machine has been used as a classifier with various kernel functions in stego image detection by many authors such as (Liu Shaohui et al., 2003; Cogranne et al., 2015; Pathak et al., 2014; Shankar et al., 2016).

Artificial Neural Networks (ANNs)

Since in the past little decade neural networks are proficiently used in stego image detection. Artificial neural networks are familiar with significant data analysis tools. It accurately captures both linear and nonlinear models and also it is said to be a powerful tool for data clustering, classification, function approximation and etc. We will see how the authors are using the ANNs in stego detection. Since ANN is a mathematical-like model that pretends the whole structure as of biological neural scheme. It adopts some of the features of the natural nervous system which is a collection of computing units called neurons. These neurons were embodied as the biological model into the conceptual component for circuits which can do the operational tasks. The simple model of the neuron is originated upon the functionality of a natural neuron. ANN comprises of an interrelated collection of artificial neurons and practices data by means of a connectionist method of reckoning. Such model illustrates tough similarity to axons and dendrites in a nervous system. Flexibility, Robustness, collective computation is the gorgeous structures of this model, owing to its self-organizing and adaptive nature. An artificial neuron consists of three interesting basic components; 1. Neurons Synapses are showed as weights. The aforementioned interrelates the neural networks and supports the connection. Here weight is assigned by a number and synapse is represented. 2. The positive value of a weight designates excitatory connection and the negative weight designates inhibitory connection. Hence all the inputs are added together and the modified by weights and it is referred as the linear combination. 3. At last, the amplitude of an output is measured by an activation function. For illustration, the yield is accepted when it is range between 0 and 1 or it could be between -1 and 1.

The structure of a network node looks like a differential equation. The connection among the nodes is either interconnected between nearest layers are interconnected with nearest neurons in the same layer. An activation value outputs from a previous layer is given as an input into the nodes of the subsequent layers. The activation value from an activation function is passed over non- linear function. If the vectors are analog in nature then squash function ID considered, on the other hand, if the vectors are binary of polar then hard – limiting non-linearity is considered. Some of the quash function are given as tanh (+1 or -1), sigmoid (0 or 1), logarithmic, exponential and Gaussian. Likewise, the network is considered either analog or discrete. The analog network is allied with continuous output whereas the discrete network is allied with two states. The discrete network can be considered as synchronous when each neuron state is updated in the network. Then again, the discrete network is considered as asynchronous, when only one particular is updated for a given time.

A feed-forward network delivers input to the following layer with no closed chain of dependence among neural states via a weight set. The entire network is set as static when the network output depends upon the current input, whereas the entire network is set a dynamic if the output depends on the past input or output. Likewise based on the time factor the network is called as adaptive or non-adaptive. In the case of adaptive the interconnection among neurons changes with time, on the other hand, the network is called as non-adaptive when it is not undergone any changes with time.

In the practical scenario, most of the patterns are not separate linearly. In order to achieve virtuous separability nonlinear classifiers are mostly used for pattern classification. The multilayer network is a nonlinear classifier (e.g. Polynomial discriminate function - pdf) since it uses hidden layer. In the case of the polynomial discriminate function, the input vector is basically preprocessed. In practical, neural networks are used for classifying the patterns by learning some samples. To learn the patterns several weight updating methods have been developed so far, that is supervised and unsupervised methods. When both input and output are considered then the problem is dealt under supervised learning methodology whereas in the case of unsupervised learning, the input will be available and target output cannot be provided. Once the sum of the excitatory inputs reaches its threshold value then a neuron is said to be fired. Until the neurons receive any input then this state always remains valid. This model can be used to hypothesis a network which can compute any logical function, but this was un-biological. To overcome such a model deficiency, a model was proposed to learn and generalize.

To scrutinize the texture of the pixel within the neighborhood plane, Lafferty et al. (2004) proposed a steganalysis method based on local binary pattern texture operator. It computes the statistics of pixels among neighbors, the correlation between neighbors. Also, first order statistics and delta among histogram bins are used as features. And back propagation neural networks are used for training and testing the clean and stego images. Likewise, neural networks are used by many authors in stego detection on different domains (Shaohui et al., 2003); Davidson et al., 2005; Sabeti et al., 2010).

Ensemble Classifier

As current steganalysis, have faith in on progressively complicated image models, so there is a need of scalable machine learning tool. To discourse the issue of complexity, an ensemble classifier is used. This background constructed as a combination of judgments of weak base learners. In Kodovský et al., (2011) Kodovský et al. (2014), Kodovský et al. (2012), Fridrich et al. (2011), Tao et al. (2003), and Pevny et al. (2010), the authors used an ensemble classifier as a fully automatized framework and the ensemble classifier research area gets bloomed up.

Ensemble classifiers consist of many individual trained base learners. From the feature space F, unpretentious classifiers are constructed based on the subspaces which are randomly selected. The dimension chosen by the random subspaces are quite smaller than the entire dimension d and thus the training complexity has greatly reduced. Ensemble classifier is finely trained by using training set and when a new unseen test image is given, each base learner will give its own decision and the final decision will be given by accumulating all the decisions given by each base learner. Since the base learner has chosen are the weak base learner, the performance was given by each base learner also weak, but the accuracy of aggregation is an improved one. This strategy will work only in the case of individual base learners are adequately miscellaneous in the sense that makes the error for an unseen new data. In the hope of increasing the mutual diversity of base learners, each base learner is trained in a bootstrap manner, whereas some samples are drawn from the training set other than the complete training set. This is termed as aggregating or bagging which may allow attaining the testing error accurately. We will go little bit deep for explain the full concept of Ensemble classifier.

As an alternative to SVM, the Fisher Linear Discriminant (FLD) ensemble classifier was initially anticipated (Cogranne et al., 2015) as a scalable learning tool which works as a promising detector in high dimensional feature spaces besides set of the huge size of training set. Assume that from an image, $f \in \mathbb{R}^d$ be a row vector of features d mined. Both training and testing set contains cover and stego image features whereas, the features of stego and cover of training set be matrices $N^{training} \times d$ size where the components of $c^{training}$ and $s^{training}$ respectively. FLD considers that between these two classes, means of features are μc_{over} and $\mu st_{ego,}$ covariance matrices are $\Sigma co_{ver a}$nd $\Sigma st_{ego o}$f size d×d. By using all these linear decisions rile is defined by:

$$R : \begin{cases} H_0 & if\ f.w^T - b < 0 \\ H_1 & if\ f.w^T - b > 0 \end{cases} \tag{1}$$

where b is a threshold, f is a row vector, the FLD determines the weight vector $w \in R^d$ which maximizes the below fisher ratio:

$$Fisher\ ratio\ F(w) : \frac{w\left(\mu_{cover} - \mu_{stego}\right)^T \left(\mu_{cover} - \mu_{stego}\right)w^T}{w\left(\Sigma_{cover} + \Sigma_{stego}\right)w^T} \tag{2}$$

Some experimental observations illustrates that the maximization of fisher ratio from the training samples hints to the resulting weight vector w.

$$w = \left(\hat{\mu}_{stego} - \hat{\mu}_{cover}\right)\left(\hat{\Sigma}_{cover} + \hat{\Sigma}_{stego}\right)^{-1} \tag{3}$$

with

$$\hat{\mu}_{cover_i} = \frac{1}{N_{training}} \sum_{n=1}^{N_{training}} cover_{n,i}^{training},$$

$$\hat{\mu}_{stego_i} = \frac{1}{N_{training}} \sum_{n=1}^{N_{training}} stego_{n,i}^{training},$$

$$\hat{\Sigma}_{\text{cover}_{n,i}} = \frac{1}{N_{training} - 1} \sum_{n=1}^{N_{training}} \left(\text{cover}_{n,i}^{training} - \hat{\mu}_{\text{cover}_i}\right)\left(\text{cover}_{n,j}^{training} - \hat{\mu}_{\text{cover}_j}\right),$$

$$\hat{\Sigma}_{stego_{n,i}} = \frac{1}{N_{training} - 1} \sum_{n=1}^{N_{training}} \left(stego_{n,i}^{training} - \hat{\mu}_{stego_i}\right)\left(stego_{n,j}^{training} - \hat{\mu}_{stego_j}\right)$$

Let I_d be an identity matrix of size $d{\times}d$, the inversion of the covariance matrix "between class" is performed directly but in most of the cases, to improve numerical stability λI_d is added with covariance matrix and hence $\hat{\Sigma}_{\text{cover}} + \hat{\Sigma}_{\text{cover}} + \lambda I_d$. In the case of feature space dimensionality d and the amount of training samples $N^{training}$, order of magnitude is similar then the covariance matrix of between-class is often ill-conditioned. Fisher Linear Discriminant ensemble is a set of L base learners which can be trained on equally randomly selected dimensional subsets of the feature space. To diversify the base learners, such an approach was initially used with decision trees. It works on the majority voting process. That is an ensemble gives a final assessment by combining all the decisions given by all the base learners by means of majority voting. The training scale of the ensemble is a good enough one because of $d_{sub} {\ll} d$. Either by using cross-validation set or bootstrapping d_{sub} and L is determined.

In some of the works, the rule of majority voting has substituted with a likelihood ratio. Once the majority voting rule is replaced with LRT then automatically the ensemble turns into a linear classifier. And also both the linear and nonlinear FLD ensemble classifier performance are same. Truly, there is no difference between linear and nonlinear when the high dimensional rich image model decision boundary is near to linear. In the current digital image steganography scenario, the linear classifier may accomplish the identical classification precision as near as the original majority voting – FLD ensemble classifier. Then it makes us rise a question as there exist any simpler approaches based on FLD. Hence four linear classifiers are there such as Ridge regression, l2 regularization of Fisher ratio, solving LLS with LSMR and LASSO regularization.

1. L2 Regularization of Fisher Ratio

The fisher ratio from L2 regularization can be accomplished by interchanging the Fisher ratio intensification with

$$w = \arg\min F\left(w\right)^{-1} + \lambda \parallel w \parallel_2^2$$

This may lead to the identical weight vector as the w which can attained using Tikhonov regularization.

$$w = \left(\hat{\mu}_{stego} - \hat{\mu}_{\text{cover}}\right)\left(\hat{\Sigma}_{\text{cover}} + \hat{\Sigma}_{stego} + \lambda I_d\right)^{-1} \tag{4}$$

2. Ridge Regression

The other name of Ridge regression is denoted as Tikhonov regularization- least square estimation. For further explaining this classifier, consider the training samples in a matrix as

$$X = \begin{pmatrix} c^{training} \\ s^{training} \end{pmatrix} \tag{5}$$

And it's label vector $y \in R^{2N^{training}}$ which defines the corresponding class of the examples as of x. Where y= (-1-1-1...+1+1+1...)^T. Its aim is to find a weighting vector w_{rr} which can minimize the squared error between actual and the estimated label.

$$w_{rr.} = \arg\min_{w \in \mathbb{R}^d} \| y - Xw^T \|_2^2 + \lambda \| w \|_2^2 \tag{6}$$

3. Solving LLS With LSMR (Least Square Minimum Residual)

On the availability of the large set of optimization methods for solving the linear system, the ridge regression can be implemented using a large optimization method called LSMR. The reason for using LSMR is, this having low computational complexity and also there is a requirement of little memory space. This may involve us in finding regularization λ and forbearance used in LSMR parameter. This greatly panels the trade-off among computational effectiveness and optimal solution.

4. LASSO Regularization

Machine learning group always prefers to use l_1 regularization because of generating the sparse solution and identifying a feature set of linear classifiers and hence it is called as LASSO (Least Absolute Shrinkage and Selection Operator).

Deep Learning

In the preceding few decades deep learning (Krizhevsky et al., 2012; Russakovsky et al., 2015; Szegedy et al., 2015) is the emerging area and it is said to be a particularly promising alternate to steganalysers depends on the rich models of the image with ensemble classifiers. Convolution Neural networks (CNN) is an approach to Deep learning which acts as steganalysers with a set of useful features and new classification procedures. Detection takes place based on 2d shape variation and also is used in many pattern recognition problems. Couchot et al.(2016) proposed a CNN based steganalysis system which entrenches fewer convolutions and larger filters in the final layer of convolution. It efficiently deals with larger payload and outperforms other steganalysis systems with same embedding key. In some steganographic schemes, DNA sequences have been used as a cover medium to hide medium to cover the secret messages. Due to DNA's complex internal structure, hidden message detection is difficult. To detect such a method the author proposed deep recurrent neural network to detect DNA steganalysis. Likewise, Wu et al. proposed deep residual learning based network to catch complex statistics and also preserves stego signal. In addition to that even though there is a cover source mismatch, Pibre et al. (2016) convolution neural network and fully connected neural network are very robust to mismatch problem and their results have been shown that very promising in detecting the stego images than the state of the art steganalysis. In (2017) Sedighi et al. proposed an optimized method for rich features. Since the availability of CNN packages, the feature set such as the projection of spatial rich features are optimized and simulated a new histogram layer from the quantized noise residuals.

Recent many published works on using CNN's mainly focus on detecting spatial domain steganography only (Shuang et al., 2007; Qian et al., 2015; Qian et al., 2016; Thai et al., 2014; Xu et al., 2016a, 2016b). Even though JPEG steganography is more conveniently used in practice, there is a gap on applying CNN for detecting such a JPEG steganography domain schemes. To fill this gap Zeng et al. (2017) proposed a hybrid CNN optimized method upon several DCT quantized sub-bands of decompressed input image files. Three convolutional layers are used in this method and also employed an average pooling that usually appears in spatial domain steganalysis. The experiment has been carried out on 14 million images collected from the Image Net Database and their results showed up that, because of using the huge number of training data, CNN outperforms the usual feature- based steganalysis methods in detecting JPEG steganography schemes. Later Xu et al. (2017) articulate that using "shallow architecture and average pooling layers are too conservative" in bringing the full strength of deep learning. Little more deeply discuss that, spatial domain steganography directly changes the pixel values of an image and hence CNN is very powerful in mining such a local pattern, run the peril of learning the hiding patterns that would ultimately damage the generality of the trained models.

To solve this, authors (Xu et al., 2017; Xu et al., 2016) designed a CNN framework to distinguish the most powerful JPEG steganography method – J-UNIWARD (JPEG universal wavelet relative distortion). The experiment has been conducted on BOSS base database images compressed with JPEG QF (Quality Factor) of 75 and 95. Each compressed image has embedded in J-UNIWARD steganography method using Gibbs simulator with all the rates of 0.1-0.4 bpnzAC (bits per non zero AC Coefficients). Their results discovered that the designed 20 layer CNN worked with batch normalization, shortcut connections for worthy gradient back propagation has more promising performance that the state-of-the-art feature based steganalysers and also 20 layers CNN has cut down error rate by 35% than the large-scale JPEG steganalysis (Zeng et al., 2017).

The architecture of the work is as follow. To project each input into 16 various frequency bands, 4×4 un-decimated DCT was used. When the study has been done in this research various DCT sizes are used such as 2×2, 4×4, 3×3, 5×5 and 8×8 but the best result was obtained in the DCT size 4×4. Also, no exact improvement has been observed when removing the highest frequency subbands or DC subband. For the feature extraction purpose, magnitudes of subbands and quantization have been used. The subbands are truncated with a global threshold value of 8 and it greatly helps to prevent some information loss. Truncation is an important step to limit the range of input data and also it attains fast convergence. Ensuring these pre-processing steps is the essential portion of the CNN encompassing 20 convolutional layers plus a global- average pooling layer. This may help the classifier to learn the optimized function to transform every preprocessed input into the 384-dimensional feature vector. To decrease the internal covariant shift and Rectified Linear Unit (ReLU), Batch Normalization (BN) has used. GPUs memory has been fit with12GB memory and single GPU and the convolution kernel used was 3×3 along the spatial dimension.

FEATURE NORMALIZATION

At present, the more promising feature set designed to steganalysis is rich models comprises of co-occurrences (joint probability mass function) of neighboring noise residuals extracted using a bulk of nonlinear and linear pixel predictors. Owing to the problem of features cure of dimensionality and more training complexity, we are in need of low complexity machine such as ensemble classifier (Kodovsky et al., 2014), regularized linear discriminates (Cogranne et al., 2015) and linear version (Cogranne et al., 2015). To achieve the better detection rate and to utilize the feature vector information without using any intricate machine learning tools is, performing a pre-processor transformation on the feature vector before given into classification. To separate the stego and cover features with a plain decision boundary non- linear feature transformation is used in Boroumand et al.(2016). This work was extended to assessing tacit feature maps in kernelized SVM with explicit transformation.

FEATURE SELECTION

In feature selection, the aim is to choose the features subgroup to form the original features to perform the best prediction scheme by confiscating the redundant and irrelevant features. This can be accomplished by appreciative the kindliness of the features in the direction of the steganographic algorithm which aids in plummeting the training time, the difficulty of the features and too aids in improving the classification/ prediction performance.

To improve the efficiency of classifiers, several feature selection methods have been discussed under three categories. 1. Filter approach, 2. Wrapper approach, 3. Hybrid approach. Filtering method assess the feature relevance depends on the numerical characteristic of information and ranks the features. Generally, features with high rank and high discriminatory capability are selected. For steganalysis, various filtering approaches have been proposed based on the distance measures such as Euclidean distance, Bhattacharya distance, and Mahalanobis distance. To remove the redundant features, information gain and mutual information are also proposed. Correlation-based Feature Selection Measures are there, it ranks the feature subsets instead of each feature. The concept behind is that, on behalf of a feature subgroup, it to be relevant each features must have the high correlation with its class variable. In some other research based on Analysis of Variance (ANOVA), the Image Quality Metrics (IQM) are ranked and the images were detected as stego or clean via multivariate regression analysis classifier.

Secondly method namely wrapper method which evaluates the feature subset effectiveness. For individually feature subgroup, the precision has been appraised and the combined features subset with maximum accuracy has been selected. In some steganalysis research, forward selection algorithm has been employed which begins with the best features and starts to add a new feature one by one, until the classifier identifies the maximum accuracy. This may help to overcome the exhaustive search need best it is not an effective one for high dimensional features. On the other hand, many research works have been done based on PSO (Particle Swarm Optimization), GA (Genetic Algorithm), ABC (Artificial Bee Colony) and etc.

The advantage of filtering method is that, its computation simplicity. It may give preference for the high dimensional feature selection as like as it provides good computational efficiency in terms of computational time and cost. Their advantage it does not depends on the classifier, that is it is difficult to know about the performance of the selected subset until a learning model is generated. On the other hand, wrapper approach gives good accuracy as it computes the performance of each feature subset and chooses the combination of feature set with maximum accuracy. The problem is that for the high dimensional feature set, it is computationally exclusive.

To overcome the problems of both wrapper and filtering approaches, hybrid approaches have gained consideration in the recent years. The idea is to use the filter approaches for selecting the feature subset and its output is given as an input into wrapper approach. In this case, the evaluation of wrapper approach is reduced the computational complexity and on the other hand, the enhanced precision may be retained. This hybrid approach has been realistic for various applications such as malware detection, steganalysis, biomedical, internet traffic classification and etc. But using hybrid approach for feature selection in steganalysis is still an unexplored area and also only less research work has been done.

On the emergent of deep learning, the usage of such a feature selection method for pattern recognition like research will be reduced because of not worrying about the size of data in the deep learning.

CONCLUSION

In this chapter, we have attempted to deliver a short introduction to machine learning algorithms used as a classifier in detecting the stego images. Many machine learning algorithms are used in the literature. Since many steganalysers try to detect the recent steganographic algorithms via a high dimensional feature set. Recently, ensemble learning and deep learning are the most promising and fastest learning methods and it is greatly free from the complexity problems. And also, even though the feature set contains lakhs of features and the training the system using lakhs of objects in the dataset, deep learning is the best tool to training such a larger of the amount of dataset. On the other hand to overcome the complexity of training time and space, handling the huge set of high dimensional features, the ensemble learning, and deep learning is the suggested one.

REFERENCES

Boroumand, M., & Fridrich, J. (2016). Boosting Steganalysis with Explicit Feature Maps. *Proceedings of 4th ACM Workshop on Information Hiding and Multimedia Security*. doi: 10.1145/2909827.2930803

Chandramouli, R., & Memon, N. (2001). Analysis of LSB based image steganography techniques. *Proceedings of ICIP 2001*. 10.1109/ICIP.2001.958299

Chanu, Singh, & Tuithung. (2012). Image Steganography and Steganalysis: A Survey. *International Journal of Computer Applications, 52*(2), 1-11.

Chen, X., Gao, G., Liu, D., & Xia, Z. (2016). Steganalysis of LSB Matching Using Characteristic Function Moment of Pixel Differences. Image Detection and Analysis Technique. *China Communications, 13*(7), 66–73. doi:10.1109/CC.2016.7559077

Cogranne, R., Denemark, T., & Fridrich, J. (2014). Theoretical model of the FLD ensemble classifier based on hypothesis testing theory. *IEEE International Workshop on Information Forensics and Security (WIFS)*, 167–172. 10.1109/WIFS.2014.7084322

Cogranne, R., & Fridrich, J. (2015). Modeling and extending the ensemble classifier for steganalysis of digital images using hypothesis testing theory. *IEEE Transactions on Information Forensics and Security, Volume, 10*(12), 2627–2642. doi:10.1109/TIFS.2015.2470220

Cogranne, R., Sedighi, V., Pevný, T., & Fridrich, J. (2015). Is Ensemble Classifier Needed for Steganalysis in High-Dimensional Feature Spaces? *IEEE International Workshop on Information Forensics and Security.* 10.1109/WIFS.2015.7368597

Couchot, J.-F., Couturier, R., Guyeux, C., & Salomon, M. (2016). *Steganalysis via a Convolutional Neural Networks using Large Convolution Filters for embedding process with same stego key.* Cornell University Library.

Davidson, Bergman, & Bartlett. (2005). An artificial neural network for wavelet steganalysis. *Proceedings of SPIE- The International Society for Optical Engineering, Mathematical method in Pattern and Image Analysis, 5916,* 1-10.

Deepa, S., & Uma Rani, R. (2016). Steganalysis on images based on the classification of image feature sets using SVM classifier. *International Journal on Computer Science and Engineering, 5*(5), 15–24.

Farid, H. (2002) Detecting hidden messages using higher-order statistical models. *Proceedings of IEEE International Conference Image Processing, 2,* 905–908. 10.1109/ICIP.2002.1040098

Farsi, H., & Shahi, A. (2014). Steganalysis of images based on spatial domain and two-dimensional JPEG array. *Journal of the Chinese Institute of EngineersVolume, 37*(8), 1055–1063. doi:10.1080/025 33839.2014.929711

Filler, T., & Fridrich, J. (2010). Gibbs Construction in Steganography. *IEEE Transactions on Information Forensics and Security, Volume, 5*(4), 705–720. doi:10.1109/TIFS.2010.2077629

Fridrich, J., & Goljan, M. (2006). On estimation of secret message length in LSB steganography in spatial domain. In Proceedings of Security, steganography, and watermarking of multimedia Contents VI. *Proceedings of the Society for Photo-Instrumentation Engineers, 5306,* 23–34. doi:10.1117/12.521350

Fridrich, J., Goljan, M., & Du, R. (2001). Detecting LSB steganography in color and gray-scale images. *IEEE MultiMedia, 8*(4), 22–28. doi:10.1109/93.959097

Fridrich, J., & Kodovský, J. (2012). Rich models for steganalysis of digital images. *IEEE Transactions on Information Forensics and Security, 7*(3), 868–882. doi:10.1109/TIFS.2012.2190402

Fridrich, J., Kodovský, J., Goljan, M., & Holub, V. (2011). Breaking HUGO – the process discovery. *Information Hiding, 13th International Workshop, 6958,* 85–101.

Fridrich, J., Kodovský, J., Goljan, M., & Holub, V. (2011). Steganalysis of content-adaptive steganography in spatial domain. *Information Hiding, 13th International Workshop, 6958,* 102–117. 10.1007/978-3-642-24178-9_8

Fridrich, J., Pevný, T., & Kodovský, J. (2007). Statistically Undetectable JPEG Steganography: Dead Ends, Challenges, and Opportunities. *Proceedings of the 9th ACM Multimedia & Security Workshop,* 3–14.

Guo, Ni, & Shi. (2014). Uniform Embedding for Efficient JPEG Steganography. *IEEE Transactions on Information Forensics and Security, 9*(5), 814–825. doi:10.1109/TIFS.2014.2312817

Guo, L., Ni, J., & Shi, Y.-Q. (2012). An Efficient JPEG Steganographic Scheme Using Uniform Embedding. *Proceedings of Fourth IEEE International Workshop on Information Forensics and Security.* 10.1109/WIFS.2012.6412644

Guoming, C., Qiang, C., Dong, Z., & Weighing, Z. (2012). *Particle swarm optimization feature selection for image steganalysis.* IEEE Computer Society.

Hastie, T., Tibshirani, R., Friedman, J., & Franklin, J. (2009). *The elements of statistical learning: data mining, inference and prediction* (2nd ed.). Springer. doi:10.1007/978-0-387-84858-7

Hetzl, S., & Mutzel, P. (2005). A Graph-Theoretic Approach to Steganography. *Communications and Multimedia Security, 9th IFIP TC-6 TC-11 International Conference, CMS 2005,* 119–128. 10.1007/11552055_12

Ho, T. K. (1995). Random decision forests. *Proceedings of International Conference on Document Analysis and Recognition,* 278–282.

Holotyak, T., Fridrich, J., & Voloshynovskiy, S. (2005). Blind statistical steganalysis of additive steganography using wavelet higher order statistics. *Proceedings of 9th IFIP Conference on Communication and Multimedia Security, LNCS 3677,* 273–274. 10.1007/11552055_31

Holub, V., & Fridrich, J. (2015). Low-Complexity Features for JPEG Steganalysis Using Undecimated DCT. *IEEE Transactions on Information Forensics and Security, 10*(2), 219–228. doi:10.1109/TIFS.2014.2364918

Holub, V., & Fridrich, J. (2015). Phase-Aware Projection Model for Steganalysis of JPEG Images. *Proceedings of SPIE, Electronic Imaging, Media Watermarking, Security, and Forensics 2015, 9409,* 1–11.

Holub, V., Fridrich, J., & Denemark, T. (2014). *Universal distortion function for steganography in an arbitrary domain.* EURASIP Journal on Information Security.

Hou, X., Zhang, T., & Xu, C. (2016). New framework for unsupervised universal steganalysis via SRISP-aided outlier detection. *Image Communication, 47C,* 72–85.

Ker, A. K. (2006). Fourth-order structural steganalysis and analysis of cover assumptions. Proceedings of SPIE 6072, Security, Steganography, and Watermarking of Multimedia Contents VIII, 6072, 1–14. doi:10.1117/12.642920

Kodovský, J., & Fridrich, J. (2011). Steganalysis in high dimensions: Fusing classifiers built on random subspaces. *Proceedings SPIE, Electronic Imaging, Media Watermarking, Security and Forensics of Multimedia XIII, 7880,* 1–13.

Kodovský, J., & Fridrich, J. (2012). Steganalysis of JPEG Images Using Rich Models. *Proceedings SPIE, Electronic Imaging, Media Watermarking, Security, and Forensics 2012, 8303.* 10.1117/12.907495

Kodovský, J., & Fridrich, J. (2012). Steganalysis of JPEG images using rich models. *Proceedings SPIE, Electronic Imaging, Media Watermarking, Security, and Forensics of Multimedia XIV.* 10.1117/12.907495

Kodovský, J., Fridrich, J., & Holub, V. (2012). Ensemble classifiers for steganalysis of digital media. *IEEE Transactions on Information Forensics and Security, 7*(2), 432–444. doi:10.1109/TIFS.2011.2175919

Krizhevsky, A., Sutskever, I., & Hinton, G. (2012). Imagenet classification with deep convolutional neural networks. Proceedings of Communications of the ACM, 60(6), 84-90.

Lafferty & Ahmed. (2004). Texture based steganalysis: results for color images. *Proceedings of SPIE, Mathematics of Data/Image Coding, compression and encryption VII with applications, 5561,* 145-151.

Lerch-Hostalot, D., & Megías, D. (2013). LSB matching steganalysis based on patterns of pixel differences and random embedding. *Computers & Security, 32,* 192–206. doi:10.1016/j.cose.2012.11.005

Lerch-Hostalot, D., & Megías, D. (2016) Unsupervised steganalysis based on artificial training sets. *Proceedings of EngApplArtifIntell, 50,* 45–59. 10.1016/j.engappai.2015.12.013

Liu, Q., Sung, A. H., Qiao, M., Chen, Z., & Ribeiro, B. (2010). An improved approach to steganalysis of JPEG images. *Information Sciences, 180*(9), 1643–1655. doi:10.1016/j.ins.2010.01.001

Liu, S., Yao, H., & Wen, G. (2003). Neural Network based steganalysis in Still Images. *Proceedings of IEEE International Conference on Multimedia and Expo (ICME),* 509-512. doi:10.1109/ICME.2003.1221665

Lyu, S., & Farid, H. (2004). Steganalysis using color wavelet statistics and one-class vector support Machines. Proceedings of SPIE security, steganography and watermarking of multimedia contents, 5306, 35–45. doi:10.1117/12.526012

Pathak & Selvakumar. (2014). Blind image steganalysis of JPEG images using feature extraction through the process of dilation. *Digital Investigation, 11,* 97–77.

Pevný, T., Filler, T., & Bas, P. (2010). Using high-dimensional image models to perform highly undetectable steganography. In *Information Hiding, 12th International Workshop, Lecture Notes in Computer Science.* Springer-Verlag. 10.1007/978-3-642-16435-4_13

Pevny, T., Fridrich, J., & Ker, A. D. (2012). From blind to quantitative Steganalysis. *IEEE Transactions on Information Forensics and Security, 7*(2), 445–454. doi:10.1109/TIFS.2011.2175918

Pibre, L., Pasquet, J., Ienco, D., & Chaumont, M. (2016). Deep learning is a good steganalysis tool when embedding key is reused for different images, even if there is a cover source-mismatch. *Proceedings of SPIE, IS&T International Symposium on Electronic Imaging, Media Watermarking, Security, and Forensics.* 10.2352/ISSN.2470-1173.2016.8.MWSF-078

Provos, N. (2001). Defending Against Statistical Steganalysis. *Proceedings of 10th USENIX Security Symposium,* 323–335.

Qian, Y., Dong, J., Wang, W., & Tan, T. (2015). Deep learning for steganalysis via convolutional neural networks. In *Proceeding of SPIE 9409.* Media Watermarking, Security, and Forensics. doi:10.1117/12.2083479

Qian, Y., Dong, J., Wang, W., & Tan, T. (2016). Learning and transferring representations for image steganalysis using convolutional neural network. *IEEE International Conference on Image Processing,* 2752–2756. DOI:10.1109/ICIP.2016.7532860

Russakovsky, O., Deng, J., Su, H., Krause, J., Satheesh, S., Ma, S., ... Li, F.-F. (2015). ImageNet large scale visual recognition challenge. *International Journal of Computer Vision, 115*(3), 211–252. doi:10.100711263-015-0816-y

Sabeti, V., Samavi, S., Mahdavi, M., & Shirani, S. (2010). Steganalysis and payload estimation of embedding in pixel differences using neural networks. *Pattern Recognition, 43*(1), 405–415. doi:10.1016/j.patcog.2009.06.006

Sajedi, H. (2016). Steganalysis based on steganography pattern discovery. *Journal of Information Security and Applications, 30*, 3–14. doi:10.1016/j.jisa.2016.04.001

Sallee, P. (2005). Model-Based Methods for Steganography and Steganalysis. *International Journal of Image and Graphics, 5*(1), 167–190. doi:10.1142/S0219467805001719

Sedighi, V., & Fridrich, J. (2017). Histogram Layer, Moving Convolutional Neural Networks Towards Feature Based Steganalysis. *Proceedings of IS&T, Electronic Imaging, Media Watermarking, Security, and Forensics.*

Shankar & Upadhyay. (2016). Performance analysis of various feature sets in calibrated blind steganalysis. *International Journal of Computer Science and Network Security, 16*(8), 29-34.

Shi, Y. Q., Sutthiwan, P., & Chen, L. (2012). Textural features for steganalysis. In *Information Hiding. 14th International Conference, IH 2012*. Springer.

Shrivastava, G., Pandey, A., & Sharma, K. (2013). Steganography and its technique: Technical overview. In *Proceedings of the Third International Conference on Trends in Information, Telecommunication and Computing* (pp. 615-620). Springer. 10.1007/978-1-4614-3363-7_74

Shuang, H. Z., & Hong, B. Z. (2007). Blind steganalysis using wavelet statistics and ANOVA. *Proceedings - International Conference on Machine Learning and Cybernetics, 5*, 2515–2519.

Song, X., Liu, F., Yang, C., Luo, X., & Zhang, Y. (2015). Steganalysis of Adaptive JPEG Steganography Using 2D Gabor Filters. *The 3rd ACM Workshop on Information Hiding and Multimedia Security (IH&MMSec '15).*

Sorina, D., Xiaolin, W., & Zhe, W. (2003). Detection of LSB steganography via sample pair analysis. *IEEE Transactions on Signal Processing, 51*(7), 1995–2007. doi:10.1109/TSP.2003.812753

Szegedy, Liu, Jia, Sermanet, Reed, Anguelov, ... Rabinovich. (2015). Going deeper with convolutions. *Proceedings of IEEE International Conference on Computer Vision and Pattern Recognition (CVPR)*, 1–9.

Tan, S., & Li, B. (2014). Stacked convolutional auto-encoders for steganalysis of digital images. *Signal and Information Processing Association Annual Summit and Conference (APSIPA)*. 10.1109/APSIPA.2014.7041565

Tao, Z., & Xijian, P. (2003). Reliable detection of LSB steganography based on the difference image histogram. *Proceedings of. IEEE International Conference on Acoustics, Speech, and Signal Processing*, 545–548.

Thai, T., Cogranne, R., & Retraint, F. (2014). Statistical Model of Quantized DCT Coefficients: Application in the Steganalysis of Jsteg Algorithm. *IEEE Transactions on Image Processing, 23*(5), 1–14. doi:10.1109/TIP.2014.2310126 PMID:24710399

Thai, T. H., Cogranne, R., & Retraint, F. (2014). Optimal Detection of OutGuess using an Accurate Model of DCT Coefficients. *Sixth IEEE International Workshop on Information Forensics and Security.* 10.1109/WIFS.2014.7084324

Upham, D. (n.d.). *Steganographic algorithm JSteg.* Retrieved from http://zooid.org/ paul/crypto/jsteg

Westfeld, A. (2001). High Capacity Despite Better Steganalysis (F5 – A Steganographic Algorithm). In *Information Hiding, 4th International Workshop* (Vol. 2137, pp. 289-302). Springer-Verlag.

Wu, S., Zhong, S., & Liu, Y. (2017). Deep residual learning for image steganalysis. *Multimedia Tools and Applications*, 1–17.

Xia, Z., Wang, X., Sun, X., Liu, Q., & Xiong, N. (2016). Steganalysis of LSB matching using differences between nonadjacent pixels. *Multimedia Tools and Applications, 75*(4), 1947–1962. doi:10.100711042-014-2381-8

Xiang, Y., & Zhang, W. H. (2012). Effective steganalysis of YASS based on statistical moments of wavelet characteristic function and Markov process. *Proceedings of International conference on computer science and electronics engineering*, 606–610. 10.1109/ICCSEE.2012.218

Xiangyang, L., Fenlin, L., Shiguo, L., Chunfang, Y., & Stefanos, G. (2011). On the typical statistic features for image blind steganalysis. *IEEE Journal on Selected Areas in Communications, 29*(7), 1404–1422. doi:10.1109/JSAC.2011.110807

Xiong, G., Ping, X., Zhang, T., & Hou, X. (2012). XiaodanHou. (2012). Image textural features for steganalysis of spatial domain steganography. *Journal of Electronic Imaging, 21*(3), 033015-1. doi:10.1117/1.JEI.21.3.033015

Xu, G. (2017). Deep Convolutional Neural Network to Detect J-UNIWARD. *Proceedings of 5th ACM Workshop Information Hiding Multimedia Security. (IH &MMSec).* 10.1145/3082031.3083236

Xu, G., Wu, H.-Z., & Shi, Y.-Q. (2016). Ensemble of CNNs for steganalysis: An empirical study. *Proceeding of 4th ACM Workshop on Information Hiding and Multimedia Security (IH&MMSec '16),* 103–107. DOI: 10.1145/2909827.2930798

Xu, G., Wu, H.-Z., & Shi, Y.-Q. (2016, May). Structural design of convolutional neural networks for steganalysis. *IEEE Signal Processing Letters, 23*(5), 708–712. doi:10.1109/LSP.2016.2548421

Xuan, G. R., Shi, Y. Q., & Gao, J. J. (2005). Steganalysis based on multiple features formed by statistical moments of wavelet characteristic functions. *Proc. 7th International Information Hiding Workshop, LNCS 3727,* 262–277. 10.1007/11558859_20

Zeng, J., Tan, S., Li, B., & Huang, J. (2017). *Large-scale JPEG image steganalysis using hybrid deep-learning framework.* arXiv: 1611.03233v2

Zhang, T., Li, W., Zhnag, Y., Zheng, E., & Ping, X. (2010). Steganalysis of LSB matching based on statistical modeling of pixel difference distributions. *Information Sciences*, *180*(23), 4685–4694. doi:10.1016/j.ins.2010.07.037

Zhang, T., & Ping, X. (2003). A Fast and Effective Steganalytic Technique AgainstJsteg-like Algorithms. *Proceedings of the ACM Symposium on Applied Computing*, 307–311.

This research was previously published in the Handbook of Research on Network Forensics and Analysis Techniques; pages 351-371, copyright year 2018 by Information Science Reference (an imprint of IGI Global).

Chapter 53
Wearable Devices Data for Activity Prediction Using Machine Learning Algorithms

Lakshmi Prayaga
University of West Florida, Pensacola, USA

Krishna Devulapalli
Indian Institute of Chemical Technology, Secunderabad, India

Chandra Prayaga
(iD) https://orcid.org/0000-0002-7534-4313
University of West Florida, Pensacola, USA

ABSTRACT

Wearable devices are contributing heavily towards the proliferation of data and creating a rich minefield for data analytics. Recent trends in the design of wearable devices include several embedded sensors which also provide useful data for many applications. This research presents results obtained from studying human-activity related data, collected from wearable devices. The activities considered for this study were working at the computer, standing and walking, standing, walking, walking up and down the stairs, and talking while walking. The research entails the use of a portion of the data to train machine learning algorithms and build a model. The rest of the data is used as test data for predicting the activity of an individual. Details of data collection, processing, and presentation are also discussed. After studying the literature and the data sets, a Random Forest machine learning algorithm was determined to be best applicable algorithm for analyzing data from wearable devices. The software used in this research includes the R statistical package and the SensorLog app.

1. INTRODUCTION AND MOTIVATION

Wearable devices can generate multiple types of data such as heart rate, accelerometer, and gyroscope values, location, etc. This data is useful across multiple disciplines, including health care, cybersecurity, user interface design, personalizing social preferences, etc. Healthcare is one such institution that

DOI: 10.4018/978-1-6684-6291-1.ch053

is leveraging this medium of data collection and performing analytics that is informative to healthcare providers, administrators, pharma companies and patients. Such analysis allows the audience in the domain of healthcare to maximize their returns either commercially or personally at an individual level.

Activity Recognition is an emerging field of research, born from the larger fields of ubiquitous computing, context-aware computing and pervasive computing (Pierluigi, Oriol & Petia, 2011; Sztyler & Stuckenschmidt, 2017). Recognizing everyday activities and its relation to overall wellness is generating a lot of interest in the research community of data scientists, pharmaceutical companies and healthcare professionals. Research also documents that monitoring physical activity in real life vs. a controlled environment provides a better context to evaluate patients and or other interested clients (Sztyler & Stuckenschmidt, 2016). The use of accelerometers and gyroscopes in wearable devices such as smartwatches and smartphones are now widely accepted for monitoring physical activity and tailoring interventions as needed (del Rosario, Redmond & Lovell, 2015; Akker, Jones, Hermens & Hermie, 2014), without purchasing expensive wearable ambulatory monitors. Smart phones have also proven to be extremely useful to monitor the activity levels of construction workers, a context which provides a wealth of information for project management related to their work (Akhavian & Behzadan, 2016).

Fitness tracking devices are gaining in popularity and new devices are entering the market at regular intervals. Wearable devices include accelerometers, Gyroscope, barometers, and altimeters to provide high-quality data which is useful for tracking posture, activity, HR, sleep, etc. (Henriksen et al., 2018). A wearable device has the potential to be integrated as an intervention to increase physical activity embedding it as a change to lifestyle (Ridgers et al., 2018; Cadmus-Bertram, 2017; Maher, Ryan, Ambrosi & Edney, 2017) Many of these devices are being used for data collection and research on various aspects related to individual health including monitoring physical activity, sleep quality, heart rate, etc. and their impact on patient health.

The literature reviewed cited above demonstrates that recent studies have analyzed accelerometer data and have investigated the data for physical activity recognition. Nevertheless, few of them have undertaken the difficult task of performing experiments out-of-the-lab. The conditions to perform experiments out-of-the-lab create the need to build easy to use and easy to wear systems to free the testers from the expensive task of labeling the activities they perform. This study attempts to address this challenge and afford the ability to generate and analyze data outside the lab in an open and free environment using data recorded by the accelerometer on wearable devices or cell phones. Data generated in such a format can be used to train models using machine learning algorithms and use the models to test new data.

Random Forest machine learning algorithm was used in this study. A review of recent literature suggests that when the Random Forest algorithm's performance was compared to other techniques such as support vector machine, C4.5 and *k*-nearest neighbor methods, Random forest was the most accurate and suitable for the analysis of data from wearable devices (Balli, Sağbaş & Peker, 2019; Henriksen et al., 2018; Zhang, Stogin & Alshurafa, 2018). Random Forest was also documented to be specifically reliable to predict the gait of a subject. (Ahamed et al., 2018) which is applicable to the current research. Random forest is one of the most popular machine learning algorithms. Machine learning algorithms are successful because they provide in general a good predictive performance, low overfitting, and easy interpretability. This interpretability is given by the fact that it is straightforward to derive the importance of each variable on the tree decision. In other words, it is easy to compute how much each variable is contributing to the decision. Random Forest algorithm has also yielded high accuracy in classification problems due to the identification of important features (Natarajan, Kumar & Selvaraj, 2018).

Data preparation and preprocessing using Random Forest involves feature selection, a process which we have used in our case and described in section 4 below. Feature selection algorithms fall into three categories: filters, wrappers, and embedded techniques. The Random forest algorithm fits into the embedded techniques category. Embedded methods combine the qualities of filter and wrapper methods. They are implemented by algorithms that have their own built-in feature selection methods. Some of the benefits of embedded methods are:

- They have a high accuracy
- They generalize better
- They are interpretable

R Language is an open source popular language for statistical analysis and for data science applications. R Language provides thousands of packages covering various applications. In the present study, the Random Forest package of R, which implements Breiman's random forest algorithm, was utilized for performing the calculations.

2. EXAMPLE USE CASES OF THIS STUDY

Studies show that nearly 40 million workers in Europe are diagnosed with Musculoskeletal disorders (MSD) attributed to their work due to repetitive movements and improper postures), and close to 40% of chronic conditions for patients over the age of 16 years was also attributed to MSD (Cammarota, 2003). Several studies have documented the efficacy and correlation of good posture in maintaining good health. McGinnis et al. (2017) cited other researchers documenting the correlation of maintaining good posture and reduction of stress levels, reduction of depression and other chronic conditions. These researchers have found that maintaining proper posture is a key element to ensure the overall quality of health of the human body. Additionally, when conditions such as fractures, muscle tears, and other bone and muscle related incidents happen, maintaining good posture is essential for speedy recovery.

When patients visit their physicians or health care providers with fractures and/or other related injuries, x-rays are used to determine the extent of the injury and appropriate treatment is provided to the patient. Healthcare providers are trained to determine the correct posture that the patient must strive to maintain to recover from the injury.

The problem, in this case, is that the patient does not know how to check if he/she is maintaining the right posture and if necessary, rectify the posture, until the next scheduled visit to the facility of the provider, who hosts expensive infrastructure and possesses the domain knowledge required to evaluate the patient. The physician then takes another set of x-rays, studies them and observes the patient's posture to determine the extent of improvement. If the posture is not conducive to a speedy recovery, the physician might again send the patient to a physiotherapist who can assist the patient to improve the posture. This cycle repeats over and over again until satisfactory results are obtained.

Ideally, it is desirable to propose a system of intervention that patients can use, in between visits to the healthcare provider, which could assist the patient in determining, and, if necessary, correcting, their posture based on some quantifiable values. This solution is two-fold in that we use machine learning algorithms for training and testing activity related data and determine the accuracy of activity prediction. In the present study, we apply the Random Forest machine learning technique to the acceleration data collected from eight volunteers' smartphones for training and testing the model. The volunteers used the SensorLog app which affords the ability to export the accelerometer data to a CSV file. Volunteers performed each of the six activities described below for five to ten minutes and uploaded the corresponding files for each activity to the researchers.

3. METHODOLOGY

The statistical data analysis package R and the SensorLog mobile app were used to analyze the data for this study. R is a popular statistical package used to apply machine learning algorithms and perform data analytics. The data for this research project is collected from an app (SensorLog) installed on the smartphone. Most raw data collected by the sensors from the wearable devices must be interpreted and transformed into a format that can be understood by the naïve user. Mobile apps are generally used for data transformation. In our study, the SensorLog app available both on the App Store and Google play store was used to collect the raw data from the wearable devices and transmit it as a CSV file via the Internet. Figures 1 to 4 provided below show the interface provided by the SensorLog app.

User Interface of the SensorLog App

The SensorLog app has a user interface that can be configured to collect specific data and also options to save the data to a particular file format. In this research the researchers collected the data and saved it as a csv file which can be downloaded or shared. The four figures below describe the user interface of the SensorLog.

Figure 1 displays the accelerometer data collected by the sensorLog app.

Figure 2 displays the screen to specify and configure the file type, recording rate, device ID etc.

Figure 3 displays the screen for the Logged Files that are available

Figure 4 displays the available options to share and or download the logged file

A description of the data collection, processing and analyzing are presented below.

3.1 Description of Data

The dataset consisting of uncalibrated accelerometer data with a sampling frequency of 30 Hz, is collected from 8 participants using their wearable devices (mobile phones) performing six activities. These activities are referred to as labels and are codified as follows

1: Working at a computer
2: Standing and walking
3: Standing
4: Walking
5: Walking up and down stairs
6: Talking while standing

For each participant, the corresponding csv file which can be downloaded contains the following information: sequential number, x acceleration, y acceleration, z acceleration and activity label. The activity label is codified as numbers 1 to 6 where each activity has a corresponding number associated with it. Working at the computer has a code of 1, Standing has a code of 3, etc.

Figure 1. SensorLog accelerometer data

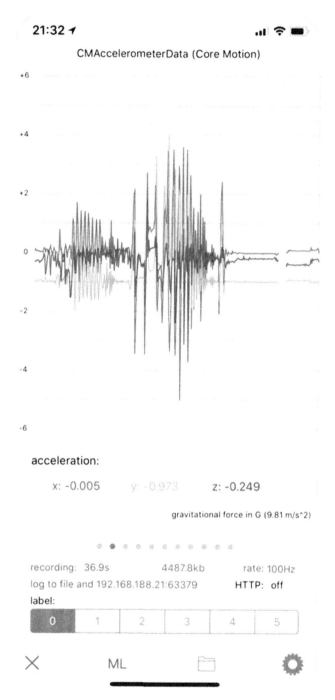

Figure 2. SensorLog configuration options

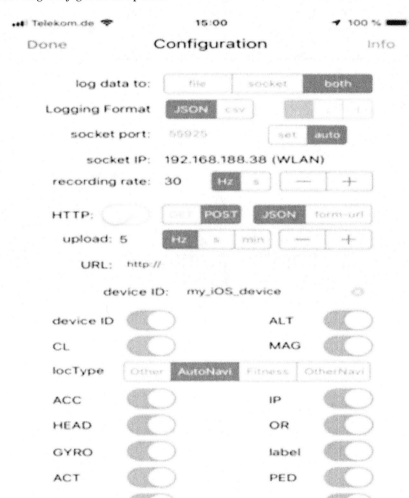

Figure 3. Files generated by SensorLog app

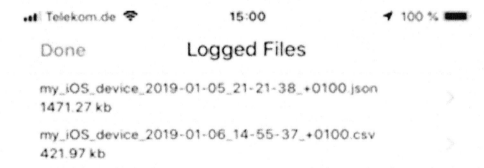

Figure 4. SensorLog file export options

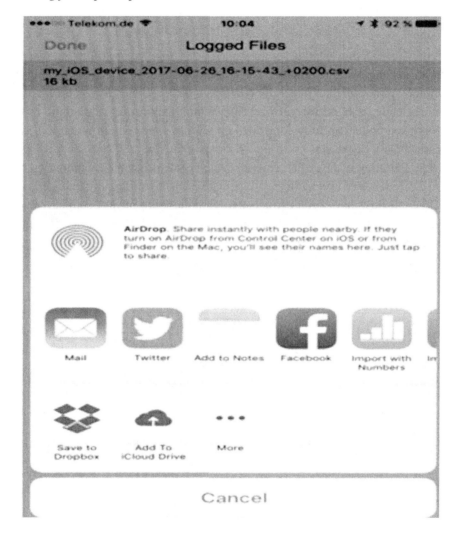

Note: In the data tables and plots in this paper, the classes are labelled according to the above list of activities

Data Preparation and Preprocessing

Table 1 presented below provides a list of variables for which raw data were collected from the wearable device corresponding to the activity - sitting at a computer.

From this list, a set of values for the following fields were used for the prediction of the activity. These include

```
LoggingTime,
LoggingSample,
AccelerometerAccelerationX(G),
```

```
AccelerometerAccelerationY(G),
AccelerometerAccelerationZ(G).
```

Acceleration data recorded in the dataset are coded according to the following mapping: [0; +30] = [-1.5g; +1.5g]. Ehatisham-ul-Haq, Azam, Naeem, Rehman and Khalid (2017) observed that the time series generated by smartphones generally contains noise generated by the participants and by the smartphones. So, the coded data is smoothed by Holt Winter exponential smoothing model. It is to be noted that data obtained under carefully controlled conditions may contain much less noise and yield much better accuracy (Tillis 2016).

As suggested by Pierluigi et al. (2011), features have been extracted by windowing of 75 samples, corresponding to 2.5 seconds of accelerometer data, with 50% of overlapping between windows. From each window, fifteen features have been extracted corresponding to means, standard deviations, minimum, maximum and median values for the three axes x, y, and z. As stated earlier, R language software was utilized for generating these new set of features.

Table 1. List of variables

loggingTime(txt)	motionUserAccelerationY(G)
loggingSample(N)	motionUserAccelerationZ(G)
locationTimestamp_since1970(s)	motionAttitudeReferenceFrame(txt)
locationLatitude(WGS84)	motionQuaternionX(R)
locationLongitude(WGS84)	motionQuaternionY(R)
locationAltitude(m)	motionQuaternionZ(R)
locationSpeed(m/s)	motionQuaternionW(R)
locationCourse(å¡)	motionGravityX(G)
locationVerticalAccuracy(m)	motionGravityY(G)
locationHorizontalAccuracy(m)	motionGravityZ(G
locationFloor(Z)	activityTimestamp_sinceReboot(s)
accelerometerTimestamp_sinceReboot(s)	activity(txt)
accelerometerAccelerationX(G)	activityActivityConfidence(Z)
accelerometerAccelerationY(G)	activityActivityStartDate(txt)
accelerometerAccelerationZ(G)	pedometerStartDate(txt)
motionTimestamp_sinceReboot(s)	pedometerNumberofSteps(N)
motionYaw(rad)	pedometerAverageActivePace(s/m)
motionRoll(rad)	pedometerCurrentPace(s/m)
motionPitch(rad)	pedometerCurrentCadence(steps/s)
motionRotationRateX(rad/s)	pedometerDistance(m)
motionRotationRateY(rad/s)	pedometerFloorAscended(N)
motionRotationRateZ(rad/s)	pedometerFloorDescended(N)
motionUserAccelerationX(G)	pedometerEndDate(txt)

3.2 Classification and Prediction of Activities

In order to classify and predict the individual's activity based on the newly derived features, the Random Forest machine learning model was utilized. For fitting Random Forest, software programs were developed using the R language.

The newly derived dataset consisting of 15 features is divided into two datasets viz., training dataset and test dataset. The training dataset is obtained by taking 80% of the randomly selected observations and the remaining 20% of the dataset is utilized as the test dataset. Random Forest model is fitted with the training dataset and tested with the test dataset. With the Random Forest model, the important variables were also identified.

4. RESULTS AND DISCUSSION

Results from the Random Forest Model are presented in Tables 2, 3 and 4. Table 2 includes the resulting OOB error and confusion matrix obtained from the Training dataset. The Confusion Matrix of the results displayed in Table 2 demonstrates the accuracy of the model. In the Confusion Matrix, the diagonal elements show the number of observations which are correctly classified for each activity, non-diagonal elements are the number of observations, which are not correctly classified. The overall accuracy of the Random Forest Model is given by Out of the Bag (OOB) estimate of error rate, which is 11.67%. This clearly demonstrates that the Random Forest Model has accurately classified all the activities with 88.33% accuracy in the training dataset.

Table 2. Random forest model results for the training dataset

	1	2	3	4	5	6
1	454	23	7	9	1	7
2	24	628	10	7	21	21
3	8	29	433	1	4	11
4	3	8	0	758	27	37
5	1	15	1	28	418	19
6	4	23	6	30	23	398

Call: randomForest(formula = activity ~ ., data = train, ntree = 500, mtry = 5)

Type of random forest: classification

Number of trees: 500

No. of variables tried at each split: 5

OOB estimate of error rate: 11.67%

The labels of the six classes listed in the top row and left column in the confusion matrix are as follows:

1: Working at Computer
2: Standing and Walking
3: Standing

4: Walking

5: Walking Up and Down Stairs

6: Talking while Standing

Prediction for Test Dataset

The results of the test dataset for the Random Forest Model are given in Table 3a, Table 3b and Table 3c. Table 3a displays the confusion matrix, Table 3b. displays the overall statistics and Table 3c. displays the statistics by class obtained from the test dataset. From the overall statistics, we observe that the overall accuracy of the model for the Test Dataset is 85.94% accurate.

Table 3a. Predictions for test dataset – confusion matrix

	1	2	3	4	5	6
1	90	4	3	0	0	5
2	13	162	4	4	8	6
3	2	4	124	0	0	2
4	1	1	0	188	9	6
5	3	2	2	8	97	9
6	3	3	2	10	9	91

Table 3b. Predictions for test dataset – overall statistics

Accuracy	0.8594
95% CI	(0.8346, 0.8818)
No Information Rate	0.24
P-Value [Acc > NIR]	< 2.2e-16
Kappa	0.8291
Mcnemar's Test P-Value	NA

Table 3c. Predictions for test dataset – statistics by class

	Class1	Class2	Class3	Class4	Class5	Class6
Sensitivity	0.8036	0.9205	0.9185	0.8952	0.7886	0.7647
Specificity	0.9843	0.9499	0.9892	0.9744	0.9681	0.9643
Pos Pred Value	0.8824	0.8223	0.9394	0.9171	0.8017	0.7712
Neg Pred Value	0.9715	0.9794	0.9852	0.9672	0.9655	0.9630
Prevalence	0.1280	0.2011	0.1543	0.2400	0.1406	0.1360
Detection Rate	0.1029	0.1851	0.1417	0.2149	0.1109	0.1040
Detection Prevalence	0.1166	0.2251	0.1509	0.2343	0.1383	0.1349
Balanced Accuracy	0.8939	0.9352	0.9539	0.9348	0.8784	0.8645

The labels of the six classes listed in the top row and left column in the confusion matrix are as follows:

1: Working at Computer

2: Standing and Walking

3: Standing

4: Walking

5: Walking Up and Down Stairs

6: Talking while Standing

The labels of the six classes are as follows:

1: Working at Computer
2: Standing and Walking
3: Standing
4: Walking
5: Walking Up and Down Stairs
6: Talking while Standing

The RandomForest package in R reports the results for the training dataset by giving the OOB estimate of error rate, and the results for the Test dataset by providing the overall statistics, as reported above.

4.2 Identifying Important Variables

The important variables identified by the Random Forest Model are given in Table 4. The MeanDecreaseGini values give the relative importance of each individual variable, which is provided under the column "Overall". From this table, it is observed that the variables ymax, ymean, xmax, which have higher MeanDecreaseGini values are the important features followed by other features. The overall OOB error for different activities as functions of the number of trees in the Random Forest model is given in Figure 5.

Figure 5. Overall OOB error for different activities

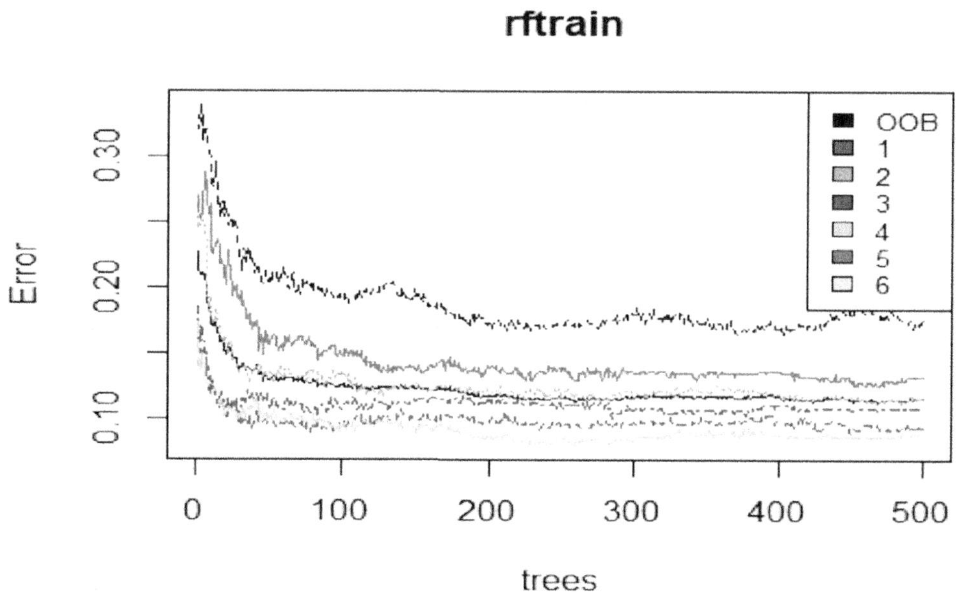

Explanation of Figure 5: The OOB (out of the Bag) error estimate is similar to that obtained by N-fold cross-validation (Hastie, Tibshirani & Friedman 2016). It steadily decreases as the number of trees are added in the model and reaches lowest values around 500 trees. The labels of the six classes are as follows:

1: Working at Computer
2: Standing and Walking
3: Standing
4: Walking
5: Walking Up and Down Stairs
6: Talking while Standing

Table 4 below lists the hierarchy of importance of the variables

Table 4. Overall variables importance

xmean	187.2409
ymean	252.3255
zmean	134.8651
xsd	200.4376
ysd	135.1334
zsd	168.6573
xmin	188.7961
ymin	219.7125
zmin	139.0769
xmax	234.8544
ymax	298.4171
zmax	181.0266
xmedian	191.5964
ymedian	211.1288
zmedian	137.1785

Figure 6 also visually displays the same hierarchy of importance of variables. The RandomForest package automatically identifies the important variables/features based on MeandecreaseGini values. Figure 6 is obtained by considering the Mean Decrease in Node impurity.

5. CONCLUSION AND FUTURE PROSPECTS

An attempt is made in this study to predict the activity of the individual by utilizing the accelerometer data obtained from smartphones. As the data is available with a frequency of 30 Hz, a window of 75 observations is taken, corresponding to two and a half seconds, with 50% overlapping. From the rolling windows, fifteen features have been extracted for the three x, y, and z accelerometer data. The Random Forest Machine Learning algorithm was utilized to predict the six activities utilizing the data. 80% of the randomly selected data was utilized as a training set and the remaining 20% of the data was utilized for testing the model. Random Forest model has identified the activities with 88.33% accuracy in the training dataset and 85.94% accuracy in the test dataset.

Figure 6. Variables importance plot

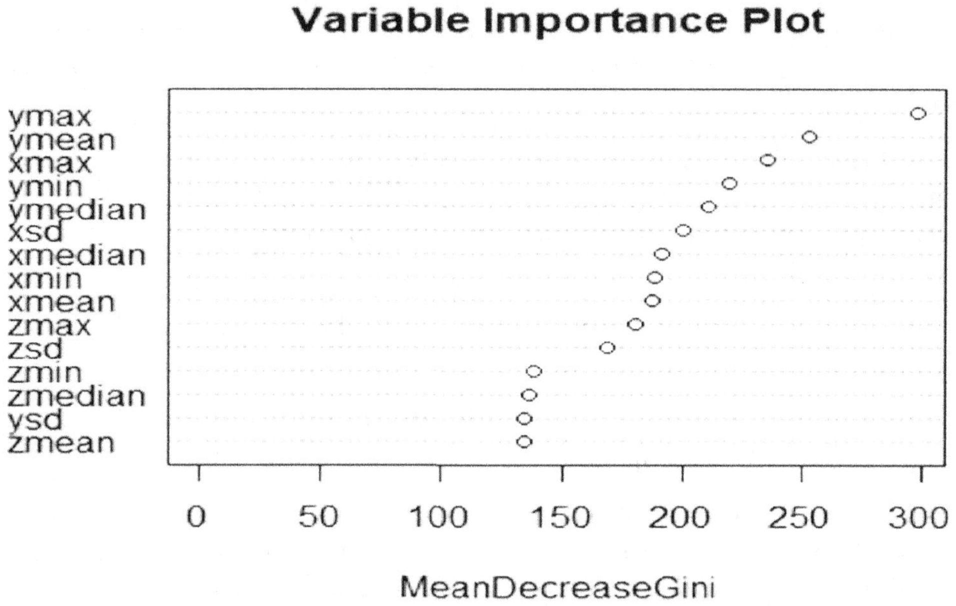

6. FUTURE WORK

Some of the limitations in this study are that a. practical usability of the study and b. extensibility. To ensure practical usability of this study the researchers plan to design user interfaces (UI) to allow users to monitor and test their own data. Examples include using a UI such as a shiny app that allows a user to upload data acquired from a wearable device, and obtain a decision on whether their activity and or posture was accurately being monitored. Data collected from such applications can be used by medical practitioners to determine the impact on the patient's health. Additionally, the researchers plan to expand this study to include a much larger population in different domains of knowledge.

REFERENCES

Ahamed, N. U., Kobsar, D., Benson, L., Clermont, C., Kohrs, R., Osis, S. T., & Ferber, R. (2018). Using wearable sensors to classify subject-specific running biomechanical gait patterns based on changes in environmental weather conditions. *PLoS One*, *13*(9), e0203839. doi:10.1371/journal.pone.0203839 PMID:30226903

Akhavian, R., & Behzadan, A.H. (2016). Smartphone-based construction workers' activity recognition and classification. *Automation in Construction*, 71, 198-209.

op den Akker, H., Jones, V. M., & Hermens, H. J. (2014). Tailoring real-time physical activity coaching systems: a literature survey and model. User modeling and user-adapted interaction, 24(5), 351-392.

Balli, S., Sağbaş, E. A., & Peker, M. (2019). Human activity recognition from smart watch sensor data using a hybrid of principal component analysis and random forest algorithm. *Measurement and Control*, *52*(1-2), 37–45. doi:10.1177/0020294018813692

Cadmus-Bertram, L. (2017). Using Fitness Trackers in Clinical Research: What Nurse Practitioners Need to Know. *The Journal for Nurse Practitioners*, *13*(1), 34–40. doi:10.1016/j.nurpra.2016.10.012 PMID:28603469

Cammarota, A. (2003), "The commission's initiative on MSDS: Recent developments in social partner consultation at the European level. *Presented at the Conference on MSDs — A Challenge for the Tele-communications Industry*, Lisbon, Portugal, October 20–21 (pp. 20-21).

del Rosario, M. B., Redmond, S. J., & Lovell, N. H. (2015). Tracking the Evolution of Smartphone Sensing for Monitoring Human Movement. *Sensors*, *15*(8), 18901–18933. doi:10.3390150818901 PMID:26263998

Hastie, T., Tibshirani, R., & Friedman, J. (2016). *The Elements of Statistical Learning: Data Mining, Inference, and Prediction* (2nd ed.). Springer.

Henriksen, A., Haugen Mikalsen, M., Woldaregay, A. Z., Muzny, M., Hartvigsen, G., Hopstock, L. A., & Grimsgaard, S. (2018). Using Fitness Trackers and Smartwatches to Measure Physical Activity in Research: Analysis of Consumer Wrist-Worn Wearables. *Journal of Medical Internet Research*, *20*(3), e110. doi:10.2196/jmir.9157 PMID:29567635

Henriksen, A., Haugen Mikalsen, M., Woldaregay, A. Z., Muzny, M., Hartvigsen, G., Hopstock, L. A., & Grimsgaard, S. (2018). Using Fitness Trackers and Smartwatches to Measure Physical Activity in Research: Analysis of Consumer Wrist-Worn Wearables. *Journal of Medical Internet Research*, *20*(3), e110. doi:10.2196/jmir.9157 PMID:29567635

Ehatisham-ul-Haq, M., Azam, M. A., Naeem, U., ur Rèhman, S., & Khalid, A. (2017). Identifying Smartphone Users based on their Activity Patterns via Mobile Sensing. *Procedia Computer Science*, *113*, 202–209.

Maher, C., Ryan, J., Ambrosi, C., & Edney, S. (2017). Users' experiences of wearable activity trackers: A cross-sectional study. *BMC Public Health*, *17*(1), 880. doi:10.118612889-017-4888-1 PMID:29141607

Natarajan, B., Sundhara Kumar, K. B., & Selvaraj, C. (2017). Empirical study of feature selection methods over classification algorithms. *International Journal of Intelligent Systems Technologies and Applications*.

Pierluigi, C., Oriol, P., & Petia, R. (2011), Human Activity Recognition from Accelerometer Data Using a Wearable Device. In *Pattern Recognition and Image Analysis: 5th Iberian Conference, IbPRIA 2011*, Las Palmas de Gran Canaria, Spain, June 8-10 (pp. 289-296).

Ridgers, N. D., Timperio, A., Brown, H., Ball, K., Macfarlane, S., Lai, S. K., ... Salmon, J. (2018). Wearable activity tracker use among Australian adolescents: Usability and acceptability study. *JMIR mHealth and uHealth*, 6(4), e86. doi:10.2196/mhealth.9199 PMID:29643054

McGinnis, R. S., DiCristofaro, S., Mahadevan, N., Sen-Gupta, E., Silva, I., Jortberg, E., ... & Patel, S. (2017, August). Longitudinal Data from Wearable Sensor System Suggests Movement Improves Standing Posture. In *Proceedings of the 41st Annual Meeting of the American Society of Biomechanics*, Boulder, CO (pp. 8-11).

Tillis, R. (2016). Machine Learning Project – random forest – Sensor Data. *RPubs*.

Zhang, S., Stogin, W., & Alshurafa, N. (2018). I sense overeating: Motif-based machine learning framework to detect overeating using wrist-worn sensing. *Information Fusion*, 41, 37–47.

Sztyler, T., & Stuckenschmidt, H. (2016). On-body localization of wearable devices: An investigation of position-aware activity recognition. In *Proceedings of the 2016 IEEE International Conference on Pervasive Computing and Communications (PerCom)*. IEEE. 10.1109/PERCOM.2016.7456521

Sztyler, T., & Stuckenschmidt, H. (2017). Online personalization of cross-subjects based activity recognition models on wearable devices. In *Proceedings of the 2017 IEEE International Conference on Pervasive Computing and Communications (PerCom)* (pp. 180-189). IEEE. 10.1109/PERCOM.2017.7917864

This research was previously published in the International Journal of Big Data and Analytics in Healthcare (IJBDAH), 4(1); pages 32-46, copyright year 2019 by IGI Publishing (an imprint of IGI Global).

Chapter 54

Machine Learning for Health Data Analytics:
A Few Case Studies of Application of Regression

Muralikrishna Iyyanki

https://orcid.org/0000-0002-4961-9010

Independent Researcher, India

Prisilla Jayanthi

Administrative Staff College of India, India

Valli Manickam

Administrative Staff College of India, India

ABSTRACT

At present, public health and population health are the key areas of major concern, and the current study highlights the significant challenges through a few case studies of application of machine learning for health data with focus on regression. Four types of machine learning methods found to be significant are supervised learning, unsupervised learning, semi-supervised learning, and reinforcement learning. In light of the case studies reported as part of the literature survey and specific exercises carried out for this chapter, it is possible to say that machine learning provides new opportunities for automatic learning in expressive models. Regression models including multiple and multivariate regression are suitable for modeling air pollution and heart disease prediction. The applicability of STATA and R packages for multiple linear regression and predictive modelling for crude birth rate and crude mortality rate is well established in the study as carried out using the data from data.gov.in. Decision tree as a class of very powerful machine learning models is applied for brain tumors. In simple terms, machine learning and data mining techniques go hand-in-hand for prediction, data modelling, and decision making. The health analytics and unpredictable growth of health databases require integration of the conventional data analysis to be paired with methods for efficient computer-assisted analysis. In the second case study, confidence interval is evaluated. Here, the statistical parameter CI is used to indicate the true range of the mean of the crude birth rate and crude mortality rate computed from the observed data.

DOI: 10.4018/978-1-6684-6291-1.ch054

1. INTRODUCTION

Data in digital form is the new oil, as being considered globally. For any developmental activity data are essential and hence data science. According to Bernard (2015) by the end of the year 2025, Forbes estimated that the digital data is quite sure to increase automatically by an order of magnitude from 4.4 ZB. On this planet, every human generates new information of 1.7 MB in every second. Innovative data mining techniques and machine learning techniques are necessary for facilitating related information through data modelling, prediction and prescription. Data mining and Machine learning have a good amount of commonality as the two transect to enhance the collection and usability of large amounts of data for analytics purposes.

According to *"Bio IT World"* statement, the predictive analysis is the future of data mining as it can be seen in advanced analytics across industries like medical applications (Agosta 2004). Arthur Samuel one of the forerunners and developer of machine learning define that "machine learning relates to the study, design and development of the algorithms that give computer's the capability to learn without being explicitly programmed". The process of unstructured data that tries to extract knowledge and/or unknown interesting patterns is defined as data mining. During this process, Machine Learning (ML) algorithms are traditionally used. ML is further associated with the query, how machines can learn, i.e., to the algorithmic part. In ML, an agent learns from rewards (data) in the environment, but not from patterns or pattern-label pairs. In data mining, the question is how to learn from patterns or pattern-label pairs. "ML techniques are fairly generic and can be applied in various settings. Data mining has emphasis on utilizing data from a domain e.g., social media, sensor data, video streams, etc. to understand some questions in that domain". New questions arise that may not be answered in the algorithmically oriented ML perspective including preprocessing of data and the complete data mining process chain (Souhila 2013 and Xavier 2016). From large historical datasets, the data mining intent is to find out unseen patterns and relationships and derive a business value. Its interest is upon uncovering relationships between two or more variables in the dataset and extracting insights. These insights include mapping the data into information and predicting outcomes from incoming events and prescribing actions. Multiple data sorting techniques can be used to achieve this target such as clustering, classification, and sequence analysis. Typically, data mining uses batch-process information to reveal a new insight at any specific point. And DM is not automated process but DM requires human involvement and cannot be implemented without humans.

2. MACHINE LEARNING [ML] AND DATA MINING [DM]

ML uses human-based algorithm and works everything without the use of humans' interference; once implemented, the outcome is accurate because the process is automated. Also, ML is capable to take the own decision and resolve the issue. Ever growing ML techniques, overwhelms problems associated with DM techniques as ML techniques are more accurate and less error prone compared to DM. This self-learning technique is not available in DM whereas ML uses self-learning algorithms to improve its performance as an intelligent task with experience over time (Brooks & Dahlke 2017). To summarize the foregoing, it can be stated the following are the definitions and differences or commonalities, if any, between ML and DM:

- "In **Machine learning**, performance is usually evaluated with respect to the ability to reproduce known knowledge, while in knowledge discovery and data mining (KDD) the key task is the discovery of previously unknown knowledge. Evaluated with respect to known knowledge, an uninformed (unsupervised) method will easily be outperformed by other supervised methods, while in a typical KDD task, supervised methods cannot be used due to the unavailability of training data" (Machine_learning, Wikipedia).
- **Data mining** is a cross-disciplinary field that has emphasis on finding out properties of data sets. There are various approaches to discover properties of data sets; among which machine learning is one of them.
- **Machine learning** is a sub-field of data science that focuses on designing algorithms that can learn from and make predictions on the data.
- **Machine learning** and Data Mining often employ similar methods. Machine learning focuses on prediction whereas data mining focuses on the unearthing of unidentified and new properties/ trends in the data. Prediction by ML is based on known properties learned from the training data. Data mining uses many machine learning methods, but with different goals; on the other hand, machine learning also employs data mining methods as unsupervised learning.

In general terms machine learning techniques can be used for data mining. However, data mining can use other techniques besides or with machine learning. As per existing analysis and protocols developed, data mining and machine learning are to be considered as each one inclusive of other and with significant overlap due to commonality of tools and techniques. The reason behind for considering at this stage that data mining and machine learning are mutually inclusive techniques with considerable overlap (supervised, unsupervised and semi-supervised learning) between both. However, there are few ML techniques like reinforcement learning that does not come under data mining which is used more for logical analysis. Further with several examples one can clearly visualize that reinforcement learning belongs to ML, but not to data mining (DM). Machine learning, and/or for that matter, data mining is essentially, the applicable methods for prediction and description of the event or phenomenon of varying dimensions and categories (Data Mining- Machine Learning, doublebyteblog). These differences are depicted in figure 1 as a schematic sketch highlighting the structure of machine learning, comprising of different learning techniques viz. supervised learning, unsupervised learning, semi-supervised learning and reinforced learning.

Supervised learning is a case of learning applicable to the efforts in which both input and output are known and thus the system is trained so as to predict output for a given input value. Supervised learning is the task of inferring a function from labeled training data and which is further used for mapping new examples. Supervised learning is one of the methods associated with machine learning which involves allocating labeled data so that a certain pattern or function can be deduced from that data. It is worth noting that supervised learning involves allocating an input object, a vector, while at the same time anticipating the most desired output value, which is referred to as the supervisory signal. The bottom-line property of supervised learning is that the input data is known and labeled appropriately. The algorithm will correctly determine the class labels for unseen instances. This leads the learning algorithm to generalize from the training data to unseen situations in a reasonable way (McNulty 2015). This explanation of supervised learning is applicable to both the tasks of data mining and machine learning.

Figure 1. Machine learning structure

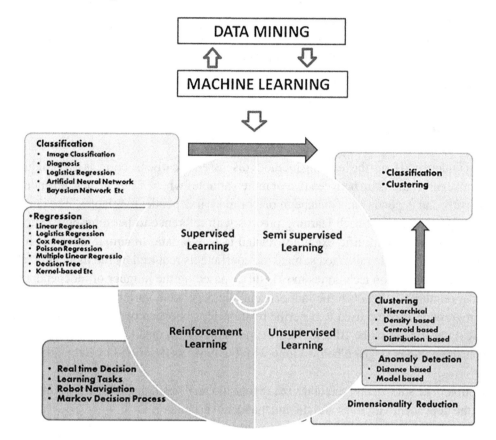

Data mining is becoming, as discussed in earlier section, essential aspect in the current world due to increased raw data where organizations need to analyze and process so that they can make sound and reliable decisions. Here data mining relates to explaining about the past and predicting the future based on analysis. Data mining helps to extract information from huge datasets. It is the procedure of mining knowledge from data. The techniques of data mining are classification, clustering, regression, association rules, sequential patterns and prediction. R-language and Oracle data mining are prominent data mining tools. The main drawback of data mining is that many analytics software is difficult to operate and requires advanced training to work upon.

The second method is unsupervised learning that determines the hidden patterns from unlabeled data; and used for exploratory data analysis. One main characteristics of unsupervised learning is that both the structures of input and output are unknown. Since the examples that are given during the learning are unlabeled, the scope for assessment of the validation of the output with reference to the real-world situation is not possible. For ex. while, applying clustering technique of unsupervised classification of a digital image, the output essentially gives clusters which represent classes in spectral domain and not feature domain. The techniques used in both the learnings appear to be similar, making the user challenging to differentiate between the two learning methods. However, there exist significant differences between supervised and unsupervised learning. In semi-supervised learning, which is a mix of supervised learning, viz., classification technique and unsupervised learning, viz., clustering technique are used.

Reinforced learning which is basically a type of machine learning and it differs from supervised learning as labelled input / output pairs need not be present, and sub-optimal actions need not be explicitly corrected. Instead, the focus is finding a balance between exploration and exploitation of current knowledge. In this context the regression techniques are very much significant for any sort of learning and modeling.

3. REGRESSION MODELS

Regression, as understood from the learning methods discussed in earlier section, is a technique for determining the statistical relationship between two or more variables where a change in a dependent variable is associated with, and depends on, a change in one or more independent variables. The comparison of machine learning algorithms of each learning process with reference to learning type / sub-types and methods is carried out with specific examples related to health data. In simple linear regression, one can use statistics on the training data to estimate the coefficients required by the model to make predictions for new data. Regression techniques mostly differ based on the number of independent variables and the type of relationship between the independent and dependent variables. For health care related application, regression is being used to describe relationships between two variables like gender, age, weight, clinical observations like BP etc. Regression analysis is considered for statistical evaluation which enables three things as given below along with the types as described by Schneider et al (2010).

- Description: The statistically method viz., regression analysis helps to describe the relationships among the dependent variables and the independent variables
- Estimation: The values of the dependent variables can be estimated from the observed values of the independent variables.
- Prognostication: Risk factors that influence the outcome can be identified, and individual prognoses can be determined.

Based on the above factors, the application of regression is given in Table 1 for a typical case study of application to a medical record. Linear regression, polynomial regression, logistic regression, proportional hazard regression, poisons regression and non –linear regression etc. are various types suitable for different types of data modeling and few of which are described below in the Table 1.

The Table 2 describes the divergence with respective to input data, complexity, real time and accuracy between supervised and unsupervised learning.

Logistic regression is a regression and / or a binary classification algorithm, producing a continuous or categorical output. Logistic regression is not a classification algorithm on its own. It is a type of classification algorithm in combination with a decision rule. It is a regression model to estimate the probability of class membership as a multilinear function of the features. Unlike in the case of conventional regression which outputs continuous number values, logistic regression transforms its output using the logistic sigmoid function to return a probability value which can be mapped to two or more discrete classes. It may be recollected here that a sigmoid function is a mathematical function having characteristic S-shaped curve or sigmoid curve. The proportional Hazard models are a class of survival models known as Cox Regression for a specific outcome case study which indeed is a method for investigating the effect of several variables on the time a specified event takes to happen. Poisson Regression is used for modeling events where the output is given as counts, to be precise, about count data. It is discrete data with non-negative integer values that counts the number of times an event occurs during a given timeframe. Count data is expressed as rate data, because the number of times an event occurs within a timeframe can be expressed as a raw count (LogisticRegression ufldl.stanford.edu).

Table 1. Machine learning algorithms [doublebyteblog]

Learning Type	Sub Type	Method	Sub Method
UNSUPERVISED	Continuous	Clustering	K means SVM PCA
		Dimensionality Reduction	
	Categorical	Association analysis	Apriori
			FP growth
		Hidden Markov Model	Markov Chain
SUPERVISED	Continuous	Regression	Linear
			Polynomial
		Decision Trees	Random Forests
			Gradient tree
	Categorical	Classification	KNN
			Trees
			Logistics Regression
			Naïve-Bayes
			SVM

Table 2. Divergence between supervised and unsupervised learning[Mujtaba & Irshad (2017)]

Factors	Unsupervised Learning	Supervised Learning
Input data	Unlabeled data and machine must categorize	Labelled data and machine must determine hidden patterns
Computational Complexity	Method of learning is less complex	Method of learning is more complex
Accuracy	For the method of learning the machine has to define and label the input data before determining the hidden patterns and functions. Hence accuracy is of major concern.	The input data is well known and labelled. The accuracy is high and it analyzes only hidden patterns in a reliable way.
Number of classes	No prior knowledge of the classes in unsupervised method is seen.	All the classes used in supervised learning are known. The aim of supervised learning is to determine the unknown cluster.
Real time learning	In real time, the learning takes all the input data for analyzing and labeling in the presence of learners which helps them to understand and classification of raw data. Real time data analysis is the most significant of this learning.	The preparing and labeling of input data are carried out off-line while the analysis of the hidden pattern is done online.

Table 3. Regression models [Schneider et al (2010)]

Type	Application	Dependent Variables	Independent variables
Linear Regression	Description of a linear relationship	Continuous(weight, blood pressure)	Independent variables can be continuous or categorical
Logistic Regression	Prediction of the probability of belonging to groups (outcome: yes / no)	Dichotomous (success of treatment: yes / no)	
Cox Regression [Proportional-Hazard Regression]	Modeling of survival data	Survival time (time from diagnosis to event)	
Poisson Regression	Modeling of counting processes	Counting data: whole numbers representing events in temporal sequences (e.g. the number of times a woman gave birth over a certain period of time)	
Multiple Linear Regression Model	Used to explain the relationship between one continuous dependent variable and two or more independent variables	Continuous (Land use, traffic, etc values)	
		Continuous (chest pain type, blood sugar, ECG etc)	Heart disease prediction

4. MULTIPLE/MULTIVARIATE REGRESSION

Multiple regressions pertain to one dependent variable and multiple independent variables whereas multivariate regression pertains to multiple dependent and multiple independent variables. Multivariate regression (MMR) is used to model the linear relationship between more than one independent variable and more than one dependent variable. MMR with more than one independent variable is referred multiple. MMR is multivariate because there is more than one dependent variable. Few case studies of multiple regressions are discussed in the next section.

Air Pollution Modeling Using Multiple Regression

In a case of development of a Multiple Linear Regression technique, a study by Mateus et al (2015) is discussed here. The objective of this study is to model air pollution to predict value of NO_2 concentration using multiple linear regressions, in which few independent variables were used for bivariate regression analysis. In this study, two independent variables viz., elevation and traffic within 150m radius are used for the multivariate regression coined as Land Use Regression model [LUR] and for the year 2001, it predicted almost 60% of NO_2. The results highlight vehicular traffic as important variable responsible to increase air pollutant levels, in the areas where cars are more such as the city center, or close to busy expressways. LUR methods are applied successfully to model annual mean concentrations of NO_2, NOx, PM2.5, and VOCs. The LUR model is designed to predict the total concentration of pollutants. The model included key independent co-variables like traffic volume, road type, land use, altitude and demography and their respective coefficients. The bivariate regression and correlation analysis were calculated on SPSS and the multivariate regression was calculated on STATA. The land use data includes nine classifications by type of use (industrial, arable, forests and water) and building patterns (enclosed, low, high, recreational). GIS software MapInfo with buffers 50, 100, 150, 250 and 500 m-radii were used to create the independent variables in 25 locations.

Results of the study by Mateus et al (2015) showed that the geographic characteristics such as altitude and traffic intensity, contribute considerably to the urban air quality. Furthermore, the LUR model is recommended for estimating outdoor concentrations at any specified location. It would support policymaking about the improvement of urban air quality. This study does not include meteorological parameters into the model.

Heart Disease Prediction Using Multiple Linear Regression Model

Heart disease kills one in three persons every day as per World Health Statistics 2012 worldwide. Researchers have developed various heart disease prediction systems to extract hidden datasets from heart disease databases. They help doctors and other medical professionals by predicting heart diseases more efficiently and accurately and thus make best clinical decisions.

In a study by Polaraju and Durgaprasad (2017), multiple linear regression analysis has been performed to predict the chance of heart disease in a case study, by the training data sets consisting of 3000 instances with 13 different attributes as given in Table 4. In this study a wide range of works have been analyzed related to heart disease prediction system using different data mining algorithms. Based on the study results given in Table 5, it was observed that multiple regression algorithm accuracy is better compared to other techniques. Typically, the methodology includes a procedure to determine whether the patient has heart disease by considering the attributes of patient data set like age, chest pain type, fasting blood sugar, rest ECG, number of major vessels colored by fluoroscopy, blood pressure, serum cholesterol, maximum heart rate achieved etc. The experiment is performed by training data set consists of 3000 instances with 13 different attributes.

Table 4. Patient's attributes [Mujtaba & Irshad (2017)]

Attributes	Description
Pid	Patient Identification
Gender	Male or Female
Age	In years
Cp	Chest pain type
Thestbps	Resting blood pressure
Chol	Serum cholesterol
Restecg	Resting Electrographic results
Fbs	Fasting blood sugar
Thalach	Maximum heart rate achieved
Exang	Exercise induced angina
Ca	Number of major vessels colored by Fluoroscopy
Obes	Obesity
Smoke	Smoking
Ecg	Electro Cardiogram

Table 5. Data set definition [Polaraju & Durgaprasad (2017)]

Parameters	Weightage	
Person	Age < 30	0.1
	>30 to <50	0.3
	Age>50 and age<70	0.7
	Age>70	0.8
Smoking	Never	0.1
	Past	0.3
	Current	0.6
Overweight	Yes	0.8
	No	0.1
Alcohol Intake	Never	0.1
	Past	0.3
	Current	0.6
High salt diet	Yes	0.9
	No	0.1
High saturated fat diet	Yes	0.9
	No	0.1
Exercise	Never	0.6
	Regular	0.1
	High if age< 30	0.1
	High if age> 50	0.6
Sedentary Lifestyle/inactivity	Yes	0.7
	No	0.1
Hereditary	Yes	0.7
	No	0.1
Bad Cholesterol	Very high >200	0.9
	High 160 to 200	0.8
	Normal < 160	0.1
Blood Pressure	Normal (130/89)	0.1
	Low (<119/79)	0.8
	High (>200/160)	0.9
Blood Sugar	High (>129 & <400)	0.5
	Normal (>90 & <120)	0.1
	Low (<90)	0.4
Heart Rate	Low (<60 bpm)	0.9
	Normal (60 to 100)	0.1
	High(> 100 bpm)	0.9

The dataset is divided into two parts with 70% of the data used for training and 30% are for testing. Based on the experimental results as shown in Table 5 (Polaraju & DurgaPrasad, 2017), it is clear that the classification accuracy of regression algorithm is better compared to other algorithms. The popular regression technique viz., multiple linear regressions analysis is performed on trained data to build a model on which test data is applied. From the experimental results it is proved that multiple linear regressions are equally appropriate for predicting heart disease chance.

STATA and R for Multiple Linear Regressions

An example of application the potential of the two software packages for multiple linear regression i.e. Stata and R for Brain Tumor severity assessment is being carried out by the authors. It is initially stated that Stata IC 15.0 is faster in computation, efficient, and has few machine learning algorithms implemented. The analysis of Odd Ratios (OR) and Confidential Interval (CI) calculations using unconditional logistics regression can be performed using Stata, this feature is not available in R. This feature helps the prediction of brain tumor but R provides a definite platform for machine learning algorithms.

5. CONFIDENCE INTERVAL: THE PREDICTIVE MODELLING FOR CRUDE BIRTH RATE AND CRUDE MORTALITY RATE

In the next case study, confidence interval is evaluated for crude birth / mortality rate by predictive modelling. Confidence interval is an interval estimate, computed from the observed data, which contain the true value of an unknown population parameter. It is known that in predictive modelling, a prediction is a single outcome value given by some input variable. In other terms, predictive modelling which is the measurement of the uncertain estimated model referred to as confidence interval, CI such as mean or standard deviation. A confidence interval is a bound on the estimate of a population variable. It is an interval statistic used to quantify the uncertainty on an estimate. In machine learning, confidence intervals can be used as a regression predictive model by Jason B (2018). Confidence intervals are a way of quantifying the uncertainty of an estimate. It provides both a lower and upper bound and likelihood on a population parameter, such as a mean, estimated from a sample of independent observations from the population. The 95% confidence interval (CI) is a range of values calculated from the data, including the true value of what one estimates about the population.

For instance, the infant death rate for a particular district, say, a residential area in the year 2000 was 6.5 per 1000 live births = (13 Infant deaths / 1989 births) x 1000 = 6.5.

The following formula is used to calculate a 95% confidence interval:

Upper Limit = (1000/n) (d + (1.96 x square root of d))

Lower Limit = (1000/n) (d - (1.96 x square root of d))

where

d = number of events upon which the rate is based
n = denominator of the rate i.e., area population for crude birth and death rates, live births for infant
    death rates.

Hence, if a 95% confidence interval was computed for that rate, an upper limit rate of 5.7 and a lower limit rate of 0.75 would be the result.

Table 6a. Crude birth rate in six different states from the year 1981 to 1995 ["data.gov.in", 2019]

Sno.	Name of States for CBR	y-1981	y-1982	y-1983	y-1984	y-1985	y-1986	y-1987	y-1988	y-1989	y-1990	y-1991	y-1992	y-1993	y-1994	y-1995
1	Andhra Pradesh	31.7	31.2	30.8	31.2	29.9	31.6	30.3	27.4	25.9	26.3	26	24.5	24.3	23.8	24.2
2	Assam	33	34.2	34.7	35.3	34.3	34.7	34.2	32.9	29.4	29.7	30.9	30.8	29.5	30.8	29.3
3	Madhya Pradesh	37.6	38.5	38.5	36.9	39.4	37.2	36.4	37	35.5	37.1	35.8	34.9	34.9	33	33.2
4	Uttar Pradesh	39.6	38.6	38.4	38.7	37.6	37.5	37.9	37.1	37	35.6	35.7	36.3	36.2	35.4	34.8
5	D&N Haveli	36.8	41.7	40.1	45.9	36.9	43.4	35.8	38.3	35.6	35.9	31.1	37.8	33.6	34.4	29.7
6	Pondi cherry	21.7	23.8	23.5	25.3	22.1	22.5	22.4	22.5	21.1	20.4	19.2	19.8	15.5	18	20.1

Table 6b. Crude birth rate in six different states from the year 1996 to 2011(continuation)

Sno	Name of States for CBR	y-1996	y-1997	y-1998	y-1999	y-2000	y-2001	y-2002	y-2003	y-2004	y-2005	y-2006	y-2007	y-2008	y-2009	y-2010	y-2011
1	Andhra Pradesh	22.8	22.5	22.4	21.7	21.3	21	20.7	20.4	19	19.1	18.9	18.7	18.4	18.3	17.9	17.5
2	Assam	27.6	28.2	27.9	27	26.9	27	26.6	26.3	25.1	25	24.6	24.3	23.9	23.6	23.2	22.8
3	Madhya Pradesh	32.3	31.9	30.7	31.1	31.4	31	30.4	30.2	29.8	29.4	29.1	28	28.2	27.7	27.3	26.9
4	Uttar Pradesh	34	33.5	32.4	32.8	32.8	32.1	31.6	31.3	30.8	30.4	30.1	29.5	29.1	28.7	28.3	27.8
5	D&N Haveli	28.9	28.2	34.1	34.2	34.9	29.5	30.4	30.3	28.8	29.4	28.1	27.8	27	27	26.6	26.1
6	Pondi cherry	18.1	18.4	18.2	17.7	17.8	17.9	17.9	17.5	17	16.2	15.7	15.1	16.4	16.5	16.7	16.1

Table 7a. Crude death rate of six states from the year 1981 to 1995

Sno	Names of States for CDR	y-1981	y-1982	y-1983	y-1984	y-1985	y-1986	y-1987	y-1988	y-1989	y-1990	y-1991	y-1992	y-1993	y-1994	y-1995
1	Andhra Pradesh	11.1	10.6	10.4	11	10.3	9.9	9.9	10.2	9.5	9.1	9.7	9.2	8.6	8.3	8.4
2	Assam	12.6	12.4	12.1	13.2	13.2	12.6	11.6	11.8	10.4	10.5	11.5	10.4	10.2	9.2	9.6
3	Madhya Pradesh	16.6	14.9	14.5	14.2	14.2	13.6	13.3	14.3	12.9	12.6	13.8	12.9	12.6	11.6	11.2
4	Uttar Pradesh	16.3	15.1	15.7	17.8	15.8	14.6	14.5	13.2	12.6	12	11.3	12.8	11.6	11	10.3
5	D&N Haveli	14.1	13.2	14	15.5	11.9	9.4	11.3	9.8	8.7	9.6	11.4	11.4	12.2	9.4	8.2
6	Pondi Cherry	7.3	6.5	8.5	8.3	7.2	8.3	8	7.9	7.8	6.2	6.6	6.8	6.3	7.5	7.6

Table 7b. Crude death rate of six states from the year 1996 to 2011(continuation)

Sno	Names of States for CDR	y-1996	y-1997	y-1998	y-1999	y-2000	y-2001	y-2002	y-2003	y-2004	y-2005	y-2006	y-2007	y-2008	y-2009	y-2010	y-2011
1	Andhra Pradesh	8.4	8.3	8.8	8.2	8.2	8.2	8.1	8	7	7.3	7.3	7.4	7.5	7.6	7.6	7.5
2	Assam	9.6	9.9	10	9.7	9.6	9.6	9.2	9.1	8.8	8.7	8.7	8.6	8.6	8.4	8.2	8
3	Madhya Pradesh	11.1	11	11.2	10.4	10.3	10.1	9.8	9.8	9.2	9	8.9	8.7	8.6	8.5	8.3	8.2
4	Uttar Pradesh	10.3	10.3	10.5	10.5	10.3	10.1	9.7	9.5	8.8	8.7	8.6	8.5	8.4	8.2	8.1	7.9
5	D&N Haveli	9.2	8.2	7.9	6.6	7.8	6.5	6.8	6.1	5.2	5.1	4.8	4.8	5.4	4.8	4.7	4.6
6	Pondi Cherry	7.1	8	7.8	6.9	6.5	7	6.7	6.3	8	7.1	7.3	7.7	7.5	7	7.4	7.2

For example, consider an area which had 20 deaths in 1979, 35 in 1980 and 28 deaths in 1981 (Jason B, 2018). If in the year 1980 population was 10,000, the three-year summary crude death rate can be computed as shown below:

$$((20 + 35 + 28) / (3 \times 10000)) \times 1000 = (83 / 30000) \times 1000 = 2.77.$$

This case study deals with the evaluation of confidence interval using crude birth rate and crude mortality rate. The data is taken from www.data.gov.in and analysis was carried out using STATA software. In most of the developing countries, malnutrition is the major cause of child mortality. The areas with better health, hygiene and sanitation facilities help in reduction in mortality rate. Literacy and the economical understanding have blended to lower the birth rate.

Table 8. Crude birth and mortality rate in India from the year (1971 -2011)

Year	Population	Crude Birth Rate	Crude Mortality Rate	Percentage Decadal Variation	Annual Exponential Growth Rate (%)
1971	548.2	41.2	19	24.8	2.2
1981	683.3	37.2	15	24.66	2.22
1991	846.4	32.5	11.4	23.87	2.16
2001	1028.7	24.8	8.9	21.54	1.97
2011	1210.9	21.8	7.1	17.7	1.63

The study calculates the confidence interval to understand the crude birth rate and crude mortality rate in India in six different states namely Andhra Pradesh, Assam, Madhya Pradesh, Uttar Pradesh and Dadra & Nagar Haveli and the data was collected from the year 1981 to 2011. The table 8 shows the decrease in crude birth rate and crude mortality rate from 1971 to 2011 with the population rise. The graph in figure 2 shows the decline in crude birth rate (21.8) and crude mortality rate (7.1) in the year 2011.
From the Table 8,

Population mean = 865.17,
SE = 2.37 with 95% CI = 860.52 to 869.83
and crude birth rate mean = 31.44,
SE = 0.07 and 95% CI = 31.30 to 31.59.
The crude mortality rate mean = 12.24,
SE = 12.16 showed 95% CI = 0.04 to 12.33.
mean = 22.49 and SE = 0.02.
The results of percentage decadal variation 95% CI = 22.44 to 22.54,
mean = 2.034 and SE = 0.002.
The results for annual exponential growth rate were 95% CI = 2.030 to 2.038,

Confidence interval (CI) computes standard errors and confidence intervals for each of the variables.

Figure 2. Graph representing crude birth rate and crude mortality rate in India

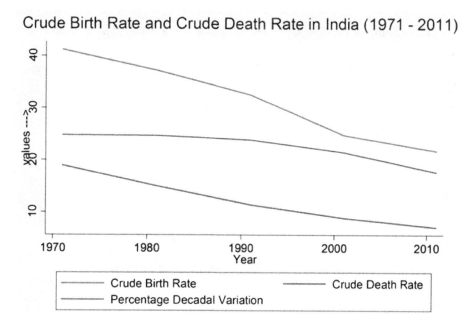

Table 9. CI of crude birth rate and mortality rate in rural and urban

Variable	Mean	Std. err	95% CI
Crude Birth rate rural	21.31	2.25	15.50-27.12
Crude Birth rate urban	19.13	2.17	13.5 -24.71
Crude Death rate rural	7.08	0.43	5.97 -8.18
Crude Death rate urban	5.18	0.49	3.90-6.46

Figure 3. Normal CI calculation screen shot

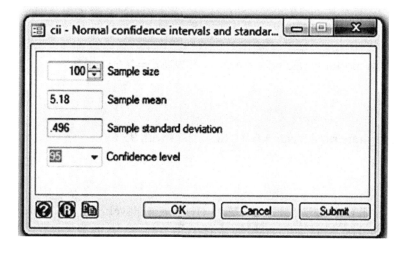

For estimation of CI the following steps are adopted:

- select Statistics > Summaries, tables, and tests > Summary and descriptive statistics > Confidence intervals.
- Enter the mean and std. error in cii dialog box as shown in figure 3 for calculating the normal CI calculation.

Hence, the value of crude birth rate urban is 95% CI = 13.5 to 24.71,

mean = 19.13 and SE = 2.17;

The assessed value of crude birth rate rural - 95% CI = 15.50 to 27.12

mean = 21.31 and SE = 2.25.

The evaluated value of crude mortality rate rural – 95% CI 5.97 to 8.18,

mean = 7.08 and SE = 0.43.

Finally, the calculated value of crude mortality rate urban - 95% CI = 3.90 to 6.46,

mean = 5.18 and SE =0 .49 shown in Table 9.

From the graph in figure 4, the results of total six states for crude birth rate

mean = 21.22, SE = 2.27 and 95% CI = 15.38 to 27.07;

The results of crude birth rate rural mean = 20.78, SE = 2.44 and 95% CI = 14.51 to 27.05 and crude birth rate urban mean = 19.90, SE = 2.41 and 95% CI = 13.69 to 26.11.

The results of total six states for crude mortality rate mean =6.3, SE = 0.58 and 95%

CI= 4.81 to 7.78;

The results of crude mortality rate urban mean = 5.29, SE = 0.60 and 95%

CI = 3.73 to 6.85.

The crude mortality rate rural mean = 6.93, SE = 0.49 with 95%

CI = 5.66 to 8.21.

The peak crude birth rate can be seen in Dadra and Nagar Haveli with 27.7 and lowest total crude mortality rate was found be 4 in Dadra and Nagar Haveli.

Table 10. Confidence interval, mean and standard error for crude birth rate in India (1981-2011)

Year	Mean	Standard Error	[95% Conf. Interval]
1981	32.53	1.59	29.19 to 35.86
1982	34.32	1.59	30.99 - 37.65
1983	33.85	1.54	30.63 - 37.06
1984	35.65	1.71	32.07 - 39.21
1985	32.58	1.54	29.35 - 35.80
1986	34.03	1.77	30.32 – 37.72
1987	32.04	1.41	29.10 - 34.98
1988	32.34	1.49	29.21 - 35.45
1989	30.66	1.48	27.55 - 33.75
1990	30.54	1.55	27.30 - 33.77
1991	28.98	1.49	25.87 - 32.09
1992	30.65	1.67	27.15 - 34.15
1993	28.27	1.90	24.30 - 32.24
1994	28.86	1.63	25.45 - 32.25
1995	28.12	1.26	25.48 - 30.76
1996	26.85	1.37	23.99 - 29.72
1997	26.66	1.30	23.94 - 29.38
1998	27.6	1.45	24.56 - 30.63
1999	27.49	1.53	24.29 - 30.69
2000	27.70	1.56	24.43 - 30.97
2001	26.25	1.29	23.55 - 28.95
2002	26.23	1.29	23.53 - 28.92
2003	25.96	1.31	23.23 - 28.70
2004	25.13	1.28	22.44 - 27.81
2005	24.90	1.35	22.08 - 27.73
2006	24.30	1.33	21.52 - 27.09
2007	23.83	1.34	21.02 - 26.62
2008	23.81	1.17	21.37 - 26.24
2009	23.68	1.14	21.31 - 26.05
2010	23.45	1.08	21.19 - 25.71
2011	22.95	1.09	20.67 - 25.23

Table 11. Confidence interval, mean and standard error for crude mortality rate in India (1981-2011)

Year	Mean	SE	95% Conf. Interval
1981	13	1.42	9.32 to 16.67
1982	12.12	1.31	8.74 - 15.49
1983	12.53	1.11	9.67 - 15.39
1984	13.33	1.36	9.81 - 16.85
1985	12.1	1.24	8.89 - 15.30
1986	11.4	1.03	8.72 - 14.07
1987	11.43	0.94	8.99 - 13.87
1988	11.2	0.96	8.72 - 13.67
1989	10.31	0.84	8.14 - 12.49
1990	10	0.94	7.58 - 12.41
1991	10.71	0.98	8.19 - 13.24
1992	10.58	0.95	8.13 - 13.03
1993	10.25	0.99	7.70 - 12.79
1994	9.5	0.64	7.86 - 11.13
1995	9.21	0.56	7.76 - 10.66
1996	9.28	0.57	7.80 - 10.76
1997	9.28	0.52	7.94 - 10.62
1998	9.36	0.57	7.88 - 10.84
1999	8.71	0.70	6.89 - 10.53
2000	8.78	0.62	7.17 - 10.39
2001	8.58	0.64	6.91 - 10.25
2002	8.38	0.57	6.91 - 9.85
2003	8.13	0.66	6.43 - 9.83
2004	7.83	0.61	6.24 - 9.41
2005	7.65	0.60	6.09 - 9.20
2006	7.6	0.63	5.97 - 9.22
2007	7.61	0.60	6.06 - 9.16
2008	7.66	0.49	6.38 - 8.94
2009	7.41	0.57	5.94 - 8.88
2010	7.38	0.55	5.95 - 8.81
2011	7.23	0.54	5.82 - 8.63

In figure 5, the graph shows the highest crude birth rate in the year 1984 with 45.9 in Dadra and Nagar Haveli and minimum in the year 2007 in Pondicherry.

Figure 4. Graph representing crude birth rate and crude mortality rate in urban and rural

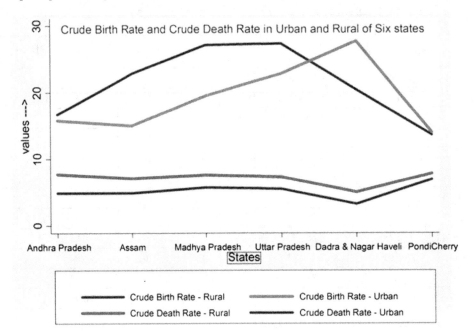

Figure 5. Graph representing crude birth rate in six different states

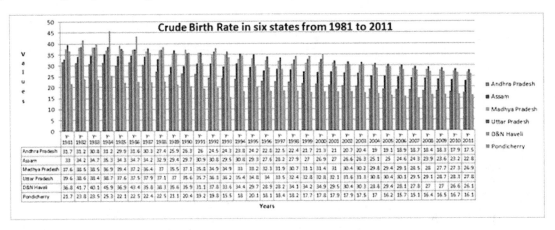

The spacing between children in the rural and urban areas implies that about half of the birth should have spacing of 36 months and above. Most of rural and urban areas now have 70 percent of births which have birth interval of about 24 months.

6. DECISION TREES: A CASE STUDY IN HEALTH CARE

Decision tree is the form of a tree structure which is built on regression or classification models. Decision Tree is a type of very powerful ML model capable of achieving high accuracy in many tasks while being highly interpretable. What makes decision trees special in the realm of ML models is really their clarity of information representation. The "knowledge" learned by a decision tree through training is directly formulated into a hierarchical structure. This structure holds and displays the knowledge in such a way that it can easily be understood, even by non-experts. Decision trees are typically a set of inputs used to create a tree with new cases. It breaks down a dataset into smaller and smaller subsets while at the same time an associated decision tree is incrementally developed. Mujtaba & Irshad (2017) did a Comparative study of existing techniques for heart diseases prediction using data mining approach. On the contrary, decision tree is widely used and practically useful method for reliable inference. For approximating any typical discrete valued target function, learned function is represented by a decision tree.

Decision Tree for Brain Tumour

For this study data in excel format is taken from Gandhi Hospital and Omega hospital. The decision tree is experimented on the unseen datasets that is highlighted by the prediction and application which decision making does. Decision trees work on huge training set and are built in parallel tractable size training datasets. Decision tree will reduce a set of rules and resolve conflict rules, and the resultant is merged into a single unit. Each case is defined by a set of attributes / features. Each training case is given the class name, and each node of the decision tree contains a conditional test that divides the training cases, and the test has two branches ('Yes' or 'No') which the result has to follow. These properties make decision trees a valuable and standard tool for classification and all it follows is the basic divide and conquer algorithm (Steven, 1994). The construction for a decision tree method adopted is below [Quinlan, 1993]:

If S represents training set and R classes denoted by $\{P_1, P_2... P_j\}$, then

- if S has one or more objects where all objects belong to a single class Pj, the decision tree is a leaf identifying class Pj.
- if S has no objects, the decision tree is a leaf itself (S).
- if S has objects that belong to a mixture of classes, then a test is chosen, based on single attribute, that has one or more mutually exclusive outcomes $\{O_1, O_2,..., O_n\}$. S is partitioned into subsets $S1, S2,..., Sn,$ where Si contains all the objects in S that have outcome O_i of the chosen test. The same method is applied recursively to each subset of training objects (Podgorelec V et al, 2002).

With huge number of inputs widely known as features tend the decision trees to overfit. In high-dimensional space, a tree with a few samples is likely to overfit, and the right ratio for samples to the number of features is neccesary. As the number of patient cases increases, the branches in the decision tree increases as shown in figure 6. The figure 6 is an output of the decision tree using python code. The leaf nodes of the tree show that it cannot be divided further and contains an output variable which is used to make a prediction. In this method, from the large training sets the dataset is broken into n subsets (Abhishek, R. 2011). A decision tree is generated on each of the subsets, and rules are generated from the decision tree. This rule sets are combined into a single rule set with conflicts among rules resolved. Decision trees are found to be reliable and scalable with its property to handle huge and large datasets in this study as it gave satisfactory result in diagnosing and predicting brain tumors. Decision tree is found to be one of the successful data mining techniques used in the disease diagnosis as per the literature and in the present case of application.

Figure 6. Decision tree diagram on brain tumor obtained through Python Application
[*See Appendix 1 and 2*]

CONCLUSION

- In the light of the few case studies reported as part of literature survey and specific exercises carried out for this paper, it is possible to say that machine learning provides new opportunities for automatically learning in expressive models.
- The demanding health services by the ever-growing population put the health sector to adopt the computer- based services. This made the entry of machine learning and artificial intelligence, and data mining techniques to unimaginable domain of predictive modelling.
- Regression Models including Multiple and Multivariate Regression techniques are suitable for modeling Air Pollution and heart disease prediction. The applicability of STATA and R packages

for multiple linear regression and predictive modelling for Crude Birth Rate and Crude Mortality Rate is well established in the present study carried out using the data from data.gov.in.

- Decision Tree is a class of very powerful Machine Learning model is applied for Brain Tumor. Machine learning is maturing promptly and requires efficient, well-knowledge and skilled persons on supervised as well as on unsupervised machine learning.

- In simple terms, machine learning techniques and data mining techniques go hand-in-hand as the data analytics tools used in the study for prediction, data modelling, and decision making.

- The health analytics and unpredictable growth of health databases require integration of the conventional data analysis to be paired with methods for efficient computer-assisted analysis. There is need for validation of computational models that are composed of multiple processing layers, which form part of deep learning efforts and are not part of this paper. Deep learning (DL), a technique in artificial neural networks is emerging as a powerful tool for machine learning, promising to reshape the future of artificial intelligence.

- Electronic health records are the source of patient information that include medical history details such as diagnosis, diagnostic exams, medications and treatment plans, immunization records, radiology images, electroencephalogram EEG, laboratory and test lab reports. As such it requires standards for maintenance of these records so as to serve as meaningful and reliable database.

REFERENCES

Abhishek, R. (2011). Computer aided detection of brain tumor in magnetic resonance images. *IACSIT International Journal of Engineering and Technology*, *3*(5), 523–532. doi:10.7763/IJET.2011.V3.280

Agosta, L. (2004, August). The future of data mining -- predictive analytics. *DM Review*.

Bernard, M. (2015). *Big Data: 20 Mind-Boggling Facts Everyone Must Read*. Retrieved September 30, 2015 from https://www.forbes.com

Brooks, R., & Dahlke, K. (2017). *Artificial Intelligence vs. Machine Learning vs. Data Mining 101 – What's the Big Difference?* Retrieved from October 6, 2017 from https://www.guavus.com

Charles, R. B. (2005). *Predictive analysis is data mining's future*. Retrieved June 5, 2005 from http://www.bio-itworld.com

Data Mining- Machine Learning. (n.d.). Retrieved from August 25, 2014. https://doublebyteblog.wordpress.com

Data Mining Tutorial: Process, Techniques, Tools & Applications. (n.d.). Retrieved from https://www.guru99.com

Jason, B. (2018). *Confidence-intervals-for-machine-learning*. Retrieved from May 28,2018. https://machinelearningmastery.com

LogisticRegression. (n.d.). Retrieved from http://ufldl.stanford.edu

Machine_learning. Relation_to_data_mining. (n.d.). Retrieved from https://en.wikipedia.org/wiki/

Mateus, H., Monica, B., & Marie, H. (2015). Land use regression as method to model air pollution. Previous results for Gothenburg/Sweden. *ScienceDirect Procedia Engineering, 115*, 21–28. doi:10.1016/j.proeng.2015.07.350

McNulty, E. (2015). *Whats-the-difference-between-supervised-and-unsupervised-learning*. Retrieved from January 8, 2015 http://dataconomy.com

Mujtaba, A. Q., & Irshad, A. M. (2017). Comparative Study of Existing Techniques for Heart Diseases Prediction Using Data Mining Approach. *Asian Journal of Computer Science and Information Technology, 7*(3), 50–56.

Podgorelec, V., Kokol, P., Stiglic, B., & Rozman, I. (2002). Decision trees: An overview and their use in medicine. [PubMed]. *Journal of Medical Systems, 26*(5), 445–463. doi:10.1023/A:1016409317640

Polaraju, K., & Durgaprasad, D. (2017). Prediction of Heart Disease using Multiple Linear Regression Model. *International Journal of Engineering Development and Research, 5*(4), 1419–1425.

Quinlan, R. J. (1993). *C4.5: programs for machine learning*. San Francisco, CA: Morgan Kaufmann Publishers Inc.

Schneider, A., Hommel, G., & Blettner, M. (2010). Linear regression analysis. In a series of part 14 on evaluation of scientific publications. [PubMed]. *Deutsches Ärzteblatt International, 107*(44), 776–782.

Souhila, S. (2013). *What is the difference between machine learning and data mining?* Retrieved October 23, 2013 from https://www.researchgate.net

Steven, L. S. (1994). *Book Review: C4.5: programs for machine learning by Ross Quinlan J., Machine Learning (16)*. Boston: Kluwer Academic Publishers.

Xavier, A. (2016). *What's the relationship between machine learning and data mining?* Retrieved January 14, 2016 from https://medium.com

This research was previously published in Challenges and Applications for Implementing Machine Learning in Computer Vision; pages 241-270, copyright year 2020 by Engineering Science Reference (an imprint of IGI Global).

APPENDIX 1

Algorithm for Computation of Information gain and Entropy of class attribute

Understanding which attribute to be placed at the root level from the dataset consisting of 'n' attributes is a challenging step. Selecting randomly a node to be the root does not solve the problem. Information gain and entropy are the standards which calculate values for every attribute. The attribute with the highest value is placed at the root. Information is the measure of purity, and entropy is the impurity measure. Information gain is the expected reduction in entropy caused by the splitting of attribute. The entropy of class attribute is calculated by the standard rule

Entropy $= -P/(P+N)\log_2(P/(P+N)) - N/(P+N)\log_2(N/(P+N))$

where P and N represent the positive and negative outcome of the class attribute (predicted column). The standard rule for information gain and entropy of an attribute is given below.

$I(P_i, N_i) = - P/(P+N)\log_2(P/(P+N)) - N/(P+N)\log_2(N/(P+N))$

Entropy attribute $= \Sigma(P_i + N_i)/(P+N) \cdot I(P_i, N_i)$

Gain = Entropy class – Entropy attribute

The gain is calculated to find which attribute has the highest value. The one with the highest value will be the root node. The analysis was carried out using python on 101 patients' reports which were collected from Gandhi Hospital (Secunderabad) and Omega Hospital (Hyderabad). Using the standards discussed above the entropy of class attribute (brain tumor) = 2.9736.

Calculating for sex attribute.

$I(P_i, N_i)$ female=0.6235.
$I(P_i, N_i)$ male=0.2076.
Entropy of the sex=0.3929.
Gain of sex=2.5807; similarly, calculate for the age; it can be split into three groups
    1.   Age≥25 and age<40.
    2.   Age≥40 and age<65.
    3.   Age≥65 and above.
$I(Pi, Ni)$ age≥ 25 and age<40=0.738.
$I(Pi, Ni)$ age>=40 and age <65=0.6722.
$I(Pi, Ni)$ age>=65 and above=0.7219.
Entropy of the age=0.600.
Gain of the age=2.3736,

considering three common and major symptoms, i.e, headache, vomiting, and seizure based on the severity and duration of the symptom on the patient, the values are assigned 0, 1, and 2.

The information gain is calculated as shown in Table 12.

Headache Severity	I(Pi, Ni)
0	0.937
1	0.175 Entropy of headache=0.5111
2	0 Gain of the headache=2.9736 – 0.5111 = 2.4625
Vomiting Severity	**I(Pi,Ni)**
0	0.8058
1	0 Entropy of vomiting=0.582
2	0 Gain of the vomiting=2.9736-0.582=2.3916
Seizure severity	**I(Pi,Ni)**
0	0.742
1	0.468 Entropy of seizure=0.651
2	0 Gain of the Seizure=2.9736-0.651=2.3226

APPENDIX 2

Source Code for Decision Tree Program

 # step 1: import all the required libraries

```
import numpy as np
import pandas as pd
from sklearn import tree
from IPython.display import Image
from sklearn.externals.six import StringIO
import pydotplus
```

#step 2: read input data and map each attribute that need to be printed

```
input_file = "HDetails.csv"
df = pd.read_csv(input_file, header = 0)
d = {'Y': 1, 'N': 0}
df['BrainTumor'] = df['BrainTumor'].map(d)
df['Headache'] = df['Headache'].map(d)
df['Vomiting'] = df['Vomiting'].map(d)
df['Seizure'] = df['Seizure'].map(d)
df['alteredbehaviour'] = df['alteredbehaviour'].map(d)
df['decreasedvision'] = df['decreasedvision'].map(d)
df['difficultyspeech'] = df['difficultyspeech'].map(d)
df['lossofconsciousness'] = df['lossofconsciousness'].map(d)
df['giddiness'] = df['giddiness'].map(d)
df['fever'] = df['fever'].map(d)
```

#step 3: assigning the types of tumor with a numeric value

```
d = {'Glioma': 1, 'Meningioma': 2, 'Parietal': 3, 'Recurrent':4}
df['TypeTumor'] = df['TypeTumor'].map(d)
d = {'M': 1,'F': 0}
df['sex'] = df['sex'].map(d)
print(df.head())
```

 # step 4: listing all the columns from the excel/csv datasheet

```
features = list(df.columns[:13])
features
y = df["BrainTumor"]
X = df[features]
```

 # step5: create the model and create the training data for the classifier / decision tree
 # install pydotplus and graphviz….Graphviz is a tool for drawing graphics using dot files. Pydot-plus is a #module to Graphviz's Dot language
 # train the classifier (decision tree) with the training data

```
clf = tree.DecisionTreeClassifier()
clf = clf.fit(X,y)
dot_data = StringIO()
tree.export_graphviz(clf,out_file = dot_data, feature_names = features)
graph = pydotplus.graph_from_dot_data(dot_data.getvalue())
print("Creating graph...")
graph.write_png('tree2.png')
from sklearn.ensemble import RandomForestClassifier
```

 # step 6: random forests algorithm, technically is an ensemble method (based on the divide-and-#conquer approach) of decision trees generated on a randomly split dataset. This collection of #decision tree classifiers is also known as the forest.

```
clf = RandomForestClassifier(n_estimators=30)
clf = clf.fit(X, y)
```

 # step 7: prints the tree

```
print (clf.predict([[82, 1, 1, 1, 1, 0, 1, 1, 0, 0, 1, 0, 1]]))
print (clf.predict([[28, 1, 2, 1, 1, 0, 0, 1, 1, 0, 0, 0, 0]]))
```

Output: Decision tree diagram on brain tumor obtained through Python Application [Fig 6]

Chapter 55
Drug Prediction in Healthcare Using Big Data and Machine Learning

Mamoon Rashid
https://orcid.org/0000-0002-8302-4571
Lovely Professional University, India & Punjabi University, India

Vishal Goyal
Punjabi University, India

Shabir Ahmad Parah
University of Kashmir, India

Harjeet Singh
Mata Gujri College, India

ABSTRACT

The healthcare system is literally losing patients due to improper diagnosis, accidents, and infections in hospitals alone. To address these challenges, the authors are proposing the drug prediction model that will act as informative guide for patients and help them for taking right medicines for the cure of particular disease. In this chapter, the authors are proposing use of Hadoop distributed file system for the storage of medical datasets related to medicinal drugs. MLLib Library of Apache Spark is to be used for initial data analysis for drug suggestions related to symptoms gathered from particular user. The model will analyze the previous history of patients for any side effects of the drug to be recommended. This proposal will consider weather and maps API from Google as well so that the patients can easily locate the nearby stores where the medicines will be available. It is believed that this proposal of research will surely eradicate the issues by prescribing the optimal drug and its availability by giving the location of the retailer of that drug near the customer.

DOI: 10.4018/978-1-6684-6291-1.ch055

INTRODUCTION

This section of chapter provides a brief outline of introduction to machine learning and health care, use of big data pipeline in health care systems and role of machine learning and big data in drug prediction. The authors have tried to provide the utility of drug discovery in terms of machine learning and big data pipeline.

Introduction to Machine Learning and Health Care

Machine Learning is presently playing major role in Health Care Systems by using various forms of data accumulated over years to derive meaningful insights. Health Care Systems are actively making use of machine learning along with Big Data Analytics to provide proper diagnosis and solutions for diseases by predicting right kinds of drugs. Whenever patient's complaint for any kind of disease, all symptoms are recorded and forwarded to computer with machine learning intelligence. Physicians usually recommend patients to undergo various tests and the inferences are carried out to resolve patient problems by using machine learning approach. For example, once the patient visits any consulting physician, the next step is to take scans in terms of X-rays and MRI's. These scans are later provided as input to machine learning models to diagnose patient problems and health condition with better results.

Use of Big Data Pipeline in Health Care Systems

The inclusion of Big Data Analytics has brought new opportunities for treating patients in the domain of drug development and precision medicines. The use of Big Data Analytics along with Machine Learning has transformed health care systems to the next level. However still Health Care systems are fighting for the right understanding of diseases and drugs. According to (Schork, N. J. 2015), only 25% patients are benefitted from the top 10% drugs which are prescribed in United States Health Care Systems. This percentage is only 2% for patients who are prescribed for cholesterol drugs. The implementation of Big Data helps in tasks for maintaining data in terms of Electronic Health Records and brings data in perfect shape for data monitoring. Big Data is playing its vital role for bringing global medical system together and allowing places and countries to get best treatments and consultation. Social media is the medium where Big Data Analytics has contributed in Health Care Systems. People speak about diseases on social networking sites like Facebook and Twitter. This kind of real data is to be analyzed for insights for various kinds of health care information's by various Big Data Techniques and help in awareness among masses at global level (Bachrach, Y. et al. 2012). The valuable insights can be drawn out of clinical data by the use of smart healthcare technology in terms of big data analytics. This process achieves success in presenting patients risk forecast. This approach will certainly replace the expensive procedures used for maintaining records for patients in Health Care Systems. Big Data Technology has allowed to store huge amounts of patient data in terms of quantity and thus to continuously analyze it for improving quality of life. Big Data Market in terms of Health Care Systems is estimated to grow its market place from 10 billion dollars in year 2016 to 27.6 billion dollars by year 2021 (Kalyan Banga, 2016). The year wise increase in Big Data markets is shown in Figure 1.

Figure 1. Year Wise Big Data Health Care Estimation from 2016 to 2021

Role of Machine Learning and Big Data in Drug Prediction

The algorithms in machine learning are becoming quite useful in the discovery of drugs and their development. In drug development methodology, machine learning plays vital role in several steps. The prediction of various kinds of compounds, the biological activity of molecules, predictions of table structures are some of the areas where the machine learning algorithms contribute in better ways (Lima, A. N. et al 2016). Machine learning procedures help in transformation of discovering of new drugs in the same way as it is used in classifying the unknown people on social networking sites. Machine learning classifies images with different experimental compounds. The compounds with same lighting speed are grouped together by the application of algorithms. Machine learning approach in terms of usage of algorithms turns to be faster and viable method that traditional approaches for getting biological insights. Drug interaction with different target molecules in body speak about its effect. The target variables and drug are bound by different intermolecular forces to leave effect on disease. However when drug interacts with non-target molecules, it can cause various complications for that body in action. Thus efforts are made to point out these kind of detections which are not favored to body and must be avoided.

The biomedical data is a huge collection of structured and unstructured data which needs to be processed and analyzed for the discovery of drugs. Usually this huge data comprises data related to molecules, drug and protein interaction and Electronic Health Records data. To get insights out of this data, various algorithms are needed which are scalable and efficient as well. These algorithms identify patterns in data for predicting various side-effects included in drugs. Big Data Pipelines are formed for running these algorithms for making entire process scalable. The correlation between machine learning and big data pipelines for health care datasets is shown in Figure 2.

BACKGROUND

(Vangsted, A. J et. al 2018) developed drug response prediction model for gene expression profiling from tumor samples. The authors in this work identified the patients with myeloma having high sensitivity for drugs for various suffering toxicity. A machine learning approach along with feature selection technique is performed for the analysis of peptides. This work has given SMO based classifier which

Figure 2. Big data and machine learning approach for health care datasets

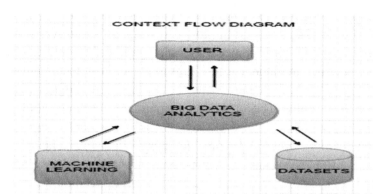

predicted the presence of lantibiotics with an accuracy of 88.5% (Poorin mohammad, N.et al., 2018). The application of artificial intelligence in health care systems was discussed in (Jiang, F. et al., 2017) for past, present and future. The work is outlined to use Artificial Intelligence for cardiology, neurology and cancer. This work has provided the detailed review for the detection and treatment of these diseases in health care systems. The real time processing of health care data has been projected in (Basco, J. A. 2017) where data from different medical related applications and mobile applications stored in Electronic Medical Records is brought in to hadoop and MongoDB environments. This work approach minimized the processing time in patient records to greater extent. (Dimitri, G. M. & Lió, P., 2017) have devised machine learning algorithm, DrugClust, which predicts the side effects in drugs. In this research, the devised machine learning algorithm first clusters the drugs on the basis of their features and then later Bayesian scores is used to predict the various side effects of drugs. The results achieved in this research are promising when evaluated by using 5-folds cross validation procedure. The computational method was proposed in (Ferdousi, R., Safdari, R., & Omidi, Y. 2017) for the prediction of drug-drug interactions. This model claims predictions of 250,000 unknown drug-drug interactions. Predictions in this model are based on similarities in drugs which are functional in nature. (Harnie, D. et al., 2017) used apache spark based pipeline for scaling target predictions in drugs using machine learning approach. The authors in this research claim a speedup factor up to 8 nodes linear in nature and thus enhancing the processing performance in drug discovery. This work basically partitioned the work among various compounds and provided intermediate results. The network bandwidth and time is saved by processing the intermediate data on the same nodes that produce it. (Khamparia, A. et al. 2015) have given a detailed study on knowledge and intelligent computing methods. This research work outlined various rule based learning and case based learnings as well. (Sukhpal Kaur et al. 2016) worked on Big Data News Clusters and managed Web News Big Data and categorizing it on the basis of text and content using different classifiers to provide the accurate news with less running time in clusters.

(Lo, Y. C. et al., 2018) have provided machine learning approach for mining chemical information from chemical databases for drug discovery. This research has provided a means of extracting and processing data related to chemical structures for identifying drugs with important biological properties. The work is tested for various machine learning models and utility of each model is discussed as well. (Chen, R., et al. 2018) have provided a detailed review of machine learning for drug target interaction prediction. This research has highlighted the various databases which are used for drug discovery. The various classification schemes are outlined as well with methods for each category. This research further discusses all the challenges of machine learning for drug target predictions. (Panteleev, J.et al. 2018) discussed the recent advancements in machine learning for drug discovery. This research outlined approaches in deep learning for synthesis and design of compounds, binding predictions and other important properties. This research concludes that machine learning aims to reduce cost, labor demands and cycle time in early levels of drug discovery. (Kolachalama, V. B., 2018) have provided the perspective of machine learning to that of medical education. The authors put emphasis on machine learning inclusion among medical students, residents and fellows. This research directs educational systems especially medical side to include machine learning in curricular time and draw valuable insights. (Lavecchia, A. 2015) has discussed the various methods and applications based on machine learning for discovery of drugs. The major focus given in this research is given to machine learning techniques for ligand based virtual screening. The limitations have been discussed in detail with opportunities and successes kept under consideration as well. (Zhang, L., 2017) summarized various deep learning approaches of machine learning along with applications for discovery of rational drugs. This research suggests that big data pipeline along with machine intelligence can be helpful guide for design and discovery of drugs. (Chen, H., 2018) discusses the remarkable achievements of drug discovery with the use of deep learning procedures. This research concludes that deep learning is having more flexibility for its architecture in comparison to machine learning and there is ease for creating neural network architectures in deep learning. However this research outlines the limitation of deep learning for its need of large training sets. (Khamparia, A. et al 2018) have proposed PCA and SVM based approach for classifying student based E-learning system. This research have used eight attributes of National Centre of Biotechnical Information in terms of Motivation, Personality, Anxiety, Style of Learning, Previous Grades, Prior Student Knowledge, Study Level and Cognitive Style for classification purposes. (M Rashid, R Chawla, 2013) discusses the measures to bring security in data storage on public clouds by providing the extended model of Role Based Access Control where the authenticated users can only access the data in terms of roles with assigned permissions and restricts the unknown users from accessing data by adding variable constraints.

(Colwell, L. J. 2018) has discussed machine learning and statistical techniques and approaches for the prediction of protein-ligand interactions in discovery of drugs. This research outlined the major difficulties and challenges for the prediction of ligands and highlighted challenges for using datasets which are unbiased for models. (Brown, N., 2018) have given overview of using big data in drug discovery. This research concludes that artificial intelligence with NLP pipelines can draw successes in the field of drug discovery. Moreover the authors have given outline to prepare models in Big Data for handling various issues in discovery of drugs. (Khamparia, A. et al. 2016) presented a model driven framework for identifying threats in E-Learning System. This research also provided case study based on petri net models for improving consistency and reliability in e-learning systems.

NOVEL APPROACH FOR DRUG PREDICTION USING BIG DATA AND MACHINE LEARNING

Nowadays medicine consuming has become day to day activities for the people who are suffering from diseases. Most of the people are not also aware of the medication prescribed by doctors or pharmacies. Sometimes patients get other kind of complications as well by taking the medicines prescribed by medical practitioners. According to Forbes, there are many reasons associated with it and some problems associated with it are given.

1. Overuse and unnecessary care accounts for high amount of money and is more common than you might imagine. Unnecessary tests and drugs explains Why Health Care Costs So Much.
2. Traditionally, health plans, Medicare and Medicaid pay providers for whatever services they deliver, regardless of whether services truly benefit the patient or not.
3. Transparency galvanizes change like nothing else. Transparency is a vital component to build an effective and efficient health care system and the lack of transparency in Indian healthcare threatens to erode public trust.
4. Awareness of the people: A lot of primary health problems can be solved if we provide effective training and the knowledge to the local population. The lack of awareness among the patients provides doctors to take benefit of "supplier induced demand" to extract money.
5. Accessibility: The rural-urban divide is enormous; therefore, proper supply chain management is indispensable. The usage technology is good for accessibility, the use of telemedicine is very helpful.

For addressing the above challenges, the authors tried to eradicate these issues somehow by prescribing the optimal drug, its usage and its availability by giving the location of the retailer of that drug near the customer. The proposal of big data pipeline along with machine learning approach for the prediction and suggestion of right drugs is shown in Figure 3.

Figure 3. Drug prediction model using big data and machine learning

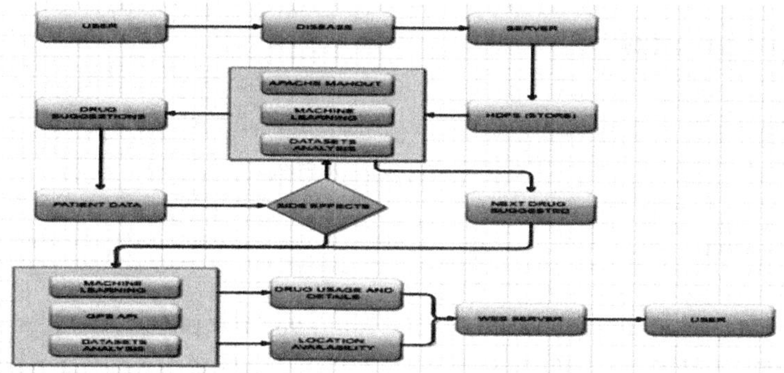

The idea is to prepare Big Data Pipeline and store Health Care Data in terms of patient's previous summary and medicines in Hadoop Distributed File System. Later when the patient will come with any kind of symptoms, machine learning algorithms are applied in terms of Mllib library of Apache Spark to provide drug suggestions keeping side effects of patient under consideration on the basis of previous log data. The machine learning approach is to be used iteratively until the best suited medicine is to be suggested for patient. Later concept of GPS API is to be added in idea which will provide the availability of location where the medicine is to be available. The various functions performed by this big data pipeline is explained in steps:

1. Drug Analysis and Prediction

Providing the transparency to the people who do not know that which medicine is good for the disease and which is not will save patients from the wrong diagnosis by the doctors. Based on the historical datasets and machine learning algorithms, optimal drug is prescribed according to the disease input by the user.

2. Side Effects Analysis

This module is for analyzing patient's data that can lead to side effects by that prescribed drug. A medicine may have a side-effect of skin-irritation. But if the patient is already having some other skin problem then taking this medicine can worsen the condition of patient.

3. Next Optimal Drug Suggestion

This module follows the side effect analysis module. If the prescribed drug leads to side effects based on the drug records and patient records, then the drug dataset is analyzed again and next optimal drug is suggested.

4. GPS API

Geo location refers to the identification of the geographic location of a user or computing device via a variety of data collection mechanisms. Typically, most geo location services use network routing addresses or internal GPS devices to determine this location. By adding the GPS API, we will be able to fetch the location of the user.

5. Drug Location Availability

Based on the user's location, drug retailers and medicinal shops near the user's location are shown to the customers.

6. Speech Recognition

Speech recognition will be implemented for the blind and the physically disabled so that they can speak the disease name and they would be suggested for the medicines which can be an antidote to their disease, especially useful for users with disability.

The drug details and usage will also be given to patient for effective use of drugs. The step procedure of drug prediction model using big data pipeline is shown in Figure 4.

The patient is required to enter disease name or symptoms to the web interface from where the data is to be fetched and stored in Hadoop Distributed File System (HDFS). Patient query is checked from the log data present on HDFS and machine learning approach is to be applied to check side effects of drug suggested. Alternate medicines are suggested in case the recommended drug is having side effects for patient.

Figure 4. Step procedure of drug prediction model using big data pipeline

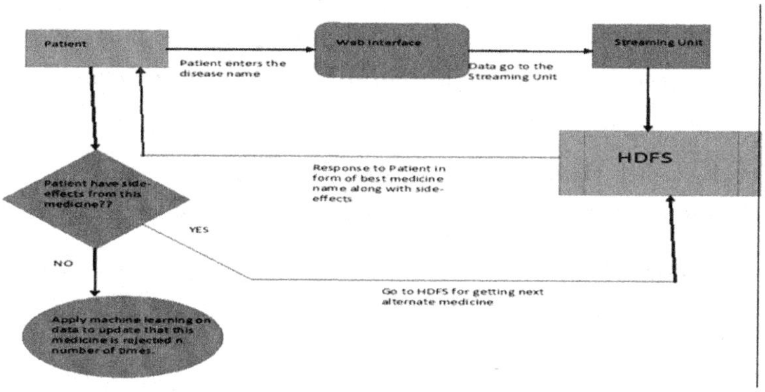

EXPECTED OUTCOME OF WORK

Save Time and Money

Going to hospital costs a great deal of time and money. You have to make an appointment in advance but sometimes still wait for hours to see doctors, and then stand in line to get your medicines. By utilizing data analytics in this model, last health records can be used to reduce diagnostic process and avoid cost-intensive treatments that they did not work in history.

Better Care

This idea will help the patients to get confirmation that they are being diagnosed for the correct disease by entering the symptoms and then getting the disease name. Now, the second problem may be that doctor have identified the diseases correctly, but medicine is not proper for it or it has some side-effects. This problem will also get solved by getting the list of medicines from HDFS for that disease. Third thing is that sometimes patients find it difficult for getting a particular medicine because it may not be available on local stores. So authors are proposing the availability of locations of various medical stores where that medicine can be found.

CONCLUSION

This chapter of research will surely eradicate the issues somehow by prescribing the optimal drug, its usage and its availability by giving the location of the retailer of that drug near the customer. This research chapter takes a step-in order to reduce various errors in medical system. It will reduce the unnecessary costs and overuse of drug which is more common in today's world. It will also bring the transparency, along with awareness regarding the details of medicines and its usage which is a vital component to build an effective and efficient health care system.

REFERENCES

Bachrach, Y., Kosinski, M., Graepel, T., Kohli, P., & Stillwell, D. (2012, June). Personality and patterns of Facebook usage. In *Proceedings of the 4th annual ACM web science conference* (pp. 24-32). ACM. 10.1145/2380718.2380722

Banga, K. (2016, October). Big Data Healthcare Market to reach $27.6bn by 2021. *Future Analytics World*. Retrieved from http://fusionanalyticsworld.com/big-data-healthcare-market-reach-27-6bn-2021/

Basco, J. A. (2017, November). Real-time analysis of healthcare using big data analytics. *IOP Conference Series. Materials Science and Engineering, 263*(4), 042056. doi:10.1088/1757-899X/263/4/042056

Brown, N., Cambruzzi, J., Cox, P. J., Davies, M., Dunbar, J., Plumbley, D., & Sheppard, D. W. (2018). Big Data in Drug Discovery. *Progress in Medicinal Chemistry, 57*, 277–356. doi:10.1016/bs.pmch.2017.12.003 PMID:29680150

Chen, H., Engkvist, O., Wang, Y., Olivecrona, M., & Blaschke, T. (2018). The rise of deep learning in drug discovery. *Drug Discovery Today, 23*(6), 1241–1250. doi:10.1016/j.drudis.2018.01.039 PMID:29366762

Chen, R., Liu, X., Jin, S., Lin, J., & Liu, J. (2018). Machine Learning for Drug-Target Interaction Prediction. *Molecules (Basel, Switzerland), 23*(9), 2208. doi:10.3390/molecules23092208 PMID:30200333

Colwell, L. J. (2018). Statistical and machine learning approaches to predicting protein-ligand interactions. *Current Opinion in Structural Biology, 49*, 123–128. doi:10.1016/j.sbi.2018.01.006 PMID:29452923

Dimitri, G. M., & Lió, P. (2017). DrugClust: A machine learning approach for drugs side effects prediction. *Computational Biology and Chemistry, 68*, 204–210. doi:10.1016/j.compbiolchem.2017.03.008 PMID:28391063

Ferdousi, R., Safdari, R., & Omidi, Y. (2017). Computational prediction of drug-drug interactions based on drugs functional similarities. *Journal of Biomedical Informatics, 70*, 54–64. doi:10.1016/j.jbi.2017.04.021 PMID:28465082

Harnie, D., Saey, M., Vapirev, A. E., Wegner, J. K., Gedich, A., Steijaert, M., & De Meuter, W. (2017). Scaling machine learning for target prediction in drug discovery using apache spark. *Future Generation Computer Systems, 67*, 409–417. doi:10.1016/j.future.2016.04.023

Jiang, F., Jiang, Y., Zhi, H., Dong, Y., Li, H., Ma, S. & Wang, Y. (2017). Artificial intelligence in healthcare: past, present and future. *Stroke and Vascular Neurology, 2*(4), 230-243.

Kaur, S., & Rashid, M. (2016). Web News Mining using Back Propagation Neural Network and Clustering using K-Means Algorithm in Big Data. *Indian Journal of Science and Technology, 9*(41). doi:10.17485/ijst/2016/v9i41/95598

Khamparia, A., & Pandey, B. (2015). Knowledge and intelligent computing methods in e-learning. *International Journal of Technology Enhanced Learning, 7*(3), 221–242. doi:10.1504/IJTEL.2015.072810

Khamparia, A., & Pandey, B. (2016). Threat driven modeling framework using petri nets for e-learning system. *SpringerPlus, 5*(1), 446. doi:10.118640064-016-2101-0 PMID:27119050

Khamparia, A., & Pandey, B. (2018). SVM and PCA Based Learning Feature Classification Approaches for E-Learning System. *International Journal of Web-Based Learning and Teaching Technologies*, *13*(2), 32–45. doi:10.4018/IJWLTT.2018040103

Kolachalama, V. B., & Garg, P. S. (2018). Machine learning and medical education. *NPJ Digital Medicine, 1*(1), 54.

Lavecchia, A. (2015). Machine-learning approaches in drug discovery: Methods and applications. *Drug Discovery Today*, *20*(3), 318–331. doi:10.1016/j.drudis.2014.10.012 PMID:25448759

Lima, A. N., Philot, E. A., Trossini, G. H. G., Scott, L. P. B., Maltarollo, V. G., & Honorio, K. M. (2016). Use of machine learning approaches for novel drug discovery. *Expert Opinion on Drug Discovery*, *11*(3), 225–239. doi:10.1517/17460441.2016.1146250 PMID:26814169

Lo, Y. C., Rensi, S. E., Torng, W., & Altman, R. B. (2018). Machine learning in chemoinformatics and drug discovery. *Drug Discovery Today*, *23*(8), 1538–1546. doi:10.1016/j.drudis.2018.05.010 PMID:29750902

Panteleev, J., Gao, H., & Jia, L. (2018). Recent applications of machine learning in medicinal chemistry. *Bioorganic & Medicinal Chemistry Letters*, *28*(17), 2807–2815. doi:10.1016/j.bmcl.2018.06.046 PMID:30122222

Poorin Mohammad, N., Hamedi, J., & Moghaddam, M. H. A. M. (2018). Sequence-based analysis and prediction of lantibiotics: a machine learning approach. *Computational Biology and Chemistry*.

Rashid, M., & Chawla, R. (2013). Securing Data Storage by Extending Role Based Access Control. *International Journal of Cloud Applications and Computing*, *3*(4), 28–37. doi:10.4018/ijcac.2013100103

Schork, N. J. (2015). Personalized medicine: Time for one-person trials. *Nature*, *520*(7549), 609–611. doi:10.1038/520609a PMID:25925459

Vangsted, A. J., Helm-Petersen, S., Cowland, J. B., Jensen, P. B., Gimsing, P., Barlogie, B., & Knudsen, S. (2018). Drug response prediction in high-risk multiple myeloma. *Gene*, *644*, 80–86. doi:10.1016/j.gene.2017.10.071 PMID:29122646

Zhang, L., Tan, J., Han, D., & Zhu, H. (2017). From machine learning to deep learning: Progress in machine intelligence for rational drug discovery. *Drug Discovery Today*, *22*(11), 1680–1685. doi:10.1016/j.drudis.2017.08.010 PMID:28881183

This research was previously published in Hidden Link Prediction in Stochastic Social Networks; pages 79-92, copyright year 2019 by Information Science Reference (an imprint of IGI Global).

Chapter 56
Smart Pollution Alert System Using Machine Learning

P. Chitra

Thiagarajar College of Engineering, India

S. Abirami

Thiagarajar College of Engineering, India

ABSTRACT

This chapter proposes a novel mobile-based pollution alert system. The level of the pollutants is available in the air quality repository. This data is updated periodically by collecting the information from the sensors placed at the monitoring stations of different regions. A model using artificial neural network (ANN) is proposed to predict the AQI values based on the present and previous values of the pollutants. The ANN model processes the normalized data and predicts whether the region is hazardous or not. A novel mobile application which could be used by the user to know about the present and future pollution level could be developed using a progressive web application development environment. This mobile application uses the location information of the user and helps the user to predict the hazardous level of the pollutants in that particular location.

INTRODUCTION

The introduction of particulates, harmful gases and other biological molecules into the Earth's atmosphere causes air pollution, which leads to disease, death and damage to humans, damage and other living organisms such as food crops. These particles and gases that pollute the atmosphere are known as air pollutant. The air pollutant causes adverse effects on human beings and their ecosystem. Sources of air pollutants are generally either anthropogenic or natural.

Air pollutants are classified as primary or secondary. A primary pollutant is emitted directly from a source, e.g. Sulfur Dioxide (SO_2), Carbon Monoxide (CO), Nitrogen Oxides (NOX), and particulate matter (PM). A secondary pollutant is not directly emitted as such, but forms when other pollutants

DOI: 10.4018/978-1-6684-6291-1.ch056

(primary pollutants) react in the atmosphere. An example of a secondary pollutant is Ozone. When hydrocarbons are emitted and they react with NO_x in presence of sunlight, they form ozone.

The secondary pollutant Ozone has critical effects on human health such as permanent lung damage, aggravated asthma, or other respiratory illnesses. Above certain limits they also cause damage to plants, reduce the crop yield, and also increase of vegetation vulnerability to diseases.

Particulate matter (PM) is the mixture of all solid and liquid particles suspended in air, many of which are hazardous. Both organic and inorganic particles, such as dust, pollen, soot, smoke, and liquid droplets are present in this mixture. Some of them such as dust, dirt, soot, or smoke, are large enough to be seen with the naked eye while the rest are so small that they can only be detected only using an electron microscope. Fine particulate matter ($PM_{2.5}$) consisting of particles with diameter 2.5 mm or smaller, is an important pollutant among others as they are capable of penetrating deeply into the lungs and cause health problems, including the decrease of lung function, development of chronic bronchitis and nonfatal heart attacks (EPA, 2005).

Sulphur dioxide is another eminent air pollutant whose source is from fossil combustion of industries and locomotives. Its effects on human beings include damage of respiratory system, particularly lung function, and can irritate the eyes. It mainly causes respiratory tract inflammations along with coughing, mucus secretion and also aggravates conditions such as asthma and chronic bronchitis. Also, wet deposition of it is acidic and causes acid rain that contains sulfuric acid. This badly affects the ecosystem by changing the nutrient balance in water and soil (EPA, 2005).

Nitrogen dioxide, another important air pollutant is part of a group of gaseous air pollutants produced as a result of road traffic and other fossil fuel combustion processes. Globally, it contributes to global warming and is the third most important greenhouse gas in the UK. Nitric Oxide (NO_x) gases react to form acid rain and smog and also contribute to the formation of fine particles (PM) and ground level ozone. All these, in turn affect human beings with their associated adverse health effects (EPA, 2005).

Periodic air quality evaluation could be the best way to monitor and control air pollution. The suitability of air for lives on earth depends upon its characteristics. The Air Quality Health Index (AQHI) is a health protection tool designed in Canada that helps to understand the impact of air quality on human health. As shown in Figure 1 it provides a number from 1 to 10+ to indicate the level of health risk associated with local air quality. As the number increases it indicates greater the health risk and suggests the needed precautions to be taken. The index describes the level of health risk associated with this number as 'low', 'moderate', 'high' or 'very high', and suggests steps that can be taken to reduce exposure. Building a forecast system to predict hourly average concentrations of the pollutants and thereby its AQHI would be an efficient system to protect the people especially the vulnerable groups on a daily basis from the negative shades of air pollution.

The three main factors that mainly influence the concentration of air pollution at a particular location are meteorological factors, the source of pollutants and the local topography of that location. Many air quality forecasting uses straightforward approaches like box models, Gaussian models and linear statistical models. Though, these models are easy to implement and allow for the fast calculation of forecasts, they fail to describe the interactions and non-linear relationship that handle the transportation and behavior of pollutants in the atmosphere.

The knowledge discovery and their interpretations from the huge amount of past air pollutant concentrations data and meteorological data seemed vital in the process of forecasting air quality. Machine learning that originated from the field of artificial intelligence has become popular in solving it. A large number of neural networks are used for forecasting air quality and are also found to be more advanta-

Figure 1. Air quality health index table

Health Risk	Air Quality Health Index	Health Messages	
		At Risk Population	General Population
Low	1 - 3	Enjoy your usual outdoor activities.	Ideal air quality for outdoor activities.
Moderate	4 - 6	Consider reducing or rescheduling strenuous activities outdoors if you are experiencing symptoms.	No need to modify your usual outdoor activities unless you experience symptoms such as coughing and throat irritation.
High	7 - 10	Reduce or reschedule strenuous activities outdoors. Children and the elderly should also take it easy.	Consider reducing or rescheduling strenuous activities outdoors if you experience symptoms such as coughing and throat irritation.
Very High	Above 10	Avoid strenuous activities outdoors. Children and the elderly should also avoid outdoor physical exertion.	Reduce or reschedule strenuous activities outdoors, especially if you experience symptoms such as coughing and throat irritation.

geous than the statistical methods. However, some of their difficulties include computational expense, multiple local minima during optimization, over fitting to noise in the data, etc. Furthermore, there are no general rules to determine the optimal size of network and learning parameters, which greatly affects the prediction performance.

Model updating is another key feature in air quality forecasting that updates and refines the model along with everyday forecasting using their latest observations. The two ways for model updating are batch learning and online learning. In batch learning, whenever new data are received, it uses the past data together with the new data and performs a retraining of the model. Therefore, batch training is computationally expensive. Online learning uses only the new data to revise the model. Generally linear models easily update with batch learning or online learning. But, for non-linear methods, online learning is difficult for many formulations such as the non-linear kernel method. Also, short time update implementation using batch learning is too expensive as a non-linear model tends to have more parameters to train and the training process is much slower compared to linear models. Hence, developing non-linear updatable models for real-time air quality forecasting is remaining essential.

Machine Learning Algorithms

Machine learning is a sub-field of Artificial Intelligence. Machine learning algorithms analyze input data to predict output values within an acceptable range. As new data is fed to these algorithms, they learn and optimize their operations to improve performance, developing intelligence over time. There are four types of machine learning algorithms: supervised, semi-supervised, unsupervised and reinforcement.

Supervised Learning

In this the model is trained using previous examples. A known dataset that includes desired inputs and outputs is fed as input and the job of the algorithm is to find a method to determine how to arrive at those inputs and outputs. In this process, the algorithm identifies patterns in data, learns from observations and makes predictions. Finally, the algorithm makes predictions and is corrected by its previous knowledge and this process continues until the algorithm achieves a high level of accuracy. Some of the common tasks followed using supervised learning is Classification, Regression and Forecasting.

- **Classification:** In this the algorithms gains knowledge from the past database and tries to determine under what category the new observations belong to. For example, when detecting credit card fraud as 'fraud' or 'safe', the program must look at existing observational data and classify the new data accordingly.
- **Regression:** In this the algorithm must infer and understand the relationships among the different variables. The regression analysis is particularly useful for forecasting/ prediction of the dependent variable using the others.

Semi-Supervised Learning

It is similar to supervised learning, but the input to the algorithm has both labeled and unlabeled data. Labeled data is essentially carries information that has meaningful tags so that the algorithm can understand the data, while unlabelled data lacks them. Using the labeled data machine learning algorithms can learn to label unlabeled data.

Unsupervised Learning

In this method of training the algorithm identify patterns from the input data. There is no meaningful information provided to the algorithm. Instead, the machine determines the correlations and relationships by analyzing available data. Through this sort of training the machine learning algorithm is left to interpret large data sets and address that data accordingly. The algorithm keeps categorizing that data into clusters in some way to describe its structure and makes it look more organized. As it learns pattern by assessing more data it gradually improves its ability to make decisions on the data. One importank task that can be performed using unsupervised learning is clustering. Clustering refers to grouping sets of similar data based on defined criteria. It for segments data into several groups and performs analysis on each data set to find patterns.

Reinforcement Learning

In reinforcement learning processes, the machine learning algorithm is provided with a set of actions, parameters and end values. By using regimented learning process it defines the rules and tries to explore different options and possibilities. It monitors and evaluates each result and determines which one is optimal based on trial and error. The algorithm is from past experiences and begins to adapt its responses to the situation in such a way to achieve the best possible result.

Online Machine Learning Algorithm

An up to date model can be obtained only if it can learn from new examples in something close to real time. Online machine learning algorithms (Figure 2) keep updating the model for every new observation made now and then. Online learning is data efficient and adaptable. It is not only fast but also has the capability to capture any new trend visible in with time.

Figure 2. Online Machine Learning Algorithm

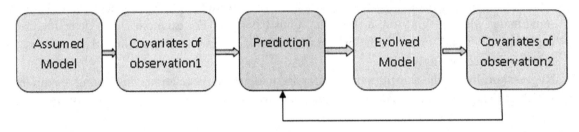

Air Pollution Alert System

Good air quality is essential for existence and survival of life on earth. With huge developments in urbanization our ecosystem is highly endangered to pollution. Many diseases and allergies affect all life on earth. Acid rain and global warming are other effects of air pollution that makes the earth an unsuitable place to live in. Proper forecasting of air quality can help people reduce their exposure on risky days and also support the law makers to set rules accordingly to counter the increasing pollution. Hence the need for an efficient and accurate air pollution alert system remains imperative in today's world.

Various machine learning algorithms are used till date for extracting knowledge from past pollutant concentration and meteorological databases that are available in large quantity for various locations. Apart from pollutant concentration and meteorological data many researches prove that the forecasting values also depend upon the location's topography, traffic, peaks etc. This knowledge discovery using machine learning (Figure 3) helps to obtain valuable patterns in the values of air quality with respect to various parameters. These patterns in turn are efficiently utilized to predict the future air quality values which can be used to alert the people when air quality value is expected to go down. This alert system mainly helps the vulnerable group of people suffering from various diseases and allergies to reduce their exposure so that they can avoid the risk of their health on those risky days. Children, older adults and those who are suffering from lung and/or heart disease are especially vulnerable to the adverse effects of air pollutants and should take special precautions when the ambient air quality crosses unhealthy levels. High AQHI readings (7-10) can cause increased asthma symptoms, such as coughing, wheezing, chest tightness and the need for increased inhaler use. Planning outdoor activities by checking the AQHI could possibly minimize the health risks. Many researches has also proved this by using the clinical database- the number of patients being admitted in hospitals everyday- as one of the parameter in machine learning algorithms for knowledge discovery (Ren et al, 2018). Hence, location specific predicted air quality values and advisories must be made widely available through air pollution alert system to people in order to reduce/avoid exposure on days having unhealthy air quality.

Figure 3. Air Pollution Alert System

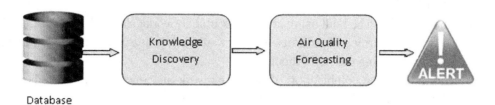

Previous Works

Standard conventional static methods like the typical SVM algorithm is not able to process the huge data that needs frequent and continuous updating (Ghaemi et al, 2018). Once a typical SVM algorithm is trained, it works as the stationary model afterward and when new training samples are available, learning has to restart again. This process is computationally expensive and time-consuming. Online algorithms are regarded as an alternative to the conventional static methods.

A semi-supervised learning approach can be used based on a co-training framework that consists of two separated classifiers (Zheng et al, 2013). One is a spatial classifier based on an artificial neural network (ANN), which takes spatially-related features (e.g., the density of POIs and length of highways) as input to model the spatial correlation between air qualities of different locations. The other is a temporal classifier based on a linear-chain conditional random field (CRF), involving temporally-related features (e.g., traffic and meteorology). The framework consists of two major parts, offline learning and online inference

Long short-term memory neural network extended (LSTME) model that inherently considers spatio-temporal correlations for air pollutant concentration prediction (Li et al, 2017). Long short term memory (LSTM) layers can be used to automatically extract inherent useful features from historical air pollutant data, and auxiliary data, including meteorological data and time stamp data. Unlike traditional RNNs, LSTM NNs are capable of learning long time series and are not affected by the vanishing gradient problem. Compared to traditional shallow models such as the SVR, ARMA and TDNN, deep learning-based models exhibit better prediction performance.

Feature selection and spatio-temporal semi supervised learning can be embedded in the input layer and the output layer of the deep learning neural network respectively (Qi et al, 2018) Feature selection and analysis is not to increase the prediction accuracy, but to discover the importance of different input features to the predictions of the neural networks, reveal the main relevant factors to the variation of air quality, and provide a proof from data science to support the air pollution's prevention and control.

Instead of updating the parameters of the prediction network, M-BP algorithm can be used to update the missing values of input data to minimize the prediction loss with the trained prediction neural network (Li et al, 2017). Without the M-BP, the model takes 5 hours to converge on a single Nvidia Titan GPU card, while with the M-BP, it takes 8 hours to converge.

In order to improve the processing speed along with required machine learning functionalities, Apache Spark can be employed on the Hadoop cluster (Asgari et al, 2017). Multinomial Naïve Bayes and Multinomial Logistic Regression algorithms are used for short-term air pollution forecasting. Predictive air quality risk map is generated for the next 24 hours for the whole city using inverse distance weighting (IDW) method.

Forecasting model can also be built using artificial neural network (ANN) (Gorai et al, 2017; Goyal et al, 2015). Two types of learning algorithms, feed forward back propagation (FFBP) and layer recurrent (LR) were used for training the ANN model.

A Neuro-Fuzzy model, the combination of neural network and fuzzy logic methods can also be used for air pollutant concentration prediction which is found to be more efficient than MLR and ANN (Mishra et al, 2016).

Big Data Analytics

The amount of data being processed for air quality prediction is enormous in terms of volume, velocity and variety (Zheng et al, 2013). Hence an organized platform is essential for integrating, dealing, validating and securing this data. Hadoop is one of the most popular framework (Figure 4) for distributed storage and processing of big data. Its capability of managing and analyzing massive amounts of structured and unstructured data quickly, reliably, flexibly and at low-cost is the main reason for its popularity (Chimmiri, 2016). Apache Hadoop has master-slave architecture. The master node manages the cluster state. The slave nodes are responsible for storing data and executing tasks assigned to them. Distributed File System (HDFS) and YARN resource manager are two important advances of Hadoop 2. HDFS is designed to store large amount of data across multiple available machines in redundant fashion. YARN is manages the distributed applications across Hadoop cluster and provide computing resources like CPU, memory and etc. The support for workloads provided by YARN enhances the power of Hadoop cluster through its iterative modeling. These models allow enterprises to realize near real-time processing og big data.

Figure 4. Hadoop architecture

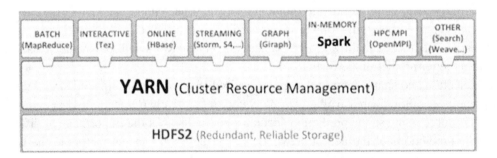

Spark

Spark is an in-memory distributed computing framework (Figure 5)for developing applications to perform general data analytics on distributed computing clusters. Spark speeds up the cluster computing processes through its in-memory feature. It processes by caching the dataset in memory and then performing computations at memory speeds and also by sharing data between subsequent iterations through memory (Kestelyn, 2013) Spark representation of a dataset is called RDD. RDD is a parallel data structure that lets users keep on intermediate results in memory, organize its partitioning to optimize data placement, and manipulate them using a rich set of operators and higher-level libraries like SparkSQL, Spark streaming, MLlib and GraphX. DAG is a finite directed graph of stages which are created based on various transformation applied to Spark RDDs. Each stage is comprised of tasks based on partitions of the RDD and these tasks should be executed on processing nodes. Spark supports YARN as cluster manager and its ability to read and write from and to HDFS enable Hadoop users to easily run Spark on their own Hadoop cluster.

Figure 5. Spark architecture

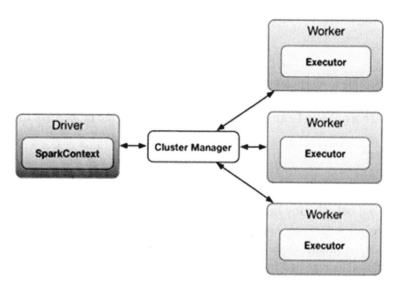

Deep Learning

A deep neural network (DNN) is an artificial neural network (ANN) with multiple hidden layers between the input and output layers (Figure 6). DNNs can model complex non-linear relationships. Deep learning can be trained in an unsupervised or supervised manner for both unsupervised and supervised learning tasks. The modern state-of-the-art deep learning is focused on training deep (many layered) neural network models using the back propagation algorithm. The most popular deep learning networks are:

- Multilayer Perceptron Networks.
- Convolutional Neural Networks.
- Long Short-Term Memory Recurrent Neural Networks.

Deep learning prototype can learn valuable representations of raw data and have spectacularly enhanced the contemporary in object detection, speech recognition, visual object recognition, and a lot of other areas. Also, deep learning models offer training scalability, stability, and generalization with big data. Due to its wide capability, Deep Learning is rapidly becoming the procedure of prime for the highest predicting precision (Ghoneim et al, 2017).

Figure 6. Deep learning architecture

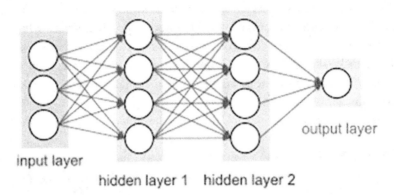

Prediction of air quality is an analysis of time series data. Traditional shallow models do not have the capacity for modeling sequential data with high accuracy rate. As time series data are more complex, high dimensional and noisy, Deep Learning is often associated with the problem of time series prediction

Proposed System

The spatial-temporal inputs considered for air quality prediction are dynamic large scale streaming, spatially expansive and behaviorally heterogeneous. Predicting air pollution under high resolution using this big dataset requires data processing technologies with high processing power and high capacity storage. In this chapter, we predict the real-time and fine-grained air quality value for an entire city based on their past air quality data reported by a limited number of existing monitor stations in the city and a variety of data sets that are observed in the city. Those observed city data could be meteorology, traffic flow, human mobility, structure of road networks, and POIs etc. Although there is no accurate relation between air quality and these factors, these models are usually based on experimental assumptions and the observed parameters that may not be applicable to all urban environments. In this chapter, we consider the meteorological data and the geographical data along with the past air quality data.

The proposed air pollution alert system (Figure 7) is a real time application that aid people to take decision regarding avoiding /reducing their exposure particularly on risky days. It provides 24 hours advanced location specific predicted values on mobile clients and website through web services. The spatial-temporal model used to predict air quality overcomes the limitation in accuracy due to the scarcity of monitoring station in urban areas.

DATA CONSIDERED FOR PREDICTION

Pollutant Data

The concentration of various pollutant collected from various monitoring stations are considered. These data is collected and is available in every air quality monitoring stations on hour basis. Due to the high cost of construction the numbers of monitoring stations are not available along all parts of a city and hence the prediction is based on the pollutant data along with how this would vary with other observed data like meteorology, traffic flow and topography of a location.

Figure 7. Flow Chart of the Proposed System

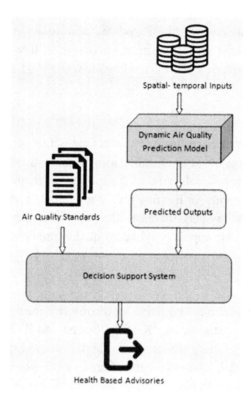

Meteorology Data

This data includes the values of wind speed, temperature and humidity for every location on hourly basis. This data is collected from the government's meteorology centre. Researches had proved that the amount of a pollutant concentration varies with these meteorology parameters.

Geographical Data

This data includes the topography features of a location such as its height, distance from the available peaks nearby, distance from the nearby roads, the traffic flow rate, various points of interests (POIs) etc. These features of a location greatly influence the concentration of the pollutants found in it. For example, the locations near to traffic roads embrace the adverse effects of air pollution.

Data Preprocessing

A more sophisticated M-BP algorithm (Li et al, 2017) capable of overcoming the missing data challenge, which provides high temporal-spatial air pollution estimation, at low computational complexity is considered. This data preprocessing is deep (has recurrent structures) and can perform sequential feature extraction automatically, which saves the step of constructing multiple classifiers. Instead of updating the parameters of the prediction network, M-BP updates the missing values of input data to minimize the prediction loss with the trained prediction neural network. Without the M-BP, the model takes 5 hours to converge on a single Nvidia Titan GPU card, while with the M-BP, it takes 8 hours to converge.

Model

Online deep learning based knowledge discovery accelerates the performance of back-propagation neural network to handle the large quantity of online air pollution streaming data taken as input for the spatial- temporal model. Hadoop based distributed computing overcomes the large amount of memory and computation power requirements for training the large scale dataset involved in air pollution forecasting. Deep Learning on Apache Spark increases the processing time of the prediction which is an indispensable need for any dynamic application like air quality prediction.

Mapper Module

The Mapper module is used to generate predictive air quality risk maps using an interpolation method. There are various interpolation methods, like Kriging, Spline and IDW (inverse distance weighting). Here, IDW method was used to create continuous and high precision spatial distribution maps for the predicted air quality values on each location for the entire city (Figure 8).

Figure 8. Mapper Module using IDW

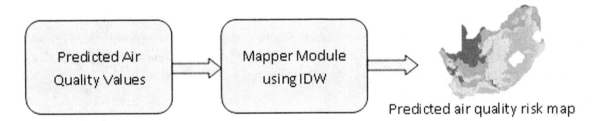

Alert System

The predictive maps and the alerts based on the air quality standards are then made available to the people via a mobile client service. The architecture of the above proposed system is as shown in Figure 9.

Figure 9. Architecture of the Proposed System

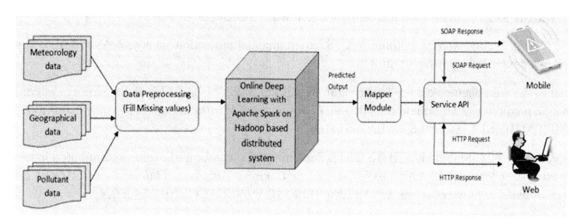

SUMMARY

Vast economic development with increase in population rise in cities has led to large environmental pollution problems involving air pollution, water pollution, noise and thermal pollution. Among these, air pollution has the most menacing effects on all life on earth. Air pollutant concentration keep increasing due to industrial, commercial and domestic sources. Various diseases, allergies, global warming and acid rains are some of the adverse outcomes of air pollution. Enhancement in computing technologies has started attracting increasing attention towards creating awareness in mitigating the adverse effects of pollution on human beings in both developing and developed countries. Accurate air quality forecasting can significantly reduce these grave effects of pollution on human beings and improvise their life standard. Hence, the need to improve air quality forecasting has become indispensable for the betterment of the society.

In this chapter, the need for air pollution alert system is summarized and its implementation using machine learning algorithm is also elaborated. The handiness on the implementation of the fine grained real time air quality prediction with advancement in big data is well justified. Apart from the recent literature study and reviews here we also proposed an air quality evaluation based on big data analytics, machine learning models and other techniques. The proposed model is well suitable for all urban environments and could play a vital role in environmental protection against air pollution.

REFERENCES

Asgari, M., Farnaghi, M., & Ghaemi, Z. (2017, September). Predictive mapping of urban air pollution using Apache Spark on a Hadoop cluster. In *Proceedings of the 2017 International Conference on Cloud and Big Data Computing* (pp. 89-93). ACM. 10.1145/3141128.3141131

Chimmiri, M. (2016). *What is hadoop?* Retrieved December 23 2016, from http://www.hadooptpoint. com/what-is-hadoop/http://www.hadooptpoint.com/what-is-hadoop/

EPA. (2005). *Six common air pollutants.* U. S. environmental protection agency. Retrieved from http:// www.epa.gov/air/urbanair/6 poll.html

Ghaemi, Z., Alimohammadi, A., & Farnaghi, M. (2018). LaSVM-based big data learning system for dynamic prediction of air pollution in Tehran. *Environmental Monitoring and Assessment, 190*(5), 300. doi:10.100710661-018-6659-6 PMID:29679160

Ghoneim, O. A., & Manjunatha, B. R. (2017, September). Forecasting of ozone concentration in smart city using deep learning. In *Advances in Computing, Communications and Informatics (ICACCI), 2017 International Conference on* (pp. 1320-1326). IEEE. 10.1109/ICACCI.2017.8126024

Gorai, A. K., & Mitra, G. (2017). A comparative study of the feed forward back propagation (FFBP) and layer recurrent (LR) neural network model for forecasting ground level ozone concentration. *Air Quality, Atmosphere & Health, 10*(2), 213–223. doi:10.100711869-016-0417-0

Goyal, P., Mishra, D., & Upadhyay, A. (2015). Forecasting of ozone episodes through statistical and artificial intelligence based models over Delhi metropolitan area. *Recent Researches in Applied Mathematics, Simulation and Modeling,* 111-120.

KestelynJ. (2013). Retrieved from http://blog.cloudera.com/blog/2013/11/putting-spark-to-use-fast-in-memory-computing-for-your-big-dataapplications/http://blog.cloudera.com/blog/2013/11/putting-spark-to-se-fast-in-memory-computing-for-your-big-data-applications/

Li, V. O., Lam, J. C., Chen, Y., & Gu, J. (2017, December). Deep learning model to estimate air pollution using m-bp to fill in missing proxy urban data. In *GLOBECOM 2017-2017 IEEE Global Communications Conference* (pp. 1-6). IEEE. 10.1109/GLOCOM.2017.8255004

Li, X., Peng, L., Yao, X., Cui, S., Hu, Y., You, C., & Chi, T. (2017). Long short-term memory neural network for air pollutant concentration predictions: Method development and evaluation. *Environmental Pollution, 231,* 997–1004. doi:10.1016/j.envpol.2017.08.114 PMID:28898956

Mishra, D., & Goyal, P. (2016). Neuro-fuzzy approach to forecast NO2 pollutants addressed to air quality dispersion model over Delhi, India. *Aerosol and Air Quality Research, 16*(1), 166–174. doi:10.4209/ aaqr.2015.04.0249

Qi, Z., Wang, T., Song, G., Hu, W., Li, X., & Zhang, Z. M. (2018). Deep Air Learning: Interpolation, Prediction, and Feature Analysis of Fine-grained Air Quality. *IEEE Transactions on Knowledge and Data Engineering, 30*(12), 2285–2297. doi:10.1109/TKDE.2018.2823740

Ren, Z., Zhu, J., Gao, Y., Yin, Q., Hu, M., Dai, L., & Li, X. (2018). Maternal exposure to ambient PM 10 during pregnancy increases the risk of congenital heart defects: Evidence from machine learning models. *The Science of the Total Environment, 630,* 1–10. doi:10.1016/j.scitotenv.2018.02.181 PMID:29471186

Srimuruganandam, B., & Nagendra, S. S. (2015). ANN-based PM prediction model for assessing the temporal variability of PM10, PM2. 5 and PM1 concentrations at an urban roadway. *International Journal of Environmental Engineering*, 7(1), 60–89. doi:10.1504/IJEE.2015.069266

Zheng, Y., Liu, F., & Hsieh, H. P. (2013, August). U-air: When urban air quality inference meets big data. In *Proceedings of the 19th ACM SIGKDD international conference on Knowledge discovery and data mining* (pp. 1436-1444). ACM. 10.1145/2487575.2488188

Chapter 57
Application of Machine Learning Methods for Passenger Demand Prediction in Transfer Stations of Istanbul's Public Transportation System

Hacer Yumurtaci Aydogmus
Alanya Alaaddin Keykubat University, Turkey

Yusuf Sait Turkan
Istanbul University-Cerrahpasa, Turkey

ABSTRACT

The rapid growth in the number of drivers and vehicles in the population and the need for easy transportation of people increases the importance of public transportation. Traffic becomes a growing problem in Istanbul which is Turkey's greatest urban settlement area. Decisions on investments and projections for the public transportation should be well planned by considering the total number of passengers and the variations in the demand on the different regions. The success of this planning is directly related to the accurate passenger demand forecasting. In this study, machine learning algorithms are tested in a real world demand forecasting problem where hourly passenger demands collected from two transfer stations of a public transportation system. The machine learning techniques are run in the WEKA software and the performance of methods are compared by MAE and RMSE statistical measures. The results show that the bagging based decision tree methods and rules methods have the best performance.

DOI: 10.4018/978-1-6684-6291-1.ch057

INTRODUCTION

Predicting what will happen in the future using the available data has always been of interest. The ability to predict the future course of a time series and the values is a continuing issue, the importance of which is still going up in various fields such as biology, physics, mathematics, engineering, economics and statistics. Studies related to public transportation hold a crucial position among studies involving estimation. Public transportation is of great importance for people's quality of social life and economic and social development of cities. In order to ensure that people reach their jobs as quickly as possible, as well as to improve their access to social services such as health and education, municipalities should provide cheap and safe public transportation within their borders. In order to establish public transportation plans and to manage public transport effectively, passenger statistics should be monitored for different regions and the amount of passengers in future periods should be estimated.

Istanbul is the greatest urban settlement area in Turkey. Traffic becomes a growing problem in Istanbul where approximately more than 800 new vehicles hit the roads and nearly 13 million passengers are transported per day. Therefore, besides the efficient management of public transportation, new public transportation investments are also of great importance. In order to make investment decisions on public transport, it is vital to accurately estimate the public transportation demands of different regions or stations. Decisions on investments and projections for the public transportation should be well planned by considering the total number of passengers and the variations in the demand on the different regions. The success of such planning is directly related to the accurate passenger demand forecasting.

Statistical methods and intelligent techniques can be used in the prediction of the public transport demand. Four-stage model, land use models and time series methods are influential classical methods. In recent years, for the estimation of passenger demands hybrid methods are used together with classical methods. In many complex transportation forecasting problems, it is hard to understand the relationships between different variables. Therefore, it is seen that artificial techniques are more preferred in recent years.

The aim of this study is to determine the effectiveness of different machine learning algorithms for prediction of passenger demand in transfer stations of a public transportation system. For this purpose, various machine learning algorithms have been tried in a real-world demand forecasting problem. To examine the forecast performance of machine learning algorithms, five-year daily passenger traffic data of two selected transfer stations in Istanbul are used in the experiment to see the prediction accuracy measured by Mean Absolute Error (MAE), Root Mean Square Error(RMSE) and Correlation Coefficient (R). The results show that some bagging (decision trees and rules) algorithms are very successful and they can even be used to predict passenger demand in transfer stations.

BACKGROUND

Passenger demand estimation problem in public transport can be categorized into long term and short term demand forecasting problems. Long-term public transport passenger forecasting is used for long-term planning, strategic decisions and investments in public transport, while short-term forecasting is more effective in operational decisions. Conventional demand forecasting methods are generally classified as univariate time series approaches and multivariate demand modeling approaches. Multivariate demand modelling approaches can be undertaken using a conventional four-step travel planning model or direct demand models. Travel planning model including the steps of trip generation, trip distribution, mode choice, and assignment has been used in many demand forecasting applications (Bar-Gera and Boyce, 2003; Blainey and Preston, 2010; Dargay et al., 2010; Jovicic and Hansen, 2003; Owen and Philips, 1987; Preston, 1991; Wardman and Tyler, 2000; Wardman, 2006).

The data driven model includes linear and nonlinear estimation methods. Time series models (Preez and Witt, 2003; Williams et al.1998) and Kalman filtering model (Ye et al., 2006) are the most common linear forecasting methods. SARIMA, which is the most known model among all time series models, can take into consideration the periodicity of the time series when estimating, which can increase the estimation success. However, the success of SARIMA is significantly reduced if the time series is non-linear.

When the studies in recent years are examined, it is seen that the most widely used methods are nonparametric regression (Clark, 2003; Smith et al., 2003), gaussian maximum likelihood model (Lin, 2001), neural network algorithm (Huang Y., and Pan, 2011; Tsung-Hsien et al., 2005) and support vector machine (Chen et al., 2011; Zhang and Xie, 2007).

In the recent studies on passenger estimation, studies on airline passenger estimation and bus passenger estimation stand out. For example, Cyril et al. (2018) used a univariate time series ARIMA model to forecast the inter-district public transport travel demand and in 2019 they studied the application of time-series method for forecasting public bus passenger demand. They used Electronic Ticketing Machines, which generated the big data, based time-series for issuing tickets and collecting fares. Suh and Ryerson (2019) built a methodology that is grounded in established airport passenger demand forecasting practices and is able to significantly improve the accuracy of aviation demand forecasting models. Efendigil and Eminler (2017) compared artificial intelligence methods and regression analysis technique. They also examined 114 academic publications in airport passenger demand and observed that artificial intelligence techniques are becoming more preferable over econometric models.

The human brain is capable of intelligent data processing, and artificial neural networks are precisely developed to mimic this data processing. In artificial neural networks, synaptic weights can be adjusted to automatically match the input-output relationship of the analyzed system through a learning process (Hagan et al. 1996; Wei and Wu 1997). It is seen that artificial intelligence techniques, especially artificial neural networks, are used in many public transportation forecasting studies (Ding and Chien 2000; Chien et al. 2002; Chen et al. 2004).

In this study, many machine learning methods have been applied to a real-life problem in one of the vital bus transfer stations of Istanbul. In this way, the most successful algorithms in these types of problems were investigated and the parameters that might lead to success and failures were investigated.

Machine Learning Techniques of Estimation

Fischer and Lehner (2013) have classified forecasting methods into three categories: time series, casual and machine learning. According to them ARIMA, multiple linear regression and exponential smoothing are time series techniques; ARMAX and multivariate linear regression are causal techniques; support vector machines, bayesian networks, neural networks and decision trees are machine learning techniques.

Machine learning is a frequently used concept and research area in recent years. This approach is applied in academic research or industrial fields. Before presenting the definition of machine learning, it would be appropriate to consider briefly the concept of learning. We can say that human life consists of what they learn. As a multi-faceted event learning processes include the acquisition of new declarative knowledge, the development of motor and cognitive skills through instruction or practice, the organization of new knowledge into general, effective representations, and the discovery of new facts and theories through observation and experimentation (Carbonell et al.,1983). Also, Laplante (2000) gave another definition for the learning as "generally, any scheme whereby experience or past actions and reactions are automatically used to change parameters in an algorithm".

The history of machine learning extends to the Neural Networks (1943) and Turing Test (1950). Basic definition of machine learning in the literature is "the field of scientific study that concentrates on induction algorithms and on other algorithms that can be said to 'learn'" (Provost and Kohavi, 1998). Beam and Kohane (2018) also presented a broad definition as "machine learning was originally described as a program that learns to perform a task or make a decision automatically from data, rather than having the behavior explicitly programmed".

Machine Learning is considered a natural outgrowth of the intersection of Statistics and Computer Science (Mitchell, 2006). Data mining and machine learning are intersect concepts.

Nowadays, machine learning methods are applied in many different fields. For example, there are many researches in the field of civil engineering (Kewalramani and Gupta, 2006; Heshmati et al., 2008; Chou and Tsai, 2012; Chou and Pham, 2013; Yumurtacı Aydogmus et al., 2015a), stock market (Choudhry and Garg, 2008; Patel et al., 2015; Shen et al., 2012), oil price forecasting (Yumurtacı Aydogmus et al., 2015b; Abdullah and Zeng, 2010), network security (Haq et al., 2015), spam detection (Crawford et al., 2015; Kolari et al., 2006), medicine (Deo, 2015; Obermeyer and Emanuel, 2016), healthcare (Chen et al., 2017); wind speed (Türkan et al., 2016; Salcedo-Sanz et al., 2011) etc.

There are two main types of machine learning: unsupervised learning and supervised learning. Unsupervised machine learning technique is "clustering" and supervised machine learning techniques are "classification" and "regression". Supervised learning trains a model on known input and output data and so that it can predict future outputs. Unsupervised learning finds hidden patterns or intrinsic structures in input data. While the classification techniques predict discrete responses (for example whether an email is genuine or spam), regression techniques predict continuous responses. Clustering is used for exploratory data analysis (gene sequence analysis, and object recognition etc.) (MathWorks, 2016).

Some of the well-known machine learning methods and the methods used in the study are as follows:

Support Vector Machines

Support Vector Machines was firstly used to solve a classification problem by Vapnik in 1995. SVM is a method, which considers the input data in an n dimension space as two sets of vectors. This method is a recently popularized method and uses structural risk minimization in problem solving along with empirical risk minimization, which is also used by ANN and other learning machines. While empirical risk minimization tries to reduce the error rate between examples, structural risk minimization lowers the error rate upper limit that could be on all examples. Thus, SVM reduce the risk of getting trapped in local extreme points in problem solving (Vapnik, 1999, as cited in Türkan et al., 2011). In classification, SVM method uses VC (Vapnik-Chervonenkis dimension) based structural risk minimization. SVM is an inductive method used in the machine learning and support vectors are defined as the vectors passing from the closest samples of the two data sets, which maximizes the distance between two samples (Türkan and Yumurtacı Aydoğmuş, 2016). SVM is a type of core-based artificial intelligence technique used to solve the regression and classification problems. It was firstly used to solve a classification problem by Vapnik in 1995. Successful forecasting studies were performed with support vector regression on the issue of time series forecasting in different fields such as production forecasting, speed of traffic flow forecasting and financial time series forecasting. (Castro-Neto et al, 2009; Hsu, et al, 2009; Huang &

Tsai, 2009; Kim, 2003; Lu, et al, 2009; Mohandes, et al, 2004; Pai& Lin, 2005; Pai, et al, 2009; Tay & Cao, 2003; Thissen et al, 2003).

Artificial Neural Network

Artificial Neural Network (ANN) has emerged as a result of the studies trying to imitate the working principle of human brain in artificial systems. Generally, ANN is a complex system consisting of the connection of various neurons in human brain, or the simple processors that artificially connect with each other at different levels of interaction (Gülez, 2008). Artificial Neural Networks (ANN) is one of artificial intelligence techniques and has a widespread use in the different areas (Kecman, 2001). ANN, unlike traditional statistical methods, does not need model assumptions and can work on any kind of non-linear function without making any prior assumptions (McNelis, 2004, as cited in Türkan et al., 2011). Many researchers concluded that ANN, which applies the Empirical Risk Minimization Principle, was more useful than traditional statistical methods (Hansen & Nelson, 1997, as cited in Türkan et al., 2011).

Multilayer Perceptron (MLP), or namely back propagation network, developed in 1986 by Rumelhart et al. The MLP works with supervisory learning principle and in the learning phase, both inputs and the corresponding outputs are shown. The task of the network is to produce output for each input. The learning rule of the MLP is the extended version of the Delta Rule, which is based on the least square method and called as Extended Delta Rule (Güllü et al., 2007).

M5P

Decision trees are the most preferred predictive method because of their high performance and easy to understand graphical interpretation (Bozkır et al., 2019).

The M5P method is strong because it implements a decision tree as much as linear regression to predict a continuous variable. Moreover, M5P implements regression trees and model trees. The M5P algorithm consists of three stages (Bragaet al., 2007):

1. Creating trees,
2. Prune the tree and
3. Smoothing the tree.

This tree model is used for numerical estimation. M5P keeps a linear regression model that predicts the class value of samples that reach each leaf. In determining which feature is best for separating the T part of the training data that reaches a specific node using the split criterion. The standard deviation of the class in T is considered a measure of the error at that node, and each feature at that node is tested by calculating the expected reduction in error. The feature selected to split maximises the expected error reduction at that node. The standard deviation reduction (SDR) calculated by the following formula is the reduction of expected errors.

$$SDR = sd\left(T\right) - \sum \frac{\left|T_i\right|}{\left|T\right|} * sd\left(T_i\right) \qquad (1)$$

Linear regression models in leaves aim to predict continuous numerical qualities. They resemble piecemeal linear functions. They eventually come together and a nonlinear function is formed. It is aimed to build a model that correlates a target value of the training cases with the values of their input qualities. The quality of the model is measured by accurately estimating the target values of situations that are not usually seen. The division process ends only when the standard deviation is a fraction smaller than the standard deviation of the original sample set, or when the number of samples remains several (Onyari and Ilunga, 2013).

Weka program provides M5P algorithm that is used to create classification and regression tree with a multivariate linear regression model where *p* stands for prime. This algorithm provides linear model as classes with some percent of approximated errors (Bhargava et al., 2013).

M5'Rules

That is the method of producing rules from trees and quite simple. It works the following way: a learning tree (in this instance the model trees) is applied to the full training data set and a pruned tree is learned. Then, the best leaf (according to some intuitions) is made into the rule, and finally the tree is discarded.

All samples covered by the rule are removed from the data set. The process is applied repeatedly to the remaining samples and operations end when all samples are covered by one or more rules. This is the basic separation and conquest strategy for the rules of learning; however, instead of creating a single rule, as usually, a full model tree is built at each stage, and its "best" leaf is made into a rule. This avoids the over-pruning potential called hasty-generalization (FW98). Unlike PART, which uses the similar strategy for categorical prediction, M5'Rules creates complete trees instead of partially discovered trees. Creating partial trees leads to more computational efficiency and does not affect the size and accuracy of the resulting rules (Holmes et al., 1999).

REP Tree Algorithm

The Reduced Error Pruning Tree applies additional reduced-error pruning as a post-processing step of the C4.5 algorithm (Gulenko et al., 2016). Fundamentally REP Tree is a quick decision tree learning and it builds a decision tree based on information benefit or reducing the variance. The basis of pruning of this algorithm is the use of "reduced error pruning" along with back over fitting. It gently sorts values for numerical attribute once and it handles the missing values with embedded method by C4.5 in fractional instances (Mohamed et al., 2012).

This algorithm was first proposed by Quinlan. In REP Tree algorithm, more than one tree is created in different iterations with the logic of regression tree. Then, the best decision trees are chosen. The algorithm is based on the following principles (Aksu ve Karaman, 2017):

1. Minimize error caused by variance,
2. The principle of knowledge acquisition with entropy.

Random Forrest Algorithm

Random Forest (RF) is the popular and very effective algorithm put forward by Breiman in 2001. This algorithm is based on model collection ideas for both regression and classification problems. The method combines the idea of bagger with random feature selection. RF's principle is to assemble many binary decision trees that are created using several bootstrap samples from the sample L (Learning) and selecting a random subset of explaining factors X at each node. Defining parameters of RF models;

1. The number of trees,
2. Number of predictors.

RF can handle large data sets, such as other tree-based methods, with numerous predictors with automatic factor selection and without factor deletion. Random forests increase the diversity among classification trees by resampling the data with modification and randomly changing the predictive variable sets over the different tree induction processes.

The RF method has advantages over other methods. These are (Naghibi et al., 2016):

1. It does not require assumptions about the distribution of explanatory factors,
2. Allows the use of categorical and numerical factors without repeating the use of indicative (or dummy) factors,
3. It can take into account interactions and nonlinear relationships between factors.

KStar

KStar is an instance-based learning algorithm that uses entropy distance measure and based on distance between instances (Malhotra and Singh, 2011). Entropy is used as distance assessment, and this property provides numerous benefits. A consistency of approach in real, symbolic, missing value attributes makes it important. A sample-based algorithm prepared for symbolic values fails on real value properties. Therefore, there is no complete theoretical basis. Approaches that succeed in the real values property are used as ad hoc approaches made to address symbolic attributes. Similar problems arise when missing values are addressed by classifiers. Generally, the missing values are considered a separate value and used instead of the average value, otherwise it is simply ignored (Madhusudana et al., 2016).

Radial Basis Function Neural Networks (RBFNetwork)

An RBFNetwork is a type of a feed-forward neural network comprised of three layers: input, hidden and output layers (Türkan et al., 2016). RBF networks consist of a three-tier architecture:

1. Input layer,
2. A single hidden layer using radial functions that give the name of the network as the event function,
3. Output layer (Çuhadar, 2013)

The operating principle of an "RBF Network" can be described as the process of determining the relationship between input and output by determining the radial-based functions with appropriate width and center values in the hidden layer based on the input data, and creating linear combinations with the appropriate weight values of the outputs produced by these functions in the output layer. RBF networks have been used as an alternative neural network to MLP, in applications involving the solution of problems such as prediction and function approximation, due to their shorter training time compared to MLP and their convergence to the best solution without local minimums (Demirkoparan et al., 2010).

Random Tree

RandomTree is also a regression-based decision tree algorithm. Trees built by RandomTree consider randomly selected attributes at each node. It performs no pruning. Also has an option to allow prediction of class probabilities based on a hold-out set (backfitting) (Witten et al., 2011). The classification works as follows (Thornton et al., 2013):

1. Random trees classifier takes vector with input property,
2. It classifies the vector with every tree in the forest and subtracts the class label, which takes the majority of the "votes".
3. In the event of a setback, the classifier's response is the average of the responses on all trees in the forest.

Bagging

Bagging or Bootstrap Aggregating improves the performance of classification models by creating various sets of the training sets and this method was proposed by Leo Breiman in 1996 (Malhotra and Singh, 2011). The bagging method is based on the procedure of mixing the outcomes of the models that result from the learning of weak training data, obtained by creating different combinations of training data, by the basic-learners. In this sense, bagging is a voting method. In Bagging, the process of creating different combinations of training data is based on the bootstrap method. This method is similar to cross-validation and is an alternative. The aim is to create multiple samples from a single sample. In the meantime, new samples are created by displacement from the original sample (Timur et al., 2011).

Locally Weighted Learning

Instance-based algorithm is used by LWL and this method assigns instance weights. LWL can be applied both classification and regression (Jiawei and Kamber, 2001, as cited in Türkan et al., 2016)

LWL depends on the distance function. There are many different approaches to define a distance function. In LWL learning, distance functions do not need to provide formal mathematical models for distance measurement. The term of scaling is used to have been reserved the weight term for the contribution of individual points (not dimensions) in the regression. Distance functions may be asymmetric and nonlinear. Thus, a distance along a given dimension may depend on whether the value of query point for the dimension is larger or smaller than the value of stored point for that dimension. The distance along a dimension may also depend on the values being compared (Atkeson et al., 1997).

Lazy IBK

Lazy IBK is also known by the K-NN (K nearest neighbor) algorithm. Lazy IBK is is an instance-based learning method for classifying objects based on the closest training examples in the feature space (Adebowale et al., 2013). Comparative study of selected data mining algorithms used for intrusion detection.

International Journal of Soft Computing and Engineering (IJSCE), 3(3), 237-241.). The amount of data/ nearest neighbors is determined by the user stated by k (Fitri, 2014). Lazy IBK has successful applications in classification problems. Solomatine et al. (2006) explored the applicability of lazy (instance-based) learning methods and results showed that lazy IBk is accurate predictor. Peng et al. (2009) developed a performance metric to evaluate the quality of classifiers for software defect prediction and according to the results Lazy IBk (K-nearest-neighbor) algorithm is among the first three methods of 13 classifier algorithms. Fitri (2014) studied to find out the best performance of Naïve Bayesian, Lazy-IBK, Zero-R and Decision Tree-J48. The test results show that the Bayesian naïve algorithm has the best accuracy in the cross-validation test mode, and Bayesian naïve algorithm and lazy IBk have the best accuracy in the percentage-validation test mode.

Problem Definition and Data Set

Today, crowded cities are overwhelming and people need transportation service during the day. For private organizations or public corporations providing transportation services, meeting customer demand at the right place at the right time is of great importance. Predicting the number of passengers (demand) is one of the most important elements for public transport management, in order to make the vehicle and personnel schedules and to determine the necessary investments. With advances in technology, faster and more efficient solutions are focused. Machine learning methods are one of the current methods for transportation management problems.

In this study, metrobus line which is the busiest passenger transportation line in Istanbul is investigated. Metrobus line, given in the Figure1, the longest public transport line in Istanbul, has a total of 45 stations, eight of which are transfer stations. This line, which connects Asia and Europe, runs 535 buses on separated roads and transports an average of 800,000 passengers per day.

Figure 1. The Metrobus Line
Source: metrobusharitasi.com, 2018

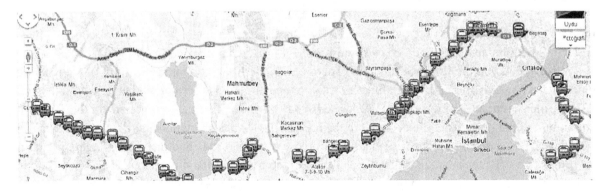

In the problem, daily and hourly the number of passenger data of five years (from 2015 to 2019 June) for two main stations were used. These stations are transfer stations and there have been no major changes in their environment in the last five years, therefore no parameter other than time data is use. The inputs for the problem are time values including year, month, day and hour. The output is the number of passengers. The stations named M1 and M2 given in the Figure2 are among the most active transfer stations with many universities and dormitories around them. There are more than 1 million records in the entire data set and in order to reduce the computing time, we limit our study with two stations. The data belonging to the first four years were used for learning stage and those belonging to the last year were used for test stage.

Figure 2. Istanbul railway network map and M1, M2 Metrobus transfer stations
Source: metrobusharitasi.com, 2018

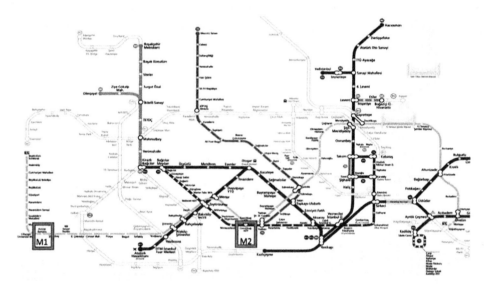

In terms of transportation, the availability of more vehicles during peak hours is one of the important factors that will ensure customer satisfaction and reduce waiting time. In order to make this planning, supervised learning was carried out with data sets and the results were presented to the corporation. Correlation coefficient, root mean square error and mean absolute error are used as statistical techniques to compare machine learning methods success.

Statistical Measures

Successes of the methods employed were compared using different statistical measures. Mean Absolute Error (MAE), Root Mean Square Error (RMSE) and Correlation Coefficient (R) are among the widely used measures that are based on the notion of "mean error". Correlation analysis is performed to determine the level and direction of relationship between two variables. Correlation coefficient takes a value between -1 and +1. Here, the absolute magnitude of numbers refers to the level of correlation between variables, and the numbers' signs (positive or negative) express the direction of correlation. The positive correlation coefficient means the rise (or decline) in the values of a variable increases (or decreases) those of the other.

$$R = \frac{n\sum yy' - \left(\sum y\right)\left(\sum y'\right)}{\sqrt{\left(\sum y^2\right) - \left(\sum y\right)^2}\sqrt{\left(\sum y'^2\right) - \left(\sum y'\right)^2}} \tag{2}$$

The relationship between the level of correlation between variables and the value the correlation coefficient may be given as follows: If it is in the range 0-0.25 the level of correlation is very weak, 0.26-0.49 weak, 0.50-0.69 medium, 0.70-0.89 strong, and 0.90-1.00 very strong. Root Mean Square Error (RMSE) is used to determine the rate of error between calculation values and model forecasts. As RMSE approaches zero, the forecasting capacity of the model increases. For the problem addressed in this paper; and, expressed in the following RMSE equation, refer to the model's forecasting results and realized values, respectively. N, on the other hand, shows the number of forecasts.

$$RMSE = \sqrt{\frac{\sum_{0-1}^{N}\left(o_i - t_i\right)^2}{N}} \tag{3}$$

Mean Absolute Error (MAE) questions the absolute error between calculation values and model forecasts. As MAE approaches zero, the forecasting capacity of the model increases. In the following equation, and refer to the model's forecasting results and realized values, respectively (Türkan et al., 2011).

$$MAE = \frac{1}{N}\sum_{Y'=1}^{N}\left|o_i - t_i\right| \tag{4}$$

RESULTS

In the study, by using machine learning methods in WEKA software platform the number of passengers in the M1 and M2 stations are predicted. The results of the prediction were compared by statistical measures R, MAE and RMSE. Learning stage was performed by using data of first 48 months, and by using data of last 5 months the test was performed. Table 1 and 2 show the results of some machine learning methods for M1 and M2 stations respectively. The methods are ranked from good to bad according to the values in the test phase.

According to the results obtained for M1 station, four of the five most successful methods are in the bagging structure (Table 1). According to values for test phase, the correlation coefficient for the eight methods was higher than 0,9 and the level of correlation is very strong. MAE and RMSE values of the first four methods are very close and there is only one passenger difference between them for MAE test values.

According to the results obtained for M2 station, three of the five most successful methods are in the bagging structure (Table 2). According to values for test phase, the correlation coefficient for the eight methods was higher than 0,9 and the level of correlation is very strong. MAE and RMSE values of the first three methods are very close and there is only three passenger difference between them for MAE test values.

Table 1. The abilities of the methods for the prediction of the number of the passengers for M1 station

Methods	Type	Train / Test	R	MAE	RMSE	Number of Instances
Bagging M5 Rules	Meta /Rules	Train	0,9049	38,4712	454,0787	34599
		Test	0,9114	239,1067	458,5407	3601
Bagging REP Tree	Meta /Trees	Train	0,9366	180,2343	374,1572	34599
		Test	0,9095	239,1950	462,8889	3601
M5 P	Trees	Train	0,9078	231,6832	447,3046	34599
		Test	0,9091	240,0613	464,6997	3601
Bagging M5 P	Meta /Trees	Train	0,9084	229,9234	446,0061	34599
		Test	0,9106	240,1593	459,8334	3601
Bagging-Lazy IBK	Meta /Lazy	Train	0,9877	75,1689	169,0644	34599
		Test	0,9011	244,1227	487,5597	3601
M5 Rules	Rules	Train	0,9044	239,5068	454,9735	34599
		Test	0,9077	245,8961	468,9580	3601
REP Tree	Trees	Train	0,9196	203,9997	419,0296	34599
		Test	0,9036	247,2436	477,4424	3601
Bagging Randomizable Filtered Classifier	Meta	Train	0,9803	103,9136	215,5580	34599
		Test	0,9070	256,7968	469,2043	3601
Random Committee	Meta	Train	0,9999	8,9139	14,6959	34599
		Test	0,8687	269,5896	571,7861	3601
Lazy IBK	Lazy	Train	1	0	0	34599
		Test	0,8686	269,895	571,9134	3601
Randomizable Filtered Classifier	Meta	Train	1	0	0	34599
		Test	0,8686	269,8950	571,9134	3601
Random Tree	Tree	Train	0,9999	10,0129	17,2456	34599
		Test	0,8687	270,0506	571,8926	3601
K Star	Lazy	Train	0,8764	384,8665	577,8713	34599
		Test	0,8781	405,6397	598,4694	3601
LWL	Lazy	Train	0,6840	510,0190	778,3020	34599
		Test	0,6987	529,1702	802,1674	3601

The MAE and RMSE values in Table 1 and 2 are shown in Figure 3 and 4 for stations M1 and M2, respectively.

The R values obtained for M1 and M2 stations are shown in Figure 5.

Table 2. The abilities of the methods for the prediction of the number of the passengers for M2 station

Methods	Type	Train / Test	R	MAE	RMSE	Number of Instances
Bagging M5 P	Meta /Trees	Train	0,9150	332,8420	585,0478	34585
		Test	0,9179	339,3311	605,8028	3601
Bagging M5 Rules	Meta /Rules	Train	0,9136	338,1297	589,6476	34585
		Test	0,9174	342,2148	607,0451	3601
M5 P	Trees	Train	0,9125	338,9278	593,1908	34585
		Test	0,9160	342,5776	613,3095	3601
M5 Rules	Rules	Train	0,9113	342,7935	597,0392	34585
		Test	0,9156	345,2501	614,1827	3601
Bagging-Lazy IBK	Meta /Lazy	Train	0,9884	108,3782	222,7395	34585
		Test	0,9003	355,7866	671,7106	3601
Bagging REP Tree	Meta /Trees	Train	0,9370	276,0961	507,1352	34585
		Test	0,9149	356,4012	614,7465	3601
REP Tree	Trees	Train	0,9201	310,5068	568,1633	34585
		Test	0,9144	363,3687	617,0568	3601
Bagging Randomizable Filtered Classifier	Meta	Train	0,9894	114,6319	215,3494	34585
		Test	0,9035	366,2529	653,6433	3601
Random Committee	Meta	Train	0,9999	14,2861	23,3542	34585
		Test	0,8691	391,0943	782,0272	3601
Random Tree	Trees	Train	0,9998	15,2580	25,6270	34585
		Test	0,8691	391,3976	782,1465	3601
Lazy IBK	Lazy	Train	1	0	0	34585
		Test	0,8690	391,6870	781,9324	3601
Randomizable Filtered Classifier	Meta	Train	1	0	0	34585
		Test	0,8252	492,6240	902,4183	3601
K Star	Lazy	Train	0,8791	483,8534	721,0367	34585
		Test	0,8756	510,1458	761,9977	3601
LWL	Lazy	Train	0,6324	851,3814	1123,4483	34585
		Test	0,6504	876,9572	1162,6019	3601

CONCLUSION

Transport is of great importance for countries for their economic and social development. Passenger transport has a critical role in enabling people to reach basic social services.

In this study, it can be concluded that machine learning methods are highly successful in the passenger flow estimation and results can be used for decisions on investments and projections for the public transportation. Furthermore, the success of the estimation was measured with the use of different inputs as well as by estimation on time basis. In this study, 5-year of data of passenger numbers is used and MAE, RMSE and R statistics are used to evaluate the machine learning methods.

Figure 3. MAE and RMSE values of test phase for M1 Metrobus transfer stations

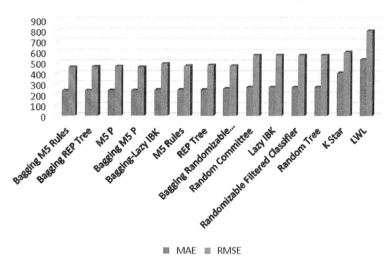

Figure 4. MAE and RMSE values of test phase for M2 Metrobus transfer stations

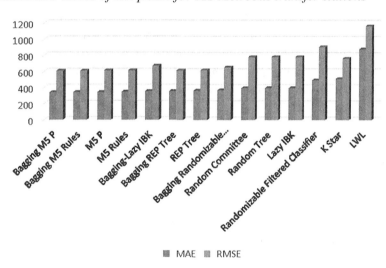

Figure 5. R values of test phase for M1 and M2 Metrobus transfer stations

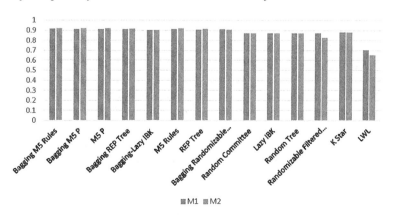

In this study, it can be concluded that the first five methods are respectively; bagging with M5Rules and M5P, M5 P, bagging with Rep Tree and Lazy IBK as seen in Table 3.

Table 3. Ranking of the first five methods for M1 and M2 stations

Methods	Type	Rank of M1 Station	Rank of M2 Station
Bagging M5 Rules	Meta /Rules	1	2
Bagging M5 P	Meta /Trees	4	1
M5 P	Trees	3	3
Bagging REP Tree	Meta /Trees	2	6
Bagging-Lazy IBK	Meta /Lazy	5	5

It is seen from the results of the study that bagging methods as ensemble learning methods have a clear superiority. In this aspect, this study also investigates the potential usage of the bagging methods. Bagging M5 Rules is superior than M5 P and RepTree. Table 3 shows that bagging ensemble learning methods and the methods-based rules and trees are quite successful in the prediction of the passenger numbers. For this reason, it can be stated that passenger number forecasting made by these methods may help in decision making for investments and projections for the public transportation.

Further studies will apply for estimating the number of passengers for future with the methods presented in this study. The number of vehicles will be scheduled by these methods. With the schedule thus obtained, labor costs, fuel costs, vehicle maintenance costs, and even the density of metrobus traffic will be reduced.

ACKNOWLEDGMENT

The authors would like to acknowledge the support of the Istanbul Metropolitan Municipality and Istanbul Electricity, Tramway and Tunnel General Management for providing the data that were used in this study.

REFERENCES

Abdullah, S. N. & Zeng, X. (2010, July). Machine learning approach for crude oil price prediction with Artificial Neural Networks-Quantitative (ANN-Q) model. In *The 2010 International Joint Conference on Neural Networks* (IJCNN) (pp. 1-8). IEEE.

Adebowale, A., Idowu, S. A., & Amarachi, A. (2013). Comparative study of selected data mining algorithms used for intrusion detection. [IJSCE]. *International Journal of Soft Computing and Engineering, 3*(3), 237–241.

Aksu, M. Ç. & Karaman, E. (n.d.). Link analysis and detection in a web site with decision trees. *Acta INFOLOGICA, 1*(2), 84-91.

Atkeson, C. G., Moore, A. W., & Schaal, S. (1997). Locally weighted learning. In *Lazy learning* (pp. 11–73). Dordrecht, The Netherlands: Springer. doi:10.1007/978-94-017-2053-3_2

Bar-Gera, H., & Boyce, D. (2003). Origin-based algorithms for combined travel forecasting models. *Transportation Research Part B: Methodological, 37*(5), 405–422. doi:10.1016/S0191-2615(02)00020-6

Beam, A. L., & Kohane, I. S. (2018). Big data and machine learning in health care. *Journal of the American Medical Association, 319*(13), 1317–1318. doi:10.1001/jama.2017.18391 PMID:29532063

Bhargava, N., Sharma, G., Bhargava, R., & Mathuria, M. (2013). Decision tree analysis on J48 algorithm for data mining. In Proceedings of International Journal of Advanced Research in Computer Science and Software Engineering, 3(6).

Blainey, S. P., & Preston, J. M. (2010). Modelling local rail demand in South Wales. *Transportation Planning and Technology, 33*(1), 55–73. doi:10.1080/03081060903429363

Bozkır, A. S., Sezer, E., & Bilge, G. (2019). *Determination of the factors influencing student's success in student selection examination (OSS) via data mining techniques. IATS'09.* Karabük Turkiye.

Braga, P. L., Oliveira, A. L., & Meira, S. R. (2007, September). Software effort estimation using machine learning techniques with robust confidence intervals. In *7th International Conference on Hybrid Intelligent Systems (HIS 2007)* (pp. 352-357). IEEE. 10.1109/HIS.2007.56

Breiman, L. (2001). Random forests. *Machine Learning, 45*(1), 5–32. doi:10.1023/A:1010933404324

Carbonell, J. G., Michalski, R. S., & Mitchell, T. M. (1983). An overview of machine learning. In *Machine learning* (pp. 3–23). Morgan Kaufmann.

Castro-Neto, M., Jeong, Y. S., Jeong, M. K., & Han, L. D. (2009). Online-SVR for shortterm traffic flow prediction under typical and atypical traffic conditions. *Expert Systems with Applications, 36*(3), 6164–6173. doi:10.1016/j.eswa.2008.07.069

Chen, M., Hao, Y., Hwang, K., Wang, L., & Wang, L. (2017). Disease prediction by machine learning over big data from healthcare communities. *IEEE Access: Practical Innovations, Open Solutions, 5,* 8869–8879. doi:10.1109/ACCESS.2017.2694446

Chen, M., Liu, X. B., Xia, J. X., & Chien, S. I. (2004). A dynamic bus-arrival time prediction model based on APC data. *Computer-Aided Civil and Infrastructure Engineering, 19,* 364–376.

Chen, Q., Li, W., & Zhao, J. (2011). The use of LS-SVM for short-term passenger flow prediction. *Transport, 26*(1), 5–10. doi:10.3846/16484142.2011.555472

Chien, I.-Jy., Ding, Y., & Wei, C. (2002). Dynamic bus arrival time prediction with artificial neural networks. *Journal of Transportation Engineering, 128*(5), 429–438.

Choudhry, R., & Garg, K. (2008). A hybrid machine learning system for stock market forecasting. *World Academy of Science, Engineering and Technology, 39*(3), 315–318.

Clark, S. (2003). Traffic prediction using multivariate nonparametric regression. *Journal of Transportation Engineering, 129*(2), 161–168.

Crawford, M., Khoshgoftaar, T. M., Prusa, J. D., Richter, A. N., & Al Najada, H. (2015). Survey of review spam detection using machine learning techniques. *Journal of Big Data*, 2(1), 23. doi:10.118640537-015-0029-9

Çuhadar, M. (2013). Modeling and forecasting inbound tourism demand to Turkey by MLP, RBF and TDNN artificial neural networks: A comparative analysis. *Journal of Yaşar University*, 8(31).

Cyril, A., Mulangi, R. H., & George, V. (2018, August). Modelling and forecasting bus passenger demand using time series method. In *2018 7th International Conference on Reliability, Infocom Technologies and Optimization (Trends and Future Directions)(ICRITO)* (pp. 460-466). IEEE.

Cyril, A., Mulangi, R. H., & George, V. (2019). Bus passenger demand modelling using time-series techniques-big data analytics. *The Open Transportation Journal, 13*(1).

Dargay, J., Clark, S., Johnson, D., Toner, J., & Wardman, M. (2010). A forecasting model for long distance travel in Great Britain. *12th World Conference on Transport Research*, Lisbon, Portugal.

Demirkoparan, F., Taştan, S., & Kaynar, O. (2010). Crude oil price forecasting with artificial neural networks. *Ege Academic Review, 10*(2), 559–573.

Deo, R. C. (2015). Machine learning in medicine. *Circulation, 132*(20), 1920–1930. doi:10.1161/CIRCULATIONAHA.115.001593 PMID:26572668

Ding, Y. & Chien, S. (2000). The prediction of bus arrival times with link-based artificial neural networks. In *Proceedings of the International Conference on Computational Intelligence & Neurosciences (CI&N)—Intelligent Transportation Systems* (pp. 730–733), Atlantic City, NJ.

Du Preez, J., & Witt, S. F. (2003). Univariate versus multivariate time series forecasting: An application to international tourism demand. *International Journal of Forecasting, 19*(3), 435–451. doi:10.1016/S0169-2070(02)00057-2

Efendigil, T., & Eminler, Ö. E. (2017). The importance of demand estimation in the aviation sector: A model to estimate airline passenger demand. *Journal of Yaşar University, 12*, 14–30.

Fischer, U., & Lehner, W. (2013). Transparent forecasting strategies in database management systems. In E. Zimányi (Ed.), *European Business Intelligence Summer School* (pp. 150–181). Cham, Switzerland: Springer. Retrieved from https://books.google.com.tr/

Fitri, S. (2014). Perbandingan Kinerja Algoritma Klasifikasi Naïve Bayesian, Lazy-Ibk, Zero-R, Dan Decision Tree-J48. *Data Manajemen dan Teknologi Informasi (DASI), 15*(1), 33.

Gulenko, A., Wallschläger, M., Schmidt, F., Kao, O., & Liu, F. (2016, December). Evaluating machine learning algorithms for anomaly detection in clouds. *In 2016 IEEE International Conference on Big Data (Big Data)* (pp. 2716-2721). IEEE.

Gulez, K. (2008). Yapay sinir ağlarının kontrol mühendisliğindeki uygulamaları (Applications of artificial neural networks in control engineering). (Lecture notes, 2008) Yıldız Teknik University. Retrieved from http://www.yildiz.edu.tr/~gulez/3k1n.pdf

Güllü, H., Pala, M., & Iyisan, R. (2007). Yapay sinir ağları ile en büyük yer ivmesinin tahmin edilmesi (Estimating the largest ground acceleration with artificial neural networks). *Sixth National Conference on Earthquake Engineering*, Istanbul, Turkey.

Hagan, M. T., Demuth, H. B., & Beale, M. (1996). *Neural network design*. Boston, MA: PWS.

Haq, N. F., Onik, A. R., Hridoy, M. A. K., Rafni, M., Shah, F. M., & Farid, D. M. (2015). Application of machine learning approaches in intrusion detection system: A survey. *IJARAI-International Journal of Advanced Research in Artificial Intelligence*, *4*(3), 9–18.

Holmes, G., Hall, M., & Prank, E. (1999, December). Generating rule sets from model trees. *In Australasian Joint Conference on Artificial Intelligence* (pp. 1-12). Berlin, Germany: Springer.

Hsu, S. H., Hsieh, J. J. P.-A., Chih, T. C., & Hsu, K. C. (2009). A two-stage architecture for stock price forecasting by integrating self-organizing map and support vector regression. *Expert Systems with Applications*, *36*(4), 7947–7951. doi:10.1016/j.eswa.2008.10.065

Huang, C. L., & Tsai, C. Y. (2009). A hybrid SOFM–SVR with a filter-based feature selection for stock market forecasting. *Expert Systems with Applications*, *36*(2), 1529–1539. doi:10.1016/j.eswa.2007.11.062

Huang, Y., & Pan, H. (2011, April). Short-term prediction of railway passenger flow based on RBF neural network. In *Proceedings of the 4th International Joint Conference on Computational Sciences and Optimization, CSO 2011* (pp. 594–597). 10.1109/CSO.2011.240

Istanbul Railway Network and Metrobus Line. Retrieved from http://www.metrobusharitasi.com/metrobus-haritasi

Jiawei, H. & Kamber, M. (2001). Data mining: concepts and techniques. San Francisco, CA: Morgan Kaufmann, 5.

Jovicic, G., & Hansen, C. O. (2003). A passenger travel demand model for Copenhagen. *Transportation Research Part A, Policy and Practice*, *37*(4), 333–349. doi:10.1016/S0965-8564(02)00019-8

Kim, K. J. (2003). Financial time series forecasting using support vector machines. *Neurocomputing*, *55*(1-2), 307–319. doi:10.1016/S0925-2312(03)00372-2

Kolari, P., Java, A., Finin, T., Oates, T., & Joshi, A. (2006, July). Detecting spam blogs: A machine learning approach. In *Proceedings of the national conference on artificial intelligence* (Vol. 21, No. 2, p. 1351). Menlo Park, CA: AAAI Press.

Laplante, P. A. (Ed.). (2000). Dictionary of computer science, engineering and technology. Boca Raton, FL: CRC Press.

Lin, W. H. (2001). A Gaussian maximum likelihood formulation for short-term forecasting of traffic flow. In *Proceedings of the 2001 IEEE Intelligent Transportation Systems* (pp. 150–155), Oakland, CA.

Lu, C. J., Lee, T. S., & Chiu, C. C. (2009). Financial time series forecasting using independent component analysis and support vector regression. *Decision Support Systems*, *47*(2), 115–125. doi:10.1016/j.dss.2009.02.001

Madhusudana, C. K., Kumar, H., & Narendranath, S. (2016). Condition monitoring of face milling tool using K-star algorithm and histogram features of vibration signal. *Engineering Science and Technology. International Journal (Toronto, Ont.)*, *19*(3), 1543–1551.

MathWorks. (2016). Introducing Machine Learning. Retrieved from https://www.academia.edu/31538731/Introducing_Machine_Learning

Mitchell, T. M. (2006). *The discipline of machine learning* (Vol. 9). Pittsburgh, PA: Carnegie Mellon University, School of Computer Science, Machine Learning Department.

Mohamed, W. N. H. W., Salleh, M. N. M., & Omar, A. H. (2012, November). A comparative study of reduced error pruning method in decision tree algorithms. In *2012 IEEE International Conference on Control System, Computing and Engineering* (pp. 392-397). IEEE. 10.1109/ICCSCE.2012.6487177

Mohandes, M. A., Halawani, T. O., Rehman, S., & Hussain, A. A. (2004). Support vector machines for wind speed prediction. *Renewable Energy*, *29*(6), 939–947. doi:10.1016/j.renene.2003.11.009

Naghibi, S. A., Pourghasemi, H. R., & Dixon, B. (2016). GIS-based groundwater potential mapping using boosted regression tree, classification and regression tree, and random forest machine learning models in Iran. *Environmental Monitoring and Assessment*, *188*(1), 44. doi:10.100710661-015-5049-6 PMID:26687087

Obermeyer, Z., & Emanuel, E. J. (2016). Predicting the future—Big data, machine learning, and clinical medicine. *The New England Journal of Medicine*, *375*(13), 1216–1219. doi:10.1056/NEJMp1606181 PMID:27682033

Onyari, E. K., & Ilunga, F. M. (2013). Application of MLP neural network and M5P model tree in predicting streamflow: A case study of Luvuvhu catchment, South Africa. *International Journal of Innovation, Management and Technology*, *4*(1), 11.

Owen, A. D., & Philips, G. D. A. (1987). An econometric investigation into the characteristics of railway passenger demand. *Journal of Transport Economics and Policy*, *21*, 231–253.

Pai, P. F., & Lin, C. S. (2005). A hybrid ARIMA and support vector machines model in stock price forecasting. *Omega*, *33*(6), 497–505. doi:10.1016/j.omega.2004.07.024

Pai, P. F., Yang, S. L., & Chang, P. T. (2009). Forecasting output of integrated circuit industry by support vector regression models with marriage honey-bees optimization algorithms. *Expert Systems with Applications*, *36*(7), 10746–10751. doi:10.1016/j.eswa.2009.02.035

Patel, J., Shah, S., Thakkar, P., & Kotecha, K. (2015). Predicting stock market index using fusion of machine learning techniques. *Expert Systems with Applications*, *42*(4), 2162–2172. doi:10.1016/j.eswa.2014.10.031

Peng, Y., Kou, G., Wang, G., Wang, H., & Ko, F. I. (2009). Empirical evaluation of classifiers for software risk management. *International Journal of Information Technology & Decision Making*, *8*(04), 749–767. doi:10.1142/S0219622009003715

Preston, J. (1991). Demand forecasting for new local rail stations and services. *Journal of Transport Economics and Policy*, *25*, 183–202.

Provost, F., & Kohavi, R. (1998). Glossary of terms. *Journal of Machine Learning*, *30*(2-3), 271–274.

Salcedo-Sanz, S., Ortiz-Garcı, E. G., Pérez-Bellido, Á. M., Portilla-Figueras, A., & Prieto, L. (2011). Short term wind speed prediction based on evolutionary support vector regression algorithms. *Expert Systems with Applications*, *38*(4), 4052–4057. doi:10.1016/j.eswa.2010.09.067

Shen, S., Jiang, H., & Zhang, T. (2012). *Stock market forecasting using machine learning algorithms* (pp. 1–5). Stanford, CA: Department of Electrical Engineering, Stanford University.

Smith, B. L., Williams, B. M., & Oswald, R. K. (2002). Comparison of parametric and nonparametric models for traffic flow forecasting. *Transportation Research Part C, Emerging Technologies*, *10*(4), 303–321. doi:10.1016/S0968-090X(02)00009-8

Solomatine, D. P., Maskey, M., & Shrestha, D. L. (2006, July). Eager and lazy learning methods in the context of hydrologic forecasting. In *The 2006 IEEE International Joint Conference on Neural Network Proceedings* (pp. 4847-4853). IEEE.

Suh, D. Y., & Ryerson, M. S. (2019). Forecast to grow: Aviation demand forecasting in an era of demand uncertainty and optimism bias. *Transportation Research Part E, Logistics and Transportation Review*, *128*, 400–416. doi:10.1016/j.tre.2019.06.016

Tay, F. E. H., & Cao, L. J. (2003). Support vector machine with adaptive parameters in financial time series forecasting. *IEEE Transactions on Neural Networks*, *14*(6), 1506–1518. doi:10.1109/TNN.2003.820556 PMID:18244595

Thissen, U., van Brakel, R., de Weijer, A. P., Melssen, W. J., & Buydens, L. M. C. (2003). Using support vector machines for time series prediction. *Chemometrics and Intelligent Laboratory Systems*, *69*(1-2), 35–49. doi:10.1016/S0169-7439(03)00111-4

Thornton, C., Hutter, F., Hoos, H. H., & Leyton-Brown, K. (2013, August). Auto-WEKA: Combined selection and hyperparameter optimization of classification algorithms. In *Proceedings of the 19th ACM SIGKDD international conference on Knowledge discovery and data mining* (pp. 847-855). ACM. 10.1145/2487575.2487629

Timur, M., Aydın, F., & Akıncı, T. Ç. (2011). The prediction of wind speed of Göztepe district of Istanbul via machine learning method. *Electronic Journal of Machine Technologies*, *8*(4), 75–80.

Tsung-Hsien, T., Chi-Kang, L., & Chien-Hung, W. (2005). Design of dynamic neural networks to forecast short-term railway passenger demand. *Journal of the Eastern Asia Society for Transportation Studies*, *6*, 1651–1666.

Türkan, Y. S., Erdal, H., Ekinci, A. (2011). *Predictive stock exchange modeling for the developing Balkan countries: An application on Istanbul stock exchange*. Vol. 4, 34-51.

Türkan, Y. S., & Yumurtacı Aydogmuş, H. (2016). Passenger demand prediction for fast ferries based on neural networks and support vector machines. *Journal of Alanya Faculty of Business*, *8*(1).

Türkan, Y. S., Yumurtacı Aydogmus, H., & Erdal, H. (2016). The prediction of the wind speed at different heights by machine learning methods. [IJOCTA]. *An International Journal of Optimization and Control: Theories & Applications*, *6*(2), 179–187.

Wardman, M. (2006). Demand for rail travel and the effects of external factors. *Transportation Research Part E, Logistics and Transportation Review, 42*(3), 129–148. doi:10.1016/j.tre.2004.07.003

Wardman, M., & Tyler, J. (2000). Rail network accessibility and the demand for inter- urban rail travel. *Transport Reviews, 20*(1), 3–24. doi:10.1080/014416400295310

Wei, C., & Wu, K. (1997). Developing intelligent freeway ramp metering control systems. In *Conf. Proc., National Science Council in Taiwan, 7C*(3), 371–389.

Weka. Retrieved from http://www.cs.waikato.ac.nz/~ml/weka/

Williams, B. M., Durvasula, P. K., & Brown, D. E. (1998). Urban free-way traffic flow prediction: Application of seasonal autoregressive integrated moving average and exponential smoothing models. *Transportation Research Record: Journal of the Transportation Research Board, 1644*(1), 132–141. doi:10.3141/1644-14

Ye, Z. R., Zhang, Y. L., & Middleton, D. R. (2006). Unscented Kalman filter method for speed estimation using single loop detector data. *Transportation Research Record: Journal of the Transportation Research Board, 1968*(1), 117–125. doi:10.1177/0361198106196800114

Yumurtacı Aydogmus, H., Ekinci, A., Erdal, H. İ., & Erdal, H. (2015b). Optimizing the monthly crude oil price forecasting accuracy via bagging ensemble models. *Journal of Economics and International Finance, 7*(5), 127–136. doi:10.5897/JEIF2014.0629

Yumurtacı Aydogmus, H., Erdal, H. İ., Karakurt, O., Namli, E., Turkan, Y. S., & Erdal, H. (2015a). A comparative assessment of bagging ensemble models for modeling concrete slump flow. *Computers and Concrete, 16*(5), 741–757. doi:10.12989/cac.2015.16.5.741

Zhang, Y., & Xie, Y. (2007). Forecasting of short-term freeway volume with v-support vector machines. *Transportation Research Record: Journal of the Transportation Research Board, 2024*(1), 92–99. doi:10.3141/2024-11

Chapter 58
Classification of Traffic Events in Mexico City Using Machine Learning and Volunteered Geographic Information

Magdalena Saldana-Perez
Instituto Politecnico Nacional, Mexico

Miguel Torres-Ruiz
Instituto Politecnico Nacional, Mexico

Marco Moreno-Ibarra
Instituto Politecnico Nacional, Mexico

ABSTRACT

Volunteer geographic information and user-generated content represents a source of updated information about what people perceive from their environment. Its analysis generates the opportunity to develop processes to study and solve social problems that affect the people's lives, merging technology and real data. One of the problems in urban areas is the traffic. Every day at big cities people lose time, money, and life quality when they get stuck in traffic jams; another urban problem derived from traffic is air pollution. In the present approach, a traffic event classification methodology is implemented to analyze VGI and internet information related to traffic events with a view to identify the main traffic problems in a city and to visualize the congested roads. The methodology uses different computing tools and algorithms to achieve the goal. To obtain the data, a social media and RSS channels are consulted. The extracted data texts are classified into seven possible traffic events, and geolocalized. In the classification, a machine learning algorithm is applied.

DOI: 10.4018/978-1-6684-6291-1.ch058

INTRODUCTION

Internet is a huge source of information. Many web sites, social media, and repositories, let programmers, analysts, and users access to information about what happens in real world. Most of the internet content is created by users. People are not aware about how much data they have been producing during the last years (Li, 2015).

Social media represent a source of information about everything that concerns people such as education, technology, health, politics, and environment, among others. One advantage of social media is that makes possible to locate people or events letting users share their location (Zhao, 2015).

Internet and social media are used to identify and solve social problems; for example, are used by social movements to ask governments for justice and information about their management. Also, are used to communicate ideas and to connect people, to share safety measures when natural disasters occur, and to propagate information about certain situations and conditions that affect people's daily activities, such as traffic, air pollution, weather, rain, among others (Adamko, 2015).

One of the purposes of people when participating in social media is to be useful for others Han et al. (2017). When a person reports something that he perceives in his environment, for example a flooding, helps others to search for alternatives in order to avoid the area and to inform authorities about the problem, looking for a response.

In social media people act as sensors, the information they provide is the sensor data; in their posts citizens communicate the events and problems they perceive on roads through short texts, photos, and images; what is more, if the user allows it, many social medias are able to obtain the persons coordinates, which helps to identify the described events. The number of publications and posts related to a certain event on internet let analysts and citizens to understand the problems magnitude, and to formulate hypotheses and solutions.

Due to the huge development and growth of cities, the problems on their roads such as traffic, air pollution, among others, have considerably increased, affecting almost all the activities developed in a city.

Every day bottlenecks, traffic jams, and car accidents affect the economical, educational, and social activities in a city; the time a person spends in traffic events also affects his health. Social media has open the opportunity to have information about the real situation on the roads, letting people who have access to this information, change their routes or itineraries when problems are reported.

The data management to obtain information about the factors that affect the social dynamics, can be achieved by different computational and statistical methods. For example, classifying messages related to a specific event, or resubmitting the messages posted by trusty sources in order to make them accessible to more people (Dou, 2013).

Some researches interested in traffic at urban areas make use of data generated by vehicles with GPS implemented device (Zhang, 2011), such data are used to predict traffic in specific study areas. Alternate to the GPS generated data, cans the social media information increase the predictions accuracy? Or the ambiguity in certain social media posts decreases the predictions accuracy? Few researching works consider it.

In the present approach we propose the integration of a social media and a web RSS service to extract posts related to traffic events in a city, such as car accidents, protest marches, traffic jams, and others, that make difficult the displacement of people and vehicles through the studied area. After the extraction of the posts, they are textually processed, and geolocated to identify the geographic place where the event is reported. Finally, a machine learning algorithm is used to classify the processed data into six different kinds of traffic problems detected on the area.

A first version of the present approach is presented in the Traffic analysis based on short texts from social media (Saldana-Perez & Moreno-Ibarra, 2016).

The paper is organized as follows; in section two we show some related works about volunteered information; in section three we depict our methodology for the data integration and its geolocation; in section four we show the obtained results. Finally, in section five we point out our conclusions, and section six presents the discussions.

RELATED WORK

In this section we describe some works and concepts related to social media, to user generated content (UGC), and to the Volunteered Geographic Information (VGI).

The explosion and acceptance of social media, the technological advances, and the people's interest in generating content has increased updated data about what happens in real world that can be used by researchers to analyze the urban dynamics, and to generate possible solutions to many urban problems (Yang et al., 2016). Every image, text, photograph, design or concept created by an individual on internet whose motivation is to communicate an idea is part of the user generated content.

Volunteered Geographic Information (VGI) includes all the information generated by users on internet with coordinates or references to geographic places that make possible the geolocation of such information (Goodchild, 2007; Lin, 2013). The main principle of VGI is that it can be produced by people with or without advanced knowledge in the area to which the information bellows. This aspect opens the opportunity to more people to participate and increases the internet contents (Jiang, 2015; Cinnamon, 2013; Goodchild, 2015; Ricker, 2014; Vidal-Filho, 2013; Resch, 2015, Utomo & Ardiyanto, 2018).

Approximately 70% of smartphone users and 73.4% of internet users have a relation with VGI data. Although the high demand of this kind of information, most of the users consult or download it, few of them are producers (Havlik, 2013).

VGI has resulted useful when natural hazards or social problems appear, the data obtained from its analysis has let researchers and aid communities perform solutions, such as in the Haití earthquake (2013) when VGI was used to map affected areas and evacuation routes, in the Mexico earthquake (2017) when VGI helped to find missing people and to identify dangerous buildings.

Social media provide internet users the resources to generate VGI. One of the main characteristics of the social media information is that it is compound of few elements that in most of the cases provide concise ideas, and that can have geographical information such as coordinates or geographical elements described on their texts. This also, has increased the generation of multiple social media services such as Foursquare, Facebook, Twitter, Instagram, among others (Yilmaz & Hero, 2018).

In the present approach the social media Twitter is consulted to extract posts about the traffic situation in the study area. Twitter is a space on internet where people has the opportunity to create, get, and share information about many different topics such as health, environment, politics, sports, and more (Park et al., 2016). One of the main characteristics of Twitters posts is that they reflect the users ideas and feelings, or information about a specific topic. Users have the option to make their tweets public or not, and they can decide to share their coordinates or not in the tweets metadata (Pernici, 2018). According to (Leetaru et al. 2013), just one percent of the tweets produced every day have the coordinates of their place of publication.

In the case of tweets without coordinates, there are options to geolocate them; some researches use geographic information systems to geo-locate tweets, some others use specialized internet services such as the geo-location service of Google Maps (Bakerman et al. 2018); also there exists some researches that implement gazetteers to geolocate tweets in specific areas (Zheng & Sun, 2018, Dredze et al., 2013; Huang & Carley, 2017; Williams & Dixon, 2017).

Due to the tweets data availability and the information of events that can be obtained from them, is evident the utility of geospatial analysis over VGI information. Nowadays the participation of geospatial analysis in the VGI and UGC has become relevant (Saldana-Perez et al., 2018).

Many researches make use of tweets to analyze what is happening at big cities, since tweets represent updated citizens reports about what they see in their surroundings. Some other researches that make use of Twitter, locate the posts related to specific topics with a view to create maps that describe the urban problems interesting for citizens and authorities in their study areas. There exists maps that represent data from real time systems which monitor different factors in big cities such as energy saving, and dynamic regulations (Paredes-Valverde, 2015).

In Lansley & Longley (2016) approach, tweets posted in London are analyzed to identify the topics that concern to the citizens in the city related to 14 categories such as traffic, sports, culture, politic, work, pollution, among others. The research results let authorities and commercial agencies to know the main topics in the center of the United Kingdom capital.

It is true that the tweets veracity must be questioned but after a process of validation these can be considered as useful or not for the research purpose (Stehman, 2018).

One of the main computing areas that has particular interest in VGI, UGC and internet data is machine learning (Koswatte, 2018). Machine learning develops algorithms to obtain relevant data from heterogeneous information, examples of the machine learning usage are the data classification, the searching of patterns between data, the regression of data, analysis of humans behavior when buying, internet searching, or consuming multimedia content, among others (Mohadab, 2018).

Traffic Data Analysis From Social Media and RSS Notes

The present approach purpose is to make use of VGI and machine learning algorithms to obtain, classify, represent and analyze the traffic situation in the proposed study area, Mexico City. The main characteristic of the designed and implemented methodology is the use of machine learning to analyze an urban problem. The obtained results are used in a second research work where the classified data are considered as a data corpus for regressions computing.

The proposed methodology analyzes vehicular traffic, one of the main problems in big cities; it can be adapted to analyze some other city problems such as air pollution, public transport problems. The methodology extracts tweets related to the traffic situation in the area, applies a text mining process over the tweets, classify them using machine learning algorithms, and finally maps the classified tweets in order to analyze the relevance of each traffic problem and the areas that it affects the most.

Comparatively to other investigations that process a specific kind of data, in this work we structure a methodology to integrate and process data form different sources to make them useful for further investigations that need a corpus of pre-processed VGI data.

The methodology consists of five stages: *Database structuring*, databases to store data are designed; *Data monitoring*, data are obtained from the web sources; *Data management*, in this stage the text mining procedure is applied; *Data classification*, using a semi-supervised machine learning algorithm data are classified; and *Geocoding, t*he coordinates of the events are identified in order to map the analyzed event. In Figure 1, is show a blocks diagram of the proposed methodology.

Figure 1.

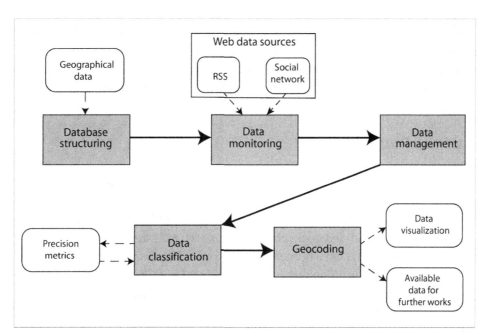

Database Structuring

In this methodology stage the databases to store the treated data are structured. Since the data used in the approach proceeds from heterogeneous sources, the stage is divided into two sub-stages, *Geographic database structuring*, and *Events database structuring*. Both databases have been structured following the relational model (Kantardzic, 2011).

Geographic Database Structuring

The Geographic database is feed with two sources, an OpenStreetMaps shapefile from the OSM repository (Osm, 2018), and a *shapefile* provided by the INEGI (National Institute of Statistics and Geographic Information in Mexico.

Form the OSM shapefile is obtained information about the roads, streets, and public transport stations. The INEGI shapefile provides information about commercial entities located on the study area, such as the number of workers in each entity, its schedules, and the description of its activities.

Three tables compound the Geographic database: *roads, transport* and *infrastructure*.

In the *table roads* is stored information about the streets and avenues in the studied area such as the name of the road, its length, the points that represent it, its beginning and ending coordinates, and the maximum number of vehicles that the road supports. The *table transport* contains information about the public transport in the area such as the coordinates and names of the bus and subway stations. The *table infrastructure* contains the information of the commercial entities in the area, its features are the same as the INEGI shapefile described above.

When working with geographic data is important to consider the following points, in order to avoid possible problems in the data processing.

- Names of the geographic elements such as streets, avenues, roads and points of interest must be normalized, this means that should not contain special characters.
- The intersection points between roads must be correct.
- Data of the geographic area must be updated when modifications are applied over their infrastructure.

Events Database Structuring

In this database are stored the posts recovered from the social media, and the RSS notes that describe traffic events in the study area.

The web sources monitoring has been limited considering the Tobler's first law of geography: "*Everything is related to everything else, but near things are more related than distant things*" (Tobler, 1970).

To treat the social media data, have been structured four tables: *usr_information* where the data of the user who published a message of interest are stored; the table *monitored_messages*, where messages recovered from the social media are stored; the table *messages_classified*, where after a text mining process the text of each message is normalized and the words of interest for the classification are identified; and finally, the table *geocoded_messages*, where the coordinates of the place where an event occurred are stored after the geocoding process.

For the RSS data, has been defined a table named *rss_data*, in this table the date, time, description, URL, latitude and longitude of the even reported in the RSS note, and its assigned classification are stored.

A fifth table named *urban_dynamics* has been structured to merge the recovered, classified, and geocoded data from the *geocoded_messages* and *rss_data* tables. The purpose of this table is to create a traffic events information data repository; this table makes possible to join the processed data from the two different monitored data sources in a normalized format. In Figure 2, are shown the fields of the *Events* database tables.

Data Monitoring

Two applications have been programmed to extract information; one of them uses the Python language program and the Twitter API to extract tweets; the other one written in PHP monitors and extract RSS notes.

Due two the differences between the consulted data sources and the applications, the data monitoring stage is divided in two sub-stages: social media monitoring, and RSS monitoring.

Figure 2.

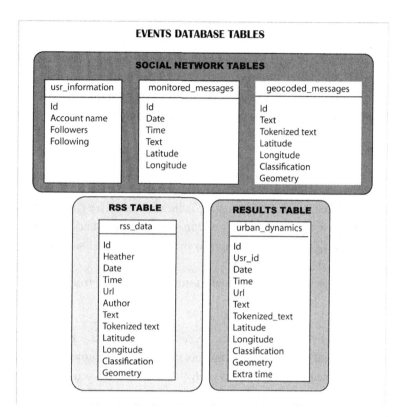

Social Media Monitoring

The messages posted in Twitter are called tweets these are 280 characters limited texts. Twitter provides a group of application interfaces for many programming languages that let them access to the tweets posted at any time in the microblogs site. The API used in this approach is the TwitterAPI (Twitterapi, 2018)

In the python program has been set a group of specific accounts to be monitored, this accounts belong to users dedicated to report the traffic conditions in the study area, their information comes from authorities and journals. Since the information they provide comes from official sources, the accounts have a large number of followers, having access to these accounts lets the application avoid repeated posts. In order to have a control about the followed users, their information is stored in the *usr_information* table.

Every time a followed account posts a tweet, this message is extracted by the programmed application and stored in the table *monitored_messages*. In the *monitored _messages* table tweets are stored preserving their original characteristics, the table represents a corpus of tweets in their original format. The monitoring of the social media is done 24 hours a day. As a future work it is considered to increase the number of monitored accounts.

RSS Monitoring

The application programmed to extract RSS notes is connected to the RSS channels of the main journals published in the study area, each time a journal posts a note the application extracts it and stores it in the table *rss_data*, dividing the note in the features of the table. The monitoring of the RSS channels is done 24 hours a day. To homogenize the extracted data to use them in the classification process, the text of the messages is treated through a text mining procedure in the data management stage.

Data Management

The main purpose of this stage is to recover useful information about traffic from the analyzed text, this is done identifying traffic related words from texts. To achieve the goal a python application programmed for the stage extracts the registries of the tables *monitored_messages* and *rss_data*, eliminates textual elements that do not provide relevant information to the approach, and store the processed text at the correspondent table in the field *tokenized_text*.

The steps of the text mining applied process are four; after the step tree, the text messages are considered processed and ready to be classified.

Step 1: Elimination of special characters. The analyzed Twitter messages are written in Spanish language, they contain special characters and accents that need to be removed in order to apply a better data analysis. Each message is treated as a vector of words if a word contains a special character (':,;.#$`'¡¿?¡/*...,) it is removed from the word, the modified word is inserted into the vector at the same the position from where it was extracted.

Step 2: Elimination of accents: In Spanish language words are written the same as they sound, so the words contain graphical accents. It is necessary to remove such accents since for many text processing tools these element may produce errors.

Step 3: Defining and removing *stop words*: One of the premises in the information recovery is to remove *stop words* from text, to make possible the extraction of relevant information. *Stop words* are all the words that usually refer to the most common ones in a language, some tools specifically avoid removing these words to support phrase search (Sidorov, 2014). Some words considered on this group are prepositions, common words, defined, and undefined articles (Silverman, 2013). On this step, we remove the *stop words* identified from the text.

Step 4: Manual classification: One of the approach purposes is to use a machine learning algorithm to classify traffic events, to make this possible a training corpus with previously classified data is needed. In this step, the third part of the treated registries is manually classified by a group of five annotators.

The annotators have been trained for the task, which consists on classify a message according to the major number of class words in its processed texts, the class words are words related to a specific traffic event.

The registry treated and its designated classification are stored at the *classified_messages*, in the field *classification*.

Step 5: First classification. To facilitate the classification of big amounts of registries a python script with multiple conditional sentences has been implemented, following the logic of the manual classification. In the script words related to each class of traffic event are grouped, the words of the processed text of each registry are analyzed and it is counted the number of class words that it contains; the class assigned to the message is the one with more words occurrences in the processed text. The registry treated and its designated classification are stored at the *classified_messages,* in the field *classification.*

The traffic event classes defined for the approach are seven, they have been proposed according to the most common traffic problems in Mexico city.

In Table 1, the classes have been described more detailed.

Table 1.

Class	Definition
Traffic	The traffic is slow, even there may be a bottle neck on the road. Some words that belong to this class are: slow, not movement, traffic jam.
Favorable	The flow is appropriate, the vehicles can move through the roads with a good average speed. Some words to reference this class are: fast, good, free road.
Accident	There is a car crash on the road or someone got injured near to the road.
Closure	The movement through the road is not possible, it has been closed by a protest march or a controlled event.
Rule	The message describes something related to governmental rules or official disposals related to vehicles.
Manager	It is a message that the VGI manager published in order to give information about the application, the message does not describe a traffic event.
unidentified	The information on the message is not enough to classify it.

After the messages classification, data are divided into two sets, the 75% of the registries is considered as the training corpus meanwhile the other 25% is considered as the test corpus. Bot corpus are used in the semi supervised classification with a machine learning algorithm.

Data Classification

In this stage a machine learning algorithm is used to classify traffic related messages in a semi supervised way. After the classification, a geocoding process is applied over the registries to make possible their visualization in a map of the study area.

In the approach the machine learning algorithm implemented is the Naïve Bayes algorithm which, is widely used in classification and filtering of text messages and e-mails.

One of the advantages of using tweets is that their limited texts reduces the searching field of elements improving the classification precision rate; also, lets to calculate the words presence probability in a message (Lantz, 2013). The classification Naïve Bayes algorithm has been implemented considering the four steps described below.

Step 1: Identifying data. In the Naïve Bayes process a python script extracts the training corpus been structured on the text mining process from the table *classified_messages*. The algorithm considers as relevant features the *id* of the registry, the *tokenized_text*, and its *classification*.

Step 2: Factorization. After the extraction of the training data, the classification of the registries is factorized; this means that the algorithm represent each label class as an integer number.

Step 3: Data dictionary. In an empty dictionary, each one of the words of the first registry is added as a key, then for the next registries the tokenized text words are compared with the dictionary ones, in case that a word of the tokenized text has not been included in the dictionary, such word is added as a new key.

The value of the words keys is the number of times that each word has appeared in the entire corpus; by this way the dictionary has the form *key:value*, where the key is the word found in the registries and its value is the number of times the word appeared in the corpus. At the final of this step, the dictionary would have all the words that are part of the registries texts (even if not all the words belong to the same registry), and the number of repetitions of each word.

Step 4: Vectorization. For the machine learning procedure it is needed that the tokenized text of the registries has the same length as the words dictionary, to achieve this, a words vector is created for each registry.

The words vector have the same length as the dictionary, each vector position represents a word in the dictionary. If a dictionary word appears in the registry text, such word position in the vector has as content the number of times that the specific word appeared in the text; if a dictionary word does not appears in the registry text its value in its vector position is zero.

After this process, the registry is represented as a numeric vector that has the same length as the dictionary. In Figure 3 is shown a diagram that illustrates the vectorization process.

Figure 3.

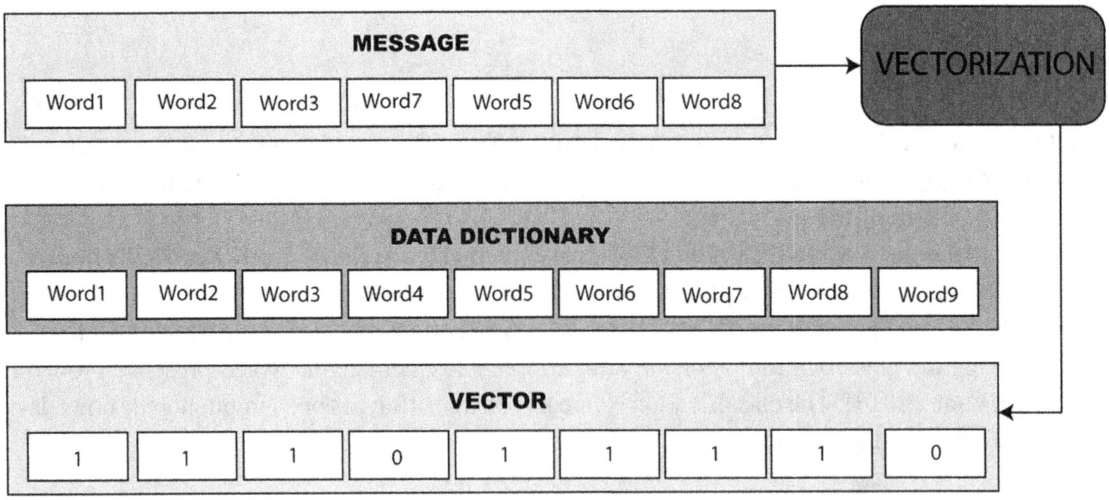

Step 5: Term-document matrix. It is possible to obtain the term-document matrix of the data corpus using the data dictionary. The words of the dictionary represent the terms, they are the fields of the matrix; meanwhile the vectors are the documents, the rows of the matrix. Inside of the matrix there are numbers that represent the number of times a word appeared in a certain registry. Most of the times the term-document matrix are sparse since the probability of occurrence of each word in all the registries is low.

Step 6: Training. In this process are considered the words from the dictionary, the belonging probability of the words to a specific class, and the probability that the registries are correctly classified according to the words they contain.

Bayes probability is based on the idea that an events probability depends on the probes at the precise moment. Naïve Bayes classification algorithm is based on two premises: the probabilities of event occurrences must be exhaustive and mutually exclusive; and that the joint probability must be considered.

Applying the Bayes theorem, it is used the Equation 1.

$$P(A_i \mid B) = \frac{P(B \mid A_i)P(A_i)}{P(B)}.$$

(1)

In Table 2, we describe the components of the equation 1.

Table 2.

Term	Meaning
B	The classification label.
A_i	The dependent event, a classification that shares features with the expected classification.
$P(B)$	Marginal probability of B, the probability that B appears at any message.
$P(A_i)$	Prior probability of event A_i
$P(B|A_i)$	Likelihood of B in event A_i
$P(A_i|B)$	Posterior probability of A_i occurrence given that B appeared.

Suppose there is needed to determine the probability that a registry describes an accident class event. It is known that a word of the message is '*closed*', the probability that '*closed*' was found in other messages classified as '*accident*' is the likelihood, the probability of the word '*closed*' to appear at any message is the marginal probability; the posterior probability is the probability of classify the message with the label A_i that represents the class '*accident*'.

Step 7: Learning. Considering that we are working with multiple words, there is used an extended classification Naïve Bayes. The algorithm is trained with the construction of a probabilities table, where there has been calculated the probability that each word of the dictionary belongs or not to each one of the defined classes (Bishop, 2006).

Any time a new registry is analyzed by the python script to be classified, the posterior probability must be calculated, with a view to determine the class where the message must be classified considering the probabilities of the words included or not on the message. This means that for the final probability, it is necessary to include the probability of presence or absence of each word in the message. This computation must be done for each class toward to identify the highest probability that would denote the correct classification of the event, in Equation 2 there is represented this calculation. In Equation 3 it is represented the final probability of classify a text as element of class 1, supposing that it has 4 words and the data dictionary has 7 words. In Table 3, are described the terms of Equation 2 and Equation 3.

$$
\begin{aligned}
&\textit{Sum of probabilities calculated for other classes} = P(Class1 \mid Pword1 \cap Pword2 \cap Pword3 \\
&\cap Pword4 \cap \neg Pword5 \cap \neg Pword6 \cap \neg Pword7) + \ldots + P(Classn \mid Pword1 \cap Pword2 \\
&\cap Pword3 \cap Pword4 \cap \neg Pword5 \cap \neg Pword6 \cap \neg Pword7)
\end{aligned} \tag{2}
$$

$$
\begin{aligned}
&P\big(text \in Class1\big) \\
&= \frac{P(Class1 \mid Pword1 \cap Pword2 \cap Pword3 \cap Pword4 \cap \neg Pword5 \cap \neg Pword6 \cap \neg Pword7)}{\textit{Sum of probabilities calculated for other classes}}
\end{aligned} \tag{3}
$$

The Naïve Bayes algorithm classifies the registry in the class with the highest probability. In the learning step the probabilistic model is structured as it was described above; this model is used also in the classification step.

Step 8: Models evaluation. Applying precision metrics to the obtained results is possible to determine if the algorithm performance is appropriate, or to identify in which points it should be improved.

To measure the precision of the Naïve Bayes algorithm applied in this research, the precision metrics of mean square error, the mean absolute error and the confusion matrix are computed.

In the confusion matrix, the columns represent the number of predictions for each class, and the rows the classified instances in the correct class; this is a useful tool to identify the classes where the algorithm presents more classification deficiencies (Bergstra, 2013).

Table 3.

Term	Meaning
Sum of Probabilities calculated for other classes	Sum of the conditional probabilities calculated for each class.
Class 1	e class that is being analyzed, there are seven different classes in this study.
Pword 1	The probability that the word 1 appears in the registry text, this probability must be calculated for every word.
¬Pword 1	The probability that the word 1 does not appears in the registry text, this probability must be calculated for every word.
$P(Class1 \mid Pword1 \cap Pword2 \ldots)$	Conditional probability of the class, it considers the intersection of the words that appear and the words that do not appear in the registry.
P(message ∈ Class 1)	Probability that the text of the registry that is being analyzed belongs to class 1.

Step 9: Final Classification. Once the algorithm has been trained with the training corpus and its deficiencies have been repaired, is time to apply the Naïve Bayes classification over the test data corpus. Below there are written the machine learning algorithm steps:

- The algorithm tokenizes the text of each registry from the test corpus,
- adds to the data dictionary the missing words,
- calculates the frequency for the new words added in the same way that the frequency of the training corpus words,
- analyzes the tokenized text to know the words that compound it,
- creates the text vectors and homogenizes their length with the dictionary length; obtains the term-document matrix.
- Based on the words of each vector and their calculated frequencies, the algorithm classifies the registries.
- Assigns a class label to the registry. In case that the registry came from the social media, the registry is stored in the table *geocoded _messages* with its machine learning assigned label, if the classified registry was a RSS note, the result would be saved in the *rss_data* table.

Geocoding

Geocoding of messages to identify the coordinates of the geographical place described in their texts is a common process, there exist different tools such as geographic information systems (GIS), and web services such as Google Maps that help developers in this work (Crooks, 2013).

In this last methodology stage are identified the geographical coordinates of the events described in the registries texts, this section is divided into two steps: *coordinates extraction* and *geometry*.

Coordinates Extraction

To obtain the coordinates of the registries the python script created for achieve the methodology stages, searches in a gazetteer of the study area the name of the streets, avenues, or points of reference provided in the text of the registries, the gazetteer returns the coordinates of the place. The application overlaps the coordinates assigned to the geographic elements, and after the spatial overlapping function, the python program obtains the coordinates of the place where the described event probably occurred. The coordinates of the event are stored in the registries fields' *latitude* and *longitude* of the table *geocoded_messages*.

The gazetteer and the geocoding process used in the approach are part of a geocoding methodology implemented in the research work of Salazar et al. (2016). This methodology has been used to geocoding the messages since it is not a purpose of the present approach.

After testing the geocoding results, we have noticed that in some cases there is an imprecision in the events location due to the length of some roads. To filter the events that were correctly geocoded from the ones that did not, the points of the coordinates are mapped in order to visualize those which location is not real. If an event was not correctly located, an external annotator geocodes the event manually, by searching the address of the registry text in Google Maps.

For the RSS data, the geocoding process is a little more complex. Most of the times the RSS registries description of the place where the event occurred is not clear or includes many details that generate confusion to the geocoding tools and gazetteers; to solve this problem, we have designated an external annotator to geocode such registries by using the Google Maps geocoding tool. The annotator searches in Google Maps the address of the RSS registry text, and saves the coordinates in the *latitude* and *longitude* fields of the *rss_data* table.

Geometry

The coordinates of all the registries are merged into a geometric point that represents the location of the event. This step is needed to visualize the events and to create new geographical features as polygons or heat maps from their analysis that can be useful for other investigations.

This step is implemented using the spatial extension PostGIS for the database manager Postgresql. Through a query to obtain the coordinates assigned to each registry, Postgis merges the both coordinates using the spatial projection of the analyzed geographic area, the resultant geometry data, the coordinates, and the classification of the event, are stored in the table *urban_dynamics*.

Results

The present approach surges from the needed to have a classification of the real traffic evens that every day affect to urban areas, as case of study has been chose the Mexico City, one of the most crowded cities in world.

Mexico City is one of the most important financial centers in Latin America, with a population around 21.2 million people, and an area of 1,485 square kilometers. It is the largest metropolitan area in the earth western hemisphere and the largest Spanish-speaking city in the world (Alba, 2015). Due to the increasing interest of people and local authorities in VGI and internet content, the use of internet as a data source for the present approach has been considered.

In the approach different computing technologies are merged to achieve the methodology purpose. For the database structuring the database manager Postgresql and its geospatial data tool Postgis are used. The analyzed data to obtain information about traffic events in the study area are posts from Twitter and RSS notes. The acquisition of the RSS notes from the main journals in the studied area is done using a PHP application programmed for that purpose; the extraction of tweets is done using Python language program.

After the extraction of data from internet and its storage in the database Events, the messages are treated as registries and processed through a text mining procedure where grammatical elements that do not provide information to classify the message are eliminated, and words of interest for the classification and geocoding of the message are identified.

Seven traffic eves class are proposed: *traffic, favorable, closure, accident, rule, manager, and unidentified*. The processed text of the registries is classified manually and using a python script to structure a training and a test corpus for the posterior machine learning data classification. Finally, the registries are classified by a semi supervised method using the machine learning algorithm Naïve Bayes. The classification algorithm is trained with the classified samples, and tested with text preprocessed registries.

In Figure 4, the points in the map represent the traffic related messages analyzed, these are registries from tables *rss_data* and *geocoded_messages*.

Regarding to the semi-supervised classification process, two different classification methods are compared, a script where the most common words that describe a class event are matched with the registries text words using conditional programming sentences, and a Naïve Bayes algorithm trained with preprocessed data.

Figure 4.

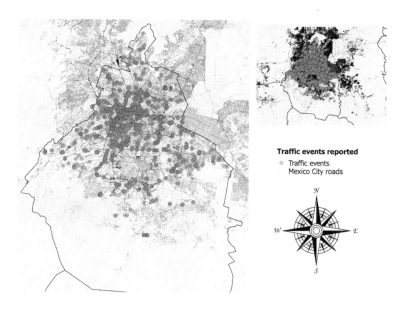

From the Naïve Bayes method good classification results were obtained, the principle of the algorithm is to learn from the training corpus those words that compound the description of each class, then analyzes the words from each registry of the test corpus and according to each class words presence or absence in the registries text classifies it.

Analyzing the precision metrics of our *Data classification* procedure, the Naïve Bayes algorithm threw an error of 0.110482 when classifying social media registries and when classifying RSS registries, it presented the highest error with a value of 0.401523; however, this error rate was lower than the first classification method, and more efficient. Another advantage of the Naïve Bayes classification is that the classification is faster, even for big amount of data.

The *urban_dynamics* table, stores the geocoded traffic events of the study area. The data can be used to be classified by using other machine learning tools.

Figure 5, shows a map where the posted traffic messages density in the studied area is shown through a heat map. The color levels change according to the number of traffic events reported in the area, if few messages were posted then the color is light; if a big amount of tweets and RSS notes describes events in the same area, its color in the heat map is dark.

To have a different perspective about the traffic situation in the study area, a map that combines a heat map and points is shown in Figure 6. The heat map represents the areas where traffic problems have been reported, meanwhile the points represent reports of the favorable class. Regarding the Figure 6, is possible to see that the number of reports about good circulation on the roads is smaller than the traffic report; this has a direct relation with the peoples interest in report problems in their city, and because when the circulation on roads is speedy people prefers to save time instead of posting the traffic conditions.

Figure 5.

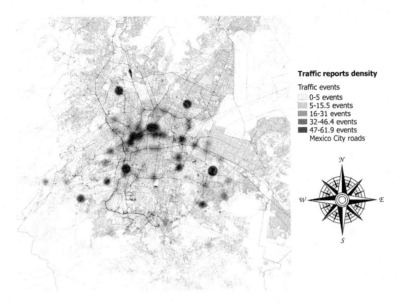

Figure 6.

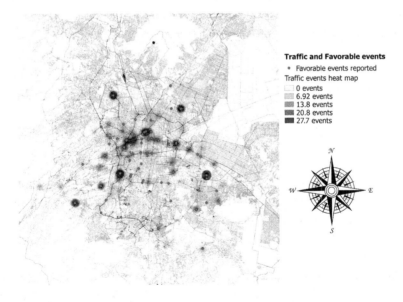

CONCLUSION

The here presented method is oriented on extracting and processing social data in order to make them compatible and available for further investigations. The integrated information concerns to the cartography of the study area, bus and subway stations, and commercial business located on its roads, and the most important, the events related to traffic and vehicular problems that occurred on the area.

The present approach is guided to analyze the traffic problems that affect urban areas using VGI and machine learning algorithms. In the approach textual and geographic information is analyzed.

The traffic problems descriptions are obtained from two web sources not related between them: a social media and a RSS service. The social media data are stored in the database named *Events*, which has five tables: *usr_information, monitored_messages, rss_data, geocoded_messages* and *urban_dynamics*.

The geographic information is obtained from shapefiles with data about the roads in the study area; such data are stored in a geospatial database compound of three tables: *roads, infrastructure* and *transport*.

After the monitoring of the web sources, the data are preprocessed by a text mining procedure in order to extract the registries relevant information. The third part of the treated registries are classified manually, the rest of the samples are classified using a script with conditional statements in order to structuring the training corpus. The 75% of the total samples is considered as the training corpus, the rest of the samples are used in the test corpus. The training and the test corpus are used in the Naive Bayes machine learning algorithm, with a view to classify automatically the registries obtained, into one of the seven classes stablished for this investigation. The classes are: *traffic, favorable, closure, accident, rule, manager, and unidentified*.

After the classification, a geocoding process is applied to the data with the purpose of get the coordinates where each event occurred and create geometric points in order to visualize the data in a map.

When all the proposed methodology stages are complete, the registries from the two processed tables *rss_data* and *geocoded _messages,* are merged into the table *urban_dynamics*; this last table represents a repository of road and traffic events that can be useful for some other classification procedures or for further investigations related to traffic. The table urban_dynamics has information of messages that describe traffic events in the study area, such as their tokenized and cleared text, its assigned classification label, the coordinates where the event occurred, and the geometry field that allows to Geographic Information Systems to represent the registries as points.

The *geographic* and the *events* databases can be useful for GIS to represent the roads of the area for which the analysis was applied, the location of bus, subway and commercial businesses located nearby the roads; and the road events that affect the correct displacement of vehicles and people of the area.

The *events* database has been structured with the purpose of creating a data repository, about the traffic events on a city that could be useful for other works, since there are many web data sources that cannot be used together but that could provide valuable information to develop new data urban systems.

DISCUSSION

The present approach analyses VGI information and internet content. The VGI information is obtained from a social media, its main characteristic is that such information represents citizens reports of the traffic situation in the study area.

VGI lets data analysis processes to have direct contact with real world studying the users reports. People reports what they perceive and consider interesting for other users and authorities. VGI lets have updated information about topics that concern to the society where the information is produced.

Machine learning is a powerful computing area, one of its main purposes is to automatize data analysis procedures learning from the data features and achieving high precision rates.

The main purpose of the presented work is to detect the main traffic problems that affect the urban dynamics at big cities, studying tweets and RSS notes posted in Mexico City. The traffic events classes have been proposed considering the different characteristics of traffic events reported in the area through Twitter. In the methodology a machine learning classification algorithm is implemented in order to merge VGI and UGC content with machine learning.

Through the methodology process tweets and RSS notes are extracted from internet, text mining processed, classified by three different tools (manually, with conditional programming, and with a ML algorithm). Finally, data are geovisualized in maps of the studied area. The maps let identify the areas with more traffic reports, and the alternative roads that can be used to avoid traffic jams in the analyzed city.

The geovisualization of the results opens to opportunity to data interpretations related with social aspects such as the areas with more traffic reports, the relation between congested areas and air pollution, the participation of citizens reporting traffic events, the alternative routes to avoid crowded roads, and how the analyzed data and designed maps can be used by authorities and organizations to keep citizens informed about the traffic situation in their neighborhood.

As results of the implemented methodology a data corpus of tweets related to traffic in their original format, and a data corpus of text processed tweets which main topic is the traffic in Mexico city are structured. Such data corpus are used in a posterior research focused in data regressions, and represent a useful data set since there are not many compendiums of traffic related information.

As further work for the approach is proposed the text processed traffic related tweets classification using different machine learning algorithms such as K Nearest Neighbors, Support vector machine, clustering, among others, to prove their efficiency and select the one with the highest precision to classify the data. Also, a real time analysis could be develop in order to analyze tweets as soon as they are posted, and to have a more accurate traffic events visualization.

The methodology presented can be adapted to work with data from other urban area as long as there exists information about its roads, and after extracting tweets and UGC from its citizens. Once the methodology is feed with the VGI and geospatial needed information, the text mining and the classification processes can be applied.

REFERENCES

Adamko, M., Navrat, P., & Kovarova, A. (2015). Personalised Recommendation of Who to Follow Based on Fellowship of Followers. *Editorial Policy, 1*.

Alba, F. (2015). International migration: Consolidation of emerging patterns. *Demos (Mexico City, Mexico)*, (13), 10–11.

Bakerman, J., Pazdernik, K., Wilson, A., Fairchild, G., & Bahran, R. (2018). Twitter Geolocation: A Hybrid Approach. *ACM Transactions on Knowledge Discovery from Data*, *12*(3), 34.

Bergstra, J., Yamins, D., & Cox, D. (2013). Making a science of model search: Hyperparameter optimization in hundreds of dimensions for vision architectures. In *Proceedings of The 30th International Conference on Machine Learning* (pp. 115-123). Academic Press.

Bishop, C. M. (2006). *Pattern recognition and machine learning*. Springer.

Cinnamon, J., & Schuurman, N. (2013). Confronting the data-divide in a time of spatial turns and volunteered geographic information. *GeoJournal*, *78*(4), 657–674. doi:10.100710708-012-9458-6

Crooks, A., Croitoru, A., Stefanidis, A., & Radzikowski, J. (2013). #Earthquake: Twitter as a distributed sensor system. *Transactions in GIS*, *17*(1), 124–147. doi:10.1111/j.1467-9671.2012.01359.x

Dou, W., Yu, L., Wang, X., Ma, Z., & Ribarsky, W. (2013). Hierarchicaltopics: Visually exploring large text collections using topic hierarchies. Visualization and Computer Graphics. *IEEE Transactions on*, *19*(12), 2002–2011. PMID:24051766

Dredze, M., Paul, M. J., Bergsma, S., & Tran, H. (2013, June). Carmen: A twitter geolocation system with applications to public health. In AAAI workshop on expanding the boundaries of health informatics using AI (HIAI) (pp. 20-24). AAAI.

Goodchild, M. F. (2015). Twenty years of progress: GIScience in 2010. *Journal of Spatial Information Science,* (1), 3-20.

Han, Y., Hong, B., Lee, H., & Kim, K. (2017). How do we Tweet? The Comparative Analysis of Twitter Usage by Message Types, Devices, and Sources. *The Journal of Social Media in Society*, *6*(1), 189–219.

Havlik, D., Egly, M., Huber, H., Kutschera, P., Falgenhauer, M., & Cizek, M. (2013). Robust and trusted crowd-sourcing and crowd-tasking in the Future Internet. In Environmental Software Systems. Fostering Information Sharing (pp. 164-176). Springer Berlin Heidelberg. doi:10.1007/978-3-642-41151-9_16

Huang, B., & Carley, K. M. (2017). *On Predicting Geolocation of Tweets using Convolutional Neural Networks*. arXiv preprint arXiv:1704.05146

Jiang, B., & Thill, J. C. (2015). Volunteered Geographic Information: Towards the establishment of a new paradigm. *Computers, Environment and Urban Systems*, *53*, 1–3. doi:10.1016/j.compenvurbsys.2015.09.011

Kantardzic, M. (2011). *Data mining: concepts, models, methods, and algorithms*. John Wiley & Sons. doi:10.1002/9781118029145

Koswatte, S., McDougall, K., & Liu, X. (2018). VGI and crowdsourced data credibility analysis using spam email detection techniques. *International Journal of Digital Earth*, *11*(5), 520–532. doi:10.1080/17538947.2017.1341558

Lansley, G., & Longley, P. A. (2016). The geography of Twitter topics in London. *Computers, Environment and Urban Systems*, *58*, 85–96. doi:10.1016/j.compenvurbsys.2016.04.002

Lantz, B. (2013). *Machine learning with R*. Packt Publishing Ltd.

Leetaru, K., Wang, S., Cao, G., Padmanabhan, A., & Shook, E. (2013). Mapping the global Twitter heartbeat: The geography of Twitter. *First Monday*, *18*(5). doi:10.5210/fm.v18i5.4366

Li, Q., Song, D., Liao, L., & Liu, L. (2015). Personalized Mention Probabilistic Ranking–Recommendation on Mention Behavior of Heterogeneous Social media. In *Web-Age Information Management* (pp. 41–52). Springer International Publishing. doi:10.1007/978-3-319-23531-8_4

Lin, W. (2013). Volunteered geographic information and networked publics? Politics of everyday mapping and spatial narratives. *GeoJournal*, *78*(6), 949–965. doi:10.100710708-013-9490-1

Mohadab, M., Bouikhalene, B., & Safi, S. (2018). *Predicting rank for scientific research papers using supervised learning*. Applied Computing and Informatics.

Osm. (n.d.). Retrieved from https://www.openstreetmap.org

Paredes-Valverde, M. A., Alor-Hernández, G., Rodríguez-González, A., Valencia-García, R., & Jiménez-Domingo, E. (2015). A systematic review of tools, languages, and methodologies for mashup development. *Software, Practice & Experience*, *45*(3), 365–397. doi:10.1002pe.2233

Pernici, B., Francalanci, C., Scalia, G., Corsi, M., Grandoni, D., & Biscardi, M. A. (2018). *Geolocating social media posts for emergency mapping*. arXiv preprint arXiv:1801.06861

Resch, B. (2013). People as sensors and collective sensing-contextual observations complementing geo-sensor network measurements. In *Progress in Location-Based Services* (pp. 391-406). Springer Berlin Heidelberg.

Resch, B., Summa, A., Sagl, G., Zeile, P., & Exner, J. P. (2015). Urban emotions—geo-semantic emotion extraction from technical sensors, human sensors and crowdsourced data. In Progress in Location-Based Services 2014 (pp. 199-212). Springer International Publishing.

Ricker, B., Daniel, S., & Hedley, N. (2014). Fuzzy Boundaries: Hybridizing Location-based Services, Volunteered Geographic Information and Geovisualization Literature. *Geography Compass*, *8*(7), 490–504. doi:10.1111/gec3.12138

Salazar, J. C., Torres, M., & Moreno, M. (2016). *Monitoreo urbano de entidades y eventos geográficos basado en censado social* (Unpublished master dissertation). Centro de Investigación en Computación, Instituto Politécnico Nacional, Mexico.

Saldana-Perez, A. M. M., & Moreno-Ibarra, M. (2016). Traffic analysis based on short texts from social media. *International Journal of Knowledge Society Research*, *7*(1), 63–79. doi:10.4018/IJKSR.2016010105

Saldana-Perez, A. M. M., Moreno-Ibarra, M. A., & Torres-Ruiz, M. J. (2018). Classification of Traffic Events Notified in Social Networks' Texts. In Encyclopedia of Information Science and Technology, Fourth Edition (pp. 6973-6984). IGI Global.

Sidorov, G., Velasquez, F., Stamatatos, E., Gelbukh, A., & Chanona-Hernández, L. (2014). Syntactic n-grams as machine learning features for natural language processing. *Expert Systems with Applications*, *41*(3), 853–860. doi:10.1016/j.eswa.2013.08.015

Silverman, K., Naik, D., Lenzo, K., & Henton, C. (2013). *U.S. Patent No. 8,583,418*. Washington, DC: U.S. Patent and Trademark Office.

Stehman, S. V., Fonte, C. C., Foody, G. M., & See, L. (2018). Using volunteered geographic information (VGI) in design-based statistical inference for area estimation and accuracy assessment of land cover. *Remote Sensing of Environment*, *212*, 47–59. doi:10.1016/j.rse.2018.04.014

Tobler, W. R. (1970). A computer movie simulating urban growth in the Detroit region. *Economic Geography*, *46*, 234–240. doi:10.2307/143141

Twitterapi. (n.d.). Retrieved from https://developer.twitter.com/en/docs/developer-utilities/twitter-libraries

Utomo, M. N. Y., Adji, T. B., & Ardiyanto, I. (2018). Geolocation Prediction in Social Media Data Using Text Analysis. *RE:view*.

Vidal-Filho, J. N., Lisboa-Filho, J., de Souza, W. D., & dos Santos, G. R. (2013). Qualitative Analysis of Volunteered Geographic Information in a Spatially Enabled Society Project. In *Computational Science and Its Applications–ICCSA 2013* (pp. 378–393). Springer Berlin Heidelberg. doi:10.1007/978-3-642-39646-5_28

Williams, E., Gray, J., & Dixon, B. (2017). Improving geolocation of social media posts. *Pervasive and Mobile Computing*, *36*, 68–79. doi:10.1016/j.pmcj.2016.09.015

Yang, L., Dong, L., & Bi, X. (2016). An improved location difference of multiple distances based nearest neighbors searching algorithm. *Optik-International Journal for Light and Electron Optics*, *127*(22), 10838–10843. doi:10.1016/j.ijleo.2016.08.091

Yılmaz, Y., & Hero, A. O. (2018). Multimodal Event Detection in Twitter Hashtag Networks. *Journal of Signal Processing Systems for Signal, Image, and Video Technology*, *90*(2), 185–200. doi:10.100711265-016-1151-4

Zhang, F., Yuan, N. J., Wilkie, D., Zheng, Y., & Xie, X. (2015). Sensing the pulse of urban refueling behavior: A perspective from taxi mobility. *ACM Transactions on Intelligent Systems and Technology*, *6*(3), 37. doi:10.1145/2644828

Zhao, Z., Cheng, Z., Hong, L., & Chi, E. H. (2015, May). Improving User Topic Interest Profiles by Behavior Factorization. In *Proceedings of the 24th International Conference on World Wide Web* (pp. 1406-1416). International World Wide Web Conferences Steering Committee. 10.1145/2736277.2741656

This research was previously published in Knowledge-Intensive Economies and Opportunities for Social, Organizational, and Technological Growth; pages 141-162, copyright year 2019 by Information Science Reference (an imprint of IGI Global).

Section 5
Organizational and Social Implications

Chapter 59
Challenges and Applications for Implementing Machine Learning in Computer Vision:
Machine Learning Applications and Approaches

Hiral R. Patel
Ganpat University, India

Ajay M Patel
AMPICS, India

Satyen M. Parikh
FCA, India

ABSTRACT

The chapter introduces machine learning and why it is important. Machine learning is generally used to find knowledge from unknown data. There are many approaches and algorithms available for performing machine learning. Different kinds of algorithms are available to find different patterns from the data. This chapter focuses on different approaches with different usage.

INTRODUCTION

The world is seeing the ongoing stream of a wide range of organized and unstructured information from internet based life, correspondence, transportation, sensors, and gadgets. World wide Data Corporation (IDC) is gauges that 180 zettabytes of information will be produced by 2025. This blast of information has offered ascend to another economy known as the Data Economy or Importance. Information is the new oil that is valuable yet helpful just when cleaned and prepared. There is a consistent fight for responsibility for between endeavors to get profits by it. The information economy with its tremendous

DOI: 10.4018/978-1-6684-6291-1.ch059

supply is empowering extraordinary development in information sciences, the field which manages extricating helpful data and bits of knowledge from the accessible information. Information science is going toward another worldview where one can instruct machines to gain from information and infer an assortment of helpful experiences. This is known as Artificial Intelligence. Man-made reasoning alludes to knowledge shown by machines that reenact human and creature insight. Computer based intelligence is utilized generally.

The following related task is performed by Artificial Intelligence.

- Self-driving vehicles
- Applications like Siri that comprehend and react to human discourse
- Google's AlphaGo AI has vanquished many Go champions, for example, Ke Jie
- Actualizing AI in chess
- Amazon ECHO item (home control chatbot gadget)
- Hilton utilizing Connie – attendant robot from IBM Watson

The general example of AI that is Amazon pulls in information from its client database to prescribe items to clients. This usefulness gets more clients. More clients produce significantly more information that assistance improves the proposals considerably further.

Alpavdin characterizes Machine Learning as- "Upgrading an execution standard utilizing precedent information and past experience".

The term Machine Learning was begat by Arthur Samuel in 1959, an American pioneer in the field of PC gaming and man-made brainpower and expressed that "it enables PCs to learn without being unambiguously modified".

Also, in 1997, Tom Mitchell gave an "all around presented" scientific and social definition that "A PC program is said to gain as a matter of fact E as for some undertaking T and some execution measure P, if its execution on T, as estimated by P, enhances with experience E.

Machine Learning is a most recent trendy expression coasting around. It has the right to, as it is a standout amongst the most intriguing subfield of Computer Science.

Data is the key idea of machine learning. Analyst can apply its calculations on information to distinguish concealed examples and addition bits of knowledge. These examples and picked up information help frameworks to learn and improve their execution.

Machine learning innovation includes the two insights and software engineering. Measurements enable one to draw deductions from the given information. To actualize proficient calculations we can likewise utilize software engineering. It speaks to the required model, and assesses the execution of the model.

Machine learning includes some progressed factual ideas, for example, demonstrating and enhancement. Displaying alludes to the conditions or likelihood dissemination for the given example information. Improvement additionally incorporates procedures used to locate the most fitting parameters for the given arrangement of information.

The information causes frameworks to learn and improve their execution. We can utilize Modern Learning innovation in a few zones, for example, counterfeit neural systems, information mining, web positioning and so forth.

In Big Data Analytics, Data mining and machine learning are the two most regularly utilized strategies. So people can get befuddled between the two however they are two distinct methodologies utilized for two unique purposes.

Here just the sight view of difference between *Data Mining and Machine Learning*. Data mining is the way toward distinguishing designs in a lot of information to investigate valuable data from those examples. It might incorporate methods of computerized reasoning, machine learning, neural systems, and measurements. The premise of information mining is genuine information. It might have taken motivation and methods from machine learning and measurements yet is put to various finishes. An individual completes information mining in a particular circumstance on a specific informational collection. The objective is to use the intensity of the different example acknowledgment procedures of machine learning.

In any case, machine learning process is a way to deal with creating man-made reasoning. We use Machine Learning calculation to build up the new calculations and strategies. These enable the machine to gain from the examined information or with experience. Most errands that need insight must have a capacity to initiate new information from encounters. Accordingly, a huge region inside AI is machine learning. This includes the investigation of calculations that can separate data without on-line human direction.

Machine Learning identifies with the investigation, structure, and improvement of the calculations. These give PCs the ability to learn without being expressly modified. Information Mining begins with unstructured information and attempts to separate learning or intriguing examples. Amid this procedure, we use machine Learning calculations.

The ability of Artificial Intelligence frameworks to take in by removing designs from information is known as Machine Learning. Machine Learning is a plan to gain from precedents and experience, without being unequivocally modified. Rather than composing code, you feed information to the nonexclusive calculation, and it fabricates rationale dependent on the information given.

Machine Learning Benefits

Give us a chance to take a gander at a portion of the advantages in this Machine Learning instructional exercise.

- Amazing Processing
- Better Decision Making and Prediction
- Faster Processing
- Precise
- Reasonable Data Management
- Reasonable
- Dissecting Complex Big Data

Highlights of Machine Learning

Give us a chance to take a gander at a portion of the highlights given beneath in this Machine Learning instructional exercise. Machine Learning is registering escalated and for the most part requires a lot of preparing information. It includes tedious preparing to enhance the learning and basic leadership of calculations.

As more information gets included, Machine Learning preparing can be mechanized for adapting new information designs and adjusting its calculation.

Machine Learning is a field which is raised out of Artificial Intelligence (AI). Applying AI, we needed to assemble better and wise machines. In any case, with the exception of couple of simple errands, for example, finding the most brief way between point A and B, we were not able program increasingly mind boggling and always advancing challenges. There was an acknowledgment that the best way to almost certainly accomplish this assignment was to give machine a chance to gain from itself. This sounds like a youngster gaining from its self. So machine learning was produced as another capacity for PCs. What's more, presently machine realizing is available in such huge numbers of sections of innovation, that we don't understand it while utilizing it.

Discovering designs in information on planet earth is conceivable just for human cerebrums. The information being extremely enormous, the time taken to register is expanded, and this is the place Machine Learning comes without hesitation, to help individuals with huge information in least time.

In the event that huge information and distributed computing are picking up significance for their commitments, machine learning as innovation breaks down those enormous lumps of information, facilitating the undertaking of information researchers in a robotized procedure and increasing equivalent significance and acknowledgment.

The procedures we use for information digging have been around for a long time, however they were not compelling as they didn't have the focused capacity to run the calculations. On the off chance that you run profound learning with access to better information, the yield we get will prompt sensational leaps forward which is machine learning.

This infers the assignments in which machine learning is concerned offers an essentially operational definition instead of characterizing the field in subjective terms. This pursues Alan Turing's proposition in his paper "Registering Machinery and Intelligence", in which the inquiry "Can machines believe?" is supplanted with the inquiry "Can machines do what we (as speculation elements) can do?"

Inside the field of information investigation, machine learning is utilized to devise complex models and calculations that loan themselves to forecast; in business use, this is known as prescient examination. These investigative models permit specialists, information researchers, designers, and examiners to "produce solid, repeatable choices and results" and reveal "concealed experiences" through gaining from authentic connections and patterns in the information set(input).

So on the off chance that you need your program to anticipate, for instance, traffic designs at a bustling convergence (errand T), you can run it through a machine learning calculation with information about past traffic designs (experience E) and, on the off chance that it has effectively "educated", it will at that point improve the situation at foreseeing future traffic designs (execution measure P).

The very unpredictable nature of some genuine issues, however, regularly implies that creating particular calculations that will tackle them superbly every time is unreasonable, if certainly feasible. Instances of machine learning issues incorporate, "Is this malignant growth?", "Which of these individuals are great companions with one another?", "Will this individual like this motion picture?" such issues are astounding focuses for Machine Learning, and in actuality machine learning has been connected such issues with extraordinary achievement.

Kinds of Machine Learning

There are three common taxonomies of Machine Learning Algorithm based on the result conclusion of the algorithm (Figure 1). The Figure 2 is also the categories of Ml Algorithms using learning Style.

The different methodologies under each category are mentioned in figure 2.

Figure 1. Kinds of ML & Categorization of ML Algorithms

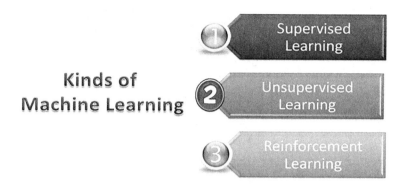

Figure 2. Categorization of ML Algorithms

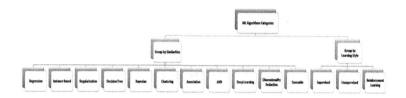

1. Supervised Learning

In regulated learning, we are given an informational index and as of now comprehend what our right yield should resemble, having the possibility that there is a connection between the information and the yield. Directed learning issues are additionally sorted into relapse and arrangement issues.

To portray the directed learning issue somewhat more formally, our objective is, given a preparation set, to get familiar with a capacity h: X → Y so that h(x) is a "decent" indicator for the comparing estimation of y. For authentic reasons, this capacity h is known as a theory. Seen pictorially, the procedure is thusly similar to what is shown in Figure 3.

At the point when the objective variable that we're endeavoring to foresee is consistent, for example, in our lodging model, we consider the learning issue a relapse issue. At the point when y can take on just few discrete qualities, (for example, if, given the living territory, we needed to anticipate if a home is a house or a condo, state), we consider it an arrangement issue.

The figure 4 shows the algorithms which are under the Supervised Learning Category of Machine Learning.

2. Unsupervised Learning

Unsupervised learning works by breaking down the information without its marks for the shrouded structures inside it, and through deciding the relationships, and for highlights that really correspond two information things. It is being utilized for bunching, dimensionality decrease, include learning, thickness estimation, and so forth.

Figure 3. Supervised Learning Style

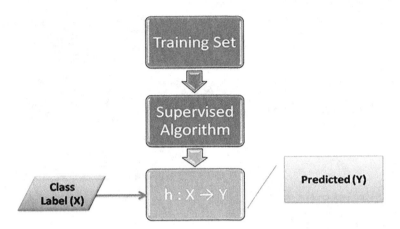

Figure 4. Supervised Learning Algorithms

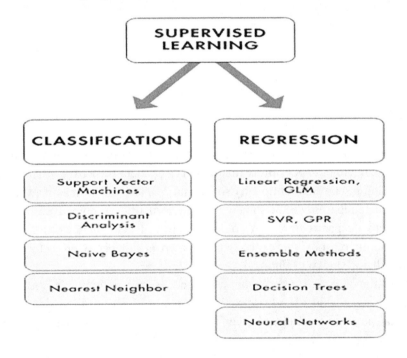

The shrouded structure once in a while called include vector, speaks to the info information such a way, that on the off chance that a similar component vector is being use to recreate the info, at that point one can do that with some satisfactory misfortune. The change in two component vectors of two data sources specifically relative to the difference in the information sources itself. Along these lines this shrouded structure or highlight vector just speaks to highlights in the information that really offer refinement to it.

In this Unsupervised Machine Learning, input information isn't marked and does not have a known outcome.

Figure 5. Unsupervised Learning Algorithms

We need to get ready model by deriving structures present in the info information. This might be to extricate general guidelines. It might be through a scientific procedure to lessen excess.

Model issues are bunching, dimensionality decrease, and affiliation rule learning.

Precedent calculations incorporate the Apriori calculation and k-Means.

3. Reinforcement Learning

Reinforcement learning is a region of Machine Learning. Reinforcement: It is tied in with making reasonable move to expand compensate in a specific circumstance. It is utilized by different programming and machines to locate the most ideal conduct or way it should take in a particular circumstance. Fortification taking in contrasts from the directed learning in a route that in regulated learning the preparation information has the appropriate response key with it so the model is prepared with the right answer itself while in Reinforcement learning, there is no answer yet the fortification specialist chooses what to do to play out the given errand. Without preparing dataset, it will undoubtedly gain from its experience.

Precedent: The issue is as per the following: We have a specialist and a reward, with numerous obstacles in the middle. The specialist should locate the most ideal way to achieve the reward. The accompanying issue clarifies the issue all the more effectively.

The figure 6 indicates robot, precious stone and flame. The objective of the robot is to get the reward that is the jewel and dodge the obstacles that is fire. The robot learns by attempting all the conceivable ways and after that picking the way which gives him the reward with the least obstacles. Each correct advance will give the robot a reward and each wrong advance will subtract the reward of the robot. The absolute reward will be determined when it achieves the last reward that is the precious stone.

Figure 6. Reinforcement Learning Example

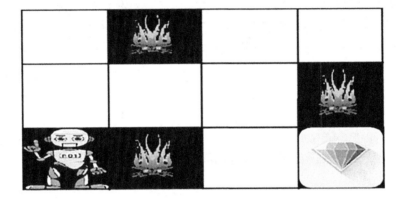

Main Points for Reinforcement Learning

Input: The information ought to be an underlying state from which the model will begin
Outcome: There are numerous conceivable output as there are assortment of answer for a specific issue
Training/Preparing: The preparation depends on the information, The model will restore a state and the client will choose to remunerate or rebuff the model dependent on its yield.

The model keeps on learning.
The best arrangement of solution is chosen dependent on the most extreme reward.

Reinforcement Learning vs. Supervised Learning

- Reinforcement Learning is tied in with settling on choices successively. In basic words we can say that the out relies upon the condition of the present information and the following information relies upon the yield of the past input where as In Supervised learning the choice is made on the underlying information or the information given toward the begin.

- In Reinforcement learning choice is reliant, So we offer names to groupings of ward decisions where as Supervised learning the choices are free of one another so names are given to every choice.
- Playing Chess is the example of Reinforcement Learning and Object Recognition is the example of Supervised Learning.

Applications of Machine Learning

One of the cutting edge developments we've seen is the making of Machine Learning. This fantastic type of man-made consciousness is as of now being utilized in different ventures and callings. For Example, Image and Speech Recognition, Medical Diagnosis, Prediction, Classification, Learning Associations, Statistical Arbitrage, Extraction, Regression.

These are this present reality Machine Learning Applications; we should see them one by one-

1. Picture Recognition

It is a standout amongst the most widely recognized AI applications. There are numerous circumstances where you can arrange the item as an advanced picture. For advanced pictures, the estimations depict the yields of every pixel in the picture. On account of a highly contrasting picture, the power of every pixel fills in as one estimation. So if a high contrast picture has N*N pixels, the all out number of pixels and thus estimation is N2.

How about we examine ANN in Machine Learning:

In the hued picture, every pixel considered as giving 3 estimations of the forces of 3 principle shading segments ie RGB. So N*N shaded picture there are 3 N2 estimations.

For face location – The classes may be face versus no face present. There may be a different classification for every individual in a database of a few people.

For character acknowledgment – We can fragment a bit of composing into littler pictures, each containing a solitary character. The classifications may comprise of the 26 letters of the English letter set, the 10 digits, and some unique characters.

2. Discourse Recognition

Discourse acknowledgment (SR) is the interpretation of verbally expressed words into content. It is otherwise called "programmed discourse acknowledgment" (ASR), "PC discourse acknowledgment", or "discourse to content" (STT).

In discourse acknowledgment, a product application perceives verbally expressed words. The estimations in this Machine Learning application may be a lot of numbers that speak to the discourse flag. We can fragment the flag into parts that contain particular words or phonemes. In each portion, we can speak to the discourse motion by the forces or vitality in various time-recurrence groups.

Despite the fact that the subtleties of flag portrayal are outside the extent of this program, we can speak to the flag by a lot of genuine qualities.

Do you think about Artificial Neural Network Model

Discourse acknowledgment, Machine Learning applications incorporate voice UIs. Voice UIs are, for example, voice dialing, call steering, domotic apparatus control. It can likewise use as straightforward information passage, arrangement of organized records, discourse to-content preparing, and plane.

3. Medicinal Diagnosis

ML gives strategies, procedures, and devices that can help in tackling symptomatic and prognostic issues in an assortment of therapeutic areas. It is being utilized for the examination of the significance of clinical parameters and of their mixes for visualization, for example expectation of ailment movement, for the extraction of medicinal information for results inquire about, for treatment arranging and support, and for in general patient administration. ML is likewise being utilized for information examination, for example, discovery of regularities in the information by properly managing blemished information, translation of consistent information utilized in the Intensive Care Unit, and for savvy disturbing bringing about successful and proficient checking.

It is contended that the effective execution of ML techniques can help the mix of PC based frameworks in the social insurance condition giving chances to encourage and upgrade crafted by therapeutic specialists and eventually to improve the effectiveness and nature of restorative consideration.

We should take a voyage through Neural Network Algorithms

In restorative conclusion, the principle intrigue is in setting up the presence of an illness pursued by its exact distinguishing proof. There is a different classification for every malady under thought and one class for situations where no illness is available. Here, AI improves the precision of restorative analysis by breaking down information of patients.

The estimations in this Machine Learning applications are ordinarily the aftereffects of certain restorative tests (precedent circulatory strain, temperature and different blood tests) or therapeutic diagnostics, (for example, medicinal pictures), nearness/nonappearance/force of different manifestations and essential physical data about the patient(age, sex, weight and so on). Based on the consequences of these estimations, the specialists slender down on the ailment exacting the patient.

4. Measurable Arbitrage

In money, measurable exchange alludes to mechanized exchanging procedures that are regular of a present moment and include countless. In such procedures, the client endeavors to execute an exchanging calculation for a lot of securities based on amounts, for example, verifiable connections and general monetary factors. These estimations can be given a role as an arrangement or estimation issue. The fundamental presumption is that costs will move towards an authentic normal.

Do you think about Kernel Functions

We apply AI strategies to acquire a file exchange methodology. Specifically, we utilize direct relapse and bolster vector relapse (SVR) onto the costs of a trade exchanged store and a surge of stocks. By utilizing foremost part examination (PCA) in lessening the component of highlight space, we watch the advantage and note the issues in the use of SVR. To create exchanging signals, we show the residuals from the past relapse as a mean returning procedure.

On account of arrangement, the classes may be sold, purchase or do nothing for every security. I the instance of estimation one may endeavor to foresee the normal return of every security over a future time skyline. For this situation, one normally needs to utilize the assessments of the normal come back to make an exchanging decision(buy, sell, and so forth.)

5. Learning Associations

Learning affiliation is the way toward forming bits of knowledge into different relationship between items. A genuine model is the way apparently inconsequential items may uncover a relationship to each other. At the point when examined in connection to purchasing practices of clients.

How about we talk about Deep learning and Neural Networks in Machine Learning

One utilization of AI Often concentrating the relationship between the items individuals purchase, which is otherwise called bin examination. On the off chance that a purchaser purchases 'X', would the person in question power to purchase 'Y' in view of a relationship that can recognize between them? This prompts the relationship that exists among fish sticks and french fries and so on when new items dispatch in the market a Knowing these connections it builds up another relationship. Realizing these connections could help in proposing the related item to the client. For a higher probability of the client getting it, It can likewise help in packaging items for a superior bundle.

This learning of relationship between items by a machine is learning affiliations. When we found a relationship by inspecting a lot of offers information, Big Data experts. It can build up a standard to infer a likelihood test in learning a contingent likelihood.

6. Arrangement

Arrangement is a procedure of putting every person from the populace under examination in numerous classes. This is recognized as autonomous factors.

View Convolutional Neural Networks Architecture

Grouping causes examiners to utilize estimations of an article to recognize the classification to which that object has a place. To set up a productive standard, investigators use information. Information comprises of numerous instances of articles with their right characterization.

For instance, before a bank chooses to dispense an advance, it evaluates clients on their capacity to reimburse the advance. By considering variables, for example, client's acquiring, age, reserve funds and monetary history we can do it. This data is taken from the past information of the credit. Henceforth, Seeker uses to make a connection between client qualities and related dangers.

7. Expectation

Consider the case of a bank registering the likelihood of any of credit candidates blaming the advance reimbursement. To figure the likelihood of the blame, the framework will initially need to order the accessible information in specific gatherings. It is portrayed by a lot of tenets recommended by the investigators.

How about we reconsider Recurrent Neural Networks

When we do the characterization, according to require we can figure the likelihood. These likelihood calculations can figure over all parts for fluctuated purposes

The present forecast is one of the most smoking AI calculations. How about we take a case of retail, prior we had the capacity to get bits of knowledge like deals report a month ago/year/5-years/Diwali/Christmas. These sort of announcing is called as verifiable detailing. In any case, as of now business is progressively keen on discovering what will be my deals one month from now/year/Diwali, and so on.

With the goal that business can take a required choice (identified with obtainment, stocks, and so on.) on time.

8. Extraction

Data Extraction (IE) is another use of AI. It is the way toward removing organized data from unstructured information. For instance pages, articles, web journals, business reports, and messages. The social database keeps up the yield delivered by the data extraction.

The procedure of extraction accepts contribution as a lot of records and delivers an organized information. This yield is in a condensed structure, for example, an exceed expectations sheet and table in a social database.

These days extraction is turning into a key in the huge information industry.

As we realize that the immense volume of information is getting created out of which the majority of the information is unstructured. The primary key test is taking care of unstructured information. Presently change of unstructured information to organized structure dependent on some example with the goal that the equivalent can put away in RDBMS.

Aside from this in current days information gathering instrument is likewise getting change. Prior we gathered information in clumps like End-of-Day (EOD)

CONCLUSION

Machine Learning is assuming control over the world-and with that, there is a developing need among organizations for experts to know the intricate details of ML. ML is figuring escalated and by and large requires a lot of preparing information. It includes dull preparing to improve the learning and basic leadership of calculations. As more information gets included, Machine Learning preparing can be computerized for adapting new information designs and adjusting its calculation.

REFERENCES

Awad, W., & Elseuofi, S. (2011). Machine Learning methods for E-mail Classification. *International Journal of Computers and Applications*, *16*(1), 39–45. doi:10.5120/1974-2646

Cao, C., Liu, F., Tan, H., Song, D., Shu, W., Li, W., ... Xie, Z. (2018). Deep Learning and Its Applications in Biomedicine. [PubMed]. *Genomics, Proteomics & Bioinformatics*, *16*(1), 17–32. doi:10.1016/j. gpb.2017.07.003

Deng & Yu. (2013). Deep Learning: Methods and Applications, Foundations and Trends R. *Signal Processing*, *7*(3-4), 197–387. doi:10.1561/2000000039

Grm, K., Štruc, V., Artiges, A., Caron, M., & Ekenel, H. (2018). Strengths and weaknesses of deep learning models for face recognition against image degradations. *IET Biometrics*, *7*(1), 81–89. doi:10.1049/iet-bmt.2017.0083

Kashyap, R. (2019a). Big Data and Global Software Engineering. In M. Rehman, A. Amin, A. Gilal, & M. Hashmani (Eds.), *Human Factors in Global Software Engineering* (pp. 131–163). Hershey, PA: IGI Global; doi:10.4018/978-1-5225-9448-2.ch006

Kashyap, R. (2019b). Sensation of Deep Learning in Image Processing Applications. In A. Hassanien, A. Darwish, & C. Chowdhary (Eds.), *Handbook of Research on Deep Learning Innovations and Trends* (pp. 72–96). Hershey, PA: IGI Global; doi:10.4018/978-1-5225-7862-8.ch005

Kashyap, R. (2019c). *Big Data Analytics Challenges and Solutions*. doi:10.1016/B978-0-12-818146-1.00002-7

Kashyap, R. (2019d). Computational Healthcare System With Image Analysis. In C. Chen & S. Cheung (Eds.), *Computational Models for Biomedical Reasoning and Problem Solving* (pp. 89–127). Hershey, PA: IGI Global; doi:10.4018/978-1-5225-7467-5.ch004

Kashyap, R. (2019e). Systematic Model for Decision Support System. In A. Mukherjee & A. Krishna (Eds.), *Interdisciplinary Approaches to Information Systems and Software Engineering* (pp. 62–98). Hershey, PA: IGI Global; doi:10.4018/978-1-5225-7784-3.ch004

Kashyap, R. (2019f). Miracles of Healthcare With Internet of Things. In J. Rodrigues, A. Gawanmeh, K. Saleem, & S. Parvin (Eds.), *Smart Devices, Applications, and Protocols for the IoT* (pp. 120–164). Hershey, PA: IGI Global; doi:10.4018/978-1-5225-7811-6.ch007

Kashyap, R. (2019g). Deep Learning: An Application in Internet of Things. In H. Purnomo (Ed.), *Computational Intelligence in the Internet of Things* (pp. 130–158). Hershey, PA: IGI Global; doi:10.4018/978-1-5225-7955-7.ch006

Kashyap, R. (2019h). Machine Learning, Data Mining for IoT-Based Systems. In G. Kaur & P. Tomar (Eds.), *Handbook of Research on Big Data and the IoT* (pp. 314–338). Hershey, PA: IGI Global; doi:10.4018/978-1-5225-7432-3.ch018

Kashyap, R. (2019i). Decision Support Systems in Aeronautics and Aerospace Industries. In T. Shmelova, Y. Sikirda, N. Rizun, D. Kucherov, & K. Dergachov (Eds.), *Automated Systems in the Aviation and Aerospace Industries* (pp. 138–165). Hershey, PA: IGI Global; doi:10.4018/978-1-5225-7709-6.ch005

Kashyap, R. (2019j). Medical Image Segmentation and Analysis. In C. Chakraborty (Ed.), *Advanced Classification Techniques for Healthcare Analysis* (pp. 132–160). Hershey, PA: IGI Global; doi:10.4018/978-1-5225-7796-6.ch007

Kashyap, R. (2019k). Big Data and High-Performance Analyses and Processes. In A. Voghera & L. La Riccia (Eds.), *Spatial Planning in the Big Data Revolution* (pp. 45–83). Hershey, PA: IGI Global; doi:10.4018/978-1-5225-7927-4.ch003

Kashyap, R. (2019l). Artificial Intelligence Systems in Aviation. In T. Shmelova, Y. Sikirda, N. Rizun, & D. Kucherov (Eds.), *Cases on Modern Computer Systems in Aviation* (pp. 1–26). Hershey, PA: IGI Global; doi:10.4018/978-1-5225-7588-7.ch001

Kashyap, R. (2020). Applications of Wireless Sensor Networks in Healthcare. In P. Mukherjee, P. Pattnaik, & S. Panda (Eds.), *IoT and WSN Applications for Modern Agricultural Advancements: Emerging Research and Opportunities* (pp. 8–40). Hershey, PA: IGI Global; doi:10.4018/978-1-5225-9004-0.ch002

Kashyap, R., & Rahamatkar, S. (2019b). Healthcare Informatics Using Modern Image Processing Approaches. In B. Singh, B. Saini, D. Singh, & A. Pandey (Eds.), *Medical Data Security for Bioengineers* (pp. 254–277). Hershey, PA: IGI Global; doi:10.4018/978-1-5225-7952-6.ch013

Litjens, G., Kooi, T., Bejnordi, B., Setio, A., Ciompi, F., Ghafoorian, M., ... Sánchez, C. I. (2017). A survey on deep learning in medical image analysis. [PubMed]. *Medical Image Analysis*, *42*, 60–88. doi:10.1016/j.media.2017.07.005

Manor, R., Mishali, L., & Geva, A. (2016). Multimodal Neural Network for Rapid Serial Visual Presentation Brain Computer Interface. [PubMed]. *Frontiers in Computational Neuroscience*, *10*. doi:10.3389/fncom.2016.00130

Najafabadi, M., Villanustre, F., Khoshgoftaar, T., Seliya, N., Wald, R., & Muharemagic, E. (2015). Deep learning applications and challenges in big data analytics. *Journal Of Big Data*, *2*(1), 1. doi:10.118640537-014-0007-7

This research was previously published in Challenges and Applications for Implementing Machine Learning in Computer Vision; pages 119-135, copyright year 2020 by Engineering Science Reference (an imprint of IGI Global).

Chapter 60
Review on Machine and Deep Learning Applications for Cyber Security

Thangavel M.
Thiagarajar College of Engineering, India

Abiramie Shree T. G. R.
Thiagarajar College of Engineering, India

Priyadharshini P.
Thiagarajar College of Engineering, India

Saranya T.
Thiagarajar College of Engineering, India

ABSTRACT

In today's world, everyone is generating a large amount of data on their own. With this amount of data generation, there is a change of security compromise of our data. This leads us to extend the security needs beyond the traditional approach which emerges the field of cyber security. Cyber security's core functionality is to protect all types of information, which includes hardware and software from cyber threats. The number of threats and attacks is increasing each year with a high difference between them. Machine learning and deep learning applications can be done to this attack, reducing the complexity to solve the problem and helping us to recover very easily. The algorithms used by both approaches are support vector machine (SVM), Bayesian algorithm, deep belief network (DBN), and deep random neural network (Deep RNN). These techniques provide better results than that of the traditional approach. The companies which use this approach in the real time scenarios are also covered in this chapter.

DOI: 10.4018/978-1-6684-6291-1.ch060

INTRODUCTION

In today's world, information is one of the most important aspects in almost every part of our life; the information is valuable for individual, organization, and country. Privacy is needed for such valuable information. Due to invention and innovation, is widespread use of device and technology, which makes people communication and industrial productions more sophisticated. This technology is not only providing sophistication to the information holders and users but also to the attackers. This same technology also ensures the attacker in many ways to launch attacks in a more creative way. Cybersecurity/information system security is the technique consists of protecting the systems, computer programs, data, and networks form attackers or unauthorized user, which are aimed for exploitation. The cybersecurity reduces the risk of cyber attacks; the cyber attacks are usually concentrating on accessing, destroying, changing the most sensitive information in order to create a risk to individual or organization. The Deep Learning and Machine Learning concept to break these constraints. The birth of Machine learning is started in conjunction with other technologies like virtual machines, test simulators, etc. This ML algorithm quickly scales the analysis process of information collected by the Sec Intel. The basic principle of the ML algorithm is it will improve its response by learning and learning. Nearly it will take 2-3 days for the security group to analyze the information provided by the Sec Intel, but the ML will take 1day at first learning, then reduce it slowly by learning and the next day it will take 12hours, and the next time it will take 8hours and so on., The effective scale analysis by ML is more times greater than the security group especially for the automated task so this is what the wonder of ML. But, Machine Learning can perform efficiently in small scale data and lower configured systems. This emerges the Deep Learning which is a subfield of the Machine learning approach. Deep Learning can perform well only in a tremendous amount of data and high configured systems. The main advantage of Deep Learning on cybersecurity is the deep neutral network process. This process deeply examines the data and for this study, the deep learning algorithm requires a vast amount of data. As we already know today's world generating googol of data than what about the future! yes, obviously it will become too large. For handling cyber security for this much amount of data the deep learning is the precise answer. Deep Learning algorithm is categorized into supervised deep learning and unsupervised deep learning. Supervised deep learning approach will predict only the targeted values from a set of data but in unsupervised approach, there are no such target values and it simply predicts all the possible values from the dataset. The usage of these two categories depends on the implementation of cybersecurity needs. The approach of deep learning to the field of cybersecurity ranges from the intrusion detection system for sensor networks and transport layer, Malicious Code Detection, Hybrid malware classification, Behaviour detection of Botnet, traffic identification and anomaly detection. Although, the application of deep learning for cybersecurity isn't easy. A report last week stated that a recent attack happened in a private organization. It was hacked during the midterms and that attack compromised access to their email accounts of their company, where they had been watched and spied by the hackers over a long time which included the details of their client. Even for an organization like this took a long time and a large amount of money to detect the intrusion and recover from the attack. A yet another report stated by Forbes, a major cyber-attack was traced in tax software which impacted people who belong to 64 countries. The attackers made an offer of 300 dollars of bitcoin for the retrieval of their hacked data as an initial payment. It gave lots of uneasiness to the government of the country as well as the individual victims who and all affected by this massive attack. So, these real-time attacks which clearly proves that the effort which we put on the safeness of our system will easily make us pay a lot of amount and time when it gets compromised.

Here, these learning techniques such as machine learning and deep learning will automatically allow our system to take necessary actions before these attacks will lead us to a critical situation. This book chapter, will tour you from the basic features of cyber security that we can offer to our data and the limitation of cybersecurity prone to the huge set of attacks that can't be handled by us within a short period of time, which enables us to use the vast use of machine learning and deep learning approach. It also helps to identify the machine learning algorithms as well as the deep learning algorithms which are also used for the real-time datasets. It also helps to identify the use of these approaches in the real-time industry problems which are taking more time to solve the problem in normal methods. It again states the application of these algorithms in all types of attacks possible in cybersecurity. These applications in cyber security will facilitate an attack-free world which we are hoping for a long period of time. This chapter covers from common cyber threats and attacks happening in the world and how these threats can be solved using machine learning and deep learning effectively and the general application of these machine learning and deep learning in real-world industrial problems and along with the conclusion.

COMMON CYBERSECURITY THREATS AND ATTACKS

The important principles of securities are confidentiality, integrity, and availability (CIA) triad. All types of information security measures should address any one of the above principles. It is a model with policy and procedure to guide information security within an organization. Confidentiality will deal with the secrecy of the information assets. It is an ability to conceal the information from the unauthorized user so the information will become senseless to the attacker. Confidentiality can be ensured by encryptions. Integrity is responsible for to maintain trustworthiness, assurance, consistency, and completeness over an entire life cycle of data. This also ensures that the data can be only modified by the legitimate user. The availability will ensure that the network is always readily available to its users, for this, the network admin will maintain bandwidth, hardware, upgrades regularly. The attacks like DOS and DDOS will affect the availability of access to the user.

Denial of Service and Distributed Denial of Service Attacks

Denial of Service attack is a cyber attack in which the attacker seeks to make a network resource unavailable to the legitimate user. The primary goal of a dos attack is not to steal the information but to slow or take down a website. The categories of resources which can be attacked by denial of service are network bandwidth, system resources, and application resources. In DDOS attacks, many computers start performing DOS attacks on the same target server. As the DOS attack is distributed over a large group of computers, it is known as a distributed denial of service attack. The DDOS attacks can take place by volume based, application based, and protocol based. In a volume-based attack, the flooding attacks can take place in a variety of forms based on which network protocol is being used to implement the attack. Floods may be through ICMP, UDP, and TCP. The application based attack will make use of the vulnerability in application to crash the server. The protocol based attack will utilize the server resource by targeting the intermediates like a firewall. The attacker may use a zombie network, which is a collection of affected or infected computers on which the attacker has silently installed the dos attacking tool. The common tool which is used by the attackers to launch dos attacks is hulk, xoic, loic, davoset ddosim-layer7 DDOS simulator, etc.

Man in the Middle Attack

Man in the Middle attack is the cyber attack where the cybercriminals launch this type of attack in two ways such as interception and decryption. The attacker will simply intercept the communication of a legitimate user. A man in the middle attack is similar to the eavesdropping where communication between two users is monitored and modified by the attacker or an unauthorized user in order to achieve some specific goals of attackers in sense of stealing or accessing the privileges of the authorized user. This is mainly done by intercepting a public key message exchange and by retransmits the message while replacing the requested key with their own. The attackers launch any one of the attacks such as IP spoofing, ARP spoofing, and DNS spoofing. The attacker may use sniffing techniques, packet injection techniques, session hijacking, SSL was stripping and many more to launch a man in the middle attacks.

Phishing Attack

Pronounced "fishing", the word origin from two words "password harvesting" or fishing for passwords. A phishing attack is also called as brand spoofing. A phishing attack is a type of attack in which the attacker can do some fraudulent attempt to obtain sensitive information of users such as user names, passwords, and credit card details. The phishing attack is a cyber-attack that uses email as a weapon. This attack is often carried out by email spoofing and instant messaging or text message. Link manipulation, website forgery; phone phishing is some of the phishing techniques. Phishing takes place by sending deceptive email, running malicious software on the user's machine, DNS based phishing, for example, host file poisoning, man-in-the-middle phishing, and ect., The causes of phishing are misleading e-mails, a vulnerability in browsers and application, limited use of digital signatures, no check of the source address and lack of user's awareness. One of the most phishing attacks happened in 2016 is the phishing email sent to the Clinton campaign chairman John Podesta's Gmail account.

Drive-by Attack

The drive-by downloads are a common method of spreading malware. A drive-by download is a program that is automatically downloaded to the user machine without any consent or user's knowledge. The drive-by downloads can be initiated by simply visiting a website or viewing HTML email messages. The attackers look for the insecure website and plant a malicious script into HTTP or PHP code on one of the pages. This script may install malware directly onto the machine of someone who visits the site, or it may take the form on an IFRAME that re-directs the victims to a site controlled by the attackers.

Password Attack

For the illegal purpose, the attackers try to obtain users password and also try to decrypt a user's password with the help of cracking programs, dictionary attacks, and password sniffers in password attacks. The password attack is the illegal purpose to gain unauthorized access. Brutus, Rainbow crack, Wfuzz, Cain and Abel, Lophtcrack, Ophcrack are some of the password cracking tools used by hackers.

Types of Password Attack

- Brute force attack.
- Rainbow table attack.
- Malware.
- Offline cracking.
- Phishing.
- Dictionary attack.
- Hash Guessing.

Dictionary Attack

Most of the passwords are chosen by the users, it is always containing a common word. The dictionary attack makes use simple file containing words that can be found in a dictionary, the attacker uses exactly the kind of words that many people use as their password.

Brute force Attack

Brute force attack is similar to that of a dictionary attack, this attack makes use of every possible letter, number, and character combination or alpha-numeric combination to guess the password. The brute force attacks involve repeated login attempts by using various numbers of tries. These attacks can take several minutes to several hours or several years depending upon the system used and also depend on the length of the password. The attacker may use a brute force attack to obtain access to a website and account in order to steal sensitive data.

Rainbow Table Attack

In a rainbow, table cryptanalysis is done very fast and effectively by calculating the hash function of every string and compares it with the system at every step. Creating a table and cracking the password is the main role of a rainbow table attack. The beauty of rainbow table needs not to know the exact string password, if the hash is matched then it will not bother about the password string matching and it will move on to the next step then is it will get authenticated.

SQL Injection Attack

SQL injection attack is one of the most serious security vulnerabilities in a web application system, mainly caused by a lack of input validation and SQL parameters. SQL injection attack will take place by executing malicious SQL statements /malicious payload by the attacker, which will control web application servers. The vulnerabilities in the web application will loss data confidentiality and data integrity. The attackers trick the SQL engine into executing unintended commands by supplying specially crafted string input, thereby gaining unauthorized access to a database so that the attacker can easily use or access the restricted data of the legitimate user. When an application uses entrusted data then SQL injection weakness will occur such as data entered into web form fields, as a part of a database query. The SQL injection utilizes weakness of applications to misguide the application into running a database backend query or command usually an application has a menu, which is used for searching personal information such as age, telephone number, sex… The application will execute an SQL query in the database backend.

```
SELECT patient_name, patient_medicine, patient_disease
WHERE patient_number = 12345.
If the user enters the number "123 or 1=1", then the SQL query passes to the
database as follows:
SELECT patient_name, patient_medicine, patient_disease
WHERE patient_number = 12345 or 1=1.
```

Cross-Site Scripting Attack

In this cross-site scripting attack, the attacker will insert the client-side code into the web pages that is executing the malicious script into a legitimate website or web application. This attack enhances hacker by utilizing greater access. The effect of a cross-site scripting attack is to redirecting the websites, stealing of cookies, showing ads in hidden IFRAMES and pop-ups. The cross-site scripting attack can take place by three types such as non-persistent, persistent, DOM-based.

Malware Attack

Malware attack is a type of cyber attack which is nothing but software is built to create damage to the target computer called malicious software. This was implanted into the target system to damage the system or to steal the information system of client, server and computer network. The growth of malware attack is increasing more nowadays and people use the word virus in the past decades but now ransomware, malware, spyware is playing more. This attack has to be taken as a serious way to solve. To launch a variety of attack the malware uses different types of delivery mechanism like Trojans, Virus, Worm. "In India usage of aadhaar cards is becoming ubiquitous and the danger is that only this mask the hackers easier to identify online, once the malware codes come into the open market, it can be repurposed by hacker anywhere in the world", Narayanan said

MACHINE LEARNING FOR CYBER SECURITY

Cyber Security's core functionality is to protect all types of information which includes hardware and software from cyber threats. These attacks are usually aimed at accessing, changing, or destroying sensitive information of any private or government sectors. In 2014, more than 60% of business networks suffer from these types of cyber-attacks which results in the decrease of the customer trust and even loss of personal details. There range a large number of cyber-attacks such as ransomware, malware, social engineering, phishing from which we can get protected using cybersecurity. The SECINTEL exchange is started to exchange between the collaboration of largest security infrastructure firms like Symantec, MacAfee, Palo Alto, etc, this exchange is dealing only about their attacks, not their solution. The idea behind this exchange is to understand how the attacks are done and what type of attacks is there so this will help the others to be aware of attack before they did. The analysis of sec Intel exchange is a time-consuming process, so Cybersecurity is influenced by the data dependencies, hardware dependencies and the problem-solving techniques that we used. Machine learning includes techniques such as Support Vector Machines and Bayesian Algorithm. These algorithms provide extra ordinal results that the normal level use of the cyber solution for those threats. The effective scale analysis by ML is more times greater than the security group especially for the automated task so this is what the wonder of ML. But Machine Learning can perform efficiently in small scale data and lower configured systems. The Machine learning helps to verify the spam mail, valid mail and seeing the features one or more frequent difference. This process automatically reduce a label and it is the major application of machine learning ML classification techniques was two types one is supervised another one is semi-supervised.

Supervised Learning

Supervised learning provides a set of label training data. They are a different type of many labels are used to verification.

Unsupervised Learning

Unsupervised learning provides a set of unlabeled training data. Labelled data is sometimes rare. The Unlabeled data set is covert to labelling data set in this process to be difficult so introduced.

Semi-supervised learning

Semi-supervised learning is both supervised and unsupervised learning. Semi-supervised learning is unlabeled data so unlabeled data as an alternative using signature generation.

Reinforcement Learning

It is full power by the artificial intelligence. The neural network used for implement reinforcement learning. It is followed by a specific type of cyber attack.

LITERATURE REVIEW OF USING MACHINE LEARNING IN CYBER SECURITY

Machine Learning in IDS

Intrusion Detection System is one of the traditional cyber security solutions. Machine Learning approach can be effectively used in Intrusion Detection System to improve its detection mechanism because in IDS the detection of intrusion events is mostly misinterpreted by the behavior or activities of the normal user. Here, it generates a large number of false positives, which complicates the process of detecting the actual attack from normal events. So, the researchers (Stroeh 2013) proposed a machine learning solution to these IDS problems. The solutions are intrusion as well as the normal events are collected, normalized and then it is fused together to form meta events. These meta events are classified based on the attributes present in them to detect the actual attacks from the normal work of the authorized users.

Figure 1 Phases of the machine learning in IDS

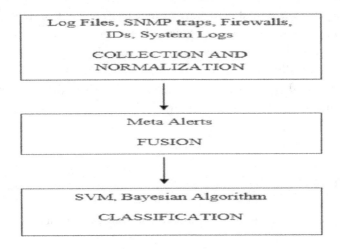

In the Figure1 Collection and Normalization phase, it takes sources to form the logs files of the system, network and firewalls to categorize them into two elements such as active and passive elements. The passive element is done by simply observing the above source file to detect the events but the active elements interact with the source events or element states. On observing the alert events from the source files, it brings three types. They are action against an object, a condition of an object and a suspicion of the state. The second phase is the fusion phase which helps to generate the meta alerts from the previous phrase. In the third phase that is the classification of the intrusion is done by the Support Vector Machine which is the latest classification technique in machine learning and Bayesian algorithm to differentiate the actual attack from the normal actions of the user. Therefore, machine learning can overcome the traditional perimeter defence in the IDS by providing quick and accurate responses to the intrusion in the system.

Machine Learning in Denial of Service Attacks

One of the popular network attacks in a cyber attack is the Denial of Service attack. This attack prevents the access of the service for the authorized users, which is done by the unauthorized person of the system. (Mukkamala, 2013) concerns the detection and prevention of Dos attack with the help of special machine learning technique Support Vector Machine. The main role is to detect the Dos attack and issues involved in identifying important input features in which Support Vector Machine classifiers reduce the input size which enhances the faster training and supports the more accurate result. Here, the log data is classified into two varieties of patterns in which one is a normal pattern and other is Dos pattern. Dos patterns cover the six different attacks possible in the system namely back, Neptune, ping of death, land, smurf, and teardrop. With the help of SVM, the normal patterns are differentiated from the Dos patterns. The authors' works on the DARPA dataset in which the input vector data is extracted from the TCP/IP dump and it is pre-processed to produce a single value data which the Dos attack pattern. The SVM in Intrusion Detection System is based on three categories such as Pre-processing, Training, and Testing. Pre-processing is focused on the process of raw data into actual patterns. In the Training phase, the SVM is trained to differentiate the normal pattern from the Dos attack patterns. Here, this differentiation is identified by two classes where one class denotes the normal data and another class denotes the data of Denial of Service attacks. The last phase which is the Testing phase and it is responsible for the detection of the Denial of Service attack accurately. From this technique, we acquired higher accuracy in a short period of time than that of the neural network techniques.

Improving Intrusion Detection System Based on Bayesian Algorithm

An IDS is a very important security mechanism to secure the information system. It should be designed in such a way to prevent unauthorized access to resources and data. A lot of machine learning algorithm has been applied to the Intrusion Detection System to enhance the efficiency and accuracy of the detection and prevention. (Dewan, 2008) proposed an intrusion detection system based on an adaptive Bayesian algorithm. These machine learning algorithms work well with a large volume of complex and dynamic audit data and make the classification of different types of attack of KDD99 benchmark intrusion detection dataset. For each attribute value, the class conditional probabilities are evaluated which is based on the occurrence of each attribute value present in the training dataset. All training dataset have unit weight, the authors first calculated the sum of weights for each attribute value in the same class. Then the authors calculated the last conditional probabilities for each attribute values by the sum of weight for each class and then the classification of test dataset took place. If the calculated value is wrong then it has to be updated with the weight of training dataset. Each test example is compared with every training example and finding out the similarity between them. If the classification is done on test example correctly then the training set weight will be unchanged again the class conditional probabilities for each attribute values are calculated for the updated training dataset. If the classification is done on test examples for the new set perfectly then the algorithm comes to an end else the algorithm takes places until it produces perfect classification from this it produces accurate and absolute classification. The naive Bayesian algorithm takes 106.7 m training time and the testing time as 26.4m but for the proposed adaptive Bayesian algorithm consumes 52.8 m as training time and 13.2 as a testing time. With this approach, the possibility of applying the machine learning based intrusion detection system commercially.

Detecting P2P Botnets Using Machine Learning

A botnet is the collection of infected devices and internet of things devices which were connected through the internet such as personal computer, servers, mobile devices, and other internet devices. These devices are controlled by the common type of malware. Even no one knows that their system is infected and controlled by malware. Detection of P2P Botnet is an uncovered area but here the authors (Garg 2013) used some machine learning techniques to detect the peer to peer [P2P] botnets. This algorithm analyses the detection rate of the classifiers which helps to detect the botnet malfunctions in the real-time environment. This method of machine learning algorithm also analyses the true positives and false positive in each class which are all advanced that of the traditional botnet detection systems.

Machine Learning Solutions to Bitcoin Threats and Attacks

The Cryptocurrency is the emerging field in which the transaction is possible between the peer to peer is possible without the intervention of any third party between them. This popular technology is also called a Blockchain. Here, the attackers can be a part of this network by creating or initiating a transaction process which appears to be a reliable person in the peer environment. This attack can also be detected with the help of machine learning algorithms. Another problem in the double spending problem where the transactions between the two peers are not either in acceptance or in rejection stage because of the presence of the lengthy blockchain. Here, this leads to the possibility of an attack by any third peer who leads to false acceptance or rejection of the transaction. Another most common attack at this point of time is the Denial of Service attack. It can also be eradicated with the help of the machine learning process at both the ends of the peer networks. Another type of attack is that the pool hoping attack, in this attack the attackers present in the place where the individual code miners are presented. The authors (Rahouti 2018) stated that these attackers get benefited due to the reward stealing from the miners who work to solve an unsolved problem. This can also be eradicated with the machine learning approach. Other possible attacks are gold finger attack and feather forking attack which are also used to cause damages to the miners as well as the peers present in the field. These attacks can also be suppressed with the help of the machine learning approach.

Machine Learning for the Internet of Things Security

This type of security can be efficiently applied with the help of the deep learning algorithm. But the working Machine Learning is combined with the Big Data can also be used to provide better results than that of the machine learning algorithm. This approach is introduced by (Kotenko 2018) where the handling of the massive amount of data generated by the IoT devices can be done with the Big Data approach. Here, the Mapper and Reducer can also be used along with the Hadoop Framework. It also includes the Hadoop Distributed File System where the handling and storing of data is possible. Then after this Machine Learning approach Support Vector Machine (SVM) is used to classify the data present in the IoT environment which reduces the possibility of threats to them. The classifier is the main role of the SVM where the normal activity of the environment is separated from the attack's intrusion data. This provides the best results also compared to the normal IDS based detection system. All possible attacks are identified with the use of the machine learning approach. But the classifier works well only in the presence of big data handling is done prior to them. Combination of the two advanced technology helps to solve all the attacks possible in the IoT environment.

Machine Learning for Security and Privacy of Data

Privacy is needed in all types of communication for the transfer or exchange of sensitive data between the source and destination. Privacy can also be achieved through the use of a machine learning approach. The researchers (Liu 2018) proposed that without the use of the data mining along with the Support Vector Machine privacy cannot be achieved precisely. Here, the sensitive data are first separated from that of the normal flow of data. These data are then fine-tuned by the use of the SVM classifiers which also helps to separate the higher priority data to provide the security along with the privacy to the data. Again, the results are massively correct than that of the traditional approach and provide better results.

Malware Classification using Self Organizing FeatureMaps and Machine Activity Data

Cyber attacks became large in recent years. These questions the liability of the authorized access too. Here, the malware classification is done which helps to differentiate the normal activities from the malicious one. The researchers (Niyaz 2014) proposed that this type of automated classification can be done with the help of Weka machine learning libraries. It helps to create a number of supervised classifiers that are tested and trained with the help of behavioral features which are CPU User Use, CPU System Use, RAM use, SWAP use, received packets, received bytes, sent packets, sent bytes, number of processes running. For doing these behavioral features, the authors produce two datasets which are clean and malicious files. Using this the feature is extracted from the classifier which is showing better classification of the malicious files from the legitimate ones.

APPLICATION OF MACHINE LEARNING

Machine learning is to collect gathering and process of data so cybersecurity can be used to detect the cyber-attack prevention to be automated. Machine learning techniques apply to many areas. Cybersecurity is a recent growing technique. The machine learning method is deploying to a wide range of problem in cybersecurity. The application of machine learning in cybersecurity like network intrusion detection system, spam detection in social network, keystrokes dynamic, smart meter energy consumption profiling.

Network Instruction Detection

Network intrusion detection system is identified as a malicious attack. This is one of the harmful attacks. Attackers must be changing tools and techniques. However, the intrusion detection system always changing in order to the attacks happening in the system which also changes the task to handle the detection of intrusion. Network instruction detection dataset is classified to the various machines learning performance. These are sequentially monitored to false negative and false positive performance.

Pros

- Response capabilities.
- Visibility.
- Defence.
- Evidence.
- Tracking of virus transmission.

Cons

- More maintenance.
- False positive.
- False negative.

Phishing Detection

One of the applications of machine learning in cybersecurity is phishing detection. Phishing is only focused on sensitive personal data to be taken. They have three types of anti-phishing methods. It is a detective, preventive and corrective. Detective solution is a continuously watch control life cycling and band monitoring. The preventive solution is Email authentication and web application security. Corrective is a forensic and investigation. Machine learning algorithm gives the solution to identifying the pattern which reveals malicious mails. The malicious content which splits into various behavior to detect whether the email is malicious or not. A cybersecurity provider named Barracuda network in which they found a machine learning technique to analyse unique pattern without human interaction. In real time this engine studies patterns for anomalous signals and gives notification to the administrator with details of phishing attack.

Pros

- User basic level trained to Bayesian filtering contents.
- It avoids a false negative statement.

Cons

- It should be the only filter for database contents so easily words are transformed.

Watering Hole

Hackers track the site in which users visit frequently. This concept is called a watering hole let us consider one example for a watering hole. Take a popular coffee shop where a number of people place their orders through the coffee shop URL. Now hackers will not attack the shop's network but they will access the coffee shop web site. Next, they will easily access the credential. Machine learning algorithms will ensure the security for the web application services. These algorithms will detect whether users are directed to malicious web sites when they are traveling to their destination path. These algorithms detect the malicious domain which helps to further solve the problem present in the URL. These methods are very effective in the watering hole attack of the system.

Webshell

Web shell is a piece of malicious code which is loaded into the web sites. This is the path for the attacker to make a modification of the directories of the server. So, the attacker can easily gain the database of the system. The e-commerce web sites might be attackers monitor to frequently in order to collect customer credit card information. Most of the attackers are from backend e-commerce platform. E-Commerce platforms mostly get affected by online payments these are expected to be more secure and confidential. So, in this process, a machine learning goal is to be wanted to detect the normal behavior of the credit card. Next, it Needs to train a machine learning model to identify normal behavior from malicious behavior. Web shell attack is noted as file less attack that relay of traditional malware.

Remote Exploitation

Remote exploitation is a final list of machine learning and cybersecurity. They are only referring to a remote attack is a malicious action. That they are focused on one or more network of computers. Their remote attacks are a target to take sensitive data and damage the machine. They can happen in various ways like denial of service, DNS poisoning, port scanning. Machine learning analyses to the behavior of system and abnormal network behavior can be identified. These algorithms trained for many data sets and it's detecting the remote exploitation attack.

Pros

- It can be managed to the thousands of cyber-attacks for at a time.
- Customer shift to after the three or four testing process.

Cons

- The main cons are mirror images of the attack.
- Distributed the malware code to be embedded.

Machine Learning for Cyber Securing in IOT

Internet of things (IOT) is a network connected object. IOT object is able to collect data from physical and virtual sensor nodes continuously and transfer to sensitive data. In this data transfer over the internet without needing human to human or human to computer interaction. Data transmitted from the communication device to remotely control device. The most possible ways of attacking are Computer attacks, data interception, and software vulnerabilities. IOT security is safeguarding for IOT device. Some of the IOT security prevent and detect the malicious attack. The security requirements are data authentication, access control, and resilience attack.

Some of the IDS algorithms applies to the detect cyber attack IOT. The author (Elrawy 2018) used a machine learning technique called Principle component analysis for detection of a cyber attack. IDS system depends on the least and most significant component. IDS based PCA used for data mining, machine learning, and statistical modelling. Misuse-based intrusion detection to detect well-known attacks. Disadvantages are network overloading and large numbers of false alarms. So, they are continuously updated to pattern and signature.

DEEP LEARNING FOR CYBER SECURITY

Machine Learning can perform efficiently in small scale data and lower configured systems. This emerges the Deep Learning which is a subfield of the Machine learning approach. Deep Learning can perform well only in a tremendous amount of data and high configured systems. The main advantage of Deep Learning on cybersecurity is the deep neural network process. This process deeply examines the data and for this study, the deep learning algorithm requires a vast amount of data. In industry, government sector, peoples and organization generating a large amount of data. For handling cyber security for this much amount of data the deep learning is the precise answer. The big companies like Google, Amazon, Microsoft, and salesforceman.com to follow deep learning technology now cybersecurity institute takes and follow them in this algorithm but deep learning is a challenging field for full helpfulness. Deep Learning algorithm is categorized into supervised deep learning and unsupervised deep learning. Supervised deep learning approach will predict only the targeted values from a set of data but in unsupervised approach, there are no such target values and it simply predicts all the possible values from the dataset. The usage of these two categories depends on the implementation of cybersecurity needs. The approach of deep learning to the field of cybersecurity ranges from the intrusion detection system for sensor networks, transport layer, Malicious Code Detection, Hybrid malware classification, Behaviour detection of Botnet, traffic identification and anomaly detection. Benefits deep learning for cybersecurity protects the plenty of data and the data are hybrid categories. It only focuses on the multivariate categorical distributions.

The Current Stage for Deep Learning in Cybersecurity

It is difficult to solve the information security problem in which need to extensive dataset labelled and if they are sometimes no such that dataset labelled. However, most of information security problem solved or significant improvement of deep learning techniques. Two areas such as improved in these techniques like malware detection and intrusion detection. Network intrusion detection system is evaluating to detect threat based on signature and rule. It is controlled to deploy at the known threat. Now, detecting the types of many anomalies using the deep learning-based system.

LITERATURE SURVEY OF USING DEEP LEARNING IN CYBER SECURITY

Deep Learning in Network Intrusion Detection System

Network Intrusion Detection System is used to detect the security compromises in any type of organization. It is the first line of defensive mechanism which can be very useful for the detection of the intrusion in the system. Here, it will also produce false results due to the time consuming and low latency of the audition of files. But it can be improved with the help of the deep learning approach which produces better results than that of the normal approach. The authors (Niyaz 2014) stated that the Network Intrusion Detection System (NIDS) can be improved with the Self-taught Learning (STL), a deep learning-based method to automate the detection system with high precise results. STL contains two stages which are used as classifiers. The first method is used to the unlabelled data which are learned the good representation of the data. Another stage is to present the data in a related form where the learning is done on the previous stage. These stages are applied to the NIDS which easily provides better results and also helps to do things well in future too. The STL classification achieves an accuracy of up to 98% than the all other classifications. In the future, this can also be used for the observation of the raw network traffic of the system which is very much advanced than that of the NIDS.

Deep Learning in Sensor Network Security

In sensor networks, a vast number of cyber attacks is possible for the malfunction of the sensor devices. Here, the intrusion or threats are also screened and monitored with the help of the IDS. (Wang 2015) proposed a deep learning-based approach to these problems. SCDNN which the combination of both Spectral Clustering and Deep Neural Network algorithms that are the clustering of data and ink subsets and the distances are calculated with the help of deep neural approach. These algorithms are applied to both the training data and the testing dataset. The sensed data are classified using DNN classifier after the clustering the data. The results of this approach not only better than that of the traditional approach but also advances the Support Vector Machine and Bayesian algorithm which are all the machine learning approaches. It also provides the facility to work for a large amount of dataset which is considerably larger than the machine learning. So, Deep learning approach is widely used for the vast dataset or project which yields best results than that of the smaller project work.

Deep Learning Approach in Detecting Threats to the IoT Environment

Internet of Things is the communication between devices to devices with human intervention. Here, a large number of attacks is possible at the gateway of the network. Most common attacks in the IoT environment are Denial of Service attacks and Denial of Sleep attacks. Denial of Service is simply the host devices are denied with flooding of requests from the attackers which restricts the host to connect with the intended devices. In Denial of Sleep attack which mostly drains the power of the sensor nodes where the sensor device lost its ability to connect with the IoT environment. Using the traffic of this environment the attackers can also read the packets and send false responses to the devices. Here, the authors (Brun 2018) used the deep random neural networks (Deep RNN) which help to understand the network attacks more precisely. The processing of this approach comparatively helps to reduce the disabling of nodes in the network with an early prediction of the attack happening in the environment. In the future, this approach can also be applicable to the Zigbee and Bluetooth devices to reduce the network attack of the ad-hoc network. Here, the attacks and intrusions are prevented with the Deep RNN technique which provides a unique solution to the core problem present in real time. The results are far best than that of the traditional machine learning approach where the Support Vector Machine is very difficult to be used in the IOT environment which is normally a large system which provides vast data with high amount of security issues. Instead of SVM, the Deep RNN approach is used to generate the efficiency of the system.

Deep Learning in Android Malware Detection

In the Android platform, large numbers of applications are developed and deployed everyday which also leads a large number of malware application with causes serious troubles to the Android OS and corrupts the data of our smartphone devices. Each malware effects are different from each other. The detection and prevention of this malware are a tedious process in cyber forensics. It can be easily done with the help of a deep learning approach. Here the researchers (Yuan 2014) proposed a model for this malware detection for Android environment which is Deep Belief Network (DBN). It consists of two phases namely Pre-training phase and propagation phase. In the pre-training phase, the learning space is given to the DBN whereas in the propagation phase the trained pre-training phases are again finely improved with supervision. The dataset which contains both normal applications as well as the malware containing applications which are fed into this DBN framework to detect the malware software's present in it. It provides a result of up to 96.4% better than that of the machine learning approach which includes

SVM, Naive Bayesian algorithm and LR. So, deep learning plays a major role in now a day's challenges to eradicating the intrusion or malware in the system.

Hybrid Malicious Code Detection Using Deep Learning

A hybrid malicious code detection using deep learning algorithm based on AutoEncoder and DBN. The autoencoder deep learning method is applied which is responsible for to reduce the dimensionality of data with nonlinear mapping, and extracting the main features of the data. The authors (Li 2013) used a Deep Belief Networks learning methods to detect malicious code. This deep belief network is consisting of multilayer restricted Boltzmann machines and a layer of BP neural network. This algorithm is based on both supervised and unsupervised learning. First, every layer of RBM is learned under unsupervised training then the output vector of the last layer of RBM is given as an input vector of BP neural network which undergoes supervised training. The outcome shows accurate detection performance and reduces the time complexity. The autoencoder consists of two parts encoder and decoder and three layers (input, output, hidden layers) here the data dimensionality reduction is defined when the hidden layer neurons are less than the number of input layer neurons and output layer neurons. The autoencoder takes place by three steps which are pretraining, unrolling and fine-tuning. The pretraining process is nothing but the output vector of each RBM hidden layer neuron is given to the input for next RBM. Connecting these independent RBM into a multilayered autoencoder is done in the unrolling process. After the pretraining process to get optimal weights the adjustment is done on initial weights further is called a Fine-tuning process. The hybrid detection algorithm will take care of digitizing and normalizing the input data, reducing the dimensionality of the data, feature mapping, DBM classifier, through the RBM learning rules the network layer is trained layer by layer, and finally the input test samples into the trained classifier to detect the malicious code and the normal code. The result of this algorithm shows greater accuracy of detecting hybrid malicious code by using the combination of AutoEncoder and DBM and this ensure the best time complexity for this model.

Deep Learning Network Based Malware Detection

Malware are increasing day by day parallel along with the evolution of technology. The detection of malware is a complex process which requires a large amount of time and works in the modern period whereas a new approach this problem is Stacked Auto-Encoders (SAEs) framework. It is used for the intelligent detection of the malware present in the network. The authors (Hardy 2015) proposed this method which contains two phases which are having both unsupervised and supervised learning a feature of SAE framework. This model is specially designed to detect the presence of malware in Windows API calls. By performing this type of detection, helps to improve the systems which are free from all the general attacks that will affect the sensitive data and also improve the performance of the system. Staked Auto-Encoders provides a wide range of classification with deep learning impact leads to the three layers in the input layer, Hidden layer, and Output layer. Each layer helps to extract the features from the data which is useful for the future application of classifier. This method also provides better results than that of the other approaches to cybersecurity.

Deep Learning Approach for Flash Malware Detection

Adobe Flash is a platform-independent software where all the multimedia is supported by them. It can also subject to a large number of attacks in recent years due to the development of technology. This software is widely used by all the users who operate on the computer. So, this can be an easy target by the attacks who all try to hack the system of the users. Recently, Casper malware which affects a large number of host systems leads to a large amount of data loss and also gives the opportunity to the hacker to earn money through this mode of attacks. To avoid this type of malware the use deep learning approach SWF is used. This method is better than that of machine learning because of the complex nature of the malware data present in today's environment. The data are first extracted as static and dynamic analysis and then the SWF classifier is applied to the system. This classifier is proposed by the authors (Jung 2015) to detect this malware in the present-day flash. This approach can also be used to detect the intrusions in the other independent platforms also. It is the additional advantage of using deep learning approach where the same classifier is used to detect the problems.

Applications for Deep Learning

The most of deep learning application apply to market, sales and finance field. Deep learning technique protects sensitive data and product from malicious code and hacker attack.

Learning-Based Detection

JavaScript code analysis is done for generating detection model. These models to be consist of deep learning techniques.

Evaluation

The malicious Java code applicable for a larger dataset which is consists of 2700 samples.

Zero-Day Attacks Detection

A zero-day attack is an ability to identify malicious code and analysis of unknown attacks.

Malware, Zero Day, and APT Detection

Deep learning is classified as malicious code without any rules. The neural network learns to identify the malicious code once identify the unknown files. In real time apply to in this process need for high accuracy. They are trained in malware detection neural network must analyse the millions of accurate malicious code classification. These are trained neural network deploy to the endpoint of the device. For example, a trained neural network would be deployed in mobile device endpoint. It is access to without network connection. So, in which that detect the malicious attacks.

Advanced Intrusion Detection and Network Anomaly Detection

Now intrusion detection system work through the grouping of anomaly detection and misuse detection techniques. These techniques are deploying to particular system network and host level. System guesses of intrusion based on deep learning techniques. Deep learning techniques analyse and filter to unknown codes. Packet analysis techniques include deep learning. These are preventing distributed denial of service, ransomware, spam, and phishing and botnet attack. It can find unusual behavior for network communication. In this method find the network communication likelihood. Network communication also selects as low likelihood.

Phishing Detection

Phishing attack already discussed previously. It is sensitive to personal data gathering techniques. Cyber-attack mostly injected to these types of method. Machine learning and deep learning is performed to pattern recognition so attack to be detected. Deep insight is a graph analysis algorithm. Deep insight text used to analyse email pattern identification and harmless mail. These are the best tool for identifying phishing attack.

Identification of Insider Threats

The pattern could be gritty to the device, user individual and network let use to deep learning techniques. Those threats in progress to be indicated are correlated data let's identify subtitles. They are modelled for application, key business system and, user behavior. The incorporate data to be a loss to deploy the file dropbox and any other cloud service. APT identification is the main added benefit for the system. It is intrusion detection, firewall, and server log and information security management event. It is could not just insider. Training material needed for the neural network could be providing an important resource.

Traffic Detection Using Deep Learning

Cyber-attack is mostly taking for source code, consumer data, important document, and software keys. Anomaly network is used to trace traffic in which that security is difficult to in this method. Now anomaly network used for communication by specific of malware based on rule-based intrusion network tools. They are transmitted of stolen encrypt with remote server traffic to occur. It is detecting the TOR traffic and analysis to traffic package. In this analyse done by a single flow of packet. Source address, source port, destination address, and destination port are involved in each flow constitutes. TOR is a safeguard for the user. TOR transfer to information hacker get access to information. The IP address cannot directly predict the in this attack. A landscape sends alert for distill network. Let us apply to deep learning method easy to detect the attack and increase the security.

CYBERSECURITY SOLUTION -INDUSTRIAL APPROACH WITH ML AND DL

HDFC Bank

Sameer ratolikar, chief information security officer of HDFC bank stated that current security technology is coupled with the power of AI which includes machine learning and deep learning in a way to move HDFC security to the next level. HDFC Bank has completed a pilot for AI-based Cyber Security Operations Centre (CSOC). The log data generated from the CSOC is then sending for processing on the AI for 8months on a cloud platform. This helps the bank to monitor insider threats. The major components of AI are machine learning and deep learning with a well-established algorithm. There are two teams, one team will manage the CSOC and the second team will focus threat hunting by writing rules for machine learning.

LogRhythm

LogRhythm is a security intelligence company (located in Boulder, Colo) that unifies SIEM security information and event management, log management, network endpoint monitoring, and forensics, and security analytics. This helps the worldwide customers to detect cyber threats before it gets breach and answers it fast. The case study on logarithm shows that regional bank required a matured security system. The logarithm will eradicate the time consumed in consolidating different data logs and points, this is done by the company by using a machine learning algorithm to profile and detect the threats, compromised accounts, misuses, and anomalies. By using machine learning it will reduce the detection time and response time for the security teams.

DarkTrace

Darktrace is located in San Francisco it is a global intelligence company in the field of cyber defence. Industry impact is that the DirectTV needed a system to provide proactive defences against data breaches and leaks of customer information. Darktrace AI platform analyses data in order to make calculations and identify patterns. The deviation from the behavior and identifying the threats is done with the use of data by machine learning technology. It helps thousands of companies across the industry to detect and fight cyber threats so that the companies use Darktraces AI-powered technology to make a detection in a better accuracy

Versive

Versive is the company founded in 2012 based on machine learning start-up and provide on-premises software, cloud service, and professional service solution. Versive is now a part of the entire company and the versive security engine is focusing on the threats that matter by identifies the bad actor, automatically understand core activities, finds the few threats. The industrial impact is the host had not to exchange the information before so, VSE alerted a bank who sent an odd volume of data from an internal to another internal host. Therefore, the backed-up on an internet-accessible server is more vulnerable to attacks. Versive helps the business team member who wasting time in identifying the threats to reducing the time or saving time by using machine learning to sort out the critical risk forms normal network activities. The machine learning also consists of a well-planned algorithm to provide the effective and appropriate result to the team and keeps the business team greatly away from the work.

Fortinet

Fortinet is an American multinational corporation headquartered. The Fortinet will develop cybersecurity software, application, and service. Industry impact of furniture manufacturer use two cloud center for hosting, they are Microsoft Azure and Amazon Web Services by making using the Fortinet security service. The Fortinet is a web application firewall that uses two layers of statistical probabilities and Machine learning to accurately detect threats.

Perimeter

PerimeterX is a cybersecurity company that prevents the automated web and mobile application from attackers. PerimeterX provides botnet detection solution for e-commerce, hospitality, media, and enterprise SaaS customer through implementing Machine learning technology. This machine learning technology analyses the sensor data to produce the risk score that identifies and tells whether a client is under risk or not.

PROBLEMS TO BE ADDRESSED

Remote Exploitation

Machine learning and deep learning in cybersecurity is remote exploitation, in which the malicious action of remote attack targets one or an entire network of the system. Due to system vulnerability, the hacker can easily exploit or steal sensitive system information with the help of malicious software. The Machine learning algorithm can be used to analyse system behavior and identifies the normal and abnormal instances which are not related to the network behavior. This machine learning algorithm trained for multiple data sets so, by self-learning from more data set it has a capability to trace before damage. The network device and management software producing company Juniper Networks using machine learning to analyse mountains of data gathered automatically. This algorithm ensures automation by learning from a huge data set and generates an appropriate prediction solution.

Predication of Unknown Ransomware

Ransomware is a type of malicious software. Mainly used to open the locked files of the user to utilize the data of the user or damage the data. The deep learning algorithm can be used to detect the unknown ransomware, for this, the data set is trained properly to provide better analyse minute behavior of ransomware. The deep learning algorithm will use both normal clean data files and a large set of ransom files for their training purpose after training, the algorithm finds out the key features of each file present in the data set. When it attacks the system, the file is checked in the trained model and the actions are implemented before it works. The cloud data protecting firm, Acronis developed their security with the aim of zero attack day by implementing machine learning to analyses the detection fast and effective.

CONCLUSION AND FUTURE WORK

As we know the technology is booming every day with new features along with an attractive name. We cannot predict the data that are in the movement and we also cannot manage the issues that rise along with them. In any field of innovation, there needs the security of data. In cybersecurity, large numbers of attacks, malware, ransom wares, viruses and trojans which are embedded along with our applications in our day to day activities. These attacks can be handled by the Intrusion Detection System and also along with the use of Intrusion Prevention System. But the time and cost spent on this process are large when compared to the use of the modern advanced domain. The Machine Learning and Deep Learning approach to the field of cyber security help to automate the process of detecting and preventing the attacks. So, this chapter covers the need for the Machine Learning and Deep Learning approach along with the effects that cause the identification of false data. Then, the survey of both fields in the cybersecurity is done by the researchers is covered which helps to identify the methods used and also helps to view the results produced by the applying of the proposed methods in the real-time dataset. Again, the approaches can also be used in the real-time application such as phishing detection, watering hole, malware detection, anomalies identification, remote exploitation and also identifying the threats. After that, the use of both machine learning and deep learning in the industrial point of view is also analysed which helps us to realize the visual use of the fields to the current cyber attacks. In the future, everything is going to be automated which does not require human interactions with them. This type of self-learning along with the solution producing strategies is delivered by both the machine learning and deep learning approach. With this, the advancement of threats will require the advancement of the technique used to handle the threats and need to recover from them.

REFERENCES

Brun, O., Yin, Y., & Gelenbe, E. (2018). *Deep learning with dense random neural network for detecting attacks against IoT-connected home environments*. Science Direct.

Elrawy, M. F., Awad, A. I., & Hamed, H. F. A. (2018). *Intrusion detection systems for IoT-based smart environments*. Springer.

Farid, D. M., & Rahman, M. Z. (2008). *Learning Intrusion Detection Based on Adaptive Bayesian Algorithm*. IEEE.

Garg, S., Singh, A. K., Sarje, A. K., & Peddoju, S. K. (2013). *Behaviour Analysis of Machine Learning Algorithms for detecting P2P Botnets*. IEEE. doi:10.1109/ICACT.2013.6710523

Hardy, W., & Chen, L., Hou, S., & Ye, Y. (2015). *A Deep Learning Framework for Intelligent Malware Detection*. Springer.

Javaid, A., Niyaz, Q., Sun, W., & Alam M. (2014). *A Deep Learning Approach for Network Intrusion Detection System*. Science Direct.

Jung, W., Kim, S., & Choi, S. (2015). *Deep Learning for Zero-day Flash Malware Detection*. IEEE.

Kotenko, I., Saenko, I., & Branitskiy, A. (2018). *Framework for Mobile Internet of Things Security Monitoring Based on Big Data Processing and Machine Learning*. IEEE. doi:10.1109/ACCESS.2018.2881998

Li, Y., Ma, R., & Jiao, R. (2013). *A hybrid malicious code detection method based on deep learning*. Springer.

Liu, Q., Li, P., & Zhao, W. (2018). *A Survey on Security Threats and defensive techniques of Machine Learning: A Data-Driven View*. IEEE.

Rahouti, M., *Kaiqi, X., & Ghani, N. (2018). Bitcoin Concepts, Threats, and Machine-Learning Security Solutions*. IEEE.

Srinivas, M. & Sung, A. H. (2013). *Detecting Denial of Service Attacks Using Support Vector Machines*. IEEE.

Stroeh, K., *Madeira, E. R. M., & Goldenstein, S. K. (2013). An approach to the correlation of security events based on machine learning techniques*. Springer Open Journal.

Wang, F., Cheng, J., & Yu, Y. (2015). *A Hybrid Spectral Clustering and Deep Neural Network Ensemble Algorithm for Intrusion Detection in Sensor Networks*. Science Direct.

Yuan, Z., Lu, Y., Wang, Z., & Xue, Y. (2014). *Droid-sec: Deep learning in android malware detection*. ACM.

This research was previously published in the Handbook of Research on Machine and Deep Learning Applications for Cyber Security; pages 42-63, copyright year 2020 by Information Science Reference (an imprint of IGI Global).

Chapter 61
Adoption of Machine Learning With Adaptive Approach for Securing CPS

Rama Mercy Sam Sigamani

Avinashilingam Institute for Home Science and Higher Education for Women, India

ABSTRACT

The cyber physical system safety and security is the major concern on the incorporated components with interface standards, communication protocols, physical operational characteristics, and real-time sensing. The seamless integration of computational and distributed physical components with intelligent mechanisms increases the adaptability, autonomy, efficiency, functionality, reliability, safety, and usability of cyber-physical systems. In IoT-enabled cyber physical systems, cyber security is an essential challenge due to IoT devices in industrial control systems. Computational intelligence algorithms have been proposed to detect and mitigate the cyber-attacks in cyber physical systems, smart grids, power systems. The various machine learning approaches towards securing CPS is observed based on the performance metrics like detection accuracy, average classification rate, false negative rate, false positive rate, processing time per packet. A unique feature of CPS is considered through structural adaptation which facilitates a self-healing CPS.

INTRODUCTION

Cyber Physical Systems (CPS)

CPSs are frameworks that connect the physical world (e.g., through sensors or actuators) with the virtual universe of data handling. They are formed from differing constituent parts that team up to make some worldwide conduct. These constituents will incorporate programming frameworks, correspondences innovation, and sensors/actuators that communicate with this present reality, frequently including installed advances.

DOI: 10.4018/978-1-6684-6291-1.ch061

An average CPS as shown in Figure 1 may:

- Monitor and control physical and hierarchical or business forms
- Be an extensive scale framework with various - and notwithstanding clashing - objectives crossing distinctive application spaces
- Require incorporation of various specialized orders and diverse application spaces
- Require a high level of constancy
- Involve generous client contribution/communication
- Continuously screen and advance its own execution
- Adapt and advance continually accordingly changes in nature, through constant (re)configuration, sending or (de)commissioning
- Require progressive choice frameworks with a high level of self-sufficiency on neighborhood, territorial, national, and worldwide dimension
- Be circulated and interconnected frameworks of frameworks

Figure 1 CPS SYSTTEM

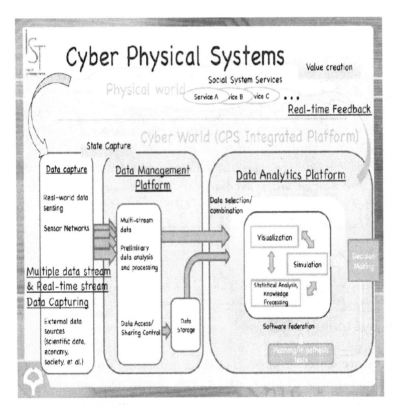

Example Application Domains

CPSs can be conveyed in a wide range of settings and application territories. Here are a few precedents:

- Improving productivity and security in homes and workplaces
- Supporting old individuals living alone.
- Monitoring security and developments of travelers in an open transport framework, or of vehicles on a street arrange.
- Optimizing crop yield and decreasing pesticide/compost use, by utilizing CPSs to distinguish and convey them just where they are required.

Figure 2 shows the CPS and embedded systems.

Figure 2 CPS AND EMBEDDED SYSTEMS

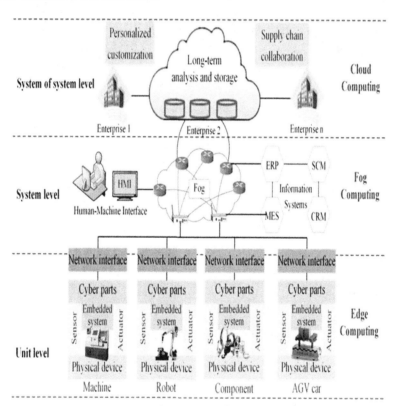

CPS and the Internet of Things

IoT and CPS share numerous difficulties, yet there are a few refinements as shown in Figure 3 IoT has a solid accentuation on interestingly recognizable and web associated gadgets and installed frameworks. CPS building has a solid accentuation on the connection among calculation and the physical world (e.g., between complex programming and equipment parts of a framework).

Figure 3 CPS – IOT

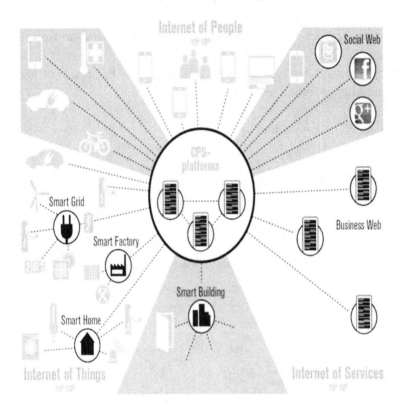

Cps Security

CPS Security Objectives

In assuring the security of cyber physical systems, there are several security objectives to achieve. They are

Confidentiality

Confidentiality means that cyber physical systems should have the capacity to prevent the disclosure to unauthorized individuals or systems. To realize confidentiality, a cyber-physical system should protect the communication channels between sensors and controllers and between the controllers and actuators from eavesdropping.

Integrity

Integrity refers to data or resources cannot be modified without authorization (Alom et al., 2015). To ensure the integrity, cyber physical systems should have the capacity to achieve the physical goals by preserving, detecting, or blocking deception attacks on the information attacks on the information sent and received by the sensors and actuators or controllers (Griffor et al., 2017). Ensuring data integrity requires the ability to detect any changes introduced (maliciously or otherwise) in the massage being communicated (Manadhata et al., 2011). Omar Al Ibrahim, et al., in Louridas et al. (2016) present some thoughts to utilize the physical unclonable functions technology to build secure coupling between cyber and physical substrates based on intrinsic physical material to achieve integrity of CPS.

Availability High availability of cyber physical system aims to always provide service by preventing computing, controls, communication corruptions due to hardware failures, system upgrades, power outages or denial-of-service attacks. Sazia Parvin, et al., proposes a multicyber framework to improve the availability of CPS based on Markov model.

Reliability

An unreliable CPS often leads to system malfunctions, service disruptions, financial losses and even human life. Leon Wu, (2014) describes a framework for benchmarking reliability of cyber physical systems. Leon Wu (2014) describe a data-centric runtime monitoring system for improving the reliability of these types of cyber physical systems, which employs automated online evaluation, working in parallel with cyber physical system to continuously conduct automated evaluation at multiple stages in the system workflow and provide real-time feedback for reliability improvement. Robert Mitchell, et al. (n.d.) analyze the effect of intrusion detection and response on the reliability of cyber physical systems and develop a probability model based on stochastic Petri nets to describe the behavior of the CPS in the presence of both malicious nodes exhibiting a range of attacker behaviors, and an intrusion detection and response system for detecting and responding to malicious events at runtime.

IMPORTANCE OF SECURITY IN CPS

CPS solutions can be stratified discussion, respectively, to introduce the solution of each layer as shown in Figure 4

Sensing Layer Security

The sensor of the sensing layer acquires the external entity information, which is constructed by these wireless sensors into the wireless sensor network. The sensor layer needs to consider the safety of the sensor network. The perceived layer of node computing, storage capacity is weak, cannot use complex encryption algorithm, so the need to design lightweight password algorithms and protocols. In order to prevent the node from being controlled, steal or tampered with, it is necessary to perform node authentication and data integrity verification. Through the expansion of the spectrum, the message priority and other security means to prevent the perception of the frequency interference. Using intrusion detection and intrusion recovery mechanism as a passive attack security measures to improve the robustness of the system.

Network Layer Security

The network layer consists of a large number of heterogeneous networks, different networks to resist security threats in different ways, so the design of the network layer security structure need to consider the network layer compatibility and consistency. Network layer security tasks include network layer identity

Figure 4 CPS Layers

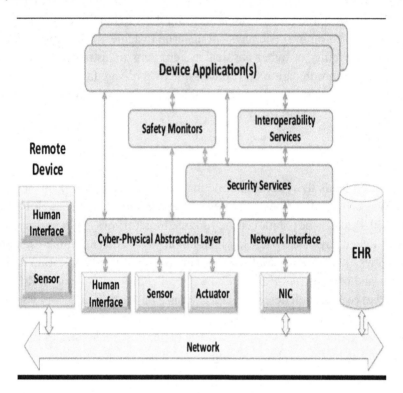

authentication, network resource access control, data transmission confidentiality and integrity, remote access security, routing system security. The security structure of the network layer has two layers: point-to-point security sub-layer and end-to-end security sublayer. Among them, the point-to-point security sub-layer guarantees the security of the data in hop-by-hop transmission. The corresponding security mechanism includes mutual authentication between nodes, hop-by-hop encryption, and cross-network authentication and so on. The end-to-terminal layer primarily implements end-to-end confidentiality and protects network availability. The corresponding security mechanisms include end-to-end authentication and secret key negotiation, secret key management and cryptographic algorithm selection, denial of service and distributed denial of service attack detection and defense, hierarchical architecture, broadcast radius limit, port interception and so on.

Collaborative Solution Security

The task of the collaborative processing layer is to collect useful data and then analyze and process the data. Therefore, the security task of this layer is to identify and delete the malicious information in the data source, collect the effective information and keep it on the basis of security. In addition, the collaborative processing layer of the synergy of the information obtained can have different sources, there may be different receivers, so in order to ensure the confidentiality and integrity of the data, the recipient and the sender need to be certified, and the information content and information sources are separated to protect the privacy of users. The security measures of the collaborative processing are as follows:

virus detection, good confidence in data sources, access control box disaster recovery, secure multi-party computing and secure cloud computing, and efficient data mining for encrypted data.

Application Control Layer Security

The application layer service is different because of the application of CPS system, and the corresponding security requirements are different. Therefore, it is necessary to provide targeted security service according to the specific application. In general, the protection of user privacy is the most common security services, such as in the medical system, the need to protect the patient's personal privacy, the patient's personal information and medical records of the contents of the need to be separated to prevent user privacy theft by outsiders. In addition, unauthorized access is prohibited, and can be secured by computer security measures to ensure this. Application control layer security measures are mainly differentiated database security services, user privacy protection mechanism, access control, security software, patches, upgrade systems.

ATTACKS ON CPS

Cyber Attack

The Internet in today's society may be a key a part of human life. We tend to use internet at home, in the office and on mobile devices anywhere and everywhere we go. It's become important to be connected to internet 24/7, to keep an eye on business, keep in bit with family and friends, and to stay up to date on news around the world. Being connected doesn't only concern with the advancement in life or business, it comes with variety of potential danger like got taken valuable knowledge, lost privacy or identity, device infected by malware. Security for any legitimate network is under threat of attack. A number of the researchers have defined these cyber attacks as cyber war (Feizollah et al., 2013) and supply some initial guidelines for future defense of cyber house. The process in the main issues with the understanding of their own network, nature of the attacker, motive of the attacker, methodology of attack, security weakness of the network to mitigate future attacks. to grasp the character of a cyber attack, it's vital to model attack earlier to form network more secure, which may be customized depending on the organization's needs (Khan et al., 2010).

A cyber attack is deliberate exploitation of pc systems, technology-dependent enterprises and networks. Cyber attacks use malicious code to alter computer code, logic or information, resulting in disruptive consequences that may compromise information and result in cybercrimes, like information and identity theft. Cyber attack is also known as a network attack (CNA). Cyber attacks occurred targeting banks and broadcasting firms in South Korea on March 20. The malware concerned in these attacks brought down multiple websites and interrupted bank transactions by overwriting the Master Boot Record (MBR) and every one the logical drives on the infected servers rendering them unusable. it was reported that thirty two thousand computers had been damaged and also the actual quantity of the financial damage has not yet been calculated. A lot of serious is that we tend to area unit likely to have greater damages in case of occurring additional attacks, since exact analysis of cause isn't done however. APT(Advanced Persistent Threat), that is becoming a big issue due to this attack, isn't a brand new way of attacking, but a kind of keyword standing for a trend of recent cyber attacks.

Moreover, cyber security measured with regards to access, integration of information, security, storage and transfer of information through electronic or different modes (Khan et al., 2010). Cyber security indicates three important factors. The methods of protecting information Technology (IT), the information itself, the information being processed and transmitted together with physical and virtual setup, the level of protection obtained by applying such measures and also the professional aspects associated (Kurakin et al., 2016).

Physical Attack

Physical attacks are inevitable threats in sensor networks. Physical attacks are relatively simple to launch and fatal in destruction. Within the simplest case, the Xun Wang, Sriram Chellappan, Wenjun Gu and Dong Yuan are with The Department of computer science and Engineering. A better attacker will detect and destroy sensors with concealment by moving across the sensor network. In any case, the end results of physical attacks are often quite fatal. The backbone of the network (the sensors themselves) is destroyed. Destruction of sensors may additionally lead to the violation of the important network paradigms. a large spectrum of impacts might result because of physical attacks and once left unaddressed, physical attacks have the potential to render the complete sensing element network mission useless. Our focus in this paper is Search-based Physical Attacks. We define search-based physical attacks as those who seek for sensors, and so physically destroy them.

The searching process is executed by means of detecting electronic, magnetic, heat signals emitted by the sensors. Once sensors are identified, the attacker physically destroys the sensors. This method is opposed to a rather blind or brute force destruction of sensors in the field (using bombs, grenades, tanks etc) that will cause casualties to the deployment field, that the attacker might want to preserve (airports, oil fields, battlefields etc. of interest to the attacker). The salient options of search based mostly physical attacks return from the power to search for and then destroy sensors. This improves the potency of the attack method, because the wrongdoer will identify and destroy important sensors (cluster-heads, knowledge aggregators etc.). The search-based wrongdoer will cause physical destruction of the sensors whereas causing minimum casualties to the field of deployment.

The small type issue of sensors, coupled with the unattended and distributed nature of their deployment exposes detector networks to a special category of attacks that might lead to the physical destruction of sensors. We tend to denote Physical Attacks as those who lead to the physical destruction of sensors, thereby rendering them for good nonoperational. During this paper we tend to model and study a representative category of physical attacks, particularly Search-Based physical attacks to know their behavior and impacts.

Our performance information clearly shows that search-based physical attacks dramatically reduce accumulative coverage, further highlighting the importance of our work. we tend to observe that the attacker parameters, namely attacker's detection ranges, accuracy and movement speed, and the sensor network parameters such as the frequencies of sensors' beacons and frequency of cluster-head rotation have vital impacts on attack effectiveness. we tend to also observe that using a hierarchical sensor network has a mixed impact on maintaining AC under attacks; on one hand, the compromised cluster-heads (in hierarchical networks) cause decrease in AC significantly; on the other hand but, the existence of cluster-heads with cluster-head rotation will mislead the attacker and create its movements less efficient. We tend to also observe that the impacts of the attacker and sensor network parameters to attack effectiveness move with each other to affect AC. Physical attacks are patent and potent threats to future detector networks. We tend to believe that viability of future detector networks is conditional their ability to resist physical attacks.

Cyber and Physical Attack

Cyber Physical Systems refer to systems that have an interaction between computers, communication channels and physical devices to solve a real world problem. Towards industry 4.0 revolution, Cyber Physical Systems presently become one among the main targets of hackers and any injury to them lead to high losses to a nation. Consistent with valid resources, many cases reported involved security breaches on Cyber Physical Systems. Understanding basic and theoretical concept of security in the digital world was discussed worldwide. Yet, security cases in relevance the cyber physical system area unit still remaining less explored. In addition, limited tools were introduced to beat security issues in Cyber Physical System. To boost understanding and introduce heaps additional security solutions for the cyber physical system, the study on this matter is highly on demand.

The world accepted that Cyber Physical Systems (CPSs) connect computers, communication devices, sensors and actuators of the physical substratum, either in heterogeneous, open, systems of systems or hybrid. Systems become additional interconnected, thereby additional advanced (Tonge et al., 2013). Computer networks currently have joined water, food, transportation, and energy because the important resource for the perform of the nationals" economy. Application of cps will be seen in several styles of industries. The common sector is oil and gas, the power grid producing, defense and public infrastructures are fully relying on the advancement of cps. Therefore, cyber physical systems security has become a matter for societal, infrastructures and economic to ever y country in the world because of the tremendous number of electronic devices that are interconnected via networks communication (Alfayyadh et al., 2010). Latest reports have shown that cyber-attacks are aimed to destroy nations systems that used for country development. CPS starts with by not simply disrupt a single enterprise or damage an isolated machine; however a target to damage infrastructures via modern dynamics threats (Biggio et al., 2014). Those forms of attacks are able to offer destruction to important infrastructures system that used in sectors such as defense, finance, health, and the public (Biggio et al., 2014). To accomplish their goals criminals, activists, or terrorists are mostly searching for new and innovative techniques and targets, thus cyber physical systems currently one of the necessary targets for the hackers (Biggio et al., 2014). Increased security risk awareness and appropriately security relevant information management offer an equally important role within the trusted infrastructure maintenance. Figure 5 shows the CPS system.

Attacks Classification

Currently, in the middle of an emergence of Cyber Physical Systems (CPS) in almost all aspects of our life, CPS are manifold and include all kinds of unmanned or remote controlled vehicles, robotized manufacturing plants, critical infrastructure such as electrical power grid and nuclear power plants, smart homes, smart cities, and many more. Based on our experience with computer and network security, CPS will become targets of adversary attacks. Attacks on CPS are neither science fiction nor the matter of the distant future. Multiple attacks on various CPS have been already performed. Currently, the most famous attack is Stuxnet. Stuxnet is considered to be the first professionally crafted attack against CPS. This attack has reportedly damaged over 1000 centrifuges at an Iranian uranium enrichment plant (Feizollah et al., 2013). Multiple further examples of attacks on various CPS have been reported or shown in the

Figure 5 CPS and its diagram

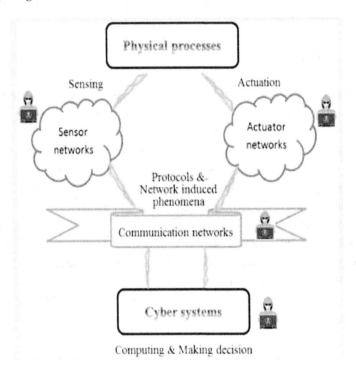

research literature. These include attacks on modern car electronics (Khan et al., 2010), attacks on remotely controlled UAVs via GPS spoofing (Kurakin et al., 2016), or even attacks which use CPS as a carrier to infect the maintenance computer (Tonge et al., 2013). There is a broad consensus among researchers that adversary goals of attacks on CPS might differ from the goals of attacks on cyber systems. For instance, many attacks on CPS would try to compromise the system's safety or physical integrity instead of data privacy usually considered in cyber-security. However, technical aspects have even more severe implications on the CPS security. Figure.5. depicts various attacks which can be performed at targets located at different system layers. It is clear that attacks will affect the attacked targets. Additionally, due to the high degree of the dependencies and interdependencies between CPS elements at different layers, secondary effects can occur at CPS elements which have not been directly attacked. These induced effects can occur at elements located in different layers or even belonging to different (cyber or physical) domains. Such cross-layer and cross-domain attacks on CPS are very intricate and barely understood so far. Below, we will use qualifier "cross-domain" as a synonym for both cross-domain and cross-layer. Figure 6 shows the layer specific attacks.

Surveying known attacks on CPS, one can notice that a significant portion exhibits cross-domain effects. This makes it extremely important to consider such attacks alongside with the conventional cyber-attacks. In order to do this, we first should be able to describe not only the single-domain but also cross-domain attacks.

Attack Categorization: The most significant feature of the proposed taxonomy is the clear distinction between Influenced Element and Victim Element. As both these dimensions are independent from each other, elements of these dimensions can belong to cyber or physical domain regardless of the domain affiliation of each other. Therefore, the description of cross-domain attacks becomes possible.

Furthermore, based on the domain of these elements, we can define following four attack categories: Cyber-to-Cyber (C2C), Cyber-to-Physical (C2P), Physical-to-Physical (P2P), and Physical-to-Cyber (P2C). These derivatives can be used to characterize attacks.

Figure 6. Layer specific attacks on CPS

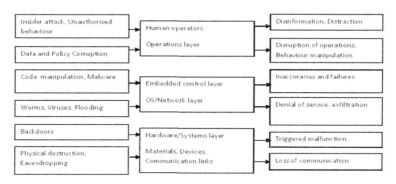

MACHINE LEARNING AND DEEP LEARNING

Fortunately, Machine Learning can aid in solving the most common tasks including regression, prediction, and classification. In the era of an extremely large amount of data and cyber security talent shortage, ML seems to be an only solution as in Figure 7.

This chapter is an introduction written to give the practical technical understanding of the current advances and future directions of ML research applied to cyber security.

Machine Learning Terminology

- **AI (Artificial Intelligence)**: A broad concept. A Science of making things smart or, in other words, human tasks performed by machines (e.g., Visual Recognition, NLP, etc.). The main point is that AI is not exactly Machine Learning or smart things. It can be a classic program installed in your robot cleaner like edge detection. Roughly speaking, AI is a thing that somehow carries out human tasks.
- **ML (Machine Learning)**: An Approach (just one of many approaches) to AI that uses a system that is capable of learning from experience. It is intended not only for AI goals (e.g., copying human behavior) but it can also reduce the efforts and/or time spent for both simple and difficult tasks like stock price prediction. In other words, ML is a system that can recognize patterns by using examples rather than by programming them. If your system learns constantly, makes decisions based on data rather than algorithms, and change its behavior, it's Machine Learning.
- **DL (Deep Learning)**: A set of Techniques for implementing Machine Learning that recognize patterns of patterns – like image recognition. The systems identify primarily object edges, a structure, an object type, and then an object itself. The point is that Deep Learning is not exactly Deep Neural Networks. There are other algorithms, which were improved to learn patterns of patterns, such as Deep Q Learning in Reinforcement task.

Figure 7. Machine learning methods

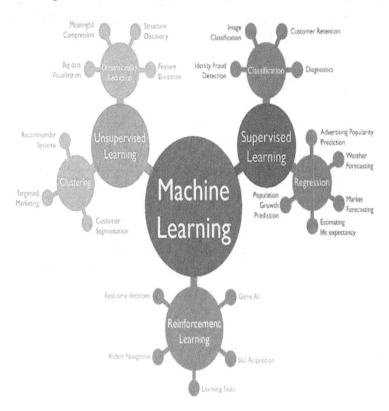

The definitions show that cyber security field refers mostly to Machine Learning (not to AI). And a large part of the tasks are not human-related. Machine learning means solving certain tasks with the use of an approach and particular methods based on data you have.

Most of the tasks are subclasses of the most common ones, which are described below:

- **Regression (or Prediction)**: A task of predicting the next value based on the previous values.
- **Classification**: A task of separating things into different categories.
- **Clustering**: Similar to classification but the classes are unknown, grouping things by their similarity.
- **Association Rule Learning (or Recommendation):** A task of recommending something based on the previous experience.
- **Dimensionality Reduction**: Or generalization, a task of searching common and most important features in multiple examples.
- **Generative Models**: A task of creating something based on the previous knowledge of the distribution.

There are different approaches in addition to these tasks.

Machine Learning Tasks and Cyber Security

Let's see examples of different methods that can be used to solve Machine Learning tasks and how they are related to cyber security tasks.

Regression

Regression (or prediction) is simple. The knowledge about the existing data is utilized to have an idea of the new data. Take an example of house prices prediction. In cybersecurity, it can be applied to fraud detection. The features (e.g., the total amount of suspicious transaction, location, etc.) determine a probability of fraudulent actions.

As for the technical aspects of regression, all methods can be divided into two large categories: Machine Learning and Deep Learning. The same is used for other tasks.

For each task, there are examples of ML and DL methods.

Deep Learning for Regression

For regression tasks, the following Deep Learning models can be used:

- Artificial Neural Network (ANN)
- Recurrent Neural Network (RNN)
- Neural Turing Machines (NTM)
- Differentiable Neural Computer (DNC)

Machine Learning for Classification

- Logistic Regression (LR)
- K-Nearest Neighbors (K-NN)
- Support Vector Machine (SVM)
- KernelSVM
- NaiveBayes
- DecisionTreeClassification
- Random Forest Classification

It's considered that methods like SVM and random forests work best. Keep in mind that there are no one-size-fits-all rules, and they probably won't operate properly for your task.

Deep Learning for Classification

- Artificial Neural Network
- Convolutional Neural Networks

Deep Learning methods work better if you have more data. But they consume more resources especially if you are planning to use it in production and re-train systems periodically.

Machine Learning for Clustering

- K-nearest neighbours (KNN)
- K-means
- Mixture model(LDA)
- DBSCn
- Bayesian
- GaussianMixtureModel
- Agglomerative
- Mean-shift

Deep Learning for Clustering

- Self-organized Maps (SOM) or Kohonen Networks

Association Rule Learning (Recommendation Systems)

Netflix and Sound Cloud recommend films or songs according to your movies or music preferences. In cyber security, this principle can be used primarily for incident response. If a company faces a wave of incidents and offers various types of responses, a system learns a type of response for a particular incident (e.g., mark it as a false positive, change a risk value, run the investigation). Risk management solutions can also have a benefit if they automatically assign risk values for new vulnerabilities or misconfigurations built on their description.

There are algorithms used for solving recommendation tasks.

Machine Learning for Association Rule Learning

- Apriori
- Euclat
- FP-Growth

Deep Learning for Association Rule Learning

- Deep Restricted Boltzmann Machine (RBM)
- Deep Belief Network (DBN)
- Stacked Auto encoder

The latest recommendation systems are based on restricted Boltzmann machines and their updated versions, such as promising deep belief networks.

Dimensionality Reduction

Dimensionality reduction or generalization is not as popular as classification, but necessary if you deal with complex systems with unlabeled data and many potential features. You can't apply clustering because typical methods restrict the number of features or they don't work. Dimensionality reduction can help handle it and cut unnecessary features. Like clustering, dimensionality reduction is usually one of the tasks in a more complex model. As to cyber security tasks, dimensionality reduction is common for face detection solutions — the ones you use in your iPhone.

Machine Learning for Dimensionality Reduction

- Principal Component Analysis (PCA)
- Singular-value decomposition (SVD)
- T-distributed Stochastic Neighbor Embedding (T-SNE)
- Linear Discriminant Analysis (LDA)
- Latent Semantic Analysis (LSA)
- Factor Analysis (FA)
- Independent Component Analysis (ICA)
- Non-negative Matrix Factorization (NMF)

Generative Models

The task of generative models differs from the above-mentioned ones. While those tasks deal with the existing information and associated decisions, generative models are designed to simulate the actual data (not decisions) based on the previous decisions.

The simple task of offensive cyber security is to generate a list of input parameters to test a particular application for Injection vulnerabilities.

Alternatively, you can have a vulnerability scanning tool for web applications. One of its modules is testing files for unauthorized access. These tests are able to mutate existing filenames to identify the new ones. For example, if a crawler detected a file called login.php, it's better to check the existence of any backup or test its copies by trying names like login_1.php, login_backup.php, login.php.2017.

Cyber Security Tasks and Machine Learning

Instead of looking at ML tasks and trying to apply them to cyber security, let's look at the common cyber security tasks and Machine Learning opportunities. There are three dimensions (Why, What, and How).

The first dimension is a goal, or a task (e.g., detects threats, predict attacks, etc.). According to Gartner's PPDR model, all security tasks can be divided into five categories:

1. Prediction;
2. Prevention;
3. Detection;
4. Response;
5. Monitoring.

Machine Learning for Network Protection

Network protection is not a single area but a set of different solutions that focus on a protocol such as Ethernet, wireless, SCADA, or even virtual networks like SDNs.

Network protection refers to well-known Intrusion Detection System (IDS) solutions. Some of them used a kind of ML years ago and mostly dealt with signature-based approaches.

ML in network security implies new solutions called Network Traffic Analytics (NTA) aimed at in-depth analysis of all the traffic at each layer and detects attacks and anomalies.

Now-a-days the construct of machine learning is used in many applications and may be a core construct for intelligent systems (Ge et al., 2017) as in Figure 8.

Figure 8 Machine Learning Types

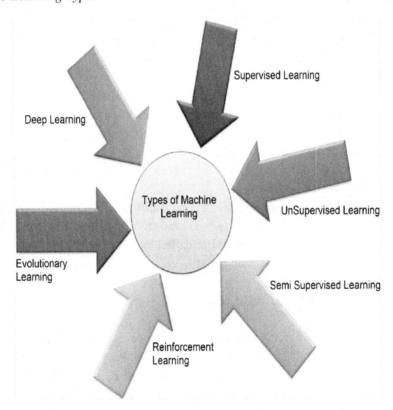

Machine learning tasks are generally classified depending on the nature of the learning "signal" or "feedback" available to a learning system.

- Supervised learning
- Unsupervised learning
- Semi-supervised Learning
- Reinforcement learning
- Multitask Learning

- Ensemble Learning
- Neural Network Learning
- Instance-Based Learning

Supervised Learning

It is the machine learning task of inferring a function from labeled training data. The training data consists of a set of training examples. A supervised learning algorithm analyzes the training data and produces an inferred function that can be utilized for mapping fresh examples. To work out on a given problem of supervised learning, one has to carry out the following steps:

1. Decide the kind of training examples. The user should decide what kind of data is to be used as a training set.
2. Collect a training set. The training set needs to be envoy of the real-world use of the function. Thus, a set of input objects is collected and corresponding outputs are also collected.
3. Decide the input feature depiction of the learned function. The accuracy of the learned function relies sturdily on how the input object is represented. Normally, the input object is altered into a feature vector that contains a number of features that are descriptive of the object. The number of features should not be too large.
4. Decide the structure of the learned function and corresponding learning algorithm.
5. Complete the design. Run the learning algorithm on the gathered training set. Some supervised learning algorithms need the user to find out certain control parameters.
6. Assess the accuracy of the learned function. After parameter adjustment and learning, the performance of the resulting function should be measured on a test set that is separate from the training set.

Unsupervised Learning

It is the machine learning task of inferring a perform to depict concealed structure from "unlabeled" information. Since the examples specified to the learner are unlabeled, there's no assessment of the accuracy of the structure that's output by the relevant algorithm which is a way of characteristic unsupervised learning from supervised learning and reinforcement learning. A central case of unsupervised learning is that the problem of density estimation in statistics [19].

Unsupervised learning used information that has no historical labels and therefore the goal is to explore the data and realize similarities between the objects. It's the technique of discovering labels from the info itself. Unsupervised learning works well on transactional information such as identify segments of consumers with similar attributes who will then be treated similarly in marketing campaigns. Or it will find the main attributes that separate customer segments from one another.

Other unsupervised learning problems are:

- Given detailed observations of distant galaxies, determine which features or combinations of features are most important in distinguishing between galaxies.
- Given a mixture of two sound sources for example, a person talking over some music, separate the two which is called the blind source separation problem.

- Given a video, isolate a moving object and categorize in relation to other moving objects which have been seen.

Typical unsupervised task is clustering where a set of inputs is divided into groups, unlike in classification; the groups are not known before. Popular unsupervised techniques include self-organizing maps, nearest-neighbor mapping, k-means clustering and singular value decomposition. These algorithms are also used to segment text topics, recommend items and identify data outliers.

Semi-Supervised Learning

In many practical learning domains such as text processing, video indexing, bioinformatics, there is large supply of unlabeled data but limited labeled data which can be expensive to generate .So semi supervised learning is used for the same applications as supervised learning but it uses both labeled and unlabeled data for training. There is a desired prediction problem but the model must learn the structures to organize the data as well as make predictions.

Semi-supervised learning is useful when the cost associated with labeling is too high to allow for a fully labeled training process. This type of learning can be used with methods such as classification, regression and prediction. Early examples of this include identifying a person's face on a web cam. Example algorithms are extensions to other flexible methods that make assumptions about how to model the unlabelled data.

DEEP LEARNING

Deep learning is a rising area of machine learning (ML) analysis. It contains multiple hidden layers of artificial neural networks. The deep learning methodology applies nonlinear transformations and model abstractions of high level in massive databases. The recent advancements in deep learning architectures inside numerous fields have already provided important contributions in AI.

A Deep Neural Network (DNN) is defined to be an artificial Neural Network (ANN) with a minimum of one hidden layers of units between the input and output layers. The additional layers provide it additional levels of abstraction, so enhancing its modeling capability. The foremost popular sorts of Deep Learning models are referred to as Convolutional Neural Nets (CNN), or just ConvNets. These space type of feed-forward artificial neural network, extensively utilized in laptop vision, wherever the individual neurons are covered in such the way that they reply to overlapping regions within the visual view. In recent times, CNN shave also been with success applied to automatic speech recognition (ASR). Deep Belief Network sand Convolutional Deep Belief Networks are another popular deep learning architectures in use.

Reinforcement Learning

A computer program interacts with a vibrant environment in which it must perform a certain goal. The program is provided feedback in terms of rewards and punishments as it navigates its problem space.

It is often used for robotics, gaming and navigation. It is the learning technique which interacts with a dynamic environment in which it must perform a certain goal without a teacher explicitly telling it whether it has come close to its goal. With reinforcement learning, the algorithm discovers through trial and error which actions yield the greatest rewards. So in the chess playing, reinforcement learning learns to play a game by playing against an opponent which performs trial and error actions to win.

Multitask Learning

Multitask learning has a simple goal of helping other learners to perform better. When multitask learning algorithms are applied on a task, it remembers the procedure how it solved the problem or how it reaches to the particular conclusion. The algorithm then uses these steps to find the solution of other similar problem or task. This helping of one algorithm to another can also be termed as inductive transfer mechanism. If the learners share their experience with each other, the learners can learn concurrently rather than individually and can be much faster [23].

Ensemble Learning

When various individual learners are combined to form only one learner then that particular type of learning is called ensemble learning. The individual learner may be Naïve Bayes, decision tree, neural network, etc. Ensemble learning is a hot topic since 1990s. It has been observed that, a collection of learners is almost always better at doing a particular job rather than individual learners. Two popular Ensemble learning techniques are given below (Jordan et al., 2015):

1. **Boosting**: Boosting is a technique in ensemble learning which is used to decrease bias and variance. Boosting creates a collection of weak learners and converts them to one strong learner. A weak learner is a classifier which is barely correlated with true classification. On the other hand, a strong learner is a type of classifier which is strongly correlated with true classification (Papernot et al., 2016).
2. **Bagging**: Bagging or bootstrap aggregating is applied where the accuracy and stability of a machine learning algorithm needs to be increased. It is applicable in classification and regression. Bagging also decreases variance and helps in handling over fitting (Papernot et al., 2016).

Neural Network Learning

The neural network (or artificial neural network or ANN) is derived from the biological concept of neurons. A neuron is a cell like structure in a brain. To understand neural network, one must understand how a neuron works. A neuron has mainly four parts .They are dendrites, nucleus, soma and axon.

The dendrites receive electrical signals. Soma processes the electrical signal. The output of the process is carried by the axon to the dendrite terminals where the output is sent to next neuron. The nucleus is the heart of the neuron. The inter-connection of neuron is called neural network where electrical impulses travel around the brain.

An artificial neural network behaves the same way. It works on three layers. The input layer takes input (much like dendrites). The hidden layer processes the input (like soma and axon). Finally, the output layer sends the calculated output (like dendrite terminals) (Abdelhamid et al., 2014) as in Figure 9.

Figure 9. Neural network

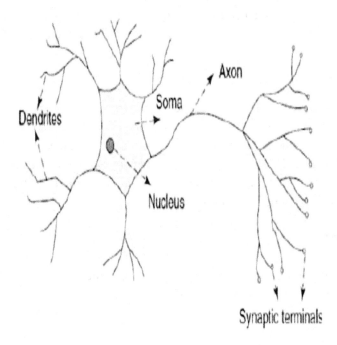

Instance-Based Learning

In instance-based learning, the learner learns a particular type of pattern. It tries to apply the same pattern to the newly fed data. Hence the name instance based. It is a type of lazy learner which waits for the test data to arrive and then act on it together with training data. The complexity of the learning algorithm increases with the size of the data. Given below is a well-known example of instance-based learning which k-nearest neighbor is (Papernot et al., 2016).

1. **K-Nearest Neighbor**: In k-nearest neighbor (or KNN), the training data (which is well-labeled) is fed into the learner. When the test data is introduced to the learner, it compares both the data. K most correlated data is taken from training set. The majority of k is taken which serves as the new class for the test data (Papernot et al., 2016).

MACHINE LEARNING ON CYBER ATTACK

ML algorithms and techniques were originally designed for stationary environments in which both the training and test data were assumed to be generated from the same distribution (Griffor et al., 2017). Increasingly, these algorithms are now being used as online learners, where they are periodically retrained for decision making in security oriented systems. Examples include fraud detection, spam filtering, and even network intrusion detection systems. In these applications, the purpose of the ML models is to prevent access from unauthorized users.

ML algorithms can be susceptible to an adept and sophisticated adversary in both the retraining and decision-making phases. Research in this area has been termed Adversarial Machine Learning and has been defined by Huang et al. as "the design of machine learning algorithms that can resist sophisticated attacks, and the study of the capabilities and limitations of attackers" (Louridas et al., 2016).

Attack Surface

The attack surface of any system is the set of points or vectors where the system is vulnerable to attack. Papernot et al. (2016) presents the attack surface of a ML system as a data processing pipeline. The four sections of their pipeline consist of an input physical domain, digital representation, ML model, and the output physical domain. The input physical domain is where input features are collected from the physical world. This could come from physical I/O hardware such as cameras or infrared sensors. This input is then processed into a digital representation, such as a JPEG image, into the system. The digital representation can then be used by the ML model to produce an output. The output can then be transferred to the output physical domain.

Threat Model

An early attempt to categorize adversarial machine learning attacks was done by Barreno et al. In their paper, they explored the security of ML and developed a taxonomy based on a three-axis model of the attack space. The first axis labeled as influence, describes the capabilities of the attacker as either causative or exploratory. Causative attacks modify the training process via influence over the training data, whereas exploratory attacks use other methods such as probing that do not affect the training data but rather attempt to gather information about the learning model. The second axis of their model is labeled as security violation and defines the goal of the adversary as either an integrity attack where the machine learner allows false negatives (intrusions into the system), or as an availability attack where the learner is subjected to a denial of service event by allowing false positives (blocking legitimate data).

The third axis, labeled as specificity, refers to the precision of the attacker's intention as either targeted or indiscriminate. An attacker with a targeted intention is attempting to degrade the machine learner's performance for a small set of data points or a particular data point. An indiscriminate attack would cause the machine learner to fail in a broader set of data. The taxonomy developed by Barreno et al. has been further developed in subsequent work and later incorporated into a framework for security evaluation. Biggio et al. (2014) provided the framework used to evaluate the security of pattern classifier algorithms in three real world examples of spam filtering, biometric authentication, and network intrusion detection.

Later the same research group evaluated the security of support vector machines using the framework in the application examples of malware detection in PDF files and image recognition of handwritten digits. The framework is also used by Mozaffari et al. to evaluate the security of six different types of ML algorithms (decision tree, rule based, naïve bayes, nearest neighbor, artificial neural network, and support vector machine) in healthcare applications. Through the use of the framework, the ML algorithms can be evaluated on the attack methods described in the next section.

Papernot et al. (2016) contributed a threat model taxonomy that represented the complexity of ML attacks. Their model showed that the complexity of an attack increased as the adversary's knowledge of the model decreased and as the adversary's goals became more targeted. The least complex attack in their taxonomy would come from an adversary that had complete knowledge of the ML model and whose goal was to reduce the confidence in the model's output. The most complex attack would come from an adversary that only had sample input and output data with a goal of forcing a specific output from a specific input.

MACHINE LEARNING SECURITY FOR CPS

In this section, security vulnerabilities of ML are considered from a CPSs view. The attack surface will be described and possible methods of attacking CPSs through their ML model are discussed. Additionally, scenarios are presented discussing how CPSs such as autonomous vehicles and drones might be attacked via these methods.

CPS Attack Surface

The attack surface of embedded systems categorized based on the layers of the system are the hardware, firmware/operating system, and application layers. Hardware layer attacks could occur both during and post production by various methods including hardware backdoors, hardware trojans, eavesdropping, fault injection, and hardware modification. Firmware and operating system layer attacks could occur by the attacker installing malicious versions of the system's firmware or drivers through updates or by attacking vulnerabilities or bugs in the underlying operating system.

Attacks to the application layer occur as attacks to the software programs or applications that the embedded system executes. Some examples include viruses, worms, software trojans, and buffer overflow attacks. As previously discussed, CPSs such as drones or autonomous vehicles are embedded systems and systems like these can also have a ML component. However, ML security is not well represented in the attack surface categorized by Papp et al. The ML component is not part of the hardware of a cyber-physical system though it can be directly influenced by the hardware or sensors. Nor is it part of the firmware or operating system, even though it can also be influenced by both the firmware and operating system. Some might consider the ML model as part of the application layer as it is generally responsible for a particular function of the system such as image identification.

However, a ML component does not fit well as a normal software application. In general, a software application or program is thought of as a group of instructions that are executed in logical steps to perform a particular task. These instructions are written by a programmer and do not change unless the program is modified by the developer. Therefore, no matter what input data the application processes, a predetermined result will be produced based on the static nature of the program instructions. This is not the case with a ML algorithm as they are not programmed but rather trained to produce an output. In the case of an online learning method such as reinforcement learning, the program output could gradually change over time.

Since ML does not fit well in the application layer, it is suggested that that the classification developed by Papp et al. be extended to cover attacks that target ML. It is proposed that a ML attack layer be added to the classification. This layer will only contain attacks (i.e., evasion and data poisoning) that are targeting the ML model of an embedded system. The extended target level categorization is presented. It is worth noting that the attack surface by Papernot et al. depicted in section 2 is contained in the ML layer. The only exception would be a possible overlap with respect to the hardware layer and the physical input and output domains described by Papernot et al.

The main difference is that these systems will operate in the physical world on a day to day basis and will have to react to real world situations. As such, these systems are likely to be online or reinforcement learners. Recently, the Israeli company Mobileye announced that it will be testing the reinforcement learning approach on roads with BMW. In this section, we briefly describe some possible attack methods.

Sensor Driver Attack

For this attack, we must assume that the attacker has some level of knowledge of the interface between the firmware drivers of the CPS and their interaction with the ML model. In this attack, an adversary would install a malicious version of a sensor's firmware driver. The malicious driver could then feed the ML model malicious or distorted data. In an online learner, this could affect the training of the model over time to produce incorrect outputs.

An example of this form of attack could be the camera firmware used for image detection. If corrupted, the driver could introduce noise into the data fed to the machine learner. This could result in images being misclassified. Or if used in an online learning situation the training of the classifier could cause the model to degrade over time. Interestingly enough this type of attack could be classified as an exploratory attack in the first case and as a causative attack in the latter case.

Adversarial Data Attack

This is an exploratory form of attack that would require no modification to the CPS whatsoever. In this method, adversarial data could be crafted and presented to the CPS via sensors in order to fool the ML model. This involve external manipulation of sensors of a CPS. Several of these sensor related attacks are detailed in work done by Petit et al. (n.d.) on automated vehicle sensors. In this work, simple laser pointers or LEDs were used to degrade the performance of cameras used for autonomous vehicles.

Additionally, fake echoes were created in the LiDAR sensors by using two transceivers. Given that previous research has shown that transferability exists between models, it's easy to see how an adversary could take the necessary steps to create and train their own model for use with camera or LiDAR sensors, then use their model and possibly some of the methods in craft adversarial examples. The adversary could then use these examples on the ML model employed by the CPS.

External Poisoning Attacks

As previously mentioned, in a poisoning attack the adversary is attempting to influence the training data of the machine learner. If we consider that CPSs like autonomous vehicles or drones are trained in an online fashion then they will be susceptible to poisoning attacks in day to day operation. A case could be surmised where an adversary devised a method to fool a camera on an automated vehicle to always think that a stop sign or impediment existed on a particular street. Over time, the existence of the projected stop sign or impediment would affect the training of the autonomous vehicle. This could result in a slower approach by the vehicle to the particular location or possibly the vehicle may reroute itself to avoid the location.

Logic Corruption Attack

This attack is very similar to other classic software or firmware attacks where malicious code is inserted into a running program. However, it must be mentioned, as it is the strongest form of attack on a ML system. In this case, the adversary would have complete control of the ML model and be able to directly manipulate the outputs, alter the feature set, or modify the underlying algorithm which could result in a change in the behavior or training of the model. It is assumed that the attacker would have a high level of knowledge about the system and access through a HW communications port in order to perform this attack. This form of attack would be causative in nature as it directly makes internal modifications to the ML model.

Need for CPS Intelligence

The incorporation of intelligence will make the CPS to be able to execute complex tasks in dynamic environments and under unforeseen conditions. To address this uncertainty of physical world, machine learning provides solutions in a statistic manner, which would always try to make optimal decisions in terms of performance such as prediction accuracy, efficiency, robustness, and other specific metrics. Among many types of machine learning methods, classification and clustering would have wide applications in CPS to identify patterns among the collected sensor data, such as anomaly detection for protecting system safety, behavior recognition for understanding surrounding environment, prediction for system optimization and planning, to name a few. In this thesis, we will propose a wide range of learning algorithms ranging from feature representation, classification and anomaly detection, and show that they can improve the learning performance for many real-life applications.

Machine Learning Algorithms in CPS

The first important part of intelligent CPS considered in this thesis is the development of advanced machine learning algorithms which is the study of how to automatically learn from past observations to make accurate predictions and decisions. The incorporation of machine learning algorithms will bring intelligence into various kinds of systems and enable them to handle uncertainty in the interaction of physical world. In below, we will briefly discuss the motivations of different types of machine learning problems in the context of CPS applications:

Feature Representation in CPS

The wide use of high-resolution sensors leads to high-dimensional data sets in many CPS. The learning performance will be reduced when the dimensionality increases for limited labeled data, which is usually referred to as the \curse of dimensionality" issue. Instead of using all features, it is better to select those most important features to reduce redundancy and irrelevancy among data, thereby improving the learning performance and reducing the computational burden as well. Most existing feature selection methods consider the dependency and relevancy among features as the rule, and their theoretical analysis is missing. An optimal feature selection rule is needed to select those features with maximum discriminative capacity for discrimination.

Machine Learning Usage In Cyber Security

Machine learning (ML) is not something new that security domain has to adapt or utilize. It has been used and is being used in various areas of cyber security. Different machine learning methods have been successfully deployed to address wide-ranging problems in computer security. Following sections highlight some applications of machine learning in cyber security such as spam detection, network intrusion detection systems and malware detection.

Spam Detection

Traditional approach of detecting spam is usage of rules also known as knowledge engineering. In this method, mails are categorized as spam- or genuine-based set of rules that are created manually either by the user. For example, a set of rules can be:

- If the subject line of an email contains words 'lottery', its spam.
- Any email from a certain address or from a pattern of addresses is spam. However, this approach is not completely effective, as a manual rule doesn't scale because of active spammers evading any manual rules. Using machine learning approach, there is no need specifying rules explicitly; instead, a decent amount of data pre-classified as spam and not spam is being used. Once a machine learning model with good generalization capabilities is learned, it can handle previously unseen spam emails and take decisions accordingly.

Network Intrusion Detection

Network intrusion detection (NID) systems are used to identify malicious network activity leading to confidentiality, integrity or availability violation of the systems in a network. Many intrusion detection systems are specifically based on machine learning techniques due to their adaptability to new and unknown attacks.

Malware Detection

Over the last few years, traditional anti-malware companies have stiff competition from new generation of endpoint security vendors that major on machine learning as a method of threat detection. Using machine learning, machines are taught how to detect threats, and, with this knowledge, the machine can detect new threats that have never been seen before. This is a huge advantage over signature-based detection which relies on recognizing malware that it has already seen.

Machine Learning and Security Information and Event Management (Siem) Solution

Security information and event management (SIEM) solutions have started leveraging machine learning into its latest versions, to make it quicker and easier to maximize the value machine data can deliver to organizations. Certain vendors are enabling companies to use predictive analytics to help improve IT, security and business operations.

Table 1. ML and Dl algorithm classification ranges

Method	Classification Accuracy %
C4.5	80%
ANN	92%
b-Clustering	95%
Intelligible SVM	93.4%
Hybrid model of hierarchical clustering	86%
SVM with RBF	80%
ANN	79%
ANN	85%
LDA-SVM and FFNN	72%
Self-organized Maps (SOM) –clustering	75%
K-means clustering	83%
Convolutional Neural Networks	95%

CONCLUSION

There is a range of different components in a system where each has particular communication input-output and its own set tasks, which provide particular challenges associated with controlling or predicting the behavior of such systems. This chapter emphasizes on securing CPSs is a hard problem, even with the recognition that the goal is not absolute security. The cross study of computing, communication, controlling and other disciplines brought a broad application prospects and more benefits to CPS, but it also brings a lot of new difficulties, such as designing of connection between different components. Thus, the better understanding of the conception and meaning of CPS, provide guidance to integrate better mechanisms with the CPS design ideas. The security objectives to be fulfilled based on possible challenges in CPS, attacks and its countermeasures are discussed based on adoption of machine learning and deep learning thus providing an intelligent CPS.

REFERENCES

Abdelhamid, N., Ayesh, A., & Thabtah, F. (2014). Phishing detection based associative classification data mining. *Expert Systems with Applications, 41*(13), 5948–5959. doi:10.1016/j.eswa.2014.03.019

Alfayyadh, B., Ponting, J., Alzomai, M., & Jøsang, A. (2010). Vulnerabilities in personal firewalls caused by poor security usability. *IEEE Int'l Conf. on Infor. Theor. and Infor. Security*, 682–688.

Alom, M. Z., Bontupalli, V., & Taha, T. M. (2015). Intrusion detection using deep belief networks. *IEEE National Aerospace and Electronics Conference (NAECON)*.

Biggio, Fumera, & Roli. (2014). Security evaluation of pattern classifiers under attack. *IEEE Transactions on Knowledge and Data Engineering, 26*(4), 984-996.

Biggio, B. (2014). *Security evaluation of support vector machines in adversarial environments. In Support Vector Machines Applications* (pp. 105–153). Springer.

Biggio. (n.d.). Evasion attacks against machine learning at test time. *Joint European Conference on Machine Learning and Knowledge Discovery in Databases*, 387-402. doi:10.1109/ICITIS.2010.5689490

Feizollah. (2013). A study of machine learning classifiers for anomaly-based mobile botnet detection. *Malaysian Journal of Computer Science*.

Friedberg, I., McLaughlin, K., Smith, P., Laverty, D., & Sezer, S. (2017). STPA-SafeSec: Safety and security analysis for cyber-physical systems. *J. Inf. Secur. Appl., 34*, 183–196.

Gardiner, J., & Nagaraja, S. (2016). On the Security of Machine Learning in Malware C8C Detection. *ACM Computing Surveys, 49*(3), 1–39. doi:10.1145/3003816

Ge. (2017). Analysis of Cyber-Physical Security Issues via Uncertainty Approaches. In *Advanced Computational Methods in Life Systems Modeling and simulation*. Springer.

Giani, A., Bitar, E., Garcia, M., McQueen, M., Khargonekar, P., & Poolla, K. (2013). Smart grid data integrity attacks. *IEEE Transactions on Smart Grid, 4*(3), 1244–1253.

Hink, R. C. B. (2014). *Machine learning for power systems disturbance and cyber-physical attacks discrimination*. IEEE ISRCS.

Hug, G., & Giampapa, J. A. (2012). Vulnerability assessment of ac state estimation with respect to false data injection cyber-attacks. *IEEE Transactions on Smart Grid, 3*(3), 1362–1370.

Jordan, M. I., & Mitchell, T. M. (2015). Machine learning: Trends, perspectives, and prospects. *Science, 349*(6245), 255–260. doi:10.1126cience.aaa8415 PMID:26185243

Khan, Baharudin, Lee, & Khan. (2010). A review of machine learning algorithms for text documents classification. *Journal of Advances in Information Technology*.

Kurakin, A., Goodfellow, I., & Bengio, S. (2016). *Adversarial examples in the physical world*. arXiv preprint arXiv: 1607.02533

Louridas, P., & Ebert, C. (2016). Machine Learning. *IEEE Software, 33*(5), 110–115. doi:10.1109/MS.2016.114

Manadhata, P. K., & Wing, J. M. (2011). An attack surface metric. *Software Engineering, IEEE Transactions on, 37*(3), 371–386. doi:10.1109/TSE.2010.60

Mitchell, R., & Chen, I.-R. (n.d.). *Effect of intrusion detection and response on reliability of cyber physical systems*. Retrieved from: http://people.cs.vt.edu/~irchen/ps/Mitchell-TR13a.pdf

Mozaffari-Kermani, M., Sur-Kolay, S., Raghunathan, A., & Jha, N. K. (2015). Systematic poisoning attacks on and defenses for machine learning in healthcare. *IEEE Journal of Biomedical and Health Informatics, 19*(6), 1893–1905. doi:10.1109/JBHI.2014.2344095 PMID:25095272

Nelson, B. (2012). Query strategies for evading convex inducing classifiers. *Journal of Machine Learning Research, 13*(May), 1293–1332.

NIST Special Publication 1500-201. (2017). NIST Framework for Cyber-Physical System: volume 1. Overview.

Papernot, N., McDaniel, P., Goodfellow, I., Jha, S., Celik, Z. B., & Swami, A. (2016). *Practical black-box attacks against deep learning systems using adversarial examples.* arXiv preprint arXiv:1602.02697

Papernot, N., McDaniel, P., Jha, S., Fredrikson, M., Celik, Z. B., & Swami, A. (2016). The limitations of deep learning in adversarial settings. In *Security and Privacy (EuroS&P), 2016 IEEE European Symposium on* (pp. 372-387). IEEE. 10.1109/EuroSP.2016.36

Papernot, N., McDaniel, P., Sinha, A., & Wellman, M. (2016). *Towards the Science of Security and Privacy in Machine Learning.* arXiv preprint arXiv:1611.03814

Pascanu, R., Stokes, J. W., Sanossian, H., Marinescu, M., & Thomas, A. (2015). Malware classification with recurrent networks. *IEEE International Conference on Acoustics, Speech and Signal Processing (ICASSP).*

Pasqualetti. (2013). Attacks detection and identification in cyber-physical security systems. *IEEE TAC, 58*(11).

Petit, J., Stottelaar, B., Feiri, M., & Kargl, F. (n.d.). *Remote attacks on automated vehicle sensors: experiments on camera and LiDAR.* Retrieved from: https://pdfs.semanticscholar.org/e06f/ef73f5bad-0489bb033f490d41a046f61878a.pdf

Sabaliauskaite. (2013). Intelligent checkers to improve attack detection in cyber-physical systems. *IEEE CyberC.*

Szegedy, C. (2014). *Intriguing properties of neural networks.* arXiv preprint arXiv: 1312.6199

Tao, L., Golikov, S., Gai, K., & Qiu, M. (2015). A reusable software component for integrated syntax and semantic validation for services computing. *9th Int'l IEEE Symposium on Service-Oriented System Engineering*, 127–132. 10.1109/SOSE.2015.10

Taylor. (2017). Security Challenges and methods for protecting critical infrastructure cyber-physical systems. *IEEE MoWNeT.*

Tonge, A., Kasture, S., & Chaudhari, S. (2013). Cyber security: Challenges for society-literature review. *IOSR Journal of Computer Engineering, 2*(12), 67–75. doi:10.9790/0661-1226775

Wang, J. (2017). *Detecting time synchronization attacks in cyber-physical security systems with machine learning techniques.* IEEE ICDCS.

Wu, L. L. (2014). *Improving system reliability for cyber-physical systems.* Columbia University. Retrieved from: https://www.researchgate.net/profile/Roger_Anderson20/publication/329044383_Leon_Wu_PhD_Thesis_Improving_System_Reliability_for_CyberPhysical_Systems_2014/links/5bf30f83299bf1124fde5df9/Leon-Wu-PhD-Thesis-Improving-System-Reliability-for-CyberPhysical-Systems-2014.pdf

This research was previously published in the Handbook of Research on Machine and Deep Learning Applications for Cyber Security; pages 388-415, copyright year 2020 by Information Science Reference (an imprint of IGI Global).

Chapter 62
Machine Learning and Its Use in E-Commerce and E-Business

Mamata Rath

 https://orcid.org/0000-0002-2277-1012

Birla Global University, India

ABSTRACT

Electronic commerce associated with highly powerful web technology and mobile communication is currently dominating the business world. Current advancements in machine learning (ML) have also further coordinated to creative business applications and e-commerce administrations to reason about complex system and better solutions. In the course of recent years, the business security and machine-learning networks have created novel strategies for secured business frameworks based on computationally learned models. With the improvement of the internet and digital marketing, every financial platform has been more secured and user friendly for monetary transactions.

INTRODUCTION

Electronic commerce associated with highly powerful web technology and mobile communication is currently dominating the Business world. While electronic commerce keeps on profoundly affecting the worldwide business condition, advancements and applications have started to concentrate more on versatile processing and the wireless We b. With this prototype comes another arrangement of issues and issues particularly identified with wireless web based business. At last, specialists and engineers must figure out what undertakings clients truly need to perform whenever from anyplace and choose how to guarantee that data and usefulness to help those errands are promptly accessible and effectively open. This paper gives a diagram of a portion of the significant advances, applications, and issues in the generally new field of wireless webbased business. Wireless online business (additionally called portable commerce or m-commerce) is the advancement, purchasing, and offering of products and ventures through electronic information correspondence arranges that interface with wireless (or versatile) gadgets. Wireless web based business is a subset of wireless figuring, which is the getting to of data

DOI: 10.4018/978-1-6684-6291-1.ch062

frameworks by wireless means. A significant number of the issues that influence wireless registering all in all likewise influence wireless online business. Technologists have been anticipating for a considerable length of time that organizations are on the cusp of a flood in profitability however, up until now, this has not occurred. Most organizations still use individuals to perform monotonous undertakings in records payable, charging, finance, claims the executives, client support, offices the board and the sky is the limit from there.

To put in a leave ask for, we need to navigate twelve stages, every one expecting to enter data the framework should definitely know or settle on a choice that the framework ought to most likely make sense of from your goal. To decide why the financial plan endured a shot for the current month, we need to troll through a hundred columns in a spreadsheet you've physically separated from your account framework. Your frameworks ought to almost certainly figure out which columns are strange and present them. When we present a buy request for another seat, we realize that Bob in obtainment needs to physically settle on a cluster of little choices to process the structure -, for example, regardless of whether your request should be sent to HR for ergonomics endorsement or would it be able to be sent directly to the money related approver.

These little choices make defers that make we and your partners less responsive than we need to be and less powerful than your organization needs we to be. We trust we will before long have much better frameworks at work. Machine learning applications will robotize the majority of the little choices that hold up procedures. It is an imperative subject on the grounds that, over the coming decade, organizations that can turn out to be progressively robotized and increasingly beneficial will surpass those that can't. Also, machine learning will be one of the key empowering influences of this change. Before we get into how machine learning can make your organization increasingly beneficial, we should look why actualizing frameworks in your organization is more troublesome than receiving frameworks in your own life. Accept your own funds for instance. We may utilize a cash the board application to follow your spending. The application reveals to we the amount we spends and what we spend it on and it makes proposals on how we could expand your investment funds. It even naturally gathers together buys to the closest dollar and puts the extra change into your investment account. Cost the executives is an altogether different involvement with work. At work, to perceive how your group is following against their financial plan, we put a demand into the money group and they hit we up the next we ek. In the event that we need to penetrate down into specific details in your financial plan, you're in a tight spot.

E-COMMERCE AND E-BUSINESS SYSTEM

Purchase and Supply Chain in E-Commerce

This primary activity Includes identifying vendors, evaluating vendors, selecting specific products, placing orders. Supply chain is part of an industry value chain that precedes a particular strategic business unit. Procurement includes all purchasing activities, plus monitoring of all elements of purchase transaction. Supply management is a term used to describe procurement activities. Portable web based business additionally incorporates the utilization of gadgets such handheld and PCs interface with figuring resources through wired synchronization. We don't consider this wired type of versatile online business in this paper mainly in light of the fact that it is probably going to be supplanted by wireless gadgets later on. Our emphasis here is on the wireless types of portable commerce.

Production Process and E-Commerce

There are three general approaches to production

1. **Make-to-Stock Items:** Made for inventory (the "stock") in anticipation of sales orders
2. **Make-to-Order Items:** Produced to fill specific customer orders
3. **Assemble-to-Order Items:** Produced using a combination of make-to-stock and make-to-order processes

Problems associated with Production are as follows.

1. Inventory problems
   a. Production manager lacks systematic method for:
      i. Meeting anticipated sales demand
      ii. Adjusting production to reflect actual sales
2. Accounting and purchasing related problems
   b. **Standard Costs**: Normal costs of manufacturing a product. Production and Accounting must periodically compare standard costs with actual costs and then adjust the accounts for the inevitable differences.

Planning in Production

Three important principles for production planning are as follows. Figure 1 represents the detail flow of information in production planning.

1. Work from sales forecast and current inventory levels to create an "aggregate" ("combined") production plan for all products
2. Break down aggregate plan into more specific production plans for individual products and smaller time intervals
3. Use production plan to determine raw material requirements.

Sales Forecasting - Whenever a sale is recorded in Sales and Distribution (SD) module, quantity sold is recorded as a consumption value for that material. Simple forecasting technique includes use of a prior period's sales and then adjust those figures for current conditions. Sales and operations planning (SOP) takes input as sales forecast provided by Marketing and gives the output of production plan designed to balance market demand with production capacity.

Marketing Strategy in E-Commerce

When creating a marketing strategy Managers must consider both the nature of their products and the nature of their potential customers. Most office furnish their product stores on the We b and believe customers organize their needs into product categories. There are Four Ps of marketing as follows and also depicted in fig.2.

- **Product**: Physical item or service that company is selling
- **Price**: Amount customer pays for product
- **Promotion**: Any means of spreading the word about product
- **Place**: Need to have products or services available in different locations

Figure 1. Production planning process

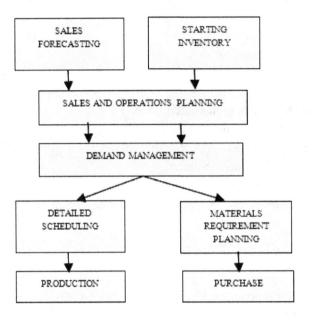

Figure 2. Four P of marketing

Different types of marketing strategies in e-commerce are as follows.

1. **Good First Step in Building a Customer-Based Marketing Strategy**: Identify groups of customers who share common characteristics
2. **Customer-Based Marketing Approaches:** More common on B2B sites than on B2C sites
3. **B2B Sellers**: More aware of the need to customize product and service offerings to match their customers' needs.
4. **Identifying Groups of Potential Customers:** The first step in selling to those customers
5. **Media Selection**: Can be critical for an online firm
6. **Challenge for Online Businesses:** Convince customers to trust them

Segmentation of Marketing Task refers to targeting specific portions of the market with advertising messages such as Segments which usually defined in terms of demographic characteristics and Micromarketing that performs marketing by targeting very small market segments. Further there can be Geographic segmentation which is done by creating different combinations of marketing efforts for each geographical group of customers or Demographic segmentation that uses age, gender, family size, income, education, religion, or ethnicity to group customers. Behavioral segmentation means creation of separate experiences for customers based on their behavior, Occasion segmentation can be done when behavioral segmentation is based on things that happen at a specific time and Usage-based market segmentation refers to customizing visitor experiences to match the site usage behavior patterns of each visitor.

Retention and Attracting Customers

In marketing some costs are involved in retention and attracting customers such as acquisition cost that refers to Money a company spends to draw one visitor to site. Conversion cost refers to Converting first-time visitor into a customer, Conversion cost means Cost of inducing one visitor to make a purchase, sign up for a subscription, or register and Retained customers are they who return to the site one or more times after making their first purchases. Marketing managers are required to have a good sense of how their companies acquire and retain customers. Further a Funnel model is used as a conceptual tool to understand the overall nature of a marketing strategy, very similar to the customer life-cycle model.

Advertisement and E-Commerce

In E-Commerce different methods are used for advertisement such as Banner ad small rectangular object on a We b page, Interactive marketing unit (IMU) ad formats which are standard banner sizes that most We b sites have voluntarily agreed to use, banner exchange network means software used for coordinates ad sharing. Sometimes banner advertising network are also used which acts as a broker betwe en advertisers and We b sites that carry ads. Following metrics are used for advertisement in the web. Cost per thousand (CPM) - Pricing metric used when a company purchases mass media advertising. Trial visit - First time a visitor loads a We b site page. Page view - Each page loaded by a visitor counts. Impression - Each time the banner ad loads.

Email-marketing are also a new methods of marketing in e-commerce. It refers to sending one e-mail message to a customer which costs less than one cent if the company already has the customer's e-mail address. Conversion rate refers to the percentage of recipients who respond to an ad or promotion. Opt-in e-mail refers to practice of sending e-mail messages to people who request information on a particular topic. Table 1. Shows Ecommerce based research and security details.

Table 1. Ecommerce based research and security details

Sl. No	Literature	Year	Ecommerce based techniques in business
1	A. Herzberg et.al	2013	TCP Ack storm DoS attack
2	A.Agah	2006	Security in wireless sensor network
3	I. Almomani et.al	2013	Logic based security architecture in multi-hop communication
4	Z. Bankovic et.al	2011	Improvinf security in WMN with reputation
5	A. Boukerche et.al	2008	Trust based security system for ubiquitous and pervasive computing
6	Abdellaui J. et.al	2018	Multi-point relay selection through estimated spatial relation in smart city
7	A. Sharma et.al	2014	Assessment of QoS based multi-cast routing protocols
8	L.Cuizhi et. al	2011	Key technologies in the development of e-commerce
9	T.Wongkhamdi et.al	2017	Mobile learning readiness in rural area
10	Tao Li et.al	2016	Privacy preserving express delivery with fine grained attribute based access control
11	W. Zhu et.al	2015	Anomaly detection on ecommerce based on variable length behaviour sequence
12	P. Parvinen et.al	2015	Ecommerce engagement and social influence
13	V. Shankara Raman et.al	2014	Enterprise systems enbling smart commerce
14	E. Seth et.al	2014	Mobile commerce with broad perspective
15	B. Fuchs et.al	2011	E-commerce and e-shopping with interactivity and individualization

The intension of e-business is to improve business exercises over the we b by accomplishing worldwide deals and achieving a bigger market gathering. In the UK, 37% of retail organizations have e-business applications on the we b and 22% of the UK populace utilize these frameworks to buy retail things (Rath et.al, 2018). It is conceivable to enhance e-business slant by extending it over to m-commerce. The development of mobile gadgets makes it conceivable to upgrade business exercises through web based business exchanges. Internet business is portrayed as a subset of e-business where online business works at the back end of the e-business condition managing electronic exchanges of the purchasing and offering procedure of e-business. Mobile gadgets can help in web based business on the grounds that the larger part of 79% of youthful grown-ups of the UK populace possesses a mobile telephone (Rath et.al, 2017). Most basic buy through mobile telephones are mobile Ringtones and benefits of up to $600 million have been created by acquiring mobile telephone Ringtones (Rath et.al, 2019). This business idea can be connected to mobile telephones, since the new third generation of mobile telephones have enhanced show screen with better hues and backings HTML content which empowers buys of CD or books on the mobile gadget straightforwardly. An ongoing study showed that 18% of respondents propose that the utilization of mobile innovation can enhance CRM action (Rath et.al, 2018). Nissan automobiles are additionally utilizing wireless PDAs to enhance their nature of administration where staff individuals furnished with their PDAs can manage client enquiries concerning save parts. The businessperson can check costs and hardware accessibility on the spot and give guide input to the client (A. Agah et.al, 2006). The utilization of mobile application programming has helped insurance agency Drive Assists in sparing street voyaging every year with the utilization of their mobile gadgets (I. Almomani et.al, 2013). The John Hopkins Hospital spared $1,000 multi day by utilizing PDAs to transfer pharmaceutical data to the drug specialists progressively and Addenbrooke's Hospital in Cambridge, UK, could finish 176 effective kidney and liver transplants on account of the forward data of organ givers by means of their

Blackberry PDAs (A. Boukerche et.al, 2008). The utilization of mobile gadgets can profit e-business applications by enhancing their efficiency rate. Mobile Commerce or m-Commerce is portrayed as the "blast" or the broad utilization of mobile applications (J. Abdellaoui et.al, 2018), or then again might be depicted as making an exchange or buy using a mobile gadget. In the business world the significance of speed and dependability of data is urgent key of accomplishment and mobile telephones can give that upper hand. A study of 400 IT chiefs recommends that 36% of representatives depend on the utilization of mobile gadgets to browse their messages, 24% utilize mobile applications to change reports while in travel and half of the organizations proposes it is fundamental to enhance mobile data transmission so as to advance mobile business applications .

TECHNOLOGICAL USAGE OF E-COMMERCE

The World Wide We b Consortium (W3C), a not-for-profit group that maintains standards for the Web. It presented its first draft form of XML in 1996; the W3C issued its first formal version recommendation in 1998. Thus, it is a much newer markup language than HTML. In 2000, the W3C released the first version of a recommendation for a new markup language called Extensible Hypertext Markup Language (XHTML).

Companies are using the Internet to connect specific software applications at one organization directly to software applications at other organizations. The W3C defines We b services as software systems that support interoperable machine-to-machine interaction over a network.

The violation of an organization's rights that occurs when a company capable of supervising the infringing activity fails to do so and obtains a financial benefit from the infringing activity.A copyright is a right granted by a government to the author or creator of a literary or artistic work. The right is for the specific length of time provided in the copyright law and gives the author or creator the sole and exclusive right to print, publish, or sell the work.

A patent is an exclusive right granted by the government to an individual to make, use, and sell an invention. In the United States, patents on inventions protect the inventor's rights for 20 years. To be patentable, an invention must be genuine, novel, useful, and not obvious given the current state of technology. In the United States, Congress enacted the Children's Online Protection Act (COPA) in 1998 to protect children from "material harmful to minors." This law was held to be unconstitutional because it unnecessarily restricted access to a substantial amount of material that is lawful, thus violating the First Amendment. Congress was more successful with the Children's Online Privacy Protection Act of 1998 (COPPA), which provides restrictions on data collection that must be followe d by electronic commerce sites aimed at children. This law does not regulate content, as COPA attempted to do, so it has not been successfully challenged on First Amendment grounds.

In 2001, Congress enacted the Children's Internet Protection Act (CIPA). CIPA requires schools that receive federal funds to install filtering software on computers in their classrooms and libraries. Filtering software is used to block access to adult content We b sites. In 2003, the Supreme Court held that CIPA was constitutional. The Internet Engineering Task Force (IETF) worked on several new protocols that could solve the limited addressing capacity of IPv4, and in 1997, approved Internet Protocol version 6 (IPv6) as the protocol that will replace IPv4.

English auctions that offer multiple units of an item for sale and allow bidders to specify the quantity they want to buy are called Yankee auctions. When the bidding concludes in a Yankee auction, the highest bidder is allotted the quantity he or she bid. If items remain after satisfying the highest bidder, those remaining items are allocated to successive lower (next highest) bidders until all items are distributed. Although all successful bidders (except possibly the lowest successful bidder) receive the quantity of items on which they bid, they only pay the price bid by the lowest successful bidder.

Web Portals are very common means of business platforms. Some companies have been successful using the general interest strategy by operating a We b portal. A portal or We b portal is a site that people use as a launching point to enter the We b (the word "portal" means"doorway"). A portal almost always includes a We b directory or search engine, but it also includes other features that help visitors find what they are looking for on the We b and thus make the We b more useful.

Most portals include features such as shopping directories, white pages and yellow pages searchable databases, free e-mail, chat rooms, file storage services, games, and personal and group calendar tools. Ex - AOL, Google. Bing

Electronic Data Interchange (EDI)

Electronic data interchange (EDI) is a computer-to-computer transfer of business information between two businesses that uses a standard format of some kind. The two businesses that are exchanging information are trading partners. Firms that exchange data in specific standard formats are said to be EDI compatible. EDI was first developed In 1987 and United Nations published first standards under the title EDI for Administration, Commerce, and Transport (EDIFACT, or UN/EDIFACT). Then in late 2000 ASC X12 organization and UN/EDIFACT group agreed to develop one common set of international standards.

Figure 3. Basic function in EDI System

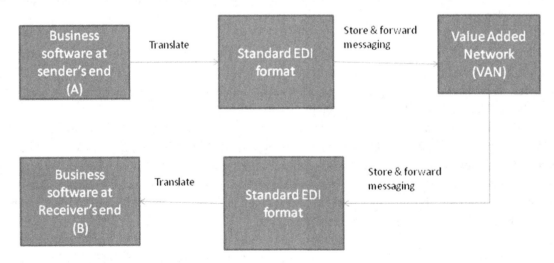

Figure 3 depicts basic function of EDI syatem. EDI Implementation can be complicated, but it can be easily understood from the following example. Consider a company that needs a replacement for one of its metal-cutting machines Paper-based purchasing process, Buyer and vendor are not using any integrated software, Information transfer between buyer and vendor is paper based. EDI replaces postal mail, fax and email. While email is also an electronic approach, the documents exchanged via email must still be handled by people rather than computers. Having people involved slows down the processing of the documents and also introduces errors. Instead, EDI documents can flow straight through to the appropriate application on the receiver's computer (e.g., the Order Management System) and processing can begin immediately. A typical manual process looks like this, with lots of paper and people involvement.

Figure 4. Direct connection EDI

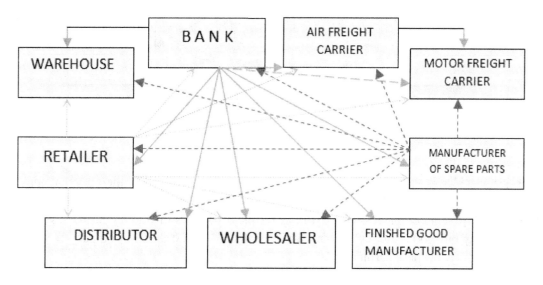

- Direct connection EDI
  - Requires each business in the network to operate its own on-site EDI translator computer
  - EDI translator computers are connected directly to each other using Modems and dial-up telephone lines or dedicated leased lines. Figures 4 and 5 depicts direct and indirect EDI.

Indirect EDI are used for business document transfer from one entity to another business entity. These are any of the documents that are typically exchanged betwe en businesses. The most common documents exchanged via EDI are purchase orders, invoices and advance ship notices. But there are many, many others such as bill of lading, customs documents, inventory documents, shipping status documents and payment documents. Because EDI documents must be processed by computers rather than humans, a standard format must be used so that the computer will be able to read and understand the documents. A standard format describes what each piece of information is and in what format (e.g., integer, decimal, mmddyy). Without a standard format, each company would send documents using its company-specific format and, much as an English-speaking person probably doesn't understand Japanese, the receiver's computer system doesn't understand the company-specific format of the sender's format.

There are several EDI standards in use today, including ANSI, EDIFACT, TRADACOMS and ebXML. And, for each standard there are many different versions, e.g., ANSI 5010 or EDIFACT version D12, Release A. When two businesses decide to exchange EDI documents, they must agree on the specific EDI standard and version.Businesses typically use an EDI translator – either as in-house software or via an

Figure 5. Indirect connection EDI

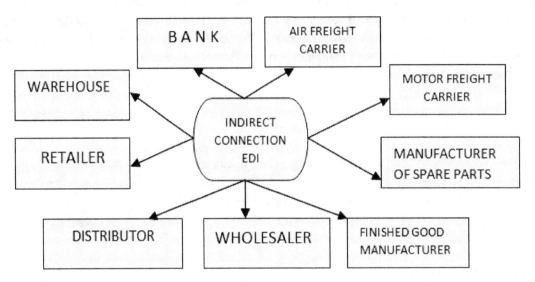

EDI service provider – to translate the EDI format so the data can be used by their internal applications and thus enable straight through processing of documents.The exchange of EDI documents is typically betwe en two different companies, referred to as business partners or trading partners. For example, Company A may buy goods from Company B. Company A sends orders to Company B. Company A and Company B are business partners.

E Mail in Business Communication

The process of using a person or computer to generate a paper form, mailing that filled form to the party,and then having another person enter the data into the trading partner's computer was slow,inefficient, expensive, redundant, and unreliable.

Digital Certificate

A digital certificate or digital ID is an attachment to an e-mail message or a program embedded in a We b page that verifies that the sender or We b site is who or what it claims to be.

A digital certificate includes six main elements, including:

- Certificate owner's identifying information, such as name, organization,
- address, and so on
- Certificate owner's public encryption key
- Dates betwe en which the certificate is valid
- Serial number of the certificate
- Name of the certificate issuer
- Digital signature of the certificate issuer

E Cash and E Wallets

Electronic cash (also called e-cash or digital cash) is a general term that describes any value storage and exchange system created by a private (nongovernmental) entity that does not use paper documents or coins and that can serve as a substitute for government-issued physical currency. A software utility that holds credit card information, owner identification and address information, and provides this data automatically at electronic commerce sites; electronic wallets can also store electronic cash. An electronic wallet (sometimes called an e-wallet), serving a function similar to a physical wallet, holds credit card numbers, electronic cash, owner identification, and owner contact information and provides that information at an electronic commerce site's checkout counter. Electronic wallets give consumers the benefit of entering their information just once, instead of having to enter their information at every site with which they want to do business.

Search Engine in the WEB

A search engine is a We b site that helps people find things on the We b. Search engines contain three major parts. The first part, called a spider, a crawler, or a robot (or simply bot), is a program that automatically searches the We b to find We b pages that might be interesting to people. When the spider finds We b pages that might interest search engine site visitors, it collects the URL of the page and information contained on the page. This information might include the page's title, key words included in the page's text, and information about other pages on that We b site. In addition to words that appear on the We b page, We b site designers can specify additional key words in the page that are hidden from the view of We b site visitors, but that are visible to spiders. These key words are enclosed in an HTML tag set called meta tags. The spider returns this information to the second part of the search engine to be stored. The storage element of a search engine is called its index or database.

Different Card Types Used in E-Commerce

Payment Cards

Businesspeople often use the term payment card as a general term to describe all types of plastic cards that consumers (and some businesses) use to make purchases. The main categories of payment cards are credit cards, debit cards, and charge cards.A credit card, such as a Visa or a MasterCard, has a spending limit based on the user's credit history; a user can pay off the entire credit card balance or pay a minimum amount each billing period. Credit card issuers charge interest on any unpaid balance.

Debit Card

A debit card looks like a credit card, but it works quite differently. Instead of charging purchases against a credit line, a debit card removes the amount of the sale from the cardholder's bank account and transfers it to the seller's bank account. Debit cards are issued by the cardholder's bank and usually carry the name of a major credit card issuer, such as Visa or MasterCard, by agreement betwe en the issuing bank and the credit card issuer. By branding their debit cards (with the Visa or MasterCard name), banks ensure that their debit cards will be accepted by merchants who recognize the credit card brand names.

Charge Card

A charge card, offered by companies such as American Express, carries no spending limit, and the entire amount charged to the card is due at the end of the billing period. Charge cards do not involve lines of credit and do not accumulate interest charges. (Note: In addition to its charge card products, American Express also offers credit cards, which do have credit limits and which do accumulate interest on unpaid balances.) In the United States, many retailers, such as department stores and oil companies that own gas stations, issue their own charge cards.

Smart Card

A smart card is a stored-value card that is a plastic card with an embedded microchip that can store information. Credit, debit, and charge cards currently store limited information on a magnetic strip. A smart card can store about 100 times the amount of information that a magnetic strip plastic card can store. A smart card can hold private user data, such as financial facts, encryption keys, account information, credit card numbers, health insurance information, medical records, and so on.

Electronic Cash in E Commerce System

Although credit cards dominate online payments today, electronic cash shows promise for the future. Electronic cash (also called e-cash or digital cash) is a general term that describes any value storage and exchange system created by a private (nongovernmental) entity that does not use paper documents or coins and that can serve as a substitute for government-issued physical currency. A significant difference betwe en electronic cash and scrip is that electronic cash can be readily exchanged for physical cash on demand. Because electronic cash is issued by private entities, there is a need for common standards among all electronic cash issuers so that one issuer's electronic cash can be accepted by another issuer. This need has not yet been met. Each issuer has its own standards and electronic cash is not universally accepted, as is government-issued physical currency.

Electronic cash has another factor in its favor: Most of the world's population does not have credit cards. Many adults cannot obtain credit cards due to minimum income requirements or past debt problems. Children and teens—eager purchasers representing a significant percentage of online buyers—are ineligible, simply because they are too young. People living in most countries other than the United States hold few credit cards because they have traditionally made their purchases in cash. For all of these people, electronic cash provides the solution to paying for online purchases. Even though there have been many failures in electronic cash, the idea of electronic cash refuses to die. Electronic cash shows particular promise in two applications: the sale of goods and services priced less than $10—the lowe r threshold for credit card payments—and the sale of all goods and services to those persons without credit cards.

Perhaps the most important characteristic of cash is convenience. If electronic cash requires special hardware or software, it is not convenient for people to use. Chances are good that people will not adopt an electronic cash system that is difficult to use. A company currently in the electronic cash business is Internet Cash.

MACHINE LEARNING APPROACHES IN E-COMMERCE AND E-BUSINESS

Machine learning permits ecommerce businesses to make a progressively customized client experience. Today, clients not just like to speak with their most loved brands by and by, howe ver they have generally expected personalization. Truth be told, an investigation by Janrain uncovered that 73% of clients are tired of being given insignificant substance. Man-made reasoning and machine learning offer retailers the capacity to customize every communication with their clients, along these lines furnishing them with a superior ordeal. Through machine learning, retailers can diminish client administration issues before they even happen. Thus, truck deserting rates ought to be lowe r and deals ought to be higher. What's more, not normal for people, client administration bots can give unprejudiced arrangements nonstop.

Machine Learning and Search

Results Improving list items offers tremendous adjustments for retailers. Machine learning can improve ecommerce indexed lists each time a client shops on the site, considering individual inclinations and buy history. Rather than utilizing customary inquiry strategies like watchword coordinating, machine learning can produce a look positioning dependent on pertinence for that specific client. This is particularly imperative for monsters, for example, eBay. With more than 800 million things recorded, the retailer is exploiting man-made reasoning and information to foresee and show the most significant list items.

Computerized Reasoning and Product Recommendation

Omnichannel is the new typical for retail, so we can anticipate that computerized reasoning should utilize not exclusively clients' advanced information, yet in addition break down their in-store conduct. Quite a long time ago, surveillance cameras were just expected to fend off shoplifters, however soon, with the assistance of face acknowledgment calculations, we may begin seeing promotions online for that new ice chest we looked at available. Machine learning can be utilized to prescribe ecommerce items as per different examples in shopping conduct, which will enable we to expand your change rates. By breaking down client information from various channels, the calculation can recognize conduct and acquiring designs which can be utilized to foresee what your clients really need. Individual customers have dependably been related with top of the line shoppers, however on account of computerized reasoning, everybody can exploit virtual ones. Open air item organization The North Face has assembled its own virtual individual customer utilizing the IBM Watson stage. The administration utilizes clients' vocal questions, shopping needs and touring plans as info and prescribes things that meet clients' criteria, but at the same time are reasonable for the area the client intends to utilize them—notwithstanding considering the we ather forecasting.

Artificial Neural Networks as Guidance for Marketing

Neural systems can gain as a matter of fact, perceive designs and anticipate patterns, so they can be utilized to discover what individuals react to, what ought to be changed and what ought to be wiped out from an advertising effort. Microsoft had the capacity to increment direct mailing open rate from 4.9% to 8.2% by utilizing BrainMaker, a neural system programming to augment returns on an advertising effort. Machine Learning Can also Eliminate Fraud.The more information we have, the less demanding it is to spot oddities. Along these lines, we can utilize machine learning to distinguish designs in information, realize what is 'ordinary' and what isn't and get advised when something isn't right. The most widely recognized application for this would be misrepresentation discovery. Retailers are frequently looked with clients who purchase vast sums utilizing stolen cards or withdraw their installments after the things have just been conveyed.

Ecommerce Targeting and Optimization of Price

Dissimilar to in a physical store where we can converse with your clients to discover what they need or need, online shops are hit with enormous measures of client information. Accordingly, client division turns out to be critical for online business, as it enables organizations to adjust their correspondence methodologies for each client. Machine learning can be utilized to comprehend your client's needs and make a customized shopping knowledge. Machine Learning can also play role in Price Optimization .Machine learning calculations can help we not just gather data in regards to valuing patterns, your rivals' costs and interest for different things, howe ver it can consolidate this data with client conduct to decide the best cost for every one of your items. Streamlining your costs will enable we to fulfill your customers just as increment your ROAS.

Product Recommendation

With the development of information, it is a standout amongst the most critical difficulties of current businesses to create information driven frameworks. Logical leaps forward in computerized reasoning (AI) have opened the entryway for a wide scope of utilizations, which can use immense measures of information into genuine business esteem. Driving AI specialist Andrew Ng says that AI is the new power as it will on a very basic level change every modern area, Forrester predicts that AI speculations will develop by 300% in 2017, and Barack Obama noticed that his successor will oversee a nation being changed by AI. Initially, the promotion around huge information and AI was very overpowering and organizations were not by any means beyond any doubt how to respond. Item suggestion is ordinarily the main thing individuals have as a top priority when they consider machine learning for online business. Highlights like "on the off chance that we like item x, we will presumably additionally like item y" have been appeared to work astoundingly we ll, and they can fill in as a significant instrument to control clients through the consistently expanding masses of choices accessible to them. Generally, suggestions have been included by hand based hard-coded item classifications, yet this is very tedious, mistake inclined, and rapidly out-dated.

Search Ranking IN Web Portals

Machine learning can help with highlights like hunt positioning, which permits arranging indexed lists by their evaluated significance. This estimation can consider frequencies of explicit hunt terms just as the specific client profile (for example age go, past item sees, expressing propensities, or past hunt terms). To put it plainly, seek calculations turn out to be less about posting all items that coordinate a given arrangement of letters, and increasingly about anticipating what clients may really need to see, notwithstanding when they probably won't know it yet. Another essential component is question extension, in which the no doubt seek term fruitions are proposed while the client is as yet composing. Aside from commonplace content based pursuit, picture based hunt is turning into an inexorably reasonable alternative. Logical advances in picture acknowledgment through profound neural systems currently give the innovation to utilize pictures of items to discover comparable things on the we b. Notwithstanding that, these techniques can be utilized to characterize outward appearances and perceive feelings. However, despite the fact that the possibility of progressively adjusting commerce administrations to the current passionate condition of a client absolutely appears to be important, organizations still have not exactly made sense of how to incorporate this.

Endeavouring to get help for clients can frequently be a significant baffling background. Clients regularly whine about exceedingly long holding up times, clarifying and re-clarify their concern on numerous occasions, inadequate guidance, or worried workers. Given the high measure of assets that are required to give solid client administration, it isn't amazing that these issues can happen. Machine learning can automatize this procedure through robots that can answer telephone calls. While past frameworks were just ready to manage a thin scope of issues and had visit false impressions, late advances in discourse acknowledgment and common language preparing by means of profound learning have made it conceivable to have a progressively adaptable and characteristic collaboration with robots. Essentially, these techniques have appeared in considering relevant data. Rather than dissecting a discourse sound or a solitary word in seclusion, present day approaches consider data from the entire information and look at it against much of the time happening designs, which has helped the exactness of machine learning models. Aside from telephone calls, machine learning can likewise add to other help stations, for example, naturally noting messages, sorting messages (for example grumbling versus question versus ask for) or offering help by means of chatbots. Chatbots specifically have motivated an assortment of AI new companies that need to change correspondence channels for promoting, counselling, or enlisting.

CONCLUSION

It is a very technical question that comes to the mind of general people that how can machine learning techniques help in electronic commerce. Many things have changed in ecommerce over the last few years and machine learning is getting more involved in such e-commerce activities more and more. Both AI (Artificial Intelligence) and ML (Machine Learning) are the future of ecommerce. AI includes the machine that can complete tasks using human cognition pattern and similar approaches, while machine learning is a section of AI that uses methods to improve the performance of the required system through learning and experiencing over a period of time. Currently, artificial intelligence and machine learning have been used entirely by global companies due to their not so available price. However, it is predicted through survey that by 2020 over 80% of all customer interactions will be handled by AI. Virtual technologies are likely to raise conversion rates and remove online shopping returns. We are already seeing those technologies being used by cosmetics, fashion and furniture companies and by the end of 2020 Augmented Reality will be generating $120 billion in revenue. The above chapter focuses on Ecommerce activities in conventional systems and how they have been improved and automated using machine learning system with special focus on areas in which the e-business has improved using ML techniques.

REFERENCES

Abdellaoui, J. E., & Berradi, H. (2018). Multipoint relay selection through estimated spatial relation in smart city environments. *2018 International Conference on Advanced Communication Technologies and Networking (CommNet)*, 1-10. 10.1109/COMMNET.2018.8360273

Abramov, R., & Herzberg, A. (2013). TCP Ack storm DoS attacks. *Computers & Security*, *33*, 12–27. doi:10.1016/j.cose.2012.09.005

Adnane, A., Bidan, C., & de Sousa Júnior, R. T. (2013). Trust-based security for the OLSR routing proto-col. *Computer Communications*, *36*(10), 1159–1171. doi:10.1016/j.comcom.2013.04.003

Agah, A., Basu, K., & Das, S. K. (2006). Security enforcement in wireless sensor networks: A framework based on non-cooperative games. *Pervasive and Mobile Computing*, *2*(2), 137–158. doi:10.1016/j.pmcj.2005.12.001

Almomani, I., Al-Banna, E., & Al-Akhras, M. (2013). Logic-Based Security Architecture for Systems Providing Multihop Communication. *International Journal of Distributed Sensor Networks*, *2013*, 1–17.

Bankovic, Z., Fraga, D., Manuel Moya, J., Carlos Vallejo, J., Malagón, P., Araujo, Á., ... Nieto-Taladriz, O. (2011). Improving security in WMNs with reputation systems and self-organizing maps. *Journal of Network and Computer Applications*, *34*(2), 455–463. doi:10.1016/j.jnca.2010.03.023

Bansal & Rishiwal. (2014). Assessment of QoS based multicast routing protocols in MANET. *2014 5th International Conference - Confluence The Next Generation Information Technology Summit (Confluence)*, 421-426.

Boukerche, A., & Ren, Y. (2008). A trust-based security system for ubiquitous and pervasive computing environments. *Computer Communications*, *31*(18), 4343–4351. doi:10.1016/j.comcom.2008.05.007

Chaturvedi, S., Mishra, V., & Mishra, N. (2017). Sentiment analysis using machine learning for business intelligence. *IEEE International Conference on Power, Control, Signals and Instrumentation Engineering (ICPCSI)*, 2162-2166. 10.1109/ICPCSI.2017.8392100

Cuizhi, L., & Yunkang, Y. (2011). A study on key technologies in the development of mobile e-commerce. *2011 International Conference on E-Business and E-Government (ICEE)*, 1-4. 10.1109/ICEBEG.2011.5886779

Feng, C., Wu, S., & Liu, N. (2017). A user-centric machine learning framework for cyber security operations center. *IEEE International Conference on Intelligence and Security Informatics (ISI)*, 173-175. 10.1109/ISI.2017.8004902

Fuchs, B., Ritz, T., Halbach, B., & Hartl, F. (2011). Blended shopping: Interactivity and individualization. *Proceedings of the International Conference on e-Business*, 1-6.

Li, Rui, & Yanchao. (2016). PriExpress: Privacy-preserving express delivery with fine-grained attribute-based access control. *2016 IEEE Conference on Communications and Network Security (CNS)*, 333-341.

Parvinen, P., Kaptein, M., Oinas-Kukkonen, H., & Cheung, C. (2015). Introduction to E-Commerce, Engagement, and Social Influence Minitrack. *2015 48th Hawaii International Conference on System Sciences*, 3257-3257. 10.1109/HICSS.2015.393

Seth, E. (2014). Mobile Commerce: A Broader Perspective. *IT Professional, 16*(3), 61–65. doi:10.1109/MITP.2014.37

Shankararaman, V., & Kit, L. E. (2014). Enterprise Systems Enabling Smart Commerce. *2014 IEEE 16th Conference on Business Informatics*, 50-53. 10.1109/CBI.2014.17

Wan, Y., & Wu, C. (2009). Fitting and Prediction for Crack Propagation Rate Based on Machine Learning Optimal Algorithm. *International Conference on E-Learning, E-Business, Enterprise Information Systems, and E-Government*, 93-96. 10.1109/EEEE.2009.31

Wongkhamdi, T., Cooharojananone, N., & Khlaisang, J. (2017). The study of mobile learning readiness in rural area: Case of North-Eastern of Thailand. *2017 International Symposium on Computers in Education (SIIE)*, 1-6. 10.1109/SIIE.2017.8259665

Zhang, S.-H., Gu, N., Lian, J.-X., & Li, S.-H. (2003). Workflow process mining based on machine learning. *Proceedings of the 2003 International Conference on Machine Learning and Cybernetics (IEEE Cat. No.03EX693)*, 2319-2323. 10.1109/ICMLC.2003.1259895

Zhao, L., & Li, F. (2008). Statistical Machine Learning in Natural Language Understanding: Object Constraint Language Translator for Business Process. *IEEE International Symposium on Knowledge Acquisition and Modeling Workshop*, 1056-1059. 10.1109/KAMW.2008.4810674

Zhu, Fu, & Han. (2015). Online anomaly detection on e-commerce based on variable-length behavior sequence. *11th International Conference on Wireless Communications, Networking and Mobile Computing (WiCOM 2015)*, 1-8.

Chapter 63
A Machine Learning Approach for Predicting Bank Customer Behavior in the Banking Industry

Siu Cheung Ho
The Hong Kong Polytechnic University, Hong Kong

Kin Chun Wong
The Hong Kong Polytechnic University, Hong Kong

Yuen Kwan Yau
The Hong Kong Polytechnic University, Hong Kong

Chi Kwan Yip
The Hong Kong Polytechnic University, Hong Kong

ABSTRACT

Currently, Chinese commercial banks are facing extremely tremendous pressure, including financial disintermediation, interest rate marketization, and internet finance. Meanwhile, increasing financial consumption demand of customers further intensifies the competition among commercial banks. Hence, it is very important to store, process, manage, and analyze the data to extract knowledge from the customer to predict their investment direction in future. Customer retention and fraud detection are the main information for the bank to predict customer behavior. It may involve the privacy data and sensitive data of the customer. Data security and data protection for the machine learning prediction is necessary before data collection. The research is focused on two parts: the first part is data security of machine learning and second part is machine learning prediction. The result is to prove the data security for the machine learning is important. Using different machining learning analysis tool to enhance the performance and reliability of machine learning applications, the customer behavior prediction accuracy can be enhanced.

DOI: 10.4018/978-1-6684-6291-1.ch063

INTRODUCTION

Banks was obliged to collect, analyze, and store massive amounts of data. But rather than viewing this as just a compliance exercise, machine learning and data science tools can transform this into a possibility to learn more about their clients to drive new revenue opportunities. In order to predict the customer behavior, we used machine learning algorithm by python to evaluate the customer segmentation for prediction. This section introduced the Chinese banking industry, the statement of problem in the banking industry, the project aim, objective and project scope, and project development schedule.

OVERVIEW OF CHINESE BANKING INDUSTRY

For banks globally, 2018 could be a pivotal year in accelerating the transformation into more strategically focused, technologically modern, and operationally agile institutions. They might remain dominant in a rapidly evolving ecosystem. According to Investopedia (Investopedia, 2018), the banking system in China used to be monolithic, with the People's Bank of China (PBC), which was the central bank, as the main entity authorized to conduct operations in that country. In the early 1980s, the government started opening up the banking system and allowed four state-owned specialized banks to accept deposits and conduct banking business. These five specialized banks were the Industrial & Commercial Bank of China (ICBC), China Construction Bank (CCB), Bank of China (BOC), Bank of Communications (BOC) and Agricultural Bank of China (ABC). The data security of machine learning was conducted before start the machine learning prediction.

In this work, supervised artificial neural network algorithm was implemented for classification purpose. First, challenge of Chinese banking industry was defined. Second, literature review for the machine learning approach and ANN model was evaluated. Third, data visualization and evaluation by using ANN algorithm had been analyzed for classifying the customer pattern. Fourth, the accuracy rate of customer behavior prediction was conducted. Lastly, after find tuning parameters by using XGB Classifier, the better result was awarded. Yaokai (Yaokai et al, 2018) expressed the most serious problems in recent years including problems of privacy leakage and denial of services. Early stage detection of cyber-attack was important and proposed different selection approach to test the performance of machine learning algorithm. The process had six stages. These were session splitting, feature extracting, feature ranking, cross validation, removing features gradually, and classifier.

CHALLENGE OF CHINESE BANKING INDUSTRY

Accuracy customer data prediction was essential for planning the business. After that, being armed with information about customer behaviors, interactions, and preferences, data specialists with the help of accurate machine learning models could unlock new revenue opportunities for banks by isolating and processing only this most relevant clients' information to improve business decision-making. This was a challenge to predict the customer pattern and behavior for planning the business in advance in this dynamic competition environment. Zhenyu (Zhenyu et al, 2018) stated that "*Machine learning is one of the most prevalent techniques in recent decades which has been widely applied in various fields. Among them, the applications that detect and defend potential adversarial attacks using machine learning method provide promising solutions in cybersecurity.*" The application of machine learning on cybersecurity and reliability and security of machine learning system was conducted and analyzed the potential security threats against a machine learning approach in three phases of testing, training and data privacy.

PROJECT AI, OBJECTIVE AND SCOPE

This project scope included the development of Artificial Neural Network (ANN) model with 10,000 record datasets to investigate and predict which of the customers were more likely to leave the bank soon. The ANN model was developed through finding the best correlations in the dataset through data visualization technique and training a classifier which could accurately predict parameter based on the customer data. Through the use of machine learning models (Deep Learning A-Z – ANN Dataset), predict customers behaviors (e.g. exit or stay), and based on their information in the bank.

PROJECT WORK SCHEDULE AND DIVISION OF LABOUR

The project summary of the project work schedule and division of labour shown in Figure 1. It was the Gantt Chart to let the entire project member to follow the project schedule. Some project tasks started in parallel. Base on the dependencies of project task in Table 1, the activity network detail was stated in Figure 1 also.

Table 1. Project work schedule and division of labour

Task Description	Description of Goals/Benchmarks
Literature review of different Machine Learning algorithms for data analysis	Select an appropriate algorithm for the selected dataset with a sound theoretical basis
Data visualization for the selected dataset	By using visual elements like charts, graphs and plots, observe trends and identify patterns in the selected dataset.
Pre-processing of the data	Pre-processing of the data includes two main steps which were data cleaning and data transformation. Data cleaning was performed through filling in missing values and removing outliers. Data transformation referred to the normalization of the data
Build an Artificial Neural Network	Build an Artificial Neural Network in python using the pre-processed data and Keras library. The network should consisted 2-3 hidden layers using appropriate activation functions. Train the model iteratively until a reasonable good accuracy was observed (e.g. 80%).
Evaluating, improving and tuning the model	Evaluate the model performance through the test dataset. Compare the predicted result to the actual result and make appropriate adjustments to the model to improve accuracy.
Report preparation	The report was clearly identified the problem statement associated with the dataset and describe how to develop an ANN model step by step. Provide an insightful evaluation of the model and digged out some hidden patterns and relations in the dataset.
Presentation slides	A brief summarization of the problem statement, the methodologies used to approach this problem and the ANN model.

Figure 1. Gantt Chart for the work schedule and division of labor

PROJECT GANTT CHART

	TASK NAME	TEAM MEMBER*	START DATE	END DATE	START ON DAY*	DURATION* (WORK DAYS)
Machine Learning - Deep Learning A-Z - ANN dataset						
1	Literature review of different Machine Learning algorithms for data analysis	A	26/11/2018	27/11/2018	0	2
2	Data visualization for the selected dataset	D, M & Q	28/11/2018	1/12/2018	2	4
3	Pre-processing of the data	D, M & Q	2/12/2018	4/12/2018	6	3
4	Build an Artificial Neural Network	J & K	5/12/2018	8/12/2018	9	4
5	Evaluating, improving and tunning the model	J & K	9/12/2018	11/12/2018	13	3
6	Report preparation	A	12/12/2018	16/12/2018	16	5
7	Presentation slides	A	14/12/2018	16/12/2018	18	3

*A - ALL, D - Dee, J - Jack, K - Kin, M - Miki , Q - Queenie

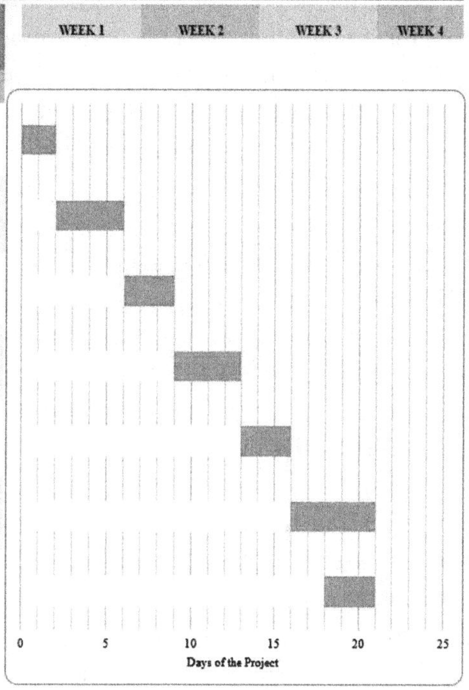

LITERATURE REVIEW

Predicting banking customer behaviors using machine learning approach to improve the prediction of customer retention in the bank was a challenging task in the worldwide banking industry. Vahid (Vahid et al., 2014) expressed that the training data and the test data was drawn from the same distribution, which was hard to be met in real world banking applications for the traditional machine learning approach. Therefore, this study evaluated the machine learning algorithms such as Artificial Neural Network (ANN) and AI platform runtime software for analyzing the workable solution to predict the customer behaviors in banking industry.

DATA SECURITY AND DATA PROTECTION

Before starting the data collection for customer behavior analysis, the data security and data protection was a critical element before using the customer data for prediction. Charles (Charles et al., 2017)) expressed the potential malicious attacks and compromised hosts may be missed in the enterprise. Machine learning was a viable approach to reduce the false positive rate and improve the productivity of Security Operation Center (SOC). Charles (Charles et al., 2017) proposed Security Information and Event Management (SIEM) System to normalize security events from different preventive technologies and flag alert to evaluate the potential malicious attacks for protecting the sensitive data in safe. Yan and J.P (Yan and J.P, 2008) introduced machine learning deals with the issue of how to build programs that improve their performance at some task through experience and suggested 6 modules to monitor the events on the computer and network such as user monitor, process monitor, network monitor, traffic monitor, file monitor and clipboard monitor. It also stated that *"Machine learning deals with the issue of how to build programs that improve their performance at some task through experience. Machine learning algorithms have proven to be of great practical value in a variety of application domains. They are particularly useful for (a) poorly understood problem domains where little knowledge exists for the humans to develop effective algorithms; (b) domains where there are large databases containing valuable implicit regularities to be discovered; or (c) domains where programs must adapt to changing conditions."* Anna and Erhan (Anna and Erhan, 2016) combined Machine Learning (ML) and Data Mining (DM) methods for analyzing the cyber security in support of intrusion detection. The complexity of ML/DM algorithms was addressed to solve problems in six phases: 1) business understanding, 2) data understanding, 3) data preparation, 4) modeling, 5) evaluation, and 6) deployment for understanding the metrics with different information. To perform anomaly detection and misuse Intrusion Detection System (IDS) was the important datasets for training and testing the systems.

Koosha (Koosha et al., 2016) formalized a machine learning algorithm for cyber forensic and protecting the possible attack from the data collection for decision making. The key process was data acquisition, feature extraction, classification and decision making. The database information was analyzed. Attack stimulation was run to validate whether the machine learning algorithm was suitable for cyber forensic and protection. Janice and Anthony (Janice and Anthony, 2016) identified the weakest areas in Internet of Things (IoT) and proposed using machine learning within an IoT gateway to help secure the system. Carla (Carla,2017) suggested the Intelligent Cyber Security Assistant (ICSA) architecture for providing intelligent assistance to a human security specialist. The information workflow was the important role in ICSA architecture. The processes were created domain specific data model, identify features, identify and implement artificial intelligence machine learning methods, and trained implementation artificial intelligence machine learning methods. Yaokai (Yaokai et al., 2018) evaluated Command & Control (C&C) communication between compromised bots and the C&C server. It was in the preparation phase of distributed attacks and found that the detection performance was generally getting better if more features were utilized. The captioned finding was the key indicator for helping to develop the machine learning algorithms.

MACHINE LEARNING ALGORITHMS

Priyanka and Nagaraj (Priyanka and Nagaraj, 2017) stated that *"Customer churn prediction in commercial bank. They used Support Vector Machine algorithm for classification purpose. To improve the performance of the SVM model random sampling method is used and F-measure is selected for evaluating predictive power in this paper. They also developed Logistic regression model and made comparisons between developed models. The results clears that the SVM model random with sampling method works bette*r." The growing importance of analytics in banking cannot be underestimated. Machine learning algorithms and data science techniques could significantly improve bank's analytics strategy since every use case in banking was closely interrelated with analytics. As the availability and variety of information was rapidly increasing, analytics was becoming more sophisticated and accurate. Mei-Fang and Gin-Yen (Mei-Fang and Gin-Yen, 2008) investigated some key factors by using regression analysis method to predict the turnover intentions in the Taiwanese retail banking sector. Define the critical issue in advance was necessary. To better evaluate the credit risk assessment in the commercial bank, empirical analysis was critical part influence for the bank to make the decision (Guo et al., 2015).

ARTIFICAL NEURAL NETWROK (ANN)

Manging the customer relationship was a crucial problem in the telecommunications industry for analysis the customer behaviour and Customer Lifetime Value (CLV) to plan the cross selling and up-selling to the customer and building up the loyality to the company that was the improtant. Artificial neural network (ANN) was proposed by using Multi- Layer Perceptron (MLP) network with Levenberg-Marquardt algorithm to predict the CLV and the prediction result was positive (Yi et al. 2008). Customer prediction was also a extremely elements what the banking industry looking for.

The potential value of available information was astonishing: the amount of meaningful data indicating actual signals, not just noise, had grown exponentially in the past few years, while the cost and size of data processors had been decreasing. Distinguishing truly relevant data from noise contributes to effective problem solving and smarter strategic decisions. Figrue 2 was the structure of Artificial Neural Network (ANN) consists of three basic layers such as input, hidden and output layer. (Priyanka and Nagaraj 2017)

Figure 2. A neuron and artificial neural network

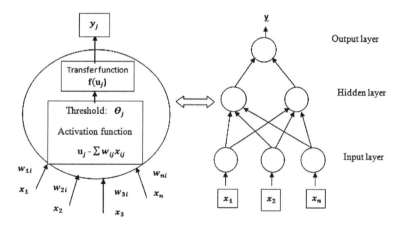

Saad (Saad et al., 2013) reviewed the cost of retaining an existing one from customer acquisition to customer retention. The results shown that "*Churn prediction has emerged as the most crucial Business Intelligence (BI) application that aims at identifying customers who are about to transfer their business to a competitor.*" ANN algorithm was used to predict the customer intention. Sanket (Sanket et al.,2018) built a multi-layered neural network for churn prediction based on customer features, support features, usage features and contextual features from data collection, pre-processing, data store, ANN classification, and then will churn or would not churn. Figure 3 was the churn neural architecture. The accuracy results were shown as 80.03%.

Figure 3. Churn neural architecture (Sanket et al., 2018)

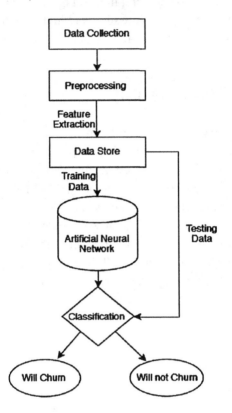

AI PLATFORM RUNTIME SOFTWARE

Yibing (Yibing et al., 2014) measured systemic risk of commercial banks in Chinese banking system by using Conditional Value-at-Risk (CoVaR) approach and extended a modified Support Vector Regression (SVR) to identify the degree of "risk externalities" for predicting systemic risk of commercials banks. Therefore, systemic prediction approach was necessary. Chang-Yun (Chang-Yun et al., 2005) stated that *"Between software architecture conception and concrete realization, semantic gap exists, the structure problem spreads to inner parts of operating system and middleware, software architecture cannot be observed and controlled by end user."* Refer to Pat Research (Pat Research, 2018), AI platform was classified as either weak AI / narrow AI, which was for a particular task or unfamiliar tasks to find out the solution. AI platform could be applied in Machine learning, automation, natural language processing and natural language understanding, and cloud infrastructure.

RESEARCH METHODOLOGY AND DATA VISUALIZATION AND EVALUATION

This chapter elaborates on the definition of data visualization, analysis the dataset of banking customer, and using ANN algorithm to evaluate the dataset through python. Data pre-processing, artificial neural network development, tuning of the artificial neural network, and data evaluation for runtime software analysis would be conducted.

DATA VISUALIZATION FOR DATASET SELECTION

The dependent variable in Table 2, the value that we are going to predict, will be the exit of the customer from the bank (binary variable 0 if the customer stays and 1 if the client exit).

Table 2. ANN dataset

Row Number	Customer Id	Surname	Credit Score	Geography	Gender	Age	Tenure	Balance	Num Of Products	HasCrCard	Is Active Member	Estimated Salary	Exited
1	15634602	Hargrave	619	France	Female	42	2	0	1	1	1	101348.88	1
2	15647311	Hill	608	Spain	Female	41	1	83807.9	1	0	1	112542.58	0
...	...	...	...	...	...	...	...	...	...	...	...	...	...

The independent variables were:

- **Credit Score:** Reliability of the customer
- **Geography:** Where is the customer from
- **Gender:** Male or Female
- Age
- **Tenure:** Number of years of customer history in the company
- **Balance:** The money in the bank account
- Number of products of the customer in the bank
- **Credit Card:** If the customer has or not the CC
- **Active:** If the customer is active or not
- **Estimated Salary:** Estimation of salary based on the entries

PRE-PROCESSING DATASET

Data pre-processing was an important step in the machine learning projects particularly applicable for data-gathering methods, it often loosely controlled, resulting in out-of-range value (Data pre-processing, 2018). Through the data visualization to analysis the dataset that had not been carefully screened for such problems could produce misleading results. The fundamental analysis results were shown in Figure 4 to Figure 25. The research method was divided in 6 steps as: Step 1: Load the Dataset Information, Step 2: Analysis the Customer Segment, Step 3: Attributes with Correlation to Retention, Step 4: Attributes without correlation to Retention, Step 5: Dataset Matrix of All Attributes, and Step 6: Outliers.

Step 1: Load the Dataset Information

Figure 4. Dataset information

```
# Importing the dataset
dataset = pd.read_csv('Churn_Modelling.csv')
```

Step 2: Analysis the Customer Segment

The basic information from Age Distribution, Top Ten Mode of Customer was come from age group of 31 – 40.

Figure 5. Age distribution

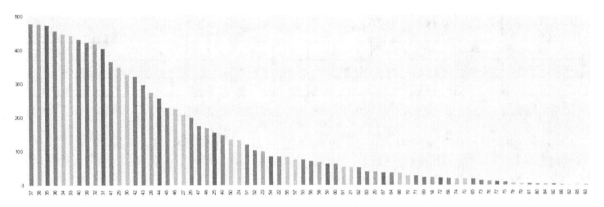

And also, they were come from France, Germany and Spain.

Figure 6. Distribution country

By plotting several graphs with different attributes against Retention, such as Age, Balance, No. of Product, Is Active Member, Estimated Salary, Credit Score and Has Credit Card, we found some attributes were correlated to Retention.

Step 3: Attributes with Correlation to Retention

1.   Age vs. Retention
     More than 2/3 of customer aged between 45 – 60 exited, and customer aged between the ages of 20 – 40, it was much more willing to keep their account.

Figure 7. Attributes with correlation to retention

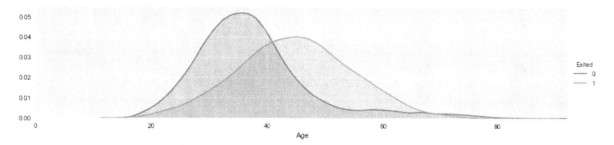

2.   Balance vs. Retention
     Customers having Zero Balance are more willing to keep their account

Figure 8. Customer Balance vs. Retention

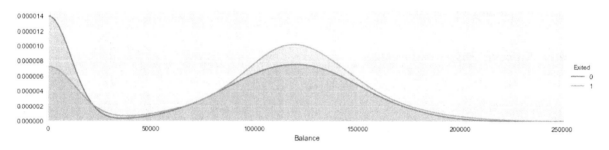

3.   No. of Product vs. Retention
     If customer had 2 Bank's Product, great chance to retain their accounts.

Figure 9. Number of Products vs. Retention

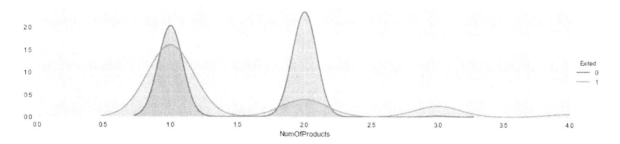

4.   Is Active Member vs. Retention
     If customer was active member, less chance to leave the bank.

Figure 10. Active Member vs. Retention

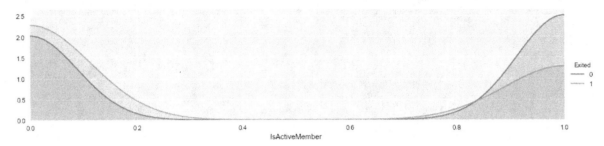

Step 4: Attributes Without Correlation to Retention

We used two curves to represent whether the customer exited or not, if two curves always overlap each other along the y-axis, it implied that attribute was not correlated to Retention.

1.   Estimated Salary vs. Retention

Figure 11. Estimated Salary vs. Retention

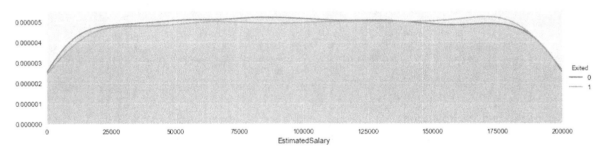

2.   Credit Score vs. Retention

Figure 12. Credit Score vs. Retention

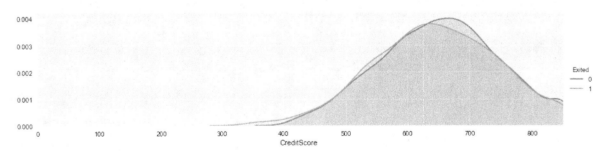

3.   Has Credit Card vs. Retention

Figure 13. Has Credit Card vs Retention

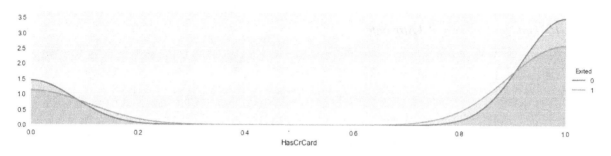

Step 5: Dataset Matrix of All Attributes

From below matrix, Age vs Exited has the largest value, this means Age of customer was the most correlated attribute to Retention.

Figure 14. Dataset Matrix of All Attributes

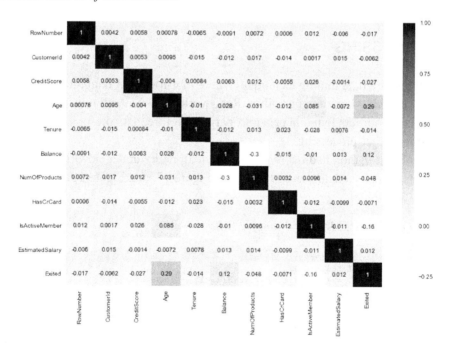

Step 6: Outliers

Usually, the accuracy of prediction was affected by some exaggerated data, thus data pre-processing was required for finding the outlier. From diagram below, two outliers were caught, one was having huge amount of Balance. Another one was having a great amount of Estimated Salary.

Figure15. Dataset Matrix of All Attributes

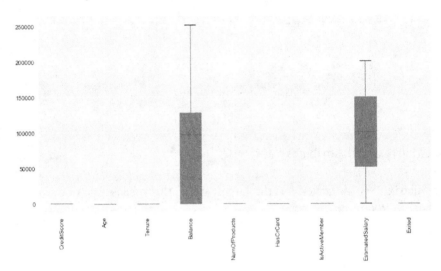

DATA PRE-PROCESSING

Data pre-processing was a data mining technique, which transform raw data into a specific format that was recognized by machine learning algorithm. Real-world data was often incomplete and contained many errors such as the outliers found in previous part. Therefore, data pre-processing was critical and must be done before further processing.

Scikit-learn library in python had many pre-built functionality under sklearn. Preprocessing which could be applied on our selected dataset as Figure 16, Figure 17, and Figure 18.

Figure 16. Convert Categorical Data to Numeric Data

```
# Encoding categorical data
X_1 = LabelEncoder()
X[:, 1] = X_1.fit_transform(X[:, 1])
X_2 = LabelEncoder()
X[:, 2] = X_2.fit_transform(X[:, 2])
onehotencoder = OneHotEncoder(categorical_features = [1])
X = onehotencoder.fit_transform(X).toarray()
X = X[:, 1:]
```

1. LabelEncoder function was used in order to convert 'Geography' and 'Gender' column to suitable numeric data

Figure 17. Data Normalisation

```
from sklearn.preprocessing import StandardScaler
StandardScaler = StandardScaler()
X_train = StandardScaler.fit_transform(X_train)
X_test = StandardScaler.transform(X_test)
```

2. StandardScaler function was used for data normalization, which scale the dataset within a specified range to prevent domination of any attribute.

Figure 18. Code of Oversampling

```
#To perform over-sampling to prevent one class dominates the other
sm  = SMOTE(random_state=42)
X, y = sm.fit_sample(X, y)
```

3. Imblearn library was imported for the implementation of SMOTE - Synthetic Minority Oversampling Technique to prevent the domination of one class over the other.

ARTIFICAL NEURAL NETWORK DEVELOPMENT

ANN was a computer program designed to process information, which was inspired by the human brain. A simple ANN model was trained with stochastic gradient descent and used to predict customer's behaviors in banking industry. Keras was a powerful easy-to-use Python library that contains complicated numerical computation libraries Theano and TensorFlow. It had many pre-built functionalities under Keras model and Keras layers which could be used for developing a neural network. With the help of this library, it was taken no more than a few of codes to define and train a neural network model. A fully-connected network structure with one hidden layer for this project was established and shown in below.

Figure 19. A Fully-connected Network Structure

```
# Initialising the ANN
classifier = Sequential()

# Adding the input layer and the hidden layers
classifier.add(Dense(units = 6, kernel_initializer = 'uniform', activation = 'relu', input_dim = 11))
classifier.add(Dense(units = 6, kernel_initializer = 'uniform', activation = 'relu'))

# Adding the output layer
classifier.add(Dense(units = 1, kernel_initializer = 'uniform', activation = 'sigmoid'))
```

The number of input variables was 11 as specified in the **input dim** argument in the first layer because we had 11 independent variables in the dataset. Fully connected layers were defined using the 'Dense' function of Keras library. The first argument was the number of neurons in the layer, the second argument was the initialization method and the third argument was the activation function.

1. The number of neurons in the hidden layer was chosen to be ½ the size of the input layer and output layer. Therefore, the **unit** argument was set to 6.
2. A uniform weight distribution was the default initialization method in Keras, which generated a small random number between 0 and 0.05 to initialize the neural network. Therefore, **kernel_initializer** argument was set to 'uniform'.
3. 'Relu' activation function was used in the first two layers to reduce the likelihood of vanishing gradient. 'Sigmoid' activation function was used in the output layer to ensure the network output was between 0 and 1 for easy mapping.

After the fully-connected network layers were defined in the previous step, the model could be compiled using the 'compile' function as below.

Figure 20. A Fully-connected Network Layer with Compile Function

```
# Compiling the ANN
classifier.compile(optimizer = 'adam', loss = 'binary_crossentropy', metrics = ['accuracy'])

# Fitting the ANN to the Training set
classifier.fit(X_train, y_train, batch_size = 10, epochs = 100)
```

Since this project was considered as a binary classification problem (e.g. exit or stay), the **loss** argument was set to 'binary_crossentropy' which could optimize the logarithmic loss for binary classification according to Keras documentations. The **optimizer** argument was chosen to be 'adam' simply for efficient computation. The model was then trained by calling the fit function using small number of iterations 100 and used a relatively small batch size of 10. These parameters were tested and modified at later stage by trial and error. After the model was fully trained, the performance of the model was evaluated using the test dataset as shown below. This gives us an overall idea of how well the model performed on new data.

Figure 21. Diagram of Accuracy of the Model

```
#Test the model on the test dataset and compute the accuracy of model

# Predicting the Test set results
y_pred = classifier.predict(X_test)
y_pred = (y_pred > 0.5)

cm = confusion_matrix(y_test, y_pred)
ascore = accuracy_score(y_test, y_pred)
print(cm)
print("Accuracy of the model is :", ascore)

[[1412  205]
 [ 301 1268]]
Accuracy of the model is :  0.8411801632140615
```

The performance of the model was concluded to be 84.11% which was considered to be reasonably good. However, fine tuning of parameters might be able to further improve the model accuracy.

TUNING OF THE ARTIFICAL NEURAL NETWORK

Parameter optimization was a big part of machine learning because that neural network was difficult to configure with a lot of parameters which need to be set. Choosing the right parameter for the neural network was critical to the model performance. Scikit-learn library in python had many pre-built machine learning algorithms to tune the parameters of Keras deep learning models. GridSearchCV class was used as the primary parameter optimization technique for this project. A dictionary of parameters evaluation had been defined in the **parameter** argument in Figure 22. Different batch size, epochs and optimizer was analyzed in order to find the optimized parameters for our model.

Figure 22. Parameter Argument

```
#Part 4 - Tuning the ANN and improving the accuracy
from keras.wrappers.scikit_learn import KerasClassifier
from sklearn.model_selection import GridSearchCV
from keras.models import Sequential
from keras.layers import Dense
def build_classifier(optimizer):
    classifier = Sequential()
    classifier.add(Dense(units = 6, kernel_initializer = 'uniform', activation = 'relu', input_dim = 11))
    classifier.add(Dense(units = 6, kernel_initializer = 'uniform', activation = 'relu'))
    classifier.add(Dense(units = 1, kernel_initializer = 'uniform', activation = 'sigmoid'))
    classifier.compile(optimizer = optimizer, loss = 'binary_crossentropy', metrics = ['accuracy'])
    return classifier
classifier = KerasClassifier(build_fn = build_classifier)
parameters = {'batch_size': [25, 32],
              'epochs': [250, 300],
              'optimizer': ['adam', 'rmsprop']}
grid_search = GridSearchCV(estimator = classifier,
                           param_grid = parameters,
                           scoring = 'accuracy',
                           cv = 10)
grid_search = grid_search.fit(X_train, y_train)
best_parameters = grid_search.best_params_
best_accuracy = grid_search.best_score_

print("Accuracy of the model is :", best_accuracy)
print("Best parameters of the model is :", best_parameters)
```

The GridSearchCV function constructed and evaluated one model for each combination of parameters. Once completed, the best result observed during the optimization procedure was accessed from the **best_score_** parameter and the **best_params_** parameter described the combination that achieved the best results.

Figure 23. Best-score-parameter and Best-params-parameter

```
Epoch 298/300
12740/12740 [==============================] - 1s 75us/step - loss: 0.3342 - acc: 0.8470
Epoch 299/300
12740/12740 [==============================] - 1s 75us/step - loss: 0.3368 - acc: 0.8464
Epoch 300/300
12740/12740 [==============================] - 1s 75us/step - loss: 0.3367 - acc: 0.8488
Accuracy of the model is : 0.8445054945054945
Best parameters of the model is : {'batch_size': 25, 'epochs': 300, 'optimizer': 'adam'}
```

In our case, the accuracy of model after tuning of parameters was 84.45% which was not much of an increase from previous step. The parameters that achieved these results were a batch size of 25, epochs of 300 and an optimizer of 'adam'. The result proved that determining suitable training and architectural parameters of an ANN model was still remained in a difficult task. Many trials and error experiments must be done in order to find the best parameter for the model.

XGBOOST

XGBoost stands for Extreme Gradient Boosting which was developed by Tianqi Chen in 2016. It was a powerful learning algorithm based on decision tree which allowed parallel and distributed computing and an optimal usage of memory resources. XGBoost used ensemble learning method which combined several machine learning algorithms into one predictive model to achieve the best possible accuracy. Therefore, XGBoost had become a widely used machine learning algorithm among data science industry. It considered as the most useful and robust solution for applying in many real-world problems.

Python already had an in-built library for XGBoost which might be easily imported. A simple XG-Boost classifier for this problem was built as shown in Figure 24.

Figure 24. XGBoost Classifier

```
import xgboost as xgb

model = xgb.XGBClassifier(max_depth = 12,random_state=7,n_estimators=100,eval_metric = 'auc' ,min_child_weight = 3
                          ,colsample_bytree = 0.75, subsample= 0.8)
model.fit(X_train, y_train)


XGBClassifier(base_score=0.5, booster='gbtree', colsample_bylevel=1,
       colsample_bytree=0.75, eval_metric='auc', gamma=0,
       learning_rate=0.1, max_delta_step=0, max_depth=12,
       min_child_weight=3, missing=None, n_estimators=100, n_jobs=1,
       nthread=None, objective='binary:logistic', random_state=7,
       reg_alpha=0, reg_lambda=1, scale_pos_weight=1, seed=None,
       silent=True, subsample=0.8)
```

Parameter Setting

- **Max_depth:** This parameter represents the depth of each tree. It was found that there's no performance gain of increasing it after it was set to 12. Therefore, this value was chosen to be 12 to simplify the model and avoid overfitting.
- **Min_child_depth:** This parameter represents minimum number of samples that a node can represent in order to be split further. Since this was an imbalanced classified problem as shown in previous chapter, therefore a value of 3 was chosen for this model.
- **Subsample:** This parameter represented the percentage of rows taken to build the tree. Typical values range between 0.8-1.0, therefore a value of 0.8 was chosen for this model.
- **Colsample_bytree:** This parameter represents the percentage of columns to be randomly samples for each tree. Typical values range between 0.5-1.0, therefore a value of 0.75 was chosen for this model.
- **N_estimators:** This parameter represents the number of trees (or rounds) in an XGBoost model. The default value for this parameter was 100.

- **Eval_metric:** This parameter represents the evaluation metrics for validation of data. "auc" was chosen for this project which stands for area under the curve.

KEY FINDING AND ANALYSIS

Through the captioned finding the accuracy had been improved using XGBoost algorithm. Confusion matrix algorithm and predicting bank customer behaviors in banking industry was discussed in this study.

CONFUSIONG MARTIX

Confusion matrix (error matrix or matching matrix) was a statistical tool used to measure the accuracy and percentage of error of our machine learning algorithm. It was a 2-dimensional table comparing predicted result and actual situation. Accuracy, type I & II Errors and other measures such as precision and recall was calculated from the confusion matrix. Accuracy, type I error and type II error were calculated as a comparison of performance for the ANN and XGBoost algorithm.

Table 3. A General Format of Confusion Matrix

		Actual Class	
		Stay	**Leave**
Predicted Class	Stay	True Positive (TP)	False Positive (FP)
	Leave	False Negative (FN)	True Negative (TN)

Table 3 shows a typical format of a confusion matrix. Given that:

$$Accuracy = \frac{TP + TN}{TP + TN + FP + FN} \quad (1)$$

$$Type\ I\ Error = \frac{FP}{TP + FP} \quad (2)$$

$$Type\ II\ Error = \frac{FN}{FN + TN} \quad (3)$$

Table 4 showed the confusion matrix of ANN model (pre-tuning). From the above table, we knew that

Accuracy = 84.12%
Type I Error = 12.68%
Type II Error = 19.18%

Table 4. Confusion Matrix of ANN Model

		Actual Class	
		Stay	**Leave**
Predicted Class	Stay	1412	205
	Leave	301	1268

Table 5. Confusion Matrix of XGBoost

		Actual Class	
		Stay	**Leave**
Predicted Class	Stay	1537	80
	Leave	174	1395

Table 5 showed the confusion matrix of the XGBoost model.

Accuracy = 92.03%
Type I Error = 4.95%
Type II Error = 11.09%

All of the above figures were stated that XGBoost had a higher accuracy and XGBoost was more predictive than ANN model with the same data.

PREDICTING BANK CUSTOMERS BEHAVIOURS IN BANKING INDUSTRY

Predicting customer behaviors in banking industry was essential for building strong profitable customer relationship through managing the customer impression and trust. ANN model was used to predict the customer behavior from the historical data to analysis the customer pattern through this single factor basic for prediction.

SINGLE-FACTOR BASIC

On a single-factor basis, it was observed from the characteristics described in part 3, these were Age, Balance and Earnings and Salary. The attributes were the most influential in deciding whether a customer would stay in the bank, supporting by plots and correlation table. However, it was observed that the correlation was not significant as the highest absolute correlation to 0.29. A single factor for prediction was evaluated to be prone to error. ANN model was hence proved a more appropriate solution.

ANN MODEL

ANN model was used to configure the application of a set of input and train by feeding the customer patterns and analysis the weights and segments for classification and prediction as well as clustering methods.

Figure 25 and Figure 26 showed the tuning parameters and results of the ANN model respectively. Using the parameters, the optimized model was concluded to 84.45% of accuracy:

- Batch size equals to 25. It was the minimum batch size of our option and suggested that as the records present were relatively small, a smaller batch size that might be led to a faster converge rate.
- There were 300 epochs. It was noted that more epochs could help drawing higher accuracy, while it might face a plateau after reaching a certain number of epochs. In this project, 300 epochs was observed and the performance was better on the same basis and that the accuracy rate was increased from 250 epochs to 300 epochs.
- Adam was the optimizer. The effect of Adam and RMSprop were usually similar. While Adam was an optimizer built on the basis of RMSprop with the addition of bias-correction and momentum. In our algorithm, Adam works was better in combination with another parameter.

Figure 25. Parameters Set for Tuning

```
#Part 4 - Tuning the ANN and improving the accuracy
from keras.wrappers.scikit_learn import KerasClassifier
from sklearn.model_selection import GridSearchCV
from keras.models import Sequential
from keras.layers import Dense
def build_classifier(optimizer):
    classifier = Sequential()
    classifier.add(Dense(units = 6, kernel_initializer = 'uniform', activation = 'relu', input_dim = 11))
    classifier.add(Dense(units = 6, kernel_initializer = 'uniform', activation = 'relu'))
    classifier.add(Dense(units = 1, kernel_initializer = 'uniform', activation = 'sigmoid'))
    classifier.compile(optimizer = optimizer, loss = 'binary_crossentropy', metrics = ['accuracy'])
    return classifier
classifier = KerasClassifier(build_fn = build_classifier)
parameters = {'batch_size': [25, 32],
              'epochs': [250, 300],
              'optimizer': ['adam', 'rmsprop']}
grid_search = GridSearchCV(estimator = classifier,
                           param_grid = parameters,
                           scoring = 'accuracy',
                           cv = 10)
grid_search = grid_search.fit(X_train, y_train)
best_parameters = grid_search.best_params_
best_accuracy = grid_search.best_score_

print("Accuracy of the model is :", best_accuracy)
print("Best parameters of the model is :", best_parameters)
```

Figure 26. Result of Tuning

```
Accuracy of the model is : 0.8445054945054945
Best parameters of the model is : {'batch_size': 25, 'epochs': 300, 'optimizer': 'adam'}
```

CONCLUSION AND RECOMMENDATION

The privacy data and sensitive data of the customer were important and must need to be secured. Data security and data protection for the machine learning prediction was necessary before data collection and analysis. Real-time analytics helped to understand the problem that held back the business, while predictive analytics aid in selecting the right technique to solve it. Significantly better results were achieved by integrating analytics into the bank workflow to avoid potential problems in advance. In this study, ANN model was used to try to predict and analyze if a customer would maintain its account in the bank, determining by the customers' information such as age and balance. The accuracy of 84.12%

accuracy had been achieved before tuning. ANN model was using unsupervised learning method to the data to analyze the dataset to cluster the customer pattern of normal and abnormal observations. This study reviewed the pros and cons of machine learning model. The parameters for prediction accuracy improvement were analyzed.

PROS AND CONS TO BE CONSIDERED

Pros and Cons evaluation was helping the decision-making for the company. It was regarded as a problem-solving activity terminated by a solution deemed to be optimal, or at least satisfactory. Table 6 was a summary to be considered (Jack V Tu, 1996).

Table 6. Pros and Cons Evaluation

Pros	Cons
❖ ANN can model non-linear data	❖ ANN model was computation intensive.
❖ Non-linear data was suggested to be significantly more challenging as it was often more difficult to seek for a statistical and mathematical explanation.	❖ It set a higher demand for the hardware requirements
❖ ANN offered a new solution for non-linear modelling on top of current solution such as non-linear regression model, which based on interpolations.	❖ ANN model might be more expensive in computation time and hardware requirement than other models.
	❖ ANN model required a relatively big data set
	❖ In order to increase the accuracy, it was required to have a minimum amount gradient updates, ANN generally tilts to be more realistic for big data.

IMPROVEMENT AND FIND TUNING PARAMETERS

XGBoost was a part of the Distributed (Deep) Machine Learning Community (DMLC) group. It became well known in the ML competition circles. This brought the library to more developers and became popular among the Kaggle community where it had been used for a large number of competitions (XG-Boost, 2018). To enhance the accuracy of the model, XGBoost was used to find tuning the parameters for evaluating the dataset. Finally, the results of accuracy were increased to 92.03% and shown in Figure 27.

PARAMETERS

Adam and RMSprop was common optimizer for ANN model. Stochastic Gradient Descent (SGD), Momentum and AdaGrad were some other optimizers that added to the parameters for tuning if computation power was adequate. A set of higher number of epochs was tested. In this case study, it was observed that more cases of epochs larger than 300 can be tested. After the model was fit and used to predict the test dataset, it was found that achievement was a much higher accuracy rate of 92%. It was also observed that this XGBoost model required much less computational power to run. It was well known that XGBoost algorithm was currently the most useful algorithm in data science.

Figure 27. Results of XGBClassifier for Improving Parameters

```
In [21]:  import xgboost as xgb

          model = xgb.XGBClassifier(max_depth = 12,random_state=7,n_estimators=100,eval_metric = 'auc' ,min_child_weight = 3
                                    ,colsample_bytree = 0.75, subsample= 0.8)
          model.fit(X_train, y_train)

Out[21]:  XGBClassifier(base_score=0.5, booster='gbtree', colsample_bylevel=1,
                colsample_bytree=0.75, eval_metric='auc', gamma=0,
                learning_rate=0.1, max_delta_step=0, max_depth=12,
                min_child_weight=3, missing=None, n_estimators=100, n_jobs=1,
                nthread=None, objective='binary:logistic', random_state=7,
                reg_alpha=0, reg_lambda=1, scale_pos_weight=1, seed=None,
                silent=True, subsample=0.8)

In [22]:  y_pred = model.predict(X_test)
          cm = confusion_matrix(y_test, y_pred)
          print(cm)
          print("Accuracy of the model is :", accuracy_score(y_test, y_pred))

          [[1537   80]
           [ 174 1395]]
          Accuracy of the model is : 0.9202762084118016
```

REFERENCES

Behbood, V., Lu, J., & Zhang, G. (2014). Fuzzy Refinement Domain Adaptation for Long Term Prediction in Banking Ecosystem. *IEEE Transactions on Industrial Informatics*, 10(2), 1637 – 1646. 10.1109/TII.2012.2232935

Buczak, A. L., & Guven, E. (2016). A Survey of Data Mining and Machine Learning Methods for Cyber Security Intrusion Detection. *IEEE Communications Surveys and Tutorials*, 18(2), 1153–1176. doi:10.1109/COMST.2015.2494502

Ca˜nedo, J., & Skjellum, A. (2016). Using machine learning to secure IoT systems. *IEEE Conference Publications*, 219 – 222. 10.1109/PST.2016.7906930

Chen, Shi, Lee, Li, & Liu. (2014). The Customer Lifetime Value Prediction in Mobile Telecommunications. *IEEE Conference Publications*, 565 – 569.

Chen, M.-F., & Lien, G.-Y. (2008). The Mediating Role of Job Stress in Predicting Retail Banking Employees' Turnover Intentions in Taiwan. *IEED Conference Publications*, 393 - 398.

Data Pre-Processing. (2018). In *Wikipedia*. Retrieved from https://en.wikipedia.org/wiki/Data_pre-processing

Deep Learning A-Z - ANN dataset. (n.d.). Retrieved from https://www.kaggle.com/filippoo/deep-learning-az-ann)

Feng, Y., Akiyama, H., Lu, L., & Sakurai, K. (2018). Feature Selection For Machine Learning-Based Early Detection of Distributed Cyber Attacks. *IEEE Conference Publications*, 173 – 180. 10.1109/DASC/PiCom/DataCom/CyberSciTec.2018.00040

Guan, Z., Bian, L., Shang, T., & Liu, J. (2018). When Machine Learning meets Security Issues: A survey. *IEEE Conference Publications*, 158 - 165. 10.1109/IISR.2018.8535799

Investopedia. (2018). *Introduction to the Chinese Banking*. Retrieved from https://www.investopedia.com/articles/economics/11/chinese-banking-system.asp

Li, C.-Y., Jiang, L., Liang, A.-N., & Liao, L.-J. (2005). A User-Centric Machine Learning Framework for Cyber Security Operations Center. *IEEE Conference Publications*, 173-175.

Luo, Y., & Tsai, J. J. P. (2008). A Framework for Extrusion Detection Using Machine Learning. *IEEE Conference Publications*, 83 – 88.

Pat Research. (2018). *Artificial Intelligence Platforms*. Retrieved from https://www.predictiveanalytic-stoday.com/artificial-intelligence-platforms/

Paul, P. S., & Dharwadkar, N. V. (2017). Analysis of Banking Data Using Machine Learning. *IEEE Conference Publications*, 876 - 881.

Qureshi, S. A., Rehman, A. S., Qamar, A. M., Kamal, A., & Rehman, A. (2013). Customer Churn Prediction Modelling Based on Behavioural Patterns Analysis using Deep Learning. *IEEE Conference Publications*, 1 - 6.

Sadeghi, K., Banerjee, A., Sohankar, J., & Gupta, S. K. S. (2016). Toward Parametric Security Analysis of Machine Learning based Cyber Forensic Biometric Systems. *IEEE International Conference on Machine Learning and Applications*, 626 – 631. 10.1109/ICMLA.2016.0110

Sayan, C. M. (2017). An Intelligent Security Assistant for Cyber Security Operations. *IEEE Conference Publications*, 375 – 376. 10.1109/FAS-W.2017.179

Tu. (1996). Advantages and disadvantages of using artificial neural networks versus logistic regression for predicting medical outcomes. *Journal of Clinical Epidemiology*. Retrieved from https://www.sciencedirect.com/science/article/pii/S0895435696000029

Wei, Yingjie, & Mu. (2015). Commercial Bank Credit Risk Evaluation Method based on Decision Tree Algorithm. *IEEE Conference Publications*, 285 -288.

XGBoost. (2018). In *Wikipedia*. Retrieved from https://en.wikipedia.org/wiki/XGBoost

This research was previously published in Machine Learning and Cognitive Science Applications in Cyber Security; pages 57-83, copyright year 2019 by Information Science Reference (an imprint of IGI Global).

Chapter 64

Data–Driven Trend Forecasting in Stock Market Using Machine Learning Techniques

Puneet Misra

https://orcid.org/0000-0003-2297-9072

University of Lucknow, Lucknow, India

Siddharth Chaurasia

https://orcid.org/0000-0002-6348-8600

University of Lucknow, Lucknow, India

ABSTRACT

Stock market movements are affected by numerous factors making it one of the most challenging problems for forecasting. This article attempts to predict the direction of movement of stock and stock indices. The study uses three classifiers - Artificial Neural Network, Random Forest and Support Vector Machine with four different representation of inputs. First representation uses raw data (open, high, low, close and volume), The second uses ten features in the form of technical indicators generated by use of technical analysis. The third and fourth portrayal presents two different ways of converting the indicator data into discrete trend data. Experimental results suggest that for raw data support vector machine provides the best results. For other representations, there is no clear winner regarding models applied, but portrayal of data by the proposed approach gave best overall results for all the models and financial series. Consistency of the results highlight the importance of feature generation and right representation of dataset to machine learning techniques.

INTRODUCTION

Financial domain presents one of the most complex fields which can be influenced by numerous factors making it susceptible to unexpected changes. Financial time series, for example, daily prices of security, index or currency, presents an example of high dimensional, non-stationary and noisy data. Due to its

DOI: 10.4018/978-1-6684-6291-1.ch064

practical importance, the analysis of financial market movements has been widely studied in the fields of finance, engineering and mathematics in the last decades (Yoo, Kim, & Jan, 2007).

Adding on to challenges inherent in data, economists have also highlighted the unpredictability of financial markets. Efficient Market Hypothesis (Fama, 1965) and Random Walk Theory (Godfrey, Granger, & Morgenstern, 1964) both signify that the market movements are random and unpredictable thus ridiculing utility of technical analysis. (Lendasse et al. 2001) references to statement by Campbell which says, "Recent econometric advances and empirical evidence seem to suggest that financial asset returns are predictable to some degree." hence, stressing on the utility of technological advancements for prediction of market.

As successful prediction in this field can result into financial gains by guiding investment decisions, the market prediction has been the forerunner in the adoption of technology. Consequently, forecasting which was considered as forte of statisticians in the last decade has seen substantial implementation of AI-based techniques like machine learning, evolutionary computation and fuzzy logic.

Complex, chaotic and noisy nature of financial data presents the challenges that require non-parametric methods which do not use a statistical assumption about its nature. Machine learning approach achieves this as no apriori knowledge about data is required (Misra & Siddharth, 2017). A lot of efforts has been made to predict the price or movement direction of the security. Still, accurate forecast of the stock price, even its movements, is not easy to achieve.

For short-term market predictions, technical analysis is widely employed as it provides a framework for taking informed investment decisions by applying a supply and demand methodology to market prices. Fundamental principles of the study of technical analysis are governed by the changes in the supply and demand of traded securities affect their current market prices (Scott, Carr, & Cremonie, 2016). Raw time series data in the form of Open, High, Low, Close and Volume (OHLCV) is utilized to compute technical indicators (TI). Mathematical nature of technical analysis enables its smooth blending with data-driven techniques which bring in insights that may not be obvious in raw data.

Attribute or feature generation and selection represent a critical aspect in the construction of the ML models. A good set of attributes derived from the financial time series will ease the process of classification (Gerlein, McGinnity, Belatreche, & Coleman, 2016). Another vital aspect after selection of attributes is to present the selected input in the format that can provide the inherent information in an interpretable form such that maximum information gain can be accomplished. This paper provides empirical evidence on the second aspect which is depiction of features in the right format as per the prediction goal.

Predictors generated by the application of technical analysis can be considered as proxies for the true but unobservable latent factors. Hence for this study, we hypothesize that the use of TIs should assist in improved prediction. The improvement can be in the form of accuracies or stability of the predicted outcomes. Moreover, trend information generated from TIs should be more appropriate for trend prediction. Hence, after selection of features, the format in which the selected inputs are offered to machine learning system may also play a crucial role in the effectiveness of the outcomes.

According to a recent study (Gerlein et al., 2016), the average accuracy of machine learning models for the task of trend prediction is around 48% to 54%. Though in this study the models used were simpler ones like C4.5, K*, Naïve Bayes (NB), JRip, OneR. Other studies too have reported accuracies in the range of 50s and 60s like (Kim, 2003), (Qian & Rasheed, 2007), (Lin, Guo, & Hu, 2013). Even after decades of research, inherent challenges in financial forecasting keeps research community alive to learn the intricacies of market forecasting and improve upon the prediction accuracy.

Literature shows that forecasting the direction is enough to execute profitable trading strategies (Ballings, Van Den Poel, Hespeels, & Gryp, 2015). Hence, the emphasis of this study is to predict the next day direction of movement instead of absolute price. Different techniques have been utilized in directional predictions. Above paper lists the researches focusing on directional forecast which indicates ANN, SVM to be preferred methods. Recently, ensembles like RF have also been tried with reasonable accuracy. Thus, this paper uses said models for next day directional forecast for three financial securities.

This study contributes to existing literature in three ways: First, it proposes an approach for directional forecast which is independent of interpretations from the finance domain. The proposed approach still provides results that are at par with an approach which utilizes financial knowledge to interpret TI values generated by mathematical formulations. Second, it extensively compares four different approaches to data presentation on three data series for next day directional forecasting. Third, extensive experimentation is carried out to evaluate the performance of machine learning models in conjunction with technical analysis for each representation of data thus highlighting the utility of ML techniques in this field of forecasting.

Rest of paper is divided into four sections. Section 2 describes the experimental setup. It provides details of the generation of four datasets used in this paper along with testing strategy of cross validation. Section 3 describes the three prediction models used in this study. Section 4 details and discusses the observed results, improvements seen with various experimental setups. Section 5 concludes the paper.

REVIEW OF LITERATURE

Stock market prediction initially was considered to be the field of statistician and econometricians. Linear models have appeared in literature since long. Some of well-known early contributions are: linear-trend prediction model, exponential smoothing model, ARIMA (autoregressive integrated moving average) and random walk models (Rather, Sastry, & Agarwal, 2017). (Atsalakis, 2014) offers a good review that covers conventional methods for financial market forecasting. Recently, machine learning and other data driven computational techniques are in focus. (Atsalakis & Valavanis, 2009) and (Cavalcante & Oliveira, 2015) provides good review of literature pertaining to market prediction for the state-of-the-art methods. Since stock data is characterized as non-linear, techniques like Artificial Neural Network (ANN), Support Vector Machine (SVM) are widely used (Atsalakis & Valavanis, 2009). Both techniques learn the patterns in different ways. ANN mimic human brain and rely on massive parallelization and iterative learning while SVM is a maximum margin classifier which searches for hyperplane in higher dimensions to distinguish between the classes. They rely on kernel function for the transformation of dimensions. Ensembles like random forests (RF) have also shown promising results and in studies like (Patel, Shah, Thakkar, & Kotecha, 2015), (Ballings et al., 2015) have outperformed single classifiers.

Neural networks are data-driven and self-adaptive that can capture nonlinear attributes of financial series without any statistical assumptions about the data. Various kinds of ANNs are proposed in literature and have been applied for financial forecasting. (Martinez, Da Hora, João, Meira, & Pappa, 2009) notices that majority of work on ANN is based on multilayer feed forward network (MLP) trained using backpropagation. Martinez et al. themselves used MLP to learn correlational patterns between technical indicators and high-low value of the stock prices. (Jasemi, Kimiagari, & Memariani, 2011) used MLP to learn not so obvious patterns in Japanese candlestick charts to identify the reversals in the stock prices. (Vanstone, Finnie, & Hahn, 2012) used MLP in conjunction with fundamental indicators in Australian stock market. Recently deep learning techniques are also being applied for the market predictions as in (Chong, Han, & Park, 2017) who used different representations of data along with deep networks and (Fischer & Krauss, 2018) who utilized LSTM (long short-term memory networks). A recent survey by (Mihaylova, 2019) provides good coverage for usage of neural network for economic and financial applications.

SVMs are statistical intelligent learning methods that have been widely used as an alternative for ANN in pattern recognition tasks. SVMs learning mechanism implements a risk function that considers the empirical error and a regularized term based on the structural risk minimization principle. In contrast to ANN which is based on the empirical risk minimization principle by minimizing the miss-classification error, SVM minimizes the structural risk by seeking to minimize an upper bound for the generalization error (Cavalcante, Brasileiro, Souza, Nobrega, & Oliveira, 2016). According to (Yuan, 2013), the solution of SVM may be global optimum, while conventional ANNs tend to produce just local optimum solution. SVM has been used for both regression and classification tasks. (Kim, 2003) used SVM to predict the direction of daily stock price change in Korean stock market. Similarly (Huang, Nakamoria, & Wang, 2005) predicted the weekly direction of movement in Japanese stock market. More recently, (Kia, Haratizadeh, & Shouraki, 2018), (Ren, Wu, & Liu, 2018) too used SVM in their work of market predictions.

Ensemble models have also been frequented in the financial domain. Ensemble allows exploring additional information and the consensus among individual classifiers that combine the predictors with the goal of improving the generalization performance when compared with an individual learning method. (Ballings et al., 2015) provide a comparative analysis of ensemble methods to individual classifiers. Random forest (RF), AdaBoost (AB) and Kernel Factory (KF) are compared against the single classifiers ANN, SVM, Logistic Regression (LoR) and KNN. Results indicated RF to be best followed by SVM. (Sun & Li, 2012) used individual SVM and compared it with ensemble of SVM and results indicated significant improvement by ensemble over individual classifier for financial distress prediction. Similarly in research by (Patel et al., 2015) and (Wei, Wu, & Yao, 2019) ensemble classifiers are shown to provide better results over individual classifiers.

Each algorithm has its own way to deal with the problem with their own limitations and strengths. Based on the above survey of the literature it can be said that no single method can be indicated as clear winner but ANN, SVM and ensembles like RF have found to perform well and have found the interest of research community. Moreover, predictions outcome cannot be solely said to be dependent on algorithms, rather representation of input data is equally important. Generation of right features and their usage too is an important aspect to achieve improved results.

Experimental Setup

In this paper, experiments are conducted in four different setups for three financial series. First, machine learning techniques are directly applied to the raw data of OHLCV. Second, various technical indicators are created as per the definition in (Kara, Acar Boyacioglu, & Baykan, 2011). Indicator values are continuous in nature and are used for market prediction. Third, based on the definitions from technical analysis, continuous values of indicators are converted to signals in the form of trend layer as in (Patel et al., 2015) to predict up or down movement by each TI. Finally, this paper proposes the conversion of continuous indicator values to discrete values in a pure machine learning way. Instead of using definitions from the domain of finance to generate the signals, the proposed method achieves the conversion of continuous to discrete values in a way that minimizes the interpretation of generated indicator values.

The proposed method for discretization still achieves the results that are at par with previous experiments as in (Patel et al., 2015) and (Kara et al., 2011) on three different datasets from Indian stock market.

While implementing different approaches from base papers for comparison purpose, instead of hand-crafting the dataset into train and test set, this paper uses cross-validation. Usage of cross-validation instils more confidence in the results as the data used for training and testing are non-overlapping and there by test results are not biased.

Prediction task has been set to next day direction of movement of the high price for stock or stock indices. Choice of prediction of high price is to minimize the impact of volatility which is evident in closing price due to closure of certain positions at the end of trading day. (Gorenc Novak & Velušček, 2016) noted that volatility seen during the last 15 minutes of closing time makes close price carry more noise due to day-end effect. The probable cause of preference for the closing price in the existing literature can be due to a definite time for it while high price for the day can occur in entire trading window. Academic literature exploring high prices for prediction are comparatively rare. e.g. (Gorenc Novak & Velušček, 2016) & (Mettenheim, H. and Breitner, M., 2012). Machine learning models using data that are more volatile will have to generate random features to adjust for noise effects that may not have any meaningful impact on the prediction outcome. Hence, in our experimentation, we have used prediction of high price direction as our target variable. Usage of high price also provide a greater window for trade targets as high prices are bound to be higher than or equal to close price.

Data for Experimentation

Three different datasets: two stock indices and one stock from the Indian stock market has been used for experimentation. Duration for the data used is from the year 2004 to 2017, i.e. 14 years. Nifty data has been taken from (https://www.nseindia.com/) while TCS stock data and S&P BSE Sensex data from (https://www.bseindia.com/). In case of TCS, this is around 13.5 as it got listed in stock exchanges in mid of 2004. S&P BSE Sensex, CNX Nifty are the two major stock indices from BSE and NSE stock exchanges. S&P BSE Sensex index consists of 30 large-cap stocks. It presents a right mix from every sector and offers a good generalization of individual sectors. Similarly, CNX Nifty is another benchmark index from Indian markets comprising of 50 major companies. One large-cap IT stock of TCS is also selected for experimentation. Both stock and indices are highly voluminous and well traded, and hence they are considered to reflect Indian economy.

Data Representation – Raw Data (DS1)

Raw data in the form of open, high, low, close and volume (OHLCV) is used for the first set of experiments. Normalization in the range of [-1, 1] is carried out to remove any bias which may come from the different scale of inputs. The pre-processing step ensures that contribution from higher scale values does not have overwhelming influence from attributes having lower scales.

Data Representation – Technical Indicators (DS2)

Technical indicators are calculated by mathematical formulas discussed in table 1. Each indicator provides an insight that may be used to gauge into future based on past price and volume action in its unique way. This representation is based on continuous values of TIs. After calculation, in order to neutralize the scaling effects, all the attributes are normalized to the range of [-1,1].

Table 1. Rules to convert continuous indicator values to signals as in (Kara et al., 2011)

Name of Indicators	Formulas
Simple n(10) day Moving Average	$\dfrac{C_t + C_{t-1} + \ldots + C_{t-9}}{n}$
Weighted n(10) day Moving Average	$\dfrac{(10)C_t + (9)C_{t-1} + \ldots + C_{t-9}}{n + (n-1) + \ldots + 1}$
Momentum	$C_t - C_{t-9}$
Stochastic K%	$\dfrac{C_t - LL_{t-(n-1)}}{HH_{t-(n-1)} - LL_{t-(n-1)}} * 100$
Stochastic D%	$\dfrac{\sum\limits_{i=0}^{n-1} K_{t-i}}{10} \%$
Relative Strength Index (RSI)	$100 - \dfrac{100}{1 + \left(\sum\limits_{i=0}^{n-1} UP_{t-i} \Big/ n\right) \Big/ \left(\sum\limits_{i=0}^{n-1} DW_{t-i} \Big/ n\right)}$
Moving Average Convergence Divergence (MACD)	$MACD(n)_{t-1} + \dfrac{2}{n+1} * \left(DIFF_t - MACD(n)_{t-1}\right)$
Larry William R%	$\dfrac{H_n - C_t}{H_n - L_n} * 100$
A/D (Accumulation/Distribution) Oscillator	$\dfrac{H_t - C_{t-1}}{H_t - L_t}$
CCI (Commodity Channel Index)	$\dfrac{M_t - SM_t}{0.015 D_t}$

Ct-Closing price, Ht-High Price, Lt-Low Price at time t.

$Diff_t = EMA(12)_t - EMA(26)_t$ EMA is Exponential Moving Average,

$$EMA(k)_t = EMA(k)_{t-1} + \alpha \times \left(C_t - EMA(k)_{t-1}\right), \alpha = 2 \big/ (k+1)$$

k = time period of k day EMA, LL_t and HH_t implies lowest low and highest high in last t days, respectively. $M_t=(H_t+L_t+C_t)/3$, $SM_t = \left(\sum_{i=1}^{n} M_{t-i+1}\right)\!\!/n$, $D_t = \left(\sum_{i=1}^{n} |M_{t-i+1} - SM_t|\right)\!\!/n$, UP_t means upward price change and DW_t is the downward price change at time t

Data Representation – Discretization into trading signals (DS3)

The third set of experiments makes use of trading signals generated by interpretation of continuous values into trading signals in form of buy or sell. Details of the signal generation rules is listed in table 2. Since the aim of the study is to predict the next day direction of movement which re-quires only trend information, such conversion of absolute values to directional values should assist in the outcome as data represented in inputs will be of a similar form as what is expected in output. Additionally, such conversion can be considered as a way of dimensionality reduction where a complex series gets converted to a more interpretable format with the usage of domain-specific knowledge.

Table 2. Rules to convert continuous indicator values to signals as in (Patel et al., 2015)

Name of indicators	Rules for Signals
Simple n (10) day Moving Average (SMA)	If $(SMA_t >= CP_t) => +1$ else -1
Weighted n(10)-day Moving Average (WMA)	If $(WMA_t >= CP_t) => +1$ else -1
Momentum (Mom)	If $(Mom_t >= 0) => +1$ else -1
Stochastic K% (STCK)	If $(STCK_t > STCK_{t-1}) => +1$ else -1
Stochastic D% (STCD)	If $(STCK_t > STCK_{t-1}) => +1$ else -1
Moving Average Convergence Divergence (MACD)	If $(MACD_t > MACD_{t-1}) => +1$ else -1
Larry William's R% (WR)	If $(WR_t > WR_{t-1}) => +1$ else -1
A/D (Accumulation/Distribution) Oscillator (AD)	If $(AD_t >= AD_{t-1}) => +1$ else -1
Relative Strength Index (RSI)	If (RSI>70) => -1; If (RSI <30) => +1; If $(30 <= RSI <= 70)$ and $(RSI_t > RSI_{t-1}) => +1$ else -1
Commodity Channel Index (CCI)	If (CCI>200) => -1; If (CCI <-200) => +1; If $(-200 <= CCI <= 200)$ and $(CCI_t > CCI_{t-1}) => +1$ else -1

Data Representation: Discretization by ML Method (DS4)

This setup proposes an approach of data representation where trading signal generation is achieved by a machine learning setup and do not make use of explicit financial interpretations as in prior setup. Hence, this approach does not require any knowledge for interpretation of generated values of TIs and can be said to be independent of the domain it is being applied.

Individual trading signals as per each TI are generated by using raw data and one indicator as input to an intermediate ML layer. In this paper linear SVM is used to generate the trend information. Choice of linear SVM is to keep intermediate layer simplistic and yet get the power of maximum margin classifier. Furthermore, since used prediction models in the final prediction layer are non-linear, this combination, in a sense also acts hybridization of linear and non-linear models. Since ten indicators are being used, this step uses ten executions. Each execution provides trend signal in form of {+1, -1} i.e. up/down. Every single indicator may interpret the current state of security price and volume differently. Hence, the signals generated by every TI will provide a prediction of the movement according to their design. This unique setup depicted in Figure 1 provides insight from every indicator which is then combined in the second step to generate the outcome. The last stage of experimentation is analogous to how traders execute their trades in the stock market by using multiple signals to reassure their price action understanding.

Figure 1. Proposed method to extract trend information

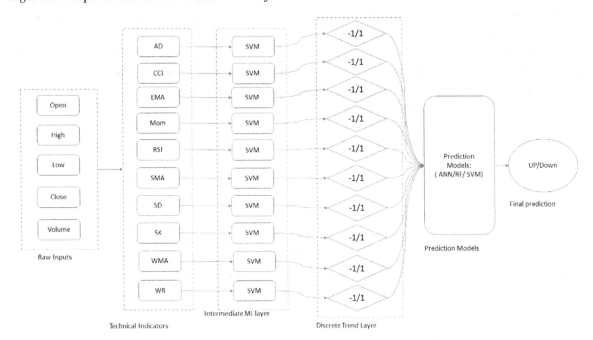

K-Fold Cross Validation

For estimating the accuracy of a classier, an estimation method needs to have low bias and low variance. While it is known that no accuracy estimation can be correct all the time, (Kohavi, 2016) in pursuit of identifying a method that is well suited for the biases and trends in typical real-world datasets showed the viability of k-fold cross validation (CV).

Scikit-learn (Pedregosa, Weiss, & Brucher, 2011) and its documentation illustrates the working of k fold cross validation as: The data is divided into k subsets. Below steps are then repeated for each of the k "folds":

- A model is trained using k-1 of the folds as training data
- The resulting model is validated on the remaining part of the data to compute the performance measure.
- Method is repeated until all the k folds are used as validation set.

The performance measure like accuracy, reported by k-fold cross-validation is averaged over the k trials to get total effectiveness of model.

This setup ensures that every data point gets to be in a validation set exactly once and be part of training set k-1 times. This significantly reduces bias as we are using most of the data for training and reduces variance as almost all of the data is being used in validation set. Interchanging the training and test sets add to the effectiveness of this method resulting in better generalization of results.

An important aspect of using cross validation is decision of k. K-fold cross-validation with moderate k values (10-20) reduces the variance while increasing the bias. As k decreases (2-5) and the sample sizes get smaller, there is variance due to the instability of the training sets them-selves, leading to an increase in variance (Kohavi, 2016).

All the experiments in this study have used k as ten as it provides right tradeoff between bias and variance in a two-class classification attempt as in this study. Moreover, grid search was done for the selection of parameters for each ML technique in the defined window of testable values which is detailed in parameter tables 3 and 4 in below sections.

Prediction Models

Artificial Neural Network (ANN), Random Forest (RF), and Support Vector Machine (SVM) are utilized to provide the final prediction. Choice of model is based on the literature survey. Results from ANN, RF and SVM, have been reported to be at par in studies like (Patel et al., 2015), (Ballings et al., 2015), (Shynkevich, McGinnity, Coleman, Li, & Belatreche, 2014) where directional prediction of the market is attempted. Reviews (Atsalakis & Valavanis, 2009) and (Cavalcante et al., 2016) provides a good insight on the soft computing and different computational approaches used for various financial pre-diction tasks like stock market prediction, forex prediction, risk analysis and so forth. These reviews also highlight the significance of selected models for market forecasting.

Artificial Neural Network

Neural network is a biologically inspired densely connected setup, which is based on the concept of parallelization. They are considered to be universal approximators which can implement a non-linear input-output mapping. Neural network trains iteratively since at each step the partial derivatives of the loss function concerning the parameters are computed to update the parameters. In an economic context, ANN allows for trading rules to be remodeled because the parameters of the change generate as an output a prediction of the future situation of the series (Farias Nazário, e Silva, Sobreiro, & Kimura, 2017). ANN has shown promising results for the directional forecast for market prediction as in (Patel et al., 2015), (Ballings et al., 2015), (Shynkevich et al., 2014).

Three-layer feedforward with backpropagation is employed in this study for the experiments as in (Patel et al. 2015) and (Kara et al. 2011). Inputs of the neural network depend on the dataset used. For raw data, input comprises of five neurons each representing OHLCV. For all other datasets, inputs comprise of ten inputs each represented by one neuron which are either direct TI values or generated signals. Output layer comprises of a single neuron indicating either up or down prediction. Hyperbolic tangent - tanh is used as activation function for all the experiments. Adam, i.e. Adaptive momentum estimation algorithm is used for updating the weights in backpropagation step. Adam calculates an exponential moving average of the gradient and the squared gradient. The decay rates for both the moments are set to 0.9 and 0.999. Initially, the learning rate is fixed at 0.1. Executions are made by keeping learning rate as constant. L2 Regularization parameter is set to 0.0001. Parameters for ANN setup that are kept floating are discussed in table 3.

The parameter setting experiments are done by evaluating various values for number of neurons in hidden layers, momentum and number of epochs. Total of 10x10x9 = 900 executions are made for each dataset. Learning rate controls the step size every time gradient descent algorithm takes towards minima. It affects the speed at which the ANN arrives at the minimum solution.

Since ANN may get stuck at local minima in pursuit of global optimal solution, momentum term is introduced to counter this limitation. Momentum is used to prevent the system from converging to a local mini-mum or saddle point. When the gradient keeps pointing in the same direction, this will increase the size of the steps taken towards the minimum. Moreover, when the gradient keeps changing direction, momentum will smooth out the variations.

Table 3. Parameters tested for ANN and their levels

Parameters	Level(s) Tested
Learning Rate	0.1
Momentum	0.1,0. 2...0.9
Number of Hidden Layer Neurons	10, 20...,100
Epochs	1000, 2000...,10000

For the final runs, all identified parameters are kept constant and learning rate is varied between 0.1 and 0.9 at an interval of 0.1 to find the optimal learning rate for parameter setting.

Support Vector Machine

SVM is mentioned to be to be one of the best methods for financial predictions in (Ballings et al., 2015). Other studies that have reported SVM to outperform ANN and RF are (Kumar & Thenmozhi, 2006), In the following section, SVM for two class classification is discussed. Concepts on this can also be found in (Patel et al., 2015) and (Lee, 2009).

(Khemchandani, Jayadeva, & Chandra, 2009) mentions that in SVM, points are classified by means of assigning them to one of two disjoint half spaces, either in the pattern space or in a higher-dimensional feature space. SVM aims to identify maximum margin hyperplane. The idea is to maximize the margin between positive and negative examples.

Given a training set (x_i, y_i) where $i \in 1,2,...,N$ such that $x_i \in R^n$ Rn and $y_i \in \{-1,+1\}$ as class labels $y_i \in \{-1,+1\}$. SVM finds an optimal separating hyper-plane with the maximum margin by solving the following optimization problem. The training vectors are implicitly mapped into a higher dimensional space by the function ϕ.

$$K\left(x_i, x_j\right) = \phi(x_i)^T \phi(x_j)$$

The decision function is defined by

$$\text{sgn}\left(\sum_{i=1}^{N} y_i \alpha_i . K(x_i, x) + \gamma\right)$$

Value of α is extracted by maximizing the below equation:

$$\sum_{i=1}^{N} \alpha_i - \frac{1}{2}\sum_{i=1}^{N}\sum_{j=1}^{N} \alpha_i \alpha_j . y_i y_j . K(x_i, x_j)$$

Such that $0 \leq \alpha_i \leq C$

$$\sum_{i=1}^{N} \alpha_i y_i = 0, i = 1, 2, ..., N$$

Two kernel functions used in the experiments in this study are radial bias (RBF) and polynomial function (poly). These are defined as:

RBF Kernel: $K(x_i, x_j) = \exp\left(-\gamma \left\| x_i - x_j \right\|^2\right)$

Polynomial Kernel: $K(x_i, x_j) = (x_i . x_j + 1)^D$

C is the regularization parameter and controls the tradeoff between misclassification of training examples against the simplicity of the decision boundary. SVM may allow some examples to be "ignored" or placed on the wrong side of the margin; this can lead to a better overall fit. C is the parameter for the soft margin cost function, which controls the influence of each individual support vector.

Table 4. Parameters tested for SVM and their levels

Parameters	Testing Levels	
	Levels (Polynomial	Levels (Radial Bias)
Regularizer Parameter (C)	0.5,1,5,10	0.5,1,5,10
Gamma in Kernel (γ)	-	0.5,1.0,1.5...,10
Degree(D)	1,2,3,4	-

Small C signifies high bias and low variance by allowing misclassification. When C is large, penalization for misclassified points is high thus signifying low bias and high variance kind of setup.

Gamma is used in case of RBF kernel and defines the distance of influence of a single training example i.e. spread of the kernel. Hence, a small gamma gives low bias and high variance while a large gamma will give higher bias and low variance.

Degree D is used for polynomial function and controls the flexibility of kernel boundary. Degree of one lead to linear separation and higher values allows more flexible decision boundaries.

Random Forest

Random forest belongs to the class of ensemble methods. The idea of ensemble learning is that a single classifier is not enough for determining the class of test data. Reason being, based on sample data, a classifier is not able to distinguish between noise and pattern. So, it performs sampling with replacement such that given n trees to be learnt are based on these dataset samples. Random Forest builds an ensemble of trees to improve upon the limited robustness and suboptimal performance of decision trees. As in (Patel et al., 2015), each tree is learnt using three features selected randomly. After creation of n trees, when testing data is used, the decision which majority of trees come up with is considered as the final output. This also avoids the problem of over-fitting.

Number of trees in the ensemble n is considered to be the parameter for random forest model. Range of 10 to 200 is tested with a gap of 10 in between. Therefore 20 treatments for each dataset is carried out before considering the best results provided by RF.

Evaluation Metrics and Results

Accuracy and F-score are used to evaluate the performance of the prediction models. Computation of both the evaluation measures requires estimating Precision and Recall which are evaluated from True Positive (TP), False Positive (FP), True Negative (TN) and False Negative (FN). Formulation of the metrics used is detailed in table 5.

Table 5. Evaluation measures used

Metric	Formula
Precision (P)	TP/(TP+FP) & TN/(TN+FN)
Recall (R)	TP/(TP+FN) & TN/(TN+FP)
F-Score	(2*P*R)/(P + R)
Accuracy	(TP+TN)/(TP+TN+FP+FN)

TN-True Negative, TP-True Positive, FP-False Positive, FN-False Negative

Figure 2 depicts the workflow of experimentation. After creation of the four datasets, brute force search i.e. grid search with cross validation is applied to find the optimal parameters for all the three models.

Use of grid search ensures that comparison is being done between the best results from each model and that are as far as possible not biased. Selected parameters then form the model parameters and are

Figure 2. Experimental setup

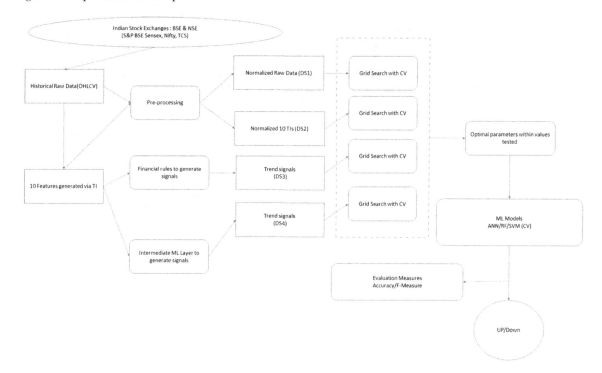

results are reported in the tables 6,7,8 &9. In order to ensure unbiased final results, all the executions have made use of tenfold cross validation.

Rest of this section discusses the results obtained and observed improvements when ML techniques are applied to four datasets. Best parameter combination is selected by brute force search. Purview of this search is limited by the selected values as per tables 3 and 4. Five executions are made for the selected best values and average results are detailed in the table 6, 7, 8 and 9. Each table also presents the parameter setting used for the obtained results.

Table 6. Results of ANN on four datasets

ANN	BSE-Sensex		Nifty		TCS	
	F-Measure	**Accuracy**	**F-Measure**	**Accuracy**	**F-Measure**	**Accuracy**
DS1	H = 10, I = 4000, M = 0.1, L = 0.2		H = 10, I = 1000, M = 0.1, L = 0.2		H = 100, I = 8000, M = 0.1, L = 0.1	
	0.5185	0.5313	0.5275	0.5541	0.5579	0. 5602
DS2	H = 100, I = 9000, M = 0.2, L = 0.1		H = 20, I = 5000, M = 0.2, L = 0.1		H = 20, I = 6000, M = 0.7, L = 0.1	
	0.7032	0.7033	0.7103	0.7105	0.6712	0.6687
DS3	H = 40, I = 7000, M = 0.1, L = 0.1		H = 10, I = 7000, M = 0.1, L = 0.1		H = 90, I = 5000, M = 0.3, L = 0.1	
	0.7069	0.7091	0.7029	0.7061	0.6794	0.6798
DS4	H = 20, I = 3000, M = 0.2, L = 0.1		H = 40, I = 1000, M = 0.1, L = 0.1		H = 100, I = 8000, M = 0.8, L = 0.1	
	0.7201	0.7208	0.7162	0.7171	0.6921	0.6934

H = number of hidden layers, I = number of epochs, M = momentum, L = Learning Rate

Table 7. Comparison of RF on four datasets

Random Forest	BSE-Sensex		Nifty		TCS	
	F-Measure	Accuracy	F-Measure	Accuracy	F-Measure	Accuracy
DS1	n = 160		n = 60		n = 140	
	0.5185	0.5313	0.5684	0.5707	0.5905	0.5873
DS2	n = 100		n = 140		n = 100	
	0.7023	0.7074	0.6958	0.6938	0.6702	0.6687
DS3	n = 10		n = 100		n = 100	
	0.7005	0.7007	0.7029	0.7061	0.6784	0.6729
DS4	n = 100		n = 140		n = 100	
	0.7212	0.7202	0.7162	0.7127	0.6978	0.6971

n = number of trees

Table 8. Comparison of SVM (RBF) on four datasets

SVM(RBF)	BSE-Sensex		Nifty		TCS	
	F-Measure	Accuracy	F-Measure	Accuracy	F-Measure	Accuracy
DS1	C = 10, G = 11.5		C = 10, G = 2.5		C = 10, G = 6.5	
	0.6215	0.6332	0.59	0.6119	0.6522	0.6582
DS2	C = 0.5, G = 0.5		C = 0.5, G = 0.5		C = 1, G = 0.5	
	0.7204	0.7253	0.7212	0.7226	0.6805	0.681
DS3	C = 0.5, G = 0.5		C = 5, G = 0.5		C = 5, G = 0.5	
	0.7093	0.7086	0.7124	0.7073	0.6758	0.6732
DS4	C = 1, G = 1		C = 0.5, G = 0.5		C = 0.5, G = 0.5	
	0.7235	0.7235	0.7183	0.7168	0.6963	0.6935

C = Regularization Parameter, G = Gamma

Table 9. Comparison of SVM(Poly) on four datasets

SVM(Poly)	BSE-Sensex		Nifty		TCS	
	F-Measure	Accuracy	F-Measure	Accuracy	F-Measure	Accuracy
DS1	C = 100, D = 1		C = 100, D = 1		C = 100, D = 1	
	0.6673	0.6884	0.6534	0.6838	0.6771	0.6833
DS2	C = 100, D = 1		C = 100, D = 1		C = 100, D = 1	
	0.7202	0.7229	0.7214	0.7205	0.6812	0.6813
DS3	C = 0.5, D = 3		C = 0.5, D = 3		C = 0.5, D = 3	
	0.7058	0.7013	0.7116	0.7073	0.6803	0.6808
DS4	C = 0.5, D = 1		C = 0.5, D = 1		C = 0.5, D = 1	
	0.7242	0.7235	0.7321	0.7252	0.6935	0.6924

C = Regularization Parameter, D = Degree

SVM with polynomial kernel presents the best results on DS1. All the models trained on DS1 show improvement when other datasets are used. Results for the models applied on DS2, which comprises of continuous values generated from ten TIs are significantly better than DS1. Thus, this improvement establishes the utility of various technical indicators for short-term predictions. These indicators help in representing raw data in a more interpretable format which help in discovering hidden patterns resulting in predictable moves. Applying technical analysis is tantamount to creating hand crafted features which bring about patterns and intelligence that help in gauging the trends.

If the purpose is to determine the trend, it makes sense to present the in-put data in the form of trend information which can be presented in discretized form. It is mentioned in (Patel et al., 2015) that pre-sentation of trend layer is the situation where each of the input parameters signify about the probable future trend, and we have the actual future trend to identify the transformation from probable trends to the correct trend. This is a step forward from converting our dataset from a non-stationary dataset to trend deterministic data-set. Models must determine the correlation between the input trends and output trend. Though it is non- linear, it is easier to create a model which can transform input trends into the out-put trend.

DS3 is created as per approach defined in (Patel et al., 2015) which is based on signal generation as per table 2. DS4 is formed by the introduction of intermediate ML layer and without any rules for signal generation. Though the construction of DS4 makes use of mathematical formulations from technical analysis, unlike DS3 approach is independent of interpretation of TIs.

Analyzing the results, performance of ML models except for SVM when applied on DS3 is better in most executions as compared to DS2 thus validating the hypothesis that it is plausible to provide trend inputs when working towards trend determination. Even in the case of SVM, results are comparable. Possible reason for SVMs unimproved results is loss of information that happens when trend information is generated. Conversion of continuous data to discrete data is like collapsing the infinite search space to a bounded space which can have only discrete values. For ML techniques, this helps in getting rid of noise and represent data in an interpretable form, for SVM which is more of a statistical method loss of information becomes heftier.

Usage of DS4 improves the result in almost all the cases over the other three representations. More-over, the results are more stable and consistent across all ML techniques.

For the creation of DS3, trading signals have been generated based on the rules as per table 2 which appears to be a naïve way of signal generation. In the domain of finance, same values can have multiple interpretations when seen in conjunction with prevailing market scenario. For e.g. in a bull market RSI value of 80 instead of 70 can be considered as a signal for overbought condition. Moreover, these levels also depend on the volatility of security under consideration. More volatile can have 80, 20 as their levels (www.investopedia.com) and (https://stockcharts.com/). Such adjustments are frequent in order to minimize the false signal generation. The idea of trend determinism layer in (Patel et al., 2015) is compelling, but its actual conversion to the trend can be improved. Either more domain information needs to be brought in for effective signal generation, or approaches which do not partake any interpre-tive conclusions from the domain can be used.

Figure 3, 4, 5 and 6 illustrates the percentage improvement achieved by DS4 over other datasets for each of the securities used in the experimentation. Improvements are seen for all the ML models though they are more significant for ANN and RF.

Figure 3. Percent change in results for ANN on four datasets

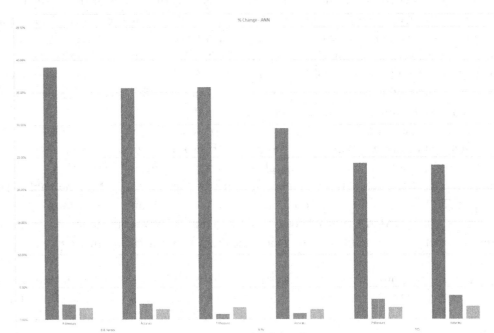

Figure 4. Percent change for random forest on four datasets

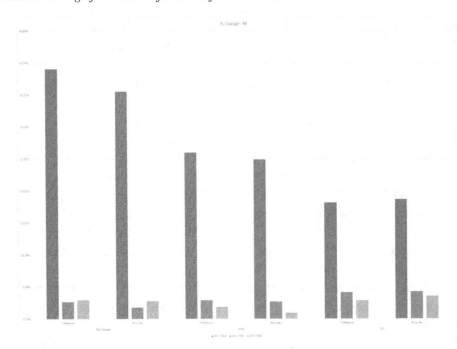

Figure 5. Percent change for SVM(RBF) on four datasets

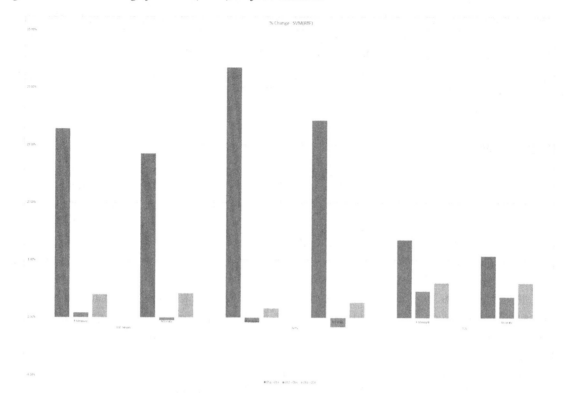

Figure 6. Percent change for SVM(Poly) on four datasets

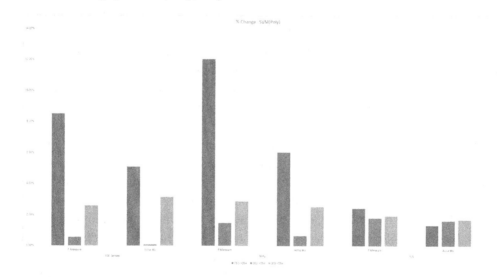

ML techniques learn from data and can generate rules and relations in different attributes. Providing them enough data enables them to learn the patterns and generate signals in the first pass. This phase generates statistical indications on the demand and supply of the security from the lenses of each TI. Second application of ML models finds the correlation in the generated signals which turns out to be an easier task as compared to finding trend information in noisy and complicated financial time series with a wide range of values.

CONCLUSION

This paper applies two non-linear single classifier ANN, SVM and one ensemble approach of RF to predict the next day direction of movement for stocks and stock indices from Indian stock market. Datasets generated in four different ways for three securities were used in the experiments. First, raw data in the form of OHLCV as extracted from stock exchanges is utilized. Second, ten technical indicators are used to generate features which provide insights into oversold and overbought positions apart from momentum and trend. Third and fourth datasets move one step ahead and convert these generated features into signals indicating up or down tendencies. Results from second, third and fourth dataset show remarkable improvement over the first approach in all the classifiers indicating the applicability of technical analysis for short-term predictions. Moreover, best and consistent performance is given by the dataset created by proposed approach hence indicating a viable solution when determination of trend is the objective. Usage of cross-validation which averages measures of fitness in prediction, to correct the optimistic nature of pre-diction of training error, ensures an accurate estimate of model prediction performance (Seni & Elder, 2010).

Experiments with raw data show SVM – polynomial function as best method while results from other ML models do not appear to be very promising. Moreover, for the three financial series i.e. S&P BSE Sensex, Nifty stock indices and TCS stock, there is a considerable deviation in accuracies for RF and ANN indicating an unstable prediction which is varying too much with data. Also, anything around 50% can be considered as random guess thus outcomes from this experiment do not look very promising and stems the unpredictability and random behavior of the stock market when raw data is utilized.

Trend information is extracted from TIs which carries innate opinions regarding probable movement direction. The proposed method of extraction of trend using intermediate ML layer is compared with other approaches where continuous TIs and rule-driven trends are extracted. Pro-posed method of data preparation outperformed the nearest competition in the range of 1-3 per cent indicating it to be a more effective way of data representation and trend extraction. Improvement is over 15% in most of the cases when compared with predictions drawn from raw in-puts. Moreover, since it is purely computational and do not bring any definitions from finance, it is comparatively straightforward to implement.

In this study, binary classification of trends, i.e. up or down movement is predicted. It may further be helpful to get the associated probabilities to provide the degree of confidence on the predictions. Higher degrees should be more consistent and may help in making informed risk-reward decisions for investments.

As one moves further into future for predictions, it gets difficult to gauge the trends and prediction accuracy tend to diminish. Further study can focus on more than just one-day predictions. Also, since the proposed approach does not use any definitions from finance, it would be worth trying to implement in other fields where information regarding trends is useful.

Machine Learning approaches are still far from being optimal solutions for financial forecasting due to the complex nature of the financial time series and market erratic behaviors and the possible presence of extreme events that can undermine any generalization or pattern found on them. Still, this study shows utility of technical analysis in conjunction with ML techniques for short term predictions. The attributes generated by technical indicators must be used in conjunction instead of isolation as different indicator provides separate signals. This is analogous to how financial analysts use technical analysis to take their trading decisions.

REFERENCES

Atsalakis, G., & Valavanis, K. (2013). Surveying stock market forecasting techniques - Part I: Conventional methods. In C. Zopounidis (Ed.), *Computation Optimization in Economics and Finance Research Compendium* (pp. 49–104). New York: Nova Science Publishers, Inc.

Atsalakis, G. S., & Valavanis, K. P. (2009). Surveying stock market forecasting techniques - Part II: Soft computing methods. *Expert Systems with Applications*, *36*(3 Part 2), 5932–5941. doi:10.1016/j.eswa.2008.07.006

Ballings, M., Van Den Poel, D., Hespeels, N., & Gryp, R. (2015). Evaluating multiple classifiers for stock price direction prediction. *Expert Systems with Applications*, *42*(20), 7046–7056. doi:10.1016/j.eswa.2015.05.013

Cavalcante, R. C., Brasileiro, R. C., Souza, V. L. F., Nobrega, J. P., & Oliveira, A. L. I. (2016). Computational Intelligence and Financial Markets: A Survey and Future Directions. *Expert Systems with Applications*, *55*, 194–211. doi:10.1016/j.eswa.2016.02.006

Cavalcante, R. C., & Oliveira, A. L. I. (2015). An approach to handle concept drift in financial time series based on Extreme Learning Machines and explicit Drift Detection. In *Proceedings of the International Joint Conference on Neural Networks*. 10.1109/IJCNN.2015.7280721

Chong, E., Han, C., & Park, F. C. (2017). Deep learning networks for stock market analysis and prediction: Methodology, data representations, and case studies. *Expert Systems with Applications*, *83*, 187–205. doi:10.1016/j.eswa.2017.04.030

Fama, E. F. (1965). The Behavior of Stock-Market Prices. *The Journal of Business*, *38*(1), 34–105. doi:10.1086/294743

Farias Nazário, R. T., Silva, J. L., Sobreiro, V. A., & Kimura, H. (2017). A literature review of technical analysis on stock markets. *The Quarterly Review of Economics and Finance*, *66*, 115–126. doi:10.1016/j.qref.2017.01.014

Fischer, T., & Krauss, C. (2018). Deep learning with long short-term memory networks for financial market predictions. *European Journal of Operational Research*, *270*(2), 654–669. doi:10.1016/j.ejor.2017.11.054

Gerlein, E. A., McGinnity, M., Belatreche, A., & Coleman, S. (2016). Evaluating machine learning classification for financial trading: An empirical approach. *Expert Systems with Applications*, *54*, 193–207. doi:10.1016/j.eswa.2016.01.018

Godfrey, M. D., Granger, C. W. J., & Morgenstern, O. (1964). The Random-Walk Hypothesis of Stock Market Behavior. *Kyklos*, *17*(1), 1–30. doi:10.1111/j.1467-6435.1964.tb02458.x

Gorenc Novak, M., & Velušček, D. (2016). Prediction of stock price movement based on daily high prices. *Quantitative Finance*, *16*(5), 793–826. doi:10.1080/14697688.2015.1070960

Huang, W., Nakamoria, Y., & Wang, S.-Y. (2005). Forecasting stock market movement direction with support vector machine. *Computers & Operations Research*, *32*(10), 2513–2522. doi:10.1016/j.cor.2004.03.016

Jasemi, M., Kimiagari, A. M., & Memariani, A. (2011). A modern neural network model to do stock market timing on the basis of the ancient investment technique of Japanese Candlestick. *Expert Systems with Applications*, *38*(4), 3884–3890. doi:10.1016/j.eswa.2010.09.049

Kara, Y., Acar Boyacioglu, M., & Baykan, Ö. K. (2011). Predicting direction of stock price index movement using artificial neural networks and support vector machines: The sample of the Istanbul Stock Exchange. *Expert Systems with Applications*, *38*(5), 5311–5319. doi:10.1016/j.eswa.2010.10.027

Khemchandani, R., Jayadeva, & Chandra, S. (2009). Knowledge based proximal support vector machines. *European Journal of Operational Research*, *195*(3), 914–923. doi:10.1016/j.ejor.2007.11.023

Kia, A. N., Haratizadeh, S., & Shouraki, S. B. (2018). A hybrid supervised semi-supervised graph-based model to predict one-day ahead movement of global stock markets and commodity prices. *Expert Systems with Applications*, *105*, 159–173. doi:10.1016/j.eswa.2018.03.037

Kim, K. (2003). Financial time series forecasting using support vector machines. *Neurocomputing*, *55*(1–2), 307–319. doi:10.1016/S0925-2312(03)00372-2

Kohavi, R. (2016). A Study of Cross-Validation and Bootstrap for Accuracy Estimation and Model Selection A Study of Cross-Validation and Bootstrap for Accuracy Estimation and Model Selection. In *Proceedings of the International Joint Conference on Artificial Intelligence* (pp. 1137–1143).

Kumar, M., & Thenmozhi, M. (2006). Forecasting Stock Index Movement: A Comparison of Support Vector Machines and Random Forest. *Indian Institute of Capital Markets 9th Capital Markets Conference Paper*. doi:10.2139srn.876544

Lee, M. C. (2009). Using support vector machine with a hybrid feature selection method to the stock trend prediction. *Expert Systems with Applications*, *36*(8), 10896–10904. doi:10.1016/j.eswa.2009.02.038

Lendasse, A., Lee, J., De Bodt, É., Wertz, V., & Verleysen, M. (2001). Dimension reduction of technical indicators for the prediction of financial time series - Application to the BEL20 Market Index. *European Journal of Economic and Social Systems*, *2*(2), 31–48. doi:10.1051/ejess:2001114

Lin, Y., Guo, H., & Hu, J. (2013). An SVM-based approach for stock market trend prediction. In *Proceedings of the International Joint Conference on Neural Networks*. 10.1109/IJCNN.2013.6706743

Martinez, L. C., Da Hora, D. N., João, J. R., Meira, W., & Pappa, G. L. (2009). From an artificial neural network to a stock market day-trading system: A case study on the BM&F BOVESPA. In *Proceedings of the International Joint Conference on Neural Networks* (pp. 2006–2013). 10.1109/IJCNN.2009.5179050

Mettenheim, H., & Breitner, M. F. (2012). Forecasting daily highs and lows of liquid assets with neural networks. In *Proceedings of the Operations Research Proceedings* (pp. 253–258). Springer Leibnitz. doi:10.1016/0377-2217(90)90174-A

Mihaylova, I. (2019). Advanced Methodologies and Technologies in Artificial Intelligence, Computer Simulation, and Human-Computer Interaction. Hershey, PA: IGI Global; doi:10.4018/978-1-5225-7368-5.ch073

Misra, P., & Siddharth. (2017). Machine learning and time series: Real world applications. In *Proceedings of the 2017 International Conference on Computing, Communication and Automation (ICCCA)* (pp. 389–394). 10.1109/CCAA.2017.8229832

Patel, J., Shah, S., Thakkar, P., & Kotecha, K. (2015). Predicting stock and stock price index movement using trend deterministic data preparation and machine learning techniques. *Expert Systems with Applications, 42*(1), 259–268. doi:10.1016/j.eswa.2014.07.040

Pedregosa, F., Weiss, R., & Brucher, M. (2011). Scikit-learn. *Machine Learning in Python, 12*, 2825–2830.

Qian, B., & Rasheed, K. (2007). Stock market prediction with multiple classifiers. *Applied Intelligence, 26*(1), 25–33. doi:10.100710489-006-0001-7

Rather, A. M., Sastry, V. N., & Agarwal, A. (2017). Stock market prediction and Portfolio selection models: A survey. *Opsearch, 54*(3), 558–579. doi:10.100712597-016-0289-y

Ren, R., Wu, D. D., & Liu, T. (2018). Forecasting Stock Market Movement Direction Using Sentiment Analysis and Support Vector Machine. *IEEE Systems Journal.* doi:10.1109/JSYST.2018.2794462

Scott, G., Carr, M., & Cremonie, M. (2016). *Technical Analysis: Modern Perspectives.* CFA Institute Research Foundation.

Seni, G., & Elder, J. (2010). *Ensemble Methods in Data Mining: Improving Accuracy Through Combining Predictions.* Morgan & Claypool Publishers. Retrieved from www.morganclaypool.com

Shynkevich, Y., McGinnity, T. M., Coleman, S., Li, Y., & Belatreche, A. (2014). Forecasting stock price directional movements using technical indicators: Investigating window size effects on one-step-ahead forecasting. In *Proceedings of the IEEE/IAFE Conference on Computational Intelligence for Financial Engineering, Proceedings (CIFEr)* (pp. 341–348). 10.1109/CIFEr.2014.6924093

Sun, J., & Li, H. (2012). Financial distress prediction using support vector machines: Ensemble vs. individual. *Applied Soft Computing, 12*(8), 2254–2265. doi:10.1016/j.asoc.2012.03.028

Vanstone, B., Finnie, G., & Hahn, T. (2012). Creating trading systems with fundamental variables and neural networks: The Aby case study. *Mathematics and Computers in Simulation, 86*, 78–91. doi:10.1016/j.matcom.2011.01.002

Wei, Z., Wu, C., B, Y. G., & Yao, Z. (2019). *Advances in Information and Communication Networks.* Springer International Publishing. doi:10.1007/978-3-030-03402-3

Yoo, P. D., Kim, M. H., & Jan, T. (2007). Machine Learning Techniques and Use of Event Information for Stock Market Prediction: A Survey and Evaluation. In *Proceedings of the International Conference on Computational Intelligence for Modelling, Control and Automation and International Conference on Intelligent Agents, Web Technologies and Internet Commerce (CIMCA-IAWTIC'06)* (Vol. 2, pp. 835–841). 10.1109/CIMCA.2005.1631572

Yuan, Y. (2013). Forecasting the movement direction of exchange rate with polynomial smooth support vector machine. *Mathematical and Computer Modelling, 57*(3–4), 932–944. doi:10.1016/j.mcm.2012.10.004

This research was previously published in the Journal of Information Technology Research (JITR), 13(1); pages 130-149, copyright year 2020 by IGI Publishing (an imprint of IGI Global).

Chapter 65

Evaluation of Pattern Based Customized Approach for Stock Market Trend Prediction With Big Data and Machine Learning Techniques

Jai Prakash Verma

https://orcid.org/0000-0001-6116-1383

Institute of Technology Nirma University, Ahmedabad, India

Sudeep Tanwar

Institute of Technology Nirma University, Ahmedabad, India

Sanjay Garg

Institute of Technology Nirma University, Ahmedabad, India

Ishit Gandhi

Institute of Technology Nirma University, Ahmedabad, India

Nikita H. Bachani

Institute of Technology Nirma University, Ahmedabad, India

ABSTRACT

The stock market is very volatile and non-stationary and generates huge volumes of data in every second. In this article, the existing machine learning algorithms are analyzed for stock market forecasting and also a new pattern-finding algorithm for forecasting stock trend is developed. Three approaches can be used to solve the problem: fundamental analysis, technical analysis, and the machine learning. Experimental analysis done in this article shows that the machine learning could be useful for investors to make profitable decisions. In order to conduct these processes, a real-time dataset has been obtained from the Indian stock market. This article learns the model from Indian National Stock Exchange (NSE) data obtained from Yahoo API to forecast stock prices and targets to make a profit over time. In this article, two separate algorithms and methodologies are analyzed to forecast stock market trends and iteratively improve the model to achieve higher accuracy. Results are showing that the proposed pattern-based customized algorithm is more accurate (10 to 15%) as compared to other two machine learning techniques, which are also increased as the time window increases.

DOI: 10.4018/978-1-6684-6291-1.ch065

INTRODUCTION

Stock market plays a major role in the economy of various countries and contributes a lot. Predicting a trend of future stock prices are widely considered and studied a topic in the area of trading, finance, statistics, computer science. Mainstream traders usually conduct fundamental analysis and technical analysis to observe stocks and make an investment decision. Fundamental analysis is a too mainstream approach which analyzes fundamental of companies such as earning, revenues, Future growth, return on equity, Profit margin and other data to decide its value and potential for future growth (Barak & Ortobelli, 2017). Whereas Technical analysis is a way of evaluating companies based on statistics of market activity such as price, volume. It uses charts and other tools to recognize the patterns that can be helpful for investment decision (Dash & Dash, 2016). Variation and volatility of stock price depend on multiple factors such as news, Social media data, and fundamentals, Production of the company, Government bonds, historical price and country's economics (Nayak et al., 2016). The feature selection significantly helps to handle overfitting. Decision Tree algorithms is applied for feature selection and it suggests a subset of stock technical indicators are critical for predicting the stock trend (Gerleni et al., 2016). It is very crucial to identify the best feature set which enhances the performance of prediction of the stock price. In order to conduct these processes, a real dataset obtained from Istanbul Stock Exchange is used with technical and macroeconomic indicators. Had investigated the ability of ANN in forecasting the daily NASDAQ stock exchange rate (Boyacioglu & Avci, 2010; Kara et al., 2011; Uygur & Tas, 2014).

In order to decide the final best feature subsets, a different number of feature subsets obtained by different filter methods is used. This approach conducts the following process: combining filter methods, applying classification and obtaining final feature subsets according to voting scheme (Pehliyanit et al., 2016). Prediction model which considers only one factor might not be accurate. There are two common methods to predict stock market prices, first one is technical analysis and the second one is fundamental value analysis. Two models are introduced as part of the research. First is daily prediction model considers both sentiment and historical data which forecasts the trend for next day. The second model is monthly prediction model considers only historical data (Nayak et al., 2016). Several networks for NASDAQ index prediction for two input datasets (four prior days and nine prior days) were developed and validated as shown in (Moghaddam, 2016) created two models. First is for Next-Day model in which 50% accuracy was obtained and second was a Long-term model in which 79% accuracy was obtained overall. Logistic Regression, SVM, Gaussian Discriminant Analysis, Quadratic Discriminant Analysis were applied and 70% of the data was used as a training data and remaining data was testing data. Overall, the highest accuracy was obtained by SVM. As a conclusion, it can be easily seen that fewer, more appropriate and stable indicators are obtained, and they produce better prediction accuracy than the full feature space (Pehliyanit et al., 2016). By considering various patterns like continuous up/down, volume traded per day and also including sentiment of the company a model has been built and tested with different stock market data available open source as shown in (Nayak et al., 2016). The performance of ANNs was evaluated using the determination coefficient (R2) and the mean square error (MSE)as shown in (Moghaddam et al., 2016). It is concluded that stock technical indicators are very effective and efficient features without any sentiment data in predicting short-term stock trend as per trend Deterministic Data Preparation Layer proposed by (Patel et al., 2015) paper exploits inherent opinion of each of the technical indicators About stock price movement.

A large amount of data available for different Stock market transactions which can be used to predict the price of a stock in advance. Traditional data analytics model for stock market price prediction basically based on some features also known as indicators. The performance of these types of traditional models is decreased when a number of indicators increases. Big Data Analytics (BDA) helps to handle such large amount of data with increasing scope of features or indicators (Attigeri et al., 2015). So, the idea is to train the machine learning model by giving features that you think which have a relationship with the dependent variable, be it next period's return, volatility, etc. With modern computing power such as BDA (Seungwoo et al., 2018), one can easily select hundreds of features from different data sources (e.g. prices, macroeconomic data, fundamental data, etc.), and the ML algorithm would figure out the relationship on its own.

Motivation

Gaps in the literature motivate us for providing the more efficient approach for stock market price prediction. As per literature, many researchers are working on SMP model with ML algorithms. As per the need and requirement of robust SMP model, here we are exploring a pattern based customized approach. Comparative analysis with other existing ML algorithms may justify the selection of an approach for pattern based SMP model. Due to the availability of a large amount of data from different stock market transactions (Volume), high-speed data generated from these transactions (Velocity), and considering of market trends and government policies (Variety), the data analysis for stock market price prediction problem consider under Big Data problem.

Research Contribution of This Paper

The primary contributions of this work are as follows:

1   We have proposed an architecture for SMP model with different components for handling a large amount of data for predicting stock market price in advance;
2   A pattern based customized approach has been proposed for stock market price prediction;
3   Performance evaluation of proposed scheme shows its superior performance over the other existing ML approaches like ANN and SVM.

The rest of the paper is organized as follows. Section 2 shows related work done by different researchers in the area of SMP. Section 3 shows the proposed research work presented in this research paper. Section 4 shows the data sources and data selection require to carry out proposed research work. Section 5 and 6 show the data preprocessing and feature selection requirement to execute the selected machine learning algorithm with this dataset. Section 7 shows the brief description of the selected machine learning algorithms for the prediction model. Section 8 shows the result analysis and discussion with justification with statistical analysis. Section 9 shows the conclusion and future enhancement in this research work.

RELATED WORK

There has been a demand to extend the stock market prediction services which help investors to take a correct decision on correct time. This section describes the previous work done by researchers in the selected domain of stock market SM prediction. Following are the contributions of various researcher done in this domain:

Nonita Sharma et al. (2017) proposed a predictive model based on machine learning algorithms for predicting stock price in 1 to 40 days in advance based on 10 years past data. This paper shows that prediction based Random Forest using LS boost gives better result compare to Support Vector Regression. The experimental analysis was based on past ten year's stock market data taken from Bombay Stock Exchange (BSE) and Nifty Sensex from Indian stock markets. Sharma et al. (2017) proposed a survey on stock market prediction systems. The study is shown in this survey paper emphasizing on the prediction model based on regression algorithms for predicting future stock prices based on past stock market data. The work published helps investors and brokers for selecting a particular DMM for SMP. Asil Oztekin et al. (2016) proposed a data analytics approach for predicting daily stock price based on past eight years data from 2007 to 2014 of Borsa Istanbul BIST Index. A comparative analysis of three machine learning algorithms adaptive neuro-fuzzy inference systems, artificial neural networks, and support vector machines based DMM is published in this paper. The measurement of the performance of algorithms was based on accuracy, sensitivity, and specificity.

Eric T. Bradlow et al. (2017) proposed a data analysis model for forecasting prices for retail market based on Big Data particularly five dimensions like a customer, location, channel, product and time. The main focus of this research is an improvement in prediction based on data quality and the analysis based on Bayesian analysis techniques. Seungwoo Jeon et al. (2018) proposed a pattern-based current stock price prediction based on historical data. The research work is done in this article identifies the pattern on stock pricing based on similar condition and parameters for the historical dataset. An ANN-based data analytical model is designed for predicting best stock price. A big data analytics framework is used to analyze the model. Jing Zhang et al. (2018) proposed an unsupervised heuristic algorithm based SMP model for prediction trends for a stock from Shenzhen Growth Enterprise Market (China) dataset. Predicted trend for a stock classified in main four classes is up, down, flat, and unknown. Up and down classes are further classified in a different level. The prediction models were based on a combination of random forests, imbalance learning and feature selection algorithms.

PROPOSED WORK

Figure – 1 shows the process flow for prediction model of the project. The research work proposed in this paper is based on a project which consists of creating a system for stock market trend prediction based on the machine learning algorithms. It is also managing stocks for a particular user profile with the functionality of add update and delete share as per current market prices. Modules of the system will include various prediction schemes, searching as well as tracking of stocks. In this research, the main task is to predict a trend for particular stock/share based on Indian stock market and a comparative analysis of three machine learning algorithms are also presented. Figure -2 shows the proposed system architecture and its different components.

Table -1 shows the abbreviations which are used for writing this research paper. Figure -2 shows the system architecture for proposed SMP model in this paper. All the components are classified as per their execution. Step -1 shows the component requires for data extraction, cleaning and preprocessing. The process attribute selection emphasizing on the feature or indicator selection for the SMP model. Step -2 showing the components required designing and implementation of DMM for stock market price prediction. As per the literature survey, many researchers are using SVM and ANN for stock market prediction. Here we are implementing a DMM in python with libraries available for SVM and ANN in the scikit-learn package. As well as a program for pattern-based recommendation system is implemented in python. Comparative study of these three algorithms is done based on the accuracy of prediction. These DMM predict yesterday's share price based on a time window of last 400 days to till the day before yesterday.

Figure 1. Process flow for the prediction model

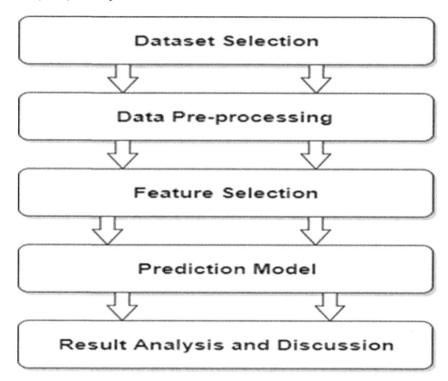

Table 1. Abbreviation

Abbreviation	Paraphrase
BDA	Big Data Analytics
SMP	Stock Market Prediction
DMM	Data Mining Model
SVM	Support Vector Machine
ANN	Artificial Neural Network
ML	Machine Learning

Figure 2. Proposed system architecture

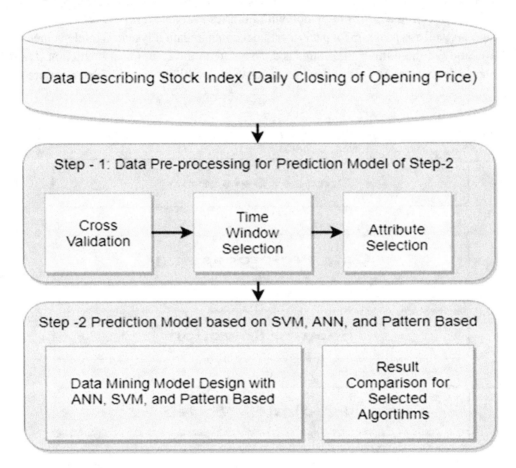

DATASET SELECTION

Getting detailed dataset for Indian stock markets NSE and BSE were not a convenient and an easy task. Dataset used in different research could not be used because the current prices of shares were required for user profile management module of this research work. Data generated for Indian stock market from NSE website and Google finance has also required some data preprocessing to make them suitable for prediction model of the project. The dataset could not provide full information for all the companies listed in that stock market. We have to specify company symbol in API to get data for specific companies. Dataset selected for India Stock Market is on the daily basis and not be available on an hourly basis or minute basis. For this research, work data are selected based on the companies registered in NSE by querying web service of the NSE. Yahoo finance also provides historical data of any company registered in NSE and BSE in CSV format. The Yahoo finance web API can be called by providing specific parameters like company symbol, type of data, and range or frequency i.e. 1y, 2m, 10d where y, m, and d stands for year, month and days respectively. Historical Stock Data available from yahoo finance and "URI:URI:/ instrument/1.0/goog/chart data;type=quote;range=1y/csv". The most commonly available attributes are Date, Open, High, Low, Close, and Volume. From Yahoo finance, we have got the historical data from all companies individually in CSV format listed in NSE in the prescribed format. Following are the sample for data received form yahoo finance API. Table 2 shows the data format for current share values.

Table 2. Data format for current share value

Date	Close	High	Low	Open	Volume
20160126	668.2600	672.3000	663.0600	667.8500	586000
20160127	823.8700	825.9000	817.8210	822.3000	6348100

DATA PREPROCESSING

Before processing or apply any data analysis algorithm with the selected dataset, the analyst wants to understand their dataset using statistical techniques or visualization. They want to first sense of the data quality, missing values, and outliers. As well as sense the major characteristics of the data like central tendency like mean, mode, median, standard deviation, etc. Data preprocessing represents the first step in the actual data analytics and aims at making sure that data is ready to be analyzed. Here Pandas a python's package for data manipulation and analysis is used for data reprocessing steps. Pandas provide a fast, flexible and robust data structure handling many data reprocessing issues like missing values, data alignment etc. Python's command "dataset.describe()" used to describe the information of each attribute of selected dataset. Following python libraries are added to the working model for data preprocessing and data analytics:

```
# Load libraries
import pandas
from pandas.plotting import scatter_matrix
import matplotlib.pyplot as plt
from sklearn import model_selection
from sklearn.metrics import classification_report
from sklearn.metrics import confusion_matrix
from sklearn.metrics import accuracy_score
from sklearn.linear_model import LogisticRegression
from sklearn.tree import DecisionTreeClassifier
from sklearn.neighbors import KNeighborsClassifier
from sklearn.discriminant_analysis import LinearDiscriminantAnalysis
from sklearn.naive_bayes import GaussianNB
from sklearn.svm import SVC
```

FEATURE SELECTION

Feature selection is an important part of machine learning. Feature selection refers to the process of reducing the inputs for processing and analysis, as well as finding the most meaningful feature. A related term, feature engineering (or feature extraction), refers to the process of extracting useful information or features from existing data. In any database, an attribute with more value of information gain serves best for analysis. The information of all attributes can be calculated using the information gain method. To decide the priority of the attributes, information gain is to be calculated for all of them, whichever attribute has the maximum gain, majorly influences the results of the dataset. Based on information gain theory the features like opening price, closing price and the average price of the day are selected as features for designing prediction model for predicting share/stock trends. These features are selected for different timespans like one month, three months, six months and one year and five years of data for analyzing with selected machine learning algorithms.

PREDICTION MODEL

The project mainly covers two main tasks first for user profile management and second for prediction of share price and trends. For second task one prediction model is designed which predicts share price for near future and recommends the information to the user. The research work proposed in this paper is a mainly comparative analysis of three machine learning algorithms which can be used for implementing the prediction model. The selected algorithms for this analysis are SVM (Support Vector Machine), ANN (Artificial Neural Network), and Pattern based Customized Algorithm. Scikit learns to provide the python libraries of many machine learning algorithms. For analyzing the selected dataset, the python libraries for SVM and ANN are used. And the program is written in python for a pattern-based customized algorithm for this comparative analysis. Following are the description of these selected three machine learning algorithms.

SVM (Support Vector Machine)

"Support Vector Machine" (SVM) is a supervised machine learning algorithm which can be used for either classification or regression challenges based on the predefined classes. However, it is mostly used in classification problems. In this algorithm, a plot each data item based on a particular share's feature as a point in n-dimensional space (where n is a number of features which have been selected) with the value of each feature being the value of a particular coordinate. After it, a classification is performed by finding the hyperplane that differentiate the two classes (classes which considering positive and negative trend for a particular share). Figure -3 shows a typical example for support vector machine algorithm.

Support Vectors are simply the coordinates of individual observation. Support Vector Machine is a frontier which best segregates the two classes by hyper-plane or line (Figure 3).

ANN (Artificial Neural Network)

ANNs (Artificial Neural Network) are digitized models of a human brain, computer programs designed to simulate the way in which human brain processes information. ANNs learn or are trained through ex-

Figure 3. Support Vector Machine algorithm

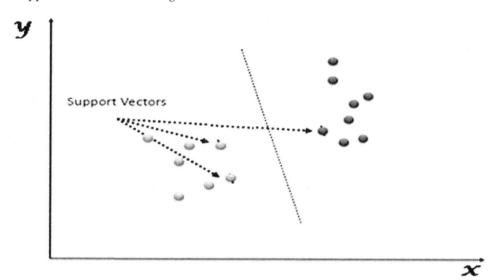

perience with appropriate learning exemplars just as people do, not from programming. Neural networks discover knowledge by detecting the patterns and relationships in data. Work presented in this paper is finding knowledge about the trends (positive or negative) for a particular share (Agatonovic-Kustrin & Beresford, 2000). Learn from observations with the dataset is the most recognized advantage of ANN. A random function is used for approximation operation in ANN algorithm. The approximation function helps to estimate the most cost-effective and ideal methods for arriving at solutions while defining computing functions or distributions. For saving execution time and cost a data sampling-based approach is applied to ANN algorithm. ANN algorithm mainly used three layers which are interconnected with their nodes. The first layer represents input neurons. Those neurons send data on to the hidden layer (middle layer), which in turn sends the output neurons to the output layer. Training an artificial neural network involves choosing from allowed models for which there are several associated algorithms (Figure 4).

Pattern-Based Customized Algorithm

The basic idea behind this algorithm is to look into past and every machine learning programmer does that to train their model. But the most important thing is pre-processing, the format of data and selection of features. Here, what we meant by 'look into past' is analyze the past data to predict the future trend. We divided past data into frames and store them as a list, against that we stored actual outcome pattern. For experimental analysis here graph frame is designed based on past 400 days u and down of a share price. Now we pass pattern for which we have to predict future trend to the algorithm and it will match this current pattern with those previously stored pattern designs, not value. Based on threshold value we get similar patterns, now we fetch each outcome pattern that we stored in each frame (Figure 5). Each outcome pattern represents either High trend (bullish trend) or low trend (bearish trend). We stored 100 for bullish trend and 0 for a bearish trend. Based on a count of 0s and 100s we could decide whether the trend is bullish or bearish.

Figure 4. Artificial Neural Network algorithm

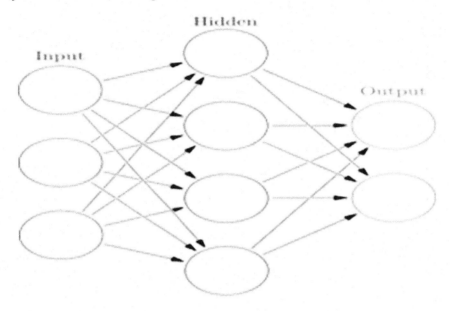

Figure 5. Pattern-based customized algorithm

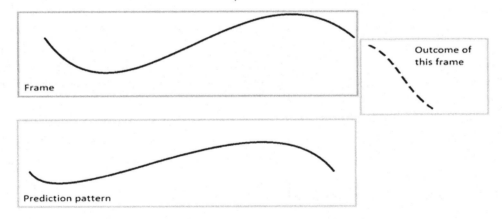

Components

Our algorithm does basically pattern matching. We can take data of past N days (where N is any number) and pass it to our algorithm. Then it will break those N days data into small chunks based on specified value X (X is a number) what we called frames. Then we have to feed algorithm with prediction pattern (prediction pattern is past M days data) by matching this prediction pattern we have to predict a stock trend, whether the market will go High or Low.

Steps which we have performed in order to fulfill the research objectives mentioned in the paper are as follows:

Step 1: Data to split into two partitions. One for the Training set and other for testing set.

Step 2: Features and labels are related from training dataset to execute the traditional model.
Step 3: Model fitting processes in executed with selected features.
Step 4: Evaluation of prediction model.
Step 5: Evaluation with respect to at least last 400 days data.

The stock market prediction web application is beneficial to the investors/traders as it fully satisfies their operational requirements. We have kept user requirements in mind before the application to make it operationally feasible. We have carefully considered the all possible operational aspects in the project.

Some of the advantages of the proposed system are:

- The stock data provided by the system is accurate and firm;
- It is kept in mind that the security features should be based on the roles of the user;
- The database used in creating the application is feasible for handling large amount.

SIMULATION ENVIRONMENT

This application is divided into two parts. First, a user interface using HTML, CSS, JavaScript, jQuery which can interact with the python Services. It is the web application which is easily reached to the user. Second, Research work in which we have implemented and analyzed two existing machine learning algorithms and pattern based customized algorithm. So, developing and analyzing this algorithm by using Scikit-Learn library in python was feasible. The system has been completely examined from all the different technical points and considerations. This application uses open source tools and technologies in the development phase except Microsoft Windows was used in the development phase. The database used in the development of the system is MySQL and server Xampp which are open source. The Stock market intraday data used currently in system obtained from Yahoo finance is totally free. Now up to this level project is financially and economically feasible. Web application for user profile management is developed in PHP and MySQL where the user can manage their stock market profile with add, delete, and update capability. For predicting stock price based on the past stock performance of that share, machine learning algorithms are used. Here Python's machine learning libraries which are implemented in Scikit-Learn package is used for comparing different algorithms.

RESULT ANALYSIS AND DISCUSSION

We have applied algorithms to stock data of five companies. As shown in Table 3, for experimentation five companies are randomly selected for comparative analysis with above mention algorithms.

After implementing algorithms, the prediction result of these companies is evaluated with the accuracy measure. Table-4, Table-5, and Table-6 show the accuracy of each five companies with different timespans are generated for each algorithm with respect to backtesting results. The backtesting is a method which can check the accuracy of method or strategy for prediction results proposed by in this research work. This method applies trading strategies or analytical method to historical data. For evaluation, the actual result (today's share vale) can be compared with the predicted results. This is how this research work producing the evaluation of prediction model and how accurate a particular model is efficient to another model.

Table 3. Selected company list

Company	Industry
MRF Ltd.	Auto tire Rubber Product
YES bank	Banks
INDUSIND bank	Banks
HDFC bank	Banks
ENGINERSIN	Consulting Services

Table 4. Prediction based on SVM with selected companies data

Company Name	1 Month	3 Month	6 Month	1 Year	5 Year
MRF	53.84%	53.85%	52.0%	40.00%	50.65%
YESBANK	57.69%	53.85%	72.0%	42.22%	50.0%
HDFCBANK	58.97%	48.72%	73.33%	42.96%	52.55%
ENGINERSIN	59.61%	54.49%	68.%	45.55%	52.07%
INDUSINDBANK	56.92%	49.74%	67.2%	46.66%	53.97%

Table 5. Prediction based on ANN with selected companies data

Company Name	1 Month	3 Month	6 Month	1 Year	5 Year
MRF	53.84%	74.36%	52.0%	57.77%	50.65%
YESBANK	57.69%	67.94%	54.0%	53.33%	50.90%
HDFCBANK	58.97%	58.97%	61.33%	51.85%	53.51%
ENGINERSIN	59.61%	62.17%	59.0%	54.45%	53.57%
INDUSINDBANK	60.0%	55.89%	62.4%	56.44%	54.51%

Data features like opening price, closing price and an average of opening and closing price of a stock are selected in this research work. By doing this we got 72.2% average accuracy. We took past 2000 days of data and 80% is training data whereas 20% is testing data. The single-threaded program took 332.512 seconds on an i5 processor and 4 GB RAM configuration laptop. Table 7 and Table 8 show the overall average prediction accuracy for all the five selected companies' data. As per the comparative analysis, the pattern based customized algorithm gives the better result compare to SVM and ANN. Figure 6 and Figure 7 also depicts the results that pattern based customized algorithm is more efficient compared to SVM and ANN.

The Table 7 and Table 8 show the average accuracy of each algorithm for five companies. Here as we can see Maximum accuracy we have obtained through a pattern-based custom algorithm which provides maximum accuracy 73.78% with % years of historical data. After that SVM can provide second best results. Result in these tables are also showing that proposed pattern based customized algorithm is more accurate (10 to 15%) compare to other two machine learning techniques, which is also increasing with the time window increases.

Table 6. Prediction based on a pattern-based customized algorithm

Company Name	1 Month	3 Month	6 Month	1 Year	5 Year
MRF	56.66%	60.34%	65.66%	69.23%	72.49%
YESBANK	58.44%	59.55%	65.79%	69.62%	72.28%
HDFCBANK	57.99%	68.63%	67.88%	72.72%	74.00%
ENGINERSIN	59.34%	71.44%	68.22%	71.41%	75.17%
INDUSINDBANK	60.61%	66.77%	69.13%	72.28%	75.22%

Table 7. Overall average prediction accuracy with the time dimension

Algorithm	1 Month	3 Months	6 Months	1 Year	5 Years
SVM	60%	66%	63.43%	43.66%	53.97%
ANN	56.92%	60%	53.71%	43%	54.81%
Pattern Based Customized algorithm	66.72%	68.14%	69.46%	73.21%	73.78%

Figure 6. Graph for overall average prediction with the time dimension

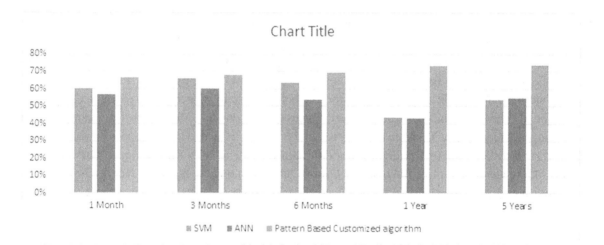

Table 8. Overall average prediction accuracy algorithm-wise

Company Name	SVM	ANN	Pattern-Based Customized Algorithm
MRF	50.068	57.724	64.876
YESBANK	55.152	56.772	65.136
HDFCBANK	55.306	56.926	68.244
ENGINERSIN	55.944	57.76	69.116
INDUSINDBANK	54.898	57.848	68.802

Figure 7. Graph for overall average prediction algorithm-wise

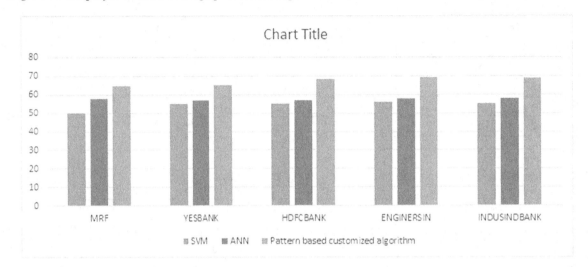

CONCLUSION AND FUTURE WORK

Forecasting financial time series data are not an easy proposition as they are found to be non-linear, volatile and fluctuating. Three methods are most widely used to analyze the stock market prediction are Fundamental Analysis, Technical Analysis and machine learning based analysis. As per survey carried out the Fundamental and Technical Analysis specifically shows little to no potential of ever producing any statistically significant result when the correct methodology is applied. In this research work, the financial time series data for stock market indices have been studied using three machine learning computing techniques. The Machine learning methods (SVM, ANN, and Pattern based customized algorithm) were then be tested on a wide range of data sources. As a result of this process, three innovative models for the above said three financial time series have been developed. The prediction model based on Pattern-based customized algorithm produced better accuracy compare to other two machine learning techniques. Prediction of the trends of the stock market based on current affair or event on news becomes more popular. Today current affairs and news feed drive the up and fall of stock market prices. Here, we are proposing the stock market prediction based on these type of unstructured and semi-structured input as for a future enhancement of this research work. Considering these types of heterogeneity of data, this problem would be considered under big data problem.

ACKNOWLEDGMENT

Authors are thankful to Ishit Gandhi, Nikita Bachani, MCA students of Institute of Technology, Nirma University Ahmedabad for contributing in the experimental analysis of SMP model and comparative analysis with ML algorithms during their Major Project.

REFERENCES

Agatonovic-Kustrin, S., & Beresford, R. (2000). Basic concepts of artificial neural network (ANN) modeling and its application in pharmaceutical research. *Journal of Pharmaceutical and Biomedical Analysis, 22*(5), 717–727. doi:10.1016/S0731-7085(99)00272-1 PMID:10815714

Attigeri, G. V., Manohara Pai, M. M., Pai, R. M., & Nayak, A. (2015). Stock market prediction: A big data approach. In TENCON 2015 - 2015 IEEE Region 10 Conference, Macao (pp. 1-5).

Barak, S., Arjmand, A., & Ortobelli, S. (2017). Fusion of multiple diverse predictors in the stock market. *Information Fusion, 36*, 90–102. doi:10.1016/j.inffus.2016.11.006

Boyacioglu, M. A., & Avci, D. (2010). An Adaptive-Network-Based Fuzzy Inference System (ANFIS) for the prediction of stock market return: The case of the Istanbul Stock Exchange. *Expert Systems with Applications, 37*(12), 7908–7912. doi:10.1016/j.eswa.2010.04.045

Bradlow, E. T., Gangwar, M., Kopalle, P., & Voleti, S. (2017). The Role of Big Data and Predictive Analytics in Retailing. *Journal of Retailing, 93*(1), 79–95. doi:10.1016/j.jretai.2016.12.004

Dash, R., & Dash, P. K. (2016). A hybrid stock trading framework integrating technical analysis with machine learning techniques. *J. Finance Data Sci., 2*(1), 42–57. doi:10.1016/j.jfds.2016.03.002

Gerlein, E. A., McGinnity, M., Belatreche, A., & Coleman, S. (2016). Evaluating machine learning classification for financial trading: An empirical approach. *Expert Systems with Applications, 54*, 193–207. doi:10.1016/j.eswa.2016.01.018

Jeon, S., Hong, B., & Chang, V. (2018). Pattern graph tracking-based stock price prediction using big data. *Future Generation Computer Systems, 80*, 171–187. doi:10.1016/j.future.2017.02.010

Kara, Y., Acar Boyacioglu, M., & Baykan, Ö. K. (2011). Predicting direction of stock price index movement using artificial neural networks and support vector machines: The sample of the Istanbul Stock Exchange. *Expert Systems with Applications, 38*(5), 5311–5319. doi:10.1016/j.eswa.2010.10.027

Moghaddam, A. H., Moghaddam, M. H., & Esfandyari, M. (2016). Stock market index prediction using artificial neural network. *Journal of Economics, Finance and Administrative Science, 21*(41), 89–93. doi:10.1016/j.jefas.2016.07.002

Nayak, A., Pai, M. M. M., & Pai, R. M. (2016). Prediction Models for Indian Stock Market. *Procedia Computer Science, 89*, 441–449. doi:10.1016/j.procs.2016.06.096

Oztekin, A., Kizilaslan, R., Freund, S., & Iseri, A. (2016). A data analytic approach to forecasting daily stock returns in an emerging market. *European Journal of Operational Research.*

Patel, J., Shah, S., Thakkar, P., & Kotecha, K. (2015). Predicting stock and stock price index movement using Trend Deterministic Data Preparation and machine learning techniques. *Expert Systems with Applications, 42*(1), 259–268. doi:10.1016/j.eswa.2014.07.040

Pehlivanlı, A. Ç., Aşıkgil, B., & Gülay, G. (2016). Indicator selection with committee decision of filter methods for stock market price trend in ISE. *Applied Soft Computing, 49*, 792–800. doi:10.1016/j.asoc.2016.09.004

Sharma, N., & Juneja, A. (2017). Combining of Random Forest Estimates using LSboost for Stock Market Index Prediction. In *2nd International Conference for Convergence in Technology (I2CT)* (pp. 1199-1202). 10.1109/I2CT.2017.8226316

Sharma, A., Bhuriya, D., & Singh, U. (2017). Survey of Stock Market Prediction Using Machine Learning Approach. In *International Conference on Electronics, Communication and Aerospace Technology ICECA* (pp. 506-509). 10.1109/ICECA.2017.8212715

Uygur, U., & Taş, O. (2014). The impacts of investor sentiment on different economic sectors: Evidence from Istanbul Stock Exchange. *Borsa Istanb. Rev., 14*(4), 236–241. doi:10.1016/j.bir.2014.08.001

Zhang, J., Cui, S., Xu, Y., Li, Q., & Li, T. (2018). A novel data-driven stock price trend prediction system. *Expert Systems with Applications, 97*, 60–69. doi:10.1016/j.eswa.2017.12.026

This research was previously published in the International Journal of Business Analytics (IJBAN), 6(3); pages 1-15, copyright year 2019 by IGI Publishing (an imprint of IGI Global).

Chapter 66
Algorithmic Machine Learning for Prediction of Stock Prices

Mirza O. Beg

National University of Computer and Emerging Sciences, Pakistan

Mubashar Nazar Awan

National University of Computer and Emerging Sciences, Pakistan

Syed Shahzaib Ali

National University of Computer and Emerging Sciences, Pakistan

ABSTRACT

Stock markets and relevant entities generate enormous amounts of data on a daily basis and are accessible from various channels such as stock exchange, economic reviews, and employer monetary reports. In recent times, machine learning techniques have proven to be very helpful in making better trading decisions. Machine learning algorithms use complex logic to observe and learn the behavior of stocks using historical data which can be used to predict future movements of the stock. Technical indicators such as rolling mean, momentum, and exponential moving average are calculated to convert the data into meaningful information. Furthermore, this information can be used to build machine learning prediction models that learn different patterns in the data and make future predictions for accurate financial forecasting. Additional factors that are being used for stock prediction include social media influences and daily news on trading stocks. Considering these qualitative and quantitative features at the same time result in improved prediction models.

INTRODUCTION

Machine Learning refers to a concept in which a machine has been programmed to learn specific patterns from historical data using powerful algorithms and make predictions in future based on the patterns it learnt. Machine learning is a branch of Artificial Intelligence (AI), the term proposed in 1959 by Arthur

DOI: 10.4018/978-1-6684-6291-1.ch066

Samuel who defined it as the ability of computers or machines to learn new rules and concepts from data without being explicitly programmed.

This idea has stretched out its effect to the financial markets because of the rapid and revolutionary advancements in Artificial Intelligence (AI) and Machine Learning (ML). Since last two decades, markets have turned out to be more inclined towards high frequency trading as compared to traditional trading schemes. Stock markets generates huge amount of information on daily basis which can be accessible from various channels such as stock exchange, economic reviews, employer monetary reports etc. Therefore, it is helpful to analyze market data and get useful insights about securities to make better trading decisions. In the past, several studies have been done to predict stock prices. Different natural inspired algorithms have been proposed for stock prediction. Genetic algorithms have been studied with neural networks (Fang et. al, 2014). Different hybrid evolutionary algorithms have been proposed (Bisoi and Dash, 2014). Five algorithms Flower Pollination Algorithm (FPA), Bat algorithm (BA), Modified Cuckoo Search (MCS), Artificial Bee Colony(ABC), and Particle Swarm Optimization (PSO) were proposed. These algorithms selected the best parameters to train and optimize Least Square- Support Vector Machine (LS-SVM). The problem with those algorithms was that they couldn't overcome the overfitting and were falling in local minima (Hegazy, Soliman, and Salam, 2015). Not only the statistical data of stocks but also the textual information can make huge effects on stocks. News articles have been used with the stock prices for prediction (Li, Xiaodong et. al, 2014). Twitter sentiment analysis has been done on stocks (Ranco et. al, 2015). By incorporating the textual information with the financial information also gives better results than models which uses financial information only (Lee, Surdeanu, MacCartney, and Jurafsky, 2014). Topic modeling has been studied where topic based sentiment analysis was done by using LDA tool (Nguyen and Shirai, 2015). The events occuring in the real world can make significant effects on stock markets. Event driven stock price prediction has been studied in detail where the information about the events was extracted from the web-scale data (Ding, Zhang, Liu, and Duan, 2014). Deep learning models have proposed by using news text (Ding, Zhang, Liu, and Duan, 2015). Following the events, the news on media and public sentiments can also change the behaviour of investors and can have great influence over stock market (Li, Qing et. al, 2014). Multiple classifiers have been trained for short term and long term stock price prediction by using the historical data stocks (open, high, low & close prices) ((Patel, Shah, Thakkar, and Kotecha, 2015) Ballings, Van den Poel, Hespeels, and Gryp, 2015).

Hedge fund traders are now more biased towards the programs that will take over their daily trading business in order to maximize returns. Quantitative hedge funds have been developing and creating different machine learning based algorithms to make trading decisions. AI based programs make statistical analysis for a security, become aware of buying and selling correlations, examine market developments, and make trading decisions based on the overall findings. As the quantity of data increases, these prediction models can enhance their overall performance through the years. That is what makes them a smart bet for stock marketplace traders seeking to take emotion out of the equation. Over the time, approaches have been enhanced, which uses sophisticated and efficient algorithms to parse the content of news feed and calculating their impact on particular company's stock price. As for a long term trading decision, news about the particular security can significantly impact its price over the time. Machine learning algorithms can be used to analyze sentiments from that information and calculate its impact on a security.

It has likewise been persuasive in instructing personal computers to drive autosand in addition, interpreting languages, and now, investors are depending on this technology to make better trading decisions. Certainly that Artificial Intelligence based trading system are making significant advances towards accomplishing the objectives and this has truly changed how we see the stock trading system.

As described earlier, there are several algorithms which has been used in the area of stock prediction, it includes Naive Bayes', Linear Regression, K-Nearest Neighbors (KNN), Neural Network, Linear Discriminant Analysis (LDA), Support Vector Machine (SVM), and Random Forest. The US stocks data has been used for the training and testing purposes. Random forest was simply the best classifier in all the previous works.

In this chapter, there is a technical analysis for prediction and trading for a shorter period (i.e. 3,4, or 5 days) instead of long term predictions. Different technical indicators has been explained for short term predictions and machine learning algorithms have been trained to predict the 5th day closing price of stocks.

DATA EXPLOITATION

Data Collection

There are plenty of sources available on the internet which provides historical data of stocks like Google finance, Yahoo finance or Quandl. They provide very easy way to pull out cleaned and formatted data either manually or by API calls through code. Data contains following attributes or columns (in days interval):

- **Date:** The date on which the information is recorded.
- **Open:** The starting price (in US Dollars) at which the trading open.
- **High:** The highest price at which the stock traded in a day.
- **Low:** The lowest price at which the stock traded in a day.
- **Volume:** Total amount of stocks traded in a day.
- **Close:** The last price at which the stock traded.
- **Adjusted Close:** Little bit different from closing price, price adjusted after stock splits or dividend payments.

Data Sources

Google Finance

Google Finance can be used to get the free historical data for most of the stocks in several frequencies in which one minute being the lowest time frame. Source [1] can be used to get the data from google finance.

- PERIOD indicate the frequency or interval (in seconds). For example, for 5 minute interval, its value should be 300 (i.e. 5 * 60)
- DAYS refers to the total number of past p days for which the data is needed.
- TICKER is the symbol of the stock (i.e. for Apple stock it should be 'AAPL')

Yahoo Finance

Yahoo Finance is another very useful resource to get historical data for several stocks in different intervals, one minute being the lowest. Source [2] can be used to download data from yahoo finance.

Finam

Finam is a website which provides useful historical data for limited but popular set of stocks. Several months of data can be downloaded even for the lowest interval or time frame (i.e. one-minute). Source [3] can be used to download the historical data from finam.

Data Preprocessing

As the matter of fact that financial data is really effective for financial analysis and research. It is considered to be perfectly recorded and formatted data as stored by computers. It's an assumption that the data is accurately and consistently recorded minute by minute without having missing data points. Actually, the stock price is not the same on all the exchanges, for a particular stock, it may be traded at NYSE (New York Stock Exchange), NASDAQ, and BATS at the same time with different prices. The actual data is made up from the combination of all different data sources and providers. The other thing is not every stock trade all the time, sometime they quit existing or trading and there is no data available for that time period. So, it should be kept in mind that data can be faulty or inconsistent containing missing or null values. Therefore, after collecting or gathering data from any reliable source, it must be checked and corrected for these errors otherwise noisy or inconsistent data would lead to a bad prediction model because the model highly depends on the quality of the data it has been trained on.

Dealing With Missing Values

As explained above, data may contain missing or null values. As this is a purely time series based challenge, it is important to deal with the missing values. Below figure shows some missing values of a stock price (i.e. no trading occurred) for some intervals.

Figure 1. Stock data with missing values

Now the challenge is to fill these values in such a way that should not negatively affect the prediction model.

Intuitively, one can think of interpolating the missing values, the fact is there is no trading done and price available for that range. Therefore, it is unwise to interpolate any random value to fill null values because doing so will have a huge negative impact on the calculation of technical indicators (Rolling mean, Daily returns, Bollinger bands etc.) which can directly affect the prediction model as it would be based on self-made data points.

The best and safe way to fill these values are to use last known values as it reflects what was going on with the data.

Figure 2. Forward/backward approach to fill missing values

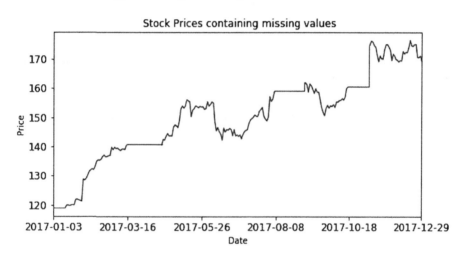

There are two steps involved known as forward fill and backward fill. As shown in the above figure, red line represents forward fill approach. All the missing prices are filled with the last known price for that stock. Similarly, green line at the start indicates backward fill operation, which eventually uses the actual starting known price to fill unknown backward values. These should be applied in a sequence such that forward fill has to done before backward fill.

Feature Engineering

One of the most important step for any good prediction model is to generate artificial features from existing features or data. Adding relevant information to the model decreases the chance of predicting incorrect prediction. A number of statistical measures can be computed using historical data which are called technical indicators. These indicators are heuristics and provides hint to buy or sell a particular stock. Use of multiple indicators at the same time is more effective than using a single indicator at a time. Also, use of technical analysis for prediction and trading for a shorter period (i.e. 3, 4, or 5 days) of time is more reliable than predicting for longer term (e.g. 5, 7, or 12 months). As over long term prediction of a stock price movement is more dependent on stock's fundamental analysis like company worth, market value, global events etc. Hence, long term analysis depends on a lot of factors which also changes over time and involves some complex decisions which should be taken by humans. On the other hand, short term prediction and high frequency trading can be done by computers by using machine learning techniques. Some useful technical indicators for short term prediction are explained as follows:

Daily Returns

It is considered to be the most effective and important statistical indicator used in financial analysis. It is simply the measurement which indicates the change in the price of the stock on t-th day compared to (t-1)-th day. It is calculated as follows:

$$Daily\ Return(t) = \frac{(price\_at\_t) - (price\_at(t-1))}{price\_at(t-1)} \tag{1}$$

Price at day t represents the t-th day adjusted closing price of the stock whereas price at day (t-1) indicates the last or previous day adjusted closing price of the stock. For example, if the current price of the stock is \$110 and the last day closing price was \$100, by putting the values in the above equation, it results in 0.1 which is equal to 10% percent. According to this, there is a +10% change (rise) in the stock price relative to previous day.

Figure 3. Daily change in APPL's stock of year 2017

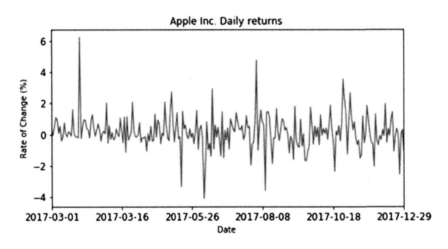

Above figure shows daily rate of change for the Apple's stock over the year of 2017.

Some other statistical measures like mean, standard deviation (how far individual measurements deviate from mean) and kurtosis (curved arching) of daily returns can also be useful for analysis. The figure below shows that how many values of daily return falls in a particular range. The mean, standard deviation and kurtosis values are 0.15, 1.12 and 5.29 respectively. In simple words, for the year 2017 average daily return of apple's stock is approximately 0.15%.

Figure 4. Distribution of daily return

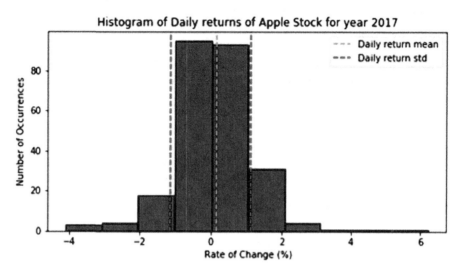

Kurtosis comes from a geek word that means curved or arching. It is the measure of extreme values on the tail of the distribution in which small or large excursions along the tail is indicated by negative (skinny tails) and positive (fat tails) kurtosis respectively. It is considered to be fat tails (positive kurtosis) when there are frequently more occurrences on the tails as compared if that was a Gaussian or normal distribution. Similarly, skinny tails (negative kurtosis) when there are less occurrences on tails. In the above figure, as the kurtosis has a positive value of 5.29. So, it is defined as fat tails or positive kurtosis.

Momentum

It is the measure of the stock's price strength or weakness over some time interval. Momentum is similar to the daily return except the one day interval is replaced with the n-th day's interval. Such that, the price change (return) is calculated as the percentage difference between the price at (t-th) day and the price at (t-n)-Th day.

$$Momentum\left(t\right) = \frac{\left(priceatt\right) - \left(priceat\left(t-n\right)\right)}{priceat\left(t-1\right)} \tag{2}$$

Rolling Mean (Simple Moving Average (SMA)

It is the average adjusted closing price of the stock over some time frame. E.g. n day's simple moving average (SMA) is the mean value of last n day's closing price with respect to t-th day. Intuitive decisions can be made by looking into the pattern of rolling mean that is how much the actual price deviates from the moving average at particular instance creating an opportunity to buy or sell.

$$RollingMean(t) = \frac{(priceatt - 1) + (priceatt - 2)... + (priceatt - n)}{n} \qquad (3)$$

The below figure shows the rolling mean or simple moving average for the 20 days (n=20) of window. Unlike the spikes shown for the price value of AAPL, the movement of the stock price can be easily perceived in rolling mean due to its smoothness.

Figure 5. Rolling mean / simple moving average (SMA)

Weighted Moving Average (WMA)

It is similar to the simple moving average (rolling mean) except the price values are given some weights on the basis of their importance that is why it is called weighted moving average. It is a weighted average or mean taken for last n prices. Usually, most recent prices are given more weight since they are significantly more important. It can be calculated as follows:

$$WMA(t) = \frac{(W*(priceatt - 1)) + ((W - 1)*(priceatt - 2))...n}{n} \qquad (4)$$

In the above equation, W indicates the weight assigned to each value of the price. It must be noted that there is a difference of 1.0 between two consecutive weights which means the rate of decrease is consistent.

Exponential Moving Average (EMA)

Unlike the weighted moving average where the decreasing rate of weights are consistent, in exponential moving average (EMA) rate of decrease in weights are exponential between two consecutive prices.

This technique shows quicker behavior than simple moving average because more weight is assigned to recent prices and less to past prices. Exponential weighted values for prices can be calculated as follows:

$$EMA(t) = \left(\left(closingprice\right) - EMA(t-1)\right) * \left(\frac{2}{n+1}\right) + EMA(t-1) \tag{5}$$

In the above equation, n represents the time frame window for which the average is be calculated and EMA (t-1) is the exponential moving average of previous day or record.

Figure 6. Exponential moving average (EMA)

Return Moving Average

It is the measure of average return value (price change) over some interval which means n days return moving average is the mean value of last 'n days return' with respect to t-th day.

$$ReturnMovingAverage(t) = \frac{Return(t-1) + Return(t-2)... + Return(t-n)}{n} \tag{6}$$

Bollinger Bands®

How much deviation from the rolling mean indicates buy/sell signal. To measure that, John Bollinger proposed a technical indicator called Bollinger bands® in 1980s which consists of two standard deviations above and below the simple moving average. For N-window moving average, an upper band should be calculated as K times N-window standard deviation added to the N-window moving average (MA + Kσ).Similarly, the lower band is defined as K times N-window standard deviation subtracted to the N-window moving average (MA - Kσ). The default value of K is 2 and N is 20, but can be changed according to the requirement and behavior of the pattern.

Figure 7. Bollinger (upper and lower) bands of Apple's stock for year 2017

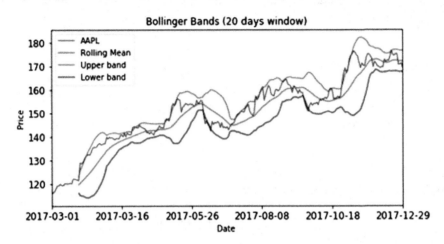

The above figure shows the visual representation of the Bollinger bands. Changing the window size and the value of K will also change the behavior of the upper and lower bands. It may be notice that some starting data points of rolling mean, lower and upper bands are not visualized, it is because of the window size which is 20. When calculating these indicators, there must be an equal number of preceding data points as the window size. People use these indicators to buy or sell stocks, the intuition is when the stock price hits or overlaps the lower band value, it is potentially considered to be the buying time as it might rise up again. Similarly, selling time is when the stock price value approaches to upper band value. But, one should not rely only on this and start trading, as there are some other factors involved which should not be over looked (e.g. sharp ratio).

Relative Strength Index (RSI)

It is one of the most popular momentum based oscillator developed by J. Welles Wilder which measures the magnitude and velocity of recent price movements. Its value oscillates between 0 and 100 which shows the trading trend for a particular security. Usually, the security/stock is considered overbought when its RSI value surpasses above 70 and oversold when the value is below 30. It is calculated as follows:

$$RSI\left(t\right) = 100 - \left[100 \ / \left(1 + \frac{Ndaysaverageupwardreturn}{Ndaysaveragedownwardreturn}\right)\right] \tag{7}$$

Where N is the total number of days or the time frame for which the value of RSI is to be calculated.

Stochastic Oscillator (%K)

It is another momentum based oscillator developed by George C in late 1950's which measures the closing trend with respect to the range of previous high and low prices over a specific period of time. In general theory, when the market trend is upward, the closing price are often near high price whereas when the market trend is downward, closing prices are near low. The formula for Stochastic Oscillator is as follows:

$$\%K\left(t\right)=100*\frac{\left(ClosingPrice\left(t-1\right)-L\left(N\right)\right)}{\left(H\left(N\right)-L\left(N\right)\right)} \tag{8}$$

In the above equation, L (N) and H(N) represents the lowest and highest price recorded for previous N days respectively.

Figure 8. Relative strength index (RSI) of Apple's stock for the year 2017

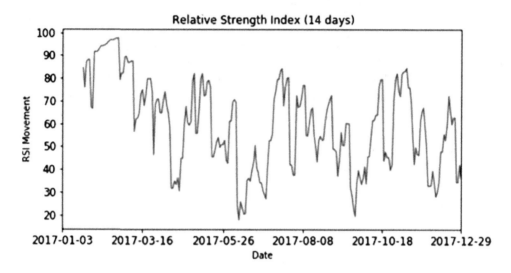

Figure 9. Stochastic oscillator %K of Apple's stock for the year 2017

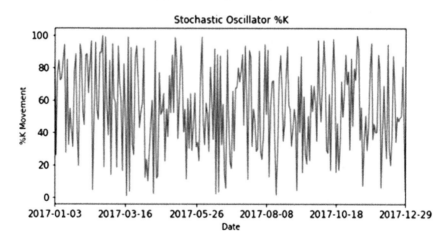

Stochastic Oscillator (%D)

It is simply the moving average (i.e. simple, weighted or exponential) of %k for D-period (time range). Usually, the three period (D=3) moving average is used to observe the market trend for buy/sell signal.

$$\%D(t) = \frac{\%k(t-1) + \%k(t-2)... + \%K(t-D)}{D}$$ (9)

Moving Average Convergence Divergence (MACD)

Another momentum oscillator developed by Gerald Appel, is calculated by subtracting the longer exponential moving average (i.e. 26 days) from shorter exponential moving average (i.e. 12 days). This way, it combines the following trend of both long and short term momentum. As the name implies, it identities the convergence and divergence of two moving averages, it converges when these two move towards each other and diverges when they move away from each other. MACD oscillates above and below the 0 for which the value of MACD is positive when the shorter EMA value is greater than the longer EMA. Positive MACD indicates that the momentum is upward. On the other hand, negative MACD indicates the downward momentum such that the value of shorter EMA diverges below the longer EMA.

$$MACD(t) = EMA(t - 12) - EMA(t - 36)$$ (10)

Number of days for shorter and longer moving averages can be varied according to the trading goals.

Accumulation/Distribution (A/D) Oscillator

An Oscillator developed by Marc Chaikin to identity the pattern of the money flow in a security. It uses stock price and its volume to analyze the supply and demand behavior of investors for a particular stock. It identifies the buying (accumulation) or selling (distribution) trend of investors by calculating the close location value and then multiplying it with corresponding volume for a given range. It is formulated as follows:

$$A/D(t) = \frac{\left(\left(ClosePrice - L(N)\right) - \left(H(N) - ClosePrice\right)\right)}{\left(H(N) - L(N)\right)} * Vol(N)$$ (11)

In above equation, L (N) and H (N) represents the lowest and highest price of last N prices. Similarly, Vol (N) indicates the total volume for a given range. The direction of A/D line indicates the buying or selling pressure for that security in a market. If the direction is upward, the chances of buying pressure prevails whereas a selling pressure for the downward movement.

Commodity Channel Index (CCI)

A technical indicator developed by Donald Lambert which indicates about the ending of existing trend or a start of a new trend. It measures the current price levels relative to the moving average over the given period of time. CCI value is high when the prices are much higher as compared to their average price and its value is relatively low when prices are low with respect to their averages. It can also be used to identify the overbought and oversold behavior of the stock in a market. The value of CCI can be calculates as follows:

$$TypicalPrice\left(t\right) = \frac{High\left(t\right) + Low\left(t\right) + Close\left(t\right)}{3} \tag{12}$$

$$CCI\left(t\right) = \frac{TypicalPrice\left(t\right) - NPeriodSMAofTypicalPrice}{NPeriodStandarddeviationofTypicalPrice} \tag{13}$$

For a given range (i.e. days, weeks, months), Commodity Channel Index can be calculated using above equation in which N represents the time period (range). High reading values of CCI (e.g. above +100) indicates the start of an upward movement whereas low readings (e.g. below -100) indicates the start of downward trend of a stock.

BUILDING ALGORITHMIC MODELS

Data Sampling for Algorithm

Before applying any algorithms on data it is very important to split the data into at least two samples called training and testing/validation. Training set is used to train the model which learns the patterns from data whereas validation set is used evaluate the performance of the model for unseen examples. If the algorithm is tested over the same data it was trained on, it would not be properly evaluated, as it already goes through all the exact training samples. The algorithm should be tested on the data which it has not seen yet. The process of evaluating model for test set is called out of sample testing.

Creating a Training Set

Independent Variables (X)

These are the input parameters like rolling mean, momentum, exponential moving average etc. computed using historical data. These are eventually the basis for prediction model, algorithm tries to learn the behavior of depended variable (i.e. rise/fall price signal) with respect to different independent variables.

Dependent Variable (Y)

The output parameter is called the dependent or predictor variable. In case of stock movement or price prediction, the dependent variable is either the rise/fall signal or the stock price of the future.

Creating a training set purely depends on the requirement of the prediction problem. To create a model which predicts the next day price movement of a stock, the training data for the machine learning algorithm should be structured in a way that the input parameters (i.e. daily returns, simple moving averages, momentum etc.) of current day should be aligned against the dependent variable Y (i.e. daily return (rise/fall signal)) of next day.

Example

Consider the following sample for training data.

Table 1.

Date	Close (X1)	Rolling Mean (X2)	Momentum (X3)	Daily Return (X4)
June, 4 2018	46.52	48.03	-5.03	-0.41 - Fall
June, 5 2018	45.37	47.44	-5.91	-2.49 - Fall
June, 6 2018	46.96	46.96	-4.81	+3.50 - Rise
June, 7 2018	46.91	46.38	-5.81	-0.10 - Fall

In order to create a training set and dependent variable for the prediction of stock movement for next day. The daily return column values has to be shifted one place above.

Table 2.

Date	Close (X1)	Rolling Mean (X2)	Momentum (X3)	Daily Return (X4)	Next Day Change (Y)
June, 4 2018	46.52	48.03	-5.03	-0.41 - Fall	Fall
June, 5 2018	45.37	47.44	-5.91	-2.49 - Fall	Rise
June, 6 2018	46.96	46.96	-4.81	+3.50 - Rise	Fall

Creating a Validation Set

Test set does not contain dependent variable Y, in fact this set is used to predict its value. Therefore, there is no preprocessing like training set is required on the test set other than calculating the predictor variables (e.g. Bollinger bands, daily return, simple moving average etc.)

Machine Learning Algorithms

This is the core step for which all the above processing have been done such that data collection, preprocessing, feature generation, and data sampling. There are several machine learning algorithms developed for different type of problems which is whether the problem is supervised or unsupervised learning. Supervised learning is the approach of creating a model using an algorithm in which it learns to map an input (X) to an output (Y) using historical data. On the other hand, unsupervised learning models are the one which create groups or clusters for similar set of items. The majority of machine learning problems are based on supervised learning.

Machine Learning model refers to a model artifact which is created in the process of learning algorithm using historical or training data. Regression and classification models are based on supervised machine learning. In regression, model predicts the future numerical (e.g. stock price) value (Y) given a set of parameters (X). On the other hand, classification model predicts the categorical value (e.g. stock movement rise/fall) based on the input data. A number of different models can be created using different machine learning algorithms.

Linear Regressions

An algorithm which finds the best value of parameters for an equation to fit the training data. For the simple linear approach, the equation is as follows:

$$y = mx + c \tag{14}$$

As it can be noted that it is the equation of line in which m and c are the parameters for which the algorithm finds the best value considering the input x (i.e. features). Whereas, y is the output/depended variable (e.g. next day stock price). It is also known as parametric modeling. For a parametric approach, there is no need for a trained model to use the historical data while prediction, as it has already learnt the best parameters for an equation to predict a value. But, the model should be retrain and update its parameter values when the new or additional training data is gathered or added.

Pros:
- ○ Easy to understand and implement.
- ○ Useful to find the relationship between variables.

Cons:
- ○ Sensitive to the anomalies or noise in a data set (i.e. outliers).
- ○ Under perform for the non-linear data set (i.e. relationship between dependent and independent variables are not linear).

K Nearest Neighbor (KNN)

It is one of the most popular machine learning technique which has an instance based and data centric approach. The algorithm predicts the Y value by taking a vote of its 'K' nearest neighbors. For example if the value of k is 3, for any new test example b, it computes the distance of b from all the training samples (by using x values) and select Y values of 3 nearest samples. Further, the maximum occurring

Y value out of those 3 is selected for example b. Unlike, linear regression where the data is not being used after the parameter finding. KNN uses or consult the historical data for every prediction it makes. This approach is hard to apply when there are large number of data points as each data point needs to be considered while prediction. But, there is no need to train a model again since it does not require any parameters (i.e. m and c) like regression based model.

Pros:
- Implementation of Algorithm is not complex.
- Easy to add new features
- Can also handle Multi-class problems

Cons:
- High computation cost for large set of data.
- As it is a distance based learning, which type of distance function should be used can be a problem to consider.
- Need to ascertain the value of K.

Decision Tree

As the name suggests, the model is based on a structure like a tree. A prediction is made by traversing the nodes of the tree one by one. On every node, there is a calculation involve on the input values (x) which eventually approaches to an outcome. A model is formed by the training algorithm in such a way that the features or input parameters which are highly correlated with an output are placed on the upper node of the tree.

Pros:
- Easily consider discrete and categorical features at the same time.
- Handle both regression and classification problems.
- Visualization and interpretation is easy.

Cons:
- Likely to over-fit as the depth of tree increases.
- Under perform for diagonal decision boundaries.

Random Forest Classifier

It is one of the most powerful algorithm which works just like the decision tree but instead of one tree, it is composed of several decision trees (weak learners) which are trained or created on random chunk of data from training set. The predictions of several models are combined to give a final result or output. It is called random because for every model a chunk of data is randomly selected from training set, further it also randomly select the limited set of features or nodes (i.e. $n = \sqrt{Total\ number\ of\ features}$) to create a decision tree for that model.

The algorithm uses a concept called bagging which is defined as creating several models from same algorithm (e.g. Support Vector Machine, K- Nearest Neighbour, Neural Net etc.) trained on a subset of randomly selected training data (known as bags of data). For a test sample prediction, all the individual predictions from models are averaged together to get the final prediction. It also helps to reduce high variance (over-fitting) while keeping the possession of bias (under-fitting).

Pros:
- Easily consider discrete and categorical features at the same time.
- Handle both regression and classification problems.
- Smartly handle multiple correlated features.
- Reduce variance and over fitting due to decorrelation between trees.

Cons:
- Likely to over-fit when the number of trees increases in case of boosted trees.
- Visualization and interpretation is not easy.

AdaBoost Classifier

AdaBoost which is a short form for adaptive boosting. Unlike the bagging approach used by random forest algorithm, it uses an adaptive boosting concept which is defined as a set of several subsequent weak learners (models) of same algorithm. Each weak learner model tries to correct the misclassifications of previous model. Thus, creating a strong learning model from several weak learners.

Ensemble Models

Combination of several algorithms for the purpose to predict something is called ensembles. It is not an algorithm but a collection of different weak learner models (i.e. KNN, Linear Regression, Random Forest etc.) combined together to build a single model. The final prediction value is calculated by using the output value of all the models. For a regression problem, the prediction value is calculated by taking the average value of the prediction of all models. Similarly, voting based approach is used for a classification problem. Use of ensemble learners often reduces the chance of over-fitting as the output is not biased on a single model or algorithm. It also minimizes the overall absolute error and improve accuracy. It should be noted that Random Forest and AdaBoost are also ensembles because instead of using several algorithms for different models, they uses the same algorithm with random data for different models.

Model Evaluation Metrics

Models are evaluated for their correctness of predictions. It is one of the major step to check how accurate the model is for future predictions of a problem. There are many evaluation metrics available for different nature of problems. Accuracy measure and Root mean square error (RMSE) are the most popular metrics for classification and regression problems respectively. In case of over-fitting, in sample (training set) error decreases and out of sample (test set) error increases.

Accuracy

In case of classification models, accuracy measure is used to evaluate model's perfection for predictions. It is the percentage of the number of correct predictions made by the model. For example, if a model correctly predicts 80 samples out of 100 then the accuracy of the model is 80%.

$$Accuracy = \frac{NumberofCorrectPredictions}{NumberofTotalPredictions} \times 100 \tag{15}$$

Root Mean Square Error (RMSE)

For a regression model which predicts a numeric value, RMSE can be used to evaluate a model. As the prediction value is numerical, accuracy metric would not be a good choice for a regression model because it gives an approximate prediction value for numerical inputs. Root mean square error is basically an average error of the overall predictions made by the model. It is calculate as follows:

$$RMSE = \sqrt{\frac{\sum \left(ActualValue\left(Y\right) - PredictedValue\left(Ytest\right)\right)^2}{TotalNumberofPredictions\left(N\right)}} \tag{16}$$

The equation above simply takes a squared difference of the actual and predicted value for all the predictions. Further, it computes square root of their mean. The square of a difference is taken to avoid negative values, as the error cannot be negative.

Bias and Variance in Models

When the model is trained, it is very important to analyze it for bias (over-fitting) and variance (under-fitting). Higher bias indicates that the model is performing too well for the training data but not on test data whereas high variance indicates that the model is not working well on training data as well as on test data. In other words, a highly over-fitted model tightly learns the training examples and fails for the testing sample. Whereas, an under-fitted model does not even understand the training examples properly. Therefore, an ideal model should have low bias and low variance.

It can be noticed in the above figure that when the number of parameters increases from 5, the difference between train and test error increases which indicates over-fitting of the model. On the other hand, when the number of parameters are set to 1 or 2, it is considered an under-fitted model.

SAMPLE USE CASE

There are two different scopes in the prediction of stocks which are to predict the actual value of the stock price for the future or to predict the stock price movement (i.e. rise or fall in price) for the future. For this particular example, the goal is to predict the 5th day closing price movement of apple's stock which is a supervised learning and classification problem.

Four years (2013-2017) of apple's daily historical data was collected from yahoo finance and preprocessed before feature generation. The following additional features (technical indicators) were generated out of data to train a learning model.

The performance of some machine learning algorithms on this data are as follows:

Figure 10. Train/test performance sample

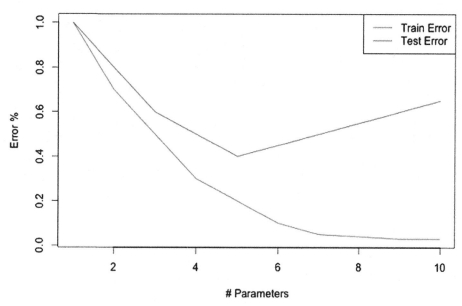

Table 3.

Technical Indicators
1. Rolling Mean (Simple Moving Average of 10 days)
2. Weighted Moving Average (10 days)
3. Relative Strength Index (RSI) of 10 days
4. Momentum (10 days)
5. Moving Average Convergence Divergence (MACD)
6. Stochastic K%
7. Stochastic D% (10 days)
8. Accumulation/Distribution (A/D) Oscillator (10 days)
9. Commodity Channel Index (CCI) of 10 days

Performance on K-Nearest Neighbors (KNN)

The algorithm is tested for its performance for different values of K and the highest accuracy (i.e. ~60%) is achieved on the test data when the value of k is set to 3. The performance of the algorithm also depends on the number of features generated and considered. It can be noted that for the training set, the accuracy of the model is 100% when the k is set to 1 that is because the testing is performed on the same data.

Figure 11. K-nearest neighbor performance on test/train data

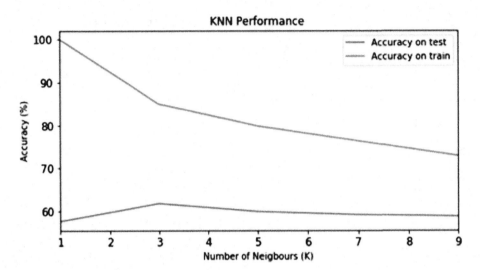

Performance on Random Forest Classifier

As compared to KNN, random forest performs slightly better when it was tested on the validation set. The performance of the model was tested on different number of trees in which the highest accuracy (i.e. ~62%) is achieved when the number of random trees were set to 160. Number of trees is a hyper parameter which vary according to the nature of the data and should be tuned with respect to training and testing data performance (i.e. low variance and bias).

Figure 12. Random forest performance on test/train data

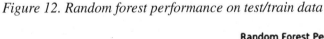

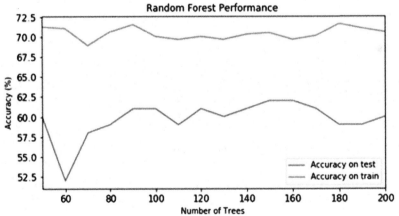

Performance on AdaBoost Classifier

The performance of AdaBoost algorithm was also tested on different number of trees and the best result (i.e. approx. 60%) on test set was achieved when the number of trees were set above 120. The algorithm does not perform better than KNN or Random Forest. This judgement is purely based on the quality of data and features generated out of historical data.

Figure 13. AdaBoostPerformance on test/train data

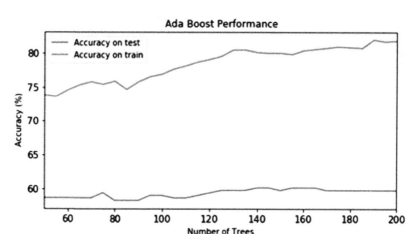

It can be noted that increasing the number of trees improve the accuracy of training set. But on the other hand, when the number of trees are increased above120. The accuracy on test set does not show much improvement which means the modelis over-fitting the training data. This behavior can be observed in AdaBoost algorithm because of its subsequent weak learner approach. Increasing the number of trees tightly learns the training set as each model (tree) tries to correct the misclassification of previous model.

FUTURE WORK

So far there has been many advancements in the field of machine learning and artificial intelligence which support and handle complex behaviors of daily stock markets. In this chapter, only technical analysis of stock market is being considered for the sake of prediction. But, there are other factors which might useful in the improvement of long term predictions. This includes the influence of social media and daily news on particular security and stock market. Recently, there has been much improvement in the area of Natural Language Processing (NLP) and Deep Learning techniques. These advancements can be really helpful in calculating and interpreting the impact of daily news on particular stock. Many implementations are there on the sentiment analysis of text. But, there is a plenty of room for its improvement in the field of financial market such that calculating the exact impact of a news on a stock. Similarly, fundamental analysis is yet another technique which evaluate the intrinsic value of a stock. Considering these qualitative and quantitative features at the same time would result in the improved prediction models.

CONCLUSION

The above use case illustrate that how artificial intelligence and machine learning techniques can play significant role in stock trading. Incorporating machine learning in trading strategies can help investors and traders to capture more alpha. Over the past some years, there have been several advancements occurred in field of machine learning according to the rate of improvement in computer performance. When dealing with the complex, non-linear and dynamic behavior of financial markets the use of more sophisticated trading algorithms is necessary. In search for methods to address these weaknesses and thanks to the advances in computing and technology, research focuses on the various tools of computational intelligence. The most popular algorithms reported in literature are Logistic Regression, K-Nearest Neighbors, Neural Networks, and Support Vector Machine. Furthermore, results of predictions can be improved by analyzing the strength and weakness of the security and taking the sentiment of its information into account.

REFERENCES

Ballings, M., Van den Poel, D., Hespeels, N., & Gryp, R. (2015). Evaluating multiple classifiers for stock price direction prediction. *Expert Systems with Applications*, 42(20), 7046–7056. doi:10.1016/j.eswa.2015.05.013

Bisoi, R., & Dash, P. K. (2014). A hybrid evolutionary dynamic neural network for stock market trend analysis and prediction using unscented Kalman filter. *Applied Soft Computing*, 19, 41–56. doi:10.1016/j.asoc.2014.01.039

Ding, X., Zhang, Y., & Liu, T., & Duan. (2015). Deep learning for event-driven stock prediction. *IJCAI (United States)*, 2327–2333.

Ding, X., Zhang, Y., Liu, T., & Duan, J. (2014). Using structured events to predict stock price movement: An empirical investigation. *Proceedings of the 2014 Conference on Empirical Methods in Natural Language Processing (EMNLP)*, 1415-1425.

Fang, Y., Fataliyev, K., Wang, L., Fu, X., & Wang, Y. (2014). Improving the genetic-algorithm-optimized wavelet neural network for stock market prediction. *International Joint Conference on Neural Networks (IJCNN)*, 3038-3042. 10.1109/IJCNN.2014.6889969

Hegazy, O., Soliman, O. S., & Salam, M. A. (2015). Comparative study between FPA, BA, MCS, ABC, and PSO algorithms in training and optimizing of LS-SVM for stock market prediction. *IJACR, 35*.

Lee, H., Surdeanu, M., MacCartney, B., & Jurafsky, D. (2014). On the Importance of Text Analysis for Stock Price Prediction. *LREC*, 1170-1175.

Li, Q., Wang, T. J., Li, P., Liu, L., Gong, Q., & Chen, Y. (2014). The effect of news and public mood on stock movements. *Information Sciences*, 278, 826–840. doi:10.1016/j.ins.2014.03.096

Li, X., Xie, H., Chen, L., Wang, J., & Deng, X. (2014). News impact on stock price return via sentiment analysis. *Knowledge-Based Systems*, 69, 14–23. doi:10.1016/j.knosys.2014.04.022

Nguyen, T., & Shirai, K. (2015). *Topic modeling based sentiment analysis on social media for stock market prediction*. Association for Computational Linguistics.

Patel, J., Shah, S., Thakkar, P., & Kotecha, K. (2015). Predicting stock and stock price index movement using trend deterministic data preparation and machine learning techniques. *Expert Systems with Applications*, *42*(1), 259–268. doi:10.1016/j.eswa.2014.07.040

Ranco, G., Aleksovski, D., Caldarelli, G., Grcar, M., & Mozetic, I. (2015). The effects of Twitter sentiment on stock price returns. *PLoS One*, *10*(9), e0138441. doi:10.1371/journal.pone.0138441 PMID:26390434

ENDNOTES

[1] https://www.google.com/finance/getprices?i=[PERIOD]&p=[DAYS]d&q=[TICKER]
[2] https://finance.yahoo.com/quote/[TICKER]
[3] https://www.finam.ru/analysis/profile041CA00007/default.asp

This research was previously published in FinTech as a Disruptive Technology for Financial Institutions; pages 142-169, copyright year 2019 by Business Science Reference (an imprint of IGI Global).

Chapter 67
Application of Machine Learning Techniques in Healthcare

Sathya D.
Kumaraguru College of Technology, India

Sudha V.
Kumaraguru College of Technology, India

Jagadeesan D.
Cherraan's Arts Science College, India

ABSTRACT

Machine learning is an approach of artificial intelligence (AI) where the machine can automatically learn and improve its performance on experience. It is not explicitly programmed; the data is fed into the generic algorithm and it builds logic based on the data provided. Traditional algorithms have to define new rules or massive rules when the pattern varies or the number of patterns increases, which reduces the accuracy or efficiency of the algorithms. But the machine learning algorithms learn new input patterns capable of handling complex situations while maintaining accuracy and efficiency. Due to its effectual benefits, machine learning algorithms are used in various domains like healthcare, industries, travel, game development, social media services, robotics, and surveillance and information security. In this chapter, the application of machine learning technique in healthcare is discussed in detail.

INTRODUCTION

In recent days, the people are using medical sensors and other health devices to monitor health status. Using the advanced medical devices the patients' health related parameters can be monitored continuously and in real time, and then processed and transferred to medical databases. This certainly improves patient's quality-of-care without disturbing their comfort and significantly reduces the hospital occupancy rates. At the same time, the enormous amount of health data collected using the sensors are difficult to analyse by the human beings. The advancement in technologies like machine learning when combined

DOI: 10.4018/978-1-6684-6291-1.ch067

with health care helps the health care to move a step ahead. Machine learning infact helps us to improve the performance in health care from experience rather than programming.

Since the health data is more sensitive and any fault may affect person's life, it has to be processed and the health problem has to be predicted quickly. The human being's cannot process the data quickly using the conventional methods. So the machine learning techniques are used in these cases to find out the disease pattern and the cause. Similarly, the machine learning techniques are used in various applications like disease diagnosing systems, drug detection, and assistive technology. The benefits of machine learning algorithm includes accuracy, decision making, quick and powerful processing, handling complex data and cost effective. The objective of this study is to explore the current applications of AI techniques in health care systems in detail.

The applications of machine learning techniques in health systems are listed below:

1. Disease Diagnosing systems
2. Remote Health Monitoring Systems
3. Drug detection and analysis
4. Assistive Technologies
5. Medical Imaging Diagnosis
6. Smart Health Records
7. Clinical Trial and Research
8. Crowd sourced Data Collection
9. Better Radiotherapy
10. Outbreak Prediction

The chapter is organized as follows: Section 1 gives the brief Introduction on the uses and applications of AI, Section 2 explains the types of disease diagnosing systems, AI system in diagnosing stroke and cancer, Section 3 describes the Remote Health monitoring systems and AI in mobile Health, WMSN and Internet of Things (IoT), Section 4 discusses the AI in drug detection and analysis, Section 5 explains the Assistive technology devices and its use, Section 6 describes the Medical Imaging diagnosis, Section 7 presents the smart health records and its use, Section 8 briefs about the Clinical trial and research, Section 9 explains the crowd sourced data collection, Section 10 illustrates the radiotherapy and Section 11 briefs on outbreak prediction.

DISEASE DIAGNOSING SYSTEMS

In most of the disease diagnosing systems the AI techniques analyses the data from medical images, genetic test reports, electrophysiological data, and clinical notes etc. The clinical notes are the unstructured data which has to be processed before analysing. The AI techniques converts the unstructured data into machine readable Electronic Medical Record (EMR), which is analysed by the machine learning techniques easily (Fei et al. 2017).

The disease diagnosing systems are using the below given types (emrj.com):

- **AI-Chatbots:** The speech recognition techniques are used in AI- Chatbots to identify disease patterns and to advise a suitable course of action for the patients.

- **Oncology:** The researchers train the algorithm using deep learning to identify cancerous tissues specifically skin cancer.
- **Pathology:** Traditionally the pathologists use the microscope to diagnose disease, as well as it involves the diagnosing using body fluids like blood, urine etc. Deep learning techniques and machine vision algorithms are used to provide speed and accurate diagnosing results.
- **Unusual Diseases:** The genetic and other rare diseases are detected using facial recognition and deep learning techniques.

In Gillies et al. (2016), AI technologies are used for analysing medical images and to convert large set of images into minable data. By the subsequent analysis of these data, it provides better decision making for the diseases like tumour. In Shin et al. (2010), the Electrodiagnosis Support System is used for clinical decision making for neural injury in the upper limb. This system provides a Graphical User Interface (GUI), which picturize the neural structure. The user can input the electromyography test results in the GUI and can get the diagnosis results.

From the above discussion, we can conclude that the medical applications using AI falls into two categories (Fei et al. 2017):

1. The machine learning techniques analyse structured data like medical images, genetic data etc to diagnose the disease.
2. The machine learning techniques analyse unstructured data using Natural Language Processing (NLP) from medical notes, medical journals. The NLP algorithms produce a machine readable structured data which can be easily analysed.

AI System to Diagnose Stroke

AI techniques are used in three stages of stroke care: Early detection of stroke, treatment, result prediction and stroke prognosis evaluation (Fei et al. 2017).

Early Detection of Stroke

A movement detecting device was developed for early stroke prediction (Villar et al. 2015). The Principle Component Analysis (PCA) and genetic finite state machine are implemented in the device. If the movement of the patient is different from the normal value then the alert will be given for stroke treatment. In Mannini et al. (2016), the wearable device is used for detecting stroke. The wearable device collects the physiological status of the patients continuously. The collected data is processed by the SVM and hidden markov model algorithms and provides accuracy about 90.5%.

For stroke diagnosis, the machine learning techniques are applied on the neuro imaging data like Magnetic Resonance Imaging (MRI) and Computed Tomography (CT) scan image. In Rehme et al. (2015), the abnormal conditions are identified using Support Vector Machine (SVM) for the patients having stroke. The accuracy of SVM on MRI data is 87.6%.

Treatment

Intravenous thrombolysis (tPA) is the only approved treatment for ischemic stroke. tPA dissolves the clot and improves the blood flow to the brain. In (Bentley et al. 2014), the SVM is used to predict whether the tPA treatment would develop any intracranial haemorrhage. The intracranial haemorrhage is the type of bleeding occurs inside the skull. The CT scan is used as the input for SVM which performs better than conventional radiology based methods. In Ye at al. (2017), the interaction trees and subgroup analysis is used to predict the tPA dosage to be given to the patient based on the patient characteristics.

Result Prediction and Stroke Prognosis Evaluation

Compared with the conventional methods machine learning techniques provides better performance in evaluating stroke prognosis. In Zhang at al. (2013), used a logistic regression to predict the result of three months treatment by analysing the physical parameters of the patients for 48 hours after getting stroke. In Asadi at. Al (2014) and Sandeep (2018), the physiological information of 107 patients is stored in a database who undergone a intra-arterial therapy. The Neural network and SVM is implemented to predict the outcome of treatment which provides 97.5% accuracy.

AI System to Diagnose Cancer

The cancer biomarkers have been used for screening, diagnosis, risk assessment, prognosis of cancer, and detection of response to treatment. Currently many newer technologies are used for disease diagnosis. For detecting breast cancer, the gene expression patterns are used to detect the prognosis of the disease. Machine learning techniques like random forest classifier and SVM classifier are used for classifying normal and abnormal tissues. The SVM accuracy is better than random forest model in same-tissue testing. The random forest classifier performs better than SVM in across-tissue testing (Henry et al. 2012).

From the study, we can conclude that AI techniques concentrate more on diseases like cancer, cardiac disease and nervous system disease.

REMOTE HEALTH MONITORING SYSTEMS

Remote health monitoring collects the physiological data of the patients using digital technologies and transmits it to the hospital or to the doctors. (cloudtweaks.com) The patient can be monitored with the parameters like blood pressure, blood sugar levels, heart rate, weight, electrocardiogram (ECG) etc. It provides the continuous monitoring of patients with better accuracy at home place. It is used for the patients who suffer from chronic diseases, post-surgery patients, elderly people, and for the patients who are bedridden.

AI in Mobile Health

Nowadays, the wireless devices are used to support the healthcare in the form of mobile health or mHealth (Sandeep 2018; Barton 2012). Mobile health applications are widely used in the areas like diagnostic disease, remote patient monitoring, surveillance on the spread of disease, emergency support, patient information management system (Barton 2012; Mohammadzadeh at al. 2014). The AI techniques are widely used in the mHealth which is the reason for the successful development of mHealth. Recently the intelligent agents are used in mHealth for communication, dynamic resource management, predicting the solutions etc. The mHealth have been successfully used in remote patient monitoring systems for adults and sport's persons, clinical decision making, emergency care. The AI techniques is used in mHealth for predicting emergency care and suggesting the first aid medication for the patients.

AI in WMSN

The application of AI is also used in the Wireless Medical Sensor Networks (WMSN). The WMSN have the collection of biosensors connected to the patient body having chronic diseases or adults who needs continuous monitoring. The WMSN is also used to continuously monitor the sports person's activities. The health data collected using wireless medical sensors are transmitted to the hospital server (Sathya et al. 2017). The data aggregation is performed at the hospital server and it is communicated to the doctor's personal digital assistant for diagnosis. The AI techniques are used in filtration of data in sensors. Instead of sending all the monitored physiological data to the hospital server. The data can be filtered using the AI techniques in the sensors and the value above the threshold value or the abnormal values can alone be send to the hospital server.

AI in IoT

The application of AI is not only used in the mHealth and WMSN it has also been extended to the smart devices. The smart devices are connected to each other to form a pervasive network is called as IoT (Islam at al. 2015; Da Xu et al. 2014). IoT is used in smart health care for the persons who need remote monitoring of health and medicine intake. The AI techniques are used in this Ambient Assisted living. The diagnosing of patient conditions and medicine intake is possible by implementing AI techniques in the Ambient Assisted living (Sandeep 2018).

The advantage of Remote Health Monitoring is listed below:

1. **Reduced Healthcare Cost:** In WMSNs and in mhealth, the patients' health related parameters can be monitored continuously and in real time, and then processed and transferred to medical databases. This certainly improves patient's quality-of-care without disturbing their comfort and significantly reduces the hospital occupancy rates.
2. **Improved Quality:** The data taken by the sensors and medical devices are highly accurate.
3. **Emergency Care:** The patient sufferings from chronic diseases are remotely monitored and any emergency conditions will be intimated immediately to the medical professionals.
4. **Disease Diagnosis:** By continuous monitoring, the identification and assessment of medications can be improved.
5. **Future Reference:** The health data collected using digital devices can be stored and used for future clinical decision making and treatments.

DRUG DETECTION AND ANALYSIS

The machine learning and natural language processing helps the drug discovery scientists to discover new drugs. The machine learning is an AI technique which becomes skilled from trained data to determine patterns and make decisions based on these patterns. Whereas the natural language processing refers to computer system which program and analyze large amount of natural language data (technologyworks. com).

Before AI techniques come into existence virtual screening, molecular modelling and predicting how drug would be non-toxic to the patient body is a difficult process. This pre-clinical test is more expensive and time consuming. But using AI we can train the compounds with known properties and learn how to do associates with the matching molecules for the required application. AI techniques are used to reduce the running of experimental labs for drug discovery and running large scale experiments.

The AI and machine learning is applied in three major areas (technologyworks.com):

1. Target Identification
2. Lead Optimization
3. Screening drug Candidates

The target identification provides validation and improves target areas for drug identification and compound screening. Lead optimization uses algorithms for simulating structure, simulating toxicity and binding. Screening drug candidate is used to assist the scientists in identifying pattern from the input image and also to identify the rare patterns from the large image datasets.

AI for Genetics and Genomics

The microarray genetic data or RNA-seq expression data can be analysed by using Supervised, semi-supervised and unsupervised machine learning algorithms (deepsense.ai). These algorithms are used to identify the genetic disease and the action of drugs. Many studies are on-going to analyse genomic data and to solve genomic sequencing problems. Finding the specific region in genomic sequencing and recognizing locations of transcriptomic sites is very difficult task in real time. Deep learning algorithms can be used for genome interpretation and analysis. The supervised heterogeneous algorithms can be used to address difficult biomedical prediction problems.

AI for Network Analysis of Biomedical Data

The analysis of genetic data would be helpful in identifying the drugs and its action (deepsense.ai). It will also be helpful for predicting the optimal combination of drugs and new drugs. The machine learning approaches for biological network analysis is used to identify the new class of genes for cancer disease. The combination of support vector machine (SVM) and machine learning assisted network interference is used to identify cancer gene pairs. This can be used to reorganise the new network for identifying key cancer genes in high dimensional data space.

ASSISTIVE TECHNOLOGIES

The Assistive technology is the life changing alternative developed for the disabled persons to make their life easier (newgenapps.com). Currently, the robots are used for disabled persons to make their life better. Robots are used by the people who are living alone. The people using the robots at home to satisfy their needs are called as home robots. The human can customize the robots to the individual needs. The home robots are used to make an emergency call to the hospital, reminding the appointments and medications.

AI in Assistive Technology

Smarter Glasses

The smarter glasses are invented by the neuroscientists and computer vision scientists in the Oxford University, UK. The smarter glass is the augmented reality glass focuses on specific part of sight. This will increase the image contrast which highlights the specific feature of an image (digitaltrends.com).

Google Glass

Google glass was introduced in the year 2013 and very useful for the visually impaired people. It assists the blind person's by describing their environment and helps to navigate. The intelligent agent has the dashboard of preferred data, maps, and the information of their surroundings. This information is helpful for the person's to know how long to travel to reach their target place (in.pcmag.com).

Cognitive Hearing Aids

The hearing aid with AI and sensors is released first time for hearing impaired patients by Livio AI (starkey.com). The head and the ear is the more appropriate place to measure our physical activity. So the Livio AI uses the 3D motion sensors like accelerometer and gyroscope to detect movements and gestures, track the activities. This hearing aid is used to help the people to treat hearing loss and also to understand and improve their overall health.

The features of Livio AI are discussed below (globenewswire.com):

1. Customizable adjustments to the sounds and programs
2. Remote controlling of the hearing aid
3. User interface with tap control
4. Hearing reality technology gives natural listening, speech clarity in the noisiest environment
5. Inertial sensors are used for fall detection.
6. Tracks the overall health and wellness.

Locked-In Syndrome

The patients with Locked-in syndrome have the full cognitive ability but they are not able to speak or move (healtheuropa.eu). The AI powered device for the locked-in syndrome patient's provides communication to the patients with eye movements.

The device tracks the eye movements by using head-mounted camera and translates into the audio communication viz a speaker (med-technews.com). The earpiece has the bone conduction element that provides the audio feedback to the user before sending to the output speaker. The device can be used without a screen, teach with personalised syntax, choose the range of output language, and can work with Bluetooth wireless technology.

Helen Paterson, speech therapist, Royal hospital, tested the device with her patient's. She said that the device is easy to wear, light weight, the patient need to move only the eyes up and down or side to side. The patient no need to have the device in front of them all the time.

Parkinson's Disease Balancing Application

Parkinson's Disease is the degenerative nerve disease that affects the motor system. The early symptoms of the disease are rigidity, shaking, difficulty in walking, slowness of movement. The advanced stages of the disease are sensory, sleepy, emotional problems, depression, anxiety. These abnormal motor symptoms are called as "parkinsonism".

The patient with Parkinson's disease suffers from loss of balance or they fall (digitaltrends.com). The University of Houston releasing the new project for the patient having loss of balance. The smarter balance system is wearable and connected with smart-phone. The smarter balance system has the special belt connected with vibrating actuators. These actuators have a customized program to map the patient movement. The patient movement is mapped like series of dots on the Smartphone. The smarter balance improves the postural stability by guiding patients through exercise. It decreases the number of falls and increases the user's confidence. The patients can have the virtual physical therapist at home which reduces the repeated visits to hospitals.

MEDICAL IMAGING DIAGNOSIS

Medical imaging is the procedure used for building a clear visual representation of the interior parts of the body that are hidden by skin and bones. This is also used for diagnosing the disease and treatment of the same. This can also be used for database construction. In a survey by IBM, it is found that about 90% of the medical database consists of images. Hence processing and analysis of medical images is a challenging task that exists in image processing.

The image diagnosing process is improved by applying Artificial Intelligence and Machine Learning algorithms. The application of machine learning to image diagnosis process dates back to 1990. In those days, the computation of the algorithm is done manually. Machine Learning algorithms are used for designing an automated image identification system and the same is presented in the market. Also, the cost of the diagnosing system and health care got reduced with the help of these technologies. One of the most significant challenges in constructing automated image diagnosing system is the data labelling and skills gap. The detailed discussion about this issue is done below.

When an image has to be processed by Machine Learning all the images must be pre processed by attaching labels to it. But including labels for all the images that are needed for constructing an innovative image recognition model is a labour-intensive process. Also, most of the medical data's are sparse. Available mining algorithms can be used for converting this sparse data set into reusable data sets. Though machine learning is applied to the medical data's by overcoming the above changes, another real life issue that exists is the knowledge level of the radiologists. Thus, to successfully apply machine learning in radiology along with automating the process, the knowledge about machine learning must be imparted to the radiologists. This skill gap can be filled by teaching the techniques to the radiologists by the data scientists.

It is predicted that in future by 2020, we may have a tool kit that automatically predict the image and serve the purpose for which it is designed. Along with improving the image diagnosing, machine learning techniques can be used to constructing a very good image acquisition system whose output can be used for further processing.

SMART HEALTH RECORDS

It is well known that prediction in medical field can be improved by applying machine learning techniques to it. But construction of medical database involves many issues. The primary issue is the collection of data. Though the above issue is addressed with the help of technologies, finding relationship among the data's is still a difficult task. Next issue is the database must include both image and genetic data. Some of the tools developed for this purpose are ePAD, and TCIA .

Personalized treatment to the patients are getting famous now-a-days. This is possible only if we have a system that stores the patient's record digitally and retrieve the needed information very quickly. Retrieval of information's can be personalized and optimized with the help of the machine learning algorithm: support vector machine.

The two constraints that are faced while applying machine learning over medical image is the heterogeneous raw data and small sample size. With the help of Electronic Health Record (EHR) and digital imaging the database size can be increased. These constraints can be solved by selecting proper data preprocessing and augmentation algorithms.

An important issue with the above proposed technique is not all the doctors are recording their prescriptions digitally and while few are not even aware of it. This drawback can be overcome by converting the characters in the hand written format to equivalent digital characters. Also, there is an ongoing research for converting the doctor's prescription and patient's health records into a digital record by applying Natural Language Processing (NLP) and ML.

Personalized treatment to the patients can be enhanced by applying predictive modelling to the EHR data. But, to apply the predictive algorithms the EHR data need to be pre-processed. This pre-processing is again a labour intensive task. A new representation is proposed in (Neil at al. 2018), for representing the EHR data created on the Fast Healthcare Interoperability Resources (FHIR) format. The application of predictive algorithms on these new formats enhances the treatment process. This proposed method is tested using the database obtained from the US academic medical centres.

From the test, it is predicted that the proposed model outperformed all the existing models. This model can be further used for creating different clinical scenarios. By applying neural network algorithms, this model is also used for retrieving relevant information about a patient.

CLINICAL TRIAL AND RESEARCH

A clinical trial is an experimental study on a person to invent new medicines. Also, it is used for deciding whether the newly invented medicine and treatment works for the purpose and does not cause any harm to the human beings when applied in future. Clinical trial plays a major role in health care as it is used for improving the research in terms of application and safety. They make researchers to learn what is working and what is not working while they are working for finding new drugs. It is also used for learning the side effects allied with the new drug, ways to manage and avoid it. Usually, clinical trials are divided into five stages. Though clinical trial procedures are speeded up, still few medicines takes even few years to reach the market. This time delay can be reduced by applying machine learning to clinical trials.

The clinical trial research can further be improvised by the application of Machine Learning. For instance, number of candidate's identification for applying clinical trial can be increased by using predictive analytics. Thus, by increasing number of participants better result can be obtained.

One of the important challenge of the clinical trial procedure lies in finding the corresponding patient for every clinical trial. Every stage in clinical trial can be improved with the help of Artificial Intelligence. The artificial intelligence algorithms can be applied to the patients record, compare it to find the matching ongoing trials. From the comparison, matching studies can be suggested. One of the main problem in following the above methodology is in maintaining the privacy and security of the patient's record. HIPAA is one of the law that is proposed for protecting the patient's record. It is difficult to apply sentiment analysis on clinical trial records. Intel proposed a solution for improving the clinical trial process using Artificial Intelligence and sensors.

Intel® Pharma Analytics Platform – the proposed solution makes use of wearable sensors to collect continuous data from the patient. On the collected data, analytics methods are applied to find important patterns and apply the suitable clinical trial on it. Few of the advantages of the above methods are: it reduces trial cost, improves data quality and improves patient experience.

Machine Learning can further be used for efficiently accessing the real-time data sets. The other applications of Machine Learning includes in identifying best trail data and aiding in maintaining electronic health records.

Machine learning algorithms can be applied on the data's collected from patients to predict the influence of the drug on the patient.

CROWDSOURCED DATA COLLECTION

Sometimes the data required for analysing and arriving for a conclusion may be insufficient. Now-a-days crowd sourcing helps the people to overcome the above constraints. Though many technologies come into the market, it is not possible for us to find relation between the big data and health care. Also, few of the health care data set lacks proper data set. But, to train a machine learning algorithm, proper data must be passed to it. This drawback is overcome with the help of crowdsourcing.

Crowdsourcing is a blooming technique that encompasses a large number of people cracking a problem or finishing a task for a single person or for an organisation. With the help of information technology, the crowd sourcing has advanced very vastly. A review of the application of crowd sourcing in health care is done in (Kerri 2018). Some of the fields in health care where crowd sourcing finds its application are surveillance; nutrition; public health and environment; education; genetics; psychology; and, general medicine/other.

The traditional way of data handling in the field like sociology and psychology are enhanced with the help of crowdsourcing and ML (Michael at al. 2011; Winter Mason at al. 2012). The following are the three advantages that are obtained by combining crowd sourcing and machine learning (allerin.com).

1. **Improves Sentiment Analysis:** The main objective of applying crowd sourcing and machine learning is to provide an impartial sentiment assessment.
2. **Improves Natural Language Processing (NLP):** In today's market, the customer review plays an important role. The existing machine learning algorithm concentrates much on the study of the reviews but not on analysing it. Thus by applying crowdsourcing in machine learning it is possible to propose an efficient algorithm for analysing the customer reviews. Initially, pre-processing of the review data is done using some machine learning algorithms. The data's that are not processed by the ML algorithms are filtered and given to the humans for processing. Then, the final analysis result is obtained from the output of the machine learning and crowd sourcing algorithms.
3. **Improves Quality of Data:** Though varieties of data are available, machine learning algorithms yields better result when they are applied to labelled data. With the help of crowd sourcing and machine learning now most of the available data's are labelled data. Also crowd sourcing helps to improve the quality of data.

BETTER RADIOTHERAPY

One of the most important technique used in the cancer treatment is the Radiation therapy. There are three specialties in the cancer treatment. They are radiation oncology, surgical oncology and medical oncology. Among the above three, radiation oncology is used in the treatment of cancer by applying radiations over the cancer cells. Also, radiation oncology is well suited for applying machine learning concepts because of the huge amount of data that can be collected in a given time period. In addition to the above application, machine learning can also be used for studying the reaction of genes over radiations. The data set available for performing predictive analysis in radiation oncology is very limited. From the available data, prediction of the accurate place for applying radiation has to be identified. The success of the identification depends upon on how well the prediction is able to differentiate between the normal and the affected place (Reid et al.). Also, with the help of AI, it possible to integrate data's from various sources.

Radiation therapy includes the following stages in the cancer treatment.

1. Patient assessment,
2. Simulation, planning,
3. Quality assurance,
4. Treatment delivery,
5. Follow-up

All the above stages can be improved by applying machine learning techniques over it. From the images obtained from the patients, it is important to find the space over which radiations must be applied.

In addition to it, the amount of radiations that need to be passed over the patients so that the purpose can be achieved with less toxic radiations. Radiation therapy when applied to the target place correctly, then it has a very powerful effect. Though radiation therapy found its application in the treatment of non-malignant disease, its most important application lies in the treatment of cancer. It makes use of waves in the treatment of cancer. Waves are nothing but the very powerful energy. Most of the cancer patients undergoing treatment will take radiation therapy treatment. Hence, there are huge amount of data available in radiation therapy. These data can be refined and information be extracted by applying ML algorithms.

In literature it is identified that there are a lot of opportunities exists in applying ML in the various phases of radiation oncology. For clinical practice, ML algorithms can be applied. A number of use cases can be supported with the help of applying ML to clinical practice. It is also inferred that an existing model can be fine-tuned to perform better on a small size dataset. In future, these technologies can save doctors time a lot.

Machine Learning has the capability to reduce the time of the radiation oncology team. Radiation oncology when combined with ML can give the world's best treatment. Machine Learning can even facilitate personalized radiation therapy treatment. One of the most important applications of radiology is the prediction of cancer. The cancer prediction process can be improved by combining imaging data with genetic data. Early prediction of cancer can be done by predicting for the existence of certain type of patterns of genes. This pattern prediction process can be improved by applying Natural Language Processing (NLP) to the genes when it is represented as characters.

OUTBREAK PREDICTION

An outbreak is an unexpected increase in number of incidents of a disease in a particular time and place. This outbreak will affect a little and localized group or some thousands of people across a continent. The outbreak may be epidemic i.e. fast spread of infectious diseases among a group of people in a very short period of time. Though the influence of outbreak is much among people, there are no formal methods proposed still now to predict the outbreak. Thus we are in need of a system that is capable of predicting the outbreaks. In this chapter, some of the existing technique used for predicting the outbreak that makes use of machine learning are discount breaks must be predicted. Outbreak prediction can be categorized in to three: probability of occurrence of particular disease; how fast it spreads and what kind of action need to be done to control the spread of the outbreak.

Epidemic diseases are the contagious diseases that spread out in a country in a particular time period when the quantity of the outbreak exceeds the minimum threshold level. Some of the well-known outbreaks are dengue, yellow fever, cholera, diphtheria, influenza, bird flu etc. By analysing the classical outbreaks, the technologist have come up with some advance methods in identifying the pattern and predicting the outbreaks. This prediction is further refined by the incoming dynamic data's.

Health predictive analysis is the new technology that is proposed for preventing contagious epidemic disease. Infectious disease spreads from affected animal or a person (Sangwon Chae at al. 2018). Here, infectious diseases are predicted using deep learning techniques. It is difficult to predict a pattern in infectious disease. Some of the disease outbreak prediction techniques are discussed in the following subsections.

Malaria Outbreak Prediction

Malaria is one of the epidemic diseases in India. It is important to predict the outbreak of this disease to prevent the life that is loosed because of it. In Vijeta (2015), a model using Machine learning is proposed. Here, two machine learning algorithms such as Support Vector Machine (SVM) and Artificial Neural Network (ANN) are used for predicting malaria disease. The data's collected from the Maharashtra state are used for training the model. The performance of these two models are compared here. As the result of the comparison, it is concluded that SVM outperforms ANN by providing more accurate results.

Another important issue that need to be addressed before applying machine learning algorithm is the incomplete data. When the collected data is incomplete, then we may not be able to derive an accurate solution. Thus, before applying the machine learning algorithm the data's need to be structured. In (emerj.com), it proposed that initially by applying decision tree algorithm, prediction for the missing values can be obtained and later map-reduce algorithm can be applied to get the results for the queries in optimal time.

Surveillance or monitoring of the outbreak of a disease is very important for a public health department. Now-a-days public health departments are allowed to access the real time data's, but from the accessed data they could not conclude anything due to the number of instances of the data. Hence, some algorithms are developed that surveys the data and gives an alarm if there are any possibility for outbreak of any diseases.

Dengue Outbreak Prediction System

Dengue is an epidemic disease that is caused by the mosquito bite. Dengue is caused by the mosquito breed Aedes. Around 30% of the world population are under risk of getting affected by dengue. By earlier prediction of dengue. It is possible to save life many peoples.

Some of the machine learning algorithms used for the dengue prediction are discussed in Rajathi at al. (2018). Here, they have compared the various data mining algorithms using the data obtained from karuna medical hospital. Decision tree algorithm is used for dengue prediction in Buczak et al. (2012). A predictive model is constructed in Thitiprayoonwongse et al. (2012) using set annotated discharge summaries as input. This model predicts the presence or absence of the dengue fever from the summary. Multivariate Poisson regression - a statistics model is used (Nandhini et al. 2016) for dengue prediction by identifying the correlation between the existing dengue cases and mosquito data. Dengue prediction in tribal area is done in Ta-Chien Chan et al. (2015) using decision tree classification algorithm.

Risk prediction model is proposed in Padet Siriyasatien et al. (2016) for predicting dengue in some small area. The model proposed here can be applied for data's from any cities. In Yuhanis Yusof et al. (2011), Least Squares Support Vector Machines (LS-SVM) is proposed for predicting dengue outbreak. This proposed method is applied in five districts of Malaysian country for dengue prediction. SVM outperforms Neural Network in performance generalization. It is proved in Qisong et al. (2008), that the Least Squares Support Vector Machines (LS-SVM) prediction model outperforms Radial Basis Function (RBF) neural network predictor and Back Propagation (BP) neural network predictor in simulation and results.

Flu Outbreak Prediction

Flu - contagious disease affected by the influenza virus. It can easily spread from one person to another person by coughing, sneezing etc. In (Sangeeta Grover et al. 2014) (Ali et al. 2018), a predictive model is proposed for predicting swine flu based on the twitter data. Like the weather forecasting, it would be of greater help when flu can be identified from the existing weather data. In (veritone.com), Roni Rosenfeld proposed one such technique. In (Hongping Hu et al. 2018), artificial tree and neural network is used for flu prediction.

CONCLUSION

Machine learning is an emerging technology that has also become a predominant technology in today's world. Now-a-days all the fields have moved up a level with the application of Machine Learning. Among them, the application of Machine Learning in health care has revolutionized this area. As discussed in this chapter, the precision and performance of many areas in health care has improved by application of this technology. The discussion in this chapter shows that the machine learning techniques will have a greater advancement in health care applications in future. We can expect the Robotic healthcare system will be used by a common man in forthcoming era.

REFERENCES

Abhigna, B. S. (2018). Crowdsourcing– A Step Towards Advanced Machine Learning. *Procedia Computer Science*, *132*, 632–642.

Alessa, A., & Faezipour, M. (2018). *Preliminary Flu Outbreak Prediction Using Efficient Twitter Posts Classification and Linear Regression with Historical CDC Reports*. Preprint. doi:10.2196/12383

Asadi, H., Dowling, R., Yan, B., & Mitchell, P. (2014). Machine learning for outcome prediction of acute ischemic stroke post intra-arterial therapy. *PLoS One*, *9*(2), e88225. doi:10.1371/journal.pone.0088225 PMID:24520356

Asadi, H., Kok, H. K., Looby, S., Brennan, P., O'Hare, A., & Thornton, J. (2016). Outcomes and complications after endovascular treatment of Brain Arteriovenous Malformations: A Prognostication Attempt using artificial Intelligence. *World Neurosurgery*, *96*, 562–569. doi:10.1016/j.wneu.2016.09.086 PMID:27693769

Barton, A. J. (2012). The regulation of mobile health applications. *BMC Medicine*, *10*(1), 46. doi:10.1186/1741-7015-10-46 PMID:22569114

Bentley, P., Ganesalingam, J., Carlton Jones, A. L., Mahady, K., Epton, S., Rinne, P., ... Rueckert, D. (2014). Prediction of stroke thrombolysis outcome using CT brain machine learning. *NeuroImage. Clinical*, *4*, 635–640. doi:10.1016/j.nicl.2014.02.003 PMID:24936414

Buczak, A. L., Koshute, P. T., Babin, S. M., Feighner, B. H., & Lewis, S. H. (2012). A data-driven epidemiological prediction method for dengue outbreaks using local and remote sensing data. *BMC Medical Informatics and Decision Making*, *12*(1), 1. doi:10.1186/1472-6947-12-124 PMID:23126401

Chae, S., Kwon, S., & Lee, D. (2018). Predicting Infectious Disease Using Deep Learning and Big Data. *International Journal of Environmental Research and Public Health*, *15*(8), 1596. doi:10.3390/ijerph15081596 PMID:30060525

Chan, T.-C., Hu, T.-H., & Hwang, J.-S. (2015). Daily forecast of dengue fever incidents for urban villages in a city. *International Journal of Health Geographics*, *14*(1), 9. doi:10.1186/1476-072X-14-9 PMID:25636965

Créquit, P., Mansouri, G., Benchoufi, M., Vivot, A., & Ravaud, P. (2018). Mapping of Crowdsourcing in Health: Systematic Review. *Journal of Medical Internet Research*, *20*(5). PMID:29764795

Da Xu, L., He, W., & Li, S. (2014). Internet of things in industries: A survey. *IEEE Transactions on Industrial Informatics*, *10*(4), 2233–2243. doi:10.1109/TII.2014.2300753

Fei, J., Yong, J., Hui, Z., Yi, D., Hao, L., Sufeng, M., ... Yongjun, W. (2017). Artificial intelligence in healthcare: Past, present and future. *Journal of Neurology, Neurosurgery, and Psychiatry*, *2*(4). Retrieved from https://emerj.com/ai-sector-overviews/machine-learning-medical-diagnostics-4-current-applications/

Gillies, R.J., Kinahan, P. E., Hricak, H. (2016). Radiomics: images are more than pictures, they are data. *Radiology*, *278*(2), 563–77.

Grover, S., & Aujla, G. S. (2014). Prediction Model for Influenza Epidemic Based on Twitter Data. *International Journal of Advanced Research in Computer and Communication Engineering*, *3*(7).

Henry, N. L., & Hayes, D. F. (2012). Cancer biomarkers. *Molecular Oncology*, *6*(2), 140–146. doi:10.1016/j.molonc.2012.01.010 PMID:22356776

Hu, H., Wang, H., Wang, F., Langley, D., Avram, A., & Liu, M. (2018). Prediction of influenza-like illness based on the improved artificial tree algorithm and artificial neural network. *Scientific Reports*, *8*(4895). PMID:29559649

Islam, S. M. R., Kwak, D., Kabir, H., Hossain, M., & Kwak, K. S. (2015). The Internet of things for health care: A comprehensive survey. *IEEE Access: Practical Innovations, Open Solutions*, *3*, 678–708. doi:10.1109/ACCESS.2015.2437951

Kerri, W. (2018). Applications of crowdsourcing in health: An overview. *Journal of Global Health*, *8*(1), 010502. doi:10.7189/jogh.08.010502 PMID:29564087

Mannini, A., Trojaniello, D., Cereatti, A., & Sabatini, A. M. (2016). A machine Learning Framework for Gait classification using inertial sensors: Application to Elderly, Post-Stroke and Huntington's Disease Patients. *Sensors (Basel)*, *16*(1), 134. doi:10.339016010134 PMID:26805847

Mason, W., & Suri, S. (2012). Conducting behavioural research on Amazon's Mechanical Turk. *Behavior Research Methods*, *44*(1), 1–23. doi:10.375813428-011-0124-6 PMID:21717266

Michael, B., Tracy, K., & Samuel, D. G. (2011). Amazon's Mechanical Turk: A new source of inexpensive, yet high-quality, data. *Perspectives on Psychological Science, 6*(1), 3–5. doi:10.1177/1745691610393980 PMID:26162106

Mitchell, T. (1997). *Machine Learning*. McGraw Hill.

Mohammadzadeh, N., & Safdari, R. (2014). Patient monitoring in mobile health: Opportunities and challenges. *Medieval Archaeology, 68*(1), 57. PMID:24783916

Nandini, V., Sriranjitha, R., & Yazhini, T. P. (2016). *Dengue detection and prediction system using data mining with frequency analysis. Computer Science & Information Technology.*

Neil, M., & Murthy, V. D. (2018). Machine learning, natural language programming, and electronic health records: The next step in the artificial intelligence journey? *The Journal of Allergy and Clinical Immunology, 141*(6), 2019–20121. doi:10.1016/j.jaci.2018.02.025 PMID:29518424

Qisong, C., Yun, W., & Xiaowei, C. (2008) Research on Customers Demand Forecasting for E-business Web Site Based on LS-SVM. *Proc. International Symposium in Electronic Commerce and Security*, 66-70.

Rajathi, N., Kanagaraj, S., Brahmanambika, R., & Manjubarkavi, K. (2018). Early Detection of Dengue Using Machine Learning Algorithms. *International Journal of Pure and Applied Mathematics, 118*(18), 3881–3887.

Rehme, A. K., Volz, L. J., Feis, D. L., Bomilcar, F., Liebig, T., Eickhoff, S. B., ... Grefkes, C. (2015). Identifying neuroimaging markers of Motor Disability in acute stroke by machine Learning Techniques. *Cereb Cortex, 25*(9), 3046–3056. doi:10.1093/cercor/bhu100 PMID:24836690

Reid, Thompson, Valdes, Fuller, Carpenter, Morin, ... Thomas, Jr. (n.d.). Artificial intelligence in radiation oncology: A specialty-wide disruptive transformation? In *Radiation and Oncology*. Elsevier.

Sandeep, R. (2018). Use of Artificial Intelligence in Healthcare Delivery. In eHealth - Making Health Care Smarter. Intechopen.

Sathya, D., & Ganesh Kumar, P. (2017). Secured Remote Health Monitoring System. *IET Healthcare Technology Letters, 4*(6), 228–232. doi:10.1049/htl.2017.0033 PMID:29383257

Shin, H., Kim, K. H., Song, C., Lee, I., Lee, K., Kang, J., & Kang, Y. K. (2010). Electrodiagnosis support system for localizing neural injury in an upper limb. *Journal of the American Medical Informatics Association, 17*(3), 345–347. doi:10.1136/jamia.2009.001594 PMID:20442155

Siriyasatien, P., Phumee, A., Ongruk, P., & Jampac, K. (2016). Analysis of significant factors for dengue fever incidence prediction. *International Journal of Pure and Applied Mathematics*, 3885. PMID:27083696

Thitiprayoonwongse, D. A., Suriyaphol, P. R., & Soonthornphisaj, N. U. (2012). Data mining of Dengue Infection using Decision Tree. *Entropy (Basel, Switzerland)*.

Vijeta, S. (2015). Malaria Outbreak Prediction Model Using Machine Learning. *International Journal of Advanced Research in Computer Engineering & Technology, 4*(12), 4415–4419.

Villar, J. R., González, S., Sedano, J., Chira, C., & Trejo-Gabriel-Galan, J. M. (2015). Improving human activity recognition and its application in early stroke diagnosis. *International Journal of Neural Systems*, 25(4), 1450036. doi:10.1142/S0129065714500361 PMID:25684369

Ye, H., Shen, H., & Dong, Y. (2017). *Using Evidence-Based medicine through Advanced Data Analytics to work toward a National Standard for Hospital-based acute ischemic Stroke treatment*. Mainland China.

Yusof, Y., & Mustaffa, Z. (2011). Dengue Outbreak Prediction: A Least Squares Support Vector Machines Approach. *International Journal of Computer Theory and Engineering*, 3(4).

Zhang, Q., Xie, Y., & Ye, P. (2013). Acute ischaemic stroke prediction from physiological time series patterns. *The Australasian Medical Journal*, 6(5), 280–286. doi:10.4066/AMJ.2013.1650 PMID:23745149

Chapter 68
Machine Learning for Emergency Department Management

Sofia Benbelkacem

Laboratoire d'Informatique d'Oran (LIO), University of Oran 1 Ahmed Ben Bella, Algeria

Farid Kadri

Big Data & Analytics Services, Institut d'Optique Graduate School, Talence, France

Baghdad Atmani

Laboratoire d'Informatique d'Oran (LIO), University of Oran 1 Ahmed Ben Bella, Algeria

Sondès Chaabane

University Polytechnique Hauts-de-France, CNRS, UMR 8201 – LAMIH, Laboratoire d'Automatique de Mécanique et d'Informatique Industrielles et Humaines, F-59313 Valenciennes, France

ABSTRACT

Nowadays, emergency department services are confronted to an increasing demand. This situation causes emergency department overcrowding which often increases the length of stay of patients and leads to strain situations. To overcome this issue, emergency department managers must predict the length of stay. In this work, the researchers propose to use machine learning techniques to set up a methodology that supports the management of emergency departments (EDs). The target of this work is to predict the length of stay of patients in the ED in order to prevent strain situations. The experiments were carried out on a real database collected from the pediatric emergency department (PED) in Lille regional hospital center, France. Different machine learning techniques have been used to build the best prediction models. The results seem better with Naive Bayes, C4.5 and SVM methods. In addition, the models based on a subset of attributes proved to be more efficient than models based on the set of attributes.

DOI: 10.4018/978-1-6684-6291-1.ch068

1. INTRODUCTION

The management of emergency departments (ED) is crucial to get medical care within appropriate time frames. However, there is an increasing demand for ED services around the world (He, Hou, Toloo, Patrick, & Fitz Gerald, 2011; Baubeau, Deville, Joubert, & Fivaz, 2000; IMNA, 2006; Cours des comptes, 2007; Kadri, Chaabane, & Tahon, 2014). This growing demand leads to the overcrowding of ED (Boyle, Beniuk, Higginson, & Atkinson, 2012). This later is manifested by a prolonged waiting time and an increasing length of stay of patients in EDs. The increased length of stay (LOS) in EDs affects the quality of treatment and prognosis by medical staff who are often overloaded thus leading to a decrease in physician job satisfaction (Rondeau & Francescutti, 2005; Lin, Hsu, Chao, Luh, Hung, & Breen, 2008); it produces violence of angry patients against staff, reduced access to emergency medical services and increase in patient mortality (Sprivulis, Da Silva, Jacobs, Frazer, & Jelinek, 2006; Alexandrescu, Bottle, Jarman, & Aylin, 2014).

The aim of this study is to anticipate the occurrence of ED overcrowding by predicting the LOS at the ED. In order to achieve this objective, the authors propose a methodology guided by data mining methods. Data mining has been used widely in various areas. Murthy, Nagadevara, & De' (2010) used data mining techniques to treat cybercrime investigation in India. The aim of this study was to identify the factors that strengthen the existing investigation methods in order to improve the success rate of cybercrimes prosecution. Wang, Yan, Chen, & Xing (2010) presented a study where they summarized the applications of data mining in the public sector. These applications have been classified into several categories including the improvement of emergency management, the management of human resources, etc. Carr, Ravi, Reddy, & Veranna (2013) used decision tree, logistic regression, multilayer perceptron and SVM to profile mobile banking users. Decision trees outperformed the other machine learning techniques. Pabreja (2017) applied various classification techniques on the educational database of a Delhi state university. They used data mining techniques to better understand strengths and weaknesses of students.

Data mining techniques allow extracting useful knowledge and regularities which may be used as a tool for decision making in such establishments, in order to respond to the needs of ED managers in their daily decision-making activities (Benbelkacem, Kadri, Chaabane, & Atmani, 2014). The main objective of this work is to propose a prediction approach based on machine learning techniques to predict the patient LOS at the pediatric emergency department in Lille regional hospital centre, France.

The remainder of this paper is organized as follows. First, machine learning techniques are presented and how it can be used in hospital emergency departments. Then, an approach for predicting patient LOS in ED is proposed. The proposed approach is then applied in the prediction of patient LOS at the PED in Lille regional hospital centre, France. Finally, the last section reviews the main conclusions of this work.

2. MACHINE LEARNING AND PREDICTING PATIENT LOS IN ED

In recent years, there has been a dramatic increase in medical data being collected (Hermon & Williams, 2014). Data sets are frequently characterized by incompleteness, incorrectness, inexactness and sparseness. These problems are quite common in the medical field. This field requires human experts with a high level of expertise and able to maintain a high degree of concentration. Therefore, the use of machine learning techniques becomes indispensable for the development of medical decision support tools that model expert behavior, clinical interpretation and analysis, and to save time for practitioners. Machine learning has been an active research field finding success in many different medical areas (Liu, Lei, Yin, Zhang, Naijun, & El-Darzi, 2006; Bolon-Canedo, Remeseiro, Alonso-Betanzos, & Campilho, 2016).

2.1. Related Work

In the related literature a significant number of machine learning methods are applied in the medical emergency area. The most common and important applications involve predictive modeling. In this regard, some research efforts made by some researchers deserve mentioning. Liu et al. (2006) applied decision trees and naive Bayesian classifiers to a geriatric hospital dataset in order to predict inpatient length of stay. Results show that naive Bayesian models performed better in comparison with the C4.5 algorithm of decision tree. So, applying naive Bayesian imputation models to handle a considerable amount of missing data can greatly increase the classification accuracy of predicting length of stay. Delen, Fuller, McCann, & Ray (2009) built a classification model to analyze the healthcare coverage using artificial neural networks and decision trees. The developed model was used to predict if an individual has healthcare coverage or not based on the specific information's about socio-demographic and lifestyle, and the importance of the various factors in the classification model. The results indicated that the most accurate classifier for this phenomenon was the multi-layer perception type of artificial neural network model. Kuruvilla & Alexander (2010) provided a predictive tool that would give advance warning to hospitals of the impending likelihood of diversion. They used logistic and multinomial regression on a real data from the Emergency Management System and 911 call data from the Metropolitan Ambulance Services Trust of Kansas City, Missouri. The proposed model illustrated the feasibility of predicting the probability of impending diversion using available information. Yang, Wei, Yuan, & Schoung (2010) proposed LOS prediction models for burn patients during three different clinical stages: admission, acute, and post-treatment. They employed the model-tree-based regression M5 and SVM regression to construct prediction models for each clinical stage. They evaluated the effectiveness of the prediction models using 1080 burn cases collected from a regional burn center in Taiwan from July 1997 to September 2002. SVM regression appears more effective than the regression technique for LOS predictions of burn patients across stages. Twagilimana (2010) presented a study that attempts to identify the variables on which depends the LOS by analyzing clinical data provided by electronic medical records from a hospital emergency department. Three analysis methodologies were identified as appropriate for this task, data mining techniques, generalized linear models and time series. Decision trees have been applied to select important variables used as input in the other models. Liu, Lin, Koh, Huang, Ser, & Ong (2011) presented an automatic prognosis system to predict the outcome of patients with heart rate variability and traditional vital signs. Extreme learning machine and support vector machine (SVM) with linear kernel were employed as predictors. The results revealed that linear SVM is able to provide the highest confidence in categorizing patients into two outcomes, death and survival. Azari, Janeja, & Mohseni (2012) proposed a data mining approach for predicting hospital length of stay. The authors formed training sets using k-means clustering and used classification techniques to identify patients who need aggressive or moderate early interventions in order to prevent prolonged stays. The results have shown that using clustering to form the training set gave better prediction results compared to non-clustering based training sets. This study also provided insight into the underlying factors that influence hospital length of stay. Schetinin, Jakaite, & Krzanowski (2013) developed a Bayesian method for predicting the survival probability of an injured patient. They used the US National Trauma Data Bank which is the major data source of records of injured patients admitted to hospitals and emergency units. They considered Bayesian inference for estimating the predictive distribution of survival. The inference was based on decision tree models which recursively split data along explanatory variables, and so practitioners can understand these models. The proposed method improved the accuracy of predictions for survival of a patient with multiple injuries. Ilayaraja & Meyyappan (2015) devised a method to predict the risk level of the patients having heart disease through frequent itemsets. Association rule mining was used to extract frequent itemsets. An experimental result showed that the developed method identifies the risk level of patients efficiently from frequent itemsets. The predictions of this method will help the medical practitioners in making diagnostic decisions to save lives of patients at risk. Salcedo-Bernal, Villamil-Giraldo, & Moreno-Barbosa (2016) explored the use of classification machine learning techniques to predict the decease of patients inside the hospital in the next 24 hours. Four predictive models have been built: logistic regression, neural networks, decision trees and nearest neighbors. This research used the clinical data of MIMICII database. The performance metrics showed that it is possible to make relatively correct predictions using sparse data and weakly correlated variables. Jothi, Rashid, & Husain (2015) presented a review study, including papers published between 2005 and 2015, in the context of data mining techniques within healthcare. The disciplines identified among the papers reviewed include: artificial intelligence, probability and statistics, and principally machine learning. The authors discussed the various classification methods used in healthcare. Classification is the discovery of a predictive learning function that classifies a data item into one of several predefined classes (Fayyad, Piatetsky-Shapiro, Smyth, & Uthurusamy, 1996). The methods widely used for classification in healthcare based on the literature (Jothi et al., 2015) are decision tree, k-nearest neighbor, Bayesian classifier, support vector and association rule.

2.2. Discussion

This review study shows that the data mining and machine learning have played a significant role in healthcare industry, especially in prediction. The Table 1 summarizes the literature review. Machine learning techniques have been applied in various fields including heart disease, healthcare coverage, hospital length of stay, geriatric, burn and injured patients.

According to the literature review listed above, better results have been provided using Bayesian methods, SVM and multi-layer perception. Working with Neural networks let to provide real time learning and it works well on numerical or categorical data. One of its weaknesses is the complexity of the network structure design. The main strength of using SVM is the ability to deal with a large variety of classification problems while its limitation is the requiring of key parameters to reach good classification results. Bayesian networks lets to resolve both classification and regression problems and also to handle missing data. The problem with using Bayesian networks is that it usually requires discretization of continuous attributes that could generate some classification issues like missing information, noise, etc. (Soofi & Awan, 2017).

From this literature review we found the most popular classification algorithms applied in healthcare systems which includes decision trees, Bayesian methods, SVM and k-NN. Decision trees are recognized to their simplicity and effectiveness while the strengths of Bayesian networks include flexible applicability. Some advantages of k-NN are that it is easy to understand and robust to noisy training data. We use these techniques to predict patient LOS in EDs.

Table 1. Machine learning techniques applied in the medical emergency area

Method	Application Field	Reference
Decision trees and Naive Bayes	Predict inpatient length of stay of geriatric patients	Liu et al., 2006
Decision trees and Neural networks	Predict if an individual has healthcare coverage	Delen et al., 2009
Logistic and Multinomial regression	Predict the probability of impending diversion in hospitals	Kuruvilla & Alexander, 2010
Model-tree-based regression and SVM	Predict length of stay of burn patients across clinical stages	Yang et al., 2010
Decision trees	Identify the variables on which depends the LOS of patients from a hospital ED	Twagilimana, 2010
SVM	Predict the outcome of patients with heart rate variability and traditional vital signs	Liu et al., 2011
k-means clustering	Predict hospital length of stay	Azari et al., 2012
Bayesian method	Predict survival probability of an injured patient	Schetinin et al., 2013
Association rule mining	Predict risk level of patients having heart disease	Ilayaraja & Meyyappan, 2015
Decision trees, k-NN, Logistic regression and Neural networks	Predict the decease of patients inside the hospital	Salcedo-Bernal et al., 2016

3. APPROACH FOR PREDICTING PATIENT LOS IN ED

Supervised machine learning is about learning to make predictions from examples of past observations (Beygelzimer, Langford, & Zadrozny, 2008). The most basic problem of machine learning can be described as follows. Let's take a training set of examples $(x_1, y_1), \ldots, (x_l, y_l)$. Each example (x_i, y_i) consists of an object x_i (typically, a vector of attributes) and its label y_i. The problem is to predict the label y_k of a new object x_k (Gammerman & Vovk, 2007).

In this paper, the authors propose a methodology for the prediction of the patient LOS in emergency departments (EDs). This methodology is based on prediction models generated by machine learning techniques. The main steps of the proposed methodology are summarized in Figure 1. The first step is collecting data from a real database outcome of the pediatric emergency department (PED) at Lille regional hospital centre, France. The next steps are pre-processing and statistical analysis. Then, feature selection method is used to find the most relevant descriptors for LOS prediction. Finally, machine learning techniques are used to develop LOS prediction models at the PED.

3.1. Data Collection

The first step is the collection of data. This step consists of several sub-steps: data sources are located, accessed, and selected. Selected data is put into a tabular format (Giudici & Jiang, 2006). The proposed approach focuses on a real data about patients of PED in order to predict their length of stay. Each patient is characterized by descriptors and its length of stay in the PED.

Figure 1. The proposed approach

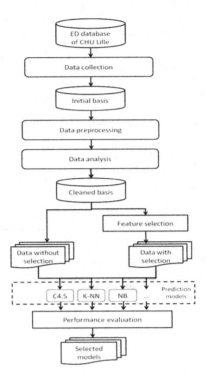

3.2. Data Preprocessing

Real-world data may be incomplete, noisy, and inconsistent, which can disguise useful patterns. The pre-processing step is required to generate quality data and improve the efficiency of data mining models (Zhang, Zhang, & Yang, 2003). This step consists of dealing with noise and missing values in the data (Cios, Pedrycz, Swiniarski, & Kurgan, 2007).

3.3. Data Analysis

In this step, a statistical analysis is made on the data; it consists of establishing statistical or functional links between the variables, in order to find the influence of certain variables or factors on the length of stay and in particular to deduce new variables. For this purpose the authors studied the number of patient arrivals at the PED.

3.4. Feature Selection

Before applying data mining techniques, irrelevant attributes needs to be filtered. The feature selection lets to evaluate the predictive ability of attributes, preferring sets of attributes that are highly correlated with the class. Feature selection methods includes Chi-square, Euclidean distance, T-test, information gain, correlation-based feature selection, Markov blanket filter, sequential forward selection, sequential backward selection, randomized hill climbing (Ladha & Deepa, 2011). In this paper the Correlation-based Feature Selection (CFS) method is used for feature selection purpose. In the literature (Hall, 1999; Hall

& Smith, 1998) it has been shown that using machine learning algorithms on data resulting from CFS could improve accuracy and comprehensibility of induced models. CFS is a simple filter algorithm that ranks feature subsets according to a correlation based heuristic evaluation function. It evaluates a subset of features by considering the individual predictive ability of each feature (Hall, 1999):

$$CFSs = \frac{k\overline{r_{cf}}}{\sqrt{k + k\left(k - 1\right)\overline{r_{ff}}}}$$

where *CFSs* is the score of a feature subset *s* containing *k* features, $\overline{r_{cf}}$ is the mean feature-class correlation $(f \in S)$, $\overline{r_{ff}}$ is the average between feature-feature correlations.

Correlation-based Feature Selection allows finding subsets of variables strongly correlated with the class and useful for class prediction.

3.5. Prediction Model

This step aims to develop a prediction model by using machine learning techniques. These techniques allow discovering useful knowledge and models from the data. To find the best models, the authors tested the most popular classification algorithms applied in healthcare systems (Jothi et al., 2015):

- Bayesian classifier: Naive Bayes (NB);
- Decision tree algorithms: C4.5, PART, RF. C4.5 is the most well-known algorithm in the literature, for building decision trees, PART is a rule induction algorithm, RF is Random Forest;
- Support vector machine (SVM);
- k-Nearest Neighbor (k-NN).

3.6. Performance Evaluation

The most suitable models chosen should offer adequate predictions. In order to evaluate models, the data used are split into two groups: 1) the training group, used to build the model and 2) the validation group, to evaluate the model. The prediction errors are usually calculated to compare the prediction models and select the best one. To evaluate the predictive abilities of the fitted models, several measures of a model's ability to fit data have been developed. The following can be cited (Prabhakar, 2013):

- **Time:** It is represented in seconds, it is the time required to complete training or modeling of a dataset;
- **Mean Absolute Error (MAE):** This is the average of the absolute value of the difference between the predicted value and the actual value:

$$MAE = \frac{1}{n}\sum_{i=1}^{n}\left|P_i - A_i\right|$$

- **Root Mean Squared Error (RMSE):** It is computed by taking the average of the squared differences between each computed value and its corresponding correct value. Root mean squared error is the square root of the mean-squared-error:

$$RMSE = \sqrt{\frac{1}{n}\sum_{i=1}^{n}\left(P_i - A_i\right)^2}$$

- **Relative Absolute Error (RAE):** Relative absolute error is defined as the summation of the difference between the predictive value and the given value, divided by the summation of the difference between the given value and average of the given value:

$$RAE = \frac{\sum_{i=1}^{n}\left|P_{ij} - A_i\right|}{\sum_{i=1}^{n}\left|A_i - A_m\right|}$$

where P_i, P_{ij} are predicted values, A_i is the actual value, A_m is the mean of all A_i and n is the number of forecasts made.

4. EXPERIMENTAL WORK AND ANALYSIS

4.1. Data Collection and Description

Lille Regional Hospital Centre (CHRU) serves four million inhabitants in Nord-Pas-de-Calais, France. The paediatric emergency department (PED) in CHRU is open 24h a day and receives 23900 patients a year on average. Besides its internal capacity, the PED shares many resources with other hospital departments such as administrative patient registration, clinical laboratory, scanner and blood Bank (Harrou, Kadri, Chaabane, Tahon, & Sun, 2015; Kadri, Pach, Chaabane, Berger, Trentesaux, Tahon, & Sallez, 2013). This study is conducted on a dataset extracted from the PED database of CHRU Lille. The authors collected data for 2011 and data for 2012 in a single database. This database includes 44992 patients. Each patient w_i is assigned a length of stay Y, which is the patient's duration in the PED. Each patient w_i is described by 12 descriptors $X_1, X_2, ..., X_{12}$. The meaning and description of the attributes are given in the Table 2.

4.2. Data Preprocessing

After the data collection, the data was cleaned which includes the elimination of duplicates, processing of atypical values and missing data, discretization of continuous attributes and selection of relevant attributes. The age of patients in the PED is around 180 months. However, there were 371 patients with an age between 181 and 1322 months (110 years) in the collected data. This data has been removed from the dataset to keep the data only under 180 months. At the end of the data preprocessing step, a cleaned base of 39661 patients was obtained.

Table 2. Attributes description

	Type	Description
X_1	Date	Arrival date at pediatric emergency service
X_2	Hour	Arrival time
X_3	String	Arrival mean
X_4	Integer	Age of patient
X_5	String	Sex of patient
X_6	String	Main diagnostic
X_7	String	Clinical classification of emergency patients (CCMU)
X_8	String	Multicentric Emergency Department Study Group (GEMSA)
X_9	Boolean	If the patient had a biology test
X_{10}	Boolean	If the patient had an echography
X_{11}	Boolean	If the patient had a radiology
X_{12}	Boolean	If the patient had a scanner
Y	Numeric	Length of stay at pediatric ED

4.3. Data Analysis

The authors studied the number of patient arrivals at the PED as follows:

- **Patient arrivals per month:** The number of arrivals per month is presented in Figure 2. The number of arrivals varies between 3500 and 4000 between January and June. On the other hand, the number of arrivals decreases between July and September). According to emergency staff, the period of the year has an influence on the LOS and especially the epidemic period that takes place between November and March. Looking at Figure 2, three different periods can be distinguished (see Table 3);

- **Daily patient arrivals:** The data used in Figure 3 represent the daily arrivals of patients in the PED between January 2011 and December 2012. The number of arrivals is about 5700 on Thursday and Saturday. The number of arrivals remains at least the rest of the week. It is noted that the number of arrivals of the patients is higher on the weekend and reaches 6335 arrivals on Sunday. Figure 4 shows the number of patients arriving on 24h on Sunday. This analysis shows that the number of patient arrivals varies according to the days of the week. Therefore, the researchers propose to add the day of arrival of the patients to the other descriptors;

- **Patient arrivals per hour:** Figure 5 shows the number of patient arrivals per hour. It is observed that the number of patient arrivals is low between midnight and 7am. From 8am the number of arrivals increases gradually and reaches approximately 2300 arrivals around 7pm. On the other hand, the number of patient arrivals decreases after 7pm. From this analysis, three separate daily periods can be deduced, which are given in Table 4.

Figure 2. Number of patient arrivals per month

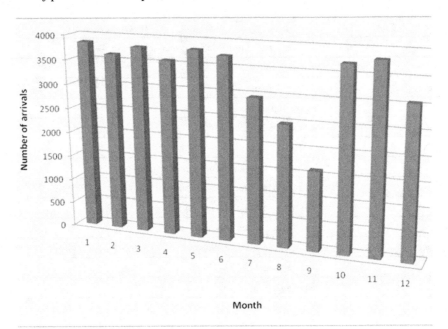

Table 3. Periods of the year

Periods	Values
Period 1	January to June
Period 2	July to September
Period 3	October to December

Figure 3. Number of daily arrivals of patients

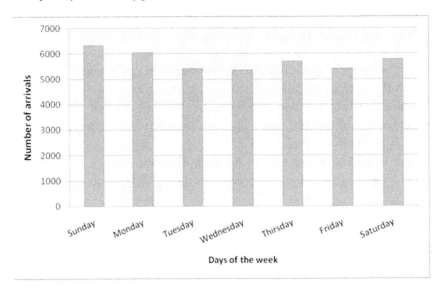

Figure 4. Number of patient arrivals on 24h on Sunday

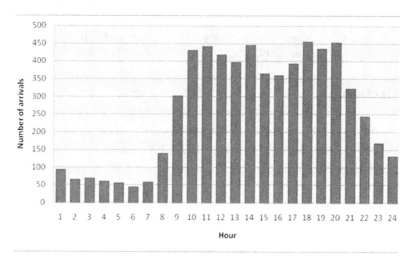

Figure 5. Number of patient arrivals per hour

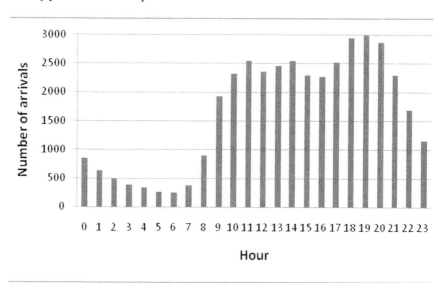

Table 4. Periods of the year

Periods	Values
Night	$0 \leq$ hour < 7
Morning	$7 \leq$ hour < 19
Evening	$19 \leq$ hour ≤ 23

Based on the statistical analysis of the data, four descriptors that influence LOS can be derived. The authors propose to add the following descriptors: X_{13}: periods of the year, X_{14}: arrival month, X_{15}: day of the week, X_{16}: periods of the day. These four new descriptors were added to the 12 attributes previously defined (Table 2). Patients are therefore described by 16 attributes.

4.4. Feature Selection

The CFS method was used to study the correlation between the variables and to choose the most relevant variables for the prediction of the patient LOS in the PED. CFS allowed selecting seven relevant features from the candidate variables (see Table 5).

Table 5. Variables before and after selection

	Before Selection	After Selection
Attributes number	16	7
Attributes	$X_1, ..., X_{16}$	$X_6, X_8, X_{10}, X_{13}, X_{14}, X_{15}, X_{16}$

4.5. Prediction Model

The next step is data modeling which is the key step of the process. To carry out the experiments, the authors used the machine learning techniques that are mainly used to solve the problem of prediction in pediatric emergencies. The prediction model has been built using the decision tree algorithm C4.5 which has been compared with other techniques: naive Bayes (NB), decision tree (PART), random forest (RF), support vector machine (SVM), k-nearest neighbor (k-NN).

C4.5 is the most well-known algorithm in the literature for building decision trees. The C4.5 algorithm (Quinlan, 1993) uses an information entropy evaluation function as selection criteria. The entropy evaluation function is calculated as follows (Lin & Chen, 2012).

- Calculate Info(S) to identify the class in the training set S:

$$Info(S) = -\sum_{i=1}^{k}\left\{\left[freq\left(C_i, S\right)/|S|\right]\log_2\left[freq\left(C_i, S\right)/|S|\right]\right\}$$

where $|S|$ is the number of cases in the training set, C_i is a class, $i = 1, 2, ..., k$, k is the number of classes, and $freq(C_i, S)$ is the number of cases in C_i.

- Calculate the expected information value, $Info_x(S)$; for feature x to partition S:

$$Info_x(S) = -\sum_{i=1}^{L}\left[\left(|S_i|/|S|\right)Info\left(S_i\right)\right]$$

where L is the number of outputs for feature x, S_i is a subset of S corresponding to the ith output, $|S|$ is the number of cases in subset S_i.

- Calculate the information gained after partitioning according to feature X:

$$Gain(X) = Info(S) - Info_s(S)$$

- Calculate the partition information value, $SplitInfo(X)$; acquired for S partitioned into L:

$$SplitInfo(X) = -\sum_{i=1}^{L}\left[\frac{|S_i|}{|S|}\log_2\frac{|S_i|}{|S|}\right]$$

- Calculate the gain ratio of $Gain(X)$ over $SplitInfo(X)$:

$$GainRatio(X) = Gain(X) / SplitInfo(X)$$

$Gain(X)$ is the quantity of information provided by X in the training set. The feature with the highest $GainRatio(X)$ is adopted as a decision tree root.

The authors evaluated the performance of prediction models with and without selection of variables. The results are given in Table 6.

Figure 6 shows that the performance of the prediction models varies between 70% and 80% with the selection of attributes.

Table 6. Accuracy of prediction models with/without feature selection

	All Variables	**Selected Variables**
C4.5	79.68	79.68
NB	79.68	79.68
PART	77.37	79.41
RF	74.17	75.09
SVM	79.68	79.68
k-NN	79.48	79.55

By comparing the performance of the different models, it is observed that the results were better with NB, C4.5 and SVM methods with an identical performance of 79.68% with or without selection of attributes. With the other methods (k-NN, PART, RF) models based on a subset of attributes (selected variables) proved to be more efficient than models based on the set of attributes (all variables). By analyzing Table 6, it can be seen that the performance is slightly improved with the selection of attributes.

Figure 6. Performance of prediction models based on selected attributes

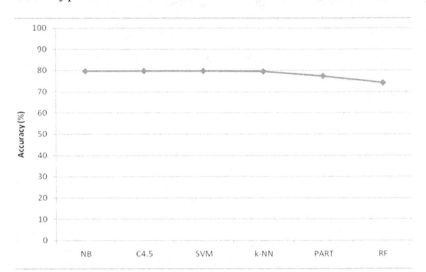

4.6. Performance Evaluation

Subsequently, the authors evaluated the prediction errors of the prediction models based on selected attributes and resulting from NB, C4.5 and SVM methods. They evaluated Mean Absolute Error (MAE), Root Mean Squared Error (RMSE) and Relative Absolute Error (RAE) prediction errors in order to assess the prediction models; they also calculated the treatment time (seconds) for each method (Table 7).

Table 7. Prediction error evaluation of prediction models

	Time	MAE	RMSE	RAE
NB	0.07	0.13	0.26	99.75
C4.5	0.62	0.13	0.26	99.98
SVM	1230.6	0.25	0.33	182.8

From Table 7 the difference between the prediction errors of NB, C4.5 and SVM algorithms can be observed. The experiments involve very commonly used error measures, MAE, RMSE. The MAE prediction error metric is also used. For the LOS prediction of patients, NB used 0.07 seconds and C4.5 used 0.62 seconds while SVM took a longer time. NB and C4.5 gave an MAE error of 0.13 and RMSE of 0.26 while SVM had an MAE of 0.25 and RMSE of 0.33. The prediction error RAE differs slightly between NB and C4.5.

Performance measures can be used to analyze predictive models. They are based on four values of the confusion table (Figure 7): true positives (*TP*), false positives (*FP*), true negatives (*TN*), false negatives (*FN*). Five performance measures are used:

- **Accuracy:** This is a rate of correct classification defined by:

$$\frac{TP + TN}{TP + TN + FP + FN}$$

- **Precision:** This is a rate of true positive classification defined by:

$$\frac{TP}{TP + FP}$$

- **Recall:** This is the evaluation and ranking of each sample based on positive class defined by:

$$\frac{TP}{TP + FN}$$

- **Kappa Statistic:** It measures the agreement of prediction with the true class labels. A score value of 1.0 signifies complete agreement, and a value greater than 0 means that the classifier is doing better than pure random behavior (Azari et al., 2012);
- **ROC:** It gives the trade-off between true positive rate defined by $TP/(TP+FN)$ (recall) and false positive rate defined by $FP/(FP+TN)$ for a given model (Han, Kamber, & Pei, 2011).

Figure 7. Format of confusion table

		Observed	
		True	**False**
Predicted	**True**	True Positive (TP)	False Postive (FP)
	False	False Negative (FN)	True Negative (TN)

Table 8 shows the performance of the prediction models obtained with each classifier in terms of accuracy, precision, recall, kappa statistic and ROC Area.

According to the Table 8, it can be seen that the maximum accuracy score is around 79.68, the precision is equal to 0.635 and the recall is 0.797 with the three methods. The ROC area belongs to 0.52 with NB while it belongs to 0.5 with C4.5 and 0.501 with SVM. According to these results, we note that using C4.5 and SVM gives a better performance for prediction models.

Table 8. Performance evaluation of LOS prediction models

	Accuracy	Precision	Recall	Kappa Statistic	ROC Area
NB	79.6803	0.635	0.797	0	0.52
C4.5	79.6828	0.635	0.797	0	0.5
SVM	79.6828	0.635	0.797	0	0.501

5. CONCLUSION

In this work, the authors exploited the machine learning techniques to implement a model of predicting the length of stay of patients in emergency department. They applied their approach to patients in the pediatric emergency department (PED) at the Lille University Hospital. Each patient is characterized by descriptors and its length of stay in the PED. After the collection of the data they made a statistical analysis which allowed finding the influence of new variables on the LOS; then they added these variables to the list of descriptors. The next steps are pre-processing and data selection. The CFS method was used to select the most relevant descriptors for LOS prediction. Subsequently, machine learning techniques were used to implement a LOS prediction model. The results were better with NB, C4.5 and SVM methods. In addition, the models based on a subset of attributes proved to be more efficient than models based on the set of attributes. The results yielded by these models could assist ED managers in their decision-making process to prevent strain situations.

Some perspectives can be considered. New experiments should be conducted. Other learning methods should be tested like neural networks in the case of deep learning approach. It is a promising learning method which has a pivotal role in providing predictive analytics solutions. The deep learning approach based on Recurrent Neural Networks (RNN) will be used in a Big Data decision support system that will allow predicting, in both batch and streaming mode, the tensions generated by the patient flow and the very long LOS in hospital systems.

REFERENCES

Alexandrescu, R., Bottle, A., Jarman, B., & Aylin, P. (2014). Classifying hospitals as mortality outliers: Logistic versus hierarchical logistic models. *Journal of Medical Systems*, *38*(5), 1–7. doi:10.100710916-014-0029-x PMID:24711175

Azari, A., Janeja, V. P., & Mohseni, A. (2012). Predicting hospital length of stay (PHLOS): A multi-tiered data mining approach. In *2012 IEEE 12th International Conference on Data Mining Workshops* (pp. 17-24).

Baubeau, D., Deville, A., Joubert, M., & Fivaz, C. (2000). *Les passages aux urgences de 1990 à 1998: Une demande croissante de soins non programmés*. Paris: DREES.

Benbelkacem, S., Kadri, F., Chaabane, S., & Atmani, B. (2014). A data mining based approach to detect strain situations in hospital emergency department systems. In *International Conference on Modeling, Optimization and Simulation*, Nancy, France.

Beygelzimer, A., Langford, J., & Zadrozny, B. (2008). Machine learning techniques - reductions between prediction quality metrics. *Performance Modeling and Engineering*, 3-28.

Bolon-Canedo, V., Remeseiro, B., Alonso-Betanzos, A., & Campilho, A. (2016). Machine learning for medical applications. In *European Symposium on Artificial Neural Networks, Computational Intelligence and Machine Learning* (pp. 225-234).

Boyle, A., Beniuk, K., Higginson, I., & Atkinson, P. (2012). Emergency department crowding: Time for interventions and policy evaluations. *Emergency Medicine International*, 1–8. doi:10.1155/2012/838610 PMID:22454772

Carr, M., Ravi, V., Reddy, G. S., & Veranna, D. (2013). Machine learning techniques applied to profile mobile banking users in India. *International Journal of Information Systems in the Service Sector*, 5(1), 82–92. doi:10.4018/jisss.2013010105

Cios, K. J., Pedrycz, W., Swiniarski, R. W., & Kurgan, L. A. (2007). *Data mining: A knowledge discovery approach*. Springer-Verlag New York, Inc.

Cours des comptes. (2007). Les urgences médicales, constats et évolution récente. *Rapport public annuel*, Février 8.

Delen, D., Fuller, C., McCann, C., & Ray, D. (2009). Analysis of healthcare coverage: A data mining approach. *Expert Systems with Applications*, 36(2), 995–1003. doi:10.1016/j.eswa.2007.10.041

Fayyad, U. M., Piatetsky-Shapiro, G., Smyth, P., & Uthurusamy, R. (1996). *Advances in knowledge discovery and data mining*. AAAI Press.

Gammerman, A., & Vovk, V. (2007). Hedging predictions in machine learning: The second computer journal lecture. *The Computer Journal*, 50(2), 151–163. doi:10.1093/comjnl/bxl065

Giudici, P., & Jiang, W. (2006). A review of: Applied data mining - statistical methods for business and industry. *IIE Transactions*, 38(12), 1131. doi:10.1080/07408170600582880

Hall, M., & Smith, L. (1998). Practical feature subset selection for machine learning. In *Proceedings of the 21st Australasian Computer Science Conference* (pp. 181-191). Springer.

Hall, M. A. (1999). *Correlation-based feature selection for machine learning* [Doctoral dissertation]. Waikato University. Retrieved from https://www.cs.waikato.ac.nz/~mhall/thesis.pdf

Han, J., Kamber, M., & Pei, J. (2011). *Data mining: Concepts and techniques*. Elsevier.

Harrou, F., Kadri, F., Chaabane, S., Tahon, C., & Sun, Y. (2015). Improved principal component analysis for anomaly detection: Application to an emergency department. *Computers & Industrial Engineering*, 88, 63–77. doi:10.1016/j.cie.2015.06.020

He, J., Hou, X., Toloo, S., Patrick, J. R., & Fitz Gerald, G. (2011). Demand for hospital emergency departments: A conceptual understanding. *World Journal of Emergency Medicine*, 2(4), 253–261. doi:10.5847/wjem.j.1920-8642.2011.04.002 PMID:25215019

Hermon, R., & Williams, P. (2014). Big data in healthcare: What is it used for? In *Australian eHealth Informatics and Security Conference*.

Ilayaraja, M., & Meyyappan, T. (2015). Efficient data mining method to predict the risk of heart diseases through frequent itemsets. *Procedia Computer Science*, *70*, 586–592. doi:10.1016/j.procs.2015.10.040

Institute of medicine committee on the future of emergency care in the U.S. (2006). Hospital-based emergency care: At the breaking point. Washington, DC: The National Academies Press.

Jothi, N., Rashid, N. A., & Husain, W. (2015). Data mining in healthcare - a review. *Procedia Computer Science*, *72*, 306–313. doi:10.1016/j.procs.2015.12.145

Kadri, F., Chaabane, S., & Tahon, C. (2014). A simulation-based decision support system to prevent and predict strain situations in emergency department systems. *Simulation Modelling Practice and Theory*, *42*, 32–52. doi:10.1016/j.simpat.2013.12.004

Kadri, F., Pach, C., Chaabane, S., Berger, T., Trentesaux, D., Tahon, C., & Sallez, Y. (2013). Modelling and management of strain situations in hospital systems using an ORCA approach. In *Proceedings of 2013 International Conference on Industrial Engineering and Systems Management* (pp. 1-9).

Kuruvilla, A., & Alexander, S. M. (2010). Predicting ambulance diversion. *International Journal of Information Systems in the Service Sector*, *2*(1), 1–10. doi:10.4018/jisss.2010093001

Ladha, L., & Deepa, T. (2011). Feature selection methods and algorithms. *International Journal on Computer Science and Engineering*, *3*(5), 1787–1797.

Lin, B. Y. J., Hsu, C. P. C., Chao, M. C., Luh, S. P., Hung, S. W., & Breen, G. M. (2008). Physician and nurse job climates in hospital-based emergency departments in Taiwan: Management and implications. *Journal of Medical Systems*, *32*(4), 269–281. doi:10.100710916-008-9132-1 PMID:18619091

Lin, S. W., & Chen, S. C. (2012). Parameter determination and feature selection for C4.5 algorithm using scatter search approach. *Soft Computing*, *16*(1), 63–75. doi:10.100700500-011-0734-z

Liu, N., Lin, Z., Koh, Z., Huang, G. B., Ser, W., & Ong, M. E. H. (2011). Patient outcome prediction with heart rate variability and vital signs. *Journal of Signal Processing Systems for Signal, Image, and Video Technology*, *64*(2), 265–278. doi:10.100711265-010-0480-y

Liu, P., Lei, L., Yin, J., Zhang, W., Naijun, W., & El-Darzi, E. (2006). Healthcare data mining: Prediction inpatient length of stay. In *2006 3rd International IEEE Conference on Intelligent Systems* (pp. 832-837).

Murthy, A. S., Nagadevara, V., & De', R. (2010). Predictive models in cybercrime investigation: An application of data mining techniques. *International Journal of Information Systems in the Service Sector*, *2*(3), 1–12. doi:10.4018/jisss.2010070101

Pabreja, K. (2017). Comparison of different classification techniques for educational data. *International Journal of Information Systems in the Service Sector*, *9*(1), 54–67. doi:10.4018/IJISSS.2017010104

Prabhakar, M. D. (2013). Prediction of software effort using artificial neural network and support vector machine. *International Journal of Advanced Research in Computer Science and Software Engineering*, *3*(3), 40–46.

Quinlan, J. R. (1993). *C4.5: Programs for machine learning*. San Francisco, CA: Morgan Kaufmann Publishers Inc.

Rondeau, K. V., & Francescutti, L. H. (2005). Emergency department overcrowding: The impact of resource scarcity on physician job satisfaction. *Journal of Healthcare Management*, *50*(5), 327–340. doi:10.1097/00115514-200509000-00009 PMID:16268411

Salcedo-Bernal, A., Villamil-Giraldo, M. P., & Moreno-Barbosa, A. D. (2016). Clinical data analysis: An opportunity to compare machine learning methods. *Procedia Computer Science*, *100*, 731–738. doi:10.1016/j.procs.2016.09.218

Schetinin, V., Jakaite, L., & Krzanowski, W. J. (2013). Prediction of survival probabilities with bayesian decision trees. *Expert Systems with Applications*, *40*(14), 5466–5476. doi:10.1016/j.eswa.2013.04.009

Soofi, A., & Awan, A. (2017). Classification techniques in machine learning: Applications and issues. *Journal of Basic and Applied Sciences*, *13*, 459–465. doi:10.6000/1927-5129.2017.13.76

Sprivulis, P. C., Da Silva, J. A., Jacobs, I. G., Frazer, A. R. L., & Jelinek, G. A. (2006). The association between hospital overcrowding and mortality among patients admitted via Western Australian emergency departments. *The Medical Journal of Australia*, *184*(5), 208–212. PMID:16515429

Twagilimana, J. (2010). Healthcare delivery in a hospital emergency department. In P. Cerrito (Ed.), *Cases on health outcomes and clinical data mining: Studies and frameworks* (pp. 275–304). Hershey, PA: IGI Global. doi:10.4018/978-1-61520-723-7.ch013

Wang, Z., Yan, R., Chen, Q., & Xing, R. (2010). Data mining in nonprofit organizations, government agencies, and other institutions. *International Journal of Information Systems in the Service Sector*, *2*(3), 42–52. doi:10.4018/jisss.2010070104

Yang, C. S., Wei, C. P., Yuan, C. C., & Schoung, J. Y. (2010). Predicting the length of hospital stay of burn patients: Comparisons of prediction accuracy among different clinical stages. *Decision Support Systems*, *50*(1), 325–335. doi:10.1016/j.dss.2010.09.001

Zhang, S., Zhang, C., & Yang, Q. (2003). Data preparation for data mining. *Applied Artificial Intelligence*, *17*(5-6), 375–381. doi:10.1080/713827180

This research was previously published in the International Journal of Information Systems in the Service Sector (IJISSS), 11(3); pages 19-36, copyright year 2019 by IGI Publishing (an imprint of IGI Global).

Chapter 69
Prediction of High–Risk Factors in Surgical Operations Using Machine Learning Techniques

Anitha N.
Kongu Engineering College, India

Devi Priya R.
Kongu Engineering College, India

ABSTRACT

Prediction of risk during surgical operations is one of the most needed and challenging processes in the healthcare domain. Many researchers use clinical assessment tools to predict perioperative outcomes and postoperative factors in surgical operations. Even though traditional model yields better results, they are not able to achieve promising accuracy due to the enormous growth of data in medical domain. Since the data size grows seamlessly every day, some of the investigators over the past decade use machine learning techniques in their model to predict the risks before and after surgery. Most of the existing systems produced better accuracy by impute missing values in dataset through some common imputation method. However, in order to increase the accuracy level further, two new techniques proposed in this chapter to handle missing values using iterative deepening random forest classifier and identification of surgical risk by using iterative deepening support vector machine. Both of the methods worked well in experimental data set and obtained promising accuracy results.

INTRODUCTION

Surgical process is the most needful one to save human life from severe complications. Many standards of practice like AST standards are available to health care providers for proper surgical treatment. Everyone believes an effective surgeon is the only responsible person for successful surgery operations. However, making an informed decision in surgical process is the challenging one even by an expert surgeon. Even though, Chand et al (2007) determined that the decision making process in surgery has evolved over

DOI: 10.4018/978-1-6684-6291-1.ch069

time, it still requires some qualitative support to treat the patients effectively and smoothly. Due to the environment pollution and vast change in weather condition, rate of infection arises rapidly. To predict the infection risk for a patient during surgery is the complicated process. Pre-operative prediction and quantification of risks will support the patient as well as doctor for safe treatment. Stonelake et al (2015) recommended the huge number of clinical assessment tools are available to predict the risk. However, to provide an optimized solution for risk identification, many researchers use AI and machine learning techniques to make an instinctive decision-making.

Nowadays, there is a rapid growth of data in all sectors and especially in medical field, it grows enormously. Massive amount of data is generated every day and needs to be stored in Electronic health record (EHRs) data warehouse. In this digital era, huge number of genetic data and medical information is stored and manipulated using Machine learning and predictive modelling techniques. To handle those massive amount of data, many researchers preferred to use machine learning and data science technologies. Hence, Ehlers et al (2017) determined that the using machine learning technique in risk prediction during surgery will accurately detect risk and help to treat patients smoothly. When compared with traditional clinical methodologies, machine learning techniques can efficiently find features and nonlinear relationships that exist among them more accurately using predictor variables. Hence, machine learning techniques is widely used in many applications of health care like identification of diabetes, prediction of risks during surgical operations etc. Some health problems can be treated only with the help of surgeries which involve decisions made on collection of sensitive values. Most of the developed countries spend around billions of cost per year for surgical complications. Hence, health care organizations need an effective predictive modeling and accurate solution to detect high-risk individuals in surgery operations.

Classification is one of the supervised learning methods and helps to predict class labels or objects. It is used in many practical applications like image classification, document classification, and speech recognition and so on. Most commonly used algorithms in classification are Naive Bayes, Logistic regression, Decision-tree, Random Forest and SVM classifiers.

Brieman in the year 2001 has recommended Random Forest classifier (RF) which is one of the standard and ensemble classification algorithms. RF uses random subspace method in which each tree is constructed independently based on random samples. Based on training samples and features, a tree is constructed and the root node decision depends upon best split value of k randomly selected variables. Random forest is a well suitable method to handle large number of features in a dataset. As well as it is an efficient process to predict the attribute values even though dataset holds missing values. RF is widely used by many researchers in various fields and produce prominent classification results in health care domain. However, the result interpretation process is vague because of random tree construction process.

Nowadays, researchers uses ensemble classifiers in all domains especially in remote sensing applications. A complete review and future scope on RF classifiers in remote sensing field is prescribed by Belgiu & Dragut (2016). RF classifier is one of the best suitable classifiers for high dimensional data. In order to achieve effective text classification, Thiago et al (2018) have proposed an improved version of Random forest classifier. They eliminate the major issue of Random forest such as over fitting problem particularly in high dimensional data by using the nearest neighborhood training set projection. Thus, the modified RF classifier works better than the other classifiers in automatic text classification process. Random forest has also outperformed well in health care domains. Zhen et al (2019) have developed an integrated approach called LSTM-based ensemble malonylation predictor (LEMP) which is the combination of RF and deep learning network with one hot encoding mechanisms. They predict malonylation sites in substrates and proved that performance of this approach was promising compared to other standard classifiers.

Customer churn prediction is one of the famous applications in that both decision tree and logistic regression have shown strong and feasible performance. Instead of using a separate classifier in prediction, the author Arno et al (2018) have proposed a hybrid approach logit leaf model (LLM)by using the above popular algorithm in order to achieve better classification. LLM approach have shown that the comprehensibility performance was improved better rather than using decision tree and logistic regression separately. Hence, Random forest classifier is one of the popular and best techniques among different classifiers. Many researchers have widely used this technique for discriminating the features. RF is a powerful classifier since it constructs multiple trees based on the random input variables and summarize the estimated values of posterior probability from each tree. RF yields better results than other classification algorithms because of its statistical properties and well supported by mathematical concepts. Sometimes, it may fail when there is no efficient feature set.

SVM classifier is one of the best and famous algorithms to classify the data which contains 'n' number of features. It represents n features in n dimensional space by plotting each data as a coordinate point. SVM classifies the data points by finding hyper plane which helps to discriminate the classes effectively. This technique always produces better results and achieves promising accuracy. So, it can be widely used in many fields like text categorization, hand-written digit recognition, tone recognition, image classification and object detection, microarray gene expression data analysis and data classification. Rakhmetulayeva et al (2018) used SVM classifiers to detect the effectiveness of drug test treatment for tuberculosis. Diagnosis is one of the time consuming process in medical application. By using SVM classifier, the model reduces the burden of doctors to some extent in making their own assumptions and intuition about disease diagnosis methodology. Prediction process is not accurate in high dimensional data. Developing prediction model with noisy features present in high dimensional data is often a more challenging process. Ghaddar& Naoum-Sawaya (2017) have used SVM classifier to perform feature selection and tested with two real life problems like tumor classification and sentiment classification. The results have proved that the model used have reduced the issues in high dimensional dataset. Even though SVM yields better results, its performance is not satisfactory when there is a noisy dataset. To overcome this limitation, instead of directly assigning the dataset to SVM model, the dataset is first preprocessed and then cross-validation is performed.

Iterative- Deepening (ID) is one of the uninformed search methods and it inherits two characteristics from Breadth First Search (BFS) and Depth First Search (DFS). DFS shows space efficiency and BFS incorporates fast searching nature. The working principle of ID method is to visit the root nodes several times and leaf node once. Thus, the ID method eventually reduces the searching space complexity from exponential to linear and cost is not so expensive.

The data collected for surgery may contain large number of features and sometimes some of their values be missing which are very crucial for providing precise treatment. Many researchers have already used machine learning methods for identifying high risk factors. But, most of the methods have ignored the missing values and make decisions only from the data that is available which creates bias in surgical operations. Also, there is a cutting edge demand in a novel method for identifying high risk factors. In order to improve the classification accuracy in risk prediction of surgical data, we have proposed a method in which hybridization of RF with Iterative Deepening (ID) method is done to impute the missing values appropriately and SVM is combined with ID method for accurate classification. Hence, the proposed system addresses the above mentioned issues using machine learning techniques and makes two contributions: (i) Treatment of missing values using Iterative Deepening Random Forest method (IDRF) and (ii) Classification using Iterative Deepening Support Vector Method (IDSVM).

The proposed system is implemented in different kinds of large surgical datasets and the predictive accuracy was found to be improved. The chapter is organized as first describes the background information, then describes the proposed system, next discusses about the results and finally provides conclusion and further enhancement options.

BACKGROUND

Surgical risk prediction is one of the most needful and crucial applications in medical domain. Many researchers have worked on this area and produced promising results by using clinical assessment tools and modern technologies like AI and machine learning. When compared to other assessment tools, machine learning algorithms performs well in predicting the risk accurately during surgical operations.

Ehlers et al (2017) predicted Adverse Events (AE) or death risks more accurately by using Naïve Bayes algorithm. This method uses around 300 predictor variables and weight of each predictor is computed probabilistically rather than assignment of some manual values to variables. Over fitting problem is reduced by partitioning the dataset randomly into equal sized samples and finally aggregating them to assess model performance. Charlson comorbidity index statistical method is used to evaluate the prediction model and outperforms well.

Wong et al (2018) have used machine learning approaches to find delirium risk for newly hospitalized patients with high-dimensional EHR data at a large academic health institution. This method uses more than 796 variables which are highly related to delirium prediction. They have developed prediction model based on five different ML algorithms. When compared with the questionnaire-based scoring system, machine learning algorithms perform well even with large number of predictor variables.

A real time diagnostic and prognostic model was developed by Meyer et al (2018) using recurrent deep neural network to predict the risk in cardiac surgery involving many static and dynamic variables. Postoperative complication risk is a type of risk that was accurately predicted from EHR data repository by using machine learning methods. This method have shown accurate predictions when patients are shifted to ICU after surgery. The model performance were validated against MIMIC-III data set and standard clinical tools. Validation results have proved that this machine learning model surpasses the traditional assessment techniques.

An automatic clinical repository system was proposed by Corey et al (2018) to predict postoperative complication risk using machine learning methods. Lasso penalized regression model is used to assess the risk among 174 clinical features. To avoid generalization problem, cross validation is performed. Finally, a prediction model is built by using random forest and extreme gradient boosted decision trees. Compared to ACS NSQIP calculator a standard clinical tool, their method performs well and end ups with a strong prediction model.

Machine Learning methods are used to develop a model to predict mortality after elective cardiac surgery. Jérôme Allyn et al (2017) used five different ML algorithms and performed feature selection using Chi-Square filtering. When compared to the single ML algorithm, the ensemble results of five different ML algorithm have shown better accuracy. To validate the model, they have used ROC and Decision Curve Analysis (DCA) and it has been proven that ML algorithms predicts more accurately than the standard clinical assessment tool namely Euro SCORE II.

Composite kernel methods are used by Soguero-Ruiz, et.al (2016) to predict the common postoperative complication Anastomosis Leakage (AL). K Nearest Neighbor (KNN) algorithm is used for missing values imputation in datasets chosen from EHR repository. Feature selection algorithm is employed to choose best features from heterogeneous dataset. The powerful kernel classifiers are observed to predict AL risk at an early stage.

Todd C et al (2018) predicted postoperative factors in Pituitary adenomas proposed by is one of the challenging processes because of its heterogeneity nature. The developed model predict the postoperative outcomes with 87% accuracy than the clinical assessment tools. Thus with the help of machine learning algorithms highly improved the patient care who have the issues of pituitary adenoma. Dogan et al (2018) developed a DNA-based precision tool to predict the risk for incident coronary heart disease. The system eventually increased the accuracy level compared to traditional model.

Even though, the existing methods with the help of machine learning techniques produce promising results, still desired accuracy in prediction of risk is not achievable. Existing methods failed to address the missing values which is a major issue in all domains especially in health care applications. Since every value contains some valuable information, if any of the values is missed in dataset, then the prediction model is not accurate. Hence, proper way of handling missing values is very important which is considered and implemented by only few researchers.

The performance assessment for cardiac surgery Prediction Model was evaluated based on the effect of imputation of missing values. Karim et al (2017) used Bland-Altman method to assess the risks generated by two different approaches namely complete cases (CC) analysis and multiple imputation (MI) analysis. As a result shown that MI analysis yielded better prediction of mortality risk. But still many of the researchers either ignored the missing values or filled with null value, even though it was an important issue in healthcare domain .Only few work have done to handle missing value in an appropriate manner. As well as in development of prediction model many of them used Naïve Bayes, random forest, logistic regression and so on. Without preprocessing of data used algorithms directly for to predict the risk in surgical operations. This may lead to failure model.

RF has been widely used in surgical risk prediction application. Alexander et al (2016) have used the RF algorithm to categorize pre-operative predictors based on its importance to classify the postoperative complications. However, the system fails to impute missing value in a proper manner. Lee et al (2018) used many algorithms like decision tree, random forest, extreme gradient boosting, support vector machine and deep learning to predict the kidney infection after cardiac surgery. It has been proven that the ensemble random forest classifier have shown highest AUC curve and lower error-rate than the other algorithms.

SVM classifier is one of the excellent tools and widely used in medical research. Some of the investigators employs SVM classifier to predict the risk during surgery. The likelihood performance assessment in perioperative cardiac events is a difficult process. Kasamatsu et al (2008) used SVM classifiers and produced better accuracy results when compared to conventional model. This technique builds an effective hyper plane so that the patients are split into different groups based on prognostic values and higher predictive accuracy is obtained than other conventional linear model.

From the existing studies, it has been realized that identification of risks which are very critical during surgery is very much essential to reduce surgical complications. Traditional clinical tests and procedures cannot predict risks accurately because of large size, heterogeneous nature and high complexity of data involved. Machine learning tools support health care providers to accurately predict the patient's high risks of surgical complications than other conventional procedures. Even then, to improve the accuracy further and to address the missingness of data issue, a hybridization approach of RF with ID and SVM with ID have been proposed. The nature of ID will search for optimal results and hence combining RF with ID will handle missing values and ID with SVM will classify the risk appropriately.

PROPOSED METHODOLOGY

The aim of the proposed system is to achieve high accuracy in prediction of high risk factors in order to reduce complications during and after surgical operations. The system performs the task by implementing these two strategies. (i) Missing value treatment using Iterative Deepening Random Forest method (IDRF) and (ii) Prediction of High risk factors using Iterative Deepening Support Vector Machine (IDSVM).

In the proposed method used six different kind of datasets and implemented in Anaconda Environment using Python package. Since, there are different kinds of datasets with complex nature, the first Step is to preprocess the experimental datasets. Among six different types of surgical datasets, thoracic and post-operative dataset contains more number of categorical attributes. The thoracic dataset consists of 470 samples and 17 features in which 14 features are categorical attributes. Likewise post-operative dataset contains 90 samples and 9 categorical features. The most important crucial process in machine learning is handling of categorical attributes. In this proposed system, "one hot encoding" mechanism is used to handle categorical attributes. This method is used to map ordinal and nominal attribute values to numeric values in a proper way.

Next step is to impute the missing values using the proposed method IDRF. Before applying dataset to IDRF first temporarily delete 25% of original values in dataset. The input for this procedure is random features selected from those missing value datasets. The split node is calculated for to decide the root node in forest. In this proposed system, iterative deepening search mechanism is used to select the best split node. Suppose the split node contains missing value means then random value is used to fill that value which is taken from non missing values in data sets. The forest construction process is iteratively repeated until terminal nodes are reached. When there is a missing value occurs during construction process the values imputed based on the grown forest node values. The above process is repeated until all the missing values imputed through the random forest method.

Once the missing imputation process is over then the next step is to predict the risk in surgical operations. To develop a predict model, the proposed system uses IDSVM method .The most important process in classification is feature selection. Thus the IDRF method is used to select the important features from dataset during the process of missing imputation. In order to perform classification first cross validation method is used to split the samples into training and testing data. Next apply SVM algorithm to dataset for prediction of high risk factors. SVM classifier accuracy is depend upon the parameter selection. Therefore we used iterative deepening method for parameter selection. After selection process is over, model is fitted using training samples and predicted using test data. Finally fitness function is used to evaluate the predicted risk with selected features. The following Figure 1 depicts the proposed model of IDRF_IDSVM for surgical risk prediction.

Iterative Deepening Random Forest Method

Many researchers have found missingness issues in healthcare datasets like EHR, MIMIC-III datasets, etc., The standard Random forest classifier method has been commonly used for missing value treatment and it is chosen for this problem because it is one of the easiest and flexible techniques among machine

Figure 1. Proposed model IDRF_IDSVM

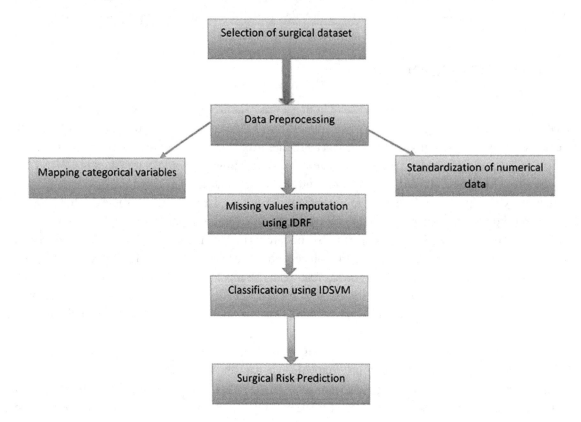

learning methods and can be used for both classification (predicting discrete attributes) and regression (predicting continuous attributes). It always produces best result from randomness of data and choses the optimum result from random data instead of searching nodes in sequential manner. Even then, there is still scope for further enhancement and hence in order to improve the accuracy further, local search mechanism called iterative deepening search method is integrated with random forest classifier. In order to yield best results, the method fixes the threshold for each feature rather than searching for the best possible nodes in the tree. The exploitative capability of the random forest method is further enhanced by searching for the right value to be distributed in the missing hole. In IDRF, Iterative deepening method works in an iterative manner and the nodes are visited multiple times so that it produces best results.

Tang and Ishwaran (2017) proposed novel random forest approaches and revealed that the RF imputation is one of the best method to handle missingness of data and improved accuracy further. It works better even when there is a noisy dataset. In medical domain, especially prediction of risk during surgical operations faces many issues in noisy data. Hence, our objective is to handle missingness of data using RF imputation method with Iterative deepening local search mechanism.

IDRF method first preimpute missing values using random values taken from non-missing data samples. Next the split node is calculated using non-missing data and the best node is found using iterative deepening method. Then, the missing values are predicted in the existing forest and the predicted values are substituted. This process is repeatedly done until terminal nodes are reached.

Figure 2. Pseudocode for iterative deepening based random forest

Input: X (m rows and n columns matrix), rmax and cmax

1: Check if there exists any column that has more than cmax missing values

2: If Yes

3:     Halt and report error

4: else

5:     log-transform the data

6: end if

7: for i = 1, ...,m do

8: if row i has more than rmax missing values then

9:     Impute missing values by random value form the non-missing data

10: else

11: if row i has at least one but no more than rmax missing values then

12:    *pos* ← *record* the positions where row i has missing values

13:    Find rows that have no missing values in column pos

14:    Calculate the split-statistic for splitting a tree node of row i with these rows

       using Iterative deepening

15:    Repeat steps 7 to 14 until terminal nodes are reached

16: end if

17: end if

18: end for

Iterative Deepening Support Vector Machine (IDSVM)

Now, the dataset contains complete records without any missing values and is ready for performing prediction. The dataset may contain many features some of which may be significant and some may be insignificant. SVM is a supervised learning technique that can be used to classify data by finding hyper planes in different classes. Classifiers can easily separate classes in linear hyper planes and not suitable for complex data. High risk factors are complex in nature. In order to handle those complex data, feature selection process is employed in IDRF missing imputation datasets. Feature Selection process is the most important process in preprocessing particularly which helps to obtain good accuracy results when there is a high dimensional dataset. SVM classifier is integrated with iterative deepening method to classify the risks in a very accurate manner and its fitness function is evaluated with the feature selected during IDRF process.

In order to identify the most significant features which carries high risks and influence surgical operations, a methodology called Iterative Deepening Support Vector Machine is proposed which is a hybrid combination of iterative deepening strategy with support vector machine. Both of the techniques work in parallel to predict the risk during surgical operations. Hence the objective of our proposed system in

Figure 3. Flow chart for iterative deepening based support vector machine

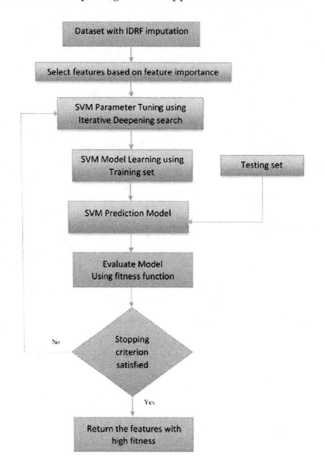

classification of risks is to use iterative deepening local search method with the SVM classifier to accurately predict high risk factors inducing surgical complications.

The process is performed iteratively and hence chances of the algorithm getting terminated without identifying the best solution is decreased to a great extent. The algorithm is run for multiple iterations and hence the solutions gets improved in each iteration. The algorithm is implemented in different kinds of surgical datasets and the risk is predicted in a very accurate manner.

EXPERIMENTAL RESULTS AND DISCUSSION

Data Set Description

Surgical datasets collected from UCI repository have been used in this proposed system to predict the risk during surgical operations. The proposed model uses six different types of surgical datasets for classification. Table 1 describes the characteristics of different data sets.

Table 1. Features overview in all six datasets

Name of the data set	Instances	Independent Attributes	Dependent Attributes
Thoracic Surgery	470	DgnCode, Fvc, Fev1, Performance Status, Pain Before Surgery, Haemoptysis Before Surgery, Dyspnoea Before Surgery, Cough Before Surgery, Weakness Before Surgery, Tnm(Size Of The Orginal Tumour), Diabetes Mellitus, Mi Upto 6 Months, Pad, Smoking, Asthma, Age At Surgery	Risk1y T stands for high risk and F stands for low risk
Breast Cancer	699	Clump Thickness, Uniformity of Cell Size, Uniformity of Cell Shape, Marginal Adhesion, Single Epithelial Cell Size, Bare Nuclei, Bland Chromatin, Normal Nucleoli and Mitoses	Identity 2 stands for benign and 4 stands for malignant
Crypo Therapy	90	Sex,Age,Time, Number_of_Warts, Area	Result_of_Treatment 0- 1-
Haberman's Surgery	306	Age of patient at time of operation, Number of positive axillary nodes detected, Patients year of operation	Survival status 1- 2-
Post-Operative Patient Data	90	L-Core(Patient's Internal Temperature In Celsius), L-Surf(Patient's Surface Temperature In Celsius), L-02 (Oxygen Saturation In Percentage), L-Bp (Last Measurement Of Blood Pressure), Surf-Stbl (Stability Of Patient's Surface Temperature), Core-Stbl (Stability Of Patient's Core Temperature), Bp-Stbl (Stability Of Patient's Blood Pressure), Comfort (Patient's Perceived Comfort At Discharge Measured As An Integer Between 0 And 20)	Decision Adm-Decs (Discharge Decision) S- A-
Lung Cancer	309	Gender,Age,Smoking, Yellow_Fingers, Anxiety, Peer_Pressure, Chronic Disease, Fatigue, Allergy, Wheezing, Alcohol Consuming, Coughing, Shortness Of Breath, Swallowing Difficulty, Chest Pain	Lung_Cancer Yes- No-

Table 2. Baseline characteristics of Habermans

BC	Age of patient at time of operation	Patients year of operation	Number of positive axillary nodes detected
count	306.000000	306.000000	306.000000
mean	52.457516	62.852941	4.026144
std	10.803452	3.249405	7.189654
min	30.000000	58.000000	0.000000
25%	44.000000	60.000000	0.000000
50%	52.000000	63.000000	1.000000
75%	60.750000	65.750000	4.000000
max	83.000000	69.000000	52.000000

The above tables represents the baseline characteristics of numeric features presented in datasets. From the above tables it was inferred that the thoracic and post-operative dataset contains many categorical attributes compared to other datasets.

Table 3. Baseline characteristics of cryotherapy

BC	sex	age	Time	Number of Warts	Type	Area	Result_of_Treatment
count	90.000000	90.000000	90.000000	90.000000	90.000000	90.000000	90.000000
mean	1.477778	28.600000	7.666667	5.511111	1.700000	85.833333	0.533333
std	0.502304	13.360852	3.406661	3.567155	0.905042	131.733153	0.501683
min	1.000000	15.000000	0.250000	1.000000	1.000000	4.000000	0.000000
25%	1.000000	18.000000	4.562500	2.000000	1.000000	20.000000	0.000000
50%	1.000000	25.500000	8.500000	5.000000	1.000000	70.000000	1.000000
75%	2.000000	35.000000	10.687500	8.000000	3.000000	100.000000	1.000000
max	2.000000	67.000000	12.000000	12.000000	3.000000	750.000000	1.000000

Table 4. Baseline Characteristics of Breast Cancer

BC	Clump Thickness	Uniformity of Cell Size	Uniformity of Cell Shape	Marginal Adhesion	Single Epithelial Cell Size	Bland Chromatin	Normal Nucleoli	Mitoses	identity
count	699.00	699.00	699.00	699.00	699.00	699.00	699.00	699.00	699.00
mean	4.417740	3.134478	3.207439	2.806867	3.216023	3.437768	2.866953	1.589413	2.689557
std	2.815741	3.051459	2.971913	2.855379	2.214300	2.438364	3.053634	1.715078	0.951273
min	1.000000	1.000000	1.000000	1.000000	1.000000	1.000000	1.000000	1.000000	2.000000
25%	2.000000	1.000000	1.000000	1.000000	2.000000	2.000000	1.000000	1.000000	2.000000
50%	4.000000	1.000000	1.000000	1.000000	2.000000	3.000000	1.000000	1.000000	2.000000
75%	6.000000	5.000000	5.000000	4.000000	4.000000	5.000000	4.000000	1.000000	4.000000
max	10.000000	10.000000	10.000000	10.000000	10.000000	10.000000	10.000000	10.000000	4.000000

Table 5. Baseline characteristics of post-operative patient dataset

BC	l_core	l_surf	l_o2	l_bp	surf_stbl	core_stbl	bp_stbl	comfort	decision
count	90	90	90	90	90	90	90	90	90
unique	3	3	2	3	2	3	3	5	4
top	mid	mid	good	mid	stable	stable	stable	10	A
freq	58	48	47	57	45	83	46	65	63

Performance Measures

In this system the five different classification measures used to evaluate the model accuracy. Definitions:

True positive (TP) = the number of cases correctly identified as patient
False positive (FP) = the number of cases incorrectly identified as patient
True negative (TN) = the number of cases correctly identified as healthy

False negative (FN) = the number of cases incorrectly identified as healthy

Table 6. Baseline characteristics of survey lung cancer dataset

BC	Age	Smo-king	Yellow Fingers	Anx-iety	Peer Pr.	Chronic Disease	Fatigue	Allergy	Wheezing	Alcohol Consuming	Coughing	Shortness of Breath	Swallo-wing Difficulty	Chest Pain
count	309.0	309.0	309.0	309.0	309.0	309.0	309.0	309.0	309.0	309.0	309.0	309.0	309.0	309.0
mean	62.67	1.563	1.569	1.498	1.501	1.504	1.673	1.556	1.556	1.556	1.579	1.640	1.469	1.556
std	8.210	0.496	0.495	0.500	0.500	0.500	0.469	0.497	0.497	0.497	0.494	0.480	0.499	0.497
min	21.00	1.0	1.0	1.0	1.0	1.0	1.0	1.0	1.0	1.0	1.0	1.0	1.0	1.0
25%	57.00	1.0	1.0	1.0	1.0	1.0	1.0	1.0	1.0	1.0	1.0	1.0	1.0	1.0
50%	62.00	2.0	2.0	2.0	2.0	2.0	2.0	2.0	2.0	2.0	2.0	2.0	2.0	2.0
75%	69.00	2.0	2.0	2.0	2.0	2.0	2.0	2.0	2.0	2.0	2.0	2.0	2.0	2.0
max	87.0	2.0	2.0	2.0	2.0	2.0	2.0	2.0	2.0	2.0	2.0	2.0	2.0	2.0

Table 7. Baseline characteristics of thoracic dataset

BC	FVC	FEV1	AGE
count	470.000000	470.000000	470.000000
mean	3.281638	4.568702	62.534043
std	0.871395	11.767857	8.706902
min	1.440000	0.960000	21.000000
25%	2.600000	1.960000	57.000000
50%	3.160000	2.400000	62.000000
75%	3.807500	3.080000	69.000000
max	6.300000	86.300000	87.000000

1. Precision also known as Positive Predictive Value (PPV) is calculated as

Precision = TP/(TP+FP)

Sometimes PPV will give biased results when there is an imbalanced classes.

2. Sensitivity/Recall also known as the True Positive rate or Recall is calculated as,

Sensitivity = TP/(TP+FN)

Since the formula doesn't contain FP and TN, Sensitivity may give you a biased result, especially for imbalanced classes.

3.   Specificity, also known as True Negative Rate is calculated as,

Specificity = TN/(TN+FP)

Since the formula does not contain FN and TP, Specificity may give you a biased result, especially for imbalanced classes.

4.   F1-Score is used to measure a test's accuracy and it lies between precision and recall. The range for F1 Score is [0, 1].

$$F1 = 2 * \frac{Precision \times Recall}{Precision + Recall}$$

5.   Accuracy Score is used to test the performance of classifiers whether it correctly classified the instances.

$$Accuracy = \frac{TP + TN}{TP + TN + FP + FN}$$

RESULT AND DISCUSSION

Experimental data sets implemented in Anaconda Environment using Python package. The four different classifiers such as Random Forest, Support Vector Machine, K-Nearest Neighbor, and Logistic Regression classifiers are used to show how the classifiers accuracy improve over by using proposed IDRF missing imputation method. The following table represents the performance measures for all data sets for four classifiers by without imputation process of missing values and with IDRF imputation process.

The above Table 8 depicts the performance measures of four different classifiers such as Random Forest, Support Vector Machine, K-Nearest Neighbor and Logistic regression without imputation of missing values and with IDRF imputation for all six data sets. From the above table 8, it is observed that the missing values in dataset have predominant effect in classification accuracy. As well as table shows that the imputation of missing values using IDRF gradually improves the prediction model accuracy. Thus, the results have shown that the performance is slightly improved for all classifiers by using the proposed method IDRF.

In order to increase the accuracy level further, feature selection process is performed using Random Forest and then these important features are used for prediction of risks using proposed method IDSVM. The following figures represents the process of feature selection for all datasets.

The following Table 9 demonstrates the classification measures for all datasets by comparing our proposed method IDRF based IDSVM (IDRF_IDSVM) with three different classifiers such as Recurrent Neural Network (RNN), least absolute shrinkage and selection operator (LASSO) penalized logistic regression and Extreme gradient boosted decision trees (EGBDT). The results depict that our proposed method performs better than the other compared classifiers by showing slight improvement in accuracy level.

Table 8. Performance measures of four different classifiers for without imputation of missing values and with using IDRF imputation for all datasets

Classifiers	Precision	Recall	F1-Score	Specificity	Accuracy
Performance Measures of Habermans dataset without missing values imputation					
RF	0.72	0.97	0.83	0.02	0.72
SVM	0.74	0.95	0.83	0.09	0.71
KNN	0.79	0.86	0.82	0.38	0.73
LR	0.86	0.40	0.54	0.83	0.51
Performance Measures of Habermans dataset with IDRF imputation					
RF	0.73	0.97	0.83	0.04	0.72
SVM	0.74	0.95	0.83	0.09	0.72
KNN	0.79	0.86	0.82	0.38	0.73
LR	0.86	0.45	0.56	0.80	0.53
Performance Measures of Cryotherapy dataset without missing values imputation					
RF	0.38	0.23	0.29	0.47	0.33
SVM	0.43	0.35	0.38	0.36	0.35
KNN	0.60	0.46	0.52	0.57	0.51
LR	0.40	0.31	0.35	0.36	0.33
Performance Measures of Cryotherapy dataset with IDRF imputation					
RF	0.40	0.24	0.30	0.40	0.35
SVM	0.44	0.35	0.40	0.33	0.38
KNN	0.62	0.48	0.53	0.50	0.53
LR	0.42	0.33	0.37	0.33	0.35
Performance Measures of Breast Cancer dataset without missing values imputation					
RF	1.00	0.96	0.98	0.98	0.96
SVM	0.78	0.97	0.86	0.10	0.76
KNN	0.76	0.72	0.74	0.25	0.61
LR	0.77	1.00	0.87	0.0	0.76
Performance Measures of Breast Cancer dataset with IDRF imputation					
RF	1.00	0.96	0.98	0.98	0.96
SVM	0.78	0.97	0.86	0.10	0.76
KNN	0.76	0.72	0.74	0.25	0.61
LR	0.77	1.00	0.87	0.0	0.76
Performance Measures of Survey Lung Cancer dataset without missing values imputation					
RF	0.88	1.00	0.93	1.0	0.87
SVM	0.96	0.95	0.96	0.73	0.92
KNN	0.89	0.99	0.94	0.15	0.88
LR	0.96	0.95	0.95	0.68	0.91
Performance Measures of Survey Lung Cancer with IDRF imputation					
RF	0.88	1.00	0.93	1.0	0.87

continues on following page

Table 8. Continued

Classifiers	Precision	Recall	F1-Score	Specificity	Accuracy
SVM	0.96	0.95	0.96	0.73	0.92
KNN	0.89	0.99	0.94	0.15	0.88
LR	0.96	0.95	0.95	0.68	0.91
Performance Measures of Thoracic dataset without missing values imputation					
RF	0.87	1.00	0.93	0.0	0.87
SVM	0.87	1.00	0.93	0.0	0.87
KNN	0.88	1.00	0.93	0.03	0.87
LR	0.88	0.98	0.93	0.06	0.86
Performance Measures of Thoracic dataset with IDRF imputation					
RF	0.87	1.00	0.93	0.0	0.87
SVM	0.87	1.00	0.93	0.0	0.87
KNN	0.88	1.00	0.93	0.03	0.87
LR	0.88	0.98	0.93	0.06	0.86
Performance Measures of Post-Operative Patient dataset without missing values imputation					
RF	0.75	0.88	0.81	0.09	0.68
SVM	0.76	0.94	0.84	0.09	0.73
KNN	0.75	0.79	0.77	0.18	0.64
LR	0.75	0.71	0.73	0.27	0.60
Performance Measures of Post-Operative Patient dataset with IDRF imputation					
RF	0.73	0.97	0.83	0.04	0.72
SVM	0.74	0.95	0.83	0.09	0.72
KNN	0.75	0.88	0.81	0.09	0.68
LR	0.76	0.72	0.74	0.25	0.61

Figure 4. Feature importances-Habermans

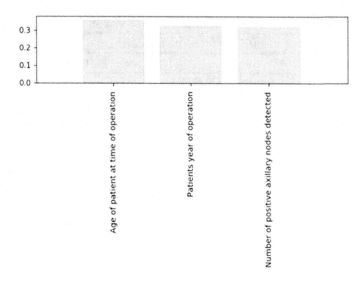

Figure 5. Feature importances-Cryotherapy

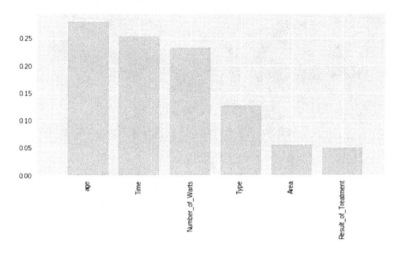

Figure 6. Feature importances-Breast Cancer

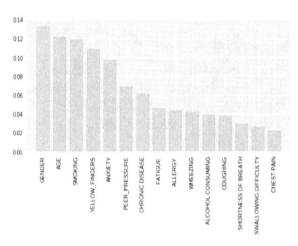

Figure 7. Feature importances-post-operative dataset

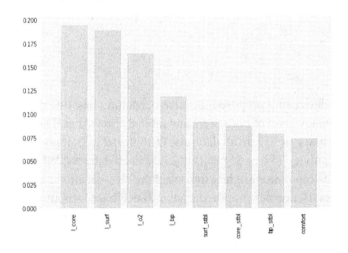

Figure 8. Feature importances-survey lung cancer

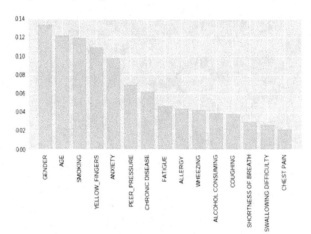

Figure 9. Feature importances-thoracic

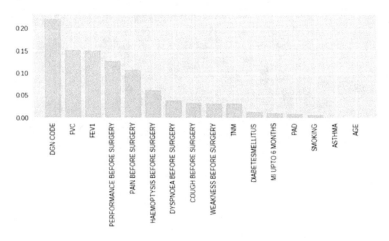

From the above table 9, it is observed that the imputation of missing values using IDRF in the datasets have produced promising results in IDSVM classification accuracy as compared to other classifiers.

DISCUSSION

Imputation of missing values using proposed Iterative deepening based Random forest (IDRF) method helps to increase the accuracy level of classifiers and table 8 shows that IDRF based classifier achieved a mean classification accuracy of 75% in all datasets. With the added support of cross validation folds in IDRF yields average Sensitivity 73% and Specificity 72% in all datasets. When compared to the existing imputation method, IDRF imputation slightly improved the classification accuracy as 5% in all data sets for all standard classifiers. Hence our proposed system IDRF based imputation of missing values have predominant effect in all standard classifiers for all datasets. IDRF method overcome the most important issues in medical domain particularly in prediction of risk during surgical operations. The results shown in the table 8 prove that the IDRF based classification with standard classifiers improves accuracy level than the other imputation based classification process. In order to further improve the accuracy level of prediction we used Iterative deepening based support vector machine. Our proposed system IDSVM produced a mean classification accuracy level of 78%.The results prove that the IDSVM works well in all types of data set and yields better results compared to standard classifiers. With the support of feature selection process IDSVM shows 5% improvement in classification accuracy compared to other

Table 9. Classification measures of different classifiers for all datasets

Classifiers	Precision	Recall	F1-Score	Specificity	Accuracy
Habermans dataset					
RNN	0.84	0.74	0.79	0.86	0.80
LASSO	0.75	0.79	0.77	0.18	0.64
EGBDT	0.75	0.71	0.73	0.27	0.60
IDRF_IDSVM	0.75	0.79	0.77	0.18	0.64
Cryotherapy dataset					
RNN	0.90	0.85	0.88	0.91	0.88
LASSO	0.75	0.88	0.81	0.09	0.68
EGBDT	0.75	0.88	0.81	0.09	0.68
IDRF_IDSVM	0.90	0.85	0.88	0.91	0.88
Breast Cancer dataset					
RNN	0.87	0.94	0.90	0.86	0.90
LASSO	0.44	0.35	0.40	0.33	0.38
EGBDT	0.62	0.48	0.53	0.50	0.53
IDRF_IDSVM	0.84	0.74	0.79	0.86	0.80
Survey Lung Cancer dataset					
RNN	0.75	0.88	0.81	0.09	0.68
LASSO	0.76	0.94	0.84	0.09	0.73
EGBDT	0.75	0.79	0.77	0.18	0.64
IDRF_IDSVM	0.75	0.71	0.73	0.27	0.60
Thoracic dataset					
RNN	0.84	0.74	0.79	0.86	0.80
LASSO	0.75	0.79	0.77	0.18	0.64
EGBDT	0.62	0.48	0.53	0.50	0.53
IDRF_IDSVM	0.84	0.74	0.79	0.86	0.80
Post-Operative Patient dataset					
RNN	0.84	0.74	0.79	0.86	0.80
LASSO	0.75	0.79	0.77	0.18	0.64
EGBDT	0.62	0.48	0.53	0.50	0.53
IDRF_IDSVM	0.87	0.94	0.90	0.86	0.90

classifiers. This method is new in the prediction of risk in surgical operations. Compared to standard classifiers IDRF based IDSVM classifiers yield better results.

CONCLUSION AND FURTHER ENHANCEMENT

Thus, two new contributions are proposed in this chapter in which the first method effectively imputes the missing values and the second one identifies high risk factors associated with surgical operations. Both these methods perform well in all the six datasets experimented and the performance measures like precision, recall, F1 score, specificity and classification accuracy of the proposed method is better than that of the state-of-the art methods. The features that are chosen for achieving better performance measures are identified as high risk factors for surgical operations. The proposed method using machine learning approaches will serve as a great boon for the doctors and clinical analysts in providing due importance to those high risk parameters. As a future work, novel deep learning architectures can be proposed to predict the factors which have close influence in the surgical operations.

REFERENCES

Allyn. (2017). *A Comparison of a Machine Learning Model with EuroSCORE II in Predicting Mortality after Elective Cardiac Surgery: A Decision Curve Analysis*. PLOS.

Belgiu, M., & Drăguţ, L (2016). Random forest in remote sensing: A review of applications and future directions. *ISPRS Journal of Photogrammetry and Remote Sensing, 114*, 24-31.

Chand, M., Armstrong, T., Britton, G., & Nash, G. F. (2007). How and why do we measure surgical risk. *Journal of the Royal Society of Medicine, 100*(11), 508–512. doi:10.1177/014107680710001113 PMID:18048708

Chen, Z., He, N., Huang, Y., Qin, W. T., Liu, X., & Li, L. (2019). Integration of A Deep Learning Classifier with A Random Forest Approach for Predicting Malonylation Sites. *Genomics, Proteomics & Bioinformatics*. PMID:30639696

Corey, K. M., Kashyap, S., Lorenzi, E., Lagoo-Deenadayalan, S. A., Heller, K., Whalen, K., ... Sendak, M. (2018). Development and validation of machine learning models to identify high-risk surgical patients using automatically curated electronic health record data (Pythia): A retrospective, single-site study'. *PLoS Medicine, 15*(11), e1002701–e1002701. doi:10.1371/journal.pmed.1002701 PMID:30481172

De Caigny, A., Coussement, K., & De Bock, K. (2018). *A New Hybrid Classification Algorithm for Customer Churn Prediction Based on Logistic Regression and Decision Trees*. Academic Press.

Dogan, M., Beach, S., Simons, R., Lendasse, A., Penaluna, B., & Philibert, R. (2018). Blood-Based Biomarkers for Predicting the Risk for Five-Year Incident Coronary Heart Disease in the Framingham Heart Study via. *Machine Learning*. PMID:30567402

Ehlers, A. P. (2017). Improved Risk Prediction Following Surgery Using Machine Learning Algorithms. *EGEMS, 5*.

Ghaddar, B., & Naoum-Sawaya, J. (2017). *High Dimensional Data Classification and Feature Selection using Support Vector Machines*. Academic Press.

Hollon. (2018). A machine learning approach to predict early outcomes after pituitary adenoma surgery. *Neurosurgical Focus, 45*(5).

Karim, M. N., Reid, C. M., Tran, L., Cochrane, A., & Billah, B. (2017). Missing Value Imputation Improves Mortality Risk Prediction Following Cardiac Surgery: An Investigation of an Australian Patient Cohort, Heart. *Lung and Circulation, 26*(3), 301–308. doi:10.1016/j.hlc.2016.06.1214 PMID:27546595

Kasamatsu, T., Hashimoto, J., Iyatomi, H., Nakahara, T., Bai, J., Kitamura, N., ... Kubo, A. (2008). *Application of Support Vector Machine Classifiers to Preoperative Risk Stratification With Myocardial Perfusion Scintigraphy*. Academic Press.

Lee. (2018). Derivation and Validation of Machine Learning Approaches to Predict Acute Kidney Injury after Cardiac Surgery. *Journal of Clinical Medicine, 7*.

Meyer, A., Zverinski, D., Pfahringer, B., Kempfert, J., Kuehne, T., Sündermann, S. H., ... Eickhoff, C. (2018). Machine learning for real-time prediction of complications in critical care: A retrospective study. *The Lancet. Respiratory Medicine, 6*(12), 905–914. doi:10.1016/S2213-2600(18)30300-X PMID:30274956

Pantanowitz, A., & Marwala, T. (2009). Missing Data Imputation Through the Use of the Random Forest Algorithm. *Proceedings of the Advances in Computational Intelligence*, 53-62. 10.1007/978-3-642-03156-4_6

Pretorius, A., Bierman, S., & Steel, S. (2016). *A meta-analysis of research in random forests for classification*. Academic Press.

Rakhmetulayeva, S. B., Duisebekova, K. S., Mamyrbekov, A. M., Kozhamzharova, D. K., Astaubayeva, G. N., & Stamkulova, K. (2018). Application of Classification Algorithm Based on SVM for Determining the Effectiveness of Treatment of Tuberculosis. Procedia Computer Science, 130, 231-238.

Razzaghi, T., Safro, I., Ewing, J., Sadrfaridpour, E., & Scott, J. (2017). *Predictive models for bariatric surgery risks with imbalanced medical datasets*. Academic Press.

Salles, T., Gonçalves, M., Rodrigues, V., & Rocha, L. (2018). Improving random forests by neighborhood projection for effective text classification. Information Systems, 77, 1-21.

Soguero-Ruiz. (2016). Predicting colorectal surgical complications using heterogeneous clinical data and kernel methods. *Journal of Biomedical Informatics, 61*, 87-96.

Stonelake, S., Thomson, P., & Suggett, N. (2015). Identification of the high risk emergency surgical patient: Which risk prediction model should be used. *Annals of Medicine and Surgery (London)*, *4*(3), 240–247. doi:10.1016/j.amsu.2015.07.004 PMID:26468369

Tang, F., & Ishwaran, H. (2017). *Random forest missing data algorithms*. Academic Press.

Wong, A., Young, A. T., Liang, A. S., Gonzales, R., Douglas, V. C., & Hadley, D. (2018). Development and validation of an electronic health record–based machine learning model to estimate delirium risk in newly hospitalized patients without known cognitive impairment. *JAMA Network Open*, *1*(4), e181018. doi:10.1001/jamanetworkopen.2018.1018 PMID:30646095

Chapter 70
Data Mining and Machine Learning Approaches in Breast Cancer Biomedical Research

Gunavathi Chellamuthu
VIT University, India

Kannimuthu S.
Karpagam College of Engineering, India

Premalatha K.
Bannari Amman Institute of Technology, India

ABSTRACT

Breast cancer is the most common invasive cancer in females worldwide. Breast cancer diagnosis and breast cancer prognosis are the two important challenges for the researchers in the medical field and also for the practitioners. If the cells in the breast start to grow without any control, it leads to cancer. Normally, the growth of the lump can be seen using x-ray. The benign and malignant breast lumps are distinguished during breast cancer diagnosis. The prognosis process predicts the period at which the breast cancer is likely to reappear in patients who have had their cancers removed. Data mining techniques and machine learning algorithms are mostly used in the whole process of breast cancer diagnosis and treatment. They utilize the large volume of breast cancer data for extracting knowledge. The application of data mining and machine learning methods in biomedical research is presently vital and crucial in efforts to transform intelligently all available data into valuable knowledge.

INTRODUCTION

Cancer is featured by an irregular, unmanageable growth that may demolish and attack the neighbouring healthy body tissues. Cancer categorization by medical practitioners and radiologists was depend on morphological and clinical characteristics and had restricted diagnostic ability in the earlier period.

DOI: 10.4018/978-1-6684-6291-1.ch070

The most prevalent and dangerous disease among the females in worldwide is breast cancer. It was found that 22.9% of evident cancers in women and 16% of all female cancers are related to breast cancer disease. 18.2% of men and women are passed away worldwide because of breast cancer (Mandelblatt et al. 2004). Researcher faces two major challenges such as Breast Cancer identification and prognosis in medical applications. Data mining techniques and machine learning algorithms are mostly used in the whole process of breast cancer diagnosis and treatment and they changed the entire process simple in nature.The benign and malignant breast lumps are distinguished during Breast Cancer diagnosis. The prognosis process predicts the period at which the breast cancer is likely to reappear in patients who have had their cancers removed. Applying data analytics and machine learning methodologies in cancer research is one of the key approaches to utilize large volume of Breast cancer data for extracting knowledge. The noteworthy methods in biotechnology and health care have shown to an outstanding production of data, such as high throughput genetic and clinical data, generated from large volume of E-health records. The application of data mining and machine learning methods in biomedical research is recently essential and crucial in efforts to convert intelligently all available data into valuable facts (Diz et al., 2015). The primary intension of the contemporary study is to take a systematic investigation of the applications of machine learning, data mining algorithms and tools in the field of Breast cancer research with reference to i) Breast cancers complications, ii) Prediction, Diagnosis and Prognosis and iii) Identification of biomarker genes.

BACKGROUND

In human body, if the cells in the breast are started to grow without any control, it leads to cancer. Normally, the growth of the lump can be seen using x-ray. The affected cells can propagate into nearby tissues or blowout all over the body. More than 100 types of cancer are identified in the medical field and it became one of the major roots of death in the world. There are many factors that influence the formation and spreading of cancers which are listed below:

1. Genetics
2. Gender
3. Age
4. Life style
5. Environment
6. Marital status

Breast cancer is the deadliest disease which is a malevolent cell development in the breast. The cancer cells extend to other parts of the body, if the patient left untreated. The occurrence of breast cancer upsurges after 40 years of age. The incidence of this disease is even high with women over age 50. Breast cancer causes deaths in women which has the second place among other diseases. According to the survey, mortality rates dropped significantly during 1992-1998 with the major decreases in younger women. Breast cancer is most prevalent in women which affect over 13% of all women in the world. There is more number of younger women vulnerable to breast cancer in most of the nations (Richie & Swanson, 2003).

Breast cancer is of two types. They are:

1. **Harmless breast lump (non-cancerous):** The texture and the size of tumor are easy to understand through the basic examination;
2. **Malignant breast lump (cancerous):** Diagnosis of clinical studies needed for predicting this kind of cancer. This type can be further categorized into:
   a. **Non-invasive:** Affected cells have not extended in other cells and tissues;
   b. **Invasive:** Affected cells have extended into the neighboring cells and tissues.

The effective treatment can be given for the patients, if we detect this kind of cancer earlier. Many attempts were executed already to identify the disease in the initial stage. But, the key cause of breast cancer is not identified by the researchers. There are some of the risks that are identified which escalate the chances of breast cancer formation in women. They are modifiable and non-modifiable factors associated with breast cancer. The modifiable factors are Women with no children, Number of abortions, Taking frequent X-Rays, Obesity, Duration of breast feeding, Age at first child birth, Alcohol consumption and Food Habits. The non-modifiable factors are Gender, Genetically having breast or ovarian cancer, Women with no children, Starting menopause after the age of 55, High breast density and Ageing.

Breast cancer has six stages. In this, stage 0 is the beginning of the disease and the stage 4 is the dangerous stage. Magnetic Resonance Imaging (MRI), Mammography, Biopsy and Positron Emission Tomography (PET) are the common methods used to identify the stage of cancer. In breast cancer research, many computer assisted diagnostic system have been developed to reduce the false-positive diagnosis. These tools are not better enough to improve the accuracy of classification, diagnosis and prognosis of breast cancer disease. This motivates us to present a machine learning and data mining based method which support oncologists in the task of breast cancer categorization, diagnosis and prognosis. These methods help oncologists in the process of classifying and diagnosing breast cancer.

Data Mining and Machine Learning

Data Mining or Knowledge Discovery from Data (KDD) is the activity of extracting useful facts from huge collection of data. The KDD process contains the actions like Data cleaning (To take away noise and inconsistent data), Data integration (To combine different datasets), Data selection (To select useful data), Data transformation (To transform data in such forms which are appropriate for data mining process), Data mining (Algorithms/processes that are used to extract patterns), Pattern evaluation (To unearth significant information extracted from data mining process), Knowledge presentation (To represent the mined knowledge for users). The Data mining functionalities can be classified into two groups. They are predictive and descriptive. Predictive mining tasks carry out induction on the present data in order to make forecasting. Descriptive data mining characterize the properties of data in target dataset (Han, Kamber, & Pei, 2011).

Machine Learning are the methods involved in dealing with huge volumes of data in the most intelligent fashion (by developing algorithms) to derive actionable patterns. The term "machine learning" is introduced by Samuel (1959). He defined Machine learning as the subfield of computer science that gives computers the ability to learn without being explicitly programmed. Another definition of machine learning is, "A computer program is said to learn from experience E with respect to some class of tasks T and performance measure P if its performance at tasks in T, as measured by P, improves with experience E" given by Mitchell (1997).

In traditional/conventional Programming, the data and program are given as input to the computer to get the output. But in machine learning, the data and output are given as input to the computer to generate a program. This program can be used further in traditional programming. Figure 1 shows the process of traditional programming and machine learning.

Figure 1. Traditional programming vs machine learning

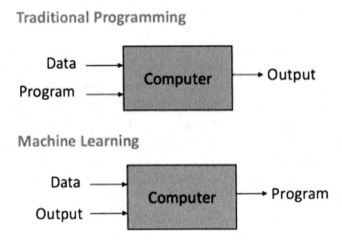

Training the machines pertain to a structural process where every phase put up an improved version of the machine. The task of teaching machines can be divided into 3 parts as shown in Figure 2.

Figure 2. Process of teaching machines

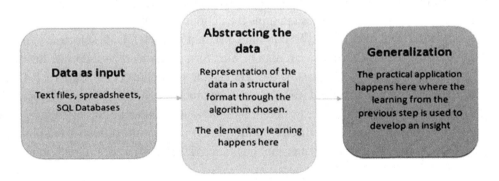

Fundamental tasks used to achieve a machine learning task are:

1. **Collecting data:** This step is the foundation for future learning, used to collect raw data. Based on the better variety, density and volume of appropriate data, the learning scenario for the machine turn out to be better;

2. **Preparation of data:** Beauty of any systematic process depends on the quality of the data used. Data analysts are in a position to invest time to find out the quality of data and take further move for solving issues such as missing data and treatment of contrast data. To examine the nuances of the data in details, exploratory analysis is used;

3. **Training process:** This task is based on selecting the relevant algorithm and representation of data in the type of the model. The dataset is separated into two groups such as training set and testing set. The first part (training data) is inputted to develop the machine learning model. The second part (test data), is used for evaluating the model;

4. **Evaluate model:** To check the accuracy, the test data is used. This task identifies the precision in the choice of the algorithm based on the outcome. The test will be better if the accuracy of model is checked to see its performance on data which was not utilized at all during model build;

5. **Improving the performance:** This task involves in selecting a diverse model altogether or bring in more variables to improve the efficiency. This is why more amount of time needs to be spent in data collection and preparation.

Each and every machine learning methods consist of three components:

*   **Representation:** This component discusses about how to represent knowledge. Decision trees, support vector machines, neural networks and graphical models are the some of the examples;
*   **Evaluation:** It is the method of evaluating the candidate programs (hypotheses). Accuracy, precision, recall, squared error and likelihood are the some of the examples;
*   **Optimization:** It is the way to improve the performance of the search process. Combinatorial optimization, constrained optimization and convex optimization are the some of the examples (Marsland, 2014).

Types of Machine Learning Algorithm

There are three kinds of machine learning algorithms. They are supervised learning, unsupervised learning and reinforcement learning.

1. **Supervised Learning:** It is used most widely in all kinds of application. The supervised learning method is similar to the learning process of a human under the guidance of a master. Based on the input and output variables given in the training dataset, the machine learning method produce a function. The function is used to forecast the value of the output parameter based on given input values. This method is called 'supervised' because the algorithm acquires knowledge by itself by using target variable. Supervised learning problems are of two types. They are Regression analysis and classification models;

2. **Unsupervised Learning:** Only input data is given without relevant output variable in unsupervised learning methods. There is no master in this concept and there are no true answers involved in this algorithm that is why it is called as unsupervised learning. These algorithms are executed to unearth and present the structure in the data. There are two categories in unsupervised learning namely Cluster analysis and Association learning. In cluster analysis, the major task is to identify the built-in groupings in the data which possess similar behaviour.The association learning problem states to find the relationships among the variables in the dataset;

3. **Reinforcement Learning:** In reinforcement learning, the algorithm finds the best possible way to achieve an objective. By interacting with the given environment it learns by itself from the consequence of its actions. It follows trial-and-error method for learning where the machine finds its suitable actions based on the history of experiences. To take accurate decisions the machine uses its best possible knowledge (Marsland, 2014).

Classification Models

Decision Tree

The classification or regression models are constructed in the form of a tree in decision tree method. The given dataset is sliced into smaller and smaller subsets. At the same time the corresponding decision tree is developed in step by step manner. Finally a tree with decision nodes and leaf nodes is achieved. Here decision node denotes the condition and leaf nodes represent a classification or a decision for the given data. The topmost node or the decision node in a tree is related to the best predictor variable. These trees are able to handle numerical and categorical data. It is assumed that at the beginning, the whole training set is considered as the root node for the decision tree. The attributes are placed either as root or internal node of the tree.

Random Forest

Random Forest is one of the machine learning techniques which is used for supervised learning tasks. It combines a group of weak models to form a powerful structure. Here, multiple trees are used as contrast to a single tree in other tree based models. For a given object with its attributes, each tree gives a label for the class and it is called as the tree "votes" for that class. Finally, the forest selects the classification that has the higher votes using all the trees. In regression, the average of the outputs of different trees is considered.

Boosting

Boosting is a collective technique that tries to produce a strong classifier from different weak classifiers. The algorithm is developed based on the regression trees. In this method, each successive tree is constructed for the prediction residuals of the earlier tree. In every step of the boosting, a best possible partitioning of the data is concluded. By using the respective means the deviations of the observed values are computed.

Support Vector Machine (SVM)

Support Vector Machines (SVM), is a classifier requires only few examples for training, and it is very intensive to the number of dimensions. SVM is considered to be a novel technique for the classification of both linear and non-linear data. SVM classification can be used to regression and classification problems. Like ANN, SVM is an example for "black-box" algorithm. SVM is most suitable algorithm for classification when compared to other algorithms. The primary task of an SVM is to separate classes with a surface that maximizes the margins between them. With the help of nonlinear mapping, the SVM converts the training dataset into a higher dimension. It finds the linear optimal separating hyperplane using the new dimension. If data is from two classes, then it is separated by a hyperplane. Hyperplane is identified by using support vectors/training tuples and margins.

K-Nearest Neighbour Classification (k-NN)

K-Nearest Neighbour method is used to construct a classification model. Based on the similarity measure it assigns a class label for the new data by considering majority voting. KNN stores the entire dataset and no learning process is needed. The prediction for a new instance is made by analysing entire training set. Normally Euclidean distance, Hamming distance, Manhattan distance and Minkowski distance measures are used for similarity checking.

Artificial Neural Networks (ANN)

The fundamental model of ANN is derived from the architecture of animal brains. ANN works based on the format of inputs and outputs. The core element of brain is neuron. It is a cell that is able to transfer and process electrical/chemical signals. Each neuron is associated with all other neuron to build a network. There is massive collection of neurons connected with each other in human brain. Every neuron possesses an input, a cell body and an output which is represented in Figure 3.

Figure 3. Structure of neuron

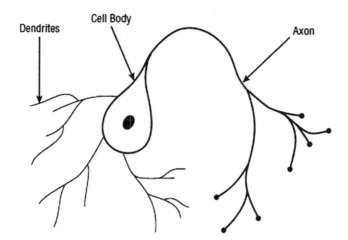

The basic component of a neural network is the perceptron. The foremost task of perceptron is to accept an input signal and it has to pass the value of the input over some form of function. It gives the result of the function. Perceptrons concentrate on the number of vector when they sent to the input. Then these values are passed to an activation function that calculates the outgoing value (Han et al., 2011).

LITERATURE REVIEW

The volume of data handled in digital and actual world is exponentially increasing over a period of time. Thus retrieving valuable information or knowledge from existing data is vital and time consuming task. Data mining contains several algorithms for unearthing useful facts from large amount of data. These methods are suitable for all kind of data that are gathered in all areas of science. Applications of data mining and machine learning techniques are realized in different domains of science like education, military, insurance, medicine, finance, telecommunication and etc.

This section discusses about the related topics that have been utilized data mining and machine learning techniques for breast cancer diagnosis and treatment. To analyze the breast cancer behavior, recurrence is used which is hardly noted in the many breast cancer related datasets. Because of this prediction, the breast cancer research became more difficult. Abreu et al. (2016) applied machine learning algorithms to predict the breast cancer recurrence. Based on the results it is proved that high accuracy is achieved by compromising sensitivity.

Oskouei et al. (2017) made an attempt to offer a complete report on the uses of KDD methods in breast cancer identification, treatment and prognosis. The major tasks in breast cancer diagnosis are presented. Chaurasia et al. (2017) used Logistic method, RepTree and RBF to analyze the breast cancer disease. From the experimental results of this work, it is understood that simple logistic classifier produces more accuracy when compared to other approaches. They used Chi-square test, Gain Ratio and Info Gain for selecting the attributes that are relevant in breast cancer diagnosis or treatment.

Kourou et al. (2015) utilized machine learning methods to classify cancer patients into low or high risk groups which can ease clinical management of patients. These methods generate predictive models which results in effective decision making. Identification of cancer disease is very important in starting stage for its proper statement. Usually DNA microarray is used to find the expression level of genes. Agrawal and Agrawal (2015) presented a detailed survey on neural network methods for cancer prediction. Even though several supervised and unsupervised machine learning methods are used for cancer prediction, neural network based methods are proved to be best in accuracy.

Mohebian et al. (2017) proposed an approach namely Hybrid Predictor of Breast Cancer Recurrence (HPBCR) for forecasting breast cancer disease. They utilized statistical feature selection methods to select discriminative features. Resultant features further refined by using Particle Swarm Optimization (PSO) with ensemble learning. The performance of the system is analysed by using cross validation methods. Experimental results show that HPBCR method performs better than other classifiers such as Decision Tree, SVM and multilayer perceptron neural network.

Liu et al. (2009) proposed a gene selection method called Recursive Feature Addition (RFA) for MAQC-II Breast Cancer dataset. In RFA, supervised learning method is combined with statistical similarity measures. RFA uses supervised learning to achieve the best training accuracy. Paulin and Santhakumaran (2011) used a neural network classifier for analysing Winconsin Dataset for Breast cancer. For training the network, back propagation network was used.

Sarvestani et al. (2010) compared the performance of different neural networks namely Multilayer Perceptron (MLP), Self-Organizing Map (SOM), Radial Basis Function (RBF) and Probabilistic Neural Network (PNN) for investigating breast cancer diagnosis problem. For training set, the RBF and PNN performed well. The experimental results support the usage of neural networks in breast cancer diagnosis.

Abdelaal et al. (2010) examined the potential use of the Support Vector Machine classifier using Tree based methods for DDSM dataset. Mammographic mass features were extracted in addition to age that distinguishes positive and negative cases. The SVM technique gives increased diagnostic accuracy in classifying the samples. Particle Swarm Optimization algorithm based classification rules are devised by Gandhi et al. (2010). The Genetic Algorithm based approach give smaller fuzzy rules with more accuracy.

Lee et al. (2001) suggested a method for classification based on rough set theory. Hierarchical granulation structure was adopted for finding the classification rules. The lower and upper approximations of rough sets are used for knowledge extraction. In their work, a testing was done using WBC dataset. This method produced minimum number of classification rules. The usage of decision trees for the detection of high-risk breast cancer groups is introduced by Anunciacao et al. (2010). The results showed that the proposed method was capable of finding substantial associations statistically by growing a decision tree and electing the best possible leaf node.

Jamarani et al. (2005) combined ANN and multiwavelet based sub band image decomposition for cancer detection. The MIAS mammographic databases and images are used for experimental purpose. Narang et al. (2012) proposed a structure that discovers the stage of cancer such as benign or malignant. They used Adaptive Resonance Theory (ART2) neural network. The clustering method was used to mine useful information and different measures like precision, recall and accuracy was analyzed.

Ammar et al. (2016) proposed a texture based feature technique called co-occurrence matrix which is extracted from MRI images for cancer treatment. They used some of the texture parameters such as cluster Shade, dissimilarity, entropy and homogeneity for their research. It was proved that those parameters measured from breast MRI can be used to assess the quality response to neoadjuvant chemotherapy. Asri et al. (2016) compared the performance of different machine learning algorithms using Wisconsin Breast Cancer (original) datasets.

Recent research focuses more on Two-gene classifiers for their easiness and realism. The algorithms that existed already uses exhaustive search that results in low time-efficiencies. Wang (2012) proposed a classification algorithm based on two-gene which uses the univariate gene selection strategy. Simple classification rules were identified based on optimal cut-points. The classification model was applied in eleven cancer gene expression datasets. A comparative study between top-scoring pair's model, greedy pair's model, Diagonal Linear Discriminant Analysis, k-Nearest Neighbour, Support Vector Machine and Random Forest was also done. It was observed that two-gene classifiers outperforms well when compared to the existing models.

EXPERIMENTAL EVALUATION

Dataset Description

There are two kind of datasets used for the experimental purpose. They are Breast Cancer Original Dataset and Breast Cancer Dataset (Diagnostics). The Breast Cancer Original Dataset contains two predictor classes namely malignant (M) and benign breast mass (B).The phenotypes for characterization are Sample ID (code number), Clump thickness, Uniformity of cell size, Uniformity of cell shape, Marginal adhesion, Single epithelial cell size, Number of bare nuclei, Bland chromatin, Number of normal nuclei, Mitosis and Classes. The dataset contains 10 Attributes and 699 Records in the dataset. The other dataset named Breast Cancer Dataset (Diagnostics) contains two predictor classes namely malignant (M) and benign breast mass (B). In the dataset the first two columns provide Sample ID and lasses (diagnosis). There were ten characteristics measured for each cell nucleus. They are Radius (mean of all distances from the centre to points on the perimeter), Texture (standard deviation of gray-scale values), Perimeter, Area, Smoothness (local variation in radius lengths), Compactness (perimeter^2 / area - 1.0), Concavity (severity of concave portions of the contour), Concave points (number of concave portions of the contour), Symmetry and Fractal dimension. There are three measures namely Mean, Standard error and Largest/worst are used for each characteristic. There are totally 32 Attributes and 569 Records used in this dataset.

Experimental Results

The Error matrix for the Decision Tree model on Breast Cancer Diagnostic (counts and proportions) is given in Table 1 and Table 2. Here, the overall error is 3.5% and Averaged class error is 4.25%.

Table 1. Error matrix for the Decision Tree model on Breast Cancer Diagnostic.csv (counts)

Actual / Predicted	B	M	Error
B	352	5	1.4
M	15	197	7.1

Table 2. Error matrix for the Decision Tree model on Breast Cancer Diagnostic.csv (proportions)

Actual / Predicted	B	M	Error
B	61.9	0.9	1.4
M	2.6	34.6	7.1

The Error matrix for the Extreme Boost model on Breast Cancer Diagnostic (counts and proportions) is given in Table 3 and Table 4. Here, the overall error is 0.4% and Averaged class error is 0.45%.

Table 3. Error matrix for the Extreme Boost model on Breast Cancer Diagnostic.csv (counts)

Actual / Predicted	B	M	Error
B	357	0	0.0
M	2	210	0.9

Table 4. Error matrix for the Extreme Boost model on Breast Cancer Diagnostic.csv (proportions)

Actual / Predicted	B	M	Error
B	62.7	0.0	0.0
M	0.4	36.9	0.9

The Error matrix for the Random Forest model on Breast Cancer Diagnostic (counts and proportions) is given in Table 5 and Table 6. Here, the overall error is 1% and Averaged class error is 1.25%.

Table 5. Error matrix for the Random Forest model on Breast Cancer Diagnostic.csv (counts)

Actual / Predicted	B	M	Error
B	355	2	0.6
M	4	208	1.9

Table 6. Error matrix for the Random Forest model on Breast Cancer Diagnostic.csv (proportions)

Actual / Predicted	B	M	Error
B	62.4	0.4	0.6
M	0.7	36.6	1.9

The Error matrix for the SVM model on Breast Cancer Diagnostic (counts and proportions) is given in Table 7 and Table 8. Here, the overall error is 1.8% and Averaged class error is 2.35%.

Table 7. Error matrix for the SVM model on Breast Cancer Diagnostic.csv (counts)

Actual / Predicted	B	M	Error
B	357	0	0
M	10	202	4.7

Table 8. Error matrix for the SVM model on Breast Cancer Diagnostic.csv (proportions)

Actual / Predicted	B	M	Error
B	62.7	0.0	0.0
M	1.8	35.5	4.7

The Error matrix for the Linear model on Breast Cancer Diagnostic (counts and proportions) is given in Table 9 and Table 10. Here, the overall error is 1.7% and Averaged class error is 1.9%.

Table 9. Error matrix for the Linear model on Breast Cancer Diagnostic.csv (counts)

Actual / Predicted	B	M	Error
B	352	5	1.4
M	5	207	2.4

Table 10. Error matrix for the Linear model on Breast Cancer Diagnostic.csv (proportions)

Actual / Predicted	B	M	Error
B	62.9	0.9	1.4
M	0.9	36.4	2.4

The Error matrix for the Neural Net model on Breast Cancer Diagnostic (counts and proportions) is given in Table 11 and Table 12. Here, the overall error is 37.3% and Averaged class error is 50%.

Table 11. Error matrix for the Neural Net model on Breast Cancer Diagnostic.csv (counts)

Actual / Predicted	B	M	Error
B	357	0	0
M	212	0	100

Table 12. Error matrix for the Neural Net model on Breast Cancer Diagnostic.csv (proportions)

Actual / Predicted	B	M	Error
B	62.7	0	0
M	37.3	0	100

Experimentation in Breast Cancer Diagnostic Dataset

The Figure 4 to Figure 19 gives the performance of different classification algorithm on Breast cancer diagnostic dataset. Figure 20 present the cost curve of different algorithms and its comparison when Breast cancer diagnostic dataset is used. Figure 21, 22 and 23 gives the Lift measure, precision/Recall values and Sensitivity/Specificity values obtained from different algorithms respectively.

Figure 4. Performance analysis of Extreme Boost in Breast Cancer Diagnostic Data Set

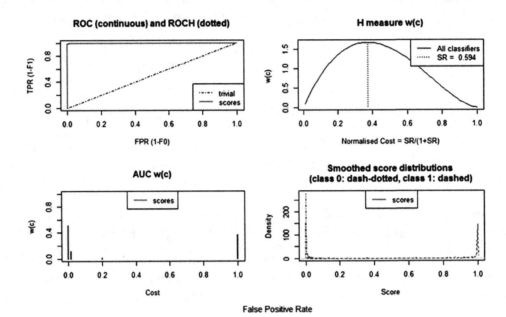

Figure 5. Performance Chart of Extreme Boost in Breast Cancer Diagnostic data

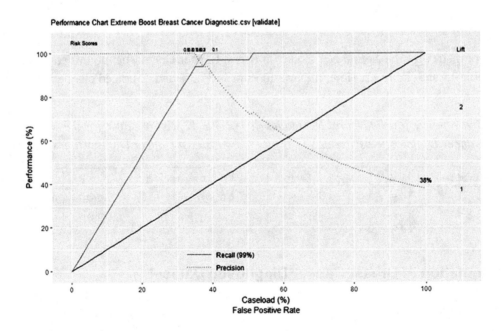

Figure 6. ROC Curve for Extreme Boost approach in Breast Cancer Diagnostic data

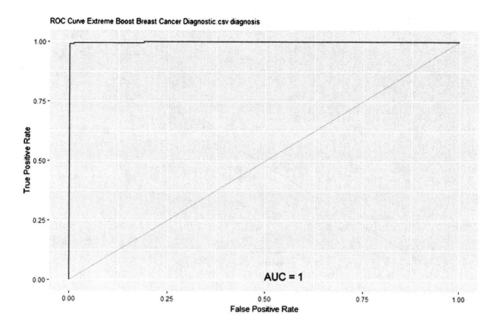

Figure 7. Performance analysis of Decision Tree in Breast Cancer Diagnostic Data Set

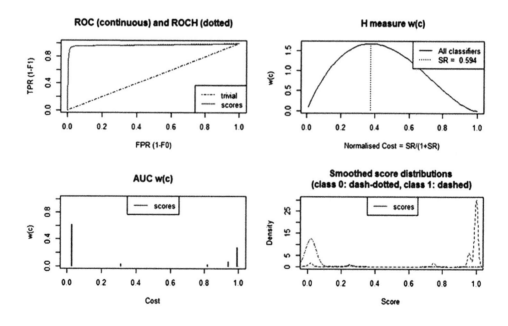

Figure 8. Performance Chart of Decision Tree in Breast Cancer Diagnostic Data

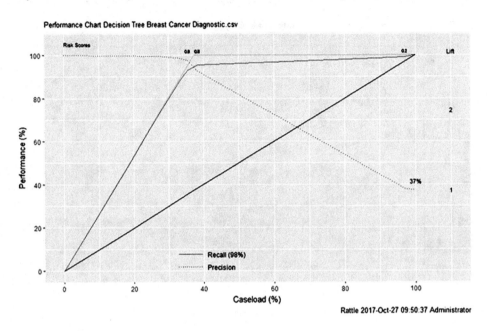

Figure 9. ROC Curve for Decision Tree approach in Breast Cancer Diagnostic data

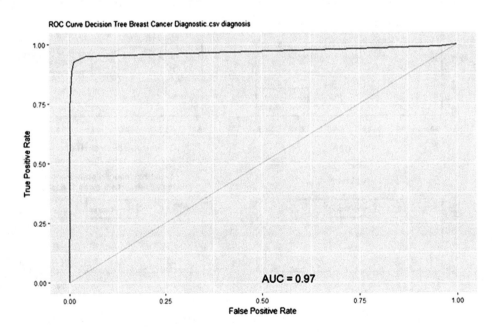

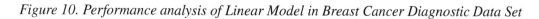

Figure 10. Performance analysis of Linear Model in Breast Cancer Diagnostic Data Set

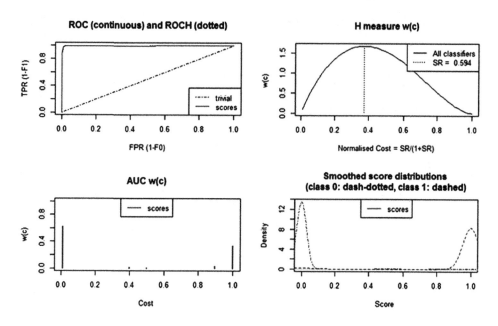

Figure 11. Performance Chart of Linear Model in Breast Cancer Diagnostic Data

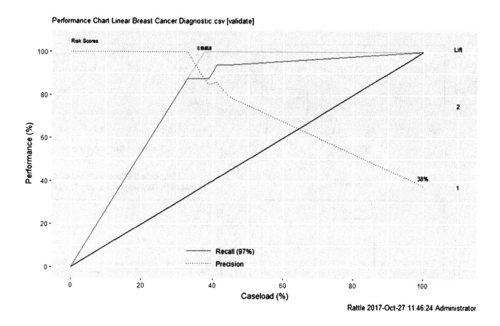

Figure 12. ROC Curve for Linear Model in Breast Cancer Diagnostic data

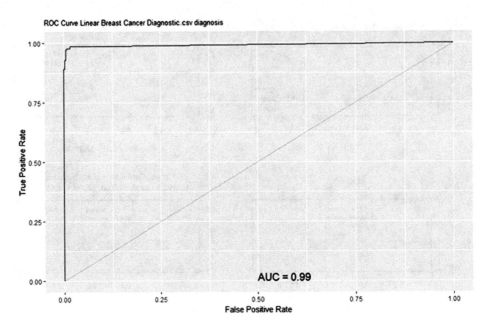

Figure 13. Performance analysis of Neural Net in Breast Cancer Diagnostic Data Set

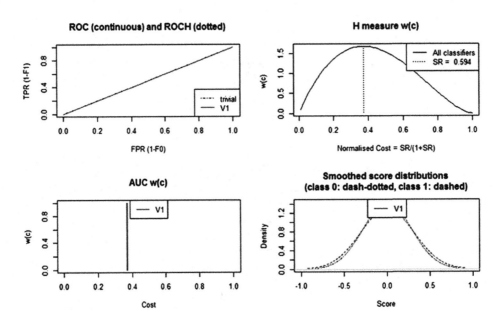

Figure 14. Performance Chart of Neural Net in Breast Cancer Diagnostic Data

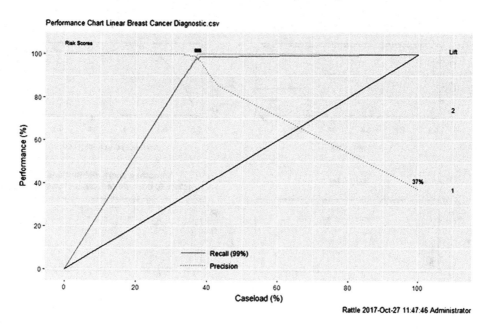

Figure 15. ROC Curve for Neural Net in Breast Cancer Diagnostic data

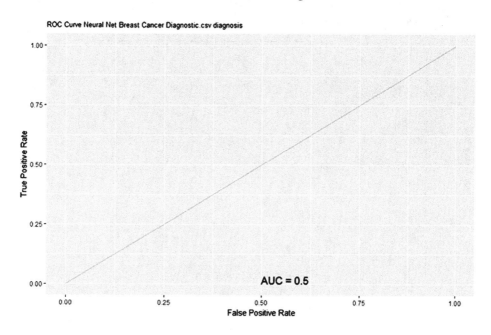

Figure 16. Performance analysis of Random Forest in Breast Cancer Diagnostic Data Set

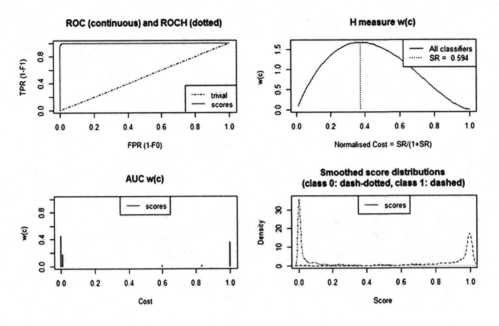

Figure 17. ROC Curve for Random Forest in Breast Cancer Diagnostic data

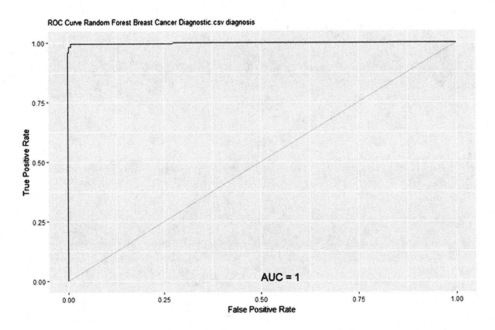

Figure 18. Performance analysis of SVM in Breast Cancer Diagnostic Data Set

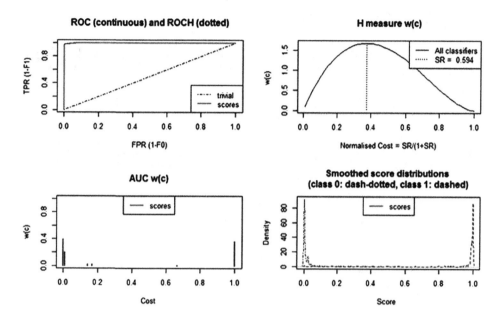

Figure 19. ROC Curve for SVM in Breast Cancer Diagnostic data

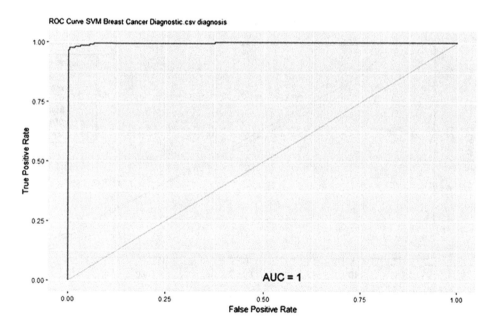

Figure 20. Cost Curve for Breast Cancer Diagnostic data on various algorithms

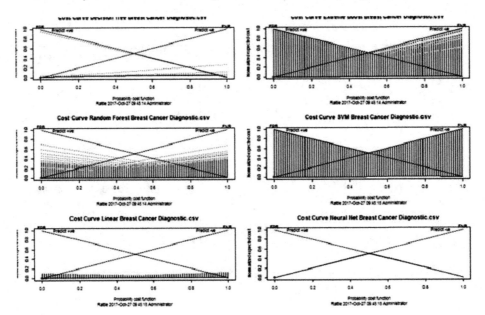

Figure 21. Lift Chart for Breast Cancer Diagnostic data on various algorithms

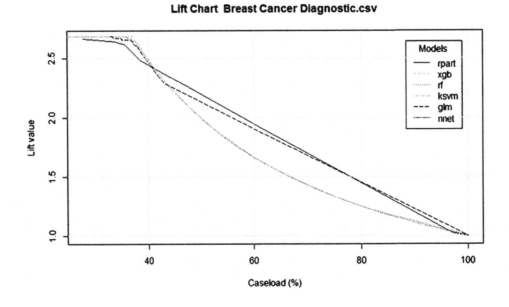

Figure 22. Precision/Recall Plot for Breast Cancer Diagnostic data on various algorithms

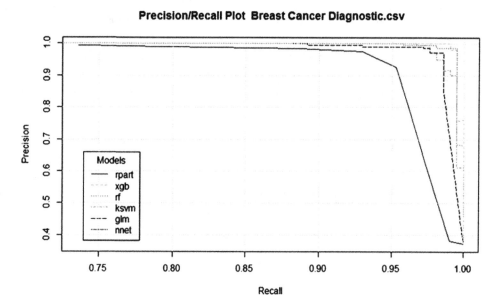

Figure 23. Sensitivity/Specificity plot for Breast Cancer Diagnostic data on various algorithms

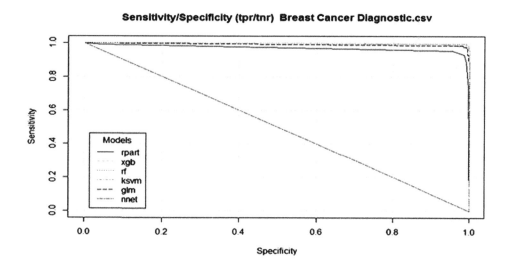

Experimentation in Breast Cancer Original

The Figure 24 to Figure 31 gives the performance of different classification algorithm on Breast cancer original dataset. Figure 32 presents the cost curve of different algorithms and its comparison when Breast cancer diagnostic dataset is used. Figure 33, 34 and 35 gives the Lift measure, precision/Recall values and Sensitivity/Specificity values obtained from different algorithms respectively.

Figure 24. Performance analysis of Decision Tree in Breast Cancer Original Data Set

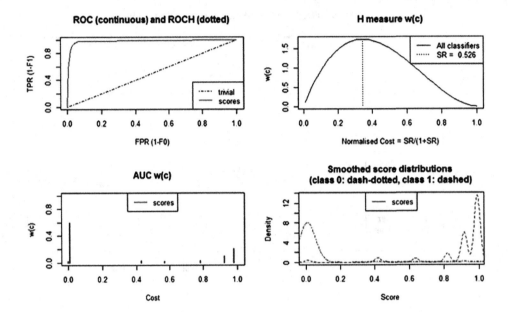

Figure 25. ROC Curve for Decision Tree in Breast Cancer Original data

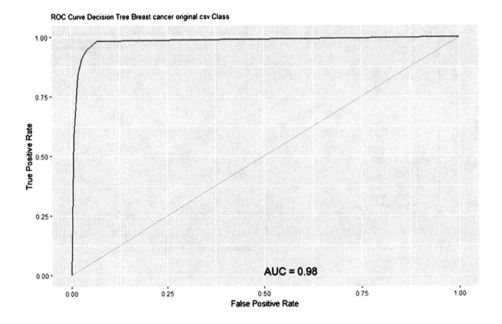

Figure 26. Performance analysis of Neural Net in Breast Cancer Original Data Set

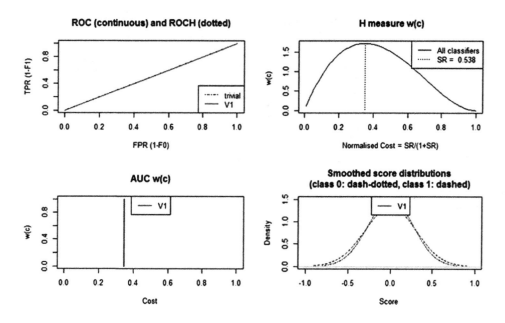

Figure 27. ROC Curve for Neural Net t in Breast Cancer Original data

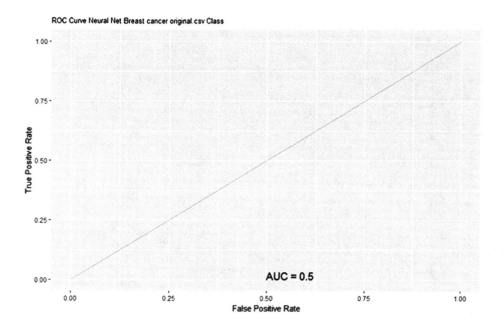

Figure 28. Performance analysis of Random Forest in Breast Cancer Original Data Set

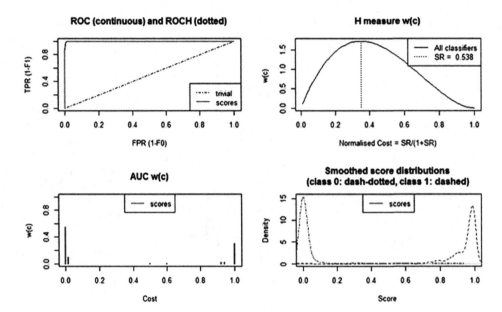

Figure 29. ROC Curve for Random Forest in Breast Cancer Original data

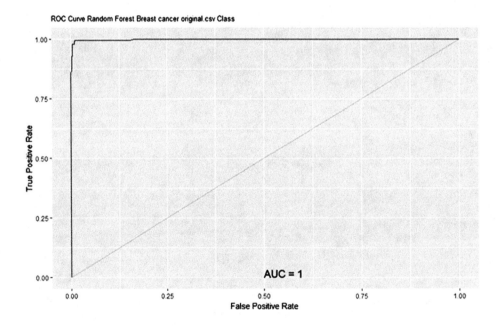

Figure 30. Performance analysis of SVM in Breast Cancer Original Data Set

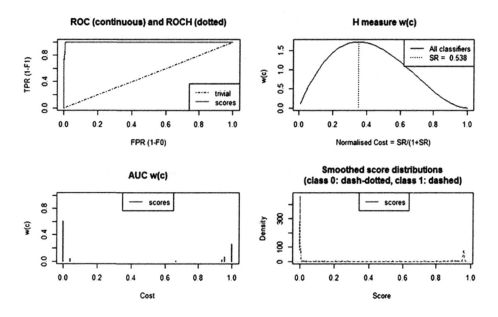

Figure 31. ROC Curve for SVM in Breast Cancer Original data

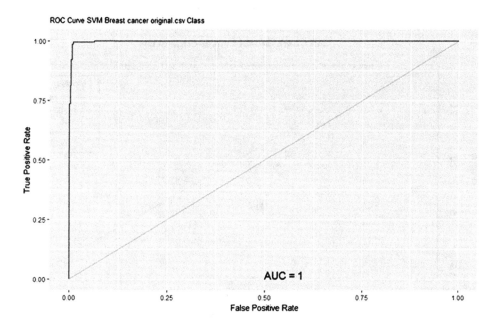

Figure 32. Cost Curve for Breast Cancer Original data on various algorithms

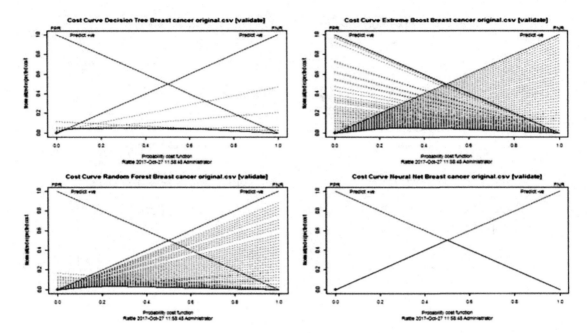

Figure 33. Lift Chart for Breast Cancer Original data on various algorithms

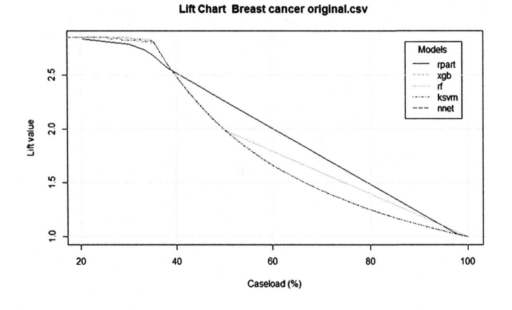

Figure 34. Precision/Recall plot for Breast Cancer Original data on various algorithms

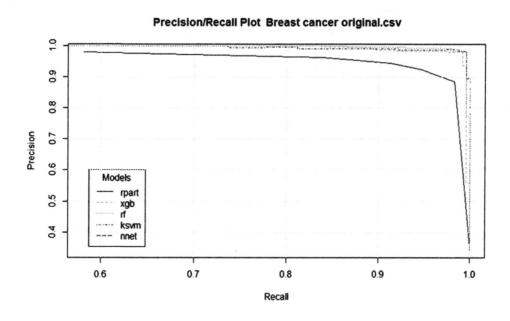

Figure 35. Sensitivity/Specificity plot for Breast Cancer Original data on various algorithms

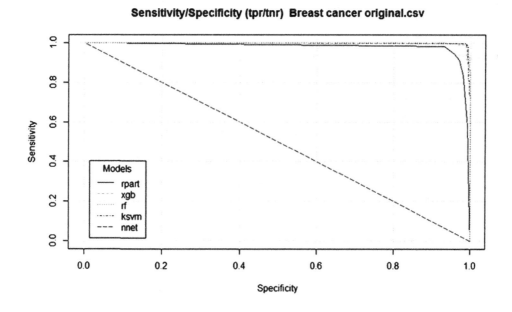

RESULTS AND DISCUSSION

In this chapter, Breast Cancer Diagnostic and Original dataset are considered for Breast Cancer Research and different classifier models such as Decision tree, Random forest, Extreme Boost, Linear model, SVM and Neural Net are employed. The performance is measured through precision/recall, sensitivity/

specificity, ROC, Lift and Risk charts. The error rate is measured for all the classifiers for Breast Cancer Diagnostic dataset. The Extreme Boost algorithm gives 99.6% accuracy with 0.4% error rate and Random Forest gives 99% accuracy with 1% error rate. The Boosting method decreases the variance of single estimation. Normally it associates numerous estimates from other models. So, the result obtained from boosting has higher stability. Random forest is an ensemble method in which a classifier is constructed by combining several different Independent base classifiers. The ensemble classifier aggregates the individual predictions to combine into a final prediction, based on a majority voting on the individual predictions.It can be shown that an ensemble of independent classifiers, each with an error rate e, when combined significantly reduces the error rate.

CONCLUSION

This chapter gives the overview of Breast cancer disease, its type and symptoms. The introduction of data mining, machine learning algorithms and types of machine learning algorithms are also presented. Two different Breast cancer dataset are taken for experimental analysis and the results were obtained. The classification methods such as Decision Tree, Extreme Boost model, Random Forest, Support Vector Machine, Linear model and Neural Network are used for analysing. The results and the performance metrics shows that Data mining concepts and Machine learning algorithms are useful in Breast cancer research. The data mining and machine learning techniques can be used for clustering and association rule mining using breast cancer dataset.

REFERENCES

Abdelaal, M. M. A., Sena, H. A., Farouq, M. W., & Salem, A. B. M. (2010, October). Using data mining for assessing diagnosis of breast cancer. In *Computer Science and Information Technology (IMCSIT), Proceedings of the 2010 International Multi conference on* (pp. 11-17). IEEE. 10.1109/IMCSIT.2010.5679647

Abreu, P. H., Santos, M. S., Abreu, M. H., Andrade, B., & Silva, D. C. (2016). Predicting breast cancer recurrence using machine learning techniques: A systematic review. *ACM Computing Surveys, 49*(3), 52. doi:10.1145/2988544

Agrawal, S., & Agrawal, J. (2015). Neural network techniques for cancer prediction: A survey. *Procedia Computer Science, 60*, 769–774. doi:10.1016/j.procs.2015.08.234

Ammar, M., Mahmoudi, S., & Stylianos, D. (2016). Breast cancer response prediction in neoadjuvant chemotherapy treatment based on texture analysis. *Procedia Computer Science, 100*, 812–817. doi:10.1016/j.procs.2016.09.229

Anunciaçao, O., Gomes, B. C., Vinga, S., Gaspar, J., Oliveira, A. L., & Rueff, J. (2010). A data mining approach for the detection of high-risk breast cancer groups. In *Advances in Bioinformatics* (pp. 43–51). Berlin: Springer. doi:10.1007/978-3-642-13214-8_6

Asri, H., Mousannif, H., Al Moatassime, H., & Noel, T. (2016). Using machine learning algorithms for breast cancer risk prediction and diagnosis. *Procedia Computer Science, 83*, 1064–1069. doi:10.1016/j.procs.2016.04.224

Chaurasia, V., & Pal, S. (2017). Data mining techniques: To predict and resolve breast cancer survivability. *International Journal of Computer Science and Mobile Computing, 3*, 10–22.

Diz, J., Marreiros, G., Freitas, A. (2015). Using Data Mining Techniques to Support Breast Cancer Diagnosis. *Proceedings of New Contributions in Information Systems and Technologies*, 689-700.

Gandhi, K. R., Karnan, M., & Kannan, S. (2010). Classification rule construction using particle swarm optimization algorithm for breast cancer data sets. In *Signal Acquisition and Processing, 2010.ICSAP'10. International Conference on* (pp. 233-237). IEEE. 10.1109/ICSAP.2010.58

Han, J., Kamber, M., & Pei, J. (2011). *Data Mining: Concepts and Techniques* (3rd ed.). Morgan Kaufmann Publishers.

Jamarani, S. M., Behnam, H., & Rezairad, G. A. (2005). Multiwavelet based neural network for breast cancer diagnosis. *GVIP, 5*, 19–21.

Kourou, K., Exarchos, T. P., Exarchos, K. P., Karamouzis, M. V., & Fotiadis, D. I. (2015). Machine learning applications in cancer prognosis and prediction. *Computational and Structural Biotechnology Journal, 13*, 8–17. doi:10.1016/j.csbj.2014.11.005 PMID:25750696

Lee, C. H., Seo, S. H., & Choi, S. C. (2001, July). Rule discovery using hierarchical classification structure with rough sets. In *IFSA World Congress and 20th NAFIPS International Conference, 2001.Joint 9th* (Vol. 1, pp. 447-452).IEEE.

Liu, Q., Sung, A. H., Chen, Z., Liu, J., Huang, X., & Deng, Y. (2009). Feature selection and classification of MAQC-II breast cancer and multiple myeloma microarray gene expression data. *PLoS One, 4*(12), e8250. doi:10.1371/journal.pone.0008250 PMID:20011240

Mandelblatt, J., Armetta, C., Robin Yabroff, K., Liang, W., & Lawrence, W. (2004). Descriptive Review of the Literature on Breast Cancer Outcomes: 1990 Through 2000. *JNCI Monographs, 2004*(33), 8–44.

Marsland, S. (2014). Machine Learning– An Algorithmic Perspective (2nd ed.). Chapman and Hall/CRC Machine Learning and Pattern Recognition Series.

Mitchell, T. M. (1997). Machine learning. McGraw-Hill International Editions Computer Science Series.

Mohebian, M. R., Marateb, H. R., Mansourian, M., Mañanas, M. A., & Mokarian, F. (2017). A hybrid computer-aided-diagnosis system for prediction of breast cancer recurrence (HPBCR) using optimized ensemble learning. *Computational and Structural Biotechnology Journal, 15*, 75–85. doi:10.1016/j.csbj.2016.11.004 PMID:28018557

Narang, S., Verma, H. K., & Sachdev, U. (2012). Breast Cancer Detection using ART2 Model of Neural Networks. *International Journal of Computers and Applications, 57*(5).

Oskouei, R. J., Kor, N. M., & Maleki, S. A. (2017). Data mining and medical world: Breast cancers' diagnosis, treatment, prognosis and challenges. *American Journal of Cancer Research*, *7*(3), 610. PMID:28401016

Paulin, F., & Santhakumaran, A. (2011). Classification of breast cancer by comparing back propagation training algorithms. *International Journal on Computer Science and Engineering*, *3*(1), 327–332.

Samuel, A. L. (1959). Some studies in machine learning using the game of checkers. *IBM Journal of Research and Development*, *3*(3), 210–229. doi:10.1147/rd.33.0210

Sarvestani, A. S., Safavi, A. A., Parandeh, N. M., & Salehi, M. (2010, October). Predicting Breast Cancer Survivability using data mining techniques. In *Software technology and Engineering (ICSTE), 2010 2nd international Conference on* (Vol. 2, pp. V2-227). IEEE. 10.1109/ICSTE.2010.5608818

Wang, X. (2012). Robust two-gene classifiers for cancer prediction. *Genomics*, *99*(2), 90–95. doi:10.1016/j.ygeno.2011.11.003 PMID:22138042

KEY TERMS AND DEFINITIONS

Classification: It is a data mining function that assigns items in a collection to target categories or classes.

Data Mining: It is the process of discovering patterns in large data sets involving methods at the intersection of machine learning, statistics, and database systems.

Machine Learning: It is a field of statistics and computer science that gives computer systems the ability to "learn" with data, without being explicitly programmed.

This research was previously published in Sentiment Analysis and Knowledge Discovery in Contemporary Business; pages 175-204, copyright year 2019 by Business Science Reference (an imprint of IGI Global).

Chapter 71
Survey of Breast Cancer Detection Using Machine Learning Techniques in Big Data

Madhuri Gupta

Jaypeee Institute of Information Technology, Noida, India

Bharat Gupta

Jaypee Institute of Information Technology, Noida, India

ABSTRACT

Cancer is a disease in which cells in body grow and divide beyond the control. Breast cancer is the second most common disease after lung cancer in women. Incredible advances in health sciences and biotechnology have prompted a huge amount of gene expression and clinical data. Machine learning techniques are improving the prior detection of breast cancer from this data. The research work carried out focuses on the application of machine learning methods, data analytic techniques, tools, and frameworks in the field of breast cancer research with respect to cancer survivability, cancer recurrence, cancer prediction and detection. Some of the widely used machine learning techniques used for detection of breast cancer are support vector machine and artificial neural network. Apache Spark data processing engine is found to be compatible with most of the machine learning frameworks.

1. INTRODUCTION

As reported by World Health Organization (WHO, 2016), breast cancer is the most prominent problem in the area of medical diagnosis, which is increasing every year. A consistent advancement in technology has been accomplished for breast cancer research (Hanahan & Weinberg, 2011). Researchers has applied different methods, for example screening and biopsy, to discover different stages of breast cancer before symptoms occur. An unprecedented amount of healthcare data (Marx, 2013) is produced by the plethora of technology such as magnetic resonance imagery (MRI), super-resolution digital microscopy, mass spectrometry, etc. These technologies mainly provide healthcare data, but their focus is not on analysis,

DOI: 10.4018/978-1-6684-6291-1.ch071

knowledge extraction or interpretation (Rider & Chawla, 2013). Therefore, there is need of data storing, data pre-processing and data management in medical research. Medical science is also ushering into the field of big data and there is a need to analyze the huge amount data by applying machine learning techniques (Mattmann, 2013). The effectiveness of big data and machine learning approaches applies appropriate methods to create efficient models for analysis. The fusion of data has significantly supported data-oriented research in breast cancer (BC) field (Dinov, 2016). It involves diagnosis and prediction of human-threatening disease.

Breast cancer detection is one of the main priorities in medical research, because mortality rate in India is growing fast (breast cancer statistics presented by Globocan Project, 2016). Here, mortality rate is the number of women who died because of breast cancer in a particular year. Breast cancer certainly generates large amount of gene expression data. So, this disease has encouraged interest in the improvement of machine learning, data analysis techniques and tools which can accurately extract information from massive data. Therefore, in breast cancer research, data analytics and machine learning approach are the main concern when it arises to management, diagnosis and other clinical aspects. Hence, it is necessary to review the current literature on data analytics and machine learning approaches in breast cancer research.

This paper has mainly 6 sections: section 2 represents an aspect of the breast cancer disease, section 3 provides the necessary background knowledge on machine learning (ML), section 4 introduces big data analytics, section 5 provides challenges, and section 6 represents conclusion and future work.

2. Breast Cancer

Cancer is a disease that causes cells in the body to grow and change uncontrollably. Breast cancer is one of them (Breast State, 2017). Majority of breast cancer cases begin in breast tissues which are made up of lobules (glands), and ducts. The remaining portion of breast is made up of lymphatic and fatty tissues. Most of the time, breast cancer is detected during breast screening or after a patient notices a lump. These breast lumps can be benign (non-cancerous) and malignant (cancerous). Breast cancer can arise in any area of the breast, the lobules, the ducts and sometimes, the tissue in between. This section deals with different types and stages of breast cancer (Breast cancer Symptoms, 2017).

Types of Breast Cancer

1. **Non-invasive:** Cancer in duct and lobules in breast, they do not spread in normal tissue within breast. It is also called pre-cancers or carcinoma in situ (CIS).
2. **Invasive**: Cancer spread in normal tissue of breast. Most breast lumps are invasive.
3. **Multifocal**: Original tumor divides itself, but remains in the same section of the breast.
4. **Multicentric**: All the tumors arise independently in different region of the breast.
5. **Recurrent:** Cancer that arise again in the same or opposite breast after a period of time when the cancer couldn't be detected.
6. **Metastatic:** Cancer spread to other portions of body. It is advanced stage cancer.
7. **Paget's disease:** In this disease, cancer cells collect around the nipple. This type of cancer, first affects the ducts of the nipple, and then spreads to the nipple.

Stages of Breast Cancer

- **Stage 0: (Tis, N0, M0).** Noninvasive cancer. This stage does not contain any symtoms or indication that the tumor cells have extent to other parts of the breast.
- **Stage 1A: (T1, N0, M0).** At this stage, tumor is small, invasive and it does not spread to the lymph nodes.
- **Stage 1B: (T1, N1, M0).** Cancer has extent only to the lymph nodes.
- **Stage IIA: (T0, N1, M0).** This stage has no evidence of cancerous tumor in the breast, only benign nodes at this stage which can spread to the axillary lymph nodes.
- **Stage IIB: (T2, N1, M0).** At this stage size of tumor cannot be larger than 50 mm and it will not spread to at most 3 axillary lymph nodes. At very next growth of cancer tumor size will increase to 50 mm.
- **Stage IIIB: (T4, N2, M0).** Size of tumor is larger than 50 mm. It does not spread to other parts of the body, only lymph nodes of under the arm can be effected and it caused swelling in the breast.
- **Stage IIIC: (any T, N3, M0).** This means tumor can be of any size, it can spread to 10 or more axillary lymph nodes but not spread to distant parts of the body.
- **Stage IV (metastatic and Recurrent).** This is a highest stage. It can be state as (any T, any N, M1) this means tumor can be of any size and it spread to other body part.

MACHINE LEARNING

Machine learning (ML) deals with the methods in which machine learns on the basis of past experiences. Mitchell has given the precise definition of ML: "A computer program is said to learn from experience E with respect to some class of tasks T and performance measure P, if its performance at tasks in T, as measured by P, improves with experience E" (Mitchell, 2006).

Machine learning process contains two phases: (1) Valuation of unknown dependencies of system on the basis of given dataset. (2) Predict the output of system on the basis of estimated dependencies. ML has also made up an interesting milestone in field of biomedical research in various uses, where a satisfactory assumption is acquired by looking over a multi-dimensional space for a dataset of biomedical samples, using distinctive algorithms (Niknejad & Petrovic, 2013).

Categories of Machine Learning Techniques

ML depends on learning system to fetch the pattern from the input dataset and give the output. ML techniques are generally classified into three classes such as (Machine learning types, 2017): Supervised learning, unsupervised learning and Reinforcement learning-

1. **Supervised Learning:** It is the widely used machine learning (Machine learning types, 2017). It contains a mapping function to map input to the output and a learning algorithm which is required to learn the mapping function. This mapping function is also known as machine learning model. It contains two type of learning tasks; classification and regression. The process of learning the system and discovering the group of input data is called classification (Liu, Ranka, & Kahveci, 2008) for example blood group. In contrast regression model predict output in form of numerical

values for example "Weight". Some of the widely used supervised techniques are: Decision Tree, Neural Network (Multilayer perceptron), K-Nearest Neighbor, Logistic Regression, and Random Forest etc.

2. **Unsupervised Learning:** In this learning, training data does not have a corresponding output variable (Machine learning types, 2017). Algorithms use to present and discover the stimulating structure in the data. It can be subdivided into association and clustering Technique. Association rule learning, determine rules which can describe a large portion of data, for example if a person buy A then he have to buy B, (Kavakiotis, Tzanis, & Vlahavas, 2014) whereas clustering is used to discover the related patterns from input dataset which is called cluster i.e. the parting of complete dataset into group of data, so that samples belongs to one group are similar (Alpaydin, 2004). Some of the widely used unsupervised machine learning techniques is K-Means and hierarchical clustering etc.

3. **Semi Supervised Learning:** It is basically combination of both supervised and non-supervised learning. This learning is mostly used when unlabeled data is more than labeled data. Some of the widely used semi supervised techniques are Support Vector Machine and Expectation Maximization (EM), etc.

4. **Reinforcement Learning:** In this learning, system has no prior knowledge. System attempts to learn by direct interaction with environment or hit and trial basis. Some of the widely used reinforcement learning techniques are Brute force method, Monte Carlo method and temporal difference method, etc.

Survey of Machine Learning Application in Breast Cancer

ML methods are involved in various complex and massive data-intensive fields, for example, prescription, cosmology, biology, etc. These methods give feasible solution to extract the information hidden in the data (Liang, Li, Chen, & Zeng, 2015). A survey of different machine learning techniques and frameworks for breast cancer detection has been done.

Techniques of Machine Learning

Some machine learning techniques which are precisely used in breast cancer diagnosis are Support Vector Machine, Neural Network, Logistic regression and random forest etc. Table 1 contain list of techniques and problem which they have solved and performance. Metrics used for measuring the performance of different techniques are accuracy, error rate, survival time, specificity, sensitivity, etc. Accuracy, specificity and sensitivity are described in terms of True Positive, True Negative, False Negative and False Positive (Zhu, Zeng & Wang, 2010).

$$\text{Accuracy} = \frac{\text{True Negative} + \text{True Positive}}{\text{True Negative} + \text{True Positive} + \text{False Negative} + \text{False Positive}} = \text{Correct valuations}$$
/ All valuations

$$\text{Specificity} = \frac{\text{True Negative}}{\text{True Negative} + \text{False Positive}} = \text{True negative valuation / All negative valuation}$$

$$\text{Sensitivity} = \frac{\text{True Positive}}{\text{True Positive} + \text{False Negative}} = \text{True positive valuation} / \text{All positive valuation}$$

Table 1. Machine learning techniques used in breast cancer diagnosis

S. no.	Machine learning techniques	Solutions	Result (%)
1	Support Vector Machine (SVM) (Xu, Zhang, Zou, Wang & Li 2012)	Breast cancer prognosis on Microarray Dataset	94.5% Accuracy
2	Multimodal Deep learning Approach (Liang, Li, Chen & Zeng 2015).	Multi-Platform Cancer Data analysis to predict survival time.	70% mean survival Time in Breast cancer
3	Single-Cell Deep Transfer Learning (Kandaswamy, Silva, Alexandre & Santos, 2016).	High-Content Analysis of Breast Cancer	77% Accuracy
4	Artificial Neural Networks (ANN) (Ayer et al., 2010).	Breast Cancer Risk Estimation	96% Accuracy
5	ANN Ensemble Kept with C4.5 Rule (Zhou & Jiang, 2003).	Health Diagnosis (Breast cancer, diabetes and hepatitis)	2.9, 24 & 14.9 Error rate resp.
6	RBF Network, Simple Logistic and RepTree (Chaurasia & Pal, 2014).	Resolve Breast Cancer Survivability and prediction of breast cancer	74.5% Accuracy
7.	Neural networks (Shaikhina &Khovanova, 2017).	Handling limited datasets in medical diagnosis	86.5% Accuracy
8.	Parallel Random Forest Technique (Chen et al., 2017).	Big Data analysis in a Spark Cloud Computing	0.2 error rate for 500 trees.
9.	ANN revisited (Ayer et al., 2010).	Breast cancer risk estimation	96% Accuracy
10.	SVM (Listgarten et al., 2004).	Predict Breast Cancer Susceptibility using nucleotide polymorphisms	69% predictive power
11.	Graph-based semi-supervised learning (Park, Ahn, Kim & Park, 2014).	Develop an Integrative gene network model to examine cancer recurrence.	Original Max 80% Accuracy
12.	SVM (Kim et al., 2012).	Breast cancer prognosis using gene signature and recurrence	89% Sensitivity 73% Specificity
13.	Graph-based semi-supervised learning (Park et al., 2013).	Prediction of breast cancer survivability using ANN, SVM and semi-supervised learning models.	Sem supervised model (76%) performed better
14.	Bayesian networks (Gevaert, Smet, Timmerman, Moreau & Moor, 2006).	Integration of clinical and microarray data to predicting the breast cancer.	85% AUC
15.	SSL Co-training Algorithm (Kim & Shin, 2013).	Prediction of Breast cancer survivability	76% Accuracy
16.	Implemented 17 SVM classifier model using LIBLINEAR (Fan, Chang, Hsieh, Wang & Lin, 2008).	Classify the Primary Sites of Cancer	62% Accuracy

The application of machine learning techniques in breast cancer research is gaining popularity because Machine learning researchers and practitioners, are building integrating intelligent algorithms and frameworks to make software work more quickly, reliably and without annoyances. Framework is a layered structure which is used to implement machine learning techniques. Some widely used frameworks (Machine learning frameworks, 2016) are described in next section

Frameworks of Machine Learning

It is the layered structure which used to implement machine learning techniques; some frameworks are required for monitoring in learning (Machine learning frameworks, 2016). Some of the general frameworks are as follows:

- **Apache Singa:** It is a distributed deep learning platform which is used to train deep learning model for large datasets. Software stack of Singa has three main modules: I/O, model and core. These models provide memory management, read and write data and model component.
- **Amazon Machine Learning:** It delivers some visualization tools and wizards for users in order to create ML models without implementing complex ML algorithms and technology. It uses the data stored in different data sources like Amazon S3, that uses to retrieve any amount of data.
- **Caffe:** It is a deep learning framework with speed, modularity and expression (Jia et al., 2014). It offers a complete toolkit for training, testing, deploying models and modification.
- **Massive Online Analysis (MOA):** It is an open source system for information stream mining (MOA, 2016). It is extendable with new stream generator, new mining algorithm and evaluation measures.
- **Scikit-Learn:** It is a ML library for python programming language. It uses Python programming framework by building on top of some existing Python packages. It contains tools for standard machine learning task such as classification, regression and clustering.

Bioinformatics data is continually increasing since more molecular data of patient is created. This molecular data comes under the category of big volume, e.g., gene expression data. Many conventional machine learning methods are not scalable and effective to handle the data with certain features such as, uncertainty, large volume, incompleteness, and heterogeneity (Luo, Wu, Gopukumar & Zhao, 2016), etc. So, ML needs to rejuvenate itself to process big data. Big data technologies are increasingly used for biomedical and health-care informatics research. Processing and analysis of massive data is performed by loading data into memory (Laney, 2001) Therefore, new techniques are required to analyze big medical data.

Big Data Analytics in Health Care Using Machine Learning

Big data is a model that converts the case-based studies to data-driven research. It is applicable in biomedical informatics domain (Belle et al., 2015) to generate better predictive models, to predict the disease accurately. It is highly required in bioinformatics because of the complex and massive volume of genomic dataset. From last decades, huge volume of clinical and biological data has been generated at an unprecedented speed, for example, electronic health records (HER) is authenticating large volume of patient data and processing of billions of DNA sequence data is speeding up every day due to new generation of sequencing technology.

Main goal of big data analytics in health care is to take benefit of the large size of data and deliver a precise intervention at the right time to the right patient. As per the survey, there are multiple technologies used together to cure the problem of big data analysis, such as data mining tools and artificial intelligence (AI), with Hadoop (Dean & Ghemawat, 2008), So, next section will describe Big Data technologies, Data processing engine and machine learning toolkits for big data.

Big Data Technologies

Biomedical researchers are facing some challenges in terms of managing, analyzing and storing, large amount of data (Margolis et al., 2014). Features of big data (size, heterogeneity and speed) need a powerful technique to fetch beneficial information to provide health-care solutions. Two main big data techniques for data analytics, are parallel computing and cloud computing-

- **Parallel Computing**: This technique is capable to execute algorithm concurrently on a set of Supercomputers or machines. Basically, it is used for big data handling. Recently, some new parallel computing models are introduced like MapReduce (Hadoop) by Google (Dean & Ghemawat, 2008).
- **Cloud Computing**: It is a distributed computing technique which permits the access to share hub of configurable computational resources through the internet (Armbrust et al., 2010). It is used to improve agility, flexibility and speed of a system. Currently, it is centered by many big data applications.

These technologies need some data processing engine to analyze big data. Some data processing engines are discussed below. These engines are intentionally made up for huge amount of data, so they are not efficient for minor projects (Landset, Khoshgoftaar, Richter & Hasanin, 2015). Hence, selection between data processing engines is based on the requirement of a particular engine. In favor to do this, it is essential to have an understanding of major engines designed for big data.

Data Processing Engines

Most of the existing tools focus on stream processing, interactive analysis and batch processing. In this section, some currently used tools are discussed for big data analysis

- **Apache Hadoop and Apache MapReduce:** Apache Hadoop and MapReduce cannot be considered as exchangeable; Hadoop is basically an open source implementation of the MapReduce concept (Dean & Ghemawat, 2008). MapReduce is a programming model that process massive data by using divide and conquers technique. MapReduce performs in two major steps: Map and Reduce, whereas Hadoop implements using two nodes: master node and worker node. In the complete scenario, Master Node divides the input data into sub problems and in Map step these problems allocates to worker nodes. Subsequently, in Reduce step, master node combines the result of all the sub problems.
- **Apache spark:** It is an open source in-memory data processing engine made for speed processing and sophisticated analytics (Apache Spark, 2016). It is designed in the bottom-up scenario to improve performance. Spark is 100x faster than Hadoop in term of speed, especially for large scale data processing due to in-memory computation and other optimizations. Apache Spark is also fast when information is stored on disk. Right now, it holds the world record for extensive scale on-disk sorting.
- **Apache Storm**: It is open source software for distributed real-time computation (Apache Storm, 2016). Storm is easy to set up and operate. It is scalable, fault-tolerant and compatible with any programming language.

- **Apache Flink**: It is an open-source stream processing engine especially for high-performing, distributed computing (Apache Flink, 2016). It performs accurate, even in the case of late-arriving data. It is easy to run on thousands of nodes with very good latency and throughput.
- **H2O**: It is the fastest in-memory data processing engine and it is also used for predictive analysis on huge amount of data (H2O, 2016). It is open source, distributed and scalable software that can run on various nodes.

Above processing engines are considered on the basis of execution model, Supported Language, associated ML tools, latency and fault tolerance (Landset et al., 2015) as shown in Table 2. Here latency represents the timestamp between initiate a job and receiving first output. Fault tolerance is the property of a system that allows continuing the working appropriately in case of failure of some of its modules. Speed may not be essential for each project.

Table 2. Comparison of processing engines on the basis of some parameter

Data Processing Engine	Current Release (June 2015)	Supported Languages	Execution Model	Associated ML Tools	In Memory Processing	Fault Tolerance	Low Latency
Spark	1.3.1	Java, R, python, Scala	Streaming, Batch	Mlib, Mahout, H2O	Yes	Yes	Yes
Map Reduce	2.7.0	Java	Batch	Mahout	No	Yes	No
Storm	0.9.4	Any	Streaming	SAMOA	Yes	Yes	Yes
Flink	0.8.1	Java, Scala	Streaming, Batch	SAMOA	Yes	Yes	Yes
H2O	3.0.0.12	Java, Scala, R, Python	Batch	H2O, Mahout, Mlib	Yes	Yes	Yes

All of the Data processing engines which are discussed in Table 2 are fault-tolerant but the approaches which they usage to achieve the output that may vary. Some mechanisms are required that can detect failures and recover after such a failure arise.

Machine Learning Frameworks for Big Data

Machine learning task does not need any special platform or library to be performed in Hadoop ecosystem (Landset et al., 2015); the expert of a regular programming can directly interact with all frameworks to get result of his source code.

There is only minimal comprehensive research is performed in several well-known frameworks. Table 3 conveys a review of four exhaustive machine learning frameworks-

- **Mahout:** is the most applicable framework for Machine Leaning and data mining. Main objective of this project is to support programmers to construct their own distributed techniques other than using already-written implementations of a library.

- **MLlib:** It is a scalable ML library. It can process common machine learning techniques such as clustering, classification, dimensionality reduction etc. It inherits some functionality of Mahout but it includes regression model.
- **H2O:** It is an Open Source Fast Scalable ML framework. It is used for brilliant techniques such as, Deep Learning, Random Forest, Gradient Boosting, Automatic Machine Learning etc. H2O is most compatible machine learning framework for deep neural networks (DNN).
- **SAMOA**: It is known as Scalable Advanced Massive Online Analysis. It is a framework for machine learning from streaming data developed by Yahoo. SAMOA is a flexible platform which can also run on stream processing engines such as, Storm, Samza and S4.

Table 3. Overview of ML frameworks

	Mahout	Mlib	H2O	SAMOA
Associated platform	MapReduce, spark (Flink and H2O in progress)	H2O, Spark	Spark, H2O and MapReduce	Storm
Interface language	Java	Java, Scala and Python	Java, Python, Scala, R	Java
Current version	0.10.1	1.3.1	3.0.0.12	0.2.0
Regression and Classification algorithms				
Naïve Bayes	Yes	Yes	Yes	
Decision tree	Yes	Yes		Yes
Logistic regression, Random Forest	Yes	Yes	Yes	
SVM		Yes		
Clustering Algorithm				
K-Mean	Yes	Yes	Yes	
Fuzzy K-Mean	Yes			
Feature selection and dimensionality reduction tools				
PCA	Yes	Yes	Yes	
Singular value decomposition	Yes	Yes		
Additional Approach				
Deep Learning	Yes		Yes	
Association rule learning	Yes	Yes		Yes
Collaborating Filtering Algorithm				
User-based CF	Yes			
Item-based CF	Yes			

Comparison of Major Machine Learning Frameworks

A comparative analysis of above machine learning frameworks is presented in Figure 1. This figure observed as a comparative rating of the frameworks, where each framework is rated as per some selection criteria which are as follows-

- **Scalability**: It represents the ability to adapt and perform under an expanded workload.
- **Speed**: Speed of a system generally affects by processing of platform and library.
- **Coverage**: It indicates the range of alternatives in the toolbox, in term of various classes of machine learning and also different executions in each class.
- **Usability**: It refers to initial setup, programming languages available, amount of documentation, on-going maintenance and user interface available etc.
- **Extensibility**: It refers to ability to extend the new functionality in the existing model.

Figure 1. Comparatives analysis of ML frameworks

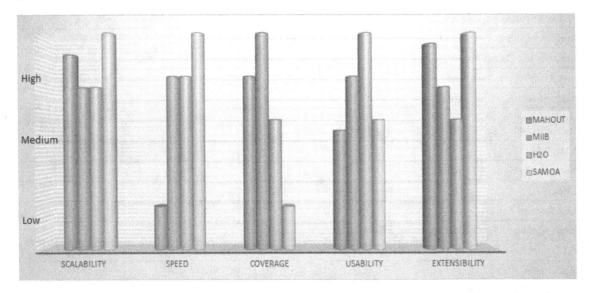

In Figure 1, X axis denotes parameter and Y axis denotes scale of performance in the form of low, medium and large.

Compatibility of Machine Learning Toolkit with Processing Engine

This section offers a detailed overview at qualities and shortcomings of the some machine learning tools for data processing via Hadoop. Figure 2, explains the associations between frameworks of machine learning, data processing engines and ML algorithms. In which Spark is most compatible with all ML techniques and frameworks.

Figure 2. Compatibility between processing engine, ML frameworks and learning algorithms (Adapted from Landset et al., 2015)

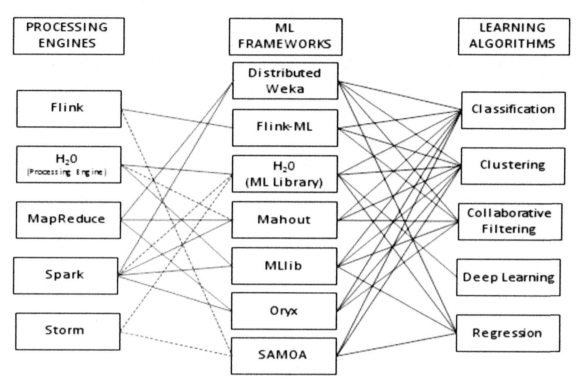

CHALLENGES

Big Data analytics has many emerging challenges; some of them are fusion of big data which constitute the way to integrate data from heterogeneous data sources (Dong, Xin & Srivastava, 2015), technique to handle the inconsistent classes in data coming from different data sources, way to identify the significance between entities from different sources, and how to resolve the conflicting data types for the same object. These challenges need to be focused to enhance the performance of big data analysis, so that the large amount of gene expression data can be processed easily and provide efficient healthcare result.

CONCLUSION

This paper focuses on breast cancer detection techniques by using machine learning in big data. Breast cancer is a genomic disease and huge amount of genomic and clinical data is produced, processed, and stored. So, big data analytics is required for improving the early detection and prediction of breast cancer. This research work discusses widely used machine learning techniques and framework for big data analytics for breast cancer detection. This paper also discusses data processing engines used for managing huge amount of data produced in breast cancer. This research work can be further extended by incorporating feature reduction techniques to improve performance metrics.

REFERENCES

Alpaydin, E. (2004). *Introduction to machine learning*. Cambridge Massachusetts London England: The MIT Press.

Flink, A. (2016). *Role of Apache Flink*. Retrieved from https://flink.apache.org/introduction.html

Spark, A. (2016). *Role of Apache Spark*. Retrieved from https://databricks.com/spark/about

Storm, A. (2016). *Role of Apache Storm*. Retrieved from http://storm.apache.org/about/integrates.html

Armbrust, M., Fox, A., Griffith, R., Joseph, A. D., Katz, R., Konwinski, A., ... Zaharia, M. (2010). A view of cloud computing. *Communications of the ACM, 53*(4), 50–58. doi:10.1145/1721654.1721672

Ayer, T., Alagoz, O., Chhatwal, J., Shavlik, J. W., Kahn, C. E. Jr, & Burnside, E. S. (2010). Breast cancer risk estimation with artificial neural networks revisited. *Cancer, 116*(14), 3310–3321. doi:10.1002/cncr.25081 PMID:20564067

Belle, A., Thiagarajan, R., Soroushmehr, S. M., Navidi, F., Beard, D. A., & Najarian, K. (2015). Big data analytics in healthcare. *BioMed Research International, 2015*, 1–16. doi:10.1155/2015/370194 PMID:26229957

Breast Cancer India. (2016). Breast Cancer Statistics presented by Globocan project. Retrieved from http://www.breastcancerindia.net/statistics/stat_global.html

Breast cancer Symptoms. (2017). Retrieved from http://www.breastcancer.org/symptoms/types

Chaurasia, V., & Pal, S. (2014). Data mining techniques: To predict and resolve breast cancer survivability. *International Journal of Computer Science and Mobile Computing, 3*(1), 10–22.

Chen, J., Li, K., Tang, Z., Bilal, K., Yu, S., Weng, C., & Li, K. (2017). A parallel random forest algorithm for big data in a Spark cloud computing environment. *IEEE Transactions on Parallel and Distributed Systems, 28*(4), 919–933. doi:10.1109/TPDS.2016.2603511

Dean, J., & Ghemawat, S. (2008). MapReduce: Simplified data processing on large clusters. *Communications of the ACM, 51*(1), 107–113. doi:10.1145/1327452.1327492

Dinov, I. D. (2016). Volume and value of big healthcare data. *Journal of Medical Statistics and Informatics, 4*(1), 3. doi:10.7243/2053-7662-4-3 PMID:26998309

Dong, X. L., & Srivastava, D. (2013, April). Big data integration. In *2013 IEEE 29th International Conference on Data Engineering (ICDE)* (pp. 1245-1248). IEEE.

Fan, R. E., Chang, K. W., Hsieh, C. J., Wang, X. R., & Lin, C. J. (2008). LIBLINEAR: A library for large linear classification. *Journal of Machine Learning Research, 9*(Aug), 1871–1874.

Gevaert, O., Smet, F. D., Timmerman, D., Moreau, Y., & Moor, B. D. (2006). Predicting the prognosis of breast cancer by integrating clinical and microarray data with Bayesian networks. *Bioinformatics (Oxford, England), 22*(14), e184–e190. doi:10.1093/bioinformatics/btl230 PMID:16873470

H2O. (2016). *Role of H2O*. Retrieved from https://github.com/h2oai/h2o-3

Hanahan, D., & Weinberg, R. A. (2011). Hallmarks of cancer: the next generation. *cell*, 144(5), 646-674.

Jia, Y., Shelhamer, E., Donahue, J., Karayev, S., Long, J., Girshick, R., ... Darrell, T. (2014, November). Caffe: Convolutional architecture for fast feature embedding. In *Proceedings of the 22nd ACM international conference on Multimedia* (pp. 675-678). ACM. 10.1145/2647868.2654889

Kandaswamy, C., Silva, L. M., Alexandre, L. A., & Santos, J. M. (2016). High-content analysis of breast cancer using single-cell deep transfer learning. *Journal of Biomolecular Screening, 21*(3), 252–259. doi:10.1177/1087057115623451 PMID:26746583

Kavakiotis, I., Tzanis, G., & Vlahavas, I. (2014). *Mining frequent patterns and association rules from biological data. Biological knowledge discovery handbook: preprocessing, mining and postprocessing of biological data. Wiley Book series on bioinformatics: computational techniques and engineering.* New Jersey, USA: Wiley-Blackwell, John Wiley & Sons Ltd.

Han, J., Kamber, M., & Pei, J. (2011). *Data mining: concepts and techniques.* Morgan Kaufmann.

Kim, J., & Shin, H. (2013). Breast cancer survivability prediction using labeled, unlabeled, and pseudo-labeled patient data. *Journal of the American Medical Informatics Association, 20*(4), 613–618. doi:10.1136/amiajnl-2012-001570 PMID:23467471

Kim, W., Kim, K. S., Lee, J. E., Noh, D. Y., Kim, S. W., Jung, Y. S., ... Park, R. W. (2012). Development of novel breast cancer recurrence prediction model using support vector machine. *Journal of Breast Cancer, 15*(2), 230–238. doi:10.4048/jbc.2012.15.2.230 PMID:22807942

Landset, S., Khoshgoftaar, T. M., Richter, A. N., & Hasanin, T. (2015). A survey of open source tools for machine learning with big data in the Hadoop ecosystem. *Journal of Big Data, 2*(1), 24. doi:10.118640537-015-0032-1

Laney, D. (2001). 3D data management: Controlling data volume, velocity and variety. *META Group Research Note, 6*, 70.

Liang, M., Li, Z., Chen, T., & Zeng, J. (2015). Integrative data analysis of multi-platform cancer data with a multimodal deep learning approach. *IEEE/ACM Transactions on Computational Biology and Bioinformatics, 12*(4), 928–937. doi:10.1109/TCBB.2014.2377729 PMID:26357333

Listgarten, J., Damaraju, S., Poulin, B., Cook, L., Dufour, J., Driga, A., ... Zanke, B. (2004). Predictive models for breast cancer susceptibility from multiple single nucleotide polymorphisms. *Clinical Cancer Research, 10*(8), 2725–2737. doi:10.1158/1078-0432.CCR-1115-03 PMID:15102677

Liu, J., Ranka, S., & Kahveci, T. (2008). Classification and feature selection algorithms for multi-class CGH data. *Intelligent Systems in Molecular Biology, 24*(13), 86–95. PMID:18586749

Luo, J., Wu, M., Gopukumar, D., & Zhao, Y. (2016). Big data application in biomedical research and health care: A literature review. *Biomedical Informatics Insights, 8*, 1. doi:10.4137/BII.S31559 PMID:26843812

Machine learning frameworks. (2016). *Description of Frameworks.* Retrieved from http://www.kdnuggets.com /2016/04/top-15-frameworks-machine-learning-experts.html

Machine Learning Types. (2017). *Machine Learning Types.* Retrieved from https://machinelearning mastery.com/ supervised-and-unsupervised-machine-learning-algorithms/

Margolis, R., Derr, L., Dunn, M., Huerta, M., Larkin, J., Sheehan, J., & Green, E. D. (2014). The National Institutes of Health's Big Data to Knowledge (BD2K) initiative: Capitalizing on biomedical big data. *Journal of the American Medical Informatics Association*, *21*(6), 957–958. doi:10.1136/amiajnl-2014-002974 PMID:25008006

Marx, V. (2013). Biology: The big challenges of big data. *Nature*, *498*(7453), 255–260. doi:10.1038/498255a PMID:23765498

Mattmann, C. A. (2013). Computing: A vision for data science. *Nature*, *493*(7433), 473–475. doi:10.1038/493473a PMID:23344342

Mitchell, T. M. (2006). *The discipline of machine learning* (Vol. 3). Carnegie Mellon University, School of Computer Science, Machine Learning Department.

MOA. (2016). *Role of MOA*. Retrieved from http://moa.cms.Waikato.ac.nz/details/

Niknejad, A., &Petrovic, D. (2013). Introduction to computational intelligence techniques and areas of their applications in medicine. *Med. Appl. Artif. Intell.*, 51.

Park, C., Ahn, J., Kim, H., & Park, S. (2014). Integrative gene network construction to analyze cancer recurrence using semi-supervised learning. *PLoS One*, *9*(1), e86309. doi:10.1371/journal.pone.0086309 PMID:24497942

Park, K., Ali, A., Kim, D., An, Y., Kim, M., & Shin, H. (2013). Robust predictive model for evaluating breast cancer survivability. *Engineering Applications of Artificial Intelligence*, *26*(9), 2194–2205. doi:10.1016/j.engappai.2013.06.013

Rider, A. K., & Chawla, N. V. (2013). An ensemble topic model for sharing healthcare data and predicting disease risk. In *Proceedings of the International Conference on Bioinformatics, Computational Biology and Biomedical Informatics* (p. 333). ACM.

Shaikhina, T., & Khovanova, N. A. (2017). Handling limited datasets with neural networks in medical applications: A small-data approach. *Artificial Intelligence in Medicine*, *75*, 51–63. doi:10.1016/j.artmed.2016.12.003 PMID:28363456

Xu, X., Zhang, Y., Zou, L., Wang, M., & Li, A. (2012). A gene signature for breast cancer prognosis using support vector machine. In *2012 5th International Conference on Biomedical Engineering and Informatics (BMEI)* (pp. 928-931). IEEE.

Zhou, Z. H., & Jiang, Y. (2003). Medical diagnosis with C4. 5 rule preceded by artificial neural network ensemble. *IEEE Transactions on Information Technology in Biomedicine*, *7*(1), 37–42. doi:10.1109/TITB.2003.808498 PMID:12670017

Zhu, W., Zeng, N., & Wang, N. (2010). Sensitivity, specificity, accuracy, associated confidence interval and ROC analysis with practical SAS implementations. In *NESUG proceedings: health care and life sciences*, Baltimore, MD.

This research was previously published in the Journal of Cases on Information Technology (JCIT), 21(3); pages 80-92, copyright year 2019 by IGI Publishing (an imprint of IGI Global).

Chapter 72
Analysis of Machine Learning Algorithms for Breast Cancer Detection

Aswathy M. A.
VIT University, India

Jagannath Mohan
ⓘ https://orcid.org/0000-0001-8953-118X
VIT Chennai, India

ABSTRACT

As per the latest health ministry registries of 2017-2018, breast cancer among women has ranked number one in India and number two in United States. Despite the fact that breast cancer affects men also, pervasiveness is lower in men than women. This is the reason breast cancer is such a vital concern among ladies. Roughly 80% of cancer malignancies emerge from epithelial cells inside breast tissues. In breast cancer spectrum, ductal carcinoma in situ (DCIS) and invasive ductal carcinoma (IDC) are considered malignant cancers that need treatment and care. This chapter mainly deals with breast cancer and machine learning (ML) applications. All through this chapter, different issues related to breast cancer prognosis and early detection and diagnostic techniques using various ML algorithms are addressed.

INTRODUCTION

During the period of 2017-2018, health ministry is predicted that the breast cancer may reach 1797900 affected patients by 2020. An article in the journal consultant 360 says that every year approximately 200,000 or above new cases of breast cancer are reporting and 40,000 or above patients are dying with breast cancer in the United States (Estape, 2018). The incidence rate of breast cancer increases with the age of patients. Mostly 50% of new breast cancer diagnoses happening at an age of 65 years and older and the incidence of breast cancer rate increases till the 80s (Sharma, 2001). Usually pathologists detect breast cancer by manually adjusting region of interest and segmenting lesions from that selected area.

DOI: 10.4018/978-1-6684-6291-1.ch072

But chances of intra and inter observability variations will be there. In that context, it is very challenging to find a method that associates automatically selecting region of interests (ROIs) and differentiating ductal carcinoma in situ (DCIS) and invasive ductal carcinoma (IDC) from other normal cancers.

Traditionally cancer detection and the treatment were identified purely on pathologist's experience. These specialists were having above 15 years of practice in the medical field and have seen many patients in similar conditions. Still the accuracy was not 100%. With the evolution of machine learning and artificial intelligence, computer aided diagnosis of different types of cancer became easy. Machine intelligence (MI) or Artificial intelligence (AI) is defined as intelligence displayed by machines and adapt to the surroundings to perform actively to achieve its goals. Here the device imitates the "cognitive" functions correlated to human minds such as learning and perception. AI has exceptional impact in the field of image processing. Machine learning is a sub discipline of artificial intelligence and both are coming under computer science branch. The subject 'Machine learning' gained immense priority among pathologists and radiologists for its benefits in global health care industry and the curiosity boosted towards how the machine learning will strengthen medical specialists in their area of work. The study in machine learning makes healthcare engineering applications straightforward in acquiring and storing patient details in a database and possible to access these databases from anywhere in the world. Smart intelligent systems are there to help doctors and pathologists to interrogate and analyses these complex datasets. An article in Technology trends point out the world market of artificial intelligence including machine learning in various fields like medical imaging, health care, recognition and identification is estimated to reach 2 billion dollars in 2023 (Massat, 2018). Thus, the branch of artificial intelligence and machine learning became a valuable sphere in the healthcare industry.

Image processing became one of the fundamental elements in biomedical and medicinal research, laboratory areas etc. Image processing succeeds in processing a three-dimensional image and converts it into a two dimensional one using numerical data analysis. According to the last 7 years' market hype, artificial intelligence techniques like machine learning and other computer vision methods will change health care medical imaging industry in the stipulations like huge productivity, improved accuracy in diagnosis and good clinical outcomes (Massat, 2018). Hence machine learning would act as a mediator in between ever-growing figure of diagnostic image screening programs despite of harsh scarcity of radiologists and pathologists in many countries. Figure 1 shows the trend of using machine learning algorithms in the world market for various applications like computer vision and deep learning.

Among the vast variety of machine learning applications, cancer detection and prognosis diagnosis at its early stage is gaining high prominence in health care industry. Many researchers and specialists like IBM Watson had invested money and time in this field to make headway but lasted with little success in the history. Now Google came up with a machine learning system that incorporates microscope which helps doctors and pathologists in cancer detection. Similarly, there are many more algorithms that help in detecting any type of cancer with the help of machine learning and deep learning. Different AI techniques like fuzzy logic (FL), genetic algorithm, and neural network can be employed to solve many problems in the biomedical field. However, each method has its own constraints and can be used in certain circumstances only. In such situations, combination of these techniques might help in solving these problems. For example, neural network is just like a "black box" to the users. Users cannot access neural network interiors for understanding parameter revision. At the same time, fuzzy logic has issues in deciding membership functions (MFs). Artificial neural networks cannot parallelize and architecture selection is difficult. Genetic algorithm has an advantage of dealing complicated parameter optimization problems. Sometimes the combination of these techniques (hybrid systems) like neurofuzzy, neural network combined with genetic algorithm etc., will guide to the optimal solution. Hence the major intension of this study is to realize different machine learning concepts, various architectures for image processing queries like segmentation, classification and pre-processing.

Repeated abscission rates for breast cancer partial mastectomy systems are as of now almost 25% because of specialists depending on unreliable techniques for assessing image specimens (Fancellu, 2019). This study is intended to find out how accurate automatic breast cancer detection from histopathology images through a set of machine learning algorithms. A patient's cancer can be characterized according to cancer stage, clinical result, and the decision of treatment by assuring oestrogen and progesterone hormone receptors and hormone epidermal growth factor 2 (HER2) (Malvia, 2017). Review and planned examinations propose that there is significant dissonance in receptor status among initial and final cancer stages. In spite of this proof and current proposals, the dissection of tissue from metastatic breast sites isn't standard practice. So, it leads to high rate of mastectomy in early breast cancer.

Figure 1. Statistics of usage of machine learning algorithms in various applications

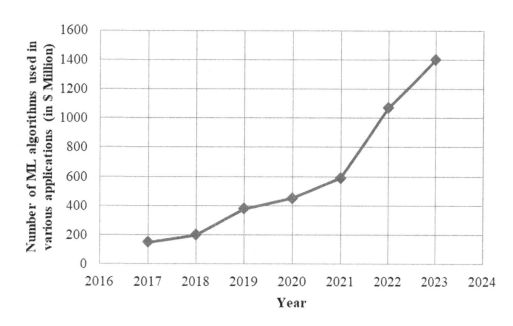

BACKGROUND AND MOTIVATION

There are many motivational reasons for researchers who are conducting studies in breast cancer field. Lynch (2017) used to observe and conduct experiments to know how exercise affects the life of a breast cancer patient, and how the lifestyle of patients impact on the further development of breast cancer. Everyone is very much interested to know about the risk factors and the surroundings that cause breast cancer like pollution, food adulteration etc. But the exciting matter is that the contributors of breast cancer are the things everyone has the ability to change. For example, overweight, lack of physical exercises and liquor consumption. Breast cancer is curable but early diagnosis makes it possible.

For many years, interpretation of microscopic images was one of the biggest challenge's humans faced. This is because microscopic images or histopathology images usually contains stain. Sometimes these stains may accumulate in one part and may be faint in color in other parts. Through the establishment of computer aided diagnosis (CAD), all these problems have been solved. Many experts in this area have tried to use professionally various techniques like machine learning, fuzzy logic, artificial neural network and genetic algorithms in order to expand the efficacy in diagnosing breast cancer. Now a days, doctors are taking much advices from pathologists and microscopic images i.e. histopathology images shows a significant role in CAD. Actually, to reduce inter and intra observer variability, pathologists need a second opinion. Here comes the significance of the CAD.

Sheshadri and Kandaswamy (2006) suggested a method for the detection of plague by using OTSU thresholding. Authors conducted the study on mini-MAIS (Mammogram Image Analysis Society) dataset. The entire study consists of segmenting the region of interest and detecting the micro calcification. Matlab software was used. Alhadidi, et al. (2007) presented a case study on mammogram images of breast cancer. The manuscript contains segmentation of cancer using watershed segmentation procedure. Elter and Held (2008) used feature extraction step with Wavelet transforms. Cell detection from histopathology images is quite difficult because of its confused structure. Existing methods uses textural features, color, contextual and edge features which are commonly known as hand-crafted low-level features. Bengio et al. (2013) suggested a new method of taking pixel level features which gives more information about shape and edge features. The deep learning (DL) technique offers the advantage of learning high level features from pixel intensities so that it will be easy for a classifier to learn and classify objects. Cruz-Roa et al. (2013) employed an autoencoder using convolutional neural network for learning image representation of histopathology images. One of the limitations of this paper was that the autoencoder has only one layer so that the high-level representation might not be accurate. Nedzved et al. (2000) recommended a segmentation method based on morphological approach for histopathology image cell detection. Al-Kofahi et al. (2010) put forwarded a hybrid model consisting graph cut binarization for nuclei count and detection.

Regarding segmentation and detection of breast cancer, histopathology images show different characteristics for various types of cancers. It includes variations in morphologies, dimensions, consistencies, and color. So, it is very hard to determine an overall pattern for histopathology image segmentation. Previously image segmentation algorithms are mainly based on texture features and their extraction, and Tashk et al. (2014) studied only about extracting these texture features. Belsare et al. (2016) suggested a segmentation method based on hyper-pixel generation. This technique was based on similarity, to develop the space-texture-color map combined with the text illustration of breast histopathology images. Xu et al. (2015) recommended a procedure based on sparse non-negative matrix factorization (SNMF) for reducing color variations in the breast images. But all these segmentation techniques lack the generality. That means all these designs are focused for peculiar types of cancer. They can't be generalizing.

With the progression of interdisciplinary fields like image processing and computer vision, a framework for cancer detection can be built by using various algorithms in machine learning. The metastatic and other harmful areas are consequently pinpoint by these systems. The oncologists are then empowered by this quantitative portrayal of the breast cancer to evaluate the prognosis, thereby analyzing customized medication, improved survival rate and enhanced personal satisfaction. Breast cancer detection system starts with segmentation and its segregation from other biological tissues. Cancer detection in metastasis stage from a segmented tissue can be done in both 2D and 3D geometries. The computer vision system has to face the challenge to extract the mathematical properties of the tumor and classify those structures into different stages. This classification task can be easily performing with the help of different classifiers like support vector machine (SVM), deep neural network, k-nn classifier etc. First there will be a concise review on the breast cancer and its various causative components. Next there will be a detailed explanation of different machine learning techniques in the breast cancer detection and last, the paper will be concluded with a detailed proposal of breast cancer detection using artificial intelligence.

STRUCTURE AND DEVELOPMENT OF THE BREAST

Breast of women has very complex structure and it is very difficult to understand the changes occurring inside the breast at each stages of body development. Breast starts to form at prenatal stage itself. Later it begins to change its shape and structure to show a feminine character from adolescence stage (Korde et al., 2010). Figure 2 shows the structure of a normal breast contains lobules, ducts, stroma, rib and other muscles (McGuire, 2016). Breast cancer is called the unwanted cellular growth inside the breast and its structures.

Breast cancer among men is very rare so that it is very difficult to study and realize in men. Less than 1% men affected with breast cancer. Usually women breasts go through many cellular and lobular transitions during adolescence, lactation and postmenopausal periods. But men don't have these changes unless changes due to the hormones viz: oestrogen and androgen (Taber et al., 2010). BRCA1 and BRCA2 are two human tumor destructive genes which are capable of repairing damaged DNA. The mutations in these hormones might cause high risk for breast cancer.

Breast cancer can be caused due to many reasons. The very important one is gene mutations as above said. The changes in BRCA1 and BRCA2 can be genetically inherited like germ line mutations that cause DNA damage. The other reasons are biological variations in the genes (somatic mutations that happen when gene changes because of some by-products reacted together due to some normal biological processes) during the life course of a person. The other reason for breast cancer is due to the external exposures like radiation, some food habits or after effects of some medical treatments.

TYPES OF BREAST CANCER

This section focused on different types of breast cancer such as invasive and non-invasive and even metastatic breast cancer (Figure 3). Cancer can happen anywhere inside breast like lobules, ducts or still in stroma or other tissues. Other than these cancers, Paget's disease which is affecting the nipple is a type of cancer. Then phyllodes lesions, metastatic cancer and molecular subtypes of breast cancer can all become life threatening.

Long Term Effects and Contentious Form of Breast Cancer

It is relentlessly increasing the rate of survival after the diagnosis of breast cancer. Of course, it is great information, however clinicians should likewise perceive this which takes out new objections to the medicinal world (Go, 2013). Breast cancer is a long-lasting disease or a disorder more than a life-threatening condition because of early diagnosis methods and therapeutic treatments. But the doctors should manage and realize the long-term abnormalities of this disease due to the various medical treat-

Figure 2. Anatomy of breast

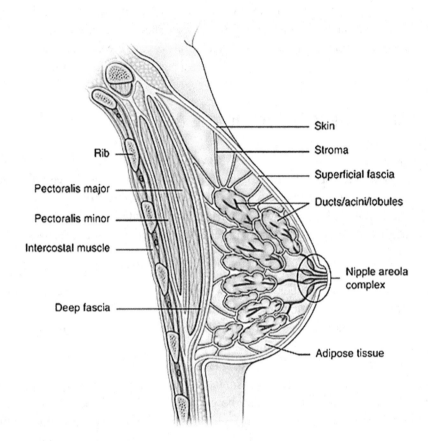

ments (Bodai & Tuso, 2015). Another important concern that demands immediate attention is in the number of teenagers (aged 25 to 38) who are affected with breast cancer is increasing. With the help of modern mammographic screening technologies and self-awareness among patients, it is easy to detect breast cancer at its early stage. But due to the most modern medical treatments, the survival rate became increased but the number of cardio vascular disease among breast cancer survivors also increased. The achievement of survival rate among breast cancer patients may leads to an unexpected increase in the death rate of patients affected with cardio vascular diseases (CVDs).

Last year many women who are breast cancer survivors cease into CVDs without prior to the stage or severity of cancer due to the various chemical treatments and diagnostic methods (Eifel et al., 2001). Recently studies have shown that CVD is a long-term effect of breast cancer (Canto, 2014). CVDs are now days became one of the foremost reasons of mortality amongst women in India. So, international specialists in oncology department undertook a special task involving cardio-oncology specialty treatments for those who are affected with breast cancer and CVDs (Albini et al., 2010). Mostly half of the breast cancer survivors do not know that they are at high risk of CVD.

Figure 3. A hierarchical diagram of various types of breast cancer

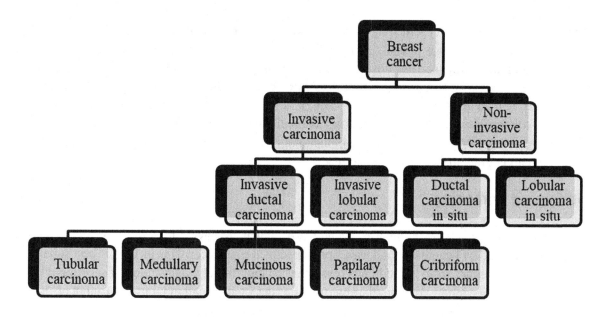

SCREENING METHODS

There are various screening methods for diagnosing breast cancer at its early stage. Screening means looking out a patient for hints of breast cancer before the symptoms start. These screening methods sometimes detect cancers which are very small in size and slowly expanding. These cancers are may be non-dangerous to the person. So, medical experts in this field are working seriously to find out people who are more prone to breast cancer. For that doctors will go through the patient's family history, exposure to radiations or other hormonal treatments during their course of life. According to their history, experts will suggest how often should the patient undergo screening tests and which screening methods are best suitable for the particular patient.

Self-Screening

Self-screening is nothing but a kind of early detection that a woman herself checking breasts for some kind of lumps or tumors or any discomfort. Studies are conducting whether self-examination is important or efficient enough to detect breast cancer early. In 2008, 400,000 women from Russia and China underwent a study on this statement. The study revealed that there is no any significant impact on early detection but women are undergoing unnecessary biopsies assuming they have breast cancer. So American Cancer Society and some other organizations not recommending self-screening instead they are advising mammography.

Digital Mammography

Mammography is the primary screening method for women that help to detect breast cancer. This method uses an X-ray radiation that is passed through the breast and a digital image is captured on a recording plate. Mammography will use a low dose radiation that won't cause any health damages. Mammography can detect small lumps that a patient cannot detect by herself but it is not effective for all age groups. For younger women and pre-menopausal women, it is less effective that their breasts are very dense. Moreover, younger breast tissues are white color in mammogram and cancer lumps are also sees as white in mammogram. So, it is difficult to read their mammogram. As age increases, breast became fattier and darker in mammogram makes them easy to read.

Ultrasound Screening

Ultrasound screening or sonography uses sound waves which are having high frequency to capture an image. This method will capture sound waves produced by a transducer. This method is best suitable to differentiate solid lumps from liquid lumps (cysts that contain liquid which are non-cancerous). Ultrasound imaging can be used to find out the abnormalities detected in mammograms. It cannot be used as a screening method by itself but can be incorporated with mammography.

Magnetic Resonance Imaging (MRI)

MRI is not a regular screening method that everyone can undergo without proper suggestion. MRI uses strong magnetic field and radio frequency waves in which a computer will capture and processes to create the image of breast tissues. MRI has a disadvantage of increased rate of false positives. Invasive breast cancers are very malignant cancers and MRI is recommending for those who are at high risk of invasive breast cancer.

Positron Emission Tomography (PET)

Positron Emission Tomography is normally used to know the normal functioning of various organs and tissues. PET scans are using a nuclear material that injects into the patient's body or a part of body. PET scans are used to detect the prognosis and metastases of breast cancer rather than detecting a mass or lump. Doctors can understand the uptake of the nuclear material as it travels through the breast tissue. These scans show the malignant lumps as "hot spots" with high density.

Thermographic Screening

Thermography is not widely acceptable for screening breast cancer due to its inefficiency in clarity of images. This screening does not contain any type involvement of radiation. So, it is purely a non-invasive type screening. Thermal imaging involves the use of a temperature sensor to determine the temperature on breast skin. Due to the abnormal multiplication of cancer cells inside breast, the blood flow and energy increases. This will cause the temperature at that particular place to increase. This temperature is detecting by the sensor. Over decades, thermography is existing. But there is no enough proof to make thermography as a better screening tool to detect breast cancer early.

OVERVIEW OF BIOPSY

The origin of the word 'Biopsy' is from Greek words: "Bios" which means "life" and "opsis" means "a view". So, Biopsy is simply "to sight a living subject". Biopsy is the last word for cancer. After all these screening methods, if something found abnormal then the doctors will suggest a biopsy. Biopsy is a clinical process that requires very keen observation and strong experience in which a tissue is taken outside from the breast and examines under a microscope for further investigation. This procedure generally carried out by pathologists. The microscopic images are called as histopathology images and the procedure is called histopathology analysis. Authors in this study mainly focused on microscopic images (histopathology images).

To visualize different tissue structures and organelles in the microscopic slides, a process called staining has to be done. Most widely acceptable staining method is Hematoxylin and eosin (H&E). Hematoxylin stain is responsible for blue shade color for nuclear structures and eosin stain is responsible for purple or pink shade to other cytoplasmic structures. For example: two H&E stained images are given below which are taken from UCSB dataset (Aswathy & Jagannath, 2017).

Figure 4. Hematoxylin and eosin (H & E) stained histopathology image specimen showing malignant characteristics

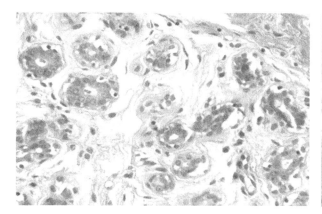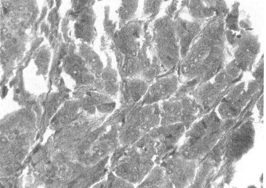

Advantages

It is impossible to view the structures inside one living subject but biopsy makes it possible by offering a section of tissue for examining. Biopsy is frequently related to cancer but in some occasions, biopsy can be used to find out other diseases and their prognosis. Biopsy can be beneficial in the following cases:

- **Cancer:** If a patient found some abnormality or lumps or lesions during screening programs, biopsy can help to figure out whether that lump is malignant or benign.
- **Gastric Ulcer:** Non-steroidal anti-inflammatory drugs (NSAIDs) are one of the root causes for ulceration in stomach. Doctors very often use bowel biopsy to diagnose stomach ulcer. Main symptoms are celiac diseases, severe abdominal pain and gastric problems.

- **Liver Cirrhosis:** Biopsy is helpful in detecting liver cancer, liver cirrhosis and fibroid in the liver. Biopsy is usually conducting when the liver is fully damaged because of alcohol consumption. In the case of hepatitis, biopsy is useful to know the response of patients against various treatments.
- **Bacterial Infection:** Biopsy also helps to locate various infections in the body and the corresponding bacteria causing it.

Rarely biopsy is conducting on transplanted organs to confirm the body is going well with the organ and there is no tendency for rejection.

HISTOPATHOLOGY IMAGE ANALYSIS

The progress of compatible and precise machine-supported systematic approaches to medical imaging allows more computational power and enhanced image evaluation. As digital scanners became more prominent the histological slides can be transformed into digital image easily. Due to this, the machine learning and computerized techniques handles digital histopathology images widely. It is well known the role of CAD algorithms in assisting radiologists. Similar way for recent years CAD algorithms is also useful in assisting pathologists for detecting tumors, lesions etc. Figure 5 depicts the workflow of histopathology image analysis that consists of several steps such as pre-processing, segmentation, feature extraction and classification.

Figure 5. Workflow of histopathology image analysis

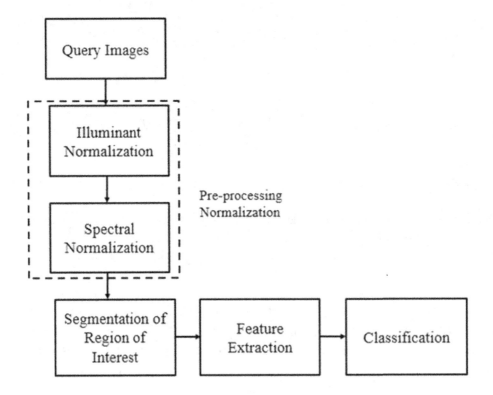

Pre-Processing Normalization

Spectral and illumination normalization is one of the biggest steps in histopathology image analysis. The normalization procedure helps in mitigating the variations in tissue specimen due to the stain and camera conditions. Illumination normalization is for correcting light variations caused due to camera fluctuations. This can be possible by calculating illumination patterns and try to match it with a reference image or by using calibration methods. Otherwise histogram matching is also a normalization method. Sometimes while staining a microscopic slide, some parts of the slide may get stained more so that the cells in that place may get clogged together makes it difficult to visualize. Most of the bright field companies now supplying a package that normalizes both light and stain variations with the help of software called one space software. Many algorithms are fully dependent on color space models. Hence, this will be helpful for such algorithms. Yang and Foran (2005) presented a LUV color space model for segmentation of histopathology images having color variations. Li et al. (2015) introduced a complete normalization technique that reduces the effect of both light and stain variations. They have used Non-Matrix factorization (NMF) and Statistical weighted histogram algorithms for the complete color normalization scheme. Some of the normalization techniques are given below:

Based on Histogram Match

The basic set of color normalization algorithms are focused on Red Green Blue (RGB) color space histogram matching. But histogram matching has one problem in which it fully avoids the regional differences of image pixel variation and local color variations. Histogram matching is very poor in preserving histological data of the image so that it leads to redundant noises for further image analysis.

Color Cue Transfer

Instead of Red, Green and Blue channels, $l\alpha\beta$ color space is there. The statistical properties like mean and variance of the query image are determined and match those with the properties of a reference image. Histopathological images are stained using more than one dye. So, after color cue transfer, the histological components of these images may get slightly changed. This difficulty can be addressed by dividing the whole image into different sections and each section having same histological details.

Spectral Matching

Initially the stain spectra of the image have been calculated by using adaptive methods or with the help of hardware. Then match those calculated spectra with that of a reference spectrum. Spectral matching has the benefit of preserving histological information. But this is possible only if color variation is due to stain variations only. If the color varied because of other reasons, the image's histological features may change after the normalization procedure.

Segmentation of the Region of Interest

Method Based on Markov Random Field (MRF)

In this method, the boundary abstraction on a saliency map conducted initially with the help of Loopy Back Propagation (LBP) algorithm on MRF. This detection method accomplished by using tensor voting. This framework can be used for both histopathology images and frames of images. LBP algorithm is usually used to find out an approximate solution for Markov random field. A saliency map is very essential to know the pixel's unique characteristics. Tensor voting is a kind of parallel marching which helps to find out features nicely. In a site, one input will communicate the message, a tensor, with its neighborhood node and assigns a vote. Hence, the site will collect all those tensor votes and evaluate and assign new tensor vote.

Watershed Segmentation With Connected Component Labeling (CCL)

Connected-component labeling is a subset of graph theory. CCL is also called as blob labeling. The sub disciplines of connected components are uniquely assigned based on a given empirical data. Connected-component labeling is usually performed with other segmentation algorithms. Watershed segmentation algorithm works well if background and foreground regions can separately mark.

Texture Segmentation

Guzmán et al. (2013) used a segmentation algorithm based on texture thresholding for the early detection of breast cancer. This algorithm was tested on several datasets of mammogram images for discriminating calcifications and small masses from background areas using morphological operations. This segmentation method is based on intensity features extracted from various machine learning algorithms.

Segmentation Algorithm Based on Feature Pyramid

Qin et al. (2018) suggested a segmentation procedure built on ResNet50-GICN-GPP feature pyramid for histopathological image segmentation. The framework consists of three points: (1) reduces the large training data size by sampling using patch wise technology (2) a multi stage GICN structure consisting different feature levels to resolve the paradox amongst classification and pixel position (3) a multi-scale feature pyramid by using average pooling along with several sizes that enables the combination of appropriate evidence on various sizes and locations. This method is purely an image semantic algorithm on ResNet50-GICN-GPP pyramid. Primarily, the image was resampled by using a patch sampling method thereby reduced the single image sample size. Then increase the training sample size. Next, a convolutional neural network (CNN) was designed on ResNet50 to acquire feature region data, then for assimilating multi-stage features, a GICN structure has been used along with a deconvolutional network. A GPP structure was finally introduced to solve the problem of neglecting minor things by GICN structures. It is also useful for acquiring the multi-scale semantic data. The anticipated feature pyramid accomplishes 63% of average segmentation accuracy on two datasets viz: Camelyon16 and Gastric WSIs Data.

Feature Extraction

Feature extraction is very essential before classification and widely used in machine learning, computer vision and image processing. The features are some informative attributes that are derived from some initial measured data and are helpful in training and testing phases. Feature extraction also helps to increase efficiency in human interpretations. On the other hand, feature extraction can be used for reducing dimensionality. An initial measured data is reduced to a new set of data for manipulation which is fully describing the original data. If the original data contains some redundant information, feature extraction reduces the redundancy and makes easy the processing of data. There is first order, second order and higher order statistic features. First order statistic features are those properties of distinct pixels neglecting the spatial relationship between neighbour pixels whereas second order and higher order statistic features are those properties collecting from two or pixels in a specific location. Some important statistical features that can be extracted are given below:

Mean

Arithmetic mean is simply referred as "mean". It is the average of all values or attributes given in a study. In image processing, mean is the average value of all neighboring pixels in a window of an image. It is calculated by summing up all the values in a sample space and then dividing the total samples by the number of samples in the space. Mathematically mean can be represented as in Equation (1).

$$\overline{X} = \frac{\sum X}{N} \tag{1}$$

where $\overline{X}$ is the mean of the population, $\sum X$ is the summation of all the samples in the population and N is the total number of samples.

Variance

Variance is a property fulfilled by a normal distribution. It is the average of squared deviation of all points in a population. It is a measure showing how far each pixel in an image from its mean. Variance gives knowledge on the pixels spread in an image. The variance represented as (σ^2) is calculated by summing up the squared distances of each sample (X) in the sample space from the mean (μ). Then this value is divided by the total number of samples in the space (N). Mathematically variance can be represented as in Equation (2).

$$\sigma^2 = \frac{\sum X^2}{N} - \mu^2 \tag{2}$$

Skewness

Skewness is a property that tells about symmetry, or the absence of equilibrium. A population or sample space is said to be balanced if the left and right portions of its center pixel is same. The normal distribution has zero skewness, and all balanced data have skewness more or less equal to zero. That means skewness can take values either positive or negative. If it is positive, it shows that the population is skewed right and otherwise it says the population is skewed left. Negative values for the skewness indicate data that are skewed left and positive values for the skewness indicate data that are skewed right. Figure 6 shows the distribution of positive and negative skewed data.

Figure 6. Positive and negative distribution of skewness

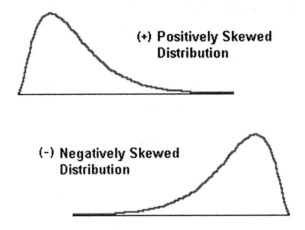

Entropy

Entropy is a measure of randomness. As an example, the entropy of gas is higher than that of a solid because particles are not free to move in a solid whereas particles are freely moving in gas. It is a thermodynamic property that measures the originality of groups with regard to the given group labels. The entropy of a set of groups can be calculated from the class distribution of the images from each group.

Kurtosis

In a frequency distribution curve, kurtosis is a measure of sharpness of the peak. Kurtosis determines the data has a peak or flat pattern compared to a normal distribution. That is, sample points having high kurtosis has sharp peak around the mean.

Contrast

Contrast is defined as the variations in the color cue that creates an image (or its representation in an image display) unique. In the view of human perception, contrast is the difference in the color hue and brightness of the substance and other substances inside the same field.

There are other geometrical features like centroid, area and gradient features like orientation can also be used for feature extraction.

Classification

In our modern life, now computer applications make possible to collect and co-ordinate flood of information at very high speed. But to manipulate all this information smoothly, the need of machine learning and deep learning techniques increased. The field of machine learning focuses on building up various algorithms for determining patterns or yield results from experimental data. Many experts from different professions and industries are implementing adaptive structures using ML to optimize several processes. Moreover, one of the biggest challenges in this category that everyone facing is information classification. Here, authors were concentrated on breast cancer classification. Some classifiers, their advantages and disadvantages, application scenario were discussed below.

Artificial Neural Network (ANN)

An artificial neural network (ANN) is constructed similarly as a human neural system. Human nervous system is responsible for remembering patterns, replicating these patterns and identify correctly next time. Figure 7 shows the typical architecture of ANN. During first phase, an artificial neural network is trained to learn some patterns. This phase is called training phase. Next stage is the testing phase. During testing phase, neural network is tested with some unknown patterns. Hence, a neural network classifier should classify these unknown patterns correctly according to the previous patterns that the neural network is trained for. Different applications are voice detection, pattern recognition, abnormality detection etc.

Figure 7. Architecture of artificial neural network

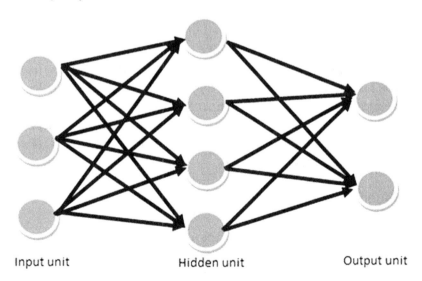

Input unit   Hidden unit   Output unit

Support Vector Machine (SVM)

SVMs are constructed on decision boundaries that are defined by decision planes. That means a decision boundary which separates two classes. Figure 8 shows an example of SVM classifier in which all red balls belongs to one class and other green balls belongs to another class. SVM normally comes under a supervised learning method. It can be used for analyzing both classification and regression problems. But SVMs are known for classification tasks. Like ANNs, SVMs are also trained with datasets which are clearly labelled one or categories. Then SVMs will build a model that categories the new data clearly. It is also called as a non-probabilistic linear binary classifier. Various applications of SVMs are handwriting categorization, image classification, permutation and combination models etc.

Figure 8. Example of SVM classifier

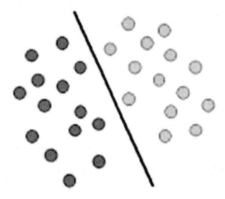

Decision Tree

Decision trees are flow charts modeled in a tree like structure that contain both decision and the corresponding consequences. Usually decision trees are employed for application like decision analysis especially operations research. But in rare cases, they can be used in machine learning applications. Three types of structures are there in a decision tree: Decision nodes that typically represent a test on an instance, a branch node that typically represents the result of a test and a leaf node that typically represents the category after calculating all attributes. The main disadvantage is that decision trees are not suitable for continuous variables.

K-Nearest Neighbour Classifier (K-NN)

K-NN algorithm is another supervised algorithm. The targets are known to us but no previous knowledge about the pattern. The K-NN model classifies the instances according to the Euclidean distance between cluster nodes. That means if an instance wants to be labelled, calculate the k values to the all clusters. Then determine the cluster to which the instance is more belongs to. The main disadvantage is that the algorithm is very time consuming. That is why k-NN classifier is called as "lazy classifier". To solve a multiclassification task, a combination of features and binary classifiers will be useful.

FUTURE RESEARCH DIRECTIONS

Around the planet, 14 million new cancer patients are diagnosed by pathologists every year. That means the uncertainty of life is increasing in millions of people every year. Pathologists are diagnosing cancer with approximately 98% accuracy. They are very good in this concern. But the biggest challenge pathologists are facing in prognosis part. For predicting the progress of disease, pathologists have only about 68% accuracy (Sayed, 2018). So, pathologists have to take next level of pathology. That is machine learning. This nucleus branch of artificial intelligence feed data first, discover patterns, then trains using the input data and finally declares a decision. Then also, the scientists have a doubt that how machine can perform better than experienced pathologists. Initially, the machines can execute things much faster than human being. Even in matter of seconds, machines will finish hundreds to thousands of biopsies whereas one biopsy itself takes 5 to 10 days for pathologists to complete. Next is about accuracy. Now days, there are a lot of data out in this world. It is very difficult to manipulate all those data by a human. But a machine can do that with the help of Internet of Things (IoT) technology. Similarly, a machine can do large number of iterations without getting tired whereas humans see this a s a tiresome task. So, future of cancer prediction is machine learning.

CONCLUSION

This chapter is fully based on machine learning, breast cancer detection and prognosis. Authors started the chapter with breast cancer statistics and motivations followed by a literature review. For better understanding on breast cancer, authors discussed the structure of breast, different types of cancer and various screening methods. The chapter only deals with histopathology images. Therefore, an overview of biopsy was explained along with histopathology image analysis using various machine learning techniques. If things are going like this, ML will replace the pathologists tomorrow. Still machine learning has way more to go in the sense that models lack enough data and absence of good bias. But machine learning is the next altitude to reach by pathology and it would provide a new dimension to the field of investigating the breast cancer.

REFERENCES

Al-Kofahi, Y., Lassoued, W., Lee, W., & Roysam, B. (2010). Improved automatic detection and segmentation of cell nuclei in histopathology images. *IEEE Transactions on Biomedical Engineering*, *57*(4), 841–852. doi:10.1109/TBME.2009.2035102 PMID:19884070

Albini, A., Pennesi, G., Donatelli, F., Cammarota, R., De Flora, S., & Noonan, D. M. (2010). Cardiotoxicity of anticancer drugs: The need for cardio-oncology and cardio-oncological prevention. *Journal of the National Cancer Institute*, *102*(1), 14–25. doi:10.1093/jnci/djp440 PMID:20007921

Alhadidi, B., Zubi, M. H., & Suleiman, H. N. (2007). Mammogram breast cancer image detection using image processing functions. *Information Technology Journal*, *6*(2), 217–221. doi:10.3923/itj.2007.217.221

Aswathy, M. A., & Jagannath, M. (2017). Detection of breast cancer on digital histopathology images: Present status and future possibilities. *Informatics in Medicine Unlocked*, *8*, 74–79. doi:10.1016/j.imu.2016.11.001

Belsare, A. D., Mushrif, M. M., Pangarkar, M. A., & Meshram, N. (2016). Breast histopathology image segmentation using spatio-colour-texture based graph partition method. *Journal of Microscopy*, *262*(3), 260–273. doi:10.1111/jmi.12361 PMID:26708167

Bengio, Y., Courville, A., & Vincent, P. (2013). Representation learning: A review and new perspectives. *IEEE Transactions on Pattern Analysis and Machine Intelligence*, *35*(8), 1798–1828. doi:10.1109/TPAMI.2013.50 PMID:23787338

Bodai, B. I., & Tuso, P. (2015). Breast cancer survivorship: A comprehensive review of long-term medical issues and lifestyle recommendations. *The Permanente Journal*, *19*(2), 48–79. doi:10.7812/TPP/14-241 PMID:25902343

Canto, J. G., & Kiefe, C. I. (2014). Age-specific analysis of breast cancer versus heart disease mortality in women. *The American Journal of Cardiology*, *113*(2), 410–411. doi:10.1016/j.amjcard.2013.08.055 PMID:24210676

Cruz-Roa, A., Gilmore, H., Basavanhally, A., Feldman, M., Ganesan, S., Shih, N. N. C., ... Madabhushi, A. (2017). Accurate and reproducible invasive breast cancer detection in whole-slide images: A Deep Learning approach for quantifying tumor extent. *Scientific Reports*, *7*(1), 46450. doi:10.1038rep46450 PMID:28418027

Eifel, P., Axelson, J. A., & Costa, J. (2001). National institutes of health consensus development conference statement: Adjuvant therapy for breast cancer. *Journal of the National Cancer Institute*, *93*(13), 979–989. doi:10.1093/jnci/93.13.979 PMID:11438563

Elter, M., & Held, C. (2008). Semi-automatic segmentation for the computer aided diagnosis of clustered microcalcifications. Proceedings of. SPIE 2008, 6915, 691524-691524.

Estapé T. (2018). Cancer in the elderly: Challenges and barriers. *Asia-Pacific Journal of Oncology Nursing*, *5*(1), 40-42.

Go, A. S., Mozaffarian, D., & Roger, V. L. (2013). Heart disease and stroke statistics -- 2013 update: A report from the American Heart Association. *Circulation*, *127*, e6–e245. PMID:23239837

Guzmán-Cabrera, R., Guzmán-Sepúlveda, J. R., Torres-Cisneros, M. D., May-Arrioja, D. A., Ruiz-Pinales, J., Ibarra-Manzano, O. G., ... Parada, A. G. (2013). Digital image processing technique for breast cancer detection. *International Journal of Thermophysics*, *34*(8-9), 1519–1531. doi:10.100710765-012-1328-4

Lynch, B. (2017). *what-motivates-our-researchers*. Retrieved from https://nbcf.org.au/news/research-blog/what-motivates-our-researchers/

Malvia, S., Bagadi, S. A., Dubey, U. S., & Saxena, S. (2017). Epidemiology of breast cancer in Indian women. *Asia Pacific Journal of Clinical Oncology*, *13*(4), 289–295. doi:10.1111/ajco.12661 PMID:28181405

Massat, M. B. (2018). A Promising future for AI in breast cancer screening. *Applied Radiology*, *47*(9), 22–25.

McGuire, K. P. (2016). Breast Anatomy and Physiology. In *Breast Disease*. Cham: Springer. doi:10.1007/978-3-319-22843-3_1

Nedzved, A., Ablameyko, S., & Pitas, I. (2006). Morphological segmentation of histology cell images. *Proceedings of IEEE International Special Topic Conference on Information Technology in Biomedicine*, 1, 500–503.

Qin, P., Chen, J., & Zeng, J. (2018). Large-scale tissue histopathology image segmentation based on feature pyramid. *EURASIP Journal on Image and Video Processing*, *75*, 1–9.

Sayed, S. (2018). *Machine learning is the future of cancer prediction*. Retrieved from https://towardsdatascience.com/machine-learning-is-the-future-of-cancer-prediction-e4d28e7e6dfa

Sharma, C. S. (2001). *India still has a low breast cancer survival rate of 66%: study*. Retrieved from https://www.livemint.com/Science/UaNco9nvoxQtxjneDS4LoO/India-still-has-a-low-breast-cancer-survival-rate-of-66-st.html

Sheshadri, H. S., & Kandaswany, A. (2006). Computer aided decision system for early detection of breast cancer. *The Indian Journal of Medical Research*, *124*(2), 149–154. PMID:17015928

Taber, J. K. A., Morisy, L. R., & Osbahr, A. J. III. (2010). Male breast cancer: Risk factors, diagnosis, and management. *Oncology Reports*, *24*(5), 1115–1120. PMID:20878100

Tashk, A., Helfroush, M. S., & Danyali, H. (2014). A novel CAD system for mitosis detection using histopathology slide images. *Journal of Medical Signals and Sensors*, *4*(2), 139–149. PMID:24761378

Xu, J., Xiang, L., Wang, G., Ganesan, S., Feldman, M., Shih, N. N. C., ... Madabhushi, A. (2015). Sparse non-negative matrix factorization (SNMF) based color unmixing for breast histopathological image analysis. *Computerized Medical Imaging and Graphics*, *46*, 20–29. doi:10.1016/j.compmedimag.2015.04.002 PMID:25958195

Yang, L., Meer, P., & Foran, D. (2005). Unsupervised segmentation based on robust estimation and color active contour models. *IEEE Transactions on Information Technology in Biomedicine*, *9*(3), 475–486. doi:10.1109/TITB.2005.847515 PMID:16167702

KEY TERMS AND DEFINITIONS

Artificial Intelligence: The intelligence revealed by computers or machines like humans show intelligence.

Biopsy: The analytical procedure through which a tissue is taken from the breast using a needle for the microscopic examination.

Breast Cancer: The abnormal and uncontrolled growth of cells inside the breast tissue.

Computer-Assisted Diagnosis: The diagnosis of a disease with the help of various computer-aided algorithms.

Haemotoxylin and Eosin (H&E): Two stains that are used for staining the biopsy specimen for clarity of tissues and other structures.

Histopathology: The analysis of a biopsy specimen under the microscope for the study of internal tissue and structures.

Normalization: The procedure used to mitigate the problems caused by the light and stain variations in a breast tissue for clear visualization.

This research was previously published in the Handbook of Research on Applications and Implementations of Machine Learning Techniques; pages 1-20, copyright year 2020 by Engineering Science Reference (an imprint of IGI Global).

Chapter 73

Early Stage Diagnosis of Eye Herpes (NAGIN) by Machine Learning and Image Processing Technique:
Detection and Recognition of Eye Herpes (NAGIN) by Using CAD System Analysis

Kakasaheb Rangnarh Nikam

HPT Arts & RYK Science College Nashik MH India, Nashik, India

ABSTRACT

Eyes are very important parts of the body. Automatic eye detection is must to diagnose various eye disease including Herpes (Nagin) in early stages. Type 1 Herpes Simplex Virus (HSV) may damaging the eye and causing permanent eyesight problems. Herpes keratitis, commonly known as eye herpes, is an inflammation of the cornea, the clear dome that covers the front part of the eye. The proposed method potentially reduce workload on eye doctors and increase the efficiency of limited healthcare resources.

INTRODUCTION

Whenever we visit Ophthalmologist (eye doctor) he/she examine our eyes with a magnifier. He may put stain on the front of our eye. It shows any irregular areas on the transparent front part of the eye (Figure 1). Due to Herpes (Nagin) Simplex infection, shows small scratch on the cornea. There is ulcer develop which called as dendritic ulcer. Dendritic means Branching.

As shown in Figure 2, ulcer is not round with a smooth edge, but like a tree with many finger-like branches. We must urgently referred to an ophthalmologist (eye specialist). They immediately start appropriate treatment.

DOI: 10.4018/978-1-6684-6291-1.ch073

Figure 1. Eye from the front

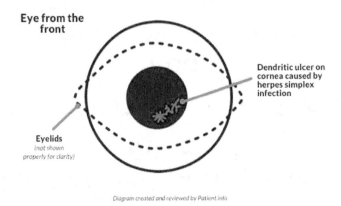

Figure 2. Levels of herpes simplex infections

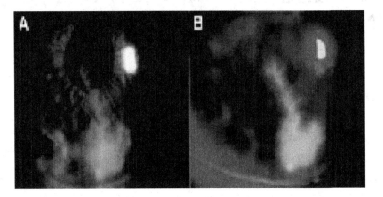

The eye is one of the most important sensory organs in the human body. Eye disease is a common health issues around the world.

If ophthalmic data is properly collected and analysis is done, it provides a way to detect Herpes (Nagin) in early stages.

Research shows "the findings in the left eye are generally likely to be more similar to those in the right eye of the same individual".

Type 1 Herpes Simplex Virus (HSV-1), eye herpes (ocular herpes) is a common, recurrent viral infection affecting the eyes. This type of herpes virus can cause inflammation and scarring of the cornea that sometimes is referred to as a cold sore on the eye.

Herpes (Nagin) "is a virus that causes cold sores, that also causes eye infections. This virus lives inside the nerves in your face and can travel down the nerves to your eye." It may damage your eye and causing permanent eyesight problems.

The purpose of paper is to study the ways available to detect Herpes (Nagin) in early stages by applying image processing techniques.

The Herpes Simplex Virus enters the body through the nose or mouth and travels into the nerves, where it may be inactive. The virus can remain dormant for years and may never wake up.

The exact cause of an outbreak is unknown, but stress-related factors such as fever, sunburn, major dental or surgical procedures and trauma are often associated with incidents.

The cornea (front part of the eye) is infected first is called as Keratitis. i.e. infection of Cornea.

When infection is in superficial layer(top) of cornea, is called epithelial keratitis.

But if dipper layer of cornea is involved, it is called stromal keratitis.

Impact After Nagin (Herpes)

Vision is good enough to drive in about 9 in 10 eyes. However severe and recurrent infections may lead to impairment vision and even severe sight impairment in some cases. Then only option is corneal transplant to restore vision.

Type 1 Herpes Simplex Virus "is a virus that causes cold sores, that also causes eye infections. This virus lives inside the nerves in our face and can travel down the nerves to our eye." Image processing is having significance for disease detection on infected eyes. With help of image processing and machine learning techniques, it is possible to automate and/or assist Ophthalmologist in diagnosis. Patients eye vision is saved if the Herpes is identified at an early stage. The regular practice consists of the acquisition and study of colour images of the eye, currently acquired non-invasively by an Ophthalmologist. With the large number of patients performing eye examinations in an ordinary way, this added work represents a time-consuming task for the Ophthalmologist, who must analyze and diagnose each one of them (Rojas et al., 2017). Figure 3 shows the virus in the eye.

Herpes simplex keratitis is an infection of the cornea caused by the herpes simplex virus (HSV). Herpes keratitis, commonly known as eye herpes, is an inflammation of the cornea, the clear dome that covers the front part of the eye. Symptoms and signs of a reactivation include eye pain, blurred vision, tearing, redness, and sensitivity to bright light. Rarely, the infection worsens and the cornea swells, making vision even more hazy.

Figure 3. Herpes virus in eye

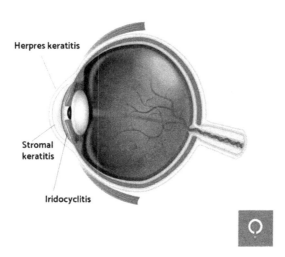

Eye Herpes Symptoms and Signs

Various signs and symptoms are associated with an ocular herpes outbreak. You may experience inflammation of the cornea, which can cause an irritation or sudden and severe ocular pain. Also, the cornea can become cloudy, leading to blurry vision.

Other characteristics of eye herpes include:

- Swelling around the eyes
- Tearing
- Recurrent eye infections
- Irritation
- Foreign body sensation
- Eye redness
- Eye sores
- Watery eye discharge

Which people are infected by (Nagin)eye herpes (Figure 4)?

- Generally, it affects about 2 to 3 people in 1000;
- People those suffered from cold sores;
- Adults of age between 30 to 40 years.

Figure 4. Eye herpes

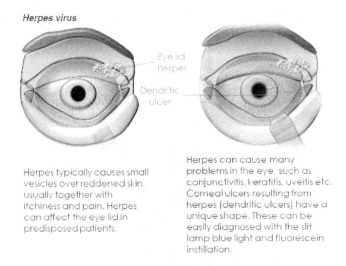

Herpes virus

Eye lid herpes

Dendritic ulcer

Herpes typically causes small vesicles over reddened skin, usually together with itchiness and pain. Herpes can affect the eye lid in predisposed patients.

Herpes can cause many problems in the eye, such as conjunctivitis, keratitis, uveitis etc. Corneal ulcers resulting from herpes (dendritic ulcers) have a unique shape. These can be easily diagnosed with the slit lamp blue light and fluorescein instillation.

LITERATURE REVIEW

Lot of studies is reported in literature for detection of eye diseases using image processing techniques. Some of the work is as follows.

Information about herpes on eye is collected from "Eye Infection Herpes Simplex", Author by Dr. Oliver Starr 23 Nov 2017.

In Year 2012, ManjulaSri Rayudu proposed," Review of Image Processing Techniques for Automatic Detection of Eye Diseases". It provides information about the application of image processing techniques for automatic detection of eye diseases. The key image processing techniques to detect eye diseases include image registration, fusion, segmentation, feature extraction, enhancement, pattern matching, image classification, analysis and statistical measurements (Yadollahi, n.d.).

Mohammadreza Yadollahi published paper on "Image segmentation for object detection" in this paper there is brief introduction of segmentation method. It is used in many scientific fields including medical imaging, object and face recognition, engineering and technology (Chitradevi & Srimathi, n.d.).

"An Overview on Image Processing Techniques", B.Chitradevi, P.Srimathi gives brief information about various methods of image processing (n.d.). Automated localization of retinal optic disk using Hough transform- The retinal fundus image is widely used in the diagnosis and treatment of various eye diseases such as diabetic retinopathy and glaucoma. The proposed methodology consists of two steps: in the first step, Region of Interest (ROI) is found by image by means of morphological processing, and in the second step, optic disk is detected using the Hough transform. We continue to work on the subject for further improvements:

- The purpose work implements a system for the improved detection of Herpes (Nagin) on eye using various image processing steps;
- This work can be useful in ophthalmology for improved detection of herpes on eye.

This Computer Aided Diagnosis (CAD) System is used as distinguished key in herpes on eye diagnosis, help for Ophthalmologist trainings and improving actual treatment.

RESEARCH OBJECTIVE

- This work can be useful in ophthalmology for improved detection of herpes on eye;
- This Computer Aided Diagnosis (CAD) System is used as distinguished key in herpes on eye diagnosis, help for Ophthalmologist trainings and improving actual treatment.

METHODOLOGY

Following block diagram shows image processing steps in proposed system Figure 7 Architecture of Herpes detection and recognition.

Procuring the Input Image

In this step, diseased images of eyes are captured to create the required database. This database has different types of eye diseases. It stored images in jpeg format. These images are then read in MATLAB using read command.

Images are typically generated by illuminating an image and absorbing the energy reflected by the objects in that scene.

Pre-Processing the Image

The colors that humans and most animals perceive in an object are determined by the nature of the light reflected from the object.

Received image should be pre -processed by performing following steps.

RGB to Grayscale

In RGB each pixel is made up of three components i.e. Red, Green and Blue. So more time and space is required for RGB. Therefore, RGB is converted to Grayscale image.

Resizing of Image

Images are resized according to the need. For resizing of images Nearest Neighbour Interpolation is used.

Color Images

- **RGB representation:** Each pixel is usually represented by a 24-bit number containing the amount of its Red (R), Green (G), and Blue (B) components;
- **Indexed representation:** A 2D array contains indices to a color palette (or look-up table, LUT).

Two Basic Components

- **Mapping Function:** Specified using a set of spatial transformation equations (and a procedure to solve them); and
- **Interpolation Methods:** Used to compute the new value of each pixel in the spatially transformed image.

Image Filtration and Enhancement

This is the process of cleaning up of an image i.e., removal of noises and highlighting some information. Median filters are used. Image enhancement includes varying brightness and contrast of image. It also includes filtering and histogram equalization. It comes under pre- processing step to enhance various features of image. i.e. Removing noise of an image. Enhancing the brightness of an image.

Image Registration

Image Registration is an important technique for change detection in retinal image diagnosis. In this process, two images are aligned onto a common coordinate system. Images may be taken at different times and with imaging devices. In medical diagnosis, it is essential to combine data from different images and for better analysis and measurements images are aligned geometrically. i.e. The image of the diseased eye is taken at different intervals of time to monitor the disease.

The sources of noise in digital images arise during image acquisition (digitization) and transmission:

- Imaging sensors can be affected by ambient conditions Interference can be added to an image during transmission;
- Spatial domain techniques are particularly useful for removing random noise;
- Frequency domain techniques are particularly useful for removing periodic noise.

Image Segmentation

According to the region of interest, the image is be divided into different parts. By this segmentation representation of the image becomes easier to analyse. FCM clustering technique is used, which is very fast and flexible than others. Image segmentation is the procedure of dividing a digital image into several regions or set of pixels. This splitting can be done by various image segmentation techniques. To be useful, these techniques must typically be combined with a domain's specific knowledge in order to effectively solve the domain's segmentation problems. i.e. Thresholding, Clustering etc.

Thresholding is usually the first step in any segmentation approach.

Feature Extraction

In feature extraction method, various attributes of the segmented image are extracted. Features like Color, Shape, and Texture are extracted using Colour Correlogram, Spatial Gray Dependency Matrix [SGDM]. Color Correlogram is used to extract color feature.

Correlogram is an image of correlation statistics.

SGDM is used to extract texture feature like Contrast, and correlation are computed for the huge content of the image.

Classification of Diseases

Classification technique is used for training and testing, to detect the type of Eye Herpes. Classification deals with associating a given input with one of the distinct class. In the given system support vector machine [SVM] is used for classification of eye disease.

The classification process is useful for early detection of Eye Herpes.

Machine Learning (ML) is constructing computer programs that develop solutions and improve with experience.

Solves problems which cannot be solved by enumerative methods or calculus-based techniques.

Machine Learning is an interdisciplinary field involving programs that improve by experience.

ML is good for problems in image processing.

The choice of the machine learning algorithm depends on the needs of the user. If the rules have to be understandable, one of the symbolic learning approaches would be preferable. If highest accuracy is more important, the Neural Network should be used.

KNN: K-Nearest Neighbor is a kind of instance-based learning, where the function is only locally approximated, and all computation is referred until classification. This technique is called lazy learning because, it does not need any training or minimal training phase. All the training data is needed only during the testing phase and this technique uses all the training data so that if we have a large data set then we need special method to work on part of data which is the algorithmic approach. Although classification is the primary application of KNN, we can also use it for density estimation also. The k-nearest neighbor algorithm is one of the simplest algorithms of all machine learning algorithms. KNN classification was formulated from the requirement to perform several analysis when reliable parametric estimates of probability densities are not known or difficult to determine.

HMM (Hidden Markov Model)

An embedded HMM - based approach for face recognition and detection uses an effective set of observation vectors gained from the 2D-DCT coefficients. The embedded HMM can sculpture the two-dimensional data finer than the one-dimensional HMM and is computationally less difficult than the two-dimensional HMM. This model is well suited for face images since it exploits important facial characteristics, structure of "states" inside each of these "super states."

Support Vector Machine (SVM) have recently become popular for classification tasks and outperform many other classifiers. Thus, it would be interesting to take Support Vector Machine into account in future comparisons.

SVM (Support Vector Machine)

In ML (Machine Learning) support vector machines (SVMs also referred as Support Vector Networks) are supervised learning models with correlated learning algorithms that learns data and determines patterns, used for regression and classification analysis (Mangai et al., n.d.). Given a set of training examples, each marked as referring to one category for one of two categories, an SVM training algorithm creates a model that divides new examples into one category or the other devising it a non-probabilistic binary linear classifier. An SVM model is a representation of the example as points in space assigned so that examples of the different categories are divided (Parul & Sharma, n.d.). In addition to performing linear classification, SVMs can expeditiously perform a nonlinear classification using the trick called the kernel trick, implicitly mapping into high dimensional feature spaces. Figure 5 Infected eye by Simplex Eye Herpes Virus.

In the proposed system, normal and herpes fundus images are input to the CAD System to extract the features. After this the classifier is applied on these extracted features to finally get the output through which the Eye Herpes is detected.

Proposed flow process of Herpes detection process shown in following figure. 6 flow of Herpes detection process.

As we understand the concepts of:

- **Image Enhancement:** Image enhancement includes varying brightness and contrast of image. It also includes filtering and histogram equalization. It comes under pre- processing step to enhance various features of image;

- **Image Registration:** Image Registration is an important technique for change detection in retinal image diagnosis. In this process, two images are aligned onto a common coordinate system. Images may be taken at different times and with imaging devices. In medical diagnosis, it is essential to combine data from different images and for better analysis and measurements images are aligned geometrically;

- **Image Fusion:** Image fusion is a process of combining information acquired from number of imaging devices. Its goal is to integrate contemporary, multi sensor, multi- temporal or multi-view information into a single image, containing all the information so as to reduce the amount of information;

- **Feature Extraction:** It is the process of identifying and extracting region of interest from the image;

- **Image Segmentation:** Segmentation is the process of dividing an image into its constituent object and group of pixels which are homogenous according to some criteria. Segmentation algorithms are area-oriented instead of pixel oriented. The main objective of image segmentation is to extract various features of image which can be merged or split;

- **Morphology:** Morphology is the science of appearance, shape and organization. Mathematical morphology is a collection of non-linear processes which can be applied to an image to remove details smaller than a certain reference shape. Various morphological operation are erosion, dilation, opening and closing. The purpose of morphological processing is primarily to remove imperfections added during segmentation;

- The basic operations are erosion and dilation;

- Using the basic operations we can perform opening and closing.

Figure 5. Infected eye by simplex eye herpes virus

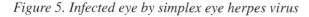
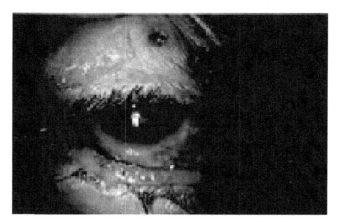

Summarised as, various image processing techniques used for the diagnosis and analysis of eye herpes are:

1. **Image Enhancement:** Removing noise of an image. Enhancing the brightness of an image;

2. **Registration:** The image of the diseased eye is taken at different intervals of time to monitor the disease;

3. **Image Fusion:** The input for image fusion is different images of eye and output is a eye with high quality;

4. **Segmentation:** Thresholding, Clustering etc.;

5. **Feature extraction:** Sobel edge detection, Canny edge detection etc.;

6. **Morphology:** Thickening the vessels of retina, Erosion, Dilation.

Figure 6. Flow chart of herpes detection process

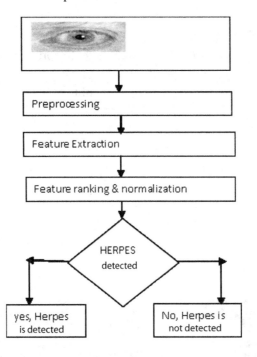

Figure 7. Architecture of herpes detection and recognition

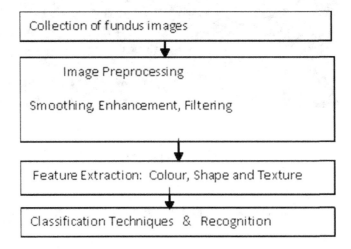

CONCLUSION

Eye Herpes (Nagin) may blind single infected eye. Various methods used by different scientists and constant research happening in this field. Here is an attempt to understand some of the techniques used till now for diagnosis of eyes using image processing and ML.

Our proposed method collects not-infected/infected eye images, performs Image Preprocessing, Image Filtration & Enhancement, Image Segmentation, Color & Feature Extraction, Recognition & Classification using SVM (Support vector Machine), and detect & recognize eye herpes (nagin).

REFERENCES

Balasundari, C.K., Ulagammal, R., Sivapriya, J., Vino Sakthiya, S. & Sathya, M. (2016). Diagnosing Retinal Diseases Using Image Processing Techniques. *International Journal of Innovative research in computer and communication engineering, 4*(4).

Chitradevi, B., & Srimathi, P. (2014). An overview on image processing techniques. *International Journal of Innovative Research in Computer, 2*(11), 6466–6472.

Devi & Murty. (n.d.). Pattern Recognition An Introduction. *Universities Press.*

Dhariwal, S. (2011). Comparative analysis of various image enhancement techniques. *International Journal of Electronics & Communication Technology, 2*(3), 91–95.

Gonzalez, R. C., Woods, R. E., & Eddins, S. L. (2004). *Digital image processing using MATLAB* (Vol. 624). Upper Saddle River, NJ: Pearson-Prentice-Hall.

Mangai, J. A., Wagle, S., & Kumar, V. S. (2013). An improved k nearest neighbor classifier using interestingness measures for medical image mining. *International Journal of Medical Health Biomedical Bioengineering and Pharmaceutical Engineering, 7*(9), 236–240.

Parul & Sharma, N. (2015). A Study on Retinal Disease Classification and Filtration Approaches. *International journal of computer science and mobile computing, 4*(5), 158-165.

Ravudu, M., Jain, V., & Kunda, M. M. R. (2012, December). Review of image processing techniques for automatic detection of eye diseases. In *2012 Sixth International Conference on Sensing Technology (ICST)* (pp. 320-325). IEEE.

Rojas, I., Joya, G., & Catala, A. (2017). *Advances in Computational Intelligence IWANN2017.* Springer.

Sekhar, S., Al-Nuaimy, W., & Nandi, A. K. (2008, May). Automated localisation of retinal optic disk using Hough transform. In *5th IEEE International Symposium on Biomedical Imaging: From Nano to Macro ISBI 2008* (pp. 1577-1580). IEEE.

Shinde, B., Mhaske, D., & Dani, A. R. (2011). Study of Image Processing, Enhancement and Restoration. *International Journal of Computer Science Issues, 8*(6), 262.

Starr, O. (2017, November 23). Eye Infection- Herpes Simplex. *Patient.*

Umesh, M. L., Mrunalini, M. M., & Shinde, S. (2016). Review of Image Processing and Machine Learning Techniques for Eye Disease Detection and Classification.

Wu, C., & Harada, K. (2011). Study on Digitization of TCM Diagnosis Applied Extraction Method of Blood Vessel. *Journal of Signal and Information Processing*, 2(4), 301.

Yadollahi, M., & Procházka, A. (2011). Image Segmentation for Object Detection. In *Proceedings of the 19th International Conference Technical Computing Prague 2011* (Vol. 129).

This research was previously published in the International Journal of Applied Evolutionary Computation (IJAEC), 10(2); pages 27-36, copyright year 2019 by IGI Publishing (an imprint of IGI Global).

Chapter 74
Machine Learning Based Program to Prevent Hospitalizations and Reduce Costs in the Colombian Statutory Health Care System

Alvaro J Riascos

University of los Andes and Quantil, Bogotá, Colombia

Natalia Serna

University of Wisconsin-Madison, Madison, USA

ABSTRACT

Health-care systems that rely on hospitalization for early patient treatment pose a financial concern for governments. In this article, the author suggests a hospitalization prevention program in which the decision of whether to intervene on a patient depends on a simple decision model and the prediction of the patient risk of an annual length-of-stay using machine learning techniques. These results show that the prevention program achieves significant cost savings relative to several base scenarios for program efficacies greater than or equal to 40% and intervention costs per patient of 100,000 to 700,000 Colombian pesos (i.e., approximately 14% to 100% of the average cost per patient in Colombia statuary health care system). This article also shows how tree-based methods outperform linear regressions when predicting an annual length-of-stay and the final model achieves a lower out-of-sample error compared to those of the Heritage Health Prize.

DOI: 10.4018/978-1-6684-6291-1.ch074

INTRODUCTION

Avoidable hospitalizations are a source of increased health expenditures in many health systems. Prolonged length-of-stay is costly for providers, insurers, and patients because it is associated to greater health service consumption and to the development of endangering states during the hospital stay. In the Colombian public health care system, the increase in health costs due to avoidable hospitalizations has raised many questions on whether insurers are implementing prevention programs and on whether such programs are effective. In this context, prediction of patient annual length-of-stay (LOS) is an important tool for resource allocation and improving patient health outcomes. Accordingly, the objectives of this paper are: predicting the annual length-of-stay of users in the public health care system in Colombia and estimating the potential cost savings of a preventive program whose main input is the annual LOS prediction.

Most of the literature on prediction of annual LOS has been developed from the providers' perspective rather than from the insurers' perspective. Many authors predict LOS using a sample of patients with specific acute conditions or physiological traits that are often unobserved by the insurer. For example, Chang et. al (2002) study individuals with cerebrovascular accident, Tu & Guerriere (1993) study patients that are admitted to the intensive care unit after having a cardiac surgery, Chertow, Burdick, Honour, Bonventre, & Bates, (2005) focus on patients with renal failure, and Clague, Craddock, Andrew, Horan, & Pendleton, (2002) analyze patients with hip fracture. Our study differs from the previous ones in the sense that we predict annual LOS using information that is symmetrical between insurers, providers, and the government. We do not focus on users with particular health conditions but analyze a representative sample of individuals in the public health care system with heterogenous demographic and morbidity characteristics. We also lack data regarding specific patient physiological traits and we extend our analysis to measuring the potential cost savings of a prevention program where the intervention is decided upon patient LOS prediction. With regard to the empirical techniques for predicting annual LOS, we use machine learning approaches similar to the ones used by Rezaei, Ahmadi, Alizadeh, & Sadoughi (2013) and Walsh et al. (2004), which include boosted trees, random forests, and artificial neural networks.

The remainder of this paper is structured as follows: after this introduction, section II describes the Colombian public health care system, section III provides the empirical framework, section IV describes our database and the data preprocessing, section V presents the results of machine learning techniques, section VI presents the impact of LOS on health costs, and section VII concludes.

The Colombian Public Health Care System

The Colombian public health care system consists of two regimes: contributory and subsidized. The first covers 44 percent of the population and the second the remaining 56 percent. Each regime has its own network of health insurers and health service providers, which are responsible for providing a predetermined benefits package to all enrollees, known as the "Plan Obligatorio de Salud" (POS). In the contributory regime, enrollees (formal employees and individual contractors) pay for health care services a compulsory monthly tariff proportional to their income, while the subsidized regime is fully funded by the government.

Contributions of enrollees in the contributory regime are collected by a government agency called FOSYGA. This agency redistributes contributions to insurers at the beginning of the year using a risk-adjusted premium per enrollee known as the "Unidad de Pago por Capitación" (UPC). The capitation premium adjusts health risks to demographic variables such as age, gender, and municipality of residence while being income neutral. Each year, all services provided must be reported to the FOSYGA in order to calculate the UPC for the next period. Our empirical analysis is based on this database of services in the contributory regime.

At the same time, insurers and health service providers negotiate bilateral contracts from a fixed menu of contract types defined by the law. Contracts in this menu define the type of payment from the insurer to the provider for attending its population of enrollees, but additional arrangements between the parties are not observed. Forms of payment include capitation and fee-for-service, which distribute risk and incentives in opposite ways between insurers and providers. The insurer bears all financial and health risks when subscribing fee-for-service contracts, while providers bear all risks in capitation contracts.

The increase in the system's health costs and risks during the last decade has made it clear that implementing and evaluating promotion and prevention programs is important to reduce costs and identify sources of cost savings, for instance, avoidable hospitalizations. As suggested in the Asociación Colombiana de Empresas de Medicina Integral [ACEMI] (2013), health care systems that rely on hospitalizations for early patient treatment, such as the Colombian health care system, are more expensive than those that use hospitalizations as a last resource.

During 2011, for every 100,000 enrollees, there were 3,500 hospitalizations in Colombia (ACEMI, 2013). Hospitalizations are more frequent in pediatric units (19,983 for every 100,000 neonatal enrollees and 8,117 for every 100,000 enrollees aged 4 or less) and some diagnosis-related groups such as the acute respiratory infection (32 percent of hospitalizations of children less than 5 years old, during 2009 to 2012, were due to respiratory infections like pneumonia or acute bronchiolitis) and the acute diarrheal disease (9 percent of hospitalizations of children less than 5 years old, during 2009 to 2012, were associated to gastrointestinal diseases) (Ministerio de Salud de Colombia, 2014).

Predicting annual patient length-of-stay is, therefore, an important tool for resource allocation and cost administration in hospitals and health insurers. Identifying the factors that increase the average patient LOS enables hospitals and insurers to engage in early interventions and prevention programs to mitigate the risk of hospitalizations.

LITERATURE AND EMPIRICAL FRAMEWORK

To predict patient LOS and evaluate a prevention program we do two things: we use machine learning techniques to address our first objective and for the second one we model a decision rule based on the predictions of the first stage, which will indicate when should a patient be intervened in order to reduce both the risk and the expected costs of being hospitalized next year. Then we measure the potential cost savings of such prevention program relative to several base scenarios.

Predicting patient LOS has motivated part of the literature of big data and machine learning in health care. Some authors use linear regression methods as in Cleary et al. (1991) and Winslow, Bode, Felton, Chen, & Meyer, (2002) by transforming the outcome variable to a logarithmic scale, ln(LOS+1). However, recent studies like Morton et al. (2014), Tanuja, Acharya, & Shailesh, (2011) and Rezaei et al. (2013) show that support vector machines, random forests and neural networks outperform multitask learning, multiple linear regression, naives bayes and decision trees models when predicting the LOS of patients with particular health conditions. On the contrary, Pendharkar & Khurana (2014) find no significant differences in the performance metrics of support vector machines and regression trees when predicting the LOS of patients in Pennsylvania federal and specialty hospitals. While Turgeman, May, & Sciulli, (2017) find that ensemble methods improve regression trees when predicting the LOS of patients at the moment of admission. In this study the authors estimate the partition criteria of the regression tree by mapping patients to a higher dimensional space using a radial basis function kernel and support vector machines. The reconciling fact about these opposite findings in the literature is that machine learning models are very context-specific when applied to health care, therefore a more general class of models and data is required.

Risk factors that increase the absolute LOS or its likelihood have also been widely documented. Kelly, Sharp, Dwane, Kelleher, & Comber, (2012) study the hospital length-of-stay of patients following a colorectal resection and find that unmarried, older patients with co-morbidities and emergency patients had longer hospital stays compared to private patients or those who are admitted to larger hospitals. Tu, Jaglal, & Naylor, (1995) analyze intensive care unit patient LOS using a risk index that controls for sex, age, surgery characteristics, and indicators of myocardial infractions, diabetes and pulmonary diseases. Patient nutrition is also regarded as a potential risk factor for hospital stay as Stratton, King, Stroud, Jackson, & Elia, (2006) indicate. Focusing on intrinsic hospital characteristics, Forster, Stiell, Wells, Lee, & Van Walraven, (2003) find that emergency department LOS is positively correlated with the hospital's occupancy rate and such correlation is heterogeneous among the percentiles of the occupancy distribution: the higher the percentile the stronger the correlation.

The importance of LOS prediction, besides providing knowledge on risk factors and guidelines on how to address them, also lies in its potential for improving hospital cost management. The relation between LOS and hospital costs seems very straightforward but availability of data has limited the number of studies that quantify it. The literature usually provides evidence of an indirect effect of hospital LOS on costs through the worsening of patients' health status. Cosgrove (2006) mentions that delayed therapy for patients undergoing major surgeries increases the risk of antimicrobial resistance which translates in increased LOS and hospital costs by about 6,000 to 30,000 US dollars. Chertow et al. (2005) also documents that patients with acute kidney injury have higher LOS and therefore an excess of hospital costs of nearly 7,500 dollars. Others report excess costs of approximately 6,000 dollars due to malnutrition and LOS Chima et al. (1997) and increased admission costs due to gastrointestinal bleeding and LOS Saltzman et al. (2011). Our study contributes to this literature in the sense that we quantify the direct monetary impact of a LOS prevention program using a model that in trained on the data of patients with different health conditions being treated under different hospitals and health insurers. Other authors concerned with measuring the impact of hospital protocols on costs include Castellanos et al. (2010) and Bayati et al. (2014). However, they focus on patients with particular health conditions or use data that comes from only one health service provider.

In an attempt to improve LOS prediction and encourage hospital programs targeted at reducing the average hospital stay, an alliance of health health service providers in United States launched during 2013 the Heritage Health Prize, a competition to predict annual days in hospital based on the claims data of the two previous years. The outcome variable for this competition was the log of LOS. Most participant teams showed machine learning techniques outperformed ordinary linear regressions. In particular, ensemble methods proved to be the best models. Milestone winners used, for example, ensembles consisting of linear combinations of boosted trees models, random forests, artificial neural networks and linear regressions, restricting the sum of coefficients to 1 and truncating negative predictions. Models were compared and evaluated using the Root Mean Squared Error (RMSE). The winning team achieved an out-of-sample RMSE of 0.4438 which is, nonetheless, 2.5 times the average log LOS of the third year of data.

To predict patient LOS in year t with claims data of t–1 and t–2, we use a panel of individuals of the contributory regime and all their associated claims from 2009 to 2011 called "Base de Suficiencia". We are interested in a regression task as the one proposed in the Heritage Health Prize and use different machine learning techniques such as: boosted trees (GMB), random forests (RF), artificial neural networks (ANN), linear regressions (OLS), and ensemble techniques (ENS).

For the second objective, we model a decision rule that indicates when do a patient has to be intervened to reduce her risk and expected cost of hospitalization, as follows.

Let $\widehat{y_i}$ be the prediction of $ln(LOS+1)$ for patient i. Since the second objective requires measuring the risk of hospitalization, we transform $\widehat{y_i}$ into a probability by estimating the logit model in Equation (1):

$$p_i = Prob\left[y_i = 1\right] = \frac{\exp\left(\beta_0 + \beta_1 \widehat{y_i}\right)}{1 + \exp\left(\beta_0 + \beta_1 \widehat{y_i}\right)} \tag{1}$$

where:

$$y_i = \begin{cases} 1 & if \quad LOS > 0 \\ 0 & if \quad LOS = 0 \end{cases} \tag{2}$$

and *LOS* is the observed annual length-of-stay.

Now suppose each insurer in the system undergoes a prevention program with an efficacy of α and a cost per patient of f. α can be interpreted as the reduction in the probability of being hospitalized next year and f *is* a fixed cost. Let g *be* a risk pool characterized by a unique combination of gender (male or female), location (urban, normal, rural), age group (0, 1-4, 5-14, 15-18, 19-44, 45-49, 50-54, 55-59, 60-64, 65-69, 70-74, and 75 or older) and long-term disease (for details of these groups see www.alvaroriascos.com\reaseach\healthEconomics). The categories in each variable will be explained in the next section. These combinations make up a total of 2088 risk pools. Let $X_g = \sum_{i \in g} x_i$ be the annual health cost of patients with LOS>0 in risk pool g calculated as the sum of the cost of all claimed services during a year and let $D_g = \sum_{i \in g} d_i$ be the sum of the number of days every patient with LOS>0 in risk pool g has been enrolled to the health system. The annual cost of hospitalizations for patients in risk pool g is:

$$c_g = 360 \times \frac{X_g}{D_g} \tag{3}$$

Table 1. Descriptive statistics of weighted annual hospitalization costs (in Colombian pesos)

Gender	Location	Age Group	Long-Term Disease	Mean Cost
Female	Urban	Age 19-44	Diabetes	1,393,861
Male	Urban	Age 19-44	Diabetes	1,053,756
Female	Urban	Age 19-44	Breast cancer	903,424
Male	Urban	Age 19-44	Hypertension	616,577
Female	Urban	Age 70-74	Lung disease	4,389,092
Male	Urban	Age 70-74	Renal disease	8,983,293

This table shows the mean annual hospitalization cost for certain risk pools weighted by the number of days enrolled. Source: Base de Suficiencia, Ministry of Health and Social Protection. Authors' calculations.

Table 1 shows the mean annual hospitalization cost for some of these risk pools. Annual hospitalization costs increase with age and, overall, are U-shaped. Costs decrease from newborns to people aged 15-18, and then increase monotonically for people aged 19 and more.

Following Bayati et. al (2014) the expected cost of hospitalization for patient i is the product between the probability of being hospitalized and the cost of hospitalization in the risk pool she belongs to:

$$C_0\left(\widehat{p_i}\right) = \widehat{p_i} c_g \tag{4}$$

If insurers undergo the prevention program for this patient, the probability of being hospitalized decreases with the program's efficacy, but hospitalization costs increase linearly with the cost of the intervention per patient. If intervened, expected health costs are:

$$C_1\left(\widehat{p_i}\right) = (1-\alpha)\widehat{p_i} c_g + f \tag{5}$$

Thus, a patient must be intervened if:

$$\pi(\widehat{p_i} \mid \alpha, f) = C_0\left(\widehat{p_i}\right) - C_1\left(\widehat{p_i}\right) \geq 0 \tag{6}$$

or if:

$$\widehat{p_i} \geq \frac{f}{\alpha c_g} \tag{7}$$

To measure the incremental cost-effectiveness of the prevention program, we compare the costs generated by a program where intervention is decided upon the inequality in expression (7) with two base scenarios: the no-intervention policy and the best uniform policy given α and f.

The first base scenario assumes the expected cost per patient is always C_0. If the inequality in (7) does not hold, the program also decides upon not intervening the patient, therefore the incremental cost-effectiveness due to this patient is zero. On the contrary, if the inequality in (7) holds, the patient is intervened, her expected cost is C_1 and the incremental cost-effectiveness relative to the no-intervention policy is C_0–C_1. Equation (8) shows the total incremental cost-effectiveness relative to the first base scenario:

$$
\begin{aligned}
CE^1 &= \sum_{i=1}^{N} \mathbb{1} \left(\widehat{p}_i \geq \frac{f}{\alpha\, c_g} \right) \pi \left(\widehat{p}_i \mid \alpha, f \right) \\
&= \sum_{i=1}^{N} \mathbb{1} \left(\widehat{p}_i \geq \frac{f}{\alpha\, c_g} \right) \left(C_0 \left(\widehat{p}_i \right) - C_1 \left(\widehat{p}_i \right) \right)
\end{aligned}
\tag{8}
$$

In the second case, the best uniform policy is the cheapest policy between no intervention and full intervention. Notice that if the best uniform policy is to intervene and inequality (7) holds for a specific patient, the incremental cost-effectiveness due to this patient is zero. The same happens when the best uniform policy is no-intervention and inequality (7) does not hold. Thus, total incremental cost-effectiveness relative to the second base scenario in the relevant cases is:

$$
CE^2 =
\begin{cases}
\displaystyle\sum_{i=1}^{N} \mathbb{1}\left(\widehat{p}_i \geq \frac{f}{\alpha\, c_g} \right)\left(C_0\left(\widehat{p}_i\right) - C_1\left(\widehat{p}_i\right) \right) & \text{if } \displaystyle\sum_{i=1}^{N} C_0\left(\widehat{p}_i\right) < \sum_{i=1}^{N} C_1\left(\widehat{p}_i\right) \\[3ex]
\displaystyle\sum_{i=1}^{N} \mathbb{1}\left(\widehat{p}_i < \frac{f}{\alpha\, c_g} \right)\left(C_1\left(\widehat{p}_i\right) - C_0\left(\widehat{p}_i\right) \right) & \text{if } \displaystyle\sum_{i=1}^{N} C_0\left(\widehat{p}_i\right) > \sum_{i=1}^{N} C_1\left(\widehat{p}_i\right)
\end{cases}
\tag{9}
$$

where $\sum_{i=1}^{N} C_0\left(\widehat{p}_i\right) < \sum_{i=1}^{N} C_1\left(\widehat{p}_i\right)$ suggests the best uniform policy is no intervention and $\sum_{i=1}^{N} C_0\left(\widehat{p}_i\right) > \sum_{i=1}^{N} C_1\left(\widehat{p}_i\right)$ suggests the best uniform policy is to intervene every patient.

THE DATA

To predict patient LOS and estimate its impact on health costs, we have the yearly claims of a sample of 5.7 million enrollees in the contributory system during 2009 to 2011. The sample was built by the Ministry of Health and Social Protection, focusing on individuals who claim at least one service per year and do not change their insurer company during the time span. For ease of computation, we choose randomly 1 million enrollees and their associated claims.

Information per individual includes: insurer to which she is enrolled, services she demands (claims) identified with a service code (CUPS by its Spanish acronym)[1], provider ID, cost per service, date, diagnosis identified with the International Classification of Diseases (ICD) Codes (10th version), length-of-stay per claim, age, gender, and municipality of residence.

The municipality of residence is categorized as urban, normal, or rural following the definition of payment geographic areas of the National Administrative Department of Statistics (DANE). The first definition integrates metropolitan areas and its adjacent municipalities, the second includes small municipalities around metropolitan areas, and the third includes peripheral municipalities. Age is also categorized in 12 groups according to the Ministry of Health and Social Protection: 0, 1-4, 5-14, 15-18, 19-44, 45-49, 50-54, 55-59, 60-64, 65-69, 70-74, and 75 or older. Finally, ICD 10 codes are categorized in 29 long-term diseases proposed by Alfonso, Riascos, & Romero, (2014).

Table 2. Descriptive statistics in the train and test sets

Variable	Train		Test		diff
	Mean	sd	Mean	sd	
Dependent variable					
LOS t	1.891	8.387	1.894	8.346	0.811
Demographics					
Male	0.445	0.497	0.446	0.497	0.432
Age 0	0.034	0.18	0.034	0.18	0.69
Age 1-4	0.054	0.225	0.054	0.226	0.388
Age 5-14	0.103	0.305	0.104	0.305	0.378
Age 15-18	0.02	0.138	0.02	0.139	0.57
Age 19-44	0.403	0.491	0.402	0.49	0.054
Age 45-49	0.082	0.275	0.082	0.275	0.745
Age 50-54	0.069	0.254	0.07	0.255	0.084
Age 55-59	0.06	0.238	0.06	0.237	0.487
Age 60-64	0.052	0.221	0.052	0.222	0.175
Age 65-69	0.041	0.199	0.041	0.199	0.687
Age 70-74	0.033	0.178	0.033	0.178	0.541
Age >75	0.048	0.214	0.048	0.214	0.985
Urban location	0.535	0.499	0.535	0.499	0.633
Normal location	0.438	0.496	0.438	0.496	0.55
Rural location	0.027	0.161	0.026	0.161	0.715
Claims' characteristics					
Average cost	29,706.10	194,898.30	30,106.10	222,212.10	0.177
Average LOS t-1	3.369	6.352	3.368	6.356	0.871
St. Dev. cost	58,556.00	292,593.70	58,462.10	285,711.20	0.819
St. Dev. LOS	5.62	18.007	5.613	19.389	0.804
LOS t-1	19.006	26.772	19.024	26.875	0.639
LOS t-1 >30	0.217	0.412	0.217	0.412	0.837
Max LOS	0.707	3.589	0.708	3.597	0.802
Second max LOS	0.15	1.333	0.149	1.351	0.591
Hemograms	0.62	1.628	0.621	1.635	0.709
Pressure tests	0.006	0.21	0.006	0.174	0.714
CTs	0.08	0.432	0.079	0.435	0.934

continues on following page

Table 2. Continued

Variable	Train		Test		diff
	Mean	sd	Mean	sd	
Creatinine tests	0.469	1.41	0.472	1.417	0.146
Thyroid tests	0.22	0.744	0.221	0.746	0.679
ER services	2.382	6.001	2.383	6.083	0.855
Ambulatory services	25.617	37.849	25.625	37.705	0.873
Hospital services	2.664	18.161	2.668	18.03	0.872
Domiciliary services	0.127	6.955	0.14	7.452	0.209
Average contribution income	1,020,238.00	291,184.20	1,020,367.00	291,343.80	0.754
St. Dev. contribution income	1,075,115.00	394,921.60	1,075,271.00	395,142.50	0.78
Drugs	10.72	20.45	10.72	20.52	0.942
N	993,857		993,711		

This table shows the mean and standard deviation of some of the features in the train and test sets. Column ``diff'' shows the p-value of the test of differences in means between both datasets. Source: Base de Suficiencia, Ministry of Health and Social Protection. Authors' calculations.

Since the data needs to be aggregated from claims-level to patient-level, we create the following features with information from $t–2$ to $t–1$: annual LOS, average LOS, maximum LOS, second maximum LOS, indicator of annual LOS greater than 30 days, standard deviation of LOS, average cost, standard deviation of cost, average income of enrollees in each insurer, standard deviation of income in each insurer, indicators of the 10 costlier diagnoses in the sample, number of hemograms, pressure tests, CTs, creatinine tests, thyroid tests, ER services, ambulatory services, hospital services, domiciliary services, drug claims, and the number of different long-term diseases affecting each patient. We also create the number of claims per month and per day of week, indicators of long-term diseases, and interactions between indicators of hospital services, ER services, domiciliary services and ambulatory services. The dependent variable is the logarithm of patient length-of-stay during year t.

To avoid over fitted predictions in the train set because models are estimated on the relevant patterns and features of this sample, we build a test set with information of a new sample of 1 million individuals chosen randomly which is mutually exclusive from the train set. Table 2 shows some descriptive statistics of both datasets and shows whether differences in variable means are significant between them. For all features reported in the table, the train and test sets are not statistically different from each other at a 95 percent confidence level. The average length-of-stay during year t is 1.89 days. Of those who claim at least one health service, 22 percent remained more than 30 days in the hospital during years $t–2$ and $t–1$. On average users claim 30 services per year, of which 83 percent correspond to ambulatory services and an average of 10.72 are due to drugs and medications. The majority of individuals live in urban municipalities and earn around 1 million Colombian pesos.

Further preprocessing of the database consists of deleting observations with more than 360 days in hospital during year t, deleting observations with more than 720 days in hospital from $t–2$ to $t–1$, and dichotomizing all categorical variables.

Results

For the prediction of patient annual LOS we use different machine learning techniques. In the case of neural networks, we set linear activation functions, one hidden layer, and estimate input weight parameters using a back-propagation algorithm. The number of neurons in the hidden layer (12) and the weight decay between layers (0.125) are chosen using repeated cross validation on a grid of values. For the boosted trees model, we use repeated cross validation to find the optimal parameters for the number of trees (8000), minimum observations in nodes (100), shrinkage (0.1), and interaction depth (2). In both models parameters are chosen to minimize the RMSE in the train set. For the random forest, we fix the number of trees to 7500. Finally, we use an ensemble method consisting of the linear combination of all the previous models, without any restriction on the sum of the coefficients. In all cases, negative predictions are truncated at zero and predictions above ln(360) are truncated at ln(360).

Table 3. Coefficients of the linear ensemble

	Dependent Variable: ln(LOS+1)
ANN	-0.058***
	(0.003)
BT	0.246***
	(0.004)
RF	0.857***
	(0.004)
OLS	-0.047***
	(0.002)
Constant	0.002*
	(0.001)
Observations	993,927
Residual Std. Error	0.559
F Statistic	291,939***

*p < \$0.1; **p < 0.05; ***p < 0.01. Source: Base de Suficiencia, Ministry of Health and Social Protection. Authors' calculations.

Table 3 shows the coefficients of the linear ensemble of the Ordinary Least Squares (OLS), Artificial Neural Network (ANN), Random Forest (RF), and Boosted Trees (BT) predictions. Standard errors in parenthesis.

Table 3 shows the coefficients of the linear combination in the ensemble. Tree-based methods have a positive correlation with the final predictor while ANN and OLS have a negative correlation.

Table 4 shows the out-of-sample Mean Absolute Error (MAE), RMSE and R-squared of different models calculated on the test set and Table 5 presents some statistics of the distribution of patient LOS generated by each model versus the observed scenario in the test set. In terms of the MAE, the linear ensemble outperforms the rest of the models while the random forest seems to be the best predictor in terms of RMSE and R-squared. Overall, models fit the data well up to the 75th percentile of the LOS distribution but prediction of higher percentiles is less accurate. The 25th and 75th percentiles of the linear ensemble prediction distribution are more similar to the corresponding percentiles of the observed distribution than that of other models. At the 25th percentile there is a difference of 0.008 days with respect to the observed distribution and of 0.452 days at the 75th percentile. However, the maximum LOS predicted by the linear ensemble is 48.8 days while the observed maximum is 360 days, which suggests the model significantly underestimates the upper tail of the distribution. On the contrary, the ANN overestimates LOS at lower percentiles and the difference between the maximum predicted LOS and the observed one is 13 days. Figure 1 shows the variation in RMSE for different percentiles of the observed LOS distribution. Tree-based methods show a lower increase in RMSE at the right tail of the distribution compared to OLS and ANN models.

Table 4. Out-of-sample model fit

Model	MAE	RMSE	R-Squared
OLS	0.4546	0.7502	0.1731
ANN	0.5032	0.7824	0.1006
RF	0.2634	0.5623	0.5354
BT	0.2721	0.572	0.5192
ENS	0.2523	0.5609	0.5179

This table shows the out-of-sample MAE, RMSE, and R-squared of different models. OLS: Ordinary Least Squares, ANN: Artificial Neural Networks, RF: Random Forest, BT: Boosted Trees, ENS: Linear ensemble. Source: Base de Suficiencia, Ministry of Health and Social Protection. Authors' calculations.

Table 5. Comparison of percentiles of patient LOS distribution

Statistic	Mean	St.Dev	Min	Pct(25)	Pct(75)	Max
Observed	0.333	0.828	0	0	0	5.889
LOS	0.338	0.318	0	0.128	0.482	5.886
ANN	0.37	0.247	0	0.229	0.753	5.851
RF	0.332	0.562	0.004	0.028	0.376	3.213
BT	0.335	0.58	0	0.022	0.39	5.886
ENS	0.334	0.605	0	0.008	0.373	3.909

This table shows the mean, standard deviation, minimum, 25th percentile, 75th percentile, and maximum of patient LOS distribution generated by each model and the observed scenario in the test set. OLS: Ordinary Least Squares, ANN: Artificial Neural Networks, RF: Random Forest, BT: Boosted Trees, ENS: Linear ensemble. Source: Base de Suficiencia, Ministry of Health and Social Protection. Authors' calculations.

Figure 1. Variation in the RMSE by percentiles of the LOS distribution (Source: Base de Suficiencia, Ministry of Health and Social Protection. Authors' calculations.)

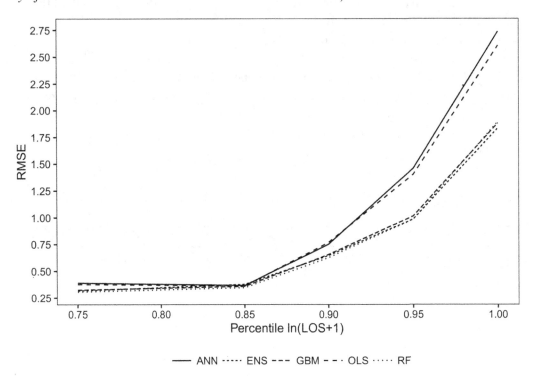

The MAE of the linear ensemble represents 75 percent of the average ln(*LOS*+1) in the test set and the RMSE 168 percent. Compared to the winning team in the Heritage Health Prize (HHP), our best model outperforms the best model in the competition, which achieves a RMSE of 0.4438 or 249 percent of the average ln(*LOS*+1) in year 3 data. However, there are several differences in the approach to LOS prediction and data preprocessing between the competition and the present study: first, in the HHP competition, training sets comprise only one year of data while we use at most two years; second, we lack information regarding the Charlson Index, lab counts, and drug counts included in the HHP; and third, we have both a larger sample of patients compared to the HHP and two additional variables related to the patient's monthly income. Despite the differences, features built for the present study and machine learning techniques are similar to the ones used by Milestone winners.

A test of model accuracy for a classification task is the Receiver Operating Characteristics Curve (ROC). In Figure 2 we build the ROC curve and calculate the area beneath it (AUC) for each model. Predicted proportions are calculated as the linear predictions divided into ln(360). The binary observed outcome takes the value of 1 if the annual LOS is greater than zero. The random forest has the highest AUC, followed by the boosted trees model and the linear ensemble: 0.932, 0.921, 0.920, respectively. Notice the linear regression outperforms the ANN and the reason is that we defined linear activation functions in the latter, so it basically amounts to estimating a regression which is linear in variables but nonlinear in parameters.

Figure 2. Prediction accuracy (Source: Base de Suficiencia, Ministry of Health and Social Protection. Authors' calculations.)

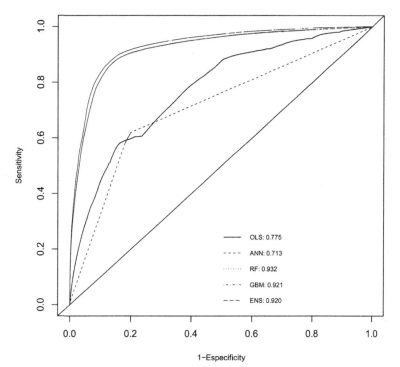

Figure 3 shows the most important predictors in the random forest model or risk factors as measured by the variation in node purity. Results shown in the figure should not be interpreted in terms of the direction of the effect but in terms of variable importance. The number of hospital services followed by the maximum LOS associated to a claim and the standard deviation of the insurer's average user income during the previous year are the most relevant predictors of next year's LOS. Comorbidities such as cardiovascular diseases and long-term pulmonary diseases explain little of the variation in annual LOS, while fixed effects for insurers K and O are more significant.

Potential Cost Savings of a Prevention Program

To measure potential cost savings of a prevention program where patient intervention is decided based on her predicted proportion as in equation (7), we estimate π for different combinations of program efficacy and intervention cost per patient. Figure 4 shows the contour plots of the cost savings per patient due to the decision rule based on predictions of the random forest versus the no intervention case, for $0 \leq \alpha \leq 1$ and $0 \leq f \leq 700,000$. The decision rule consists of assigning $C1_t$ o patient i *if* the inequality in equation (7) holds and $C0_o$ therwise. For every combination of efficacy and intervention cost, the decision rule based on the predictive model generates significant cost savings per patient. An intervention that costs 200,000 pesos per patient generates 40,000 pesos of cost savings per patient if program efficacy is greater than or equal to 30%. For intervention costs greater than that, the savings amount per patient can only be attainable with greater program efficacy compared to the no intervention case.

Figure 3. Risk factors in the random forest model (Source: Base de Suficiencia, Ministry of Health and Social Protection. Authors' calculations.)

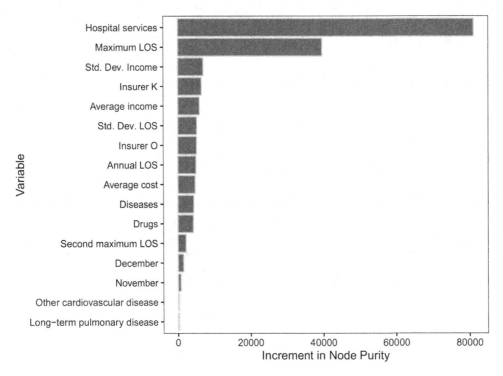

Figure 4. Cost savings over no-intervention policy (Source: Base de Suficiencia, Ministry of Health and Social Protection. Authors' calculations.)

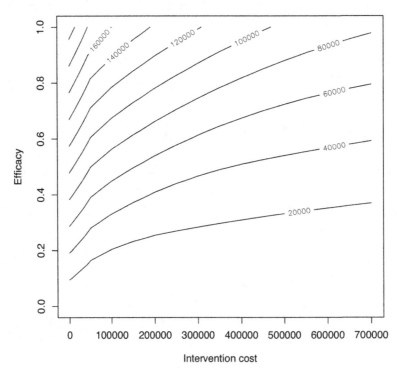

In Figure 5 we show the contour plots of the cost savings per patient due to the decision rule versus the best uniform policy for each combination of α and f. The best uniform policy is the policy that generates the highest cost saving conditional on α and f *bet*ween intervening all patients (assigning C1 $_t$o all patients) and not intervening them (assigning C0 $_t$o all patients). For intervention costs less than 50,000 pesos per patient and efficacies greater than 10%, it is cheaper to intervene all patients than to use the decision rule. The best uniform policy in this case would generate 10,000 pesos of cost savings per patient. However, when the intervention cost increases, benefits of using the decision rule are greater than the best uniform policy, and in any case greater than no intervention at all for program efficacies of more than 20%. If program efficacy falls from this threshold for any intervention cost then the program is not beneficial since it would be better to simply not intervene any patient.

These results suggest that for any intervention cost from 100,000 to 700,000 pesos per patient and with efficacies greater than 40%, an automated decision rule based on predictive modeling is an important source of cost savings for every insurer in Colombia's contributory health care system. The decision rule and results presented in this section account for patient heterogeneity in two ways: first, the predictive model is trained on patient demographic and morbidity characteristics and second, annual health costs are allowed to vary per patient.

Figure 5. Cost savings over best uniform policy (Source: Base de Suficiencia, Ministry of Health and Social Protection. Authors' calculations.)

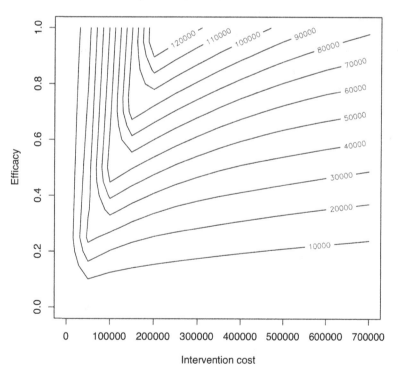

CONCLUSION

Hospitalizations are one of the main sources of health costs in Colombia's public health care system. Relying on hospitalizations for patient treatment increases the risk of bed shortages in hospitals and the risk of worse health outcomes in patients. Predicting annual patient length-of-stay is, therefore, an important tool for cost administration and resource allocation for insurers and providers. In this paper we use machine learning techniques to predict annual patient LOS based on their characteristics from previous years. We show tree-based models such as boosted trees, random forests and an ensemble of their predictions outperform linear models and artificial neural networks, in measures like the RMSE, MAE and R-squared. Relative to the average LOS in our sample, we achieve lower error rates compared to the results obtained by the winning team of the Heritage Health Prize, although there are differences in the way our data is processed. Compared to several international efforts in predicting annual LOS, our best model is highly predictive and suitable for every agent in Colombia's health care market, since it is trained with information that is symmetric between the providers, the insurers, and the government.

Using the predictions of the model we build a decision rule that suggests when to intervene a patient to prevent her hospitalization and achieve cost savings. To measure potential cost savings we compute the difference in total annual health costs between a prevention program whose intervention decision relies on the predictions of the model and the best uniform policy that consists of intervening all patients or not intervening them, conditional on the percentage of program efficacy and the intervention cost per patient. Results suggest Colombia's contributory health care system would achieve significant cost savings if insurers implemented prevention programs based on predictive modeling with efficacies of more than 40% and for any intervention cost between 100,000 and 700,000 pesos per patient.

This article contributes to the growing literature of machine learning in health care and provides evidence that is crucial for the understanding of sources of increased health expenditures that are undermining Colombia's health market financial stability.

REFERENCES

Alfonso, E., Riascos, A., & Romero, M. (2013). The performance of risk adjustment models in Colombia competitive health insurance market.

Asociación Colombiana de Empresas de Medicina Integral. (2013). *Cifras e indicadores del Sistema de Salud*. Bogotá, Colombia.

Bayati, M., Braverman, M., Gillam, M., Mack, K. M., Ruiz, G., Smith, M. S., & Horvitz, E. (2014). Data-Driven decisions for reducing readmissions for heart failure: General methodology and case study. *PLoS One*, *9*(10), 1–9. doi:10.1371/journal.pone.0109264 PMID:25295524

Castellanos-Ortega, A., Borja, S., Garcia-Astudillo, L. A., Holanda, M. S., Ortiz, F., Llorca, J., & Delgado-Rodriguez, M. (2010). Impact of the Surviving Sepsis Campaign protocols on hospital length of stay and mortality in septic shock patients: Results of a three-year follow-up quasi- experimental study. *Critical Care Medicine*, *38*(4), 1036–1043. doi:10.1097/CCM.0b013e3181d455b6 PMID:20154597

Chang, K. C., Tseng, M. C., Weng, H. H., Lin, Y. H., Liou, C. W., & Tan, T. Y. (2002). Prediction of Length of Stay of First-Ever Ischemic Stroke. *Stroke*, *33*(11), 2670–2674. doi:10.1161/01. STR.0000034396.68980.39 PMID:12411659

Chertow, G. M., Burdick, E., Honour, M., Bonventre, J. V., & Bates, D. W. (2005). Acute Kidney Injury, Mortality, Length of Stay, and Costos in Hospitalized Patients. *Journal of the American Society of Nephrology*, *16*(11), 3365–3370. doi:10.1681/ASN.2004090740 PMID:16177006

Chima, C. S., Barco, K., Dewitt, M. L., Maeda, M., Teran, J. C., & Mullen, K. D. (1997). Relationship of Nutritional Status to Length of Stay, Hospital Costs, and Discharge Status of Patients Hospitalized in the Medicine Service. *Journal of the American Dietetic Association*, *97*(9), 975–978. doi:10.1016/ S0002-8223(97)00235-6 PMID:9284874

Clague, J. E., Craddock, E., Andrew, G., Horan, M. A., & Pendleton, N. (2002). Predictors of outcome following hip fracture. Admission time predicts length of stay and in-hospital mortality. *International Journal of Care Injured*, *33*(1), 1–6. doi:10.1016/S0020-1383(01)00142-5 PMID:11879824

Cleary, P. D., Greenfield, S., Mulley, A. G., Pauker, S. G., Schroeder, S. A., & Mcneil, B. J. (1991). Variations in length of stay and outcomes for six medical and surgical conditions in Massachusetts and California. *Journal of the American Medical Association*, *266*(1), 73–79. doi:10.1001/jama.1991.03470010077034 PMID:2046132

Cosgrove, S. E. (2006). The relationship between antomicrobial resistance and patient outcomes: Mortality, length of hospital stay, and health care costs. *Clinical Infectious Diseases*, *45*(Suppl. 2), S82–S89. doi:10.1086/499406 PMID:16355321

Forster, A. J., Stiell, I., Wells, G., Lee, A. J., & Van Walraven, C. (2003). The effect of hospital occupancy on emergency department length of stay and patient disposition. *Academic Emergency Medicine*, *10*(2), 127–133. doi:10.1197/aemj.10.2.127 PMID:12574009

Kelly, M., Sharp, L., Dwane, F., Kelleher, T., & Comber, H. (2012). Factors predicting hospital length-of-stay and readmission after colorectal resection: A population-based study of elective and emergency admissions. *BMC Health Services Research*, *12*(1), 1–12. doi:10.1186/1472-6963-12-77 PMID:22448728

Ministerio de Salud de Colombia. (2014). *Análisis de Situación de Salud*. Bogotá, Colombia.

Morton, A., Maarzban, E., Giannoulis, G., Patel, A., Aparasu, R., & Kakadiaris, I. (2014). A comparison of supervised machine learning techniques for predicting short-term in-hospital length of stay among diabetic patients. In *13th International Conference on Machine Learning and Applications*.

Pendharkar, P., & Khurana, H. (2014). Machine learning techniques for predicting hospital length of stay in pennsylvania federal and specialty hospitals. *International Journal of Computer Science and Applications*, *11*, 45–56.

Rezaei, P. H., Ahmadi, M., Alizadeh, S., & Sadoughi, F. (2013). Use of Data Mining Techniques to Determine and Predict Length of Stay of Cardiac Patients. *Healthcare Informatics Research*, *19*(2), 121–129. doi:10.4258/hir.2013.19.2.121 PMID:23882417

Saltzman, J. R., Tabak, Y. P., Hyett, B. H., Sun, X., Travis, A. C., & Johannes, R. S. (2011). A simple risk score accurately predicts in-hospital mortality, length of stay, and cost in acute upper GI bleeding. *Gastrointestinal Endoscopy*, *74*(6), 1225–1229. doi:10.1016/j.gie.2011.06.024 PMID:21907980

Stratton, R. J., King, C. L., Stroud, M. A., Jackson, A. A., & Elia, M. (2006). Malnutrition universal screening tool predicts morality and length of hospital stay in acutely ill elderly. *British Journal of Nutrition*, *95*(02), 325–330. doi:10.1079/BJN20051622 PMID:16469149

Tanuja, S., Acharya, D. U., & Shailesh, K. R. (2011). Comparison of different data mining techniques to predict hospital length of stay. *Journal of Pharmaceutical and Biomedical Sciences*, *7*, 1–4.

Tu, J. V., & Guerriere, M. R. (1993). Use of a Neural Network as a Predictive Instrument for Length of Stay in the Intensive Care Unit Following Cardiac Surgery. *Computers and Biomedical Research, an International Journal*, *26*(3), 220–229. doi:10.1006/cbmr.1993.1015 PMID:8325002

Tu, J. V., Jaglal, S. B., & Naylor, C. D. (1995). Multicenter validation of a risk index for mortality, intensive care unit stay, and overall hospital length of stay after cardiac surgery. *Circulation*, *91*(3), 677–684. doi:10.1161/01.CIR.91.3.677 PMID:7828293

Turgeman, L., May, J. H., & Sciulli, R. (2017). Insights from a machine learning model for predicting the hospital length of stay at the time of admission. *Expert Systems with Applications*, *78*, 376–385. doi:10.1016/j.eswa.2017.02.023

Walsh, P., Cunningham, P., Rothenberg, S. J., O'Doherty, S., Hoey, H., & Healy, R. (2004). An artificial neural network ensemble to predict disposition and length of stay in children presenting with bronchiolitis. *European Journal of Emergency Medicine*, *11*, 259–264. doi:10.1097/00063110-200410000-00004 PMID:15359198

Winslow, C., Bode, R. K., Felton, D., Chen, D., & Meyer, P. R. Jr. (2002). Impact of Respiratory Complications on Length of Stay and Hospital Costs in Acute Cervical Spine Injury. *CHEST Journal*, *121*(5), 1548–1554. doi:10.1378/chest.121.5.1548 PMID:12006442

ENDNOTES

[1]   CUPS stands for "Código Único de Procedimientos" and is a dictionary of all services, procedures, and drugs included in the colombian benefits package.

This research was previously published in the International Journal of Knowledge Discovery in Bioinformatics (IJKDB), 8(2); pages 44-64, copyright year 2018 by IGI Publishing (an imprint of IGI Global).

Section 6
Emerging Trends

Chapter 75
Current Trends:
Machine Learning and AI in IoT

Jayanthi Jagannathan
Sona College of Technology, India

Anitha Elavarasi S.
Sona College of Technology, India

ABSTRACT

This chapter addresses the key role of machine learning and artificial intelligence for various applications of the internet of things. The following are the most significant applications of IoT: (1) manufacturing industry: automation of industries is on the rise; there is an urge for analyzing the energy in the process industry; (2) anomaly detection: to detect the existing fault and abnormality in functioning by using ML algorithms thereby avoiding the adverse effect during its operation; (3) smart campus: in-order to efficiently handle the energy in buildings, smart campus systems are developed; (4) improving product decisions: with the help of the predictive analytics system products are designed and developed based on the user's requirements and usability; (5) healthcare industry: IoT with machine learning provides numerous ways for the betterment of the human wellbeing. In this chapter, the most predominant approaches to machine learning that can be useful in the IoT applications to achieve a significant set of outcomes will be discussed.

INTRODUCTION

The Internet of Things (IoT) is the network of various physical devices in-order to exchange data and take appropriate action. In recent years the growth in technology enhances the communication between different devices are made much easier. It is estimated that there will be 30 billion devices by 2020 [Nordrum et al ., 2016]. Some of the IoT applications include automated vehicles, home automation, remote health monitoring etc. In-order to make these devices work in a smarter way or to make IoT applications more intelligent there is need for analyzing the huge amount of data using machine learning algorithm [Mahdavinejad et al., 2016]. Machine learning refers to the set of techniques meant to deal

DOI: 10.4018/978-1-6684-6291-1.ch075

with huge data in the most intelligent way in order to derive actionable insights. Figure 1 refers to the confluence of different fields such as IoT, artificial intelligence and big data

Internet of Things

The Internet of Things (IoT), refers to the collection of inter connected everyday objects over the Internet and also to one another. It provides users with smarter and smoother experiences. Internet of Things is mainly being driven by various sensors that would possibly sense the real world data, some of the widely used sensors are temperature, pressure, gas, smoke, IR, image sensors etc. IoT platform could deliver plenty of functionalities with the intelligence by combining a set of sensors and a communication networks. Thus it could able to improve and achieve effectiveness in their autonomous functionality.

The data that is flowing across the network and devices are being stored and the same is being processed, to derive the required insights. The various stakeholders who are in need of those insights will be served on time. The data sharing is done in a secured way, only the authorized users permitted to use the same.

Let us take a worlds well know Tesla vehicles as an example. The sensors mounted in and around the car senses variety of data and derive many fact values based on the perception from the environment. Then it uploads data into a huge database. The data is further processed and send necessary signals to other vehicles or other parts.

Figure 1. Confluence of IoT, artificial intelligence and big data

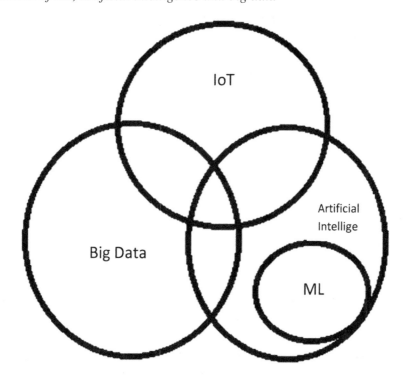

Machine Learning

Machine Learning (ML) is one of the hottest domains of the computer science field that proves the ability of a computer system to "learn" with data, with / without being explicitly trained. It is one of the most essential applications of artificial intelligence. It concentrates on the development of set of programs that can enable data access and make them learn by themselves.

The ultimate view point of ML is to automate the data analysis process with the help of algorithms that are enabled with continuous learning skill. Hence ML refers to the set of techniques meant to deal with huge data in the most intelligent way in order to derive actionable insights. There are three major types of algorithms much useful are (i) Supervised (Task driven) (ii) Unsupervised (Data Driven) (iii) Reinforcement learning(learns to react to an environment)

FOREMOST USES OF MACHINE LEARNING IN IOT

- **Clustering of Data:** Clustering deals with grouping objects which are similar to each other based on an objective measure. Binary Classification (positive or negative), Logistic Regression (discrete outcome), K-Means for clustering the data are some prevalent algorithms that's being useful in clustering in Machine Learning. From any real time data to identify certain behavioral analysis is possible. Example: Medical data, data from the devices such as gyroscope, accelerometer etc.
- **Anomaly Detection:** Anomaly detection is a technique used to identify uncommon patterns that do not conform to anticipated behavior, called outliers. It finds many applications in business, from intrusion detection (identifying abnormal patterns in network traffic that could sign a hack) to system health monitoring (spotting a malignant tumor in a scan report), and from fraud detection in credit card transactions.
- **Prediction of Data Trends:** Predictive analytics utilizes historical data to predict future happenings. Usually, historical data is used to build a mathematical model that captures significant trends. The predictive model is then used on present data to predict what will happen next, or to suggest activities to be taken to achieve the optimal outcomes.

STANDARD MACHINE LEARNING ALGORITHMS USED IN IOT APPLICATIONS

- **K-Nearest Neighbour (k-NN):** K nearest neighbours is a simple algorithm that considers all available cases and classifies new cases based on a similarity measure / distance functions. K-nearest neighbor classifier is one of the supervised classifier for performing pattern classification task. Knn address the pattern recognition problems and also the best option for deal with some of the classification related tasks. The simple edition of the K-nearest neighbor classifier algorithms is to predict the target label by finding the nearest neighbor class. The closest class will be identified using the distance measures like Euclidean distance. In an IoT application, to check whether all the sensors used for an application works normally or abnormally can be figure out using K-NN approach [3]. The average reading of neighbouring sensor can be calculated using any of the measures like Euclidean distance and hence the malfunction of the sensor node is can be predicted. Hence it can be useful at the appropriate places in an IoT environment to provide better solutions.

K-Nearest Neighbor (Knn) Algorithm Pseudocode

Let (X_i, C_i) where $i = 1, 2......, n$ be data points.

  X_i denotes feature values & C_i denotes labels for X_i for each i.

  Assuming the number of classes as 'c'

  $_{Ci} \in \{1, 2, 3, ..., c\}$ for all values of i

  Let x be a point for which label is not known, and like to find the label class using k-nearest neighbor algorithms.

Pseudocode of Knn Algorithm

1. Calculate "$d(x, x_i)$" $i = 1, 2, ..., n$; where **d** denotes the Euclidean distance between the points.
2. Arrange the calculated **n** Euclidean distances in non-decreasing order.
3. Let **k** be a +ve integer, take the first **k** distances from this sorted list.
4. Find those **k**-points corresponding to these **k**-distances.
5. Let k_i denotes the number of points belonging to the ith class among **k** points i.e. $k \geq 0$
6. If $k_i > k_j \; \forall \; i \neq j$ then put x in class i.

Decision Tree (DT): A decision tree is a graph that uses a branching method to show every possible outcome of a decision. In a health care industry, to classify the severity of the diseases based on certain parameter, decision tree algorithm can be employed. Apart from this reliability of the sensor node can be identified using the features such as mean time to failure, mean time to restore. Decision Tree algorithm belongs to the folks of supervised learning algorithms. Decision tree algorithm can be used for resolving regression and classification problems too.

The main aim of classification is to predict the target class (Yes/ No). If the trained model is for predicting any of two target classes. It is known as binary classification. The main goal of regression algorithms is to predict the discrete or a continues value. In some cases, the predicted value can be used to identify the linear relationship between the attributes.

The general motive of using Decision Tree is to create a training model which can be useful to predict class or value of target variables by learning decision rules inferred from prior data(training data).Each internal node of the tree corresponds to an attribute, and each leaf node corresponds to a class label.

In decision trees, for predicting a class label for a record, it must be started from the root of the tree. Then compare the values of the root attribute with record's attribute. On the basis of comparison, the branch corresponding to that value and jump to the next node will be followed.

Pseudocode of Decision Tree Algorithm

1. Place the best attribute of the dataset at the root of the tree.
2. Split the training set into subsets. Subsets should be made in such a way that each subset contains data with the same value for an attribute.
3. Repeat step 1 and step 2 on each subset until you find leaf nodes in all the branches of the tree.

Neural Networks (NNs): Neural networks can learn from multiple perceptron and take appropriate decisions which make them suitable for several challenging application. This can be used to recognize a pattern, to predict someone's behavior, recognizing objects etc. It can be more useful in many industrial sectors including medical fields, logistics tracking, smart cities and automobiles where IoT plays vital role. NN's would be useful in the classification of normal and threat patterns on an IoT Network.

Support Vector Machines (SVMs): Support Vector Machine" (SVM) is a supervised machine learning algorithm which can be applied for both classification and regression challenges. However, it is widely used in to providing solution to classification problems. In an IoT application, to check the proper functioning of the sensors SVM can be applied to identify its behavior (normal / malicious). This can be done by correlating the temporal and spatial information of a node and its reading are plotted in the feature space. SVM partition this into various part and a new reading can be classified based on the gap it is going to possesses.

Support vector machine which is a supervised learning algorithm[3]. When a dataset contains features and class labels both then Support Vector Machine can be used For a dataset consisting of features set and labels set, an SVM classifier builds a model to predict classes for new examples. It assigns new example/data points to one of the classes. If there are only 2 classes then it can be called as a Binary SVM Classifier.

Types of SVM classifiers:

1. Linear SVM Classifier
2. Non-Linear SVM Classifier

Svm Linear Classifier

In the linear classifier model, it is assumed that training examples plotted in space. These data points are expected to be separated by an evident gap. It predicts a straight hyperplane dividing two classes. The main focus while drawing the hyperplane is on maximizing the distance from hyperplane to the nearest data point of either class. The drawn hyperplane is called as a maximum-margin hyperplane.

SVM Non-Linear Classifier

In the real world, the dataset is generally dispersed up to some extent. To solve this problem separation of data into different classes on the basis of a straight linear hyperplane can't be considered a good choice. For this Vapnik suggested creating Non-Linear Classifiers by applying the kernel trick to maximum-margin hyperplanes. In Non-Linear SVM Classification, data points plotted in a higher dimensional space.

- **3.5 Principal Component Analysis (PCA):** The main aim of PCA is data compression and dimensionality reduction. This helps in reducing the amount of data that is transmitted among various sensor nodes by filtering the unwanted data. Moreover it could able to simplify the problem solving approach to a greater extend as it considers/ selects only few parameters for making a decision.

APPLICATIONS

- **Manufacturing Industry**: Automation of industries is in rise, there is an urge for analyzing the energy in process industry. It needs the monitoring and diagnosis of systems in order to perform in a better and efficient manner. Monostori 2014 describes a Cyber-Physical Production Systems. The parallel development of computer science, information and communication technologies on one side and of manufacturing on the other side and their mutual influence paved ways to *Cyber-Physical Systems* (CPS). CPS is a computational entities interconnected with physical world to gathers and process data / information via internet. Autonomous cars, robotic surgery, intelligent buildings are few examples of CPS system. *Cyber-Physical Production Systems (CPPSs)*, relies on the development of computer science, information, communication technologies and manufacturing. CPPS consist of both autonomous and cooperative elements across domains such as production and logistics sub system with an establishment of man machine communication. CPPS operates on a decentralized manner. Few of the CPPSs in manufacturing industry include:
- **Intelligent manufacturing systems (IMS)**: Expected to solve unseen or unpredicted problem.
- **Biological manufacturing systems (BMS):** Develops system based on biologically inspired ideas
- Reconfigurable manufacturing systems (RMS)
- **Digital Factories (DF):** Mapping of business processes into digital
- **Holonic Manufacturing Systems (HMS):** agent-based manufacturing system with properties of autonomy and cooperation

The growth of CPPS paves way to more versatile and enormous expectation. The partial fulfilment of these expectations would represent real challenges. Monostori 2014 list few of the common R&D challenges in CPPS systems as:

- Context-adaptive and autonomous systems.
- Cooperative production systems
- Identification and prediction of dynamical systems
- Robust scheduling
- Fusion of real and virtual systems.
- Human-machine symbiosis.

Anomaly Detection: To detect the existing fault and abnormality in functioning by using the ML algorithms thereby avoiding the adverse effect during its operation. The fast growing popularity of IoT led to various devices released with vulnerability which leads to different kind of attack. DIoT is a a system for **D**etecting compromised **IoT** devices [Nguyen, Thien Duc, et al., 2018]. It uses a self-learning approach (autonomous) which combines device type identification and device type specifications to classify devices based on their communicative profile and thereby detect any anomalous behavior. It detects the compromised node in a much faster and effectively (94%) manner with very few false alarms. It classify IoT malware attack into three stages as: (1) intrusion: gain unauthorized access (2) infection: attacker upload malicious code to infect the device and (3) monetization: malware takes malicious action like DDoS attack. Some of the challenges faced on anomaly detection are: (1) Dynamic threat landscape, (2) Resource limitations, (3) IoT device heterogeneity, (4) Scarcity of communications and (5) False alarms.

The growth of Internet of Things (IoT) paved ways to a number of benefits. At the same time it has various security vulnerabilities associated with it. Now a day's organization employs BYOIoT(bringing their own IoT devices) which has raised the security issues[Meidan, Yair, et al, 2017]. Therefore organization needs an intelligent system to identify the suspicious devices which are connected to the network. Suspicious IoT devices are identified using the random forest machine learning algorithm. Two major types of attacks commonly seen are:(1) Untargeted: In this approach the various IoT device are infected by malware. Cross contamination is an example of untargeted attack and (2) specifically targeted: Attacker intentionally fix the malware to the IoT device their by gaining the data in future. Such type of attack requires excellent hacking skills. Supply chain attack is an example of specifically targeted attack. The security policy of an organization should check the various IoT devices which are connected to the network by monitoring the traffic. It should check for the data origination, type of IoT device and whether it is authorized or not. If the device is found to be unauthorized appropriate action should be taken.

The Approach employed by Meidan, Yair et al, 2017 will initialize a set of authorized IoT device and structured set of traffic data are defined. Authorized IoT device are identified by using the classifier algorithm (Machine learning algorithm) by taking the TCP/IP data traffic. The classifier selected for this purpose is Random forest. It combines decision tree induction with ensemble learning. Once the classifier is trained, new streams of data traffic is given and checked whether the device is authorized one or not. Some of the common limitations are (1) the Approach is tested on a particular circumstance; if the device varies on organization then more generalized approach has to be devised. (2) The present approach describes only about TCP/IP communication technology. It does not focus on Bluetooth or Zigbee protocol and (3) the data being collected represent only normal behavior. Exceptional cases are to be considered and classifier has to be trained accordingly.

- **Smart Campus**: In-order to efficiently handle the energy in buildings, smart campus systems is developed. Whenever the user is not using the resource properly the system will intimate and make them used it in an efficient manner. Resource such as switching off the computer system, laptop, tube lights, fan can be controlled by the user mobile phone itself.

Smart Home

Home can be monitored by the data produced from various sensors fixed inside the home to make it smart [Shafie-Khah et al 2016]. For example, novel demand response (DR) methods can be useful, or customers can be alerted in the case where pollution is above its usual limit through monitoring different parameters. Cutting-edge of IoT technology facilitates smart homes and appliances including smart TVs, home security system, lighting control, fire detection, and temperature monitoring. The sensors of these appliances monitor the conditions and environment and send surveillance data to a central controller at home which enables the householder to continuously monitor and control the home even from outside and make the best decision under every circumstance [Li et al 2011].

Smart City

The main goal of a smart city is to keep the city connected together and ensure proper functioning of each subsystem with the help of information technology. The factor that facilitates the development of a city includes communicating systems, network automation and technology for measurement. Smart metering integrated Internet of Things (IoT) architecture employed in smart city applications. This can be called as Advanced Metering Infrastructures (AMI) [Lloret, Jaime, et al., 2016] . It involves communication protocol, the data format, the data gathering and big data based decision system for efficient management of electricity, water and gas their by having balance between demand and consumption. AMI act as vital role in resource (electricity, water and gas) distribution networks. The components of AMI system include hardware for communication, display, controller, sensor and software for data managements and decision support system. It provides two way communications. The author proposes a three layer approach where Layer 1 comprises of various hardware components such as meters, hub, gateway etc. Layer 2 comprises of devices responsible for receiving data at the utility side and layer 3 handles decision support system using artificial intelligent and billing system. In-order to process huge volumes of data collected through smart meters, author employs spark. By using Spark machine learning library we can performs operation likes prediction, identifying incidents and categorizing user. Three models has been formulated, (1) First model predicts the future consumption and categorize into short and medium term (2) Second model givens an alarm when something goes wrong. And (3) Apply K-means unsupervised machine learning algorithm to categorize user/ customer based on their resource consumption. Two main problem with this system are (1) false fraud incident may arise i.e. if the users consumption patterns vary an anomaly is identified (2) issues related to the data privacy i.e. based on the user behavior data are collected and analyzed pattern are extracted. Real time data may leads to privacy issues.

Meeting the essential needs of the citizens is a tough process because of the density of the population and it must be addressed by providing the ICT based IoT services. Therefore, there has been a significant development of digital devices, such as sensors, actuators, smart phones and smart appliances that motivates the vast commercial intentions of the Internet of Things (IoT). It is always likely to interconnect all devices and build communications between them through the Internet [Rathore et al 2016]. It is very mandatory to gather the information for daily management and long term planning of the city growth.

For example the real time information about any public or private transportation services must be tracked and the necessary data should be generated further analysis and based on which the decisions will be taken. The parameters that would help to track would be location, parking spaces, traffic history, pollution of different categories and areas, energy consumption etc. should be gathered constantly. IoT played a vital role in addressing these types of issues [Rathore et al., 2015]

In order to achieve higher efficiency in smart grid communications a two-way relay network with an orthogonal frequency division multiple accesses is proposed [Zhu et al ., 2015]. The global grid infrastructures are useful in connecting the smart and self-configuring devices. IoT has set of real objects that are distributed in nature .It has limited storage capacity and processing speed. It is aiming for improved reliability, performance and security of the IoT infrastructure of the smart cities [Botta et al ., 2016]. Table 1 represents the various IoT network layers and its functionality.

Actual IoT Applications for Smart Cities

The IoT uses the Internet to merge various heterogeneous things. Accordingly and for providing the ease of access, all existing things have to be linked to the Internet. The reason behind this is that smart cities include sensor networks and connection of intelligent appliances to the internet is essential to remotely monitor their treatment such as power usage monitoring to improve the electricity usage, light management, air conditioner management. To get this aim, sensors are able to be extended at various locations to gather and analyze data for utilization improvement. Botta et al 2016 illustrates the major

Table 1. IoT network Layers and its functionality

LAYERS	FUNCTIONS	DEVICES
PERCEPTION LAYER	Identify, detect objects, gather information, and interchange information with other devices through the Internet communication networks	Radio Frequency Identification Devices (RFID), cameras, sensors, Global Positioning Systems (GPS)
NETWORK LAYER	Forwarding data from the perception layer to the application layer under the checks of devices' capabilities, network limitation and the applications' is the job of the network layer.	Bluetooth and ZigBee which are used to carry the information from perception devices to a nearby gateway based on the competences of the communicating events [Jaradat et al 2015]. Basically a short distance service. WiFi, 2G, 3G, 4G, and Power Line Communication (PLC) carry the information over long distances based on the application.
APPLICATION LAYER	The information is received and processed for taking better decisions	smart homes, smart cities, power system monitoring, demand-side energy management, synchronization of distributed power storage, and integration of renewable energy generators [Hancke et al 2012]

utilizations of the IoT for a smart city. The key aims in this field of knowledge are expressed in the following subsections.

- **Improving Product Decisions:** Products are developed based on the user's requirements. With the help of the predictive analytics system products are designed and developed based on the user's requirements and usability. A supply chain is the linked network of people, organizations, resources, deeds, and technologies tangled in the manufacturing and sale of a product or service. A supply chain begins with the delivery of raw materials from a supplier to a manufacturer in the first phase and ends with the delivery of the finished product or service to the end consumer in the second phase. Supply Chain Management (SCM) [1] superintends each and every point of a company's product or service, starting from initial conception to the final sale. The well managed SCM could increase the company revenue, decrease the costs. The success of any business is inseparably linked to the enactment of the supply chain.

More than fifty percent of major new business processes will incorporate some element of IoT by 2020. Maximum of 26 billion internet-connected 'smart' devices will be installed, generating some $300 billion by the end this decade. A thirty-fold increase in internet-connected physical devices will significantly amend the operation of any supply chain operates. Many globalized industries would recognize the revolution of IoT, predominantly in manufacturing, retailing and service industries. Many distributions are focused on identifying, locating, and tracking the status of assets. 58% to 77% of surveyed organizations use locating objects, containers, and personnel as the top fundamental functions of IoT solutions

The postal services use smart mailboxes in remote areas to see whether they're empty and to avoid a unwanted journey before collection. Temperature sensitive pharmaceutical products are being monitored with sensors to confirm product reliability after leaving the warehouse. Data from such sensors can be integrated with business information systems to deliver rich business intelligence. Retailers combine the physical store online presence, to improve the visibility of data at the vital points in the supply chain. A platform on a truck can transfer messages presenting exactly what products, sizes and style differences are included, not to mention the temperature or humidity goods are being transported in. Sensors are even useful in locating the specific products and staff in large

Sensors can even be used to locate the whereabouts of products and staff in large warehouse and even on the road to compute the time of arrival. Automated data capture provides real-time prominence of stock and eludes manual counting and human errors. A bidirectional remote communication is enabled with embedded sensor technologies, which is spread over one million elevators worldwide. The captured data would help technicians to make out their decisions from remote and also can also possible to initiate repair options [2]. This will definitely increase the machine uptime and customer service. The IoT is having a control over supply chain to device the external environment. Unlike previous generations of passive sensors, the IoT will allow a supply chain to control the external environment and accomplish decisions. IoT not only can transfer data about features such as the temperature and application of the machine, but also can change equipment settings and process workflow to improve performance.

The current warehouses [Steve Banker 2014] may operate manually, semi-automatically or fully automatically by " re-intellectualize" the existing control systems for handling data coming from sensors installed. The forklift is extremely reliant on the operator. The innovative smart forklift comprises sensors for speed control, anti-slip technology, and collision detection among devices and sensors. When a forklift is integrated to a Warehouse Management System, it can able to move faster and improve the productivity. Speed control is also done to ensure safety. For example, RFID tags positioned in the floor can indicate the forklift that certain warehouse section is profoundly passage by workers, and then the forklift is agreed an automatic speed limit when near to this section. The greatest cutting-edge forklifts are put up with real-time location systems that allow drivers to progress to a stated location and pick up (or put down) a load without the need for drivers to probe the location to verify that they have picked up (or delivered) the correct load.

As Phil Van Vormer clarifies, the Internet of Things (IoT) expresses the real-time prominence of the inventory. Without real-time status, inventory management trusts on predicting "Lack of real-time visibility means impossible to know about the expend time of drivers with load, even if they prefer the utmost operative route and whether enhancements could be made to how pallets flow all over the warehouse." Besides the internet of things improves inventory counting: "Manual data collection influences inventory disorder. Too many warehouse operators spend a disparate amount of time for chasing missing or misplaced pallets as a result of data entry errors. It is overcome in the connected warehouse, such problems are removed since every single pallet is tracked to the sub inch. Sensors effectively replaces the human portion, possibly leading to 100 percent inventory accuracy."

Supply chain management (SCM) [Machado et at 2016] accomplishes to enhance processes and association with other companies in the supply chain (suppliers and customers) in order to build extra value. When SCM is already profoundly supported by numerous IT solutions, the Internet of Things can be of boundless value by providing further information. One of the main challenges in SCM is reducing the bullwhip effect. A major reason of the bullwhip effect is information alteration. For a better information flow, the Internet of Things is able to activate all appropriate players in the supply chain upon the trade of a product. In customary processes, information on demand was only passed to one's direct downstream companion instead of distributing this information with the whole chain. Fifteen new sophisticated RFID chips used in the Internet of Things permit the recording of all types of manufacturing information, production date, expiry date, warranty period, after sales details consenting real time and more efficient supply chain management. If its possible to have a real-time aspect in the supply chain operation, production capacity can be higher, that leads to more productivity with the same investment.

- **Healthcare Industry:** IoT with machine learning provides numerous ways for the betterment of the human wellbeing. Early diseases prediction is possible with the help of continuous monitoring and taking appropriate decision at right time. Recently, IoT has become more useful in the healthcare domain. In the Healthcare field IoT can analyze data send by the connected devices through cloud services to the medical practitioners. When the features of IoT is integrated into medical devices improves the quality and service of care for patients especially elderly people and kids [Darshan et at 2015]. IoT in healthcare can maintain patient's health record and make them accessible at anytime from anywhere. The wearable technology plays vital role in patient health monitoring service. This would help doctors to do remote monitoring and services. Since it is possible to assess over internet, on time needy service can be provided and patients life are saved.

Most of the countries are having only poor healthcare infrastructure and to extend and improve their facility further portable communication devices can be utilized. Since it is almost everyone are using portable devices for communication and it is also economical, can be used for good cause like healthcare services. The provision for monitoring the patient in the real time as well as all real time data of the patient is also analyzed and different insights are derived [Dhar et at 2014]. This will definitely help the doctors to take the clinical decisions in a faster way.

Improving the effectiveness of healthcare and the need of providing excellence care to patients is one of the thought-provoking things of modern society. Active healthcare be contingent on rapidity and correctness, supporting many people and a vast series of devices which are involving with IoT. Hence, IoT has become more useful in the area of healthcare[Catarinucci et al 2015]. Figure 1 represents a model of an IoT for healthcare domain which consist of various sensor to monitor the patient details and takes appropriate steps during emergency time.

Figure 2. Model of an IoT in healthcare domain

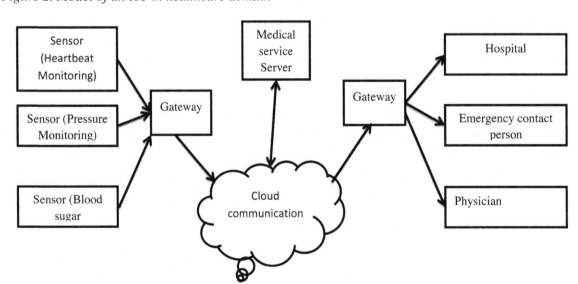

IoT focused sensor can be used to monitor patients in an uninterrupted mode. The patient needs close care due to their bodily status, which is a noninvasive monitoring. Every patient connected in the network is closely monitored for their physiological as well as physical information that need to be analyzed using the gateways. All the relevant information will be stored cloud. Further the information will be processed for the diagnosis and prediction of disease. This will support the medical practitioners to improve their decision with quality care and reduced cost [Niewolny 2013].

L. Catarinucci *et al* 2015 proposed an IoT-aware architecture for smart healthcare systems . An IoT aware smart architecture for automatic monitoring and tracking of patient's personal, and biomedical data is implemented for the patients within hospitals and nursing institutes. A smart hospital system (SHS) is established, which be dependent on different technologies, precisely RFID, WSN. Smart mobiles phones are interoperating through a constrained application protocol (CoAP)/IPv6over low-power wireless personal area network (6LoWPAN)/REST infrastructure. In real time,SHS can collect,both environmental factors and patient's physiological boundary related information through an ultra-low-power hybrid sensing network (HSN) which is composed of 6 LoWPAN nodes integrating the UHF RFID functionalities. The data which is sensed, is delivered to a control center where an advanced monitoring application (MA) makes these things easily accessible by both the local and remote users via REST web service.

A term personalized healthcare [Kulkarni et at 2014] is derived based on the unique characteristics of an individual which includes biological, behavioral, social and cultural practice of well-being. This enables each and every person to follow the simple healthcare norm of "the correct care for the correct person at the correct time", which leads to better outcomes and improvement in fulfilment thus making healthcare cost-effective. A viable service focuses on the prevention, early pathology detection, and homecare instead of the costly clinical one. It verifies the overall well-being to anticipate needs and confirm agreement to healthcare plans. Internet of Things prospects to manage the personalized care services and can maintain a digital identity for every individual. Different equipment is used in healthcare, to communicate and to make the ubiquitous system-of-system. The classifications of IoT based personalized healthcare systems are Clinical care and Remote Monitoring.

EMR is a digital form of regular paper-based medical file records of an individual. EMR systems support to make available quick access to health care info remotely, at anytime and anywhere with the accessibility of IoT technology [Mohd Ibrahim Bhat et al 2017]. EMR takes away the process of structured or unstructured paper form, which could be cumbersome to access at a glance. In this paper, a patient's medical information is entered into an EMR system of health centre in the first instance. The EMR of the patient will be updated continuously throughout his or her stay in the health centre, and linked to an RFID tag. The EMR of the patient includes the following stored information: patient's biodata, diagnostic information (from medical devices such as ECG device), medical history, prescriptions, laboratory results, blood pressure results, vital signs and medical bills. Whenever a patient seeks medical care in the health centre, the doctors will retrieve the health information of the patient from the EMR system through the use of RFID technology. Then, the retrieved information would help in to analyse and diagnose the patient's illness. Doctors can further take expert advice by sharing the information with consulting specialists if the need arises. This system ensures structure, efficiency and security because no other patient can use another's medical file.

CONCLUSION

In this chapter the most predominant approaches of machine learning that can be useful in the IoT applications to achieve significant set of outcomes will be discussed. This would guide researchers and business people to have an idea and to implement their needs in a better way. It can also help them to find out the feasibility and issues to be addressed in the project.

REFERENCES

Bank, S. (2014). *Warehouse Management Systems & Warehouse Control Systems in the Age of the Internet of Things*. SupplyChain247.

Botta, A., de Donato, W., Persico, V., & Pescapé, A. (2016). Integration of Cloud computing and Internet of Things: A survey. *Future Generation Computer Systems, 56*, 684–700. doi:10.1016/j.future.2015.09.021

Catarinucci, L. (2015). An IoT-Aware Architecture for Smart Healthcare Systems. IEEE Internet of Things Journal, 2(6), 515-526. doi:10.1109/JIOT.2015.2417684

Darshan, K. R., & Anandakumar, K. R. (2015). A Comprehensive Review on Usage of Internet of Things (IoT) in Healthcare System. *International Conference on Emerging Research in Electronics, Computer Science and Technology (ICERECT)*, 132-136, 374–380. 10.1109/ERECT.2015.7499001

Dhar, K., Bhunia, S. S., & Mukherjee, N. (2014). Interference Aware Scheduling of Sensors in IoT Enabled Health-Care Monitoring System. *Fourth International Conference of Emerging Applications of Information Technology*, 152-157. 10.1109/EAIT.2014.50

Hancke, G., Silva, B., & Hancke, G. Jr. (2012). The Role of Advanced Sensing in Smart Cities. *Sensors (Basel), 13*(1), 393–425. doi:10.3390130100393 PMID:23271603

Jaradat, M., Jarrah, M., Bousselham, A., Jararweh, Y., & Al-Ayyoub, M. (2015). The Internet of Energy: Smart Sensor Networks and Big Data Management for Smart Grid. *Procedia Computer Science, 56*, 592–597. doi:10.1016/j.procs.2015.07.250

Kulkarni, A., & Sathe, S. (2014). Healthcare applications of the Internet of Things: A Review. *International Journal of Computer Science and Information Technologies, 5*(5), 6229–6232.

Li, X., Lu, R., Liang, X., Shen, X., Chen, J., & Lin, X. (2011). Smart community: An internet of things application. *IEEE Communications Magazine, 49*(11), 68–75. doi:10.1109/MCOM.2011.6069711

Lloret, J., Tomas, J., Canovas, A., & Parra, L. (2016). An integrated IoT architecture for smart metering. *IEEE Communications Magazine, 54*(12), 50–57. doi:10.1109/MCOM.2016.1600647CM

Machado, H., & Shah, K. (2016). *Internet of Things (IoT) impacts on Supply Chain*. machado2016internet.

Mahdavinejad, M. S. (2017). *Machine learning for Internet of Things data analysis: A survey*. Digital Communications and Networks.

Meidan, Y. (2017). *Detection of Unauthorized IoT Devices Using Machine Learning Techniques*. arXiv preprint arXiv:1709.04647.

Monostori, L. (2014). Cyber-physical production systems: Roots, expectations and R&D challenges. *Procedia Cirp, 17*, 9–13. doi:10.1016/j.procir.2014.03.115

Nguyen, T. D. (2018). *IoT: A Crowdsourced Self-learning Approach for Detecting Compromised IoT Devices*. arXiv preprint arXiv:1804.07474.

Niewolny. (2013). *How the Internet of Things Is Revolutionizing Healthcare*. Freescale Semiconductors.

Nordrum, A. (2016). *Popular Internet of Things Forecast of 50 Billion Devices by 2020 Is Outdated*. IEEE.

Rathore, M. M., Ahmad, A., Paul, A., & Rho, S. (2016). Urban planning and building smart cities based on the Internet of Things using Big Data analytics. *Computer Networks, 101*, 63–80. doi:10.1016/j.comnet.2015.12.023

Shafie-Khah, M., Heydarian-Forushani, E., Osório, G. J., Gil, F. A. S., Aghaei, J., Barani, M., & Catalão, J. P. S. (2016). Optimal Behavior of Electric Vehicle Parking Lots as Demand Response Aggregation Agents. *IEEE Transactions on Smart Grid, 7*(6), 2654–2665. doi:10.1109/TSG.2015.2496796

Zhu, C., Leung, V.C.M., Shu, L., & Ngai, E.C.H. (2015). Green Internet of Things for Smart World. *IEEE Access, 3*, 2151–2162.

This research was previously published in Integrating the Internet of Things Into Software Engineering Practices; pages 181-198, copyright year 2019 by Engineering Science Reference (an imprint of IGI Global).

Chapter 76

Artificial Intelligence, Machine Learning, Automation, Robotics, Future of Work and Future of Humanity:
A Review and Research Agenda

Weiyu Wang

Missouri University of Science and Technology, USA

Keng Siau

City University of Hong Kong, Hong Kong SAR

ABSTRACT

The exponential advancement in artificial intelligence (AI), machine learning, robotics, and automation are rapidly transforming industries and societies across the world. The way we work, the way we live, and the way we interact with others are expected to be transformed at a speed and scale beyond anything we have observed in human history. This new industrial revolution is expected, on one hand, to enhance and improve our lives and societies. On the other hand, it has the potential to cause major upheavals in our way of life and our societal norms. The window of opportunity to understand the impact of these technologies and to preempt their negative effects is closing rapidly. Humanity needs to be proactive, rather than reactive, in managing this new industrial revolution. This article looks at the promises, challenges, and future research directions of these transformative technologies. Not only are the technological aspects investigated, but behavioral, societal, policy, and governance issues are reviewed as well. This research contributes to the ongoing discussions and debates about AI, automation, machine learning, and robotics. It is hoped that this article will heighten awareness of the importance of understanding these disruptive technologies as a basis for formulating policies and regulations that can maximize the benefits of these advancements for humanity and, at the same time, curtail potential dangers and negative impacts.

DOI: 10.4018/978-1-6684-6291-1.ch076

INTRODUCTION

With the rapid advancement in artificial intelligence (AI), machine learning, automation, and robotics, many jobs are at risk of being replaced by AI and AI-based automation technology. Job replacement, however, is not a new phenomenon. The loss of jobs caused by technological change is termed "technological unemployment" (Peter, 2017). Some jobs, that have disappeared as technology has advanced, include switchboard operators, elevator operators, and typists. The disappearance of obsolete jobs that have been replaced by technologies, is referred to as "technological job obliteration," each time an industrial revolution has occurred, people have been concerned about technological unemployment and technological job obliteration.

The steam engines in the first industrial revolution resulted in the transition from manual production to a machine industry. Many manual agricultural jobs were replaced by machines. The second industrial revolution enabled mass production by employing electric power and improving job automation, while the third industrial revolution further improved automated production by using electronics and information technology. With the development of AI and machine learning, as well as a fusion of technologies (such as the Internet of things, big data, robotics, virtual reality, 3-D printing, and quantum computing), the fourth industrial revolution has arrived (Bloem et al., 2014). These technologies are blurring the lines between physical, biological, and digital spheres. Further, the speed of technological breakthroughs has no historical precedent. What are the differences between this time and the past industrial revolutions? What about the future of work and humanity? In the past technological revolutions, the physical strength and speed of humans were overtaken by machines. In the fourth industrial revolution, not only are a human's physical strength and speed inferior to machines in certain jobs, but a human's cognitive abilities in some fields are also surpassed by machines. The latter makes the fourth industrial revolution particularly disturbing and unsettling.

According to a Pew Research Center survey, 63% of participants were hopeful that the expanding role of AI would leave us better off, but they worried that AI would negatively transform and affect society at the same time (Mack, 2018). The focus of this research is to analyze the impact of AI, machine learning, automation, and robotics, and their effect on the future of work and humanity. This article is structured as follows: the next section provides introductions to AI, machine learning, automation, and robotics. Then, we analyze the promises and benefits provided by these technologies. Challenges poses by these technologies are also discussed. Finally, a research agenda is proposed that emphasizes the need for academia, industry, and government to pay attention to and prepare for these rapidly advancing technologies.

Artificial Intelligence (AI)

AI is an umbrella concept that influences and is influenced by many disciplines, such as computer science, engineering, biology, psychology, mathematics, statistics, logic, philosophy, business, and linguistics (Buchanan, 2005; Kumar et al., 2016). AI can encompass anything from Apple Siri to Amazon Go, and from self-driving cars to autonomous weapons. Generally, AI can be classified into weak AI and strong AI. Weak AI, also known as narrow AI, excels in specific tasks. Most advancements in AI, that have been achieved to date, can be classified as weak AI, such as Google Assistance and Alpha Go. Researchers from different domains are, however, competing to create a strong AI (also called human-level artificial general intelligence or artificial super intelligence), which will process multiple tasks proficiently. A strong AI is the controversial and contentious concept. Many transhumanists believe that a strong AI can have self-awareness and become the equivalent of human intelligence. Once a strong AI becomes a reality, an intelligence explosion will be precipitated and technological singularity may be unavoidable. Superintelligence may emerge almost immediately after that (Müller & Bostrom, 2016). Superintelligence can be loosely defined as "any intellect that greatly exceeds the cognitive performance of humans in virtually all domains of interest" (Bostrom, 2014, p. 22). In other words, a strong AI would be able to outperform humans in nearly every cognitive task.

Automation

According to the Google dictionary, automation is the use of automatic equipment in a manufacturing system or other production process. In Wikipedia, automation is defined as "the technology by which a process or procedure is performed without human assistance." Basically, automation is a system or technology that automates some work that was previously done by humans. Parasuraman and Riley (1997, p. 2) defined automation as "the execution by a machine agent (usually a computer) of a function that has previously been carried out by a human". According to their analysis, automation changes over time and once automation is completely realized, it will be considered a machine. In another word, today's automation could be tomorrow's machine. Lee and See (2004, p. 50) define automation in a more detailed way. According to their definition, automation is a technology that "actively selects data, transforms information, makes decisions, or controls processes", as well as exhibiting potential to extend human performance and improve safety. Although automation has been defined in different ways, the common theme is that automation frees humans from time-consuming and repetitive tasks, whether the tasks involve physical functions and/or cognitive functions.

Automation usually follows pre-programmed 'rules' (Evans, 2017). Its purpose is to let machines perform monotonous tasks and free humans to focus on more complex, creative, and emotional tasks. Dishwashers, bar-code scanners, and automated assembly lines are examples of the application of automation.

Machine Learning

Arthur Samuel (2000) coined "machine learning" in 1959 and defined it as a field of study that enables computers to learn without being explicitly programmed. Although this definition is rather vague, it indicates a significant feature of machine learning – it does not follow pre-programmed "rules". In general, machine learning is an automated process that enables machines to analyze a huge data set, recognize patterns, and learn from the data to provide support for predictions and decision making. "Reinforcement machine learning", like the one used in AlphaGo Zero, starts from scratch with only the rules of the game, Go. It learned by adjusting actions, based on continuous feedback, and AlphaGo Zero achieved unbelievable results (i.e. probably the best Go "player" in the world at the moment) in a very short period of time (i.e. a few days). It discovered Go moves that were not known in the game's 3,000-4,000 years history. Reinforcement machine learning can also bypass human biases that may reside in data when using big data for training. Machine learning can be regarded as the automation of cognitive functions (Parasuraman & Riley, 1997), or the automation of knowledge work (Chui et al., 2016). AlphaGo and self-driving cars are products of machine learning, especially reinforcement learning. The drawback in machine learning, at the moment, is that the inner working of these self-learning machines is a black box, which makes it difficult to understand and explain the reasoning process and to justify the recommendations. As a result, trusting these machines is a challenge. Further, machine learning using big data can be susceptible to human biases that are inherent in the data (Lewis & Monett, 2017). People tend to only trust a system when the reasoning process is known and interpretable.

Robotics

Robotics is the technology used to develop machines, called robots, that can replicate human actions. Robots are given different names, according to their functions, such as military robots, agricultural robots, medical robots, and domestic robots. They are not necessarily like humans, since many are designed to carry out repetitive and dangerous tasks, rather than to perform high-precision and creative activities. Designers like to make robots resemble humans in appearance, which helps make them more easily accepted. Many robots can walk and talk like humans and perform tasks, such as lifting objects and carrying heavy loads. Artificial intelligent robots are also expected to learn by themselves, behave like humans, and even have the potential to surpass humans. In this case, a robot is actually an automation of physical functions (Parasuraman & Riley, 1997) and is directed by machine learning.

PROMISES AND BENEFITS

AI, in conjunction with other technologies, has the potential to address some of the biggest challenges that society faces. AI has enormous potential in business, manufacturing, healthcare, education, military, and many other areas. Numerous innovations have been developed using AI-based technology, such as facial recognition and self-driving cars. These applications require AI systems to interact with the real world and to make automatic decisions.

Self-Driving Vehicles and Drones

Through self-driving technology, it is expected that self-driving vehicles could reduce traffic accidents and deaths. In addition to land-based vehicles, self-driving technology has also enabled development of unmanned drones. Drones have become popular in various businesses and governmental organizations, especially in areas that are difficult for humans to reach or to perform efficiently, such as scanning an unreachable military base and quick deliveries at rush hours. Goldman Sachs estimates that "global militaries will spend $70 billion on drones by 2020, and these drones will play a vital role in the resolution of future conflicts and in replacing human pilots (Joshi, 2017).

AI in Education

The natural language processing capability of AI would benefit people who cannot read and write, and who cannot use computers (Prado, 2015). It is reported that artificial intelligence in U.S. education will grow by 47.5% from 2017 -2021 (Marr, 2018). AI can help release teachers from repetitive tasks such as grading and allow teachers to focus more on professional work (Siau, 2018). Besides, it is better to expose students to this technology early since they are highly likely to work with AI in the future. AI tools can also help make global classrooms available to all, including students who are not able to attend school. To stay up-to-date and ensure progress in our continuously changing world, these applications also need to support continuous life-long learning or never-ending learning (Stoica et al., 2017).

AI in Manufacturing and Factory Automation

AI has brought many benefits to the manufacturing industry, such as real-time maintenance of equipment and virtual design. For example, a generative design can be applied during manufacturing. Designer input design goals and the software can explore all possible permutations of a solution, quickly generate design alternatives, and enable the testing of their feasibility. It is possible to accomplish 50,000 days of engineering in one day (Insights team, 2018). There is no doubt that AI holds the key to future manufacturing growth.

AI in HR

AI streamlines human resource processes in many ways. Compared with humans, AI programs can sift through thousands of applications faster and more efficiently, with less unconscious bias. By identifying the traits of successful employees, AI can increase the chance of a company hiring the most qualified candidates which, in turn, will increase productivity and retention rates. It can also release human workers from repetitive paper work and providing answers to common questions. AI can also help to enhance diversity and inclusion in organizations. A word of caution, however, machine learning typically uses large data sets to learn and the data sets will have inherent biases from humans.

AI in Cybersecurity

Cybersecurity algorithms are critical to address the tsunami of cyberattacks. Cybersecurity analytics intelligence can help identify a possible attack before it actually takes place. Using AI and machine learning to help detect and respond to threats can ease the anxiety of cyber workers. In addition, AI can improve the efficiency of identifying threats, reduce the time needed to respond to incidents, and alert anomalous behavior in real time. Companies are already incorporating AI into every aspect of cybersecurity, including cyberintruder identification, prevention, threats detection, and risk analysis. This enables the redirection of human efforts to more critical activities.

AI in Military

AI benefits the military industry on many ways. For instance, combining AI autonomy with computer vision can impact the defense industry by enhancing decision-making and efficiency of soldiers. AI, along with virtual reality, are poised to be a game-changer for military planners, logistics, and military field use. Advances in AI are also enabling significant leaps forward in radio frequency systems. For facial recognition, AI is able to recognize a thermal image captured of a person's face in low-light conditions. Soldiers, who work in covert operations at night, may benefit from this development. AI in the military, however, is a very controversial topic, and many AI researchers and scientists are urging a ban on using AI as a killing machine.

AI at Home

AI is not only changing our workplace, but it is also changing the way we live in our homes. A connected home, combined with AI driven home automation, can take care of almost all daily chores done by humans, such as turning off lights, closing doors, monitoring temperature, playing music, and cleaning floors. Further, AI-powered home automation can reduce the energy consumption by controlling smart thermostats, lighting sensors, and smart plugs. The application of facial recognition algorithms can help detect break-ins and call for emergency services, thereby eliminating the need for human monitoring. Privacy is an issue in this domain.

AI in Health Care

AI-based applications can help improve patients' and elders' health conditions and the quality of their lives. Prime applications of AI in health care include monitoring medicine, treating chronic illness, diagnosing diseases, and surgery support. The National Bureau of Labor Statistics projects that the number of home health aides will grow by 38% over the next 10 years and the length of hospital stays will decrease due personalized rehabilitation and in-home therapy (Stanford University, 2016). From 2012 to 2017, healthcare-AI funding has reached $2.14 billion. AI-based applications in the medical field have achieved many successes, including mining social media to infer health risks, machine learning to predict risky patients, and robotics to support surgery (Hamet and Tremblay, 2017). In the palliative care field, studies show that only 20 percent of Americans spend their final days at home because of the shortage of palliative care professionals, although 80 percent of Americans prefer to be at home (Newby, 2018). AI can also help in predicting and identifying patients who have the most urgent needs for palliative care. From symptom diagnoses to clinical decision support, algorithms that leverage AI have made headlines in terms of accuracy and speed.

AI in Finance

AI in healthcare has a direct impact on finance too. According to Accenture analysis, the AI health market will grow by $6.6 billion by 2021, which can potentially create $150 billion in annual savings for the U.S. healthcare economy by 2026. Unlike traditional finance systems that are based on manually set rules and analytics, the AI-based system is shown to be more effective in detecting financial malfeasance with respect to accuracy and completeness. AI can help fight financial crimes, such as credit card fraud, anti-money laundering, and synthetic identity theft (Chen et al., 2004). Financial Technology (FinTech) is emerging as a transformative and strategic initiative for the financial industry (Siau et al., 2018).

AI and Hazardous Environment

The use of AI in a hazardous environment is growing because intelligent machines and systems are reliable and practical (Ema et al., 2016), and are better able to perform dangerous and laborious tasks than humans (Robert, 2017; Kumar et al., 2016). AI and robotics are designed and used to make safer working environments in fields such as nuclear energy, deep mining, and deep-sea operations. On one hand, robots are useful in situations where humans cannot be sent. On the other hand, AI can send quick and more accurate warnings. For instance, robots were used in the June 2010 Gulf of Mexico oil cleanup. With the help of robotics, human laborers can be freed from harsh and unsafe conditions, such as super high temperatures and freezing cold temperatures, extreme humidity, chemical risks, and nuclear radiation.

CHALLENGES AND ISSUES

Although AI has great potential as a cutting-edge technology, it poses significant risks for users and society. The risks mainly come from privacy concerns, data security, explicity, and transparency of algorithms, job replacement, trust and adoption, and ethical and governance issues. The concern is that the more advanced the AI is, the more risks it will bring to humanity and society. For instance, AI may make a decision that people cannot control and understand. Besides, AI may create unemployment and widen the inequality of wealth (Siau and Wang, 2018). Many big names in science and technology have recently expressed concerns about the risks posed by AI, partly because many AI milestones, which experts have generally viewed as being decades away, have been reached. Numerous AI researchers believe that human-level AI will happen before 2060 (Tegmark, 2016). Figure 1 depicts the four groups of challenges and issues that face AI.

Figure 1. Challenges and issues

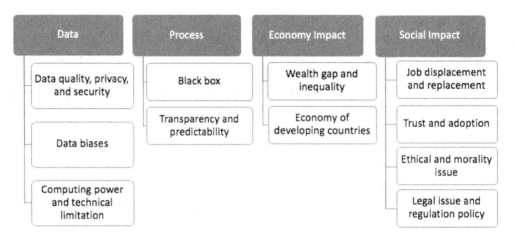

Data Quality, Privacy, and Security

To power AI technology, such as the deep learning systems, large volumes of quality data are needed. Almost all of the application domains, in which deep learning is successful, have had the ability to access mountains of data (LeCun, 2015), such as the Google Assistant and Apple Siri. Neil Lawrence, a professor at the University of Sheffield and on Amazon's AI team, said that data for AI is like coal for the early years of the industrial revolution; and big tech firms, like Google, Microsoft, and Facebook, are today's coal mines (Vincent, 2016). However, there are many smaller startups that have good ideas but are not able to access to data to support their ideas.

In addition to the quantity and quality of data, data security and privacy are very important (Chen and Zhao, 2012). With more data exposed in society and businesses, there is a higher chance that the data may be misused. For instance, to increase the accuracy of the healthcare system's performance, lots of data, including patients' sensitive information, are needed. Sensitive information is that information, which if publicly disclosed, could harm an individual socially and financially (Bansal and Gefen, 2015). A health record contains sensitive information. If that information is not adequately protected in a computer system, an unreliable individual or institution could gain access to that information and harm a patient, financially or personally.

Further, AI systems can cause serious damage if used maliciously. Cybersecurity is becoming even more critical when adversaries have accessed to and are using AI. Artificial super intelligence is a huge unknown risk. Many prominent scientists (e.g. Stephen Hawking) and technology executives (e.g. Elon Musk) are sounding the alarm. For instance, being asked to eradicate cancer in the world, an AI system may derive a solution that can accomplish the task, which could be killing everyone in the world (Bossmann, 2016).

The phones that we use every day may also pose risks to our privacy. Security experts warn that phones may listen, record, and process everything people say, and use private conversations to target ads or for other things. Many people have shared experiences that, even they never google or email about a specific product, they sometimes receive ads just a few hours after they have mentioned it in a casual conversion with others.

Data Biases and Technical Limitation

As mentioned earlier, one concern is human biases inherent in data (DeMartino et al., 2006). This issue is significant in risk assessment modeling, which can provide a decision as to whether a person should be convicted of a crime or rejected or approved for a loan. It is illegal to consider factors like race and gender in such cases. However, algorithms may be imbued with racial, gender, and other biases. For instance, Northpointe says its COMPAS algorithm does not include race as a variable when making recommendations on sentencing. However, in an investigation by ProPublica, journalists found evidence of racial bias, suggesting that COMPAS was likely biased to some age and racial groups (Snow, 2017). The biased data, fed into an algorithm, can also lead to unintentional discrimination in the delivery of care. For instance, the Framingham Heart Study evaluated cardiovascular event risk using data from predominantly white populations. This led to flawed clinical recommendations for nonwhite populations (Newby, 2018).

Today, AI algorithms are already routinely being used to make vital financial, medical, and legal decisions. If the bias lurking inside AI algorithms is not recognized, then there are likely to be negative consequences. Further, some individuals, who realize that algorithms may pose a risk of bias, are more interested in the bottom line than in rooting out biases (Knight, 2017).

From a technical perspective, the data challenge will be exacerbated by Moore's Law, which constrains the amount of data that AI-based technologies can store and process. It is claimed that the amount of data generated by the Internet of Everything devices for 2018 is almost 50x the estimated traffic in 2015 (Stoica, 2017). By 2025, the magnitude of improvements in the computer throughput requirements for processing the aggregate output of all genome sequences in the world will require that computation resources be at least doubled every year (Stoica, 2017).

"Black Box", Transparency, and Predictability

Although machine learning is creating brilliant tools, it is hard to explain the inner processing of machine learning. The "black box" inside its algorithms makes it mysterious, even to its creators and leads to significant information asymmetries among AI experts, users, and other stakeholders (Snoek et al. 2012). Using neural networks as an example, they are usually inscrutable to observers, and the reason why they reach certain decisions usually remains unexplained and unpredictable. Predictability is "the belief that the software artifact will do what it is claimed to do without adding anything malicious on top of it" (Paravastu et al., 2014, p. 34). AI systems that are predictable are naturally more dependable. Those systems can provide users with expected outcomes. In addition, these outcomes can be understood and interpreted by users. The "black-box" in ML algorithms, however, limits people's ability to understand the technology and outcomes, thereby hindering their trust in the system. To increase the transparency of AI, not only should the algorithm be transparent, but computational questions also need to be answered. For instance, what data are used, how these data are collected, and at which point do humans become involved in the decision-making process. Currently, the question as to whether a human can control the AI system is a big concern. As AI controls our cars, airplanes, and trading systems, we need to make certain that the AI system always does exactly what we want it to do. For example, Singapore has established principles that underpin the AI framework, so that decisions made by, or with the help of AI, should be explainable, transparent, and fair to consumers (Tan, 2019).

The more intelligent a machine is, the riskier it is that we will lose control of the machine (Spong, 1995). For instance, lethal autonomous weapons are programmed to fight and kill. In the hands of the wrong person, or when the weapons are out of human control, then these weapons may easily cause mass casualties. In order to avoid being thwarted by an enemy, these weapons are designed to be difficult to "turn off", which increases the risk of losing control in a combative situation. Further, as AI advances and becomes a strong AI, it may have goals that are not consistent with human goals. For instance, if a guest asks a self-driving taxi to drive to the airport as fast as possible, the taxi may not follow traffic rules, but reach the airport at the fastest speed. This is not what the customer wants, but that is literally what the customer asked for. More seriously, the strong AI may wreak havoc on our ecosystem and society as a side effect when achieving its goal.

Wealth Gap and Inequality

AI enables companies to drastically cut down on relying on a human workforce. Individuals who have ownership in AI-driven companies will increase in wealth, while the unemployed individuals will lose their source of income. A widening wealth gap has already happened. In 2014, the three largest companies in Detroit and the three largest companies in Silicon Valley generated roughly the same revenues, but Silicon Valley had 10 times fewer employees (Bossmann, 2016).

In other words, if robots and AI do most of the work and keep production high, then goods and services will be plentiful. This leads to new questions: How to distribute those goods and services to people who do not work and make no contribution? Should the robots be taxed? Universal Basic Income (UBI) was proposed to solve this problem. Although it appears to offer a simple and attractive solution, the feasibility of UBI is uncertain. Further, it may give rise to other problems, such as laziness and mental healthcare issues. UBI may discourage people from seeking retraining and reemployment, and domestic taxpayers may also flee (Re-educating Rita, 2019). As Ray Dalio said, it is "far better and it's possible to find ways for making most of these people productive" (Clifford, 2018).

Economy of Developing Countries

One of the direct threats posed by AI systems on the economy is unemployment. Industrial automation makes it harder for emerging economies, such as those in Africa and South America, to achieve economic growth. Many underdeveloped and developing countries offer cheaper labor in manufacturing areas, which enables them to grow and develop. However, factory automation has significantly decreased the need for companies to outsource their productions to countries with cheaper human labor. For the large body of less educated workers, countries may need to build unique, human-centered service industries (Re-educating Rita, 2019), which may be difficult.

Worse, developing countries may need to rely on the AI systems or robots that were created in developed countries. Also, the algorithms and databases that underlie the AI system may not apply to the conditions in developing countries. These countries have to carve out their own niches within the AI landscape (Lee, 2018), which is challenging.

Job Displacement and Replacement

Deloitte, in partnership with Oxford University, suggests that 35% of jobs will be at risk during the next 20 years (Wakefield, 2016). Scholars at Oxford University estimate that "no less than 47% of all-American jobs and 54% of those in Europe are at a high risk of being usurped by machines" (Bregman, 2017). McKinsey claims that as many as 700 million jobs could be gone by 2030. PwC suggests that 30% of those in the UK could be automated, compared to 38% in the US, 21% in Japan, and 77% in China (Rise of the robots, 2018). Foxconn, for example, which manufactures components for major brands, including Apple, recently replaced around 60,000 Chinese workers with robots. Historian Yuval Noah Harari (2016) wrote in his book that AI will create a 'useless class' of humans, who will be not only unemployed but also unemployable.

Even though AI does many tasks, that only humans could do previously, and has already replaced humans in many jobs, such as insurance assessment, accounting, truck driving, and healthcare assistants, people believe that new jobs or human-robot cooperative opportunities will be created. At least, jobs for humans will not simply disappear.

Jobs that are of a high risk of being replaced by AI are those that are routine, repetitive, and predictable. For instance, some toll booth operators have already been replaced by automated systems such as E-ZPass, cashiers have been replaced by Kiosks in McDonald's and Wendy's, and Amazon Go does not even have a checkout line or cash register. Other AI-based technologies, such as self-driving cars and IBM Watson, are still some way off, although they have been proved to be able to automatize jobs such as truck drivers and diagnosticians (Sherman, 2015).

Researchers noted that wages and educational attainments have exhibited a negative relationship with the probability of computerization (AI-based automation). Much manufacturing work, that requires moderate training and that once employed vast numbers of workers without college degrees, has disappeared, by either being shipped abroad or offloaded to robots and computers (TE, 2019). Jobs that require creative intelligence, social intelligence, strategy, and empathy are jobs with the lowest probability of computerization (Frey and Osborne, 2017). However, because AI is advancing rapidly and the job landscape is continuously changing, humans will need to figure out how to find meaning in non-labor activities and learn new ways to contribute to society.

Trust and Adoption

Trust is crucial in interpersonal relationships, human-technology interactions, and other relationships (Siau et al., 2004). It plays an important role in the adoption of new technology (Siau and Shen, 2003). Although AI's speed and capacity of processing are far beyond that of humans, it is not always competent, fair, neutral, and controllable. The risks of AI, such as AI biases and fatal self-driving car accidents, have created concerns about whether to trust AI, and to what extent. The black box in AI and machine learning algorithms have also influenced their credibility, because it is harder for people to trust what they do not understand and cannot control. Another concern that hinders people's ability to trust AI is "singularity." Once AI surpasses human intelligence, we will not be the most intelligent beings on earth anymore!

Ethical and Morality Issues

Although the concept of "machine ethics" has been proposed since 2006 (Anderson and Anderson, 2006), consideration of AI ethics is still in the infancy stage. Many researchers believe that AI is a long way from having consciousness and being comparable to humans and, consequently, there is no rush to consider the ethical issue. But AI, combined with other smart technology such as robotics, has already shown its potential in business, healthcare, and society. For instance, health robots now can diagnosis diseases and help in surgery. Who should take responsibility for a failed surgery in which a human doctor and a health robot worked together?

Currently, AI mainly refers to a weak AI, where its performance is primarily involved with training data and programming algorithms. Human experts, such as data owners and programmers, play an important role in training AI, and human users are crucial in manipulating AI-based applications. Two aspects that may cause an ethical issue for AI are AI features (Timmermans et al. 2010) and human factors (Larson, 2017). From the perspective of AI's features, it is possible for AI to get access to personal information without a host's knowledge. This is supported by research which has shown that AI can "generate audio that sounds like speech to machine learning algorithms but not to humans" (Carlini and Wagner, 2017). In addition, machine learning and deep learning are not always transparent upon inspection. The black-box in AI algorithms hinders human interpretation and expectations and may result in the evolution of AI that is without guidance or control (Wang and Siau, 2018). Worse, this may give rise to the risks of malicious utilization. From the perspective of human factors, the most significant is human bias. A weak AI, as discussed previously, relies mostly on training data. The existing biases in training data may be learned by the AI system and displayed in real applications. The second aspect is accountability, which leads to "the problem of many hands" (Timmermans et al., 2010). Who should be responsible for an undesirable consequence when using an AI system--the programmer, the data owner, the end user, or the AI per se? Besides the above two aspects, how to treat an AI system that has emotions and feelings is another consideration. For instance, would it be ethical to deploy robots into a dangerous environment?

Legal Issues and Regulation Policy

Many countries are actively creating legal conditions for the development of AI. In late March 2018, France presented new national artificial intelligence strategy, involving 1.5 billion Euros over the next 5 years, to support research in the AI field (Karliuk, 2018). The strategy aimed at four specific sectors: healthcare, transport, environment and environmental protection, and security. In the European Union, Civil Law Rules on Robotics marked the first step towards the regulation of AI. The resolution was not a binding document, but a number of recommendations were made to the European Commission on possible actions in the area of artificial intelligence, not only with regard to civil law, but also related to the ethical aspects of robotics (Karliuk, 2018). The UK's House of Lords also recommended the development of an ethical code of conduct for AI. The UK's upper chamber of parliament suggested that there be assurance that AI would be used in the public interests and that it would not be used to exploit or manipulate them (Teffer, 2018). Europe pins hope on AI ethics in the global AI race. However, although it is agreed that AI-specific laws should be adopted quickly, not many people know what those laws should look like.

RESEARCH AGENDA

Based on the above discussion, this paper proposes a research agenda with four streams, as shown in Table 1.

Table 1. Research agenda

Technique
• Computing power and technical challenges • Superintelligence • Emotional intelligence and personalized AI
Governance
• AI biases • AI governance and policy • Ethical issues and moral standards
Economy
• Economics model with AI
Human-Technology symbiosis
• Trust in AI • Adoption of AI • Human augmentation • Human-Machine/Robot interaction • Education and re-training

Computing Power and Technical Challenges

Before AI's potential can be achieved, many hurdles must be overcome. Computing power is a fundamental one (Franklin et al., 1997; Markoff, 2016). Machine learning requires a huge number of calculations, which should be completed very quickly. The concept, idea, and theory of AI have existed for more than 60 years, but the huge breakthroughs have only begun in the last few years. Many people have had good ideas, but there was not enough computing power to implement them. In the short term, cloud computing and massively-parallel processing systems can provide support but, as data volumes continue to grow and algorithms become more complex, a new generation of computing infrastructure is essential. Quantum computing is one such effort, and intensive research in this area is crucial.

The real world is changing rapidly. An AI system must be able to handle the fast-changing environment and be applicable to a different context quickly and safely, even when the environment or situation has never been encountered before. Continuous learning is important (Stoica, 2017).

Actually, AI is not one technology, but a set of technologies. To benefit the most from AI, many related technologies need to be advanced rapidly as well. Research concerned with the Internet of things, reinforcement learning, natural language processing, text analytics, and generative models are all crucial.

Superintelligence

Many well-known scientists and technology executives have expressed their concerns about AI, especially strong AI. Bill Gates called AI "a huge challenge" and something to "worry about". Stephen Hawking has warned about AI ending humanity. Elon Musk has likened AI to "summoning up the demon". Their references to AI refer to superintelligence, the intellect that can exceed the cognitive performance of humans, has consciousness, and can redesign itself at an ever-increasing rate. The biggest risks of superintelligence are its competence in enabling itself to accomplish its goals, and causing trouble when the goal is not aligned with human goals (Soares and Fallenstein, 2014). Some experts, however, are optimistic, believing that humans will always be the authors of whatever happens. Although the future is uncertain, we need to be certain about what kind of future we can expect. We believe that superintelligence should be just below human intelligence, playing the role of assistant and helper rather than the superintendent. How to create superintelligence that won't harm humans? What are the technical standards and ethical standards for superintelligence? We should have a blueprint before we start making it.

Another big concern is about the existential threat of AI to humanity. People believe that AI could someday result in human extinction, or some other unrecoverable global catastrophe (Bostrom, 2014). This is an under-researched area. Although many researchers and experts believe that superintelligence may be achieved "within a generation" (Hornigold, 2018), the research on safety issues is still in the infancy stage and lags behind.

Emotional Intelligence and Personalized AI

In the long run, an AI system which makes a user-specific decision that takes into account user behavior and preferences will be increasingly the focus. For instance, a virtual assistant learns the accent of its owner, the user, and the face-recognition software is already smart enough to analyze the smallest details of human facial expressions. Further, natural language processing algorithms help to figure out the human sentimental and emotional state from the audio (Alassarela, 2017). Big data and advanced algorithms enable AI to understand us better than we know ourselves. Personalized AI is easier for establishing an emotional connection with a human, and affecting a users' economic and psychological well-being. This area is developing rapidly and has huge potential.

AI Biases

AI systems are only as good as the data we put into them. As reinforcement learning and deep learning are more widely used, the AI system will continue to be trained to use the data. Once biased data are used, however, bias will become an ongoing problem (Verghese et al., 2018). Biases find their way into AI systems that are used to make decisions by many, from governments to businesses to academies. How can bias be eliminated from the data? How can algorithms be written that can eliminate bias? How can biased data be distinguished from good data? All of these questions remain to be answered.

AI Governance and Policy

Given that the threats of AI are indisputably real, governance and regulation are inevitable and necessary. In the last 1-2 years, academics, technology companies, and governments have begun to concentrate on setting standards and guidelines for AI. Transparency, responsibility, human control, biases, and ethics have received the most attention (Wang and Siau, 2018b), and should certainly be considered when setting up a legal framework and policies related to AI. Google, partnered with Microsoft, IBM, Apple, Facebook, and Amazon, has set up a partnership to provide a "trusted and expert point of contact" on the ethical and governance issues. Governments are beginning to respond too. For instance, Germany is drafting a set of ethical guidelines for driverless cars. Good governance would help build trust in AI and benefit economy and society to a maximum extent.

Ethical Issues and Moral Standards

As AI and robotics continue to advance, they will inevitably affect human lives. Human-machine interactions and human-robot interactions will grow significantly. As Torrance (2011) mentioned, an ethical agent can be classified in two categories: ethical productivity and ethical receptivity. In a human-robot interaction, an AI-based robot could either be an ethical producer (such as robots that assist in a surgery) or be ethical recipients (such as military robots that are commanded to dispose of a bomb). To study the ethical issues related to AI, from these two different perspectives, is essential.

Human ethics today are not perfect. On one hand, a human cannot solve all the recognized ethical issues. On the other hand, a human cannot recognize all the ethical issues. As early as 2007, Anderson and Anderson indicated that "The ultimate goal of machine ethics is to create a machine that itself follows an ideal ethical principle or set of principles" (p. 15). Without comprehensive and unbiased ethical standards, how can humans train a machine to be ethical? Further, how can we make sure that intelligent machines understand ethical standards in the same way that we do? To answer these two questions, additional research is needed. First, one should learn about current ethical standards and the proper ethical standards that are needed to train intelligent machines. Second, one should learn how to reduce information asymmetries between AI programmers and ethical standards makers.

While attempting to formulate ethical standards for AI and intelligent machines, researchers should try to understand existing ethical principles better. Thus, they will be able to contribute to the application of ethical principles to academic activities and help train programmers build an ethical AI, as well as build the AI ethically (Wang and Siau, 2018).

Economics Model With AI

PwC estimates that AI could add $15.7trn to the global economy by 2030. How will AI impact economic growth? How will AI help save costs? What changes will AI bring to the global economy? Bill Gates said recently that the law of supply and demand is over. Traditionally, the Gross Domestic Product, used as a benchmark for an economy's well-being, does not calculate investment in intangible elements, such as research and development (Konchitchki and Patatoukas, 2014). But today, as technical companies and technical products occupy a large market share, this economic model should change. On one hand, the cost of software-based products does not increase as quantities increase, which is the foundation of the law of supply and demand. On the other hand, the tools used by companies to measure intangible assets are behind the times. To get a complete picture of our economy, a new economic model should be created.

Further, the Internet of things makes the world smaller. Economic activities have merged globally rather than being limited to a company or a country. It is important to always keep an eye on global economic trends. The large increase in income inequality, caused by AI, is another big concern (Jenkins 2017). Wealth will be gathered by those who control AI and robots. Meanwhile, human workers will be replaced by those technologies because their labor costs are much higher than the costs for robot workers. Bill Gates once said that robots that take human jobs should pay taxes. But researchers believe that taxing robots is only a short-term solution (Gasteiger and Prettner, 2017). Retraining people for a new job environment is one solution. Another suggestion is the Universal Basic Income (UBI) (Sage and Diamond, 2017). Is the UBI a good idea? Research needs to be done before answering this question.

Trust in AI

Considering the potential risks that exist when trust in AI is hindered, the question of how to build such trust must be seriously considered. Many studies concerning trust have been conducted (Siau and Shen, 2003, Siau and Wang, 2018). To study trust in AI, the focus should be to identify the difference between AI and other things, such as a human, an organization, e-commerce, and machines. A trust-building model is necessary for appropriate development of that trust. Case studies and behavioral studies can be employed more in research about trust building.

Adoption of AI

As AI becomes smarter and more useful, to what extent should humans adopt it? From an individual perspective, AI can benefit humanity, especially with doing routine or dangerous tasks. Although people would be happy to adopt a robotic vacuum cleaner, the McDonald's Kiosk, and Amazon Alexa but, to what extent people would like to adopt autonomous weapons or robot doctors? From an industry perspective, a survey showed that AI adoption in 2017 remained relatively low with ta majority of the major success stories coming from the largest tech players in the industry (e.g., Google, Baidu, Apple) (Rayo, 2018). The most significant reasons include the experimental status of AI application, its lack of use, and insufficient financial commitment. To increase the adoption of AI, research should focus on building an adoption model of AI.

A Technology Acceptance Model (TAM) can provide some useful insights. TAM is a preeminent theory of technology acceptance in Information System research (Gefen et al., 2003). TAM indicates that acceptance of a new information technology is determined by its perceived usefulness (PU) and the perceived ease of use (PEOU) (Holden and Karsh 2010). PU and PEOU should also be considered as contributors to trust building (Pavlou and Gefen, 2004; Harris and Goode, 2004; Vance et al., 2008).

Human Augmentation

As AI-based robotics develop further, the future human can be stronger, faster, and less prone to injury. Human capacities may be extended beyond innate physiological levels. For instance, robotics has already advanced wearable supernumerary limbs and enabled additional limbs to extend physical abilities beyond traditional limits (Parietti and Asada, 2016). This area has been a great benefit for disabled individuals.

Human-Machine/Robot Interaction

With the development of Natural Language Processing, the Internet of Things, eye-tracking, and neurotechnology, the interactions between humans and machines exist everywhere. As robotics advances, it becomes more and more important to develop a robot that is not solely functional, but also mindful of its users (Sheridan, 2016). One study found that top doctors made erroneous decisions in 3.5% of cases, while state-of-the-art AI had an error rate of 7.5%; when the two are combined, the error rate can drop to 0.5%. In addition to the technologies that support human-machine interaction, the way and method in which humans interact with machines should also be studied. The motivation behind interaction (Robert, 2018), privacy concerns of human workers, and the trust between humans and robots are important research topics.

Education and Re-Training

Jobs that require fewer skills and contain routine tasks are easier to automate. Ownet, a consultancy company, has developed an AI tool that can scan 10,000 contracts in 50 seconds, which would cost a human 3,300 hours. Deloitte believes that 39% of legal roles could be automated within a decade, and another study indicates that 95% of accountants could lose their jobs. From construction workers to journalists, AI has shown the potential to do some parts of their jobs. PWC says that individuals with only a few educational qualifications are more vulnerable than PhD-touting scientists (Rise of the robots, 2018). From this perspective, education and re-training would make a significant contribution.

Although traditional job positions may disappear, and their required skills be useless in the future, new job categories could be created and some skills, such as programming and human-machine interaction, would become very important. According to the Royal Society, 58,000 data science jobs are being created every year in the UK alone, and it is hard to find qualified people to fill them. It is reported that 70 percent of the fastest-growing skills are new to the index and 65 percent of children will end up in jobs that do not exist yet (Kasriel, 2018).

What kind of education should be provided? What type of course structure would be proper for a future career plan? What retraining should be provided so that human workers remain competent to compete in the job market? John Hawksworth, the PWC's chief economist, said "If, back in the 1980s, when I was leaving university, someone had told me they were going to be a web designer, I wouldn't have known what on Earth they were talking about because that job didn't exist" (Rise of the robots, 2018, p. 16). In this case, we can expect that entirely new skills will be emerging in the future, bringing challenges to transform education. Besides, jobs requiring the human touches, such as nurses, artists, and social workers, seem less likely to be replaced by AI. In addition to teaching knowledge and professional skills, education and re-training should pay more attention to the training of social skills, creativity, and human skills. In other words, the benefits of automation and robotics should be used to help fund continuous education and retraining.

CONCLUSION

Distilling a generally-accepted definition of what qualifies as artificial intelligence (AI) has been attempted for many decades. One reason why a definition is hard to get is that AI is not a single technology, but a consolidation of many disciplines. From machine learning to robotics, to natural language processing and the Internet of Things, AI plays an important role in the modern technology world and has merged into our daily life. Consequently, many problems should be considered in conducting research on AI. The research agenda proposed in this paper lists some potential directions for future study. Although the technical aspects of AI, such as reinforcement learning and generative models, deserve much attention, the research agenda also focuses on the impact of AI and on topics that are closely related to human work, society, and humanity. The future of work and the future of humanity are at least as important, if not more important, than the technical aspects of AI.

REFERENCES

Alasaarela, M. (2017). The rise of emotionally intelligent AI. *Macine Learnings*. Retrieved from https://machinelearnings.co/the-rise-of-emotionally-intelligent-ai-fb9a814a630e

Anderson, M., & Anderson, S. L. (2006). Guest Editors' Introduction: Machine Ethics. *IEEE Intelligent Systems*, *21*(4), 10–11. doi:10.1109/MIS.2006.70

Anderson, M., & Anderson, S. L. (2007). The status of machine ethics: A report from the AAAI Symposium. *Minds and Machines*, *17*(1), 1–10. doi:10.100711023-007-9053-7

Bansal, G., & Gefen, D. (2015). The role of privacy assurance mechanisms in building trust and the moderating role of privacy concern. *European Journal of Information Systems*, *24*(6), 624–644. doi:10.1057/ejis.2014.41

Bloem, J., Van Doorn, M., Duivestein, S., Excoffier, D., Maas, R., & Van Ommeren, E. (2014). The Fourth Industrial Revolution—Things to Tighten the Link between IT and OT. In *Sogeti VINT2014*.

Bossmann, J. (2016). Top 9 ethical issues in artificial intelligence. *World Economic Forum*. Retrieved from https://www.weforum.org/agenda/2016/10/top-10-ethical-issues-in-artificial-intelligence/

Bostrom, N. (2014). *Superintelligence: Paths, dangers, strategies*. OUP Oxford.

Bregman, R. (2017). A growing number of people think their job is useless. Time to rethink the meaning of work. *World Economic Forum*. Retrieved from https://www.weforum.org/agenda/2017/04/why-its-time-to-rethink-the-meaning-of-work/

Buchanan, B. G. (2005). A (very) brief history of artificial intelligence. *AI Magazine, 26*(4), 53–60. Retrieved from http://libproxy.mst.edu:2048/login?url=https://search-proquest-com.libproxy.mst.edu/docview/208132026?accountid=14594

Carlini, N., & Wagner, D. (2017). Towards evaluating the robustness of neural networks. In *Proceedings of the 2017 IEEE Symposium on* Security and Privacy (SP) (pp. 39-57).

Chen, D., & Zhao, H. (2012). Data security and privacy protection issues in cloud computing. *In 2012 International Conference on Computer Science and Electronics Engineering (ICCSEE)* (Vol. 1, pp. 647-651). IEEE.

Chen, H., Chung, W., Xu, J. J., Wang, G., Qin, Y., & Chau, M. (2004). Crime data mining: A general framework and some examples. *Computer, 37*(4), 50–56. doi:10.1109/MC.2004.1297301

Chui, M., Manyika, J., & Miremadi, M. (2016). Where machines could replace humans—and where they can't (yet). *McKinsey Digital*. Retrieved from https://www.mckinsey.com/where-machines-could-replace-humans

Clifford, C. (2018). Billionaire Ray Dalio: A.I. is widening the wealth gap, 'national emergency should be declared.' *CNBC*. Retrieved from https://www.cnbc.com/2018/07/06/bridgewaters-dalio-posts-on-ai-wealth-gap-capitalism-on-facebook.html

De Martino, B., Kumaran, D., Seymour, B., & Dolan, R. J. (2006). Frames, biases, and rational decision-making in the human brain. *Science, 313*(5787), 684–687. doi:10.1126cience.1128356 PMID:16888142

Ema, A., Akiya, N., Osawa, H., Hattori, H., Oie, S., Ichise, R., ... Miyano, N. (2016). Future relations between humans and artificial intelligence: A stakeholder opinion survey in Japan. *IEEE Technology and Society Magazine, 35*(4), 68–75. doi:10.1109/MTS.2016.2618719

Evans, D. (2017). So, what's the Real Difference Between AI and Automation? *Medium*. Retrieved from https://medium.com/the-real-difference-between-ai-and-automation

Franklin, S., Wolpert, S., McKay, S. R., & Christian, W. (1997). Artificial minds. *Computers in Physics, 11*(3), 258–259. doi:10.1063/1.4822552

Frey, C. B., & Osborne, M. A. (2017). The future of employment: How susceptible are jobs to computerization? *Technological Forecasting and Social Change, 114*, 254–280. doi:10.1016/j.techfore.2016.08.019

Gasteiger, E., & Prettner, K. (2017). A note on automation, stagnation, and the implications of a robot tax.

Gefen, D., Karahanna, E., & Straub, D. W. (2003). Trust and TAM in online shopping: An integrated model. *Management Information Systems Quarterly, 27*(1), 51–90. doi:10.2307/30036519

Hamet, P., & Tremblay, J. (2017). Artificial intelligence in medicine. *Metabolism: Clinical and Experimental, 69*, S36–S40. doi:10.1016/j.metabol.2017.01.011 PMID:28126242

Harari, Y. N. (2016). *Homo Deus: A brief history of tomorrow*. Random House.

Harris, L. C., & Goode, M. M. (2004). The four levels of loyalty and the pivotal role of trust: A study of online service dynamics. *Journal of Retailing, 80*(2), 139–158. doi:10.1016/j.jretai.2004.04.002

Holden, R. J., & Karsh, B. T. (2010). The technology acceptance model: Its past and its future in health-care. *Journal of Biomedical Informatics*, *43*(1), 159–172. doi:10.1016/j.jbi.2009.07.002 PMID:19615467

Hornigold, T. (2018). When Will We Finally Achieve True Artificial Intelligence. *SingularityHub*. Retrieved from https://singularityhub.com/2018/01/01/when-will-we-finally-achieve-true-artificial-intelligence/#sm.00001azv7jc2gld26qgto4a94uxnr

Insights team. (2018). How AI Builds A Better Manufacturing Process. *Forbes*. Retrieved from https://www.forbes.com/sites/insights-intelai/2018/07/17/how-ai-builds-a-better-manufacturing-process/#6a4975641e84

Joshi, D. (2017). Exploring the latest drone technology for commercial, industrial and military drone uses. *Business Insider*. Retrieved from https://www.businessinsider.com/drone-technology-uses-2017-7

Karliuk, M. (2018). The ethical and legal issues of artificial intelligence. *Modern Diplomacy*. Retrieved from https://moderndiplomacy.eu/2018/04/24/the-ethical-and-legal-issues-of-artificial-intelligence/

Kasriel, S. (2018). The future of work won't be about college degrees, it will be about job skills. *CNBC*. Retrieved from https://www.cnbc.com/2018/10/31/the-future-of-work-wont-be-about-degrees-it-will-be-about-skills.html

Knight, W. (2017). Biased algorithms are everywhere, and no one seems to care. *MIT Technology Review*. Retrieved from https://www.technologyreview.com/s/608248/biased-algorithms-are-everywhere-and-no-one-seems-to-care/

Konchitchki, Y., & Patatoukas, P. N. (2014). Accounting earnings and gross domestic product. *Journal of Accounting and Economics*, *57*(1), 76–88. doi:10.1016/j.jacceco.2013.10.001

Kumar, N., Kharkwal, N., Kohli, R., & Choudhary, S. 2016, February. Ethical aspects and future of artificial intelligence. In *Proceedings of the 2016 International Conference on Innovation and Challenges in Cyber Security (ICICCS-INBUSH)* (pp. 111-114). IEEE. 10.1109/ICICCS.2016.7542339

Larson, B. N. (2017). Gender as a variable in natural-language processing: Ethical considerations. Retrieved from https://scholarship.law.tamu.edu/facscholar/832

LeCun, Y., Bengio, Y., & Hinton, G. (2015). Deep learning. *Nature*, *521*(7553), 436–444. doi:10.1038/nature14539 PMID:26017442

Lee, J. D., & See, K. A. (2004). Trust in automation: Designing for appropriate reliance. *Human Factors*, *46*(1), 50–80. doi:10.1518/hfes.46.1.50.30392 PMID:15151155

Lee, K. F. (2018). AI could devastate the developing world. Bloomberg Opinion. *Bloomberg*. Retrieved from https://www.bloomberg.com/opinion/articles/2018-09-17/artificial-intelligence-threatens-jobs-in-developing-world

Lewis, C., & Monett, D. (2017). AI & Machine Learning Black Boxes: The Need for Transparency and Accountability. *KDnuggets*. Retrieved from https://www.kdnuggets.com/2017/04/ai-machine-learning-black-boxes-transparency-accountability.html

Mack, E. (2018). These 27 expert predictions about artificial intelligence will both disturb and excite you. *Inc*. Retrieved from https://www.inc.com/eric-mack/heres-27-expert-predictions-on-how-youll-live-with-artificial-intelligence-in-near-future.html

Markoff, J. (2016). *Machines of loving grace: The quest for common ground between humans and robots*. HarperCollins Publishers.

Marr, B. (2018). How Is AI Used in Education -- Real World Examples of Today And A Peek Into The Future? *Forbes*. Retrieved from https://www.forbes.com/sites/bernardmarr/2018/07/25/how-is-ai-used-in-education-real-world-examples-of-today-and-a-peek-into-the-future/#4855bdf6586e

Müller, V. C., & Bostrom, N. (2016). Future progress in artificial intelligence: A survey of expertopinion. In *Fundamental issues of artificial intelligence* (pp. 553–570). Springer International Publishing. doi:10.1007/978-3-319-26485-1_33

Newby, K. (2018). Compassionate intelligence - Can machine learning bring more humanity to health care? *Stanford Medicine*. Retrieved from http://stanmed.stanford.edu/2018summer/artificial-intelligence-puts-humanity-health-care.html

Parasuraman, R., & Riley, V. (1997). Humans and automation: Use, misuse, disuse, abuse. *Human Factors*, *39*(2), 230–253. doi:10.1518/001872097778543886

Paravastu, N., Gefen, D., & Creason, S. B. (2014). Understanding trust in IT artifacts: An evaluation of the impact of trustworthiness and trust on satisfaction with antiviral software. *ACM SIGMIS Database: the DATABASE for Advances in Information Systems*, *45*(4), 30–50. doi:10.1145/2691517.2691520

Parietti, F., & Asada, H. (2016). Supernumerary robotic limbs for human body support. *IEEE Transactions on Robotics*, *32*(2), 301–311. doi:10.1109/TRO.2016.2520486

Pavlou, P. A., & Gefen, D. (2004). Building effective online marketplaces with institution-based trust. *Information Systems Research*, *15*(1), 37–59. doi:10.1287/isre.1040.0015

Peters, M. A. (2017). Technological unemployment: Educating for the fourth industrial revolution. *Educational Philosophy and Theory*, *49*(1), 1–6. doi:10.1080/00131857.2016.1177412

Prado, G. M. D. (2015). 18 Artificial intelligence researchers reveal the profound changes coming to our lives. *Business Insider*. Retrieved from http://www.businessinsider.com/researchers-predictions-future-artificial-intelligence-2015-10/

PwC. (2016). Global data and analytics survey - big decisions. Retrieved from https://www.pwc.com/us/en/analytics/big-decision-survey.html

Rayo, E. A. (2018). AI and ML Adoption Survey Results from Applied Artificial Intelligence Conference 2017. *Emerj*. Retrieved from https://www.techemergence.com/ai-and-ml-adoption-survey-results-from-applied-artificial-intelligence-conference-2017/

Re-educating Rita-Artificial intelligence will have implications for policymakers in education, welfare and geopolitics. (2019). *The Economist*. Retrieved from https://www.economist.com/special-report/2016/06/25/re-educating-rita

Robert, L. P. (2017). The Growing Problem of Humanizing Robots. *International Robotics & Automation Journal*, *3*(1), 00043. doi:10.15406/iratj.2017.03.00043

Robert, L. P. (2018). Motivational theory of human robot teamwork. *Int Rob Auto J.*, *4*(4), 248–251. doi:10.15406/iratj.2018.04.00131

Sage, D., & Diamond, P. (2017). Europe's New Social Reality: The Case Against Universal Basic Income. *Europe's New Social Reality*.

Samuel, A. L. (2000). Some studies in machine learning using the game of checkers. *IBM Journal of research and development*, *44*(1.2), 206-226.

Sheridan, T. B. (2016). Human–robot interaction: Status and challenges. *Human Factors*, *58*(4), 525–532. doi:10.1177/0018720816644364 PMID:27098262

Siau, K. (2018). Education in the Age of Artificial Intelligence: How will Technology Shape Learning? *The Global Analyst*, *7*(3), 22–24.

Siau, K., Hilgers, M., Chen, L., Liu, S., Nah, F., Hall, R., & Flachsbart, B. (2018). FinTech Empowerment: Data Science, Artificial Intelligence, and Machine Learning. *Cutter Business Technology Journal*, *31*(11/12), 12–18.

Siau, K., & Shen, Z. (2003). Building customer trust in mobile commerce. *Communications of the ACM*, *46*(4), 91–94. doi:10.1145/641205.641211

Siau, K., Sheng, H., Nah, F., & Davis, S. (2004). A qualitative investigation on consumer trust in mobile commerce. *International Journal of Electronic Business*, *2*(3), 283–300. doi:10.1504/IJEB.2004.005143

Siau, K., & Wang, W. (2018). Building Trust in Artificial Intelligence, Machine Learning, and Robotics. *Cutter Business Technology Journal*, *31*(2), 47–53.

Snoek, J., Larochelle, H., & Adams, R. P. (2012). Practical bayesian optimization of machine learning algorithms. *Advances in Neural Information Processing Systems*, 2951–2959.

Snow, J. (2017). New research aims to solve the problem of AI bias in 'black box' algorithms. *MIT Technology Review*. Retrieved from https://www.technologyreview.com/s/609338/new-research-aims-to-solve-the-problem-of-ai-bias-in-black-box-algorithms/

Soares, N., & Fallenstein, B. (2014). Aligning superintelligence with human interests: A technical research agenda. *Machine Intelligence Research Institute (MIRI)*.

Spong, M. W. (1995). The swing up control problem for the acrobot. *IEEE control systems*, *15*(1), 49-55.

Stoica, I., Song, D., Popa, R. A., Patterson, D., Mahoney, M. W., Katz, R., . . . Abbeel, P. (2017). A berkeley view of systems challenges for ai. arXiv:1712.05855

Stone, P., Brooks, R., Brynjolfsson, E., Calo, R., Etzioni, O., Hager, G., . . . Teller, A. (2016). Artificial Intelligence and Life in 2030. In *One Hundred Year Study on Artificial Intelligence*. Retrieved from http://ai100.stanford.edu/2016-report

Tan, S. (2019). Singapore releases framework on how AI can be ethically used. *The Straits Times*. Retrieved from https://www.straitstimes.com/singapore/singapore-releases-model-governance-framework-for-ai

Teffer, P. (2018). EU in race to set global artificial intelligence ethics standards. *EU observer*. Retrieved from https://euobserver.com/science/141681

Tegmark, M. (2016). Benefits and risks of artificial intelligence. *The Future of Life Institute*. Retrieved from https://futureoflife.org/background/benefits-risks-of-artificial-intelligence/

The outlook is dim for Americans without college degrees. (2019). *The Economists*. Retrieved from https://www.economist.com/finance-and-economics/2019/01/10/the-outlook-is-dim-for-americans-without-college-degrees

Timmermans, J., Stahl, B. C., Ikonen, V., & Bozdag, E. 2010. The ethics of cloud computing: A conceptual review. In Proceedings of the *IEEE Second International Conference* on Cloud Computing Technology and Science (pp. 614-620). IEEE.

Torrance, S. (2011). Machine ethics and the idea of a more-than-human moral world. *Machine Ethics*, 115-137.

Vance, A., Elie-Dit-Cosaque, C., & Straub, D. W. (2008). Examining trust in information technology artifacts: The effects of system quality and culture. *Journal of Management Information Systems*, *24*(4), 73–100. doi:10.2753/MIS0742-1222240403

Verghese, A., Shah, N. H., & Harrington, R. A. (2018). What this computer needs a physician: Humanism and artificial intelligence. *Journal of the American Medical Association*, *319*(1), 19–20. doi:10.1001/jama.2017.19198 PMID:29261830

Vincent, J. (2016). These are three of the biggest problems facing today's AI. *The Verge*. Retrieved from https://www.theverge.com/2016/10/10/13224930/ai-deep-learning-limitations-drawbacks

Wakefield, J. (2016). Foxconn replaces 60,000 factory workers with robots. *BBC*. Retrieved from http://www.bbc.com/news/technology-36376966?SThisFB

Wang, W., & Siau, K. (2018a). Ethical and Moral Issues with AI. In *AMCIS 2018 Conference*.

Wang, W., & Siau, K. (2018b). Artificial Intelligence: A Study on Governance, Policies, and Regulations. In *MWAIS 2018 Conference*.

Wright, M. (2018). Rise of the sew-bots: Asian factory workers feel chill winds of automation. *Ethical Corporation*. Retrieved from http://www.ethicalcorp.com/rise-sewbots-asian-factory-workers-feel-chill-winds-automation

This research was previously published in the Journal of Database Management (JDM), 30(1); pages 61-79, copyright year 2019 by IGI Publishing (an imprint of IGI Global).

Chapter 77
Big Data and Machine Learning:
A Way to Improve Outcomes in Population Health Management

Fernando Enrique Lopez Martinez
University of Oviedo, Spain

Edward Rolando Núñez-Valdez
University of Oviedo, Spain

ABSTRACT

IoT, big data, and artificial intelligence are currently three of the most relevant and trending pieces for innovation and predictive analysis in healthcare. Many healthcare organizations are already working on developing their own home-centric data collection networks and intelligent big data analytics systems based on machine-learning principles. The benefit of using IoT, big data, and artificial intelligence for community and population health is better health outcomes for the population and communities. The new generation of machine-learning algorithms can use large standardized data sets generated in healthcare to improve the effectiveness of public health interventions. A lot of these data come from sensors, devices, electronic health records (EHR), data generated by public health nurses, mobile data, social media, and the internet. This chapter shows a high-level implementation of a complete solution of IoT, big data, and machine learning implemented in the city of Cartagena, Colombia for hypertensive patients by using an eHealth sensor and Amazon Web Services components.

INTRODUCTION

Big Data and artificial intelligence are currently two of the most important and trending pieces for innovation and predictive analysis in health care. For big data, Internet of Things (IoT) is one of the primary sources for data acquisition nowadays in health care, allowing patients with network connectivity to send and receive data in real-time to patient-centric platforms that collect and monitor patient information. The health care industry represents significant opportunities for machine learning (ML), big data and

DOI: 10.4018/978-1-6684-6291-1.ch077

IoT. These paradigms, tools, and techniques are helping providers around the world to produce better outcomes for patients, communities and population health management.

Because many health care organizations are already working on developing their own intelligent big data analytics systems based on machine learning principles, this paper will discuss how these two components are the new pillars of population health management, value-based care and upcoming challenges in health care.

We are experiencing a new era of information in health care, a decade of progress in digitalization of medical records, usage of health wearables and monitoring devices. Electronic pharmaceutical services, insurance claims, conversations about health in social media and years of research of organizations aggregating data in electronic databases has generated according to Harvard business review magazine since 2012, 2.5 quintillion terabytes of data every day. This vast amount of data generated and collected comes in multiple forms making the extraction and integration a real challenge. The actual value of big data and IoT can be captured easily in health care and is very important to review how this data can be usable, searchable and actionable by the health care industry and specifically in the area of population health management. This collection, integration, and treatment of data will require collaboration between the public and private sector to enable the research community to better access, manage, and utilize IoT objects (smart devices, sensors, smart beds, etc.) and big data.

IoT is gaining more attention every day, and the demand for intelligent and connected devices provides a new level of opportunities to collect data at home and improve the interaction with the health care professionals.

On the other hand, generating new knowledge and predictive analysis is where Machine learning takes action in our article. The generation of machine learning (ML) algorithms that can use these immense data sets generated in health care and collected by interconnected devices might improve the quality and efficiency in several health care areas such as readmissions, treatment optimization, and population health management.

This article will show how the primary goal of health care data analytics is the combination of technologies, strategies, and techniques that allow analyzing clinical data from different sources to determine appropriate insights to improve the outcome of health care and to improve population health management. This article also shows how transforming this knowledge into practice is another challenge, this will require a change in current practices and most important practice-changing decisions.

For several years researchers have been working with health care organizations trying to improve the process of data collection, data aggregation, data analysis and decision-making process. A lot of them has succeeded enabling clinicians and health care facilities to generate insights from big data and the use of machine learning algorithms straight to the care of an individual patient or to a group of people by analyzing the data of their treatment, their socio – economic environment and their health habits. The expectation is to show what is out there that works and for whom, the complexities, needs, and challenges.

BACKGROUND

Population health management is the aggregation of patient data across multiple health information technology resources, the analysis of that data and the actions that care providers can use to improve clinical and financial outcomes of a group of individuals (Kindig, 2003). A population health management objective is to give real-time insights to health providers based on clinical, operational and financial data from a population and provides analytics to improve efficiency and patient care.

The first challenge is to aggregate and normalize the enormous amount of data across different EHR platforms and external sources like wearables and sensors. The data in health care is typically so vast and complex that it is hard to manage with traditional data management methods (Priyanka, 2014) and some of this data by its nature needs to be collected and analyzed in real-time. When the data exceeds the traditional capacity of conventional database systems, and it is generated and collected too fast, the concept of big data appears in the scene. Big data is a term that describes large volumes of high velocity, complex and variable data that requires advanced techniques and technologies to enable the capture, storage, distribution, management and analysis of the information (TechAmerica Foundation paper, 2012). Big data in health care is massive amounts of generated genomic, clinical, behavioral, business, and financial data. And, information generated from sensors and wearable's devices. Internet of Things (IoT), is a powerful paradigm that provides to healthcare, tools, and mechanism for data acquisition, data gathering and data transferring (Mustafa Abdullah, 2016). This healthcare monitoring includes body and environmental sensors, communication and networking devices and processing and analyzing nodes.

Population health management usually requires the collection of heterogeneous data from multiple sources plus the application of advanced analytics models to improve clinical operations and public health. These advanced analytics models refer to predictive modeling and transformation of this data into actionable information.

Colombia is creating personalized care programs to reduce healthcare costs to the government, reduce the number of hospitalizations in healthcare facilities and to reduce the number of patients in the emergency rooms. To do what has been mentioned before, the government is providing incentives to use technology for patient monitoring at their homes. Several research groups are creating Wireless Body Area Networks (WBAN) and Wireless Personal Area Networks (WPAN) to track and monitor population health. The data generated in this networks are large in volume, and some of the research groups need assistance and supervision on how to retrieve and analyze patient's information in real time, and how to generate meaningful statistics and visualizations with this data.

Big data analytics has been used in personalized care in different countries (Patidar, 2017) with a huge success with sensors and wireless networks in patient's health monitoring. This information in the form of "big data" is complex to analyze and store and requires specialized frameworks and architectures to be manipulated, treated and obtain insights of it.

IoT IN POPULATION HEALTH

Internet of Things (IoT) has been used in healthcare since the 2000s but just recently is taking the importance it deserves. Health care professionals know the potential and value that comes from patient data about personal health. IoT provides a perfect tool to observing patient behavior thru the use of personal health devices and sensors, allowing healthcare providers to monitor patient's health proactively. Health care is taking advantage of IoT to gather patient's information from various devices and integrate and analyze that information to provide insights and recommendations for healthy behaviors.

The devices used in IoT in health care can be categorized in:

- **Clinical Monitoring:** Are integrated and discrete sensors and signal conditioning technology used for study monitoring at the healthcare facility (Dan S Karbing, 2017). Some samples are Smart beds, Smart pumps, Smart monitors, ECG Patient Monitoring, Pulse transit time capture with many different methodologies such as bio potential and optical sensors, Respiration Measurement.

- **At Home Monitoring:** Are all wearable and sensors that can measure critical physiological indicators such as activity levels, sleep, blood pressure, heart rate, EEG and ECG at the patient's home. Some samples are, glucose monitor, oximetry monitor, weight and blood glucose monitors

- **Personal Health:** All personal devices used to track and monitor personal health. Some samples are, smart watches to monitor resting heart rate (RHR), heart rate (HR), recovery time, V02 max, movement, sleep, wireless-connected scale to measure weight, fat mass, bone mass, muscle mass, water and blood pressure monitors.

- **Ingestible Devices:** these are all kind of ingestible sensors that wirelessly reports body's vital signs (Raed Shubair, 2017). Some samples are, sensors to track what drugs patients have taken, sensors that can measure pH, temperature, and pressure and can transmit those measurements to an external data receiver.

The interest of this chapter is in the suite of wearable and sensors that can be combined and deployed in a nonclinical home (home monitoring) setting used for remote data collection and monitoring.

Hospitals are looking for strategies to minimize costs of the patient care (Itamir de Morais, 2017), and IoT provides a broad range of opportunities to offer patient monitoring at home. Smart home environments can use a network of sensors connected via Zigbee wireless (Ghamari, 2016) to a local hub that connects to the internet to transmit the data collected by the sensors to a cloud-based big data platform that will clean, transform and analyze this data. The previously mentioned network is called Wireless Body Area Network (WBAN) as described in (Bo Yu, 2009). This type of network will facilitate the early detection and prevention of several diseases by a continuous monitoring of health conditions. All the data gathered by this devices and sensors like an electrocardiogram (ECG), electroencephalography (EEG), respiratory rate, body temperature and movement will be collected and communicated to a base station wirelessly to be further analyzed and processed.

APPLICATIONS OF BIG DATA IN POPULATION HEALTH

Population health management is the aggregation of health care data across multiple health information technology systems and the analysis of this data to improve health care outcomes. The use of big data can generate multiple benefits as follows:

1. **Earlier Disease Detection:** Nowadays a lot of sensors are being used to monitor patient health, these sensors produce a vast amount of information that can be aggregated and analyzed in real-time. This analysis can predict disease outbreaks and detect early development of infections.
2. **Fraud Detection and Prevention:** Big data predictive analytics can be used by health care payers to check the accuracy of claims and payments and to verify compliance with Medical policies (Remus, 2012).
3. **Personalized Patient Care:** Health care is moving from disease-centered model to a patient-centered model (Yang, 2014). Data from medical evidence and electronic medical records (EMR)

are needed, and big data will facilitate aggregate and analyze this personalized patient care data to improve clinical outcome.

4. **Genomics Analytics:** A huge number of diseases are genetic in nature, genomic data can provide a better understanding of these diseases and conventional data-driven technologies can't treat this complex type of data.

5. **Clinical Outcomes Analytics:** Collection of data from clinical systems, clinical operations, and financial systems through big data provide improvements in health outcomes (Helm-Murtagh, 2014).

6. **Smart Health and Wellbeing:** With the current sensor technologies the adoption of wearable's devices and smart home environments the amount of data collected from patients and their conditions need big data technologies to turn this massive amount of data in useful information having a profound impact on population health.

Figure 1 shows a conceptual architecture of big data analytics that includes the Hadoop and MapReduce framework capable of storage and analyzes different types of medical data and intelligent, functional machine learning (ML) modules for diagnosis and analysis (Ngufor & Wojtusiak, 2013).

Figure 1. An applied conceptual architecture of big data analytics (Raghupathi and Raghupathi, 2014)

In this architecture, Hive will support queries in HiveQL which will be compiled into map-reduce jobs that will be executed using Hadoop. Hive will provide the initial data mining, log processing, and document indexing and initial predictive modeling. For data storage will be utilized Hadoop Distributed File System (HDFS).

MACHINE LEARNING AND CLINICAL PREDICTION MODELS

While massive data is becoming very familiar in health care, data mining and machine learning (ML) techniques can be implemented to generate knowledge from this data and machine learning has a significant opportunity to be applied in population health management. However, health care organizations before investing in Machine learning (ML) technologies should have a clear and concrete idea of how they will use it to improve health outcomes and a better population health management.

Based on the formal definition of Machine learning stated by (Mitchell, 1986). "*A computer program is said to learn from experience E with respect to some class of tasks T and performance measure P if its performance at tasks in T, as measured by P, improves with experience E*". is clear that ML refers to a particular type of algorithm that can learn from data in order to create a general model that produce accurate predictions.

Machine learning algorithms were designed and used to analyze medical data sets (Kononenko, 2001). And still today ML provides several tools for intelligent data analysis. There are three types of learning, supervised, unsupervised, and semi-supervised learning. This chapter will focus on the first type. In supervised learning, the data contains the response to be modeled, and the goal is to predict the value of the hidden data. Through the years advance ML methods have been used to analyze clinical data sets, and clinical prediction models are one of the most important branches of health care data analytics, the following is a list of the learning methods that have been used successfully for clinical prediction tasks:

1. **Linear Regression:** Is a supervised regression where the dependent variable or outcome is assumed to be a linear combination of the attributes with corresponding estimated regression parameters as explicated in (Trevor, 2009).
2. **Logistic Regression:** Supervised two class and multi-class classification. This binary classification method assumes that there is a linear relationship between the features and the log-odds of the probabilities as explicated in (Dreiseitl, 2002).
3. **Bayesian Models:** Supervised two class and multiclass classification model. Bayesian model is one of the most important principles in probability and mathematical statistics; it provides a link between the posterior likelihood and the prior probability. Is possible to see the probability changes before and after accounting for a particular random event. This theorem is explained in details in (Kononenko, 2007).
4. **Decision Trees:** Supervised two class and multi-class classification. One of the most widely used clinical prediction model (Aspinall, 1979). The prediction is made by asking a series of questions about a test record and based on the answers; the test record falls into a smaller subgroup where the individuals are similar to each other concerning the predicted outcome as explained in (Long, 1993).
5. **Artificial Neural Networks:** Supervised regression. This method is inspired by biological neural systems. Simple artificial nodes called "neurons" are combined via a weighted connection to form a network that simulates a biological neural network as explained in (Dreiseitl, 2002) and (Rosenblatt, 1958).

There are many other methods and future trends where ML in medical diagnosis could take place. The important part here is that with all the advance in computer technology and devices to collect data researchers have a lot of opportunities to improve health outcomes and the medical diagnosis that will affect population health management positively.

PROJECT IMPLEMENTATION

An initial one home monitoring platform has been implemented in Cartagena, Colombia to track and monitor hypertensive data for one patient and validate the infrastructure. For this research, a total of

150 family's homes were selected, and one hypertensive patient for each home has been chosen for the study to use the sensor shield device. Figure 2 shows the architecture utilized for this project and the following are the specifications of the data and the platforms.

- **Location:** Cartagena, Colombia
- **Universities Contributing:** University of Cartagena (Colombia) and University of Oviedo (Spain).
- **Healthcare Facility Contributing:** Clinic of Caribbean
- **The Object of the Study:** Track and treat Hypertension population in Cartagena Colombia.
- **Initial Features for Study:** Age, Race, Height, Weight, Blood pressure, daily step count, BMI index.
- **IoT Infrastructure:**
  - Arduino Uno R3
  - e-health sensor shield v2.0 (Arduino compatible)
  - Radio signal supported (BT, ZigBee, 4G / 3G / GPRS)
  - Oxygen in the blood (SPO2) sensor
  - Body temperature sensor
  - Sphygmomanometer sensor
  - DHT22 sensor (ambient humidity and temperature)
  - XBee breakout board
  - XBee 2mW Wire Antenna - Series 2
  - Raspberry Pi 2
  - Antenna Wireless Network Dongle
- **Big Data Frameworks:** Hadoop & Spark Amazon EMR
- **Machine Learning:** Amazon Machine Learning Platform.
- **Result:** A Data Analytics visualization tool and a healthcare dashboard will be created that will enable clinicians, and healthcare executives improve their decision support process for a hypertensive population.

The high-level diagram in Figure 2 shows the basic WPBN and the AWS (Amazon Web Services) services that were configured for this project. AWS IoT is a managed cloud platform that allows IoT gateways communicate easily and securely to AWS, and to gather device data based on business rules that should be defined. AWS IoT has been integrated to Amazon S3 (Amazon Simple Storage Service) to store the data from the IoT sensors and devices. Then, an EMR cluster is created to pull the data from S3 and use Hive and Hue to analyze and display the data collected from the devices. Once the data is stored in a Hive table, some transformations are needed it to prepare and clean the data. In the last step, Amazon ML is used to create and train an ML model using Amazon EMR as the data source. The trained ML model will be used to generate predictions for the test data set, and this is output back to another S3 bucket. A web application will be created to create the dashboards based on the generated prediction to support population health management decisions.

Figure 2. IoT, big data and ML infrastructure

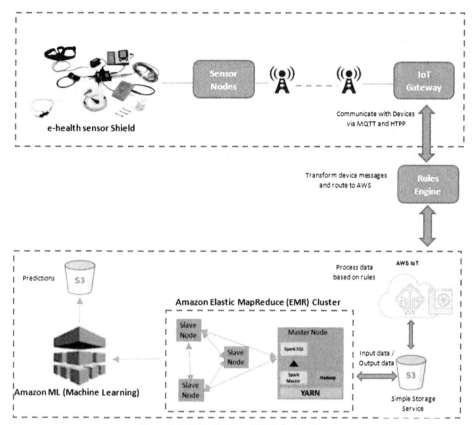

Figure 2. IoT, Big Data and ML Infrastructure

RECOMMENDATIONS

The collection and transmission of health care related data in a WBAN network is a challenge, the designers of this type of environments should keep in mind that this information is private and confidential. Encryption technologies must be used in the transmission between sensors and monitoring devices, and healthcare professional must be sure this information is protected from not authorized access. In addition, big data and machine learning allow performing sophisticated data analysis in the medical diagnosis and health care outcomes based on the secured collected data. Healthcare institutions should take advantage of all the new technologies and systems that have emerged to help medical providers to find interesting and complex relationships in clinical data to improve population health management. Technological research groups need to create strategic alliances with Clinical research groups to gain clinical knowledge and exploit the technical and practical possibilities of IoT, big data frameworks and machine learning methods applied to the medical field. This type of technology has a measurable impact on population Health allowing health care providers improve health outcomes in their communities.

FUTURE RESEARCH DIRECTIONS

The Colombian government is providing incentives to clinical research groups in Cartagena to explore technological opportunities and learn about different technologies like IEEE 802.15.4, Bluetooth devices, low-power wireless technology, Radio-Frequency Identification (RFID), and ZigBee networks to promote the building and use of WBANs for home-centric patient monitoring. Big data frameworks and machine learning methods should be incorporated in prevention and management of chronic diseases. The researchers will help improve population health management in Colombia using these technologies to aggregate data and provide a comprehensive clinical picture of an individual in a population group in the city of Cartagena, using this data to track and improve health outcomes while trying to lower the costs of health care treatments. The research will provide a general picture of the population health to health care providers and the government to identify care gaps, disease outbreaks and patient treatment deficiencies within the patient population in Cartagena.

The creation of clinical prediction models for health care institutions in Cartagena, Colombia could make a tremendous impact in terms of diagnosis and treatment of diseases. In order to promote this type of research, Cartagena local government is giving incentives to research projects that includes linear regression, logistic regression, Bayesian models and neuronal networks in the solution of clinical health care problems. This incentives also includes any other machine learning model not mentioned in this chapter that can be adapted to the health care domain.

FUTURE WORK

Scientists in Cartagena, Colombia are working with healthcare facilities and local government to implement WBAN networks for patient tracking and monitoring, and the implementation of an artificial intelligence (AI) platform for detection and diagnostic of diseases in the population. The vital objective is to create a technological platform that integrate all electronic medical record (EMR) systems from different healthcare facilities in Cartagena and all the collected patient information thru the WBAN networks. This clinical information will be accessed by authorized users (health physicians) at any time and from anywhere. Population health management in Cartagena will be improved by the analytical tools provided on this platform that will allow healthcare stake holders and physicians to identify value and opportunities to improve healthcare outcomes in the population.

CONCLUSION

Population health management is the collection and aggregation of health care data across multiple health information technology systems and the analysis of this data to improve health care outcomes. In this definition was only include data collection and aggregation but there are other components like patient stratification, care coordination, patient engagement, performance and reporting and administration of the new value-based model.

IoT, data collection, data aggregation, and analytics are at the center of all other components, and these are the pillar because the data drive clinical decisions and strategies to turn information into actionable insights supported by IoT technologies, big data frameworks and machine learning methods. Data analytics has been heavily used in the past few years and are continuing gaining importance and interest at all levels. Some of the interest areas where data analytics is gaining importance are pervasive health, health care fraud detection, pharmaceutical discoveries, computer-aided diagnosis, mobile imaging for biomedical applications and clinical decision support systems (CDSS). Another key component in this field of research is the support of health care institutions. Due to the privacy of the clinical data, this research work in the health care data analytics field should be done with a particular hospital or health care facility. There are a wide variety of public repositories in health care to validate the models, but it is important to validate the models with data collected from the nominated study population. Hardware, software, and communication technologies are no excuses anymore. Nowadays these technologies to collect and analyze health care data have significantly increased, allowing solutions to collect high volumes of data and process them in real-time, producing real-time analysis and insights.

The chapter points to articles that provide more details about IoT technologies and how effectively use Big data and prediction models in Clinical environments to improve health outcomes.

ACKNOWLEDGMENT

This research was supported by the Organization Sysdevelopment LLC. USA; University of Oviedo, Spain.

REFERENCES

Aspinall, M. J. (1979). Use of a decision tree to improve accuracy of diagnosis. *Nurs Res.*, *28*(3), 182–185. PMID:254902

Dreiseitl, S., & Ohno-Machado, L. (2002). Logistic regression and artificial neural network classification models: A methodology review. *Journal of Biomedical Informatics*, *35*(5-6), 352–359. doi:10.1016/S1532-0464(03)00034-0 PMID:12968784

e-Health Sensor Platform V2.0 for Arduino and Raspberry Pi. (n.d.). Retrieved from https://e-class.teilar.gr/modules/document/file.php/CS103/IOT%20-%20SENSORS%20-%20ACTUATORS/e-Health%20Sensor%20Platform%20V2.pdf

Ghamari, M., Janko, B., Sherratt, R. S., Harwin, W., Piechockic, R., & Soltanpur, C. (2016). A Survey on Wireless Body Area Networks for eHealthcare Systems in Residential Environments. *Sensors (Basel)*, *16*(6), 831. doi:10.339016060831 PMID:27338377

Hastie, T., Tibshirani, R., & Friedman, J. (2009). *Elements of Statistical Learning: Data Mining, Inference and Prediction* (2nd ed.). New York: Springer-Verlag. doi:10.1007/978-0-387-84858-7

Helm-Murtagh, S. C. (2014). Use of Big Data by Blue Cross and Blue Shield of North Carolina. *NCMJ*, *75*, 195–197. PMID:24830494

Itamir de Morais, B. F., & Gibeon, S. A. J. (2017). IoT-Based Healthcare Applications: A Review. Lecture Notes in Computer Science. Doi:10.1007/978-3-319-62407-5_4

Karbing, Rees, & Jaffe. (2017). *Journal of Clinical Monitoring and Computing 2016 end of year summary*. Doi:10.1007/s10877-017-0008-0

Kindig, D., & Stoddart, G. (2003). *What Is Population Health*. American Journal of Public Health, *93*(3), 380–383.

Kononenko, I. (2001). Machine learning for medical diagnosis: History, state of the art and perspective. *Artif Intell Med., 23*(1), 89-109.

Kononenko, I. (2007). Inductive and Bayesian Learning. In *Medical Diagnosis* (pp. 317–337). Journal Applied Artificial Intelligence.

Long, W. J., Griffith, J. L., Selker, H. P., & D'Agostino, R. B. (1993). A comparison of logistic regression to decision-tree induction in a medical domain. *Computers and Biomedical Research, an International Journal, 26*(1), 74–97. doi:10.1006/cbmr.1993.1005 PMID:8444029

Mitchell, T. M., Carbonell, J. G., & Michalski, R. S. (1986). *Machine Learning: A Guide to Current Research* (1st ed.). The Springer International Series in Engineering and Computer Science. Original. doi:10.1007/978-1-4613-2279-5

Ngufor, C., & Wojtusiak, J. (2013). *Learning from Large-Scale Distributed Health Data: An Approximate Logistic Regression Approach*. Academic Press.

Patidar, P., Praneeta, S., Kataria, R., & Vidhyasagar, B. S. (2017). Analysis of Multi-Disease & Prediction of Suitable Drug for Healthcare Application using Big data. *International Journal of Research in Applied Science & Engineering Technology, 5*(4).

Priyanka, K., & Kulennavar, N. (2014). A survey on big data analytics in health care. *Int. J. Comput. Sci.Inform. Technologies, 5*, 5865–5868.

Remus & Kennedy. (2012). Special Focus on Nursing Informatics. *Innovation in Transformative Nursing Leadership: Nursing Informatics Competencies and Roles*, 14-26. doi:10.12927/cjnl.2012.23260

Review on Internet of Things (IoT) in Healthcare. (n.d.). Available from: https://www.researchgate.net/publication/309718253_A_Review_on_Internet_of_Things_IoT_in_Healthcare

Rosenblatt, F. (1958). The Perceptron: A Theory of Statistical Separability in Cognitive Systems (Project Para). Buffalo, NY: Cornell Aeronautical Laboratory.

Shubair & Kiourti. (2017). *In-Body Devices for Wireless Biotelemetry: Implants and ingestibles*. Special Session organized at the 2017 IEEE AP-S Symposium on Antennas and Propagation and USNC-URSI Radio Science Meeting (AP-S/URSI 2017), San Diego, CA.

Tech America Foundation. (2012). *Demystifying Big Data: TechAmerica Foundation paper*. Retrieved from http://www1.unece.org/stat/platform/pages/viewpage.action?pageId=80053387

Yang, S., Njoku, M., & Mackenzie, C. F. (2014). 'Big data' approaches to trauma outcome prediction and autonomous resuscitation. *British Journal of Hospital Medicine, 75*(11), 637–641. doi:10.12968/hmed.2014.75.11.637 PMID:25383434

Yu, B. (2009). *Wireless Body Area Networks for Healthcare: A Feasibility Study.* Available from: https://www.ieee.org/documents/Yu_Final_Published_Paper_March2009.pdf

KEY TERMS AND DEFINITIONS

Arduino: Is an open source electronic platform to build interactive projects receiving inputs from sensors and controlling actions by using the development environment.

AWS: Is Amazon Web Services, a platform that offers on-demand cloud computing.

Big Data: Extremely large data sets, generated by humans, applications, or machines.

Cloud Computing: Is the practice of using remote servers and services hosted on the internet to store, manage, and process data.

Data Mining: Specific algorithms for extracting patterns from data.

Descriptive Analytics: Technology that focuses less on the precise details of every piece of data, and instead focuses on an overall description.

Disease: Is a disorder of a function in a human or a particular abnormal condition.

Electronic Health Record: An electronic health record contains your health information.

Hadoop: Open-source framework for processing a large volume of data in a clustered environment.

Hypertension: Is an abnormally high blood pressure.

IoT: Internet of things is the interconnection of physical devices that enable these devices to collect and exchange data.

Machine Learning: Computer programs that automatically improve with experience.

Population Health: Population health is defined as the health outcomes of a group of individuals, including the distribution of such outcomes within the group.

Predictive Analytics: Technology that learns from experience to predict the future behavior of individuals in order to drive better decisions.

Prescriptive Analytics: Generally follows prediction, in that actions can be prescribed based on what has been collected from predictive modeling.

Raspberry Pi: Is a small single-board computer.

Sensor: Is a device that detects or measures a physical property.

Chapter 78
The Role and Applications of Machine Learning in Future Self-Organizing Cellular Networks

Paulo Valente Klaine
University of Glasgow, UK

Oluwakayode Onireti
University of Glasgow, UK

Richard Demo Souza
Federal University of Santa Catarina (UFSC), Brazil

Muhammad Ali Imran
University of Glasgow, UK

ABSTRACT

In this chapter, a brief overview of the role and applications of machine learning (ML) algorithms in future wireless cellular networks is presented, more specifically, in the context of self-organizing networks (SONs). SON is a promising and innovative concept, in which future networks are expected to analyze and use historical data in order to improve and adapt themselves to the network conditions. For this to be possible, however, algorithms that are capable of extracting patterns from data and learn from previous actions are necessary. This chapter highlights the utilization and possible applications of ML algorithms in future cellular networks. A brief introduction of ML and SON is presented, followed by an analysis of current state of the art solutions involving ML in SON. Lastly, guidelines on the utilization of intelligent algorithms in SON and future research trends in the area are highlighted and conclusions are drawn.

DOI: 10.4018/978-1-6684-6291-1.ch078

INTRODUCTION

In the last couple of years, mobile wireless networks have become an essential part of our lives, due to a broad range of applications and services that are available. Nowadays, people are able to do business on the go, by performing teleconferences whenever and wherever needed, watch or listen to their favorite videos and music on the fly, talk to distant relatives, stream audio/video whenever a special event happens, instantly upload photos or videos about their daily lives in social media, and many more (Aliu, Imran, Imran, & Evans, 2013).

In the future, however, this demand is expected to be much larger, with the advents of new technologies being developed, such as ultra-high definition videos, Virtual Reality (VR) applications, the Internet of Things (IoT); Machine-to-Machine (M2M) communications; cloud computing, and various other services that are unimaginable today. In addition, not only new technologies will need to be addressed by the Next Generation of Mobile Networks (NGMN), but also the ever increasing demand of users in terms of both capacity and better services (Huawei, Technologies Co., 2016), (Samsung Electronics Co., 2015). Some of the requirements that are present in the current state-of-the-art literature of NGMNs are (P. Fettweis, 2012), (G. Andrews, et al., 2014) (Huawei, Technologies Co., 2016):

- Address the exponential growth required in both coverage and capacity;
- Provide better Quality of Service and Experience (QoS and QoE) to end users;
- Support the coexistence with other radio technologies;
- Provide peak data rates higher than 10Gbps;
- Support latency lower than one millisecond (enabling the concept of tactile internet);
- Support ultra-high reliability and network energy efficiency.

From these requirements, it is clear that NGMNs are under a heavy pressure in order to address current limitations of present mobile networks and to push their performance to a next level, allowing all these requirements and new technologies to become a reality in the near future. In order to address the expected exponential growth required in both coverage and capacity, one major shift that will probably occur in NGMNs is the network densification process, in which operators are expected to deploy a wide range of small cells in order to cover a relatively small area (G. Andrews, et al., 2014), (Alsedairy, Qi, Imran, Imran, & Evans, 2015). Although the densification process is probably going to solve some of the future cellular network problems, this process will require an even bigger change in paradigm on how future cellular networks are organized. The dense deployment of small cells will result in an exponential increase in terms of network complexity, while also increasing the total network CAPital and OPerational EXpenditures (CAPEX and OPEX), affecting the whole network in terms of configuration, optimization and healing (Valente Klaine, Imran, Onireti, & Demo Souza, 2017).

In order to address these issues created by the densification process, one possible solution is the addition of more intelligence in the network, by using algorithms that rely on data collected by operators and traffic patterns, such as Machine Learning (ML) algorithms. In addition, ML solutions would also address other network issues by simplifying the coordination, configuration and optimization procedures of the network, minimizing the network complexity, energy consumed and expenditures, while also enabling autonomous network healing (Imran, Zoha, & Abu-Dayya, 2014), (Aliu, Imran, Imran, & Evans, 2013). Furthermore, ML algorithms would also be a key enabler to new types of applications that today are unimaginable, ranging from the autonomous configuration of a new Base Station (BS) and network topology, optimization and allocation of backhaul resources, user mobility tracking and prediction, to fully enabling the concept of Self Organizing Networks (SONs) (Valente Klaine, Imran, Onireti, & Demo Souza, 2017).

Hence, the objective of this chapter is to provide the readers with a clear view of why ML is necessary for future networks, in particular, on how ML can enable the concept of SON. In addition, the authors also present a brief definition of the concept of SON, including its three main functions: self-configuration, self-optimization and self-healing. Furthermore, the authors also present the readers with some of the current state-of-the-art applications using ML applied in wireless cellular networks, in order to enable SON. Lastly, the authors will also comment on the suitability of each ML technique for each SON use case, while also providing the readers with some future research directions and a brief conclusion, highlighting the important role that ML will have in future wireless networks.

More specifically, the objectives of the chapter are:

- Provide the readers with a clear understanding of current cellular networks limitations.
- Provide the readers with a clear definition of Self Organizing Network (SON) and its subdivisions, mainly: self-configuration, self-optimization, and self-healing.
- Provide readers with a clear motivation of why ML is necessary for future networks and how it can enable future services.
- Provide current state-of-the-art examples of applications of intelligent solutions in cellular networks, highlighting which algorithm was utilized and which problem it aimed to tackle.
- Provide general guidelines on when to use some ML algorithms for each SON function.
- Provide future research trends and directions that are expected to be seen in the near future in the area of SON.

MOTIVATION

From the previous section, it is evident that the requirements that NGMNs must address are quite stringent. However, first, before trying to tackle these requirements, NGMNs should also be able to overcome current limitations of present cellular networks. Current methods today lack the adaptability and flexibility required in order to become feasible solutions for future cellular networks (Imran, Zoha, & Abu-Dayya, 2014). One simple example is the process of a BS configuration. Whenever a new BS is deployed in a network, hundreds of parameters need to be manually configured by expert engineers in order for it to become operable. These parameters can be basic operational parameters, such as IP address, default gateway address, BS identifier, the configuration of the neighbor cell list of the new BS, as well as its neighbors, and radio parameters, such as transmit power, handover (HO) parameters, like hysteresis and Time-To-Trigger (TTT), antenna azimuth and down-tilt angles, etc. (Valente Klaine, Imran, Onireti, & Demo Souza, 2017).

As it can be seen, just the simple task of adding a new BS in a network requires a lot of expertise and manual work, which is not the ideal approach. In addition, most of these parameters can also be sub-optimally configured, as the radio parameters of a BS can also affect the total network coverage or its overall topology. One can think of as an example, if the operator configures the power of the new BS too high, this will have an impact on nearby BSs, as their coverage area will be reduced and interference will increase. Thus, a simple miscalculation or change in network conditions can be disastrous.

This simple example also highlights that a static configuration of parameters is not necessarily the best solution. As the network constantly changes, it is also necessary to constantly optimize and adjust the parameters previously configured. However, as it is with the configuration process, the optimization process of a network, nowadays, also relies on manual intervention and the constant monitor of performance indicators of the network in order to determine which parameters of a cell need to be updated and by how much (Imran, Zoha, & Abu-Dayya, 2014).

Lastly, another example that points at the inefficiency of current methods is when a failure occurs in the network. Nowadays, current mobile networks are reactive (a failure happens and the mobile operators react to the failure by responding appropriately) (Farooq, Parwez, & Imran, 2015). This requires network operators to constantly monitor the network in terms of certain Key Performance Indicators (KPIs), which results in operators collecting huge amounts of data. This data then needs to be manually analyzed by expert engineers in order to determine the exact time and cause of the failure, and later the operator must then send experts to the failure location in order to fix it. This is extremely inefficient, as it can take a lot of time for the failure to be resolved, causing disruption in service, making customers unhappy and generating less revenue for the operator. Thus, from the three examples provided, it is clear that new paradigms are necessary in order to automate and make current mobile networks more efficient, and that is where ML algorithms can be extremely effective.

Machine Learning Definition and Categories

ML is the science of making computers take decisions without being explicitly programmed to do so (Simon, 2013). This is done by programming a set of algorithms that analyze a given set of data and try to make predictions about it. Depending on how learning is performed, these algorithms are classified differently, mainly into three broad categories: supervised learning, unsupervised learning and reinforcement learning.

Supervised Learning

In supervised learning, the algorithms require a data set that has information about both input and output data. As the name suggests, their process of learning is similar to having a supervisor, or a teacher, supervising the learning process. The teacher knows the answers (output) for every input data, and as the algorithm iteratively makes predictions during its training process, the teacher corrects it. More formally, supervised learning can be defined as algorithms that based on the input and output relationship of the data, learn a model that best represents the data and is able to make predictions for newly, unseen data examples (Kotsiantis, Zaharakis, & Pintelas, 2007), (Friedman, Hastie, & Tibshirani, 2001).

In addition, supervised learning algorithms are also split into two main categories, which varies according to the type of the output variable. If the output variable is a discrete variable, such as a class, for example: "Red", "Blue", or "Cat" and "Dog", the supervised learning problem is referred to as a *classification* problem. On the other hand, if the output variable is a real or a continuous value, such as the value of a house, or the birth rate of a certain region, then the supervised problem is considered as a *regression* problem (Friedman, Hastie, & Tibshirani, 2001).

Examples of algorithms from supervised learning range from very simple functions, such as linear regression, logistic regression, *k*-Nearest Neighbors, decision trees, Support Vector Machines (SVM), to more complex ones, such as neural networks, and its variations, like convolutional neural networks and deep neural networks (LeCun, Bengio, & & Hinton, 2015).

Unsupervised Learning

Unsupervised learning, on the other hand, does not have the luxury of having a supervisor in order to aid the learning process. In this case, a data set with only input labels is provided (there is no information about the correct labels for the data, so a teacher would be of no help). In this case, an algorithm is given an unlabeled data set and its goal is to correctly learn a model that best represents the dataset (Friedman, Hastie, & Tibshirani, 2001). Due to its nature of trying to estimate a model for data without labels, unsupervised learning algorithms consist mainly of clustering algorithms, such as *K*-Means, Self Organizing Maps (SOM), and anomaly detectors.

Reinforcement Learning

Differently than the previous two techniques, Reinforcement Learning (RL) is a ML technique based on a goal seeking approach (Sutton & Barto, 1998). In contrast to other ML techniques, such as supervised learning, in which the system learns by analyzing examples provided by a supervisor, in RL, the learner must discover which actions to take by trying them (Sutton & Barto, 1998), (Kaelbling, Littman, & Moore, 1996).

In RL, a system, called an agent, interacts with its surroundings, the environment. Then, based on the agent's current state, its desired goal, and the environment's conditions, the agent takes an action. After that, the agent receives a reward, if the action taken was good, or a penalty, if it was bad. The main goal of a RL system is to maximize its total reward. In order to achieve this, the agent must not only exploit the best actions currently known but also explore new actions, in order to determine if there are better possible actions to be taken. This trade-off is known as the exploration-exploitation trade-off (Sutton & Barto, 1998), (Kaelbling, Littman, & Moore, 1996).

RL can be divided, mainly, into three categories (Sutton & Barto, 1998):

1. **Dynamic Programming (DP):** In which the agent has a perfect model of the environment, given by a Markov Decision Process (MDP), and the goal is to learn the optimal policies in order to choose the best actions.
2. **Monte Carlo (MC) Methods:** In this case, it is not assumed that there is complete knowledge about the environment. Thus, the agent must learn either online, by experiencing the environment, or through simulated experiences, in which the environment is represented by a very simple model.
3. **Temporal-Difference Learning (TD Learning):** Which can be defined as a combination of MC methods and DP. Just like MC methods, TD Learning agents can learn directly from their experience with the environment, without the need of the complete environment's dynamics. Furthermore, similar to DP, TD algorithms update their estimates (either a policy or a value function) based on other learned estimates, or in other words, they are capable of bootstrapping.

Some examples of RL algorithms include armed bandit problems, Q-Learning, and SARSA (Sutton & Barto, 1998).

Figure 1 shows how ML is divided into the three main branches and its algorithms.

Figure 1. Block diagram showing the three main branches of ML and some of its algorithms

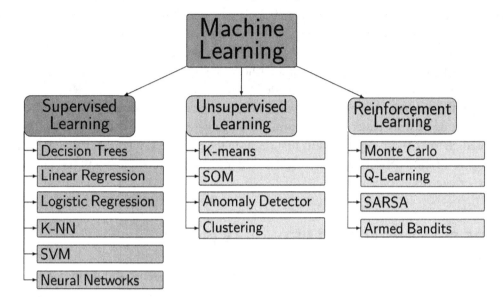

Machine Learning as an Enabler of SON

As it can be seen from the previous sections, there are lots of different algorithms that can be used, depending on the type of data available and application that is needed. In addition, since operators already collect a huge amount of data daily from their networks, it is only expected that in the near future such data can be leveraged to its full potential, moving away from manual solutions, which are both time and cost ineffective.

In addition, by deploying ML algorithms, new types of services and applications can be enabled. One example in the realm of SON can be the prediction of user mobility. By tracking each user of the network via intelligent algorithms, the network is able to predict whenever and wherever a user will be. This, in its turn, can be translated into gains in terms of control signals, in which the network is able to allocate resources in advance (before the user actually moves to the next cell) and reduce the signaling costs associated with HO, for example (Mohamed, et al., 2015).

Another interesting example can be the autonomous configuration of a mobile network from ground zero. This can be done with the usage of mobile BSs, such as truck BSs, or drones, for example, and intelligent solutions could then determine the best positions for the BSs to be, in order to maximize coverage area or minimize the number of users in an outage. This scenario can be extremely useful not only in self-configuration cases, as a planning strategy for network operators, but also in emergencies, in which a network has been destroyed and a new network must be deployed as quickly and as efficient as possible (Erdelj, Natalizio, Chowdhury, & Akyildiz, 2017). Thus, in this latter scenario, agility and adaptability are crucial, rendering intelligent solutions, depending on ML algorithms, essential in order to become a reality.

Another problem that can be solved by the analysis of data and the usage of ML algorithms can be to make current cellular networks more energy efficient. For example, by analyzing traffic patterns during different times of the day and different days of the week, operators could determine whenever it is best to turn on or off certain BSs in order to save energy, while also minimizing the number of unsatisfied users (Onireti, Mohamed, Pervaiz, & Imran, 2017). Since it is often not trivial for human experts to determine intrinsic relationships in data, especially whenever there is such a huge amount of data, as is the case of mobile networks, ML solutions are essential in order to explore these hidden correlations and determine which BS to turn on and off and for how long.

Lastly, another key concept that can be enabled through the use of ML is the detection and mitigation of faults in the network. As previously mentioned, current cellular networks are reactive, but in the future, by analyzing network patterns and historical data gathered from the network, ML algorithms will be able to predict, to a certain degree, faults that occur in the network (Farooq, Parwez, & Imran, 2015). This will enable a future network to become proactive instead of reactive and will provide a better and seamless experience to mobile users.

WHAT ARE SELF ORGANIZING NETWORKS (SON)?

The idea of self-organization is mainly inspired from biological systems and nature, in which certain species show a certain behavior in order to adapt themselves to the environment they are inserted in and achieve a particular objective. For example, a group of flocking birds is able to maintain organization without hitting one another when rapidly flying in different directions, or a group of ants is able to autonomously organize themselves in order to bring the food back to their hive (Aliu, Imran, Imran, & Evans, 2013).

Thus, based on this underlying principle of self-organization and intelligence, the idea of SON can be defined as an adaptive and autonomous network, that is not only able to maintain or achieve its desired objectives, but also that is scalable, stable and agile enough to do so (Aliu, Imran, Imran, & Evans, 2013) (Valente Klaine, Imran, Onireti, & Demo Souza, 2017). These networks are not only able to autonomously decide when and which actions to take, based on the analysis of historical data collected and their continuous interaction with the environment, but also able to improve their performance online, as the network runs.

Cellular SON can be divided into three main categories, and they are jointly referred to as *self-x* functions, they are: self-configuration, self-optimization, and self-healing (Aliu, Imran, Imran, & Evans, 2013), (Valente Klaine, Imran, Onireti, & Demo Souza, 2017).

Self-Configuration

The self-configuration function can be defined as the process of configuring all parameters necessary in order to make a network operable, such as the location of BSs in a network, software parameters of a BS, such as IP address and main gateway, network policies, topology and radio parameters, like antenna down-tilt and azimuth angles and transmission power.

The process of self-configuration can be done in several stages of a network. Most commonly, network operators would use it as a planning tool, in order to determine what the best parameters of a newly deployed network are. However, self-configuration can also be deployed when the network is already operable, by automatically configuring a newly deployed BS, for example. Additionally, self-configuration can also be utilized whenever a disaster happens and most of the network is disrupted. In this scenario, self-configuration algorithms could determine the best new positions of newly deployed BSs in order to restore service to the affected area (Erdelj, Natalizio, Chowdhury, & Akyildiz, 2017).

Self-Optimization

Another branch of SON is the self-optimization function. As the name implies, self-optimization is performed in order to continuously optimize and tune network parameters, while the network is operable. This procedure is performed due to the changes that can happen in the network, such as user mobility, high traffic demands at a specific location or time of the day, events taking place in a city, etc. In addition, by continuously monitoring the network, self-optimization algorithms are able to use reported measurements combined with historical data previously gathered and ensure that the network objectives are maintained and that its overall performance is near optimal (Aliu, Imran, Imran, & Evans, 2013).

Some examples of self-optimization functions can be in terms of caching content at BSs; backhaul congestion optimization; coverage and capacity; user mobility and HO parameters, and network energy efficiency, to name a few (Valente Klaine, Imran, Onireti, & Demo Souza, 2017).

Self-Healing

Finally yet importantly, is the self-healing function. This function, as the self-optimization one, is performed while the network is operational, as it must constantly monitor the network and its data in order to predict, detect, and classify faults as they occur. In addition, self-healing functions must also mitigate the effects that failures can have in mobile networks, not only by detecting and predicting when a failure is going to happen, but also by triggering the appropriate mechanisms in order to mitigate the effect that the fault can have in the network (Valente Klaine, Imran, Onireti, & Demo Souza, 2017).

Examples of self-healing functions can be the prediction of when a failure is likely to occur and pinpoint the BS that is most likely to fail. Another example can be the management of cell outages, in which whenever an outage happens, the appropriate self-healing function should be triggered so that the neighboring BSs can adjust their radio parameters in order to cover the out of coverage area, while the fault is not resolved.

Use Cases of Self-x Functions

Additionally, each *self-x* function can also be further divided into sub-functions, normally known as *use cases*. Figure 2 shows an outline of the most commonly found SON use cases in the recent literature.

As it can be seen, future networks are not only expected to address several issues that are commonly found in current cellular networks, but also act as an enabler for future technologies and domains that do not exist today.

MACHINE LEARNING APPLICATIONS IN SON

From the previous sections, it can be seen that intelligence in future networks is a promising concept. However, since each SON function and its respective use cases have different requirements and rely on

Figure 2. SON Use cases
adapted from (Valente Klaine, Imran, Onireti, & Demo Souza, 2017)

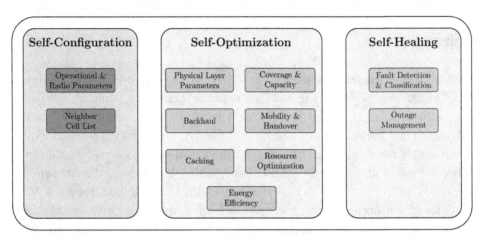

different types of data, demanding different types of ML solutions, some ML algorithms are more suitable for different *self-x* functions (Valente Klaine, Imran, Onireti, & Demo Souza, 2017).

In this section, first, some examples of applications of ML algorithms in each SON function will be analyzed and commented upon, highlighting which problem it aimed to tackle, how it was implemented and its results. Then, the authors would like to comment on the suitability of ML techniques for each SON use case, highlighting which techniques are more appropriate for which type of problem, while also giving some recommendations on which type of ML technique to use for every SON function.

Machine Learning in Self-Configuration

Although the concept of SON has been around for a while, the area of self-configuration is still underexplored. However, despite this fact, there are some interesting works covering the autonomous configuration of parameters of BSs.

Operational and Radio Parameters

The first step into configuring a new network should be the configuration of BSs basic parameters, such as IP address, main gateway, cell identifier and network topology. In addition, the configuration of BSs radio parameters is also important in order to allow users to connect to it. Examples of radio parameters are transmission power, in terms of both data and pilot symbols, antenna down-tilt and azimuth angles and HO parameters. Regarding the configuration of these parameters, a few examples can be found in the literature.

The work in (Binzer & Landstorfer, 2000), for example, proposes a solution based in Self Organizing Maps in order to configure and optimize network parameters of a Code Division Multiple Access (CDMA) network. The proposed solution aimed to determine not only planning parameters of a network, such as the number of BSs required in a certain area and their positions, but also radio parameters, such as the antenna's beam pattern and its transmit power.

Another work in this domain is the work in (Safdar, Hasbulah, & Rehan, 2015), in which the authors propose a RL approach to determine the best routing protocols for a cognitive radio network. The proposed intelligent algorithm, based on Q-Learning, has as its main goal to minimize the overall end-to-end delay of the network, while also maximizing its throughput. Results show that the intelligent algorithm outperforms current non-intelligent solutions by reducing the protocol overhead and end-to-end delay, while also increasing the package delivery ratio.

In (Razavi, Klein, & Claussen, 2010), the authors propose a RL algorithm combined with fuzzy logic to configure the down-tilt angle of BSs antennas in order to adjust the coverage and capacity of each cell. In order to test their proposed algorithm, first, the authors randomly set the down-tilt angles of each BS. After that, the proposed algorithm was enabled in order for it to learn the best possible configuration of the antenna's angle. The proposed solution was compared with another fuzzy logic solution (Evolutionary Learning of Fuzzy rules, ELF) and the results showed that the intelligent RL approach was able to learn the optimal down-tilt angle for this scenario.

Another solution that also combines the concepts of RL with fuzzy logic is the work in (Islam & Mitschele-Thiel, 2012). The proposed approach is very similar to the one previously mentioned, but in this case, despite the authors also trying to configure and learn the best down-tilt angle of antennas, they also consider different sources of noise in the data, such as thermal noise and receiver noise.

Neighbor Cell List (NCL)

Another important parameter to be configured whenever a new network must be deployed is the list of neighbors that a BS will communicate to. This is essential in order to establish HOs and for the network topology. For example, whenever a new BS is added to the network, this new BS should be capable of autonomously sensing and discovering its nearest neighbors, in order to add them to a list and be able to communicate to them. In addition, the other BSs that the new BS is now connected to must also add it to their list, otherwise, no communication will be possible.

However, despite its importance, this use-case of self-configuration has seen no usage of ML algorithms in recent years. Most solutions used still rely on the usage of feedback controllers and simple thresholds based on the distance between BSs or the perceived SINR (Valente Klaine, Imran, Onireti, & Demo Souza, 2017). Thus, the authors would like to emphasize that this area of SON is still an open issue and that further research should focus on it.

Table 1 shows a summary of the proposed ML solutions in the area of self-configuration.

Table 1. Application of ML algorithms in self-configuration

	Supervised Learning	Unsupervised Learning	Reinforcement Learning	Miscellaneous
Operational & Radio Parameters	✗	✓	✓	✗
Neighbor Cell List	✗	✗	✗	✗

Machine Learning in Self-Optimization

In contrast to self-configuration, which has received very few attention in the past couple years, self-optimization, on the other hand, is a very active research area, mainly due to a large number of parameters that can be adjusted and optimized. Since a network environment is not static with changes occurring in a network all the time, a wireless network might have to adjust its initially configured parameters in order to adapt itself and keep its objectives. Thus, self-optimization will play vital role in future cellular networks.

Physical Layer Parameters

One important aspect of future cellular networks is the optimization of physical layer parameters of communication. Nowadays, before the transmission of data begins, the transmitter must send to the receiver the communication parameters that it is going to use. Such parameters include the type of modulation and coding, type of waveform, FFT size and Cyclic Prefix (CP) length, to name a few (Su, 2013), (Lichtman, Headley, & Reed, 2014).

This is far from ideal, as any abrupt changes in the channel or network conditions may require a change in one of these parameters, requiring the transmitter to send them again to the receiver. Consequentially, this can waste a lot of bandwidth, while also increasing communication delay and signaling cost (Lichtman, Headley, & Reed, 2014). Thus, autonomous methods that attempt to dynamically learn or blindly estimate the transmitter's parameters at the receiver side are welcomed.

One example of such solution is the work in (Lichtman, Headley, & Reed, 2014), in which the authors attempt to determine at the receiver side which type of single carrier modulation was sent by the transmitter considering the effect of IQ imbalance. In this solution, the authors compare three different types of supervised learning methods, mainly K-NN, SVM and decision trees. Results show that the supervised learning methods are able to perform well in terms of classifying different types of modulation techniques, while also being able to compensate for the IQ imbalances introduced at the receiver side.

Another interesting work in the area of physical layer optimization is the work in (Dörner, Cammerer, Hoydis, & Brink, 2017), in which the authors design a whole communication system using nothing but neural networks and deep learning. The authors approach demonstrates that it is entirely possible to create a communication system in which the whole physical layer processing is performed by neural networks.

Backhaul Parameters

Another critical parameter that can be optimized is the backhaul connection of BSs, that is, the connection between the BSs and the core network. Some works that perform this optimization include the works in (Jaber M., Imran, Tafazolli, & Tukmanov, A Distributed SON-Based User-Centric Backhaul Provisioning Scheme, 2016), (Jaber M., Imran, Tafazolli, & Tukmanov, A Multiple Attribute User-Centric Backhaul Provisioning Scheme Using Distributed SON, 2016), (Jaber M., Imran, Tafazolli, & Tukmanov, 2015), in which a shift in current cellular network cell association paradigm is proposed.

Current cell association procedures look only at the Radio Access Network (RAN) parameters, such as the received signal power and Signal-to-Interference-plus-Noise Ratio (SINR). In the future, however, looking only at RAN parameters might not be enough in order to satisfy users, as the backhaul of the mobile network can become the bottleneck (Jaber M., Imran, Tafazolli, & Tukmanov, A Distributed

SON-Based User-Centric Backhaul Provisioning Scheme, 2016). Thus, solutions that look at this end-to-end connectivity, between the core network and user and not only the RAN parameters can be suitable.

In this sense, the authors propose to use RL in order to optimize the user cell association and improve overall user QoS in terms of throughput, latency and resiliency. The algorithm, based on Q-Learning, aims to tune the Cell Range Extension Offset (CREOs) of small cells so that users can connect to the small cell that has the backhaul that would better match a user needs (for example, if a user requires low latency, it would tend to connect to a backhaul that provides low latency, etc.). Results show that the proposed solution is capable of improving overall satisfaction, at the cost of a minor reduction in total cumulative throughput.

Caching

Due to the exponential growth in mobile devices and the rising popularity of social networks and multimedia services, video streaming will compose a huge part of the mobile network traffic. In 2016, it was already accounted that 60% of total mobile traffic came from mobile video, and this number is expected to be around 80% by 2021 (Index, 2017). Thus, in order to address this huge demand, caching must be provided in all levels of the network, but the questions of what, where and how to cache, remain.

In this context, some works that investigate the impact of caching in mobile networks is the work in (Bastug, Bennis, & Debbah, 2014), in which the authors propose two different solutions for the caching problem. The first one is based on collaborative filtering, a type of supervised learning technique that tries to build a model from a source's past behavior considering not only that source's data but also data from other similar sources. By using this algorithm, the authors were able to develop a caching solution that alleviated backhaul congestion.

The second solution proposed by them considered a scenario involving D2D communications, in which specific users would have contents cached into their devices so that it could be shared with other users. By using an unsupervised learning algorithm, *K*-means, the authors were able to cluster users into different groups and dynamically distribute content in the clusters.

Coverage and Capacity

In order to cope with the increasing traffic, it is essential that network coverage and capacity is constantly optimized in future networks. Based on that, several works propose intelligent solutions in order to tackle this problem.

One possible solution is the work proposed in (Debono & Buhagiar, 2005), in which the authors utilize the unsupervised learning technique, SOM, in order to achieve better network coverage. Their proposed algorithm would first try to optimize the number of BSs inside a cluster and then optimize each BSs antenna's parameters. The authors also propose two different scenarios, one in which only cluster sizes are changed, and another in which both cluster sizes and antenna parameters are optimized. Another approach to the coverage and capacity optimization problem is the work in (Ho, Ashraf, & Claussen, 2009), in which a Genetic Algorithm is proposed to minimize network coverage holes, perform load balancing and minimize pilot channel transmit power.

Mobility and Handover

The process of changing the communication channel in an on-going call is known as HO. HOs are of extreme importance in mobile networks due to the mobility of its users. Without this procedure, mobility could not be supported, as connections would not survive the process of changing cells. Thus, in order to optimize and improve the performance of future cellular networks, it is vital that NGMNs are able to predict user's movement in order to better manage network resources (Valente Klaine, Imran, Onireti, & Demo Souza, 2017). Figure 3 shows an example of how ML algorithms can be used in order to track user mobility.

Figure 3. A user moving through the network from point A to point B. In this case, historical data from the user could be leveraged in order to predict for different days of the week, or different times of the day, the route the user is most likely to take.

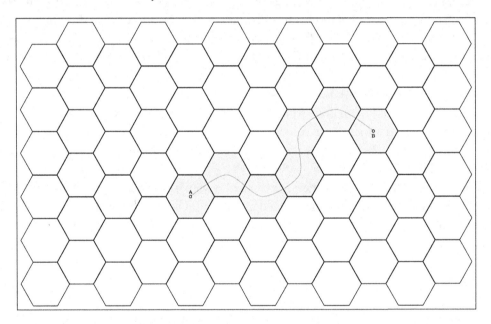

One recent work in the area of mobility prediction is the work in (Mohamed, Onireti, Imran, Imran, & Tafazolli, 2017), in which the authors propose a discrete Markov chain in order to predict the next cell a user will be. The proposed solution is shown to be signaling efficient, being able to minimize overhead signals and HO latency.

Another solution in the realm of HO optimization is the optimization of HO parameters, such as the work in (Sinclair, Harle, Glover, Irvine, & Atkinson, 2013). In this work, the authors proposed a SOM in order to optimize two critical HO parameters, hysteresis and TTT, and achieve a balance between unnecessary HOs and call drop rates. Results show that the proposed solution is able to significantly reduce the number of unnecessary HOs and dropped calls by up to 70%.

Resource Allocation and Load Balancing

Another critical aspect of future mobile networks is the provisioning and allocation of network resources. Additionally, since traffic is usually unevenly distributed in mobile networks, solutions that are also able to intelligently manage and balance traffic load are also welcomed.

In this sense, solutions such as (Dirani & Altman, 2011), propose a framework for uplink transmission of mobile users in a LTE network in order to reduce blocking rates and file transfer times. The proposed solution relies on Q-Learning combined with Fuzzy Logic to dynamically optimize Radio Resource Management (RRM) functions and it is able to provide gains in terms of network capacity and user-perceived quality in data applications. Another work regarding the use case of load balancing is the work in (Bassoy, Jaber, Imran, & Xiao, 2016), in which the authors utilize a clustering algorithm, in a network with separated control and data planes in order to reduce high load on cells in hotspot areas and improve user satisfaction rates.

Energy Efficiency

In the future, with the increasing number of BSs being deployed by operators, the huge amount of devices connected to the network, as well as the development of cloud solutions and network function virtualization, the total energy consumption of wireless networks is expected to largely increase (Alsedairy, Qi, Imran, Imran, & Evans, 2015). Thus, intelligent solutions that are able to improve the network energy efficiency, providing a greener network in order not only to reduce operator's costs but most importantly, to benefit the natural environment are necessary.

In this context, a work that utilizes RL, more specifically Q-Learning, in order to determine which BSs to turn on or off and to improve the energy efficiency of mobile networks was proposed in (Miozzo, Giupponi, Rossi, & Dini, 2017). Another interesting approach to the energy optimization problem is the work in (Wang, Cheng, & Tsai, 2016). In this paper, the authors utilize a supervised learning algorithm, polynomial regression, combined with data collected by the network in order to improve the total cell throughput and energy efficiency of an ultra-dense small cell network. Results show that the proposed solution is able to improve throughput by 50% and energy efficiency by 135% when compared to other approaches.

Table 2 summarizes the ML methods utilized in state-of-the-art research in the area of self-optimization.

Machine Learning in Self-Healing

Another area that has received quite some attention in the last couple of years is the area of self-healing. Due to its critical nature, as whenever a fault happens in a network its service is disrupted, self-healing functions must be precise, in order to detect or predict faults in advance and not generate false alarms, while also being agile in order to trigger the appropriate mechanisms and mitigate the effects of the failure (Onireti, et al., 2016).

Due to its critical nature, several research groups focus on the autonomous detection of faults, their classification and the management of two of the most common faults in a mobile network, cell outage and sleeping cell management. In the next couple of sub-sections, some examples of state-of-the-art solutions in self-healing will be presented.

Table 2. Application of ML algorithms in self-optimization

	Supervised Learning	Unsupervised Learning	Reinforcement Learning	Miscellaneous
Physical Layer	✓	✗	✗	✗
Backhaul	✗	✗	✓	✗
Caching	✓	✓	✗	✗
Coverage & Capacity	✗	✓	✗	✓
Mobility & Handover	✗	✓	✗	✓
Resource Allocation & Load Balancing	✗	✓	✓	✗
Energy Efficiency	✓	✗	✓	✗

Fault Detection and Classification

The first thing that a self-healing function must be able to do is to perform the detection of a fault. This includes determining where a fault has happened and when it has happened. In addition, in the case of proactive networks, instead of predicting when a fault has happened, the network can try and predict the likelihood of a fault happening in the next couple hours, for example (Valente Klaine, Imran, Onireti, & Demo Souza, 2017). Furthermore, not only the detection of a fault is important, but also its classification plays a crucial role in self-healing, as correctly classifying a fault, allows the correct mechanisms to be triggered in order to solve it.

In the context of proactive networks, one possible solution is the work proposed in (Farooq, Parwez, & Imran, 2015), in which the authors utilize a continuous time Markov chains combined with exponential distributions to model the reliability behavior of BSs. The proposed solution is evaluated in three different scenarios and in all of them the primary objective is to predict the occurrence of faults in the network based on historical data. Their results show that the proposed solution is able to learn to predict certain faults and reduce network recovery time, improving the overall network reliability.

Another approach to fault detection is the work in (Hashmi, Darbandi, & Imran, 2017). In this work, the authors compare five different unsupervised learning techniques in order to detect faults in mobile networks. Through the use of extensive data analysis, the proposed solutions are capable of extracting network trends and tackle similar faults in the future. Thus, the paper shows that the algorithms are capable of minimizing network recovery time and operational costs, paving the way for future self-healing approaches.

Other solutions, such as (Wang, Zhang, & Zhang, 2011) propose a framework based on transfer learning (which consists of applying a learning algorithm in a similar task and then using this already pre-trained model in a new task) in order to classify faults in femtocells. By leveraging the historical data of other femtocells, the authors are able to build a model in which two independent classifiers are trained and used as voters in the fault classification model. The proposed solution is compared with other approaches and their results show that their transfer learning approach is able to have higher accuracy than other methods.

Outage and Sleeping Cell Management

Lastly, one of the most common faults that can happen in a network is a cell being in an outage. Another particular type of problem in the outage realm is also the sleeping cell problem, in which an outage cell is not shown to the operator (users are not able to connect to that cell, but from the operator's perspective, the cell appears to be fully operable). Both these scenarios are equally important and have seen a great deal of attention recently, due to the increased scalability and complexity issues expected in NGMNs (Valente Klaine, Imran, Onireti, & Demo Souza, 2017). Figure 4 shows an example on how ML algorithms will be able to detect that an outage has happened in the network and in which location and automatically trigger the correct functions, so that the outage effects can be mitigated.

Figure 4. Use case of outage management, in which the central site of a network goes in outage (a). Based on that, the appropriate mechanisms are triggered and the neighbor BSs adjust their transmit powers in order to cover the outage area (b), adapted from (Valente Klaine, Imran, Onireti, & Demo Souza, 2017).

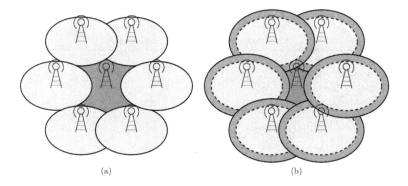

(a)   (b)

One example of cell outage management includes the work in (Onireti, et al., 2016). In this work, the authors consider a framework with distinct control and data planes and propose an algorithm that is able to detect cell outages in both planes. The authors utilize both supervised and unsupervised techniques to perform outage detection and in order to perform outage compensation (mitigate the outage effects), the authors consider a RL approach in order to adjust antenna gains and transmit powers.

Regarding sleeping cell management, one example is the work in (Chernov, Chernogorov, Petrov, & Ristaniemi, 2014), in which a data mining framework focused on the detection of sleeping cells caused mainly by the failure of random access channel is presented. The proposed algorithm, based on supervised learning (K-Nearest Neighbors) is utilized, together with dimension reduction techniques in order to assign scores for possible cells in a sleeping state. According to each cell score, the algorithm is shown to be able to detect whenever a cell is in a sleeping state or not.

Table 3 presents the ML solutions found in the area of self-healing.

Guidelines on the Application of ML in SON

From the previous sections, it could be seen that certain algorithms are utilized more predominantly in one use case than the other, this is no coincidence, as depending on the type of data and the requirements needed, some ML algorithms are more suitable for the job than others. In (Valente Klaine, Imran, Onireti, & Demo Souza, 2017), the authors provide a detailed view and comparison of different ML solutions in terms of certain SON metrics, such as scalability, algorithm training, response and convergence time, the amount of training data needed and its accuracy.

For example, certain use cases of self-configuration, such as the planning of BSs location, or the configuration of network topology do not require a very stringent time to be computed. Thus, offline solutions that explore a wide range of possibilities and possible solutions, such as genetic algorithms, or more complex heuristics could be used. On the other hand, use cases such as mobility prediction or fault detection, which require almost instantaneous responses, would not benefit from these approaches, hence, solutions that have a lower response time would be required, such as supervised or unsupervised learning.

Based on these two simple examples, it is clear that the choice of ML algorithm should be done carefully, as it can have a big impact on the problem being tackled.

Table 3. Application of ML algorithms in self-healing

	Supervised Learning	Unsupervised Learning	Reinforcement Learning	Miscellaneous
Fault Detection & Classification	✓	✓	✗	✓
Outage & Sleeping Cell Management	✓	✓	✓	✗

FUTURE TRENDS

As it could be seen, intelligence in future mobile networks is expected to play a huge role, from being able to solve current limitations of present cellular networks, to creating and enabling new types of services. However, despite the great amount of work being done in the past couple years in the area of SON, there are still some open issues and challenges that need to be addressed (Valente Klaine, Imran, Onireti, & Demo Souza, 2017).

Challenges in Self-Configuration

As it could be seen from the self-configuration section, this SON function is still underexplored, with few intelligent solutions being applied in order to solve its use cases. Hence, several challenges in this function are still present, such as how to autonomously configure a mobile network in scenarios with an ultra-dense deployment of BSs? In the future, BSs are expected to be deployed not only by the network operators but by regular users as well. Hence, some questions remain on how to autonomously and intelligently configure these nodes out of the control of the operator and how to efficiently integrate them into the network (Valente Klaine, Imran, Onireti, & Demo Souza, 2017).

In addition, a specific uncharted area in self-configuration is also the automatic configuration of NCLs, which plays a vital role in the configuration of the network and its topology. However, despite its importance, no work using ML algorithms in this use case was found and still simple solutions involving threshold-based or feedback controllers are still dominant.

Lastly, another area that is still not well covered in the realm of self-configuration is the reconfiguration of a network after natural disasters have occurred. In this context, the development of ML solutions that are able to rapidly and intelligently reconfigure a network from zero is essential in order to not only re-establish network service, but also to save human lives (Erdelj, Natalizio, Chowdhury, & Akyildiz, 2017).

Challenges in Self-Optimization

Despite self-optimization being a well-explored area, some issues still remain. In particular, use cases such as the optimization of backhaul resources are essential for future cellular networks, as the backhaul is expected to be the main bottleneck of future networks, instead of the RAN (Jaber M., Imran, Tafazolli, & Tukmanov, A Distributed SON-Based User-Centric Backhaul Provisioning Scheme, 2016). Hence, solutions that are able to optimize current backhaul links, without the need of upgrading all of them are welcomed.

Another area that can be further explored is the area of caching, in which the determination of which contents to cache and at which BSs still play a major role. In addition, in order to meet the stringent requirements in delay for NGMNs, caching contents at the edge of the network based on data collected from each cell in different times of the day can also be explored (Bastug, Bennis, & Debbah, 2014).

Finally, another use case that can play major role in future mobile networks is the optimization of physical layer parameters. Most of the current solutions attempt to blindly estimate the transmitter parameters at the receiver side considering only single carrier waveforms (Lichtman, Headley, & Reed, 2014). However, in the future, as multi-carrier waveforms, such as Orthogonal Frequency Division Multiplexing and its variants, are expected to play a major role, it is essential that the prediction of physical layer parameters can be done in multi-carrier systems.

Challenges in Self-Healing

In terms of self-healing functions, as it could be seen, most of them still rely on the concept of a reactive network, trying to learn from previous historical data in order to automatically detect and classify a fault in the network in order to trigger the appropriate mechanisms that will mitigate its effects. However, as already mentioned in this chapter, a major shift is required in future networks, in which networks are expected to become proactive instead of reactive. In this sense, the deployment of ML solutions in order to try and predict with a high level of certainty whenever faults are likely to occur in a mobile network is still needed.

CONCLUSION

In this chapter, a clear view of why ML is necessary for future networks was presented. In this context, the authors highlighted the importance of intelligent solutions in future networks as not only a solution in order to overcome current cellular networks obstacles but also as an enabler for future services and applications that today are unimaginable. With the advents of smart cities, vehicles, personal assistants and the ever increasing demand for better services, it is essential that NGMNs shift their paradigms, in order to keep on par with other state-of-the-art systems. Thus, artificial intelligence and ML algorithms are expected to play a huge role in the future of SONs.

Furthermore, for future networks to become a reality, a change in paradigm is also necessary for them to become just operable. As it is expected, in the future, thousands of small cells will be deployed in a mobile network, some without the control of the operator, thousands of cells and their parameters will need to be configured, optimized and monitored in order to detect and classify failures in a network. Thus, if all of these are done as the way it is done today, future networks are infeasible, as the amount of data generated and collected daily will be immense. Thus, in order to leverage the full potential of data analytics using all of this massive data collected by the network, intelligent solutions that rely on data analysis, such as ML algorithms are essential in order to enable SON.

ACKNOWLEDGMENT

This research was supported by the DARE project grant (No. EP/P028764/1) under the EPSRC's Global Challenges Research Fund (GCRF) allocation.

The authors would also like to thank CNPq (Brazil) for the support for this work.

REFERENCES

Aliu, O., Imran, A., Imran, M., & Evans, B. (2013). A survey of self organisation in future cellular networks. *IEEE Communications Surveys and Tutorials, 15*(1), 336–361. doi:10.1109/SURV.2012.021312.00116

Alsedairy, T., Qi, Y., Imran, A., Imran, M., & Evans, B. (2015). Self organising cloud cells: A resource efficient network densification strategy. *Transactions on Emerging Telecommunications Technologies, 26*(8), 1096–1107. doi:10.1002/ett.2824

Andrews, G., Buzzi, S., Choi, W., Hanly, S. V., Lozano, A., Soong, A. C. K., & Zhang, J. C. (2014). What will 5G be? *IEEE Journal on Selected Areas in Communications, 32*(6), 1065–1082. doi:10.1109/JSAC.2014.2328098

Bassoy, S., Jaber, M., Imran, M. A., & Xiao, P. (2016). Load Aware Self-Organising User-Centric Dynamic CoMP Clustering for 5G Networks. *IEEE Access: Practical Innovations, Open Solutions, 4*, 2895–2906. doi:10.1109/ACCESS.2016.2569824

Bastug, E., Bennis, M., & Debbah, M. (2014). Living on the edge: The role of proactive caching in 5G wireless networks. *IEEE Communications Magazine, 52*(8), 82–89. doi:10.1109/MCOM.2014.6871674

Binzer, T., & Landstorfer, F. (2000). Radio network planning with neural networks. In *Vehicular Technology Conference Fall 2000. IEEE VTS Fall VTC2000. 52nd Vehicular Technology Conference* (pp. 811-817). Boston: IEEE. 10.1109/VETECF.2000.887116

Chernov, S., Chernogorov, F., Petrov, D., & Ristaniemi, T. (2014). Data mining framework for random access failure detection in LTE networks. In *2014 IEEE 25th Annual International Symposium on Personal, Indoor, and Mobile Radio Communication (PIMRC)* (pp. 1-6). Washington, DC: IEEE.

Debono, C., & Buhagiar, J. (2005). Cellular network coverage optimization through the application of self-organizing neural networks. In *IEEE 62nd Vehicular Technology Conference, 2005. VTC-2005-Fall* (pp. 1-5). Dallas, TX: IEEE.

Dirani, M., & Altman, Z. (2011). Self-organizing networks in next generation radio access networks: Application to fractional power control. *Computer Networks*, *55*(2), 431–438. doi:10.1016/j.comnet.2010.08.012

Dörner, S., Cammerer, S., Hoydis, J., & Brink, S. T. (2017). Deep Learning Based Communication Over the Air. *IEEE Journal of Selected Topics in Signal Processing*, 132–143.

Erdelj, M., Natalizio, E., Chowdhury, K. R., & Akyildiz, I. F. (2017). Help from the Sky: Leveraging UAVs for Disaster Management. *IEEE Pervasive Computing*, *16*(1), 24–32. doi:10.1109/MPRV.2017.11

Farooq, H., Parwez, M. S., & Imran, A. (2015). Continuous Time Markov Chain Based Reliability Analysis for Future Cellular Networks. In *2015 IEEE Global Communications Conference (GLOBECOM)* (pp. 1-5). San Diego, CA: IEEE. 10.1109/GLOCOM.2015.7417594

Fettweis, G. (2012). A 5G wireless communications vision. *Microwave Journal*, 24–36.

Friedman, J., Hastie, T., & Tibshirani, R. (2001). *The elements of statistical learning*. New York: Springer.

Hashmi, U. S., Darbandi, A., & Imran, A. (2017). Enabling proactive self-healing by data mining network failure logs. In *2017 International Conference on Computing, Networking and Communications (ICNC)* (pp. 1-7). Santa Clara, CA: IEEE. 10.1109/ICCNC.2017.7876181

Ho, L. T., Ashraf, I., & Claussen, H. (2009). Evolving femtocell coverage optimization algorithms using genetic programming. In *IEEE 20th International Symposium on Personal, Indoor and Mobile Radio Communications, 2009* (pp. 1-5). Tokyo, Japan: IEEE.

Huawei, Technologies Co. (2016). *5G opening up new business opportunities*. Shenzhen: Huawei Technologies Co.

Imran, A., Zoha, A., & Abu-Dayya, A. (2014). Challenges in 5G: How to empower SON with big data for enabling 5G. *IEEE Network*, *28*(6), 27–33. doi:10.1109/MNET.2014.6963801

Index, C. (2017). *Global Mobile Data Traffic Forecast Update*. San Jose, CA: Cisco White Paper.

Islam, M. N., & Mitschele-Thiel, A. (2012). Reinforcement learning strategies for self-organized coverage and capacity optimization. In *IEEE Wireless Communications and Networking Conference (WCNC), 2012* (pp. 1-6). Shanghai, China: IEEE. 10.1109/WCNC.2012.6214281

Jaber, M., Imran, M., Tafazolli, R., & Tukmanov, A. (2015). An adaptive backhaul-aware cell range extension approach. In *IEEE International Conference on Communication Workshop (ICCW), 2015* (pp. 1-6). London, UK: IEEE. 10.1109/ICCW.2015.7247158

Jaber, M., Imran, M. A., Tafazolli, R., & Tukmanov, A. (2016). A Distributed SON-Based User-Centric Backhaul Provisioning Scheme. *IEEE Access: Practical Innovations, Open Solutions*, *4*, 2314–1330. doi:10.1109/ACCESS.2016.2566958

Jaber, M., Imran, M. A., Tafazolli, R., & Tukmanov, A. (2016). A Multiple Attribute User-Centric Backhaul Provisioning Scheme Using Distributed SON. In *IEEE Global Communications Conference (GLOBECOM)*, 2016 (pp. 1-6). Washington, DC: IEEE. 10.1109/GLOCOM.2016.7841518

Kaelbling, L., Littman, M., & Moore, A. (1996). Reinforcement learning: A survey. *Journal of Artificial Intelligence Research*, 4, 237–285. doi:10.1613/jair.301

Kotsiantis, S., Zaharakis, I., & Pintelas, P. (2007). Supervised machine learning: A review of classification techniques. In *Proceedings of the 2007 conference on Emerging Artificial Intelligence Applications in Computer Engineering*, (pp. 3-24). Amsterdam: Academic Press.

LeCun, Y., Bengio, Y., & Hinton, G. (2015). Deep learning. *Nature*, *521*(7553), 436–444. doi:10.1038/nature14539 PMID:26017442

Lichtman, M., Headley, W. C., & Reed, J. H. (2014). Automatic Modulation Classification under IQ Imbalance Using Supervised Learning. In *IEEE Military Communications Conference, MILCOM 2013* (pp. 1-6). San Diego, CA: IEEE.

Miozzo, M., Giupponi, L., Rossi, M., & Dini, P. (2017). *Switch-On/Off Policies for Energy Harvesting Small Cells through Distributed Q-Learning. In 2017 IEEE Wireless Communications and Networking Conference Workshops (WCNCW)* (pp. 1–6). San Francisco, CA: IEEE.

Mohamed, A., Onireti, O., Hoseinitabatabaei, S. A., Imran, M., Imran, A., & Tafazolli, R. (2015). Mobility prediction for handover management in cellular networks with control/data separation. In *2015 IEEE International Conference on Communications (ICC)* (pp. 1-6). London, UK: IEEE. 10.1109/ICC.2015.7248939

Mohamed, A., Onireti, O., Imran, M. A., Imran, A., & Tafazolli, R. (2017). Predictive and Core-Network Efficient RRC Signalling for Active State Handover in RANs With Control/Data Separation. *IEEE Transactions on Wireless Communications*, *16*(3), 1423–1436. doi:10.1109/TWC.2016.2644608

Onireti, O., Mohamed, A., Pervaiz, H., & Imran, M. (2017). Analytical approach to base station sleep mode power consumption and sleep depth. In *2017 IEEE 28th Annual International Symposium on Personal, Indoor, and Mobile Radio Communications (PIMRC)* (pp. 1-7). Montreal, Canada: IEEE.

Onireti, O., Zoha, A., Moysen, J., Imran, A., Giupponi, L., Imran, M. A., & Abu-Dayya, A. (2016). A Cell Outage Management Framework for Dense Heterogeneous Networks. *IEEE Transactions on Vehicular Technology*, *65*(4), 2097–2113. doi:10.1109/TVT.2015.2431371

Razavi, R., Klein, S., & Claussen, H. (2010). A Fuzzy reinforcement learning approach for self-optimization of coverage in LTE networks. *Bell Labs Technical Journal*, *15*(3), 153–175. doi:10.1002/bltj.20463

Safdar, T., Hasbulah, H., & Rehan, M. (2015). Effect of Reinforcement Learning on Routing of Cognitive Radio Ad-Hoc Networks. In *International Symposium on Mathematical Sciences and Computing Research (iSMSC)* (pp. 1-7). Ipon, Malaysia: IEEE. 10.1109/ISMSC.2015.7594025

Samsung Electronics Co. (2015). *5G Vision*. Samsung Electronics Co.

Simon, P. (2013). *Too Big to Ignore: the Business Case for Big Data*. John Wiley & Sons.

Sinclair, N., Harle, D., Glover, I. A., Irvine, J., & Atkinson, R. C. (2013). An Advanced SOM Algorithm Applied to Handover Management Within LTE. *IEEE Transactions on Vehicular Technology, 62*(5), 1883–1894. doi:10.1109/TVT.2013.2251922

Su, W. (2013). Feature Space Analysis of Modulation Classification Using Very High-Order Statistics. *IEEE Communications Letters, 17*(9), 1688–1691. doi:10.1109/LCOMM.2013.080613.130070

Sutton, R., & Barto, A. (1998). *Reinforcement Learning: An Introduction.* Cambridge, MA: MIT Press.

Valente Klaine, P., Imran, M., Onireti, O., & Demo Souza, R. (2017). A Survey of Machine Learning Techniques Applied to Self-Organizing Cellular Networks. *IEEE Communications Surveys and Tutorials, 19*(4), 2392–2431. doi:10.1109/COMST.2017.2727878

Wang, L.-C., Cheng, S.-H., & Tsai, A.-H. (2016). Bi-SON: Big-Data Self Organizing Network for Energy Efficient Ultra-Dense Small Cells. In *2016 IEEE 84th Vehicular Technology Conference (VTC-Fall)* (pp. 1-5). Montreal, Canada: IEEE.

Wang, W., Zhang, J., & Zhang, Q. (2011). Transfer Learning Based Diagnosis for Configuration Troubleshooting in Self-Organizing Femtocell Networks. In *2011 IEEE Global Telecommunications Conference (GLOBECOM 2011)* (pp. 1-5). Kathmandu, Nepal: IEEE. 10.1109/GLOCOM.2011.6133802

ADDITIONAL READING

Fan, B., Leng, S., & Yang, K. (2016). A dynamic bandwidth allocation algorithm in mobile networks with big data of users and networks. *IEEE Network, 30*(1), 6–10. doi:10.1109/MNET.2016.7389824

Farooq, H., & Imran, A. (2017). Spatiotemporal mobility prediction in proactive self-organizing cellular networks. *IEEE Communications Letters, 21*(2), 370–373. doi:10.1109/LCOMM.2016.2623276

Gomez-Andrades, A., Barco, R., Munoz, P., & Serrano, I. (2017). Data analytics for diagnosing the RF condition in self-organizing networks. *IEEE Transactions on Mobile Computing, 16*(6), 1587–1600. doi:10.1109/TMC.2016.2601919

Mehta, M., Rane, N., Karandikar, A., Imran, M. A., & Evans, B. G. (2016). A self-organized resource allocation scheme for heterogeneous macro-femto networks. *Wireless Communications and Mobile Computing, 16*(3), 330–342. doi:10.1002/wcm.2518

Wang, W., Liao, Q., & Zhang, Q. (2014). COD: A cooperative cell outage detection architecture for self-organizing femtocell networks. *IEEE Transactions on Wireless Communications, 13*(11), 6007–6014. doi:10.1109/TWC.2014.2360865

Wang, X., Chen, M., Taleb, T., Ksentini, A., & Leung, V. (2014). Cache in the air: Exploiting content caching and delivery techniques for 5G systems. *IEEE Communications Magazine, 52*(2), 131–139. doi:10.1109/MCOM.2014.6736753

Zheng, K., Yang, Z., Zhang, K., Chatzimisios, P., Yang, K., & Xiang, W. (2016). Big data-driven optimization for mobile networks toward 5G. *IEEE Network, 30*(1), 44–51. doi:10.1109/MNET.2016.7389830

Zoha, A., Saeed, A., Imran, A., Imran, M. A., & Abu-Dayya, A. (2016). A learning-based approach for autonomous outage detection and coverage optimization. *Transactions on Emerging Telecommunications Technologies*, 27(3), 439–450. doi:10.1002/ett.2971

KEY TERMS AND DEFINITIONS

Machine Learning: Class of algorithms that analyze data and make predictions about it.

Mobile Networks: Radio communication network, in which the last hop of the network is wireless.

Reinforcement Learning: Algorithms that learn from their own experience with the environment.

Self-Configuration: Autonomous configuration of network parameters in order for a network to become operable.

Self-Healing: Autonomous detection, classification, and management of failures in a mobile network, so that the effects of a fault can be mitigated.

Self-Optimization: The process of autonomously adjusting network parameters so that the network performance can be back to near optimum.

Self-Organizing Cellular Networks: Mobile networks that are capable of autonomously adapting itself to changes in their environment, while maintaining its desired objectives.

Supervised Learning: Class of machine learning algorithms that rely on the knowledge of an external supervisor in order to learn.

Unsupervised Learning: A class of machine learning algorithms that, given a set of unlabeled data, is capable of learning a function that best represents the model.

This research was previously published in Next-Generation Wireless Networks Meet Advanced Machine Learning Applications; pages 1-23, copyright year 2019 by Information Science Reference (an imprint of IGI Global).

Index

C

N

T

U

V

W

Z

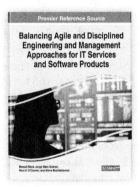

Ensure Quality Research is Introduced to the Academic Community

Become an Evaluator for IGI Global Authored Book Projects

Premier Reference Source

Stabilizing Currency and Preserving Economic Sovereignty Using the Grondona System

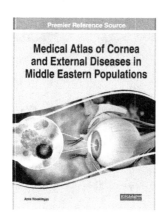

Premier Reference Source

Medical Atlas of Cornea and External Diseases in Middle Eastern Populations

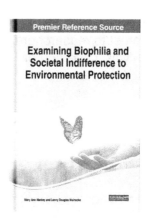

Premier Reference Source

Examining Biophilia and Societal Indifference to Environmental Protection

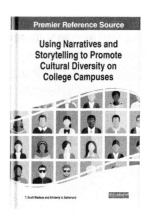

Premier Reference Source

Using Narratives and Storytelling to Promote Cultural Diversity on College Campuses

The overall success of an authored book project is dependent on quality and timely manuscript evaluations.

Applications and Inquiries may be sent to:
development@igi-global.com

Applicants must have a doctorate (or equivalent degree) as well as publishing, research, and reviewing experience. Authored Book Evaluators are appointed for one-year terms and are expected to complete at least three evaluations per term. Upon successful completion of this term, evaluators can be considered for an additional term.

If you have a colleague that may be interested in this opportunity, we encourage you to share this information with them.

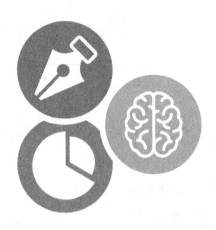

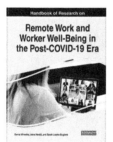

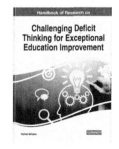

Have Your Work Published and Freely Accessible
Open Access Publishing

With the industry shifting from the more traditional publication models to an open access (OA) publication model, publishers are finding that OA publishing has many benefits that are awarded to authors and editors of published work.

Freely Share
Your Research

Higher Discoverability
& Citation Impact

Rigorous & Expedited
Publishing Process

Increased
Advancement &
Collaboration

Acquire & Open

When your library acquires an IGI Global e-Book and/or e-Journal Collection, your faculty's published work will be considered for immediate conversion to Open Access *(CC BY License)*, at no additional cost to the library or its faculty *(cost only applies to the e-Collection content being acquired)*, through our popular **Transformative Open Access (Read & Publish) Initiative**.

Provide Up To
100%
OA APC or
CPC Funding

Funding to
Convert or
Start a Journal to
**Platinum
OA**

Support for
Funding an
**OA
Reference
Book**

IGI Global publications are found in a number of prestigious indices, including Web of Science™, Scopus®, Compendex, and PsycINFO®. The selection criteria is very strict and to ensure that journals and books are accepted into the major indexes, IGI Global closely monitors publications against the criteria that the indexes provide to publishers.

Printed in the United States
by Baker & Taylor Publisher Services